W9-DAR-489

MATHEMATICAL THEORY OF COMPUTATION

McGRAW-HILL COMPUTER SCIENCE SERIES

RICHARD W. HAMMING
Bell Telephone Laboratories

EDWARD A. FEIGENBAUM
Stanford University

Bell and Newell *Computer Structures: Readings and Examples*
Cole *Introduction to Computing*
Donovan *Systems Programming*
Gear *Computer Organization and Programming*
Givone *Introduction to Switching Circuit Theory*
Hamming *Computers and Society*
Hamming *Introduction to Applied Numerical Analysis*
Hellerman *Digital Computer System Principles*
Kain *Automata Theory: Machines and Languages*
Kohavi *Switching and Finite Automata Theory*
Liu *Introduction to Combinatorial Mathematics*
Madnick and Donovan *Operating Systems*
Manna *Mathematical Theory of Computation*
Newman and Sproull *Principles of Interactive Computer Graphics*
Nilsson *Artificial Intelligence*
Ralston *Introduction to Programming and Computer Science*
Rosen *Programming Systems and Languages*
Salton *Automatic Information Organization and Retrieval*
Stone *Introduction to Computer Organization and Data Structures*
Watson *Timesharing System Design Concepts*
Wegner *Programming Languages, Information Structures, and Machine Organization*

ZOHAR MANNA

Applied Mathematics Department
Weizmann Institute of Science
Rehovot, Israel

Mathematical Theory of Computation

McGRAW-HILL BOOK COMPANY

New York St. Louis San Francisco Düsseldorf Johannesburg
Kuala Lumpur London Mexico Montreal New Delhi
Panama Paris São Paulo Singapore Sydney Tokyo Toronto

TO NITZA

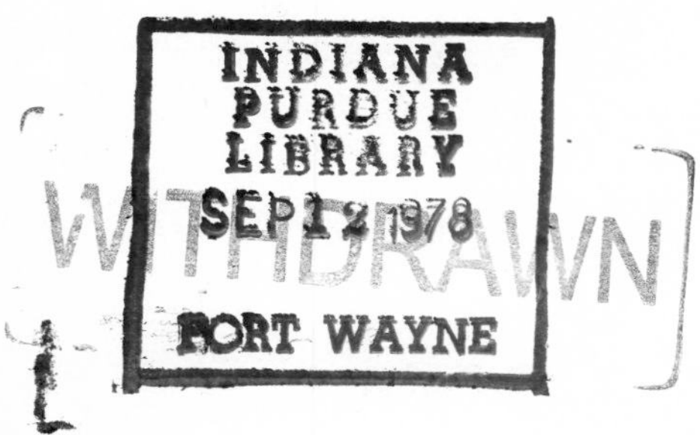

MATHEMATICAL THEORY OF COMPUTATION

34567890 KPKP 7987

This book was set in Times Roman.
The editors were Richard F. Dojny and Michael Gardner;
the designer was Nicholas Krenitsky;
the production supervisor was Sam Ratkewitch.
The drawings were done by Keter, Inc.
Kingsport Press, Inc., was printer and binder.

Library of Congress Cataloging in Publication Data

Manna, Zohar.
Mathematical theory of computation.
(McGraw-Hill computer science series)
Includes bibliographical references.
1. Electronic digital computers—Programming.
2. Debugging in computer science. I. Title.
QA76.6. M356 001.6'425 73-12753
ISBN 0-07-039910-7

CONTENTS

PREFACE ix

CHAPTER 1 COMPUTABILITY **1**

INTRODUCTION 1

1-1 FINITE AUTOMATA 2
1-1.1 Regular Expressions 3
1-1.2 Finite Automata 7
1-1.3 Transition Graphs 9
1-1.4 Kleene's Theorem 11
1-1.5 The Equivalence Theorem 17

1-2 TURING MACHINES 20
1-2.1 Turing Machines 21
1-2.2 Post Machines 24
1-2.3 Finite Machines with Pushdown Stores 29
1-2.4 Nondeterminism 35

1-3 TURING MACHINES AS ACCEPTORS 37
1-3.1 Recursively Enumerable Sets 38
1-3.2 Recursive Sets 39
1-3.3 Formal Languages 41

1-4 TURING MACHINES AS GENERATORS 43
1-4.1 Primitive Recursive Functions 45
1-4.2 Partial Recursive Functions 50

1-5 TURING MACHINES AS ALGORITHMS 53
1-5.1 Solvability of Classes of Yes/No Problems 54
1-5.2 The Halting Problem of Turing Machines 56
1-5.3 The Word Problem of Semi-Thue Systems 58
1-5.4 Post Correspondence Problem 60
1-5.5 Partial Solvability of Classes of Yes/No Problems 64

BIBLIOGRAPHIC REMARKS 67
REFERENCES 68
PROBLEMS 70

CHAPTER 2 PREDICATE CALCULUS 77

INTRODUCTION 77

2-1 BASIC NOTIONS 81
2-1.1 Syntax 81
2-1.2 Semantics (Interpretations) 85
2-1.3 Valid Wffs 90
2-1.4 Equivalence of Wffs 95
2-1.5 Normal Forms of Wffs 101
2-1.6 The Validity Problem 105

2-2 NATURAL DEDUCTION 108
2-2.1 Rules for the Connectives 110
2-2.2 Rules for the Quantifiers 115
2-2.3 Rules for the Operators 122

2-3 THE RESOLUTION METHOD 125
2-3.1 Clause Form 125
2-3.2 Herbrand's Procedures 130
2-3.3 The Unification Algorithm 136
2-3.4 The Resolution Rule 140

BIBLIOGRAPHIC REMARKS 145
REFERENCES 146
PROBLEMS 147

CHAPTER 3 VERIFICATION OF PROGRAMS 161

INTRODUCTION 161

3-1 FLOWCHART PROGRAMS 161
3-1.1 Partial Correctness 170
3-1.2 Termination 182

3-2 FLOWCHART PROGRAMS WITH ARRAYS 189
3-2.1 Partial Correctness 189
3-2.2 Termination 195

3-3 ALGOL-LIKE PROGRAMS 202
3-3.1 While Programs 203
3-3.2 Partial Correctness 205
3-3.3 Total Correctness 211

BIBLIOGRAPHIC REMARKS 218
REFERENCES 220
PROBLEMS 223

CHAPTER 4 FLOWCHART SCHEMAS 241

INTRODUCTION 241

4-1 BASIC NOTIONS 242
4-1.1 Syntax 242
4-1.2 Semantics (Interpretations) 244
4-1.3 Basic Properties 248
4-1.4 Herbrand Interpretations 260

4-2 DECISION PROBLEMS 262
4-2.1 Unsolvability of the Basic Properties 264
4-2.2 Free Schemas 268
4-2.3 Tree Schemas 274
4-2.4 Ianov Schemas 284

4-3 FORMALIZATION IN PREDICATE CALCULUS 294
4-3.1 The Algorithm 295
4-3.2 Formalization of Properties of Flowchart Programs 307
4-3.3 Formalization of Properties of Flowchart Schemas 311

4-4 TRANSLATION PROBLEMS 317
4-4.1 Recursive Schemas 319
4-4.2 Flowchart Schemas versus Recursive Schemas 322

BIBLIOGRAPHIC REMARKS 334
REFERENCES 335
PROBLEMS 337

CHAPTER 5 THE FIXPOINT THEORY OF PROGRAMS 356

INTRODUCTION 356

5-1 FUNCTIONS AND FUNCTIONALS 357
5-1.1 Monotonic Functions 359
5-1.2 Continuous Functionals 366
5-1.3 Fixpoints of Functionals 369

5-2 RECURSIVE PROGRAMS 374
5-2.1 Computation Rules 375
5-2.2 Fixpoint Computation Rules 384
5-2.3 Systems of Recursive Definitions 389

5-3 VERIFICATION METHODS 392
5-3.1 Stepwise Computational Induction 393
5-3.2 Complete Computational Induction 400
5-3.3 Fixpoint Induction 403
5-3.4 Structural Induction 408

BIBLIOGRAPHIC REMARKS 415
REFERENCES 416
PROBLEMS 418

INDEXES 431
NAME INDEX
SUBJECT INDEX

PREFACE

What is *mathematical theory of computation*? I am sure that no two computer scientists would define this concept in exactly the same way. Following John McCarthy's pioneer paper "A Basis for a Mathematical Theory of Computation,"† I consider it to be the theory which attempts to formalize our understanding of computation, and in particular to make the *art* of verifying computer programs (the famous debugging technique) into a *science*.

In this book I attempted to treat both the practical and the theoretical aspects of the theory. To make the book self-contained, I included selected concepts of computability theory and mathematical logic.

My aim was to introduce these topics to a wide variety of readers: junior-senior undergraduate students, first-year graduate students, as well as motivated programmers. I deliberately omitted tedious details and stated some results without proofs, using the spare space for giving extra examples. My intention was to give an overview of the methods and the results related to this field, rather than a standard mathematical textbook of the style "definition-theorem-proof." I therefore ask the forgiveness of my more theoretical-minded readers for preferring clarity over formality.

Numerous papers in mathematical theory of computation have been published during the last few years, and activity in the area is increasing every year. As a result, one of my main problems in writing this book was

† In P. Braffort and D. Hirschberg (eds.), "Computer Programming and Formal Systems," North-Holland Publishing Company, Amsterdam, 1962.

to decide what should be included in an introductory text in this area. I used two criteria for making this decision. First, I included only material that I feel every computer scientist should know, based mainly on my experience in teaching the mathematical theory of computation courses at Stanford University and the Weizmann Institute for the last few years. Second, because of the introductory nature of this text, I did not include topics which I expect will undergo major changes and upheavals in the near future. A few such topics are: automatic program synthesis, the logic of partial functions, and verification techniques for large-scale computer programs (such as compilers), as well as parallel programs.

Most of the chapters are self-contained. Neither chapter 1 nor chapter 2 requires any prerequisites with the exception that section 1-5 is necessary to the understanding of section 2-1.6. The reader interested in the practical aspect of the field should be aware that only sections 2-1.1 and 2-1.2 are prerequisites for chapters 3 and 5, which contain the more applicable techniques. Chapter 4, which is more theoretical in nature, requires both sections 1-5 and 2-1 for its understanding.

I added to each chapter some bibliographic remarks and references. My intention was to include in the bibliographic remarks and references only what I consider to be the most relevant papers and books on each topic, rather than trying to list all existing publications. I added also to each chapter a selected set of about 20 to 30 problems (* indicates a hard problem). I consider these problems an essential part of the text and strongly urge the reader to attempt to solve at least some of them.

Many people contributed directly or indirectly to the completion of this book. Thanks are due first to David Cooper, Robert Floyd, and John McCarthy, who introduced me to this field. Thanks are also due to my colleagues for their most helpful comments and suggestions on different versions of the manuscript. I am most indebted in this way to Peter Andrews, Edward Ashcroft, Jean-Marie Cadiou, Ashok Chandra, Nissim Francesz, Shmuel Katz, Lockwood Morris, Stephen Ness, David Plaisted, Amir Pnueli, Adi Shamir, Mark Smith, and Jean Vuillemin. Special thanks are due to John McCarthy and Lester Earnest for their consistent encouragement while I wrote this book. And finally, I am indebted to Phyllis Winkler who very patiently typed the numerous drafts of the manuscript.

ZOHAR MANNA

MATHEMATICAL THEORY OF COMPUTATION

CHAPTER 1

Computability

Introduction

In the last few decades substantial effort has been made to define a *computing device* that will be general enough to compute every "computable" function. In 1936 Turing suggested the use of a machine, since then called a *Turing machine*, which is considered to be the *most general computing device*. It was hypothesized by Church [Church's thesis (1936)] that any computable function can be computed by a Turing machine. Since our notion of computable function is not mathematically precise, we can never hope to prove Church's thesis formally. However, from the definition of a Turing machine, it is apparent that any computation that can be described by means of a Turing machine can be mechanically carried out; and conversely, any computation that can be performed on a modern-day digital computer can be described by means of a Turing machine. Moreover, all other general computing devices that have been proposed [e.g., by Church (1936), Kleene (1936), and Post (1936)]† have been shown to have the same computing capability as Turing machines, which strengthens our belief in Church's thesis.

In this chapter we discuss several machines, such as Post machines and finite machines with pushdown stores, which have the same computing capability as Turing machines. We emphasize that there are actually three different ways to look at a Turing machine: (1) as an *acceptor* (accepts a recursive or a recursively enumerable set), (2) as a *generator* (computes a total recursive or a partial recursive function), and (3) as an *algorithm* (solves or partially solves a class of yes/no problems).

We devote most of this chapter to discussing the class of Turing machines (the "most general possible" computing device); however, for purposes of comparison, in the first section we discuss the "simplest possible" computing device, namely, the *finite automaton*.

† All three papers appear in the collection by Davis (1965).

1-1 FINITE AUTOMATA

Let Σ be any finite set of symbols, called an *alphabet*; the symbols are called the *letters* of the alphabet. A *word* (*string*) *over* Σ is any finite sequence of letters from Σ. The *empty word*, denoted by Λ, is the word consisting of no letters. Σ^* denotes the set of all words over Σ, including the empty word Λ. Thus, if $\Sigma = \{a, b\}$, then $\Sigma^* = \{\Lambda, a, b, aa, ab, ba, bb, aaa, \ldots\}$. ϕ denotes the empty set $\{\ \}$, that is, the set consisting of no words.†

We define the *product* (*concatenation*) UV of two subsets U, V of Σ^* by

$$UV = \{x | x = uv, u \text{ is in } U \text{ and } v \text{ is in } V\}$$

That is, each word in the set UV is formed by concatenating a word in U with a word in V. As an example, if $U = \{a, ab, aab\}$ and $V = \{b, bb\}$, then the set UV is $\{ab, abb, abbb, aabb, aabbb\}$. Note that the word *abb* is obtained in two ways: (1) as *a* concatenated with *bb*, and (2) as *ab* concatenated with *b*. The set VU is $\{ba, bab, baab, bba, bbab, bbaab\}$. Note that $UV \neq VU$, which shows that the product operation is not commutative. However, the product operation is associative, i.e., for any subsets U, V, and W of Σ^*, $(UV)W = U(VW)$.

The *closure* (*star*) of a set S, denoted by S^*, is the set consisting of the empty word and all words formed by concatenating a finite number of words in S. Thus if $S = \{ab, bb\}$, then

$$S^* = \{\Lambda, ab, bb, abab, abbb, bbab, bbbb, ababab, \ldots\}.$$

An alternative definition is

$$S^* = S^0 \cup S^1 \cup S^2 \cup S^3 \cup \ldots,$$

where $S^0 = \{\Lambda\}$, and $S^i = S^{i-1}S$, for $i > 0$.

We shall now discuss a special class of sets of words over Σ, called *regular sets*. The class of regular sets over Σ is defined recursively as follows:

1. Every *finite* set of words over Σ (including ϕ, the empty set) is a regular set.
2. If U and V are regular sets over Σ, so are their union $U \cup V$ and product UV.
3. If S is a regular set over Σ, so is its closure S^*.

This means that no set is regular unless it can be obtained by a finite number

† Note the difference between Λ, $\{\ \}$, and $\{\Lambda\}$; Λ is a *word* (the empty word); $\{\ \}$ is a *set of words* (the set consisting of no words); and $\{\Lambda\}$ is a *set of words* (the set consisting of a single word, the empty word Λ).

of applications of 1 to 3. In other words, the class of regular sets over Σ is the smallest class containing all finite sets of words over Σ and closed under union, product, and star.

Let $\Sigma = \{a, b\}$. For example, we shall show that the set of all words over Σ containing either two consecutive a's or two consecutive b's, and the set of all words over Σ containing an even number of a's and an even number of b's, are regular sets over Σ. On the other hand, we shall show that the set $\{a^n b^n | n \geqq 0\}$ (that is, the set of all words which consists of n a's followed by n b's for any $n \geqq 0$) is not a regular set over Σ. Similarly, it can be shown that the sets $\{a^n b a^n | n \geqq 0\}$ and $\{a^{n^2} | n \geqq 0\}$ are not regular sets over Σ.†

In this section we describe three different ways of expressing regular sets. A subset of Σ^* is regular *if and only if*: (1) it can be expressed by some *regular expression*, (2) it is accepted by some *finite automaton*, or (3) it is accepted by some *transition graph*. Finally we prove that there is an algorithm to determine whether or not two given regular sets over Σ (expressed by any one of the above forms) are equal, which is one of the most important results concerning regular sets.

1-1.1 Regular Expressions

We consider first the representation of regular sets by regular expressions. This representation is of special interest since it allows algebraic manipulations with regular sets. The class of *regular expressions over* Σ is defined recursively as follows:

1. Λ and ϕ are regular expressions over Σ.
2. Every letter $\sigma \in \Sigma$ is a regular expression over Σ.
3. If R_1 and R_2 are regular expressions over Σ, so are $(R_1 + R_2)$, $(R_1 \cdot R_2)$, and $(R_1)^*$.

For example, if $\Sigma = \{a, b\}$, then $(((a + (b \cdot a)))^* \cdot a)$ is a regular expression over Σ.

Every regular expression R over Σ describes a set $\tilde{R}$ of words over Σ, that is, $\tilde{R} \subseteq \Sigma^*$, defined recursively as follows:

1. If $R = \Lambda$, then $\tilde{R} = \{\Lambda\}$, that is, the set consisting of the empty word Λ; if $R = \phi$, then $\tilde{R} = \phi$, that is the empty set.

† Note the difference between a *word,* for example, *bbaba*, a *set of words,* for example, $\{a^n b^n | n \geqq 0\}$, and a *class of sets of words,* for example, $\{\{a^n | n \geqq 0\}, \{a^n b^n | n \geqq 0\}, \{a^n b^n a^n | n \geqq 0\}, \{a^n b^n a^n b^n | n \geqq 0\}, \ldots\}$.

2. If $R = \sigma$, then $\tilde{R} = \{\sigma\}$, that is, the set consisting of the letter σ.
3. Let R_1 and R_2 be regular expressions over Σ which describe the set of words $\tilde{R}_1$ and $\tilde{R}_2$, respectively:

   If $R = (R_1 + R_2)$, then $\tilde{R} = \tilde{R}_1 \cup \tilde{R}_2 = \{x | x \in \tilde{R}_1 \text{ or } x \in \tilde{R}_2\}$, that is, set union.
   If $R = (R_1 \cdot R_2)$, then $\tilde{R} = \tilde{R}_1\tilde{R}_2 = \{xy | x \in \tilde{R}_1 \text{ and } y \in \tilde{R}_2\}$, that is set product.
   If $R = (R_1)^*$, then $\tilde{R} = \tilde{R}_1^* = \{\Lambda\} \cup \{x | x$ obtained by concatenating a finite number of words in $\tilde{R}_1\}$, that is, set closure.

Parentheses may be omitted from a regular expression when their omission can cause no confusion. There are several rules for the restoration of omitted parentheses: '$*$' is more binding than '$\cdot$' or '$+$', that is, '$*$' is always attached to the smallest possible scope (Λ, ϕ, a letter, or a parenthesized expression), and '$\cdot$' is more binding than '$+$'. The '$\cdot$' is always omitted. For example, $a + ba^*$ stands for $(a + (b \cdot (a)^*))$, and $(a + ba)^*a$ stands for $(((a + (b \cdot a)))^* \cdot a)$. Whenever there are two or more consecutive '$\cdot$', the parentheses are associated to the left, and the same is true for '$+$'. For example, aba stands for $((a \cdot b) \cdot a)$, and $a^*(aa + bb)^*b$ stands for $(((a)^* \cdot (((a \cdot a) + (b \cdot b)))^*) \cdot b)$.

EXAMPLE 1-1
Consider the following regular expressions over $\Sigma = \{a, b\}$.

R	$\tilde{R}$
ba^*	All words over Σ beginning with a b followed only by a's.
$a^*ba^*ba^*$	All words over Σ containing exactly two b's.
$(a + b)^*$	All words over Σ.
$(a + b)^*(aa + bb)(a + b)^*$	All words over Σ containing two consecutive a's or two consecutive b's.

$[aa + bb + (ab + ba)(aa + bb)^* (ab + ba)]^*$	All words over Σ containing an even number of a's and an even number of b's.
$(b + abb)^*$	All words over Σ in which every a is immediately followed by at least two b's.

□

From the definition of regular expressions, it is straightforward that *a set is regular over Σ if and only if it can be expressed by a regular expression over Σ*. Note that a regular set may be described by more than one regular expression. For example, the set of all words over $\Sigma = \{a, b\}$ with alternating a's and b's (starting and ending with b) can be described by the expression $b(ab)^*$ as well as by $(ba)^*b$. *Two regular expressions R_1 and R_2 over Σ are said to be equivalent (notation: $R_1 = R_2$) if and only if $\tilde{R}_1 = \tilde{R}_2$*; thus, $b(ab)^*$ and $(ba)^*b$ are equivalent. Later in this section we shall describe an algorithm to determine whether or not two given regular expressions are equivalent. In certain cases, the equivalence of two regular expressions can be shown by the use of known identities. Some of the more interesting identities are listed below. For simplicity, we let $R_1 \subseteq R_2$ stand for $\tilde{R}_1 \subseteq \tilde{R}_2$ and $w \in R$ stand for $w \in \tilde{R}$.

For any regular expressions R, S, and T over Σ:

1. $R + S = S + R, \quad R + \phi = \phi + R, \quad R + R = R,$
   $(R + S) + T = R + (S + T).$
2. $R\Lambda = \Lambda R = R, \quad R\phi = \phi R = \phi, \quad (RS)T = R(ST)$
   Note that generally $RS \neq SR$.
3. $R(S + T) = RS + RT, \quad (S + T)R = SR + TR.$
4. $R^* = R^*R^* = (R^*)^* = (\Lambda + R)^*, \quad \phi^* = \Lambda^* = \Lambda.$
5. $R^* = \Lambda + R + R^2 + \ldots + R^k + R^{k+1}R^* \; (k \geq 0)$
   special case: $R^* = \Lambda + RR^*$.
6. $(R + S)^* = (R^* + S^*)^* = (R^*S^*)^* = (R^*S)^*R^* = R^*(SR^*)^*$
   Note that generally $(R + S)^* \neq R^* + S^*$.
7. $R^*R = RR^*, \quad R(SR)^* = (RS)^*R.$
8. $(R^*S)^* = \Lambda + (R + S)^*S, \quad (RS^*)^* = \Lambda + R(R + S)^*.$

9. (*Arden rule*) Suppose $\Lambda \notin S$; then†

$$R = SR + T \quad \text{if and only if} \quad R = S^*T$$

$$R = RS + T \quad \text{if and only if} \quad R = TS^*$$

Most of these identities can be proved by a general technique which is sometimes called *proof by reparsing*. Let us illustrate the technique by proving that $R(SR)^* = (RS)^*R$ (identity 7). Consider any word $w \in R(SR)^*$ that is $w = r_0(s_1r_1)(s_2r_2) \ldots (s_nr_n)$ for some $n \geqq 0$, where each $r_i \in R$ and each $s_i \in S$. By reparsing the last expression (using the fact that concatenation is associative), we establish that $w = (r_0s_1)(r_1s_2) \ldots (r_{n-1}s_n)r_n$; therefore, $w \in (RS)^*R$. Since w is arbitrarily selected, this implies that $R(SR)^* \subseteq (RS)^*R$; similarly, we show $R(SR)^* \supseteq (RS)^*R$, and this establishes the identity.

Another common method for proving such identities is simply to use previously known identities. For example, $R = S^*T$ *implies* $R = SR + T$ (identity 9) since $R = S^*T \overset{(5)}{=} (\Lambda + SS^*)T \overset{(3)}{=} \Lambda T + SS^*T \overset{(2)}{=} T + SR \overset{(1)}{=} SR + T$.

Finally let us prove that *if* $\Lambda \notin S$ *and* $R = SR + T$, *then* $R = S^*T$. We note first that if $R = SR + T$ and we repeatedly replace R by $SR + T$, we obtain (after using identities 2 and 3 above)

$$R = SR + T = S^2R + (ST + T) = S^3R + (S^2T + ST + T) = \cdots$$
$$= S^{k+1}R + (S^kT + S^{k-1}T + \cdots + ST + T) \qquad \text{for } k \geqq 0$$

First we show that $R \subseteq S^*T$. Let $x \in R$ and suppose $|x| = l$.‡ Then we consider the equality $R = S^{l+1}R + (S^lT + S^{l-1}T + \cdots + ST + T)$. Since $\Lambda \notin S$, every word in $S^{l+1}R$ must have at least $l + 1$ symbols; therefore $x \notin S^{l+1}R$. But since $x \in R$, it follows that $x \in (S^lT + S^{l-1}T + \ldots + ST + T)$; therefore, $x \in S^*T$. To show that $S^*T \subseteq R$, we let $x \in S^*T$. Then there must exist $i \geqq 0$ such that $x \in S^iT$. However, the equality $R = S^{i+1}R + (S^iT + S^{i-1}T + \ldots + ST + T)$ implies that $R \supseteq S^iT$, therefore, $x \in R$.

† The condition $\Lambda \notin S$ is required in both cases only to show the implication from left to right.

‡ For any word x, $|x|$ indicates the number of symbols in x; in particular, $|\Lambda| = 0$. $|x|$ is sometimes called *the length of* x.

We shall now demonstrate the use of the above identities for proving equivalence of regular expressions.

EXAMPLE 1-2

We prove the following:

$$(b + aa^*b) + (b + aa^*b)(a + ba^*b)^*(a + ba^*b) = a^*b(a + ba^*b)^*$$

$$(b + aa^*b) + (b + aa^*b)(a + ba^*b)^*(a + ba^*b)$$
$$\overset{(3)}{=} (b + aa^*b)[\Lambda + (a + ba^*b)^*(a + ba^*b)]$$
$$\overset{(5)}{=} (b + aa^*b)(a + ba^*b)^*$$
$$\overset{(3)}{=} (\Lambda + aa^*)b(a + ba^*b)^*$$
$$\overset{(5)}{=} a^*b(a + ba^*b)^*$$

□

1-1.2 Finite Automata

A *finite automaton A over* Σ, where $\Sigma = \{\sigma_1, \sigma_2, \ldots, \sigma_n\}$, is a finite directed graph† in which every vertex has n arrows leading out from it, with each arrow labeled by a distinct σ_i $(1 \leq i \leq n)$. There is one vertex, labeled by a '$-$' sign, called the *initial vertex*, and a (possibly empty) set of vertices, labeled by a '$+$' sign, called the *final vertices* (the initial vertex may also be a final vertex). The vertices are sometimes called *states*.

For a word $w \in \Sigma^*$, a *w path* from vertex i to vertex j in A is a path from i to j such that the concatenation of the labels along this path form the word w. (Note that the path may intersect the same vertex more than once.) A word $w \in \Sigma^*$ is said to be *accepted* by the finite automaton A if the w path from the initial vertex leads to a final one. The empty word Λ is accepted by A if and only if the initial vertex is also final. The set of words accepted by a finite automaton A is denoted by $\tilde{A}$. Kleene's theorem (introduced in Sec. 1-1.4) implies that *a set is regular over* Σ *if and only if it is accepted by some finite automaton over* Σ.

† A *finite directed graph* consists of a finite set of elements (called *vertices*) and a finite set of ordered pairs (v, v') of vertices (called *arrows*). An arrow (v, v') is expressed as (v)→(v'). A finite sequence of (not necessarily distinct) vertices $v_1, v_2, \ldots, v_k$ is said to be a *path from* v_1 *to* v_k if each ordered pair (v_i, v_{i+1}), $1 \leq i < k$, is an arrow of the graph.

EXAMPLE 1-3

Consider the following finite automata over $\Sigma = \{a, b\}$. We use the notation that an arrow of the form ○ —a, b→ ○ stands for the two arrows

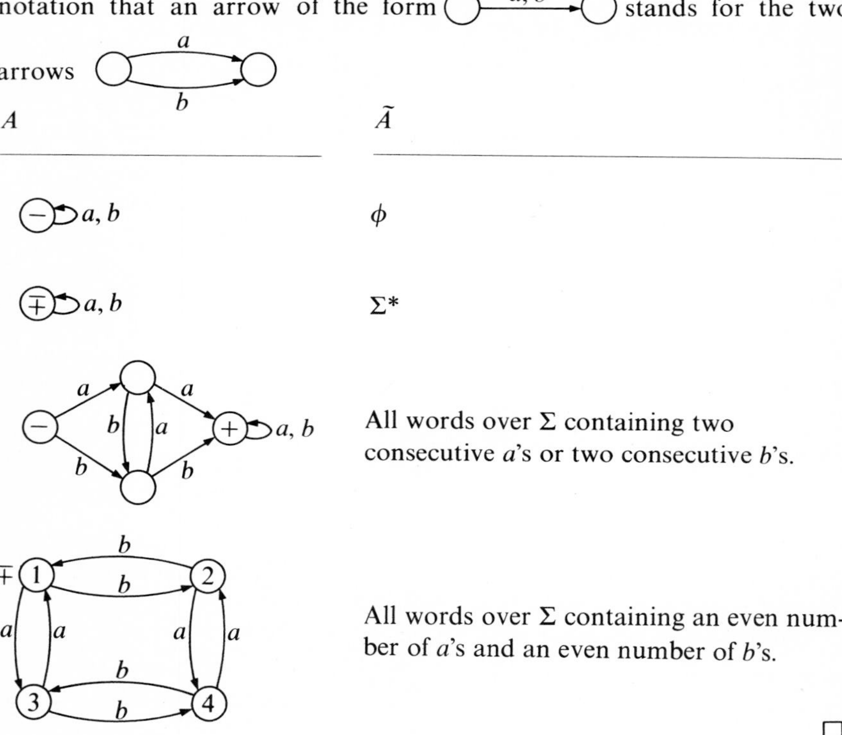

□

How do we know that the above $\tilde{A}$'s are correct? One possible way for giving an informal proof of $\tilde{A}$ is by associating with each vertex i a set S_i of all words w for which the w path from the initial vertex leads to i. Our choice of S_i's is validated by comparing each S_i with the S_j's of all vertices j leading by a single arrow to i. The union of all the S_i's for the final vertices is $\tilde{A}$. For example, the appropriate set of S_i's for the last automaton in Example 1-3 is

S_1: All words with an even number of a's and an even number of b's
S_2: All words with an even number of a's and an odd number of b's
S_3: All words with an odd number of a's and an even number of b's
S_4: All words with an odd number of a's and an odd number of b's

We can use the fact that every regular set is acceptable by some finite automaton to prove that certain sets are not regular. For example, we show that $\{a^n b^n | n \geq 0\}$ *is not a regular set over* $\Sigma = \{a, b\}$. For suppose it is a regular set; then there must exist a finite automaton A such that $\tilde{A} = \{a^n b^n | n \geqq 0\}$. Let us assume that A has N states, $N > 0$. Consider the word $a^N b^N$. Since the word is accepted by A and its length is greater than the number of vertices in A, it follows that there must exist in A at least one loop of a's or at least one loop of b's†, which enables A to accept the word $a^N b^N$. Suppose it is a loop of a's of length k, where $k > 0$. Then since we can go through the loop i times for any $i \geqq 0$, it follows that A must also accept all words of the form $a^{N+ik} b^N$ (for $i \geqq 0$), which contradicts the fact that $\tilde{A} = \{a^n b^n | n \geqq 0\}$.

1-1.3 Transition Graphs

We shall now introduce a generalization of the notion of finite automata, called *transition graphs*, by which it is much more convenient to express regular sets. We show, however, that although the class of finite automata is a proper subclass of the class of transition graphs, every regular set that is accepted by a transition graph is also accepted by some finite automaton.

A *transition graph T over Σ* is a finite directed graph in which every arrow is labeled by some word $w \in \Sigma^*$ (possibly the empty word Λ). There is at least one vertex, labeled by a '$-$' sign (such vertices are called *initial vertices*), and a (possibly empty) set of vertices, labeled by a '$+$' sign (called the *final vertices*). A vertex can be both initial and final.

For a word $w \in \Sigma^*$, a *w path* from vertex i to vertex j in T is a finite path from i to j such that the concatenation of the labels on the arrows along this path form the word w (ignoring the Λ's, if any). A word $w \in \Sigma^*$ is said to be *accepted* by a transition graph T if there exists a w path from an initial vertex to a final one. The empty word Λ is accepted by T if there is a vertex in T which is both initial and final or if a Λ path leads from an initial vertex to a final one. The set of words accepted by a transition graph T is denoted by $\tilde{T}$. Kleene's theorem (introduced in Sec. 1-1.4) implies that *a set is regular over Σ if and only if it is accepted by some transition graph over Σ.*

Note that every finite automaton is a transition graph, but not vice versa. One of the key differences between the two is that a finite automaton is *deterministic* in the sense that for every word $w \in \Sigma^*$ and vertex i there is a unique w path leading from i. On the other hand, a transition graph is *nondeterministic* because it may have more than one w path leading from i (or none at all).

† A loop of σ's, where $\sigma \in \Sigma$, is a path in which the first vertex is identical to the last one and such that all its arrows are labeled by σ.

EXAMPLE 1-4

Consider the following transition graphs over $\Sigma = \{a, b\}$.

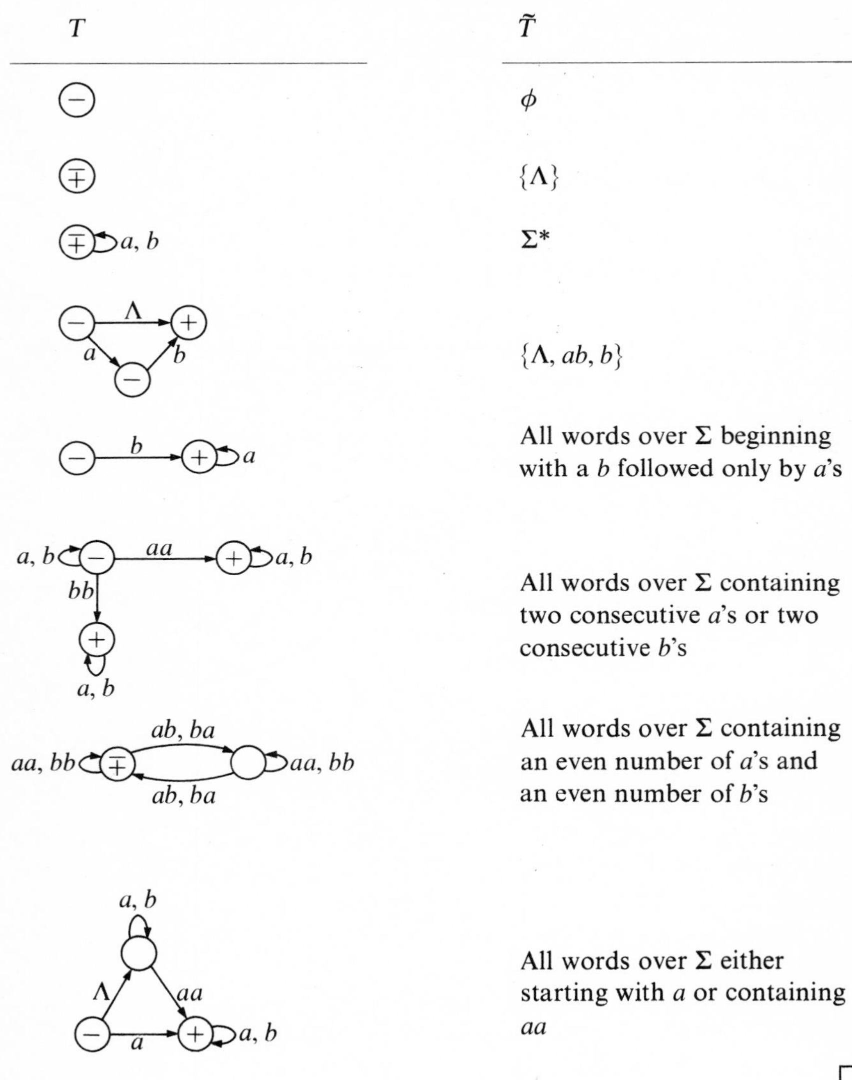

T
T̃
a, b
φ
{Λ}
Σ*
Λ
a
b
{Λ, ab, b}
b
a
All words over Σ beginning with a b followed only by a's
a, b
aa
a, b
bb
a, b
All words over Σ containing two consecutive a's or two consecutive b's
ab, ba
aa, bb
aa, bb
ab, ba
All words over Σ containing an even number of a's and an even number of b's
a, b
Λ
aa
a
a, b
All words over Σ either starting with a or containing aa

□

1-1.4 Kleene's Theorem

THEOREM 1-1 (Kleene). (1) *For every transition graph T over Σ there exists a regular expression R over Σ such that $\tilde{R} = \tilde{T}$*; (2) *for every regular expression R over Σ there exists a finite automaton A over Σ such that $\tilde{A} = \tilde{R}$.*

Because every finite automaton is a transition graph, it follows from the theorem that: (1) a set is regular over Σ if and only if it is accepted by some finite automaton over Σ, and (2) a set is regular over Σ if and only if it is accepted by some transition graph over Σ.

Proof (part 1). We describe briefly an algorithm for constructing for a given transition graph T a regular expression R such that $\tilde{R} = \tilde{T}$. For the purpose of this proof, we introduce the notion of a *generalized transition graph*, which is a transition graph in which the arrows may be labeled by regular expressions rather than just by words.

First, add to the given transition graph T a new vertex, called x, and Λ arrows leading from x to all the initial vertices of T. Similarly, add another new vertex, called y, and Λ arrows leading from all the final vertices of T to y. Let x be the only initial vertex in the modified transition graph, and y the only final vertex.

We now proceed step by step and eliminate all vertices of T until only the new vertices x and y are left. During the elimination process, the arrows and their labels are modified. The arrows may be labeled by regular expressions, i.e., we construct generalized transition graphs. The generalized transition graph which is constructed after each step still accepts the same set of words as the original T. The process terminates when we obtain a generalized transition graph with only two vertices, x and y, of the form:

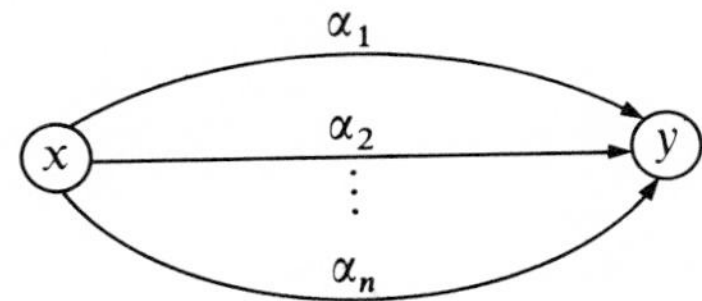

Then $\alpha_1 + \alpha_2 + \cdots + \alpha_n$ is the desired regular expression R.

The elimination process is straightforward. Suppose, for example, we want to eliminate vertex 3 in a generalized transition graph, where the arrows leading to and from vertex 3 are of the form

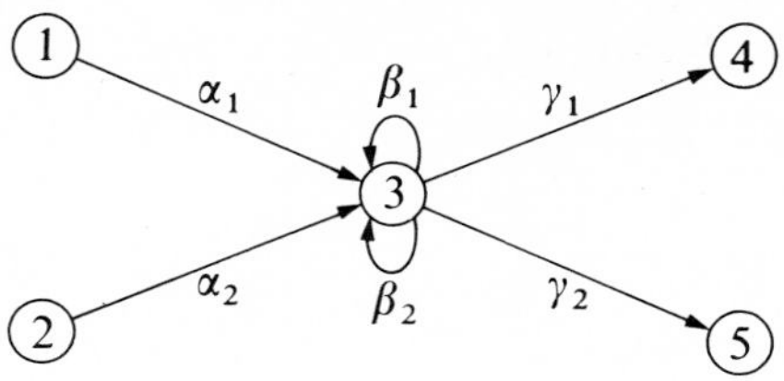

($\alpha_1, \alpha_2, \beta_1, \beta_2, \gamma_1$, and γ_2 are regular expressions.) To eliminate vertex 3 from the generalized transition graph, we replace that part by

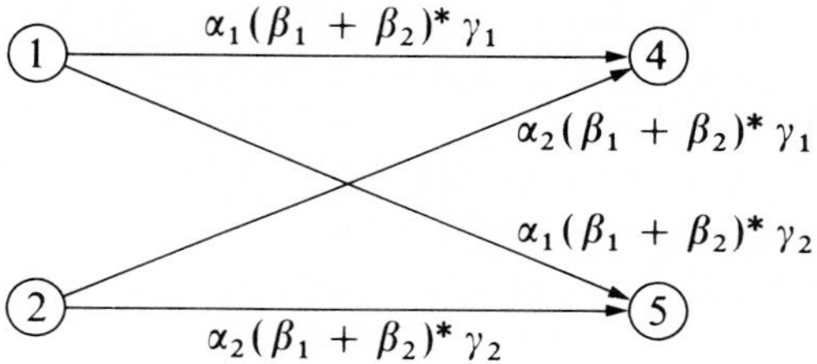

In the special case that vertices 1 and 4 are identical, we shall actually get

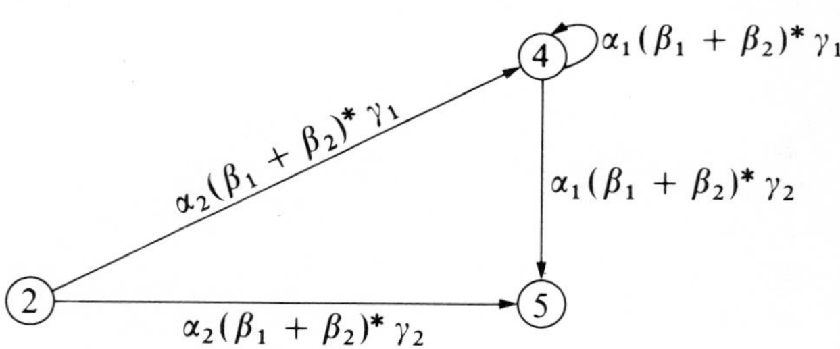

Let us illustrate the process before proceeding with the proof of part 2 of Theorem 1-1.

EXAMPLE 1-5

Consider the following transition graph T_0, which accepts the set of all words over $\Sigma = \{a, b\}$ with an even number of a's and an even number of b's.

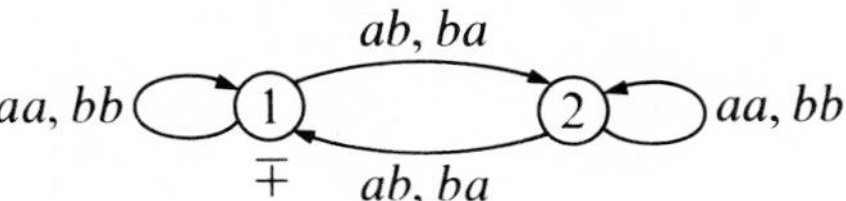

First we add the new vertices x and y. Since vertex 1 is both an initial and a final vertex of T_0, we add an Λ arrow leading from x to 1 and an Λ arrow leading from 1 to y. The corresponding generalized transition graph is

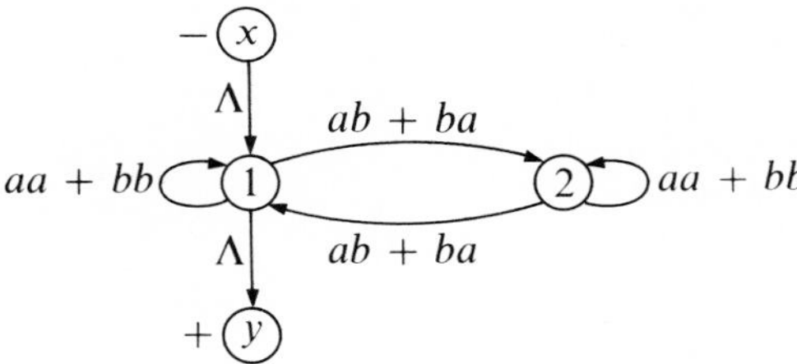

Eliminating vertex 2, we obtain

$-x$

Λ

$aa + bb$ (1) $(ab + ba)(aa + bb)^*(ab + ba)$

Λ

$+y$

Finally, eliminating vertex 1, we obtain

$-x$

$[aa + bb + (ab + ba)(aa + bb)^*(ab + ba)]^*$

$+y$

Thus the desired regular expression R_0 (that is, $\tilde{R}_0 = \tilde{T}_0$) is

$$[aa + bb + (ab + ba)(aa + bb)^*(ab + ba)]^*.$$

□

Proof (part 2) We now describe briefly an algorithm (known as the *subset method*) for constructing for a given regular expression R a finite automaton A such that $\tilde{A} = \tilde{R}$. We proceed in three steps.

Step 1. First we construct a transition graph T such that $\tilde{T} = \tilde{R}$. We start with a generalized transition graph of the form

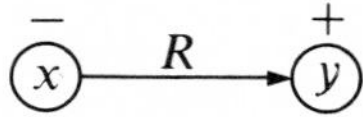

We successively split R by adding new vertices and arrows, until all arrows are labeled just by letters or Λ. The following rules are used:

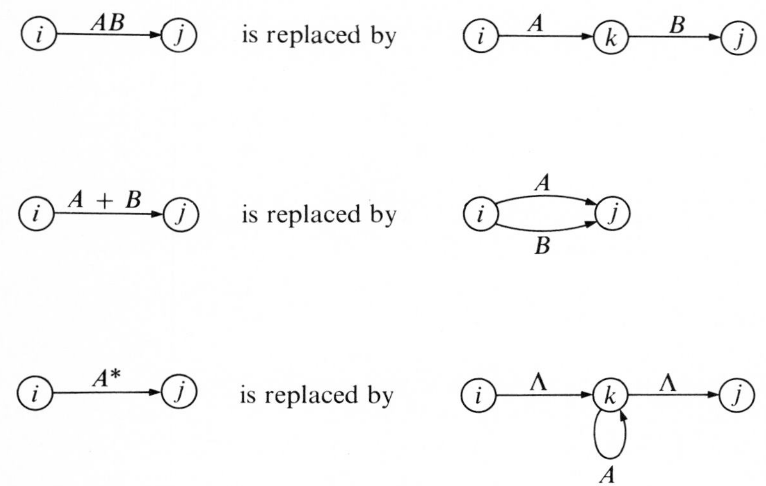

Note that in the final transition graph, x is still the only initial vertex and y is the only final vertex. In practice, often an appropriate simple transition graph can be constructed in a straightforward way without using the above inductive steps.

Step 2. Let T be the transition graph generated in Step 1. Now we construct the *transition table* of T; for simplicity we assume that $\Sigma = \{a, b\}$.

Let M be any subset of vertices of T. For any word $w \in \Sigma^*$ we define M_w to be the subset of all vertices of T reachable by a w path from some vertex of M. For example, M_{ab} consists of all vertices of T reachable by an ab path from some vertex of M, or, equivalently, all vertices of T reachable by a b path from some vertex of M_a.

The transition table of T consists of three columns. The elements of the table are subsets of vertices of T (possibly the empty set). The subset in the upper-left-hand corner of the table (first row, column 1) is $\{x\}_\Lambda$, that is, the subset which consists of the initial vertex x and all vertices of T reachable by a Λ path from x. In general, for any row of the table, if the subset M is in column 1, then we add M_a (that is, the set of vertices of T reachable by an a path from some vertex of M) in column 2 and M_b (that is, the set of vertices of T reachable by a b path from some vertex of M) in column 3. If M_a does not occur previously in column 1, we place it in column 1 of the next row and repeat the process. We treat M_b similarly.

The process is terminated when there are no new subsets in columns 2 and 3 of the table that do not occur in column 1. The process must always terminate because all subsets in column 1 are distinct and there are only finitely many distinct subsets of the finite set of vertices of T.

Step 3. Finally we use the transition table to construct the desired finite automaton A. The finite automaton A is constructed as follows. For every subset M in column 1 of the table there corresponds a vertex $\overline{M}$ in A. From every vertex $\overline{M}$ in A there is an a arrow leading to vertex $\overline{M}_a$ and a b arrow leading to vertex $\overline{M}_b$. The vertex $\overline{\{x\}}_\Lambda$ (that is, the vertex corresponding to the subset in the upper-left-hand corner of the table) is the only initial vertex of A. A vertex $\overline{M}$ of A is final if and only if M contains a final vertex of T.

We leave it to the reader to verify that a word $w \in \Sigma^*$ is accepted by T if and only if it is accepted by A. The following example illustrates the method.

EXAMPLE 1-6

Consider the regular expression R

$$(a + b)^* (aa + bb)(a + b)^*$$

which describes the set of all words over $\Sigma = \{a, b\}$ containing either two consecutive a's or two consecutive b's. We proceed to construct a finite automaton A that will accept the same set of words.

Step 1. The corresponding transition graph T is constructed as follows:

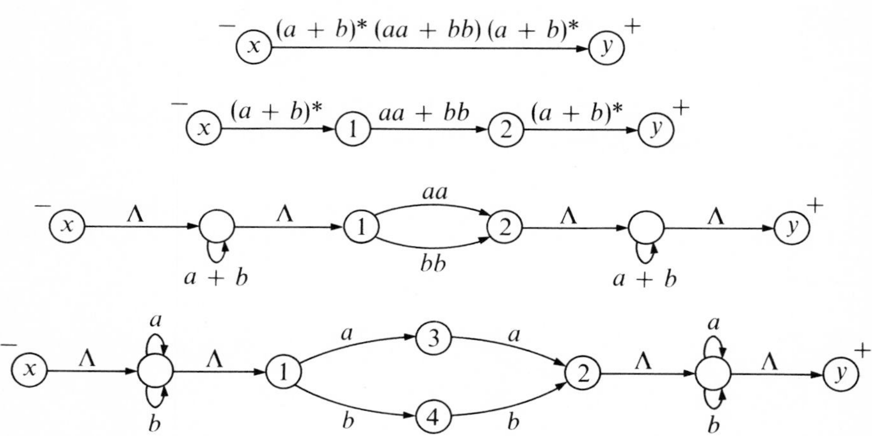

This is the desired transition graph. Clearly it can be simplified to

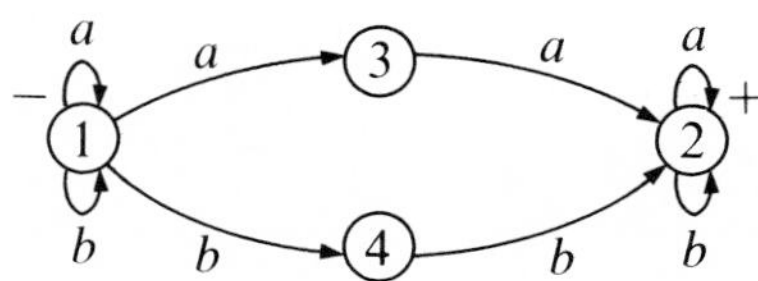

Step 2. The corresponding transition table is

M	M_a	M_b
$\{1\}$	$\{1, 3\}$	$\{1, 4\}$
$\{1, 3\}$	$\{1, 3, 2\}$	$\{1, 4\}$
$\{1, 4\}$	$\{1, 3\}$	$\{1, 4, 2\}$
$\{1, 3, 2\}$	$\{1, 3, 2\}$	$\{1, 4, 2\}$
$\{1, 4, 2\}$	$\{1, 3, 2\}$	$\{1, 4, 2\}$

Step 3. The desired finite automaton A is

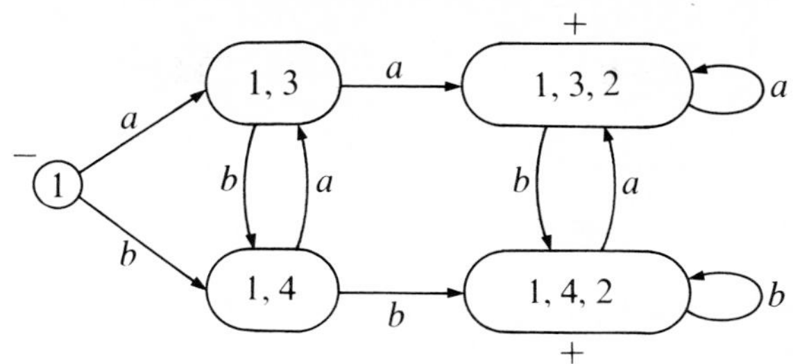

Note that it is possible to simplify the finite automaton to obtain

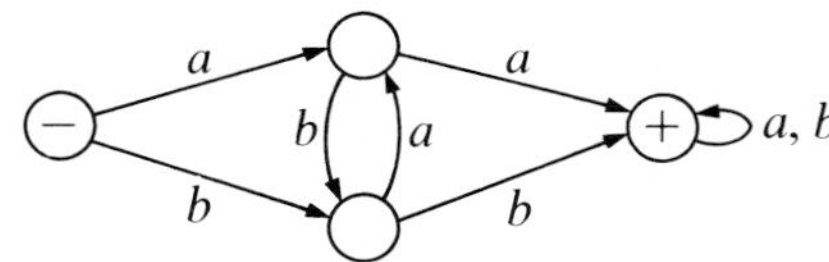

□

1-1.5 The Equivalence Theorem

We shall conclude this section with an important theorem.

THEOREM 1-2 (Moore). *There is an algorithm to determine whether or not two finite automata A and A' over Σ are equivalent (that is, $\tilde{A} = \tilde{A}'$).*

Proof. Given two finite automata A and A' over Σ. Suppose for simplicity that $\Sigma = \{a, b\}$. First we rename the vertices of A and A' so that all vertices are distinct. Let x and x' be the initial vertices of A and A', respectively.

To decide whether or not A and A' are equivalent, we construct a *comparison table* which consists of three columns. The elements of the table are pairs of vertices (v, v'), where v is a vertex of A and v' is a vertex of A'. The pair in the upper-left-hand corner of the table (first row, column 1) is (x, x'). In general, for any row of the table, if the pair (v, v') is in column 1, then we add in column 2 the pair of vertices (v_a, v'_a), where the a arrow from v leads to v_a in A and the a arrow from v' leads to v'_a in A'. Similarly, in column 3 we add the pair of vertices (v_b, v'_b), where the b arrow from v leads to v_b in A and the b arrow from v' leads to v'_b in A'. If (v_a, v'_a) does not occur previously in column 1, we place it in column 1 of the next row and repeat the process; we treat (v_b, v'_b) similarly.

If we reach a pair (v, v') in the table for which v is a final vertex of A and v' is a nonfinal vertex of A' or vice versa, we stop the process: *A and A' are not equivalent.* Otherwise, the process is terminated when there are no new pairs in columns 2 and 3 of the table that do not occur in column 1.

In this case *A and A′ are equivalent*. We leave it to the reader to verify these claims. The process must always terminate because all pairs in column 1 are distinct pairs and there are only finitely many distinct pairs of the vertices of A and A'.

Q.E.D.

EXAMPLE 1-7

1. Consider the following two finite automata A and A' over $\Sigma = \{a, b\}$ described in Fig. 1-1.

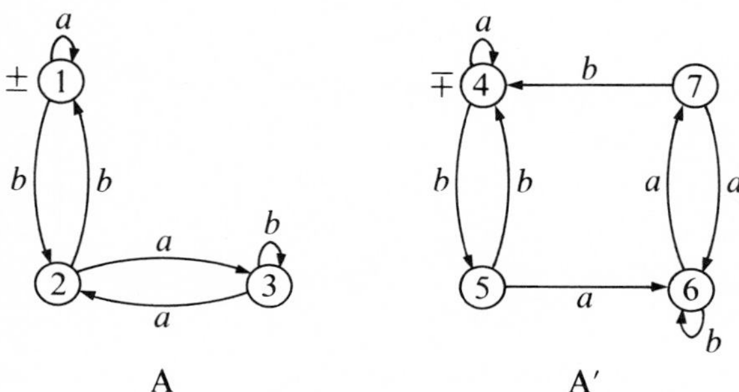

Figure 1-1 The finite automata A and A'.

They are equivalent because the corresponding comparison table is

(v, v')	(v_a, v'_a)	(v_b, v'_b)
(1, 4)	(1, 4)	(2, 5)
(2, 5)	(3, 6)	(1, 4)
(3, 6)	(2, 7)	(3, 6)
(2, 7)	(3, 6)	(1, 4)

There are no pairs in columns 2 and 3 that do not occur in column 1.

2. Consider the two finite automata B and B' described in Fig. 1-2.

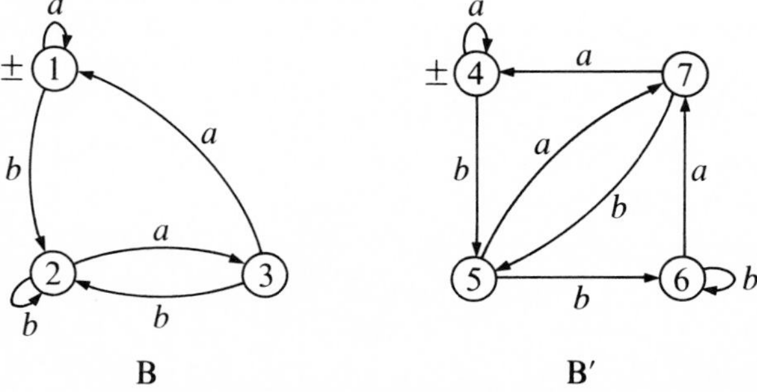

Figure 1-2 The finite automata B and B'.

They are equivalent because the corresponding comparison table is

(v, v')	(v_a, v'_a)	(v_b, v'_b)
(1, 4)	(1, 4)	(2, 5)
(2, 5)	(3, 7)	(2, 6)
(3, 7)	(1, 4)	(2, 5)
(2, 6)	(3, 7)	(2, 6)

Again, there are no pairs in columns 2 and 3 that do not occur in column 1.

3. Consider the two finite automata A and B' described in Fig. 1-3.

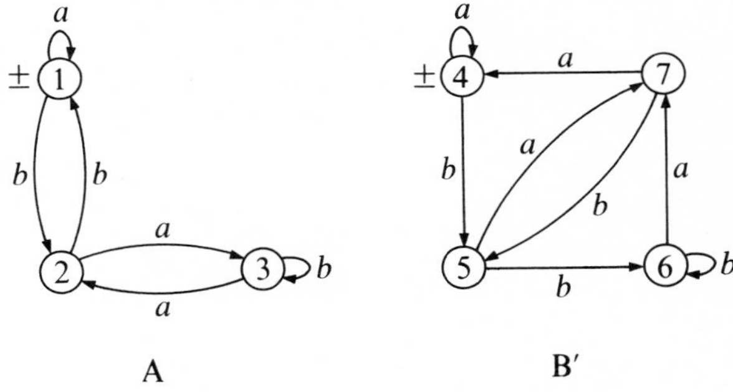

Figure 1-3 The finite automata A and B'.

They are *not* equivalent because the corresponding comparison table is

(v, v')	(v_a, v'_a)	(v_b, v'_b)
(1, 4)	(1, 4)	(2, 5)
(2, 5)	(3, 7)	<u>(1, 6)</u>

Note that 1 is a final vertex of A while 6 is a nonfinal vertex of B'. Since this pair was obtained by applying the letter b twice, the table actually shows us, not only that A and B' are not equivalent, but also that an appropriate counterexample is the word bb.

It can be shown that A accepts the set of all words which are the binary representation of natural numbers divisible by 3, where a stands for 0 and b stands for 1. (Such numbers with leading 0's on the left are also accepted.) The corresponding sets S_1, S_2, and S_3 contain all words representing binary numbers which, after division by 3, yield remainders 0, 1, and 2, respectively. The automaton B' accepts the set of all words which are the binary representation of natural numbers divisible by 4. The corresponding sets S_4, S_5, S_6, and S_7 contain all words representing binary numbers which, after division by 4, yield remainders 0, 1, 3, and 2, respectively.

□

1-2 TURING MACHINES

In this section we define three classes of machines over a given alphabet Σ: *Turing machines*, *Post machines*, and *finite machines with pushdown stores*. Each of these machines can be applied to any word $w \in \Sigma^*$ as input. It can stop in two different ways—by accepting w or rejecting w—or it can loop forever. For such a machine M over Σ, we denote the set of all words over Σ accepted by M by $accept(M)$, the set of all words over Σ rejected by M by $reject(M)$, and the set of all words over Σ for which M loops by $loop(M)$. It is clear that for any given machine M over Σ, the three sets of words $accept(M)$, $reject(M)$, and $loop(M)$ are disjoint and that $accept(M) \cup reject(M) \cup loop(M) = \Sigma^*$.

Two such machines M_1 and M_2 over Σ are said to be *equivalent* if $accept(M_1) = accept(M_2)$ and, clearly, $reject(M_1) \cup loop(M_1) = reject(M_2) \cup loop(M_2)$. A class $\mathscr{M}_1$ of machines is said to have the *same power* as a class $\mathscr{M}_2$ of machines, $\mathscr{M}_1 = \mathscr{M}_2$, if for every machine in $\mathscr{M}_1$ there is an equivalent machine in $\mathscr{M}_2$, and vice versa. We also say that a class $\mathscr{M}_1$ of machines is *more powerful* than a class $\mathscr{M}_2$, $\mathscr{M}_1 > \mathscr{M}_2$, if for every machine in $\mathscr{M}_2$ there is an equivalent machine in $\mathscr{M}_1$, but not vice versa.

We shall show that the three classes of machines—Turing, Post and finite machines with two pushdown stores—have the same power. We finally emphasize that the introduction of a *nondeterministic mechanism* to these machines does not add anything to their power.

We make use of three basic functions defined over Σ^*:

head(x): gives the head (leftmost letter) of the word x

tail(x): gives the tail of the word x (that is, x with the leftmost letter removed)

$\sigma \cdot x$: concatenates the letter σ and the word x.

For example, if $\Sigma = \{a, b\}$, then $head(abb) = a$, $tail(abb) = bb$, and $a \cdot bb = abb$. We agree that $head(\Lambda) = tail(\Lambda) = \Lambda$. Note that by definition $head(\sigma) = \sigma$, $tail(\sigma) = \Lambda$, and $\sigma \cdot \Lambda = \sigma$ for all $\sigma \in \Sigma$.

For simplicity, we present most of the results for the alphabet $\Sigma = \{a, b\}$; however, all the results hold as well for any alphabet with two or more letters.†

† In this chapter we never discuss the special case of an alphabet consisting of a single letter.

1-2.1 Turing Machines

Specifications for Turing machines have been given in various ways in the literature. In our model, a *Turing machine M over an alphabet* Σ consists of three parts:

1. A *tape* which is divided into cells. The tape has a leftmost cell but is infinite to the right. Each cell of the tape holds exactly one tape symbol. The *tape symbols* include the letters of the given alphabet Σ, the letters of a finite auxiliary alphabet V, and the special blank symbol Δ. All symbols are distinct.

2. A *tape head* which scans one cell of the tape at a time. It can move; in each move the head prints a symbol on the tape cell scanned, replacing what was written there, and moves one cell left or right.

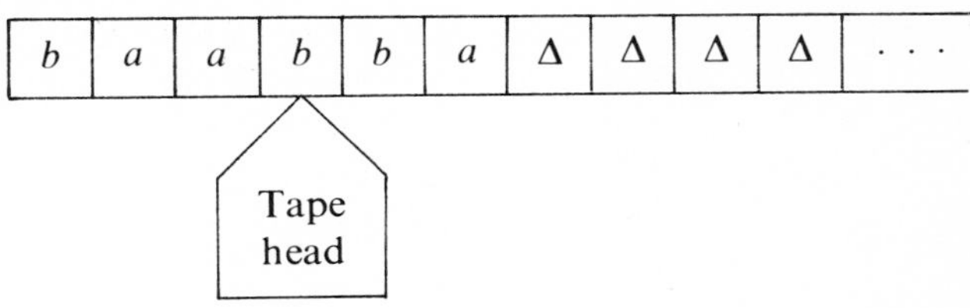

3. A *program* which is a finite directed graph (the vertices are called *states*). There is always one *start state*, denoted by START, and a (possibly empty) subset of *halt states*, denoted by HALT. Each arrow is of the form

$$(i) \xrightarrow{(\alpha,\, \beta,\, \gamma)} (j)$$

where $\alpha \in \Sigma \cup V \cup \{\Delta\}$, $\beta \in \Sigma \cup V \cup \{\Delta\}$, and $\gamma \in \{L, R\}$. This indicates that, if during a computation we are in vertex (state) i and the tape head scans the symbol α, then we proceed to vertex (state) j while the tape head prints the symbol β in the scanned cell and then moves one cell left or right, depending whether γ is L or R. All arrows leading from the same vertex i must have distinct α's.

Initially, the given input word w over Σ is on the left-hand side of the tape, where the remaining infinity of cells hold the blank symbol Δ, and the tape head is scanning the leftmost cell. The execution proceeds as instructed by the program, beginning with the START state. If we eventually reach a HALT state, the computation is halted and we say that the input word w is *accepted* by the Turing machine. If we reach a state i of the form

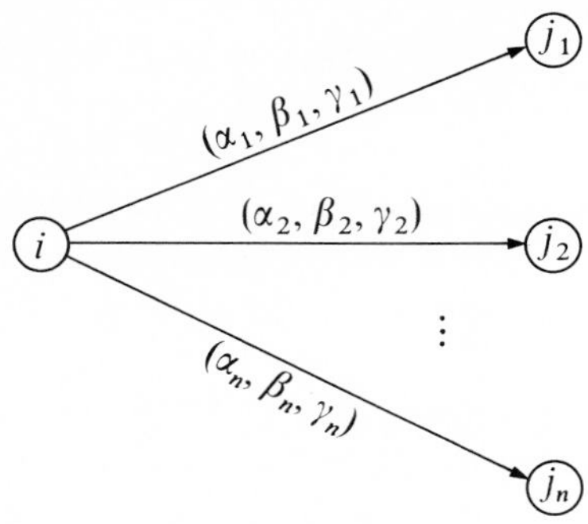

where the symbol scanned by the tape head is different from $\alpha_1, \alpha_2, \ldots,$ and α_n, there is no way to proceed with the computation. In this case therefore, the computation is halted and we say that the input word w is *rejected* by the Turing machine. The other case where the computation is halted and the input word is said to be *rejected* by the Turing machine is when the tape head scans the leftmost cell and is instructed to do a left move.

EXAMPLE 1-8

The Turing machine M_1 over $\Sigma = \{a, b\}$ (shown in Fig. 1-4) accepts every word of the form a^nb^n, $n \geqq 0$, and rejects all other words over Σ; that is, $accept(M_1) = \{a^nb^n | n \geqq 0\}$, $reject(M_1) = \Sigma^* - accept(M_1)$, and $loop(M_1) = \phi$. Here $V = \{A, B\}$. [Note that the specification of β and γ in (Δ, Δ, R) are irrelevant for the performance of this program.]

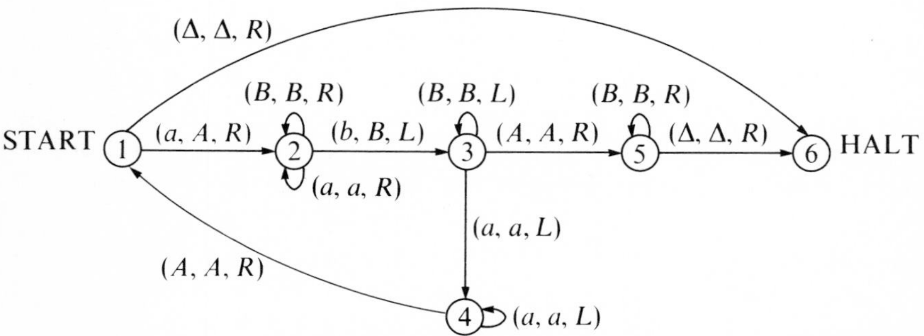

Figure 1-4 The Turing machine M_1 that accepts $\{a^nb^n | n \geqq 0\}$.

Starting from state 1, we move right. The leftmost occurrence of a is replaced by A, and then the leftmost occurrence of b is replaced by B; from state 3 we go back to the new leftmost occurrence of a and start again with state 1. This loop is repeated n times. When we reach state 5, all n a's have been replaced by A's and the leftmost n b's by B's. If the symbol to the right of the nth B is Δ (blank), the input word is accepted.

The following sequence illustrates how the Turing machine acts with input $aabb$:

$$\overset{\textcircled{1}}{\underset{\uparrow}{a}abb\Delta} \xRightarrow{(a,\,A,\,R)} \overset{\textcircled{2}}{A\underset{\uparrow}{a}bb\Delta} \xRightarrow{(a,\,a,\,R)} \overset{\textcircled{2}}{Aa\underset{\uparrow}{b}b\Delta} \xRightarrow{(b,\,B,\,L)} \overset{\textcircled{3}}{A\underset{\uparrow}{a}Bb\Delta} \xRightarrow{(a,\,a,\,L)}$$

$$\overset{\textcircled{4}}{\underset{\uparrow}{A}aBb\Delta} \xRightarrow{(A,\,A,\,R)} \overset{\textcircled{1}}{A\underset{\uparrow}{a}Bb\Delta} \xRightarrow{(a,\,A,\,R)} \overset{\textcircled{2}}{AA\underset{\uparrow}{B}b\Delta} \xRightarrow{(B,\,B,\,R)} \overset{\textcircled{2}}{AAB\underset{\uparrow}{b}\Delta} \xRightarrow{(b,\,B,\,L)}$$

$$\overset{\textcircled{3}}{AA\underset{\uparrow}{B}B\Delta} \xRightarrow{(B,\,B,\,L)} \overset{\textcircled{3}}{A\underset{\uparrow}{A}BB\Delta} \xRightarrow{(A,\,A,\,R)} \overset{\textcircled{5}}{AA\underset{\uparrow}{B}B\Delta} \xRightarrow{(B,\,B,\,R)} \overset{\textcircled{5}}{AAB\underset{\uparrow}{B}\Delta} \xRightarrow{(B,\,B,\,R)} \overset{\textcircled{5}}{AABB\underset{\uparrow}{\Delta}}$$

Here, a string of the form $A\underset{\uparrow}{a}Bb\Delta$ indicates the tape (ignoring the infinite sequence of blanks to the right), and the arrow indicates the current symbol scanned by the tape head. A labeled arrow such as $\xRightarrow{(a,A,R)}$ indicates which instruction of the program is performed, and a circled number such as $\textcircled{1}$ indicates the current state.

Note that the above argument justifies only that every word of the form $a^n b^n$ is acceptable by M_1. The other direction must be justified separately, that is, that every word acceptable by M_1 must be of the form $a^n b^n$.

□

1-2.2 Post Machines

A *Post machine M over* $\Sigma = \{a, b\}$ is a *flow-diagram*† with one variable x, which may have as a value any word over $\{a, b, \#\}$, where $\#$ is a special auxiliary symbol. Each statement in the flow-diagram has one of the following forms:

1. START statement (exactly one)

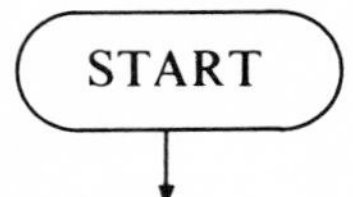

2. HALT statements

3. TEST statement

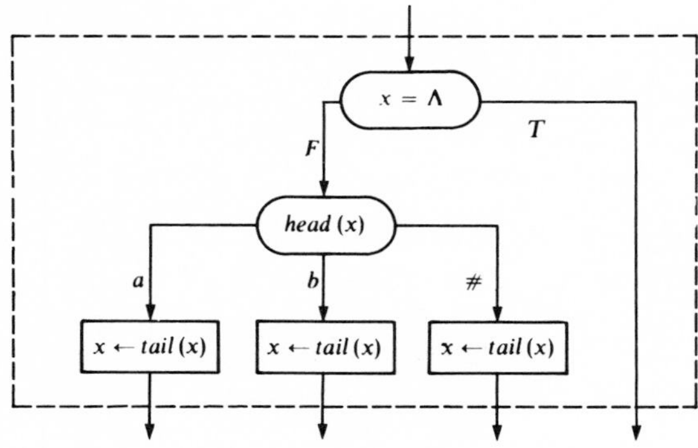

or in short‡

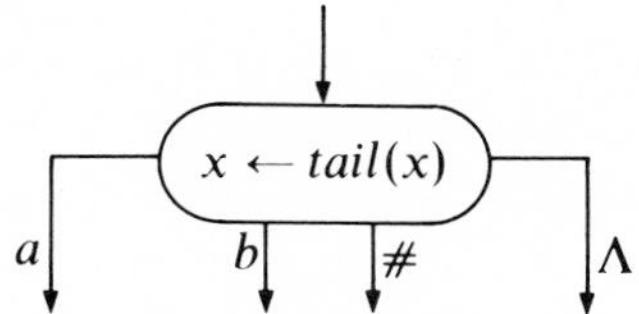

4. ASSIGNMENT statements

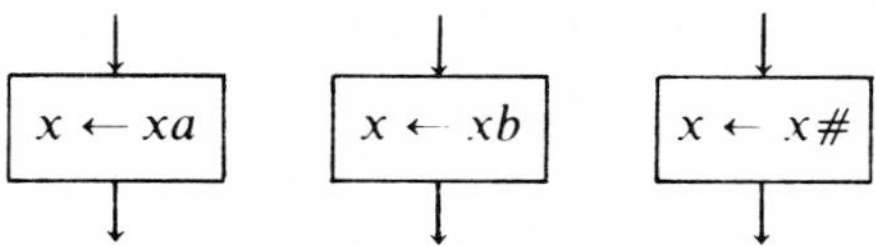

† A *flow-diagram* is a finite directed graph in which each vertex consists of a statement. We always allow the *JOIN statement* for combining two or more arrows into a single one.

‡Note that for a general n-letter alphabet $\Sigma = \{\sigma_1, \sigma_2, \ldots, \sigma_n\}$, a TEST statement would have $n + 2$ exits labeled by $\sigma_1, \sigma_2, \ldots, \sigma_n, \#, \Lambda$.

Thus the TEST statement checks the leftmost letter of x, $head(x)$, and deletes it after making the decision. The only ASSIGNMENT statements allowed are to concatenate a letter (a, b, or #) to the right of x.

A word w over Σ is said to be *accepted/rejected* by a Post machine M if the computation of M starting with input $x = w$ eventually reaches an ACCEPT/REJECT halt.

EXAMPLE 1-9

The Post machine M_2 over $\Sigma = \{a, b\}$ described in Fig. 1-5 accepts every word over Σ of the form $a^n b^n$, $n \geqq 0$, and rejects all other words over Σ; that is, $accept(M_2) = \{a^n b^n | n \geqq 0\}$, $reject(M_2) = \Sigma^* - accept(M_2)$, and $loop(M_2) = \phi$.

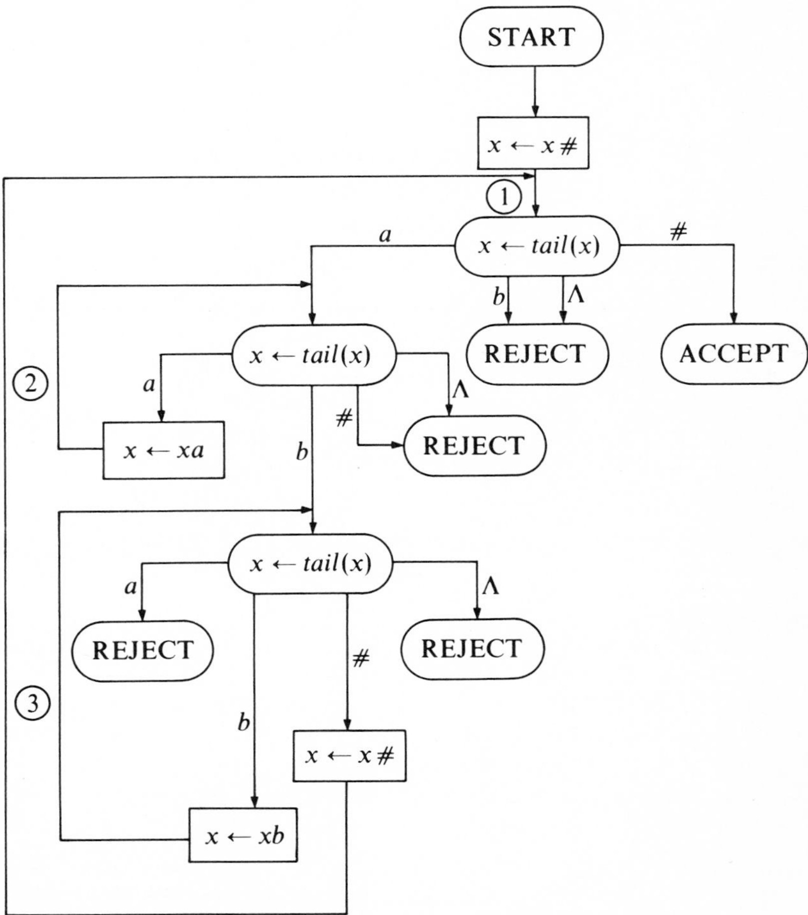

Figure 1-5 The Post Machine M_2 that accepts $\{a^n b^n | n \geqq 0\}$.

Suppose $x = a^n b^n$ for some $n \geqq 0$. The key point is that whenever we reach point 1, we have the word $a^i b^i\#$ in x, $0 \leqq i \leqq n$. Now if we find an a on the left of x, we go $i - 1$ times around loop 2 until we obtain $b^i \# a^{i-1}$; then we go $i - 1$ times around loop 3 until we obtain $\# a^{i-1} b^{i-1}$; finally we move the $\#$ symbol to obtain $a^{i-1} b^{i-1}\#$ and repeat the process from point 1. Note that there is only one ACCEPT statement, which corresponds to the case that we reach point 1 with only $\#$ in x (that is, $i = 0$).

□

EXAMPLE 1-10

Consider the Post machine M_3 over $\Sigma = \{a, b\}$ shown in Fig. 1-6. Here

$accept(M_3) = \{$all words over Σ with the same number of a's and b's$\}$
$reject(M_3) = \{$all words over Σ where the difference between the number of a's and b's is 1$\}$
$loop(M_3) = \{$all words over Σ where the difference between the number of a's and b's is more than 1$\}$

For example, $ab \in accept(M_3)$, $aba \in reject(M_3)$, while $aaba \in loop(M_3)$.

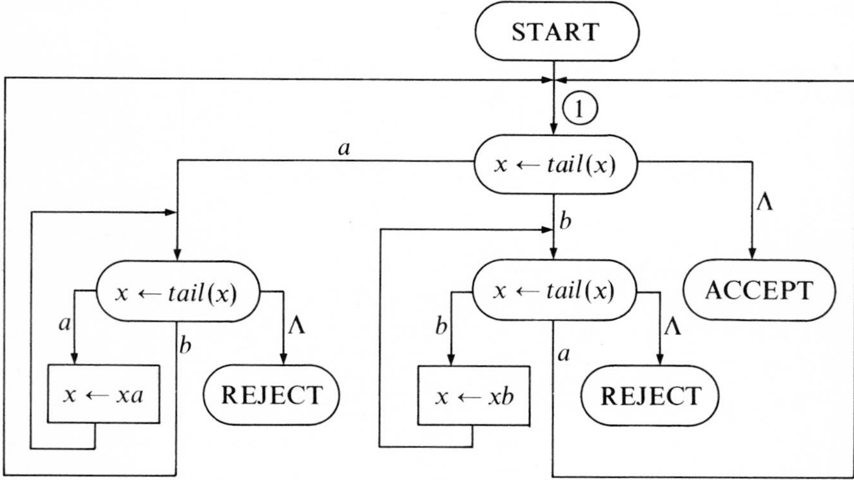

Figure 1-6 The Post machine M_3 that accepts all words with the same number of a's and b's.

Note that we have not used the special symbol $\#$, and therefore we ignored the $\#$ exit from the tests. The main test is at point 1: if $head(x) = a$, then we keep searching for a letter b to be eliminated, while if $head(x) = b$, then we keep searching for a letter a.

□

THEOREM 1-3 (Post) *The class of Post machines over Σ has the same power as the class of Turing machines over Σ.*

That is, for every Post machine over Σ there is an equivalent Turing machine over Σ and vice versa.

Proof. First we show that every Turing machine over $\Sigma = \{a, b\}$ can be simulated by an equivalent Post machine over $\Sigma = \{a, b\}$. The main idea behind this simulation is that the contents of the tape and the position of the tape head at any stage of the computation of the Turing machine are expressed as values of the variable x in the Post machine.

For example, if at some stage of the computation of the Turing machine the tape is of the form

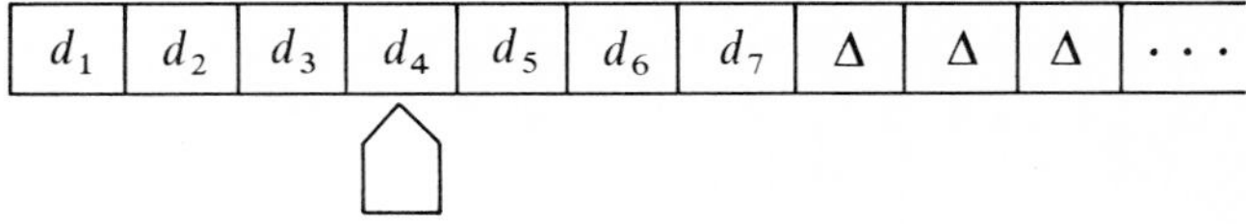

where each $d_i \in \Sigma \cup V \cup \{\Delta\}$ and the tape head scans the symbol d_4, then this situation is expressed in the Post machine by

$$x = d_4 d_5 d_6 d_7 \# d_1 d_2 d_3$$

In other words, the infinite string of Δ's is ignored and the string $d_1 d_2 \ldots d_7$ is rotated in such a way that the leftmost symbol of x is the one scanned by the tape head of the Turing machine. The special symbol $\#$ is used to indicate the *breakpoint* of the string. Now, suppose we have $x = d_4 d_5 d_6 d_7 \# d_1 d_2 d_3$ and the next move of the Turing machine is (d_4, β, R); then the contents of x are changed by the Post machine to

$$x = d_5 d_6 d_7 \# d_1 d_2 d_3 \beta$$

If $x = d_4 d_5 d_6 d_7 \# d_1 d_2 d_3$ and the next move of the Turing machine is (d_4, β, L) then the contents of x are changed to

$$x = d_3 \beta d_5 d_6 d_7 \# d_1 d_2$$

However, there are two important special cases: The first case occurs when we have $x = d_7 \# d_1 d_2 \ldots d_6$ and the next move of the Turing machine is (d_7, β, R); then we have to change x by the Post machine to $x = \# d_1 d_2 \ldots d_6 \beta$ ($\#$ is the leftmost symbol of x). This means that the next symbol to be scanned by the tape head of the Turing machine is the first Δ (blank) to the right of d_7. Therefore in this case we change the value of x to $x = \Delta \# d_1 d_2 \ldots d_6 \beta$. The second case occurs when we reach a situation where $x = d_1 d_2 \ldots d_7 \#$ ($\#$ is the rightmost symbol of x) and the next move of the Turing machine is (d_1, β, L). This case happens when the tape head of the Turing machine scans the leftmost symbol of the tape and we are instructed to make a left move. Therefore, in this case we shall go to a *REJECT* halt in the Post machine.

Note that the Post machine obtained is over $\Sigma \cup V \cup \{\Delta\}$ rather than just over Σ. We can overcome this difficulty by using a standard encoding technique: If there are l symbols in $\Sigma \cup V \cup \{\Delta\}$, where $2^{n-1} < l \leqq 2^n$, then each one of these symbols is encoded as a word of length n over $\Sigma = \{a, b\}$. For example, if $\Sigma \cup V \cup \{\Delta\} = \{a', b', A, B, C, D, \Delta\}$, then each one of these symbols is encoded as a word of three a's and b's: $a' = aaa$, $b' = aab$, $A = aba$, $B = abb$, $C = baa$, $D = bab$, and $\Delta = bba$. Now, rather than looking, for example, for A as the leftmost letter of x, we shall look for the string aba on the left of x; similarly, rather than adding the letter A to the right of x, we shall add the string aba; and so forth.

The translation for any given Post machine over $\Sigma = \{a, b\}$ into an equivalent Turing machine over $\Sigma = \{a, b\}$ is much simpler. The current value of x during the computation of the Post machine, say, $x = d_1 d_2 d_3 d_4 \# d_5 d_6$, is expressed in the tape of the Turing machine as

$$\Delta\Delta \ldots \Delta d_1 d_2 d_3 d_4 \# d_5 d_6 \Delta\Delta \ldots$$

The two main operations of the Turing machine are either replacing d_1 by Δ (*deleting the leftmost symbol of* x) or replacing the Δ to the right of d_6 by a new letter (*adding a letter to the right of* x).†

Q.E.D.

† Note that the input word $w = \sigma_1 \sigma_2 \ldots \sigma_k$ must be stored initially in the tape of the Turing machine with an additional Δ to the left, that is, $\Delta \sigma_1 \sigma_2 \ldots \sigma_k$. This is necessary in order to be able to reach σ_1 by left moves without encountering a *REJECT* halt.

1-2.3 Finite Machines with Pushdown Stores

A *finite machine M over* $\Sigma = \{a, b\}$ is a flow-diagram with one variable x in which each statement is of one of the following forms. (The variable x may have as value any word over $\{a, b\}$.)

1. START statement (exactly one)

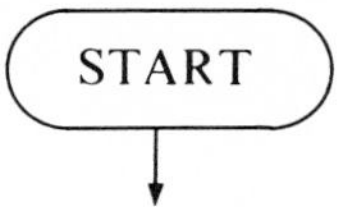

2. HALT statements

3. TEST statement

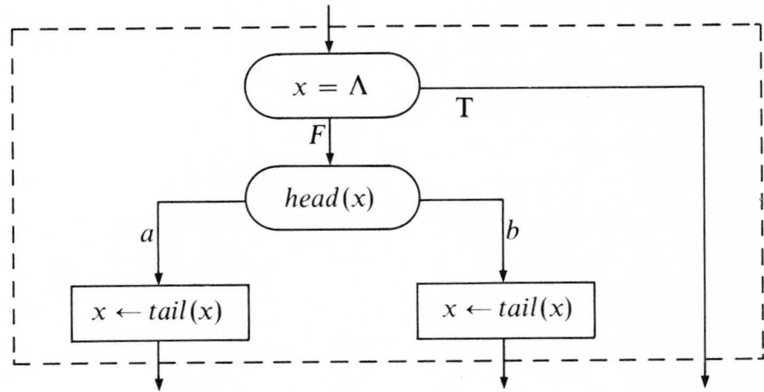

or for short

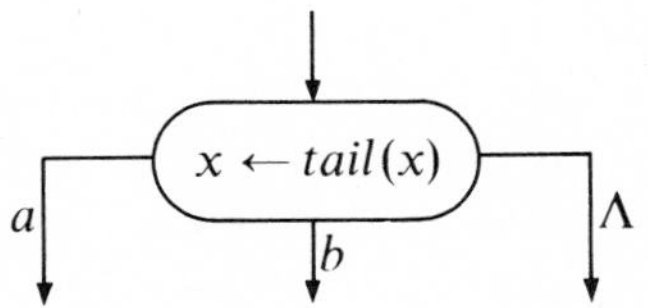

A variable y_i is said to be a *pushdown store over* $\Sigma = \{a, b\}$ if all the operations applied to y_i are of the form

1. TEST y_i

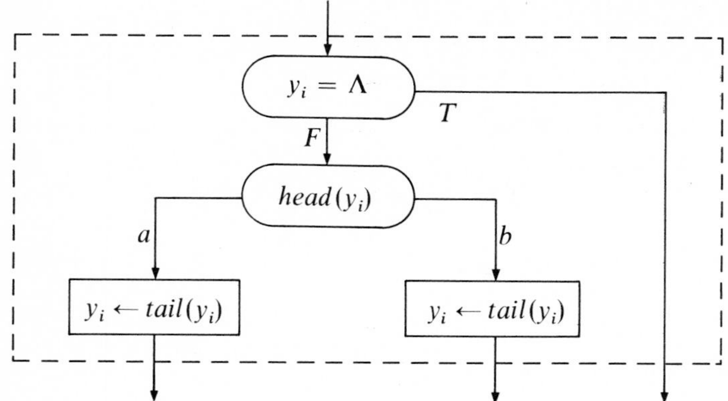

or for short

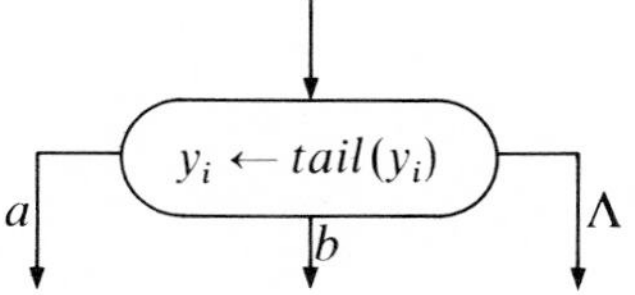

2. ASSIGN TO y_i

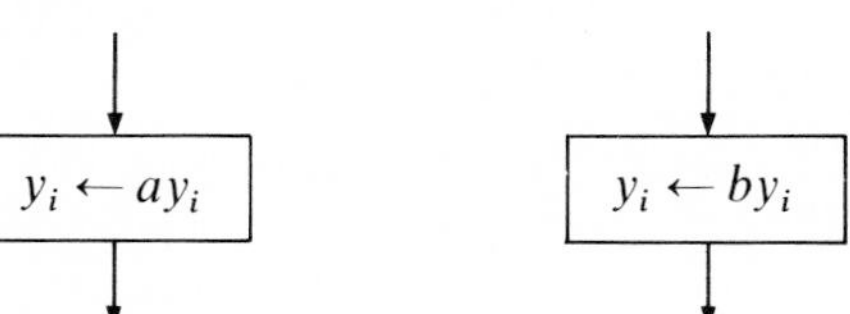

Although the Post machines seem to be very "similar" to the finite machines with one pushdown store, there is a vast difference between the two. In a Post machine, not only may we read and erase letters on the left of x, but also we may write new letters on the *right* of x. Thus, in a Post machine, as the ends of x undergo modification, the information in x circulates slowly from right to left. In a pushdown store we may write only on the *left* of y_i. Thus, while a pushdown store manipulates the string in y_i in a "last-in–first-out" manner, a Post machine manipulates the string in x in a "first-in–first-out" manner.

A word w over Σ is said to be *accepted/rejected* by a finite machine M (with or without pushdown stores) over Σ if the computation of M starting with input $x = w$ eventually reaches an ACCEPT/REJECT halt. All the pushdown stores are assumed to contain the empty word Λ initially.

EXAMPLE 1-11

The finite machine M_4 with one pushdown store y, described in Fig. 1-7, accepts every word over Σ of the form $a^n b^n$, $n \geqq 0$, and rejects all other words over Σ; that is, $accept(M_4) = \{a^n b^n | n \geqq 0\}$, and $reject(M_4) = \Sigma^* - accept(M_4)$.

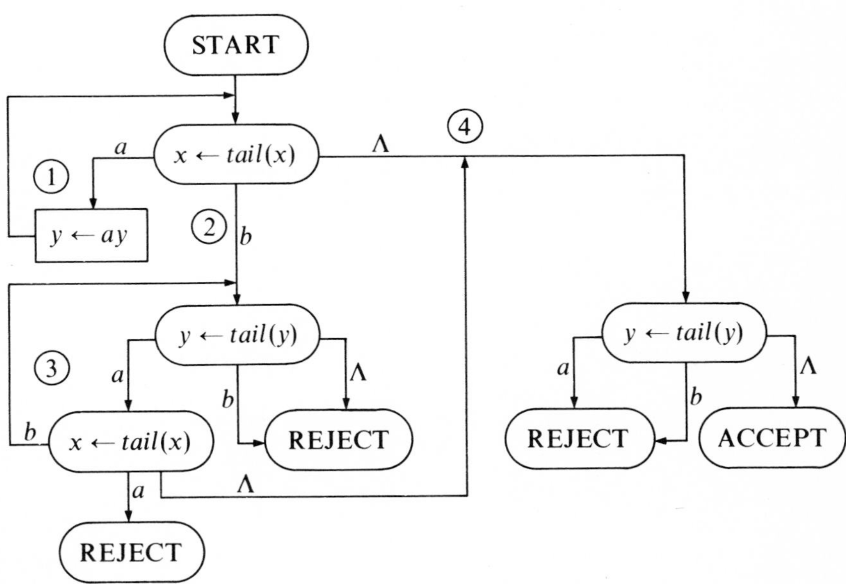

Figure 1-7 The finite machine M_4 with one pushdown store that accepts $\{a^n b^n | n \geqq 0\}$.

Suppose that $x = a^n b^n$. First we move the a's from x to y so that at point 2, a^n is stored in y while b^{n-1} is still in x. Then in loop 3 we eliminate the a's from y and the b's from x, comparing their numbers, until both x and y are empty at point 4.

□

EXAMPLE 1-12

The finite machine M_5 with two pushdown stores y_1 and y_2, described in Fig. 1-8, accepts every word of Σ of the form $a^n b^n a^n$, $n \geqq 0$, and rejects all other words over Σ; that is, $accept(M_5) = \{a^n b^n a^n | n \geqq 0\}$, and $reject(M_5) = \Sigma^* - accept(M_5)$.

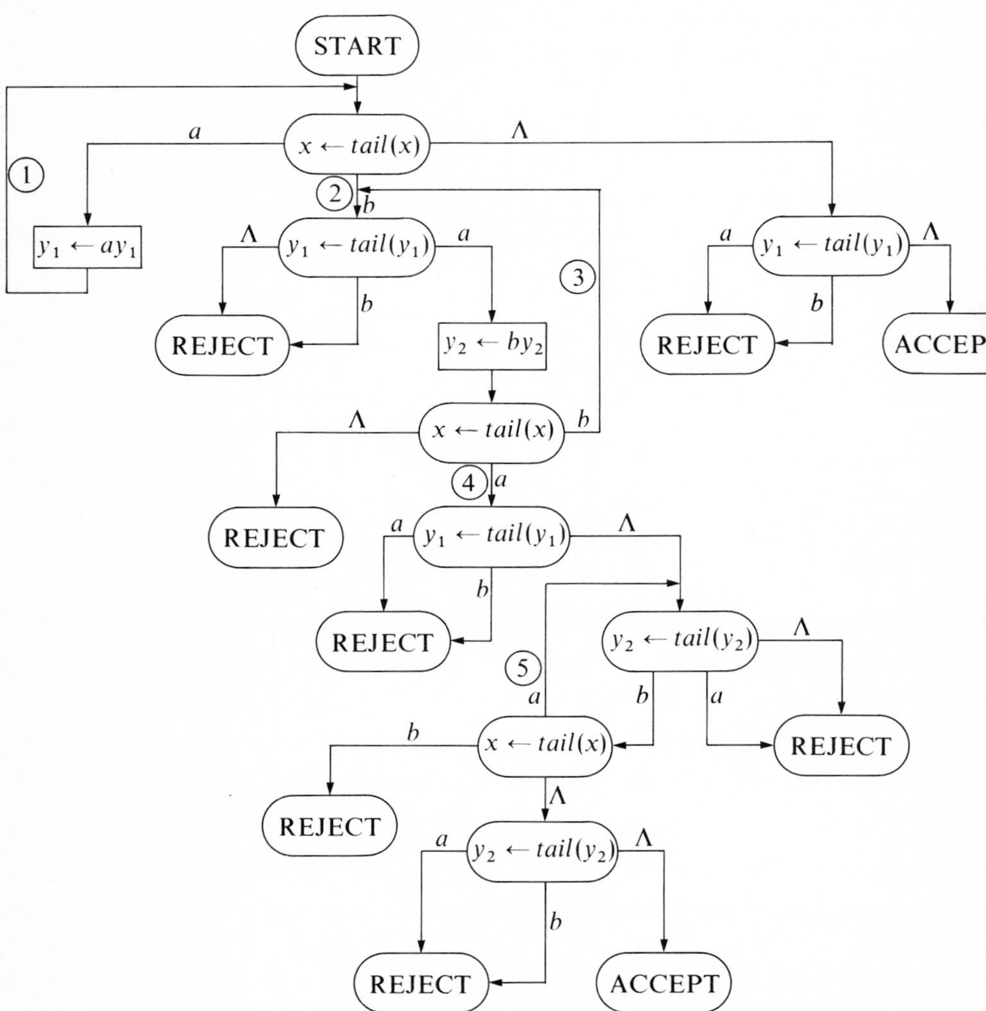

Figure 1-8 The finite machine M_5 with two pushdown stores that accepts $\{a^n b^n a^n | n \geqq 0\}$.

Suppose that $x = a^n b^n a^n$. First, in loop 1 we move the left a's from x to y_1 so that at point 2 we have a^n in y_1 and $b^{n-1}a^n$ in x. Then, in loop 3 we move the b's from x to y_2, comparing at the same time the number of a's in y_1 and the number of b's in x, so that at point 4 we have b^n in y_2 and a^{n-1} in x (y_1 is empty). Finally, in loop 5 we remove the b's from y_2 and the a's from x, comparing their numbers, until both x and y_2 are empty.

□

We are now interested in investigating whether or not the addition of pushdown stores really increases the power of the class of finite machines. We note that for a fixed alphabet Σ:

1. The class of finite machines (with no pushdown stores) has the same power as the class of finite automata introduced in Sec. 1-1.2. In other words, a set S over Σ is regular if and only if $S = accept(M)$ for some finite machine M over Σ with no pushdown stores.
2. The class of finite machines with one pushdown store is more powerful than the class of finite machines with no pushdown stores. For example, there is no finite machine over $\Sigma = \{a, b\}$ with no pushdown stores that is equivalent to the finite machine M_4 with one pushdown store described in Example 1-11.
3. The class of finite machines with two pushdown stores is more powerful than the class of finite machines with only one pushdown store. For example, there is no finite machine over $\Sigma = \{a, b\}$ with one pushdown store that is equivalent to the finite machine M_5 with two pushdown stores described in Example 1-12.
4. For $n \geqq 2$, the class of finite machines with n pushdown stores has exactly the same power as the class of finite machines with two pushdown stores.

It can be shown that the class of finite machines with two pushdown stores has exactly the same power as the class of Post machines, or equivalently, the class of Turing machines.

THEOREM 1-4 (Minsky). *The class of finite machines over Σ with two pushdown stores has the same power as the class of Turing machines over Σ.*

That is, for every finite machine over Σ with two pushdown stores, there is an equivalent Turing machine over Σ and vice versa.

Proof. For any given Turing machine over Σ, we can construct an equivalent finite machine over Σ with two pushdown stores y_1 and y_2. The finite machine simulates the operations of the Turing machine in such a way that at any stage of the computation y_1 has the contents of the tape to the left of the tape head (including the symbol being scanned) and y_2 has the contents of the tape to the right of the tape head (ignoring the infinite string of Δ's). For example, if the tape is

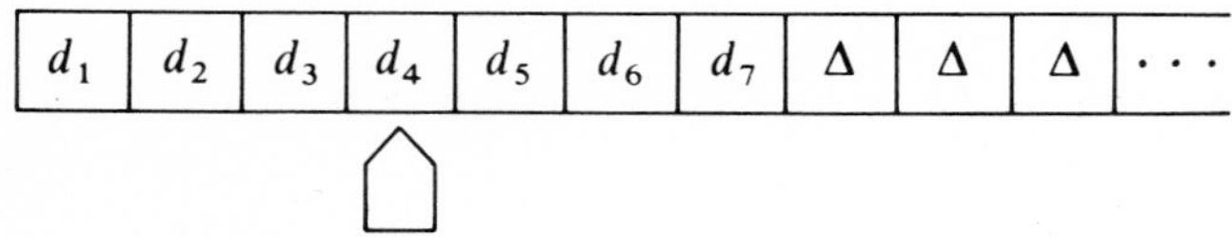

and the symbol being scanned is d_4, then

$$y_1 = d_4 d_3 d_2 d_1 \qquad \text{and} \qquad y_2 = d_5 d_6 d_7$$

Note that the left part of the tape is stored in y_1 in reverse order so that the symbol being scanned by the tape head is the leftmost symbol of y_1.

Now, we can simulate the moves of the Turing machine by modifying the leftmost symbols of y_1 and y_2. For example, if the next move of the Turing machine is (d_4, β, R), then the contents of y_1 and y_2 will be changed to

$$y_1 = d_5 \beta d_3 d_2 d_1 \qquad \text{and} \qquad y_2 = d_6 d_7$$

If, instead, the next move is (d_4, β, L), then the contents of y_1 and y_2 will be changed to

$$y_1 = d_3 d_2 d_1. \qquad \text{and} \qquad y_2 = d_5 d_6 d_7$$

As in the proof of Theorem 1-3, there are two special cases that should be treated separately: The first case occurs when the tape head reaches d_7 (that is, $y_2 = \Lambda$) and is instructed to make a right move; and the second case occurs when the tape head reaches d_1 (that is, $y_1 = d_1$) and is instructed to make a left move.

Conversely, for every finite machine over Σ with two pushdown stores we can construct an equivalent Turing machine over Σ. The current value of y_1 is stored in the odd cells and the current value of y_2 is stored in the even cells of the tape (or vice versa). If the input word w is of length k, say, $w = \sigma_1 \sigma_2 \ldots \sigma_k$, then the leftmost $k + 2$ cells of the tape are reserved to store the current value of x (with Δ on the left and the special symbol # on the right). For example, if the input word is $w = \sigma_1 \sigma_2 \sigma_3 \sigma_4 \sigma_5$ and at some stage of the computation of the finite machine we have

$$x = \sigma_3\sigma_4\sigma_5$$
$$y_1 = d_1d_2d_3d_4$$
$$y_2 = e_1e_2$$

then the corresponding tape in the Turing machine is

Δ	Δ	Δ	σ_3	σ_4	σ_5	#	d_1	e_1	d_2	e_2	d_3	Δ	d_4	Δ	Δ	Δ	⋯

Now, the operations on y_1 and y_2 of the finite machine are simulated by applying the corresponding operations on the even and odd cells of the tape to the right of #.

Q.E.D.

1-2.4 Nondeterminism

An important generalization of the notion of machines discussed above is obtained by considering nondeterministic machines. A *nondeterministic machine* is a machine which may have in its flow-diagram *choice branches* of the form

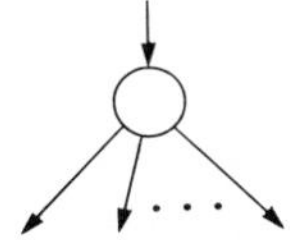

That is, whenever we reach upon computation such a choice branch, we may choose *arbitrarily* any one of the possible exits and proceed with the computation as usual. For Turing machines we introduce nondeterminism, not by using choice branches, but just by removing the restriction that "all arrows leading from the same state i must have distinct α's."

A word $w \in \Sigma^*$ is said to be *accepted* by a nondeterministic Turing machine, Post machine, or finite machine M (with or without pushdown stores) over Σ if *there exists* a computation of M starting with input $x = w$ which eventually reaches an ACCEPT halt. If w is not accepted but there is a computation leading to a REJECT halt, then w is said to be *rejected*; otherwise, $w \in loop(M)$.

EXAMPLE 1-13

The nondeterministic finite machine M_6 with one pushdown store y, described in Fig. 1-9, accepts every word over $\Sigma = \{a, b\}$ of the form ww^R, where w^R stands for the word w reversed, and rejects all other words over Σ; that is, $accept(M_6) = \{ww^R | w \in \{a, b\}^*\}$, and $reject(M_6) = \Sigma^* - accept(M_6)$. Thus, $accept(M_6)$ includes, for example, the words Λ, *aa*, *babbab*, *bbbabbabbb*, and so forth.

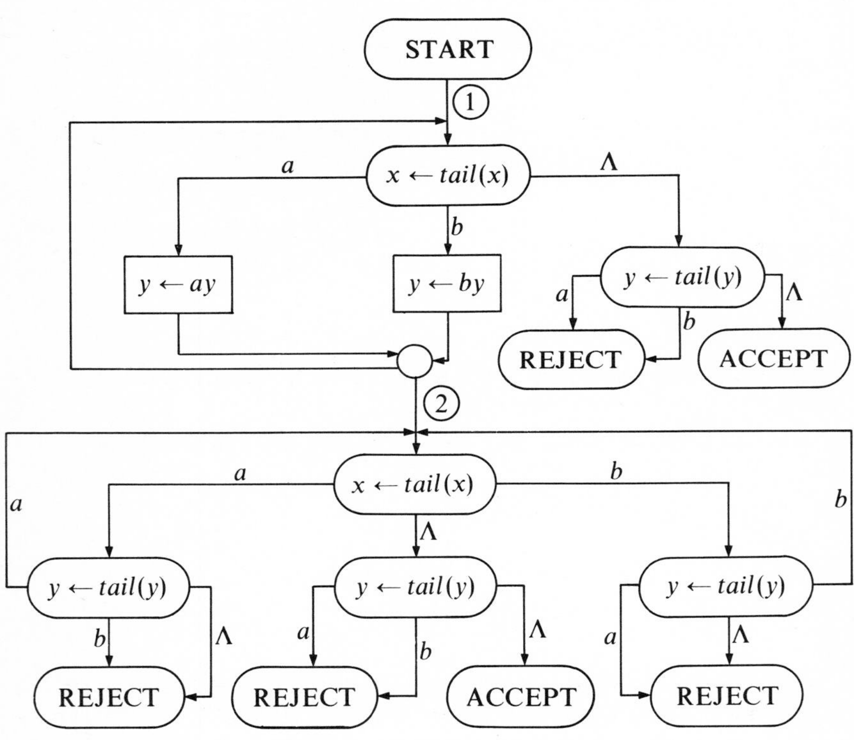

Figure 1-9 The nondeterministic finite machine M_6 that accepts $\{ww^R | w \in \{a, b\}^*\}$.

Suppose that $x = ww^R$. We begin to scan w at point 1 and scan w^R at point 2. However, there is one major difficulty: While we are scanning x from left to right, there is no way to recognize the *breakpoint*, i.e., the point when we finish scanning w and begin scanning w^R. We use a *choice branch* to overcome this difficulty. Whenever we reach the choice branch, we consider both cases at once: We may choose to go back to point 1 (that is, we are still scanning w), or we may choose to go to point 2 (that is, we are at the breakpoint) arbitrarily.

□

A natural question that may be asked is "Does the use of nondeterminism really increase the power of the class of machines?" It can be shown that *the classes of nondeterministic Turing machines, nondeterministic Post machines, and nondeterministic finite machines with two or more pushdown stores have the same power as the class of Turing machines.* The relation between the different classes of finite machines over the same alphabet Σ can be summarized as follows:

{Finite automata}
||
{Finite machines with no pushdown stores}
||
{Nondeterministic finite machines with no pushdown stores}
∧
{Finite machines with one pushdown store}
∧
{Nondeterministic finite machines with one pushdown store}
∧
{Finite machines with two pushdown stores}
||
{Nondeterministic finite machines with two pushdown stores}
||
{Turing machines}

Note the following:

1. There is no nondeterministic finite machine with no pushdown stores that is equivalent to the finite machine M_4 with one pushdown store (Example 1-11).

2. There is no finite machine with one pushdown store that is equivalent to the nondeterministic finite machine M_6 with one pushdown store (Example 1-13).

3. There is no nondeterministic finite machine with one pushdown store that is equivalent to the finite machine M_5 with two pushdown stores (Example 1-12).

1-3. TURING MACHINES AS ACCEPTORS

In this section we introduce two new classes of sets of words over an alphabet Σ: *recursively enumerable sets* and *recursive sets.* These are very rich classes of sets; actually, the intention is to have these classes rich enough to include exactly those sets of words over Σ which are partially acceptable or acceptable by any computing device. Since by Church's thesis, a Turing machine is the most general computing device, it is quite natural that we define the two classes by means of Turing machines.

We define a set S of words over Σ to be recursively enumerable if there is a Turing machine M over Σ which accepts every word in S and either rejects or loops for every word in $\Sigma^* - S$; that is, $accept(M) = S$, and $reject(M) \cup loop(M) = \Sigma^* - S$. However, the main drawback is that if we apply the machine to some word w in $\Sigma^* - S$, there is no guarantee as to how the machine will behave: It may reject w or loop forever. Therefore we also introduce the class of recursive sets, which is a proper subclass of the class of recursively enumerable sets.

We define a set S of words over Σ to be recursive if there is a Turing machine M over Σ which accepts every word in S and rejects every word in $\Sigma^* - S$; that is, $accept(M) = S$, $reject(M) = \Sigma^* - S$, and $loop(M) = \phi$. There is a very important relation between the class of recursively enumerable sets and the class of recursive sets: *a set S over Σ is recursive if and only if both S and $\Sigma^* - S$ are recursively enumerable.*

1-3.1 Recursively Enumerable Sets

Alternative definitions for a set S of words over Σ to be *recursively enumerable* are:

1. There is a Turing machine which accepts every word in S and either rejects or loops for every word in $\Sigma^* - S$.
2. There is a Post machine which accepts every word in S and either rejects or loops for every word in $\Sigma^* - S$.
3. There is a finite machine with two pushdown stores which accepts every word in S and either rejects or loops for every word in $\Sigma^* - S$.

EXAMPLE 1-14

Examples 1-8, 1-10, and 1-12 imply that the following sets of words over $\Sigma = \{a, b\}$ are recursively enumerable: $\{a^n b^n | n \geq 0\}$, {all words over Σ with the same number of a's and b's}, and $\{a^n b^n a^n | n \geq 0\}$.

□

Although the class of recursively enumerable sets is very rich, *there exist sets of words over* $\Sigma = \{a, b\}$ *that are not recursively enumerable.* We now demonstrate such a set of words. All words in $\{a, b\}^*$ can be ordered by the *natural lexicographic* order

$$\Lambda, a, b, aa, ab, ba, bb, aaa, aab, aba, abb, baa, bab, bba, bbb, aaaa, aaab, \ldots$$

that is, the words are ordered by length and lexicographically within each length. Thus it makes sense to talk about the jth string x_j in $\{a, b\}^*$. Every Turing machine over $\Sigma = \{a, b\}$ can be encoded (see Prob. 1-13) as a string in $\{a, b\}^*$ in such a way that each string in $\{a, b\}^*$ represents a Turing machine and vice versa. Therefore we can talk about the jth Turing machine T_j over $\Sigma = \{a, b\}$, that is, the one represented by the jth string in $\{a, b\}^*$,

Consider now the set

$$L_1 = \{x_j | x_j \text{ is not accepted by } T_j\}$$

Clearly, L_1 could not be accepted by any Turing machine. If it were, let T_j be a Turing machine accepting L_1. Then, by definition of L_1, $x_j \in L_1$ if and only if x_j is not accepted by T_j. But since T_j accepts L_1, we obtain the contradiction that x_j is accepted by T_j if and only if x_j is not accepted by T_j. Thus, there is no Turing machine accepting L_1; that is, L_1 *is not a recursively enumerable set.*

1-3.2 Recursive Sets

Alternative definitions for a set S of words over Σ to be *recursive* are:

1. There is a Turing machine which accepts every word in S and rejects every word in $\Sigma^* - S$.
2. There is a Post machine which accepts every word in S and rejects every word in $\Sigma^* - S$.
3. There is a finite machine with two pushdown stores which accepts every word in S and rejects every word in $\Sigma^* - S$.

EXAMPLE 1-15

Examples 1-8 and 1-12 imply that the following sets of words over $\Sigma = \{a, b\}$ are recursive: $\{a^n b^n | n \geqq 0\}$ and $\{a^n b^n a^n | n \geqq 0\}$.

□

The most important results regarding recursive sets are:

1. *If a set over* Σ *is recursive, then its complement* $\Sigma^* - S$ *is also recursive.*† If S is a recursive set over Σ, then there is a Post machine M which always halts and accepts all words in S and rejects all words in $\Sigma^* - S$. Construct a Post machine M' from M by interchanging the ACCEPT and REJECT halts. Clearly M' accepts all words in $\Sigma^* - S$ and rejects all words in S.

2. *A set* S *over* Σ *is recursive if and only if both* S *and* $\Sigma^* - S$ *are recursively enumerable.* (*a*) If S is recursive, then (by result 1 above) $\Sigma^* - S$ is recursive; and clearly if S and $\Sigma^* - S$ are recursive, then S and $\Sigma^* - S$ are recursively enumerable. (*b*) If S and $\Sigma^* - S$ are recursively enumerable, there must exist Turing machines M_1 and M_2 over Σ which accept S and $\Sigma^* - S$, respectively. M_1 and M_2 can be used to construct a new Turing machine M which simulates the computations of M_1 and M_2‡ in such a way that M accepts all words in S and rejects all words in $\Sigma^* - S$; that is, S is a recursive set. Note that the contents of the tape of M must be organized in such a way that at any given time it contains six pieces of information: the contents of the tapes of M_1 and M_2, the location of the tape heads of M_1 and M_2, and the current states of M_1 and M_2.

3. *The class of recursively enumerable sets over* Σ *properly includes the class of all recursive sets over* Σ. It is clear that every recursive set is recursively enumerable. We shall show that there exists a recursively enumerable set over Σ that is not recursive. For this purpose, let x_i denote the ith word in $\{a, b\}^*$ and T_i the ith Turing machine over $\Sigma = \{a, b\}$, and consider the set $L_2 = \{x_i | x_i \text{ is accepted by } T_i\}$. (*a*) L_2 is a recursively enumerable set because a Turing machine T can be constructed that will accept all words in L_2. For any given word $w \in \Sigma^*$, T will start to generate the words $x_1, x_2, x_3, \ldots$, and test each word generated until it finds the word $x_i = w$, thereby determining that w is the ith word in the enumeration. Then T generates T_i, the ith Turing machine, and simulates its operation. Therefore w is accepted by T if and only if $x_i = w$ is accepted by T_i. (*b*) L_2 is not a recursive set since $\Sigma^* - L_2 = L_1$ and L_1 is not recursively enumerable, as has been shown.

† However, there are recursively enumerable sets of words over Σ such that their complement is not recursively enumerable.

‡ The simulations of M_1 and M_2 are done "in parallel" (by applying alternately one move from each machine) so that neither requires the termination of the other in order to have its behavior completely simulated.

1-3.3 Formal Languages

A *type-0 grammar G over* Σ consists of the following:

1. A finite (nonempty) set V of distinct symbols (not in Σ), called *variables*, containing one distinguished symbol S, called the *start variable*.
2. A finite set P of *productions* in which each production is of the form

$$\alpha \to \beta \qquad \text{where } \alpha \in (V \cup \Sigma)^{+} \text{ and } \beta \in (V \cup \Sigma)^{*}\dagger$$

A word $w \in \Sigma^*$ is said to be *generated* by G if there is a finite sequence of words over $V \cup \Sigma$

$$w_0 \Rightarrow w_1 \Rightarrow w_2 \Rightarrow \cdots \Rightarrow w_n \qquad n \geqq 1$$

such that w_0 is the start variable S, $w_n = w$, and w_{i+1} is obtained from w_i, $0 \leqq i < n$, by replacing some occurrence of a substring α (which is the left-hand side of some production of P) in w_i by the corresponding β (which is the right-hand side of that production).‡ The set of all words generated by G is called the *language generated by G*.

EXAMPLE 1-16
Let $\Sigma = \{a, b\}$. Consider the grammar G_1 where $V = \{S\}$ and $P = \{S \to aSb, S \to ab\}$. By applying the first production $n - 1$ times followed by an application of the second production, we have

$$S \Rightarrow aSb \Rightarrow a^2Sb^2 \Rightarrow a^3Sb^3 \Rightarrow \cdots \Rightarrow a^{n-1}Sb^{n-1} \Rightarrow a^nb^n$$

It is clear that these are the only words generated by the grammar. Thus the language generated by the grammar G_1 is

$$\{a^nb^n | n \geqq 1\}$$

□

EXAMPLE 1-17
Let $\Sigma = \{a, b\}$. Consider the grammar G_2, where $V = \{A, B, S\}$ and P consists of six productions:

1 $S \to aSBA$
2 $S \to abA$
3 $AB \to BA$
4 $bB \to bb$
5 $bA \to ba$
6 $aA \to aa$

† $(V \cup \Sigma)^+$ stands for all words over $V \cup \Sigma$ except Λ (the empty word); that is, $(V \cup \Sigma)^+ = (V \cup \Sigma)^* - \{\Lambda\}$.

‡ α is a substring in w_i if and only if there exists words u, v (possibly empty) such that $u\alpha v = w_i$; w_{i+1} is then the word $u\beta v$.

The language generated by the grammar G_2 is

$$\{a^n b^n a^n | n \geqq 1\}$$

To obtain $a^n b^n a^n$, for some $n \geqq 1$, first we apply $n - 1$ times production 1 to obtain $a^{n-1}S(BA)^{n-1}$; then we use production 2 once to obtain $a^n bA(BA)^{n-1}$. Production 3 enables us to rearrange the B's and A's to obtain $a^n bB^{n-1}A^n$. Next we use $n - 1$ times production 4 to obtain $a^n b^n A^n$; then we use production 5 once to obtain $a^n b^n aA^{n-1}$. Finally, we use $n - 1$ times production 6 to obtain $a^n b^n a^n$.

Now, let us show that no other words over Σ can be generated by the grammar G_2. At the beginning we can apply only production 1 (and possibly production 3) until production 2 is applied the first time. At this point we have $a^n b$ followed by some string of n A's and $n - 1$ B's (in any order). (Now we can apply productions 3 to 6, but in each step it is always true that the left part of the word consists of a's and b's while the right part consists of A's and B's.) Next we must apply $n - 1$ times production 4 (and possibly production 3) to obtain the word $a^n b^n A^n$. The only other production we could possibly apply is production 5. However, in this case sooner or later we would have to eliminate aB in the word; but there is no such production in P, and so we must obtain the word $a^n b^n A^n$. The only way we can proceed now is by applying production 5 once and then applying $n - 1$ times production 6 to obtain the word $a^n b^n a^n$.

□

A set of words over Σ is called *type-0 language* if it can be generated by some type-0 grammar over Σ. We have the following theorem.

THEOREM 1-5 (Chomsky). *A set of words over Σ is recursively enumerable if and only if it is a type-0 language.*

Certain restrictions can be made on the nature of the productions of a type-0 grammar to give three other types of grammars. A grammar is said to be of

1. *Type-1(context-sensitive)* if for every production $\alpha \rightarrow \beta$ in P

$$|\alpha| \leqq |\beta|†$$

2. *Type-2(context-free)* if for every production $\alpha \rightarrow \beta$ in P

$$\alpha \in V \qquad \text{and} \qquad \beta \in (V \cup \Sigma)^+$$

3. *Type-3(regular)* if every production in P is of the form

$$A \rightarrow \sigma B \qquad \text{or} \qquad A \rightarrow \sigma$$

where $A, B \in V$ and $\sigma \in \Sigma$.

† Recall that $|x|$ stands for the length of the string (i.e., the number of letters in x); in particular, $|\Lambda| = 0$.

In any one of the above grammars we allow also the use of a special production, $S \to \Lambda$, but only if S (the start symbol) does not occur in the right-hand side of any production in P.

Correspondingly we define a set of words over Σ to be a *language of type-i*, $1 \leqq i \leqq 3$ (or *context-sensitive*, *context-free*, and *regular* language, respectively), if it can be generated by some type-i grammar. The following table summarizes the inclusion relations between the classes of sets over Σ discussed so far.

{Type-0 languages} = {recursively enumerable sets}
= {all sets accepted by some finite machine with two pushdown stores}

∪

{Recursive sets}

∪

{Type-1 languages}

∪

{Type-2 languages} = {all sets accepted by some nondeterministic finite machine with one pushdown store}

∪

{Type-3 languages} = {regular sets}
= {all sets accepted by some finite machine with no pushdown stores}

All the above inclusions are actually proper since for $\Sigma = \{a, b\}$ [see, for example, Hopcroft and Ullman (1969)].

1. $L_2 = \{x_i | x_i$ is accepted by $T_i\}$ is a type-0 language but not a recursive set.
2. $\{x_i | x_i$ is not generated by the ith type-1 grammar$\}$† is a recursive set but not a type-1 language.
3. $\{a^n b^n a^n | n \geqq 1\}$ is a type-1 but not a type-2 language.
4. $\{a^n b^n | n \geqq 1\}$ is a type-2 but not a type-3 language.

1-4 TURING MACHINES AS GENERATORS

In this section we introduce a class of n-ary partial functions ($n \geqq 1$), called *Turing computable functions*, mapping n-tuples of words over Σ into

† Note that in order to carry out the enumeration of type-1 grammars over $\Sigma = \{a, b\}$, we must consider only type-1 grammars with variables from $V = \{v_1, v_2, v_3, \ldots\}$; that is, if the grammar has n variables, they must be $v_1, v_2, \ldots, v_n$.

words over Σ. This is a very rich class of functions; actually, the intention is to have this class rich enough to include exactly all computable n-ary partial functions mapping n-tuples of words over Σ into words over Σ. Again, since, by Church's thesis, a Turing machine is the most general computing device, it is quite natural that we define the class by means of Turing machines.

A partial function† $f(x_1, \ldots, x_n)$, $n \geqq 1$, mapping n-tuples of words over $\Sigma = \{a, b\}$ into words over Σ, is said to be *Turing computable* if there is a Turing machine M over $\{a, b, *\}$ which behaves as follows: For every n-tuple $(w_1, \ldots, w_n)$ of words over Σ, M takes the string $w_1 * \ldots * w_n$ as input and

1. If $f(w_1, \ldots, w_n)$ is undefined, then M will loop forever.
2. If $f(w_1, \ldots, w_n)$ is defined, then M will eventually halt (either rejecting or accepting the input) with a tape containing the value of $f(w_1, \ldots, w_n)$ *followed only by* Δ*'s.*

EXAMPLE 1-18

The Turing machine M_7 over $\{a, b, *\}$, described in Fig. 1-10, computes the concatenation function over $\Sigma = \{a, b\}$: It takes a pair of words (w_1, w_2) as input and yields the word $w_1 w_2$ as output. For example, if $w_1 = abaa$

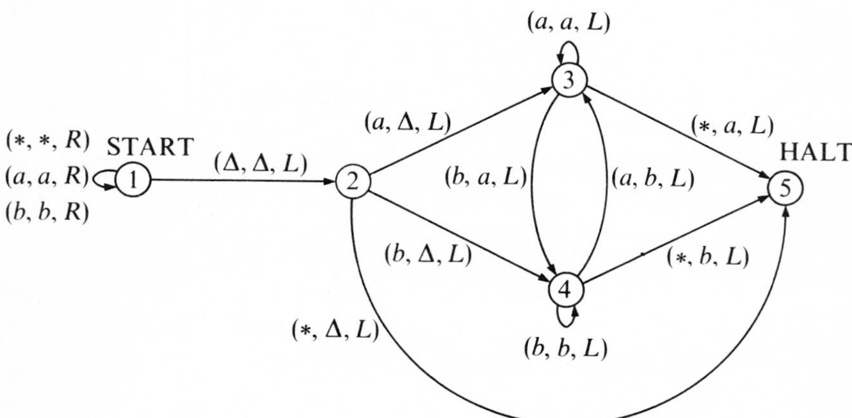

Figure 1-10 The Turing machine M_7 that computes the concatenation function.

† The words *partial function* indicate that $f(w_1, \ldots, w_n)$ may be undefined for some n-tuple of words $(w_1, \ldots, w_n)$ over Σ, in contrast with a *total function* for which $f(w_1, \ldots, w_n)$ is defined (and yields a word in Σ) for all possible n-tuples of words over Σ.

and $w_2 = bbab$, then the input and output tapes look like this:

Input tape	a	b	a	a	$*$	b	b	a	b	Δ	Δ	Δ	$\cdots$
Output tape	a	b	a	a	b	b	a	b	Δ	Δ	Δ	Δ	$\cdots$

We start with state 1 and scan the input tape moving right until we reach the first Δ symbol (state 2). Now we move left until we reach the $*$ symbol (state 5). While we are moving to the left, we read each symbol on the tape cell, remember it, move one cell to the left, and print it on the new cell. We are at state 3 whenever we have to remember the symbol a, and at state 4 whenever we have to remember the symbol b.

□

In this section we give an alternative definition of the class of Turing computable functions; that is, we show that a function is Turing computable if and only if it is a *partial recursive* function. First we shall discuss the class of *primitive recursive* functions, which is a proper subclass of the class of partial recursive functions. Virtually all functions of practical value are primitive recursive.

1-4.1 Primitive Recursive Functions

Every n-ary ($n \geqq 1$) primitive recursive function is a total function mapping n-tuples of words over Σ into words over Σ, but not every such total function is a primitive recursive function. The class of all primitive recursive functions over an alphabet $\Sigma = \{a, b\}$ is defined as follows:

1. *Base functions:*

   $nil(x) = \Lambda$ (that is, for every argument $x \in \Sigma^*$, the value of $nil(x)$ is Λ, the empty word)

   $consa(x) = ax$
   $consb(x) = bx$

   These are primitive recursive functions over Σ.
2. *Composition:*
   If $h, g_1, \ldots, g_m$ are primitive recursive functions over Σ, then so is the n-ary function f defined by

   $$f(x_1, \ldots, x_n) = h(g_1(x_1, \ldots, x_n), \ldots, g_m(x_1, \ldots, x_n))$$

(In each g_i some of the arguments may be absent.)

3. *Primitive recursion:*

If g, h_1, and h_2 are primitive recursive functions over Σ, then so is the n-ary function f defined by

(*a*) If $n = 1$,

$$\begin{aligned} f(\Lambda) &= w \qquad \text{(any word } w \text{ of } \Sigma^*) \\ f(ax) &= h_1(x, f(x)) \\ f(bx) &= h_2(x, f(x)) \end{aligned}$$

(In h_1 and h_2 some of the arguments may be absent.)

(*b*) If $n \geqq 2$,

$$\begin{aligned} f(\Lambda, x_2, \ldots, x_n) &= g(x_2, \ldots, x_n) \\ f(ax_1, x_2, \ldots, x_n) &= h_1(x_1, x_2, \ldots, x_n, f(x_1, x_2, \ldots, x_n)) \\ f(bx_1, x_2, \ldots, x_n) &= h_2(x_1, x_2, \ldots, x_n, f(x_1, x_2, \ldots, x_n)) \end{aligned}$$

(In h_1 and h_2 some of the arguments may be absent.)

EXAMPLE 1-19

The following are primitive recursive functions over $\Sigma = \{a, b\}$.

1. The constant functions a and b, where $a(x) = a$ and $b(x) = b$ for all x, are primitive recursive because, by composition,

$$\begin{aligned} a(x) &= consa(nil(x)) \\ b(x) &= consb(nil(x)) \end{aligned}$$

2. The identity function *iden*, where $iden(x) = x$ for all x, is primitive recursive because by primitive recursion (case $n = 1$),

$$\begin{aligned} iden(\Lambda) &= \Lambda \\ iden(ax) &= consa(x) \\ iden(bx) &= consb(x) \end{aligned}$$

3. The concatenation function *append*, where $append(x_1, x_2) = x_1x_2$ for all x_1 and x_2 [that is, $append(x_1, x_2)$ concatenates the words x_1 and x_2 into one word x_1x_2] is primitive recursive because, by primitive recursion (case $n = 2$),

$$\begin{aligned} append(\Lambda, x_2) &= iden(x_2) \\ append(ax_1, x_2) &= consa(append(x_1, x_2)) \\ append(bx_1, x_2) &= consb(append(x_1, x_2)) \end{aligned}$$

4. The *head* and *tail* functions, where $head(x) =$ "the leftmost letter of x" and $tail(x) =$ "the word x after removing the leftmost letter" [$head(\Lambda) =$

Λ and $tail(\Lambda) = \Lambda$], are primitive recursive because, by primitive recursion (case $n = 1$),

$$\begin{aligned} head(\Lambda) &= \Lambda & tail(\Lambda) &= \Lambda \\ head(ax) &= a(x) & tail(ax) &= iden(x) \\ head(bx) &= b(x) & tail(bx) &= iden(x) \end{aligned}$$

5. The *reverse* function, where $reverse(x)$ = "the letters of x in reversed order," is a primitive recursive because, by primitive recursion (case $n = 1$),

$$\begin{aligned} reverse(\Lambda) &= \Lambda \\ reverse(ax) &= append(reverse(x), a(x)) \\ reverse(bx) &= append(reverse(x), b(x)) \end{aligned}$$

6. The *right* and *left* functions, where $right(x)$ = "the rightmost letter of x" and $left(x)$ = "the word x after removing the rightmost letter" [$right(\Lambda) = left(\Lambda) = \Lambda$], are primitive recursive because, by composition,

$$right(x) = head(reverse(x))$$

$$left(x) = reverse(tail(reverse(x)))$$

7. The next-string function $next(x)$ = "the next word in the natural lexicographic order" is primitive recursive because

$$next(x) = reverse(nextl(reverse(x)))$$

where

$$\begin{aligned} nextl(\Lambda) &= a \\ nextl(ax) &= consb(x) \\ nextl(bx) &= consa(nextl(x)) \end{aligned}$$

8. The conditional function $cond(x_1, x_2, x_3)$ = "if $x_1 \neq \Lambda$ then x_2 else x_3" is primitive recursive because, by primitive recursion (case $n = 3$),

$$\begin{aligned} cond(\Lambda, x_2, x_3) &= iden(x_3) \\ cond(ax_1, x_2, x_3) &= iden(x_2) \\ cond(bx_1, x_2, x_3) &= iden(x_2) \end{aligned}$$

9. The predecessor function $pred(x)$ = "the predecessor of x in the natural lexicographic ordering" [$pred(\Lambda) = \Lambda$] is primitive recursive because

$$pred(x) = reverse(predl(reverse(x)))$$

where

$$\begin{aligned} predl(\Lambda) &= \Lambda \\ predl(ax) &= cond(x, consb(predl(x)), nil(x)) \\ predl(bx) &= consa(x) \end{aligned}$$

□

For abbreviation, from now on we shall write Λ, x, a, and b where $nil(x)$, $iden(x)$, $a(x)$, and $b(x)$, respectively, are required.

So far we have defined the class of primitive recursive functions over Σ; we proceed to define the class of primitive recursive predicates. A total predicate† $p(x_1, \ldots, x_n)$, $n \geqq 1$, mapping n-tuples of words over Σ into $\{true, false\}$ is said to be a *primitive recursive predicate* if the function defined by

$$\begin{array}{lll} \Lambda & \text{if} & p(x_1, \ldots, x_n) = false \\ a & \text{if} & p(x_1, \ldots, x_n) = true \end{array}$$

is primitive recursive. This function is called the *characteristic function of p* and is denoted by $f_p(x_1, \ldots, x_n)$.

EXAMPLE 1-20

1. The predicates *true* and *false*, where $true(x) = true$ and $false(x) = false$ for all x, are primitive recursive predicates because their characteristic functions $a(x)$ and $nil(x)$ are primitive recursive functions.

2. The predicate *null*, where $null(x) =$ "is $x = \Lambda$?" is a primitive recursive predicate because its characteristic function f is primitive recursive:

$$f(\Lambda) = a \qquad \text{and} \qquad f(ax) = f(bx) = \Lambda$$

3. The predicate $eqa(x) =$ "is $x = a$?" is a primitive recursive predicate because its characteristic function is

$$f(x) = cond(x, cond(pred(x), \Lambda, a), \Lambda)$$

The predicate $eqb(x) =$ "is $x = b$?" is also a primitive recursive predicate because

$$eqb(x) = eqa(pred(x))$$

□

We shall now introduce several interesting results related to primitive recursive functions and primitive recursive predicates. We let $\bar{x}$ stand for $(x_1, \ldots, x_n)$.

1. *If-then-else*:

If $p(\bar{x})$ is a primitive recursive predicate and $f(\bar{x})$ and $g(\bar{x})$ are primitive recursive functions, then the function

† A predicate is actually a function but one which yields for every n-tuple of words over Σ not a word over Σ, but *true* or *false*.

$$\textit{if } p(\bar{x}) \textit{ then } f(\bar{x}) \textit{ else } g(\bar{x}) \qquad \text{that is,} \quad \begin{cases} f(\bar{x}) & \text{if} \quad p(\bar{x}) = \textit{true} \\ g(\bar{x}) & \text{if} \quad p(\bar{x}) = \textit{false} \end{cases}$$

is primitive recursive.

In general, if $p_1(\bar{x}), p_2(\bar{x}), \ldots, p_{m-1}(\bar{x})$ are primitive recursive predicates, and $g_1(\bar{x}), g_2(\bar{x}), \ldots, g_m(\bar{x})$ are primitive recursive functions, then the function

$$\begin{aligned} &\textit{if } p_1(\bar{x}) \textit{ then } g_1(\bar{x}) \\ &\qquad \textit{else if } p_2(\bar{x}) \textit{ then } g_2(\bar{x}) \\ &\qquad\qquad \textit{else} \ldots \textit{if } p_{m-1}(\bar{x}) \textit{ then } g_{m-1}(\bar{x}) \\ &\qquad\qquad\qquad \textit{else } g_m(\bar{x}) \end{aligned}$$

is primitive recursive. Note that the function is identical to

$$\begin{aligned} &\textit{cond}(f_{p_1}(\bar{x}), g_1(\bar{x}), \textit{cond}(f_{p_2}(\bar{x}), g_2(\bar{x}), \ldots, \\ &\qquad\qquad \textit{cond}(f_{p_{m-1}}(\bar{x}), g_{m-1}(\bar{x}), g_m(\bar{x}))\ldots)) \end{aligned}$$

where $f_{p_i}(\bar{x})$ is the characteristic function of p_i for $1 \leqq i \leqq m - 1$.

2. *Propositional connectives*:
If $p(\bar{x})$, $q(\bar{x})$, and $r(\bar{x})$ are primitive recursive predicates, then so are the following predicates:

$$\sim p(\bar{x}) \qquad \begin{cases} \textit{true} & \text{if } p(\bar{x}) = \textit{false} \\ \textit{false} & \text{otherwise} \end{cases}$$

$$p(\bar{x}) \vee q(\bar{x}) \qquad \begin{cases} \textit{true} & \text{if } p(\bar{x}) = \textit{true}, \text{ or } q(\bar{x}) = \textit{true}, \text{ or both} \\ \textit{false} & \text{otherwise} \end{cases}$$

$$p(\bar{x}) \wedge q(\bar{x}) \qquad \begin{cases} \textit{true} & \text{if } p(\bar{x}) = q(\bar{x}) = \textit{true} \\ \textit{false} & \text{otherwise} \end{cases}$$

$$p(\bar{x}) \equiv q(\bar{x}) \qquad \begin{cases} \textit{true} & \text{if } p(\bar{x}) = q(\bar{x}) = \textit{true} \text{ or } p(\bar{x}) = q(\bar{x}) = \textit{false} \\ \textit{false} & \text{otherwise} \end{cases}$$

The characteristic functions of the first two predicates are

$$f_{\sim p}(\bar{x}) \qquad \textit{if null}(f_p(\bar{x})) \textit{ then } a \textit{ else } \Lambda$$

$$f_{p \vee q}(\bar{x}) \qquad \textit{if null}(\textit{append}(f_p(\bar{x}), f_q(\bar{x}))) \textit{ then } \Lambda \textit{ else } a$$

Therefore $\sim$ p and p $\vee$ q are primitive recursive predicates. The other two predicates are also primitive recursive since

$$\begin{aligned} p(\bar{x}) \wedge q(\bar{x}) \quad &\text{is} \quad \sim((\sim p(\bar{x})) \vee (\sim q(\bar{x}))) \\ p(\bar{x}) \equiv q(\bar{x}) \quad &\text{is} \quad (p(\bar{x}) \vee \sim q(\bar{x})) \wedge (q(\bar{x}) \vee \sim p(\bar{x})) \end{aligned}$$

Three very useful primitive recursive functions are *code*, *decode*, and *sub*, where $code(x) = a^i$ and $decode(a^i) = x$ iff x is the ith word in the natural lexicographic ordering ($i \geqq 0$) and $sub(a^i, a^j) = a^{i-j}$ (if $i \geqq j$). In all other cases *decode* and *sub* are defined (arbitrarily) to be Λ. In Prob. 1-17 the reader is asked to prove that these functions are indeed primitive recursive. We shall now illustrate two applications of these functions.

3. *Bounded minimization*:

If the predicate $p(\bar{x}, y)$ is primitive recursive, then so is the function $f(\bar{x}, z)$ which is defined as follows:

> The value of $f(\bar{x}, z)$ is the *first* word y of Σ^* in the natural lexicographic order (that is, Λ, a, b, aa, ab, ba, bb, aaa, . . .) such that $p(\bar{x}, y) =$ *true* or $y = z$. For all y' preceding y ($y \neq \Lambda$) in this order, $p(\bar{x}, y') =$ *false* and $y' \neq z$.

Note that the test $y = z$ ensures that the function obtained is always defined; that is, f is a total function. For brevity, we shall denote this definition by

$$f(\bar{x}, z) = h(\Lambda, \bar{x}, z) \textit{ where}$$
$$h(y, \bar{x}, z) \Leftarrow \textit{if } p(\bar{x}, y) \vee y = z \textit{ then } y \textit{ else } h(next(y), \bar{x}, z)$$

$f(\bar{x}, z)$ is primitive recursive because

$$f(\bar{x}, z) = g(code(z), \bar{x}, code(z))$$

where

$$g(\Lambda, \bar{x}, t) = decode(t)$$
$$g(as, \bar{x}, t) = \textit{if } p(\bar{x}, decode(sub(t, as)))$$
$$\textit{then } decode(sub(t, as)) \textit{ else } g(s, \bar{x}, t)$$

$g(bs, \bar{x}, t)$ can be defined arbitrarily.

4. *Equality predicate*:

The equality predicate $equal(x, y) =$ "is $x = y$?" is a primitive recursive predicate because it can be expressed as

$$equal(x, y) = null(append(sub(code(x), code(y)), sub(code(y), code(x))))$$

1-4.2 Partial Recursive Functions

The class of all partial recursive functions over an alphabet $\Sigma = \{a, b\}$ is defined as follows:

1. *Base functions*:
   $nil(x)$, $consa(x)$ and $consb(x)$ are partial recursive functions over Σ.

2. *Composition*:
   If $h, g_1, \ldots, g_m$ are partial recursive functions over Σ, then so is the n-ary function f defined by composition.†
3. *Primitive recursion*:
   If g, h_1, and h_2 are partial recursive functions over Σ, then so is the n-ary function f defined by primitive recursion. For $n = 1$ we allow f to be defined also as

$$\begin{aligned} f(\Lambda) &= \text{undefined} \\ f(ax) &= h_1(x, f(x)) \\ f(bx) &= h_2(x, f(x)) \end{aligned}$$

   (In h_1 and h_2 some of the arguments may be absent.)
4. (*Unbounded*) *minimization*:
   If p is a partial recursive predicate,‡ then the function f defined by

$$\begin{aligned} f(\bar{x}) &= h(\bar{x}, \Lambda) \textit{ where} \\ h(\bar{x}, y) &\Leftarrow \textit{if } p(\bar{x}, y) \textit{ then } y \textit{ else } h(\bar{x}, \textit{next}(y)) \end{aligned}$$

   is partial recursive. In other words, the value of $f(\bar{x})$ is the *first* word y of Σ^* in the natural lexicographic order (that is, $\Lambda, a, b, aa, ab, ba, bb, aaa, aab, \ldots$) such that $p(\bar{x}, y) = \textit{true}$; for all y' preceding y in this order $p(\bar{x}, y') = \textit{false}$. In all other cases, that is, if $p(\bar{x}, y) = \textit{false}$ for all $y \in \Sigma^*$, or $p(\bar{x}, y)$ is undefined for some y and for all y' preceding y in this order $p(\bar{x}, y') = \textit{false}$, then the value of $f(\bar{x})$ is undefined.

EXAMPLE 1-21

1. The *uhead* and *utail* functions, where $\textit{uhead}(x) =$ "the leftmost letter of a nonempty word x" and $\textit{utail}(x) =$ "the tail of a nonempty word x obtained by removing the leftmost letter" [$\textit{uhead}(\Lambda) = \textit{utail}(\Lambda) =$ undefined], are partial recursive functions because they can be defined by primitive recursion:

$$\begin{aligned} \textit{uhead}(\Lambda) &= \text{undefined} & \textit{utail}(\Lambda) &= \text{undefined} \\ \textit{uhead}(ax) &= a & \textit{utail}(ax) &= x \\ \textit{uhead}(bx) &= b & \textit{utail}(bx) &= x \end{aligned}$$

† Since a partial recursive function may be undefined for some arguments, a composition of partial recursive functions may require the value of such a function for undefined arguments. We agree that any partial function is undefined whenever at least one of its arguments is undefined.

‡ That is the characteristic function $f_p(\bar{x})$ is a partial recursive function, where $f_p(\bar{x})$ is defined as

$$f_p(\bar{x}) = \begin{cases} \Lambda & \text{if } p(\bar{x}) = \textit{false} \\ a & \text{if } p(\bar{x}) = \textit{true} \\ \text{undefined} & \text{if } p(\bar{x}) \text{ is undefined} \end{cases}$$

2. The function *undef*(x) which is undefined for every string x is a partial recursive function because it can be defined by minimization with p being *false*(x) or alternatively using primitive recursion:

$$undef(\Lambda) = \text{undefined}$$
$$undef(ax) = undef(bx) = undef(x)$$

3. The function *half*, where $half(x) = y$ iff $append(y, y) = x$ [$half(x)$ is undefined if no such y exists], is a partial recursive function because, by minimization,

$$half(x) = h(x, \Lambda) \quad where$$
$$h(x, y) \Leftarrow if\ equal(append(y, y), x)\ then\ y\ else\ h(x, next(y))$$

□

One very surprising result related to partial recursive functions is that every partial recursive function can be obtained by applying the minimization rule *at most once*, and even in this case it suffices to use a predicate p which is primitive recursive (not necessarily partial recursive). Our interest in the class of partial recursive functions is due to the following important result (which we shall present without proof).

THEOREM 1-6 (Kleene). *An n-ary partial function mapping n-tuples of words over Σ into words over Σ is partial recursive if and only if it is Turing computable.*

A partial recursive function that is total (defined for all arguments) is called a *total recursive function.* The relation between the various classes of functions over Σ (that is, mapping n-tuples of words over Σ into words over Σ) can be summarized as follows:

$$\{\text{All functions over } \Sigma\}$$
$$\cup$$
$$\{\text{Partial recursive functions}\} = \{\text{Turing computable functions}\}$$
$$\cup$$
$$\{\text{Total recursive functions}\}$$
$$\cup$$
$$\{\text{Primitive recursive functions}\}$$

All the above inclusions are proper inclusions. To show that the top inclusion is proper we consider the set $L_1 = \{x_i | x_i \text{ is not accepted by } T_i\}$. Since this set is not recursively enumerable (see Sec. 1-3.1), it follows that any function, which is defined for every $x \in L_1$ and undefined for every $x \notin L_1$, is not Turing computable; therefore, by Theorem 1-6, this function is not partially recursive.

It is also straightforward that the class of partial recursive functions properly includes the class of all total recursive functions (see Example 1-21).

Ackermann's function $A(x)$ over Σ is the classic example of a total recursive function that is not primitive recursive. $A(x)$ is equal to $f(x, x)$, where f is defined recursively as follows [see, for example, Hermes (1967)]:

$$f(x_1, x_2) = \begin{cases} ax_2 & \text{if } x_1 = \Lambda \\ f(tail(x_1), a) & \text{if } x_1 \neq \Lambda \text{ and } x_2 = \Lambda \\ f(tail(x_1), f(x_1, tail(x_2))) & \text{if } x_1 \neq \Lambda \text{ and } x_2 \neq \Lambda \end{cases}$$

The main point in the proof that $A(x)$ is not a primitive recursive function is that for every unary primitive recursive function g there exists a word $w \in \Sigma^*$ such that $A(w)$ yields a longer word than that of $g(w)$, which implies that $A(x)$ cannot be a primitive recursive function.

1-5 TURING MACHINES AS ALGORITHMS

In mathematics we often consider classes of *yes/no problems*, i.e., problems for which the answer is always either "yes" or "no," and investigate whether or not there is any algorithm (computing device) for solving (or at least partially solving) all the problems in the class. By Church's thesis, a Turing machine can be considered to be the most general possible computing device, and this suggests formalizing the common vague notion of "solvability" of classes of yes/no problems by means of Turing machines.

We say that a class of yes/no problems is *solvable* (*decidable*) if there is some fixed algorithm (Turing machine) which for any problem in the class as input will determine the solution to the problem; i.e., the algorithm *always halts* with a correct "yes" or "no" answer. (A "yes" answer is obtained by reaching an ACCEPT halt, while a "no" answer is obtained by reaching a REJECT halt.) If no such algorithm (Turing machine) exists, we say that the class of problems is *unsolvable* (*undecidable*). Note, however, that the unsolvability of a class of problems does not mean that we cannot determine the answer to a specific problem in the class by a Turing machine.

An important task of theoreticians in computer science is to indicate unsolvable classes of yes/no problems to prevent computer scientists from looking for nonexisting algorithms. One of the most famous unsolvable classes of yes/no problems is *Hilbert's tenth problem*. In 1901 Hilbert†

† David Hilbert, "Mathematical Problems," *Bull. Am. Math. Soc.*, **8**: 437–479 (1901).

listed a group of problems which were to stand as a challenge to future generations of mathematicians. The tenth problem in this group is to find an algorithm that takes an arbitrary polynomial equation $P(x_1, \ldots, x_n) = 0$ with integer coefficients as input and determines whether or not the equation has a solution in integers. This was an open problem for about seventy years. In 1970, Matijasevič† showed that there cannot exist such an algorithm, in other words, that *Hilbert's tenth problem is unsolvable.*

Unfortunately many interesting classes of yes/no problems are unsolvable. This suggests introducing a weaker notion of algorithms which will only *partially* solve the problems in the class in the sense that for any problem in the class as input: if the answer to the problem is "yes," the algorithm will eventually halt with a "yes" answer, but if the answer is "no," the algorithm may supply no answer at all! More precisely, a class of yes/no problems is said to be *partially solvable* (*partially decidable*) if there is an algorithm (Turing machine) that will take any problem in the class as input and (1) if the answer to the problem is "yes," the algorithm will eventually reach an ACCEPT halt, but (2) if the answer to the problem is "no," the algorithm either reaches a REJECT halt or never halts. This definition of solvability is clearly weaker than the original one in the sense that if a class of yes/no problems is solvable, then it is also partially solvable. However, this weaker notion of solvability is very important because many unsolvable classes of problems can be shown to be partially solvable.

At this point the reader will probably wonder how we can give a yes/no problem as input to an algorithm (Turing machine). This is purely an encoding problem. We shall be very vague regarding this problem and comment only that we restrict our yes/no problems to those that can be represented by some suitable encoding as words over $\Sigma = \{a, b\}$.

1-5.1 Solvability of Classes of Yes/No Problems

There are several interesting classes of yes/no problems related to the material discussed previously in this chapter which are solvable. For example:

1. *The equivalence problem of finite automata is solvable*; that is, there is an algorithm that takes any pair of finite automata A and A' over $\Sigma = \{a, b\}$ as input and determines whether or not A is equivalent to A'.

2. *The word problem of context-sensitive grammars is solvable*; that is, there is an algorithm that takes any context-sensitive grammar G over

† Ju. V. Matijasevič, "Enumerable Sets are Diophantine," *Sov. Math. Dokl.*, **11**(2):354–358 (1970).

$\Sigma = \{a, b\}$ and any word $w \in \Sigma^*$ as input and determines whether or not w is in the language generated by G.

In the following sections we present several classes of yes/no problems which are unsolvable. The first and most important unsolvable class of problems is known as the *halting problem of Turing machines.* It can be shown that there is no algorithm that takes an arbitrary Turing machine M over $\Sigma = \{a, b\}$ and an arbitrary word $w \in \Sigma^*$ as input and always determines whether or not M would halt if it were given input w. This result is proved later by contradiction showing that if there did exist such an algorithm, then we could conclude that there exists a Turing machine B over $\Sigma = \{a, b\}$ such that B halts for input $d(B)$ if and only if B does not halt for input $d(B)$, where $d(B) \in \Sigma^*$ is the encoded description of B as a word over Σ.

Using the unsolvability of the halting problem of Turing machines, we can prove many other classes of problems to be unsolvable by reducing the halting problem of Turing machines to those classes. More precisely, we say that a class $\mathscr{P}$ of yes/no problems is *reducible* to another class $\mathscr{P}'$ of yes/no problems if there is a Turing machine that takes any problem $P \in \mathscr{P}$ as input and yields some problem $P' \in \mathscr{P}'$ as output such that the answer to problem P is "yes" if and only if the answer to problem P' is "yes." We call such a Turing machine a *reduction Turing machine from* $\mathscr{P}$ *to* $\mathscr{P}'$.

Now, suppose we show that $\mathscr{P}$ is reducible to $\mathscr{P}'$. Then, if $\mathscr{P}'$ is solvable, we can combine the reduction Turing machine from $\mathscr{P}$ to $\mathscr{P}'$ and the algorithm for solving $\mathscr{P}'$ to form an algorithm for solving $\mathscr{P}$. Thus, *if* $\mathscr{P}$ *is reducible to* $\mathscr{P}'$ *and* $\mathscr{P}'$ *is solvable, so is* $\mathscr{P}$; in other words, if $\mathscr{P}$ *is reducible to* $\mathscr{P}'$ *and* $\mathscr{P}$ *is unsolvable, so is* $\mathscr{P}'$. In particular, since we already know that the halting problem (HP) of Turing machines is unsolvable, it follows that for every class $\mathscr{P}'$ of yes/no problems, if HP is reducible to $\mathscr{P}'$, then $\mathscr{P}'$ is unsolvable.

Using this reduction technique, we show two classes of yes/no problems to be unsolvable:

1. *The word problem of semi-Thue systems is unsolvable.*
2. *The Post correspondence problem is unsolvable.*

Note that if $\mathscr{P}$ is a class of yes/no problems and $\mathscr{P}'$ is a subclass of $\mathscr{P}$ (that is, every problem in $\mathscr{P}'$ is a problem in $\mathscr{P}$), then it is clear that if $\mathscr{P}$ is solvable, so is $\mathscr{P}'$, and if $\mathscr{P}'$ is unsolvable, so is $\mathscr{P}$.

1-5.2 The Halting Problem of Turing Machines

The HP of Turing machines over $\Sigma = \{a, b\}$ is actually a class of yes/no problems and can be stated as follows: Given an arbitrary Turing machine M over $\Sigma = \{a, b\}$ and an arbitrary word $w \in \Sigma^*$, does M halt for input w? We have the following theorem.

THEOREM 1-7 (Turing). *The halting problem of Turing machines is unsolvable.*

That is, there is no algorithm that takes an arbitrary Turing machine M over $\Sigma = \{a, b\}$ and word $w \in \Sigma^*$ as input and determines whether or not M halts for input w.

Proof (Minsky). Again we shall be vague regarding the encoding problem. We denote simply by $d(M)$ and $d(M) * w$ the encoded description of M and (M, w), respectively, as strings over $\Sigma = \{a, b\}$.

The proof is by contradiction. Suppose there exists such an algorithm (Turing machine), say, A. Then for every input $d(M) * w$ to A, we have: If M halts for input w, then A reaches an ACCEPT halt; if M does not halt for input w, then A reaches a REJECT halt. That is,

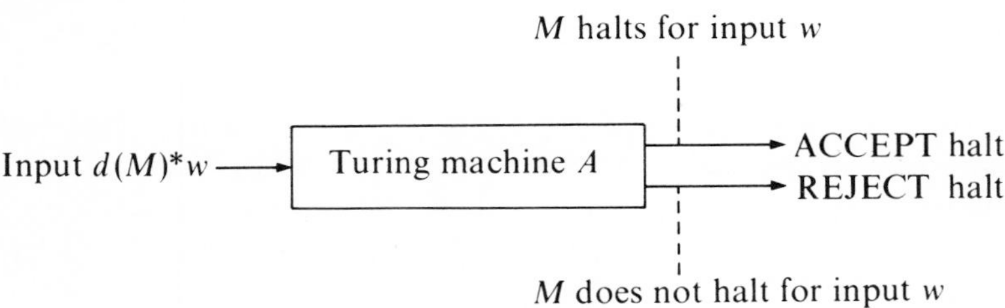

Now we can construct the Turing machine B which takes $d(M)$ as input and proceeds as follows: First, it copies the input to obtain $d(M) * d(M)$, and then it applies the Turing machine A on $d(M) * d(M)$ as input, with one modification—whenever A is supposed to reach an ACCEPT halt, instead B will loop forever. Considering the original behavior of A, we obtain

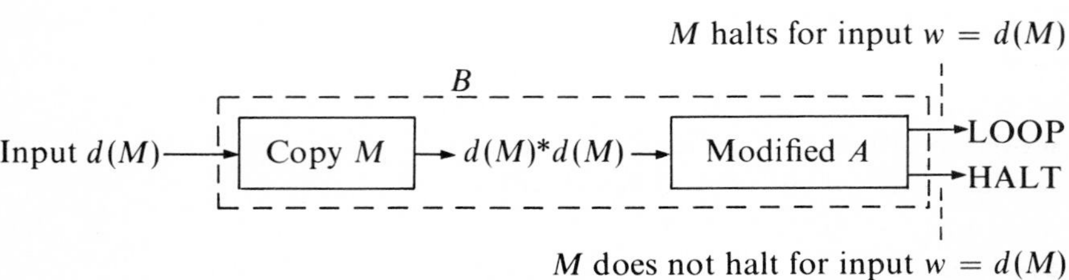

The above discussion holds true for an arbitrary Turing machine M over $\Sigma = \{a, b\}$. Since B itself is such a Turing machine, we let $M = B$; then, replacing B for M in the above figure, we obtain

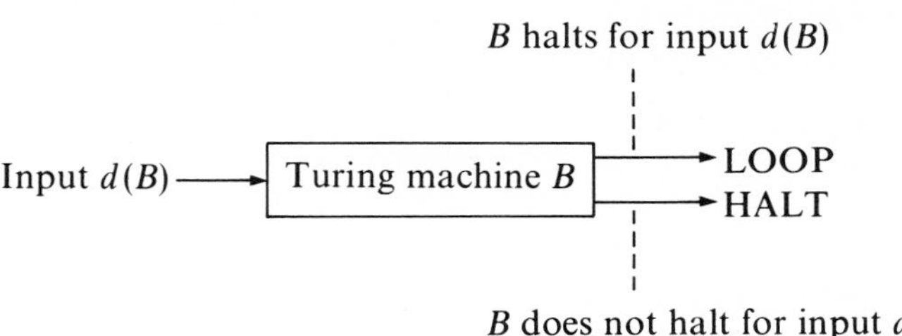

Thus, B halts for input $d(B)$ if and only if B does not halt for input $d(B)$. Contradiction.

Q.E.D.

There are two interesting variations of the halting problem of Turing machines:

1. *The empty-word halting problem of Turing machines is unsolvable.* That is, there is no algorithm that takes an arbitrary Turing machinge M over $\Sigma = \{a, b\}$ as input and determines whether or not M halts for input Λ (the empty word).

2. *The uniform halting problem of Turing machines is unsolvable.* That is, there is no algorithm that takes an arbitrary Turing machine M over $\Sigma = \{a, b\}$ as input and determines whether or not M halts for *every* input.

Both results can be proved easily by the reduction technique.

1. We show that the halting problem of Turing machines is reducible to the *empty-word halting problem of Turing machines.* In this case the reduction algorithm takes any Turing machine M over $\Sigma = \{a, b\}$ and any word $w \in \Sigma^*$ as input and yields a Turing machine M' over $\Sigma = \{a, b\}$ which first generates the word w onto the tape and then applies M to it. Thus, M halts for input w if and only if M' halts for input Λ (the empty word).

2. We show that the halting problem of Turing machines is reducible to the *uniform halting problem of Turing machines.* In this case the reduction algorithm takes any Turing machine M over $\Sigma = \{a, b\}$ and any word $w \in \Sigma^*$ as input and yields a Turing machine M' over $\Sigma = \{a, b\}$ which first clears the input tape to Δ's, then generates the word w onto the tape, and finally applies M. Thus, M halts for input w if and only if M' halts for every input.

From the discussions in previous sections it is clear that one can show the following (by using either the proof of Theorem 1-7 or the reduction technique).

1. *The halting problem of Post machines is unsolvable.* That is, there is no algorithm that takes an arbitrary Post machine M over $\Sigma = \{a, b\}$ and word $w \in \Sigma^*$ as input and determines whether or not M halts for input w.

2. *The halting problem of finite machines with two pushdown stores is unsolvable.* That is, there is no algorithm that takes an arbitrary finite machine M over $\Sigma = \{a, b\}$ with two pushdown stores and word $w \in \Sigma^*$ as input and determines whether or not M halts for input w.

3. *The totality problem of partial recursive functions is unsolvable.* That is, there is no algorithm that takes a definition of a partial recursive function f over $\Sigma = \{a, b\}$ as input and determines whether or not f is total.

4. *The recursiveness problem of type-0 grammars is unsolvable.* That is, there is no algorithm that takes an arbitrary type-0 grammar G over $\Sigma = \{a, b\}$ as input and determines whether or not the language generated by G is recursive.

1-5.3 The Word Problem of Semi-Thue Systems

A *semi-Thue system S over* $\Sigma = \{a, b\}$ consists of a set of k, $k \geqq 1$, ordered pairs (α_i, β_i) of words over Σ; that is,

$$S = \{(\alpha_1, \beta_1), (\alpha_2, \beta_2), \ldots, (\alpha_k, \beta_k)\}$$

For two words $x, y \in \Sigma^*$, we say that *y is derivable from x in S* if there exists a sequence of words over Σ

$$w_0, w_1, w_2, \ldots, w_n \qquad n \geqq 0$$

such that w_0 is x, w_n is y and w_{i+1} is obtained from w_i, $0 \leqq i < n$, by replacing some occurrence of a substring α_j (which is the left-hand side of some pair in S) in w_i by the corresponding β_j (which is the right-hand side of that pair).

The *word problem (WP) of semi-Thue systems over* $\Sigma = \{a, b\}$ is a class of yes/no problems which can be stated as follows: Given an arbitrary semi-Thue system S over $\Sigma = \{a, b\}$ and two arbitrary words $x, y \in \Sigma^*$, is y derivable from x in S?

EXAMPLE 1-22

Consider the semi-Thue system $S = \{(ba, ab), (aab, \Lambda)\}$ over $\Sigma = \{a, b\}$. Then Λ is derivable from $x \in \Sigma^*$ in S if and only if x has twice as many a's as it has b's; for example, Λ is derivable from *baaaba* but not from *baaab*.

□

We have the following theorem.

THEOREM 1-8 (Post). *The word problem of semi-Thue systems over* $\Sigma = \{a, b\}$ *is unsolvable.*

That is, there is no algorithm that takes an arbitrary semi-Thue system S over $\Sigma = \{a, b\}$ and words $x, y \in \Sigma^*$ as input and determines whether or not y is derivable from x in S.

Proof. We show that the HP of Post machines is reducible to the WP of semi-Thue systems. For an arbitrary Post machine M over $\Sigma = \{a, b\}$ and input word $w \in \Sigma^*$, we construct a semi-Thue system S over $\Sigma = \{a, b\}$ and a pair of words $x, y \in \Sigma^*$ such that M halts for input w if and only if y is derivable from x in S. In this proof we make use of the fact that we can consider, without loss of generality, only Post machines where TEST statements must have the form

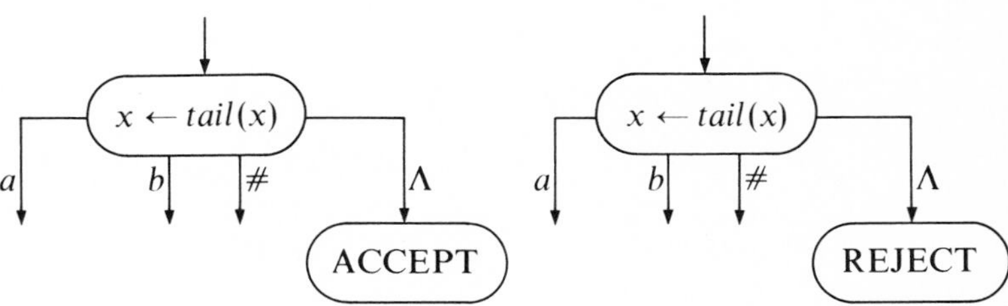

and there are no other HALT statements. That is, for every Post machine over Σ there exists an equivalent Post machine over Σ having only such TEST statements.

Suppose the Post machine M has m TEST and ASSIGNMENT statements labeled by $B_1, B_2, \ldots, B_m$. Let B_0 be the START statement. Suppose also that $w = \sigma_1\sigma_2 \ldots \sigma_n$. Then take

$$x = B_0 \vdash \sigma_1\sigma_2 \ldots \sigma_n \dashv$$
$$y = \Lambda$$

The list of ordered pairs of S is constructed as follows:

1. B_0 yields (B_0, B_1)

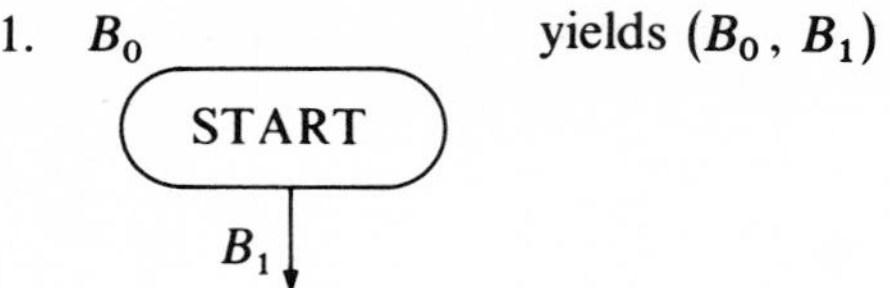

2.

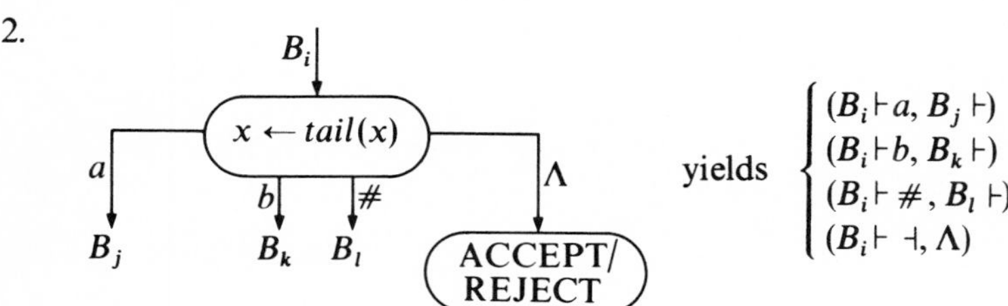

yields $\begin{cases} (B_i \vdash a, B_j \vdash) \\ (B_i \vdash b, B_k \vdash) \\ (B_i \vdash \#, B_l \vdash) \\ (B_i \vdash \dashv, \Lambda) \end{cases}$

3. B_i

$x \leftarrow x\sigma$ yields $(\dashv B_i, \sigma \dashv B_j)$

B_j

where $\sigma \in \{a, b, \#\}$.

4. Cycling: $\begin{cases} (\sigma B_i, B_i\sigma) \\ (B_i\sigma, \sigma B_i) \end{cases}$

for all $\sigma \in \{a, b, \#, \vdash, \dashv\}$ and $1 \leqq i \leqq m$.

It is straightforward to see that M halts for input w if and only if y is derivable from x in S.

Note that the alphabet of the semi-Thue system S that we have constructed is actually $\{a, b, \#, \vdash, \dashv\} \cup \{B_0, B_1, \ldots, B_m\}$. However, with "suitable" encoding one can construct a semi-Thue system S' over $\Sigma = \{a, b\}$ and words $x', y' \in \Sigma^*$ such that M halts for input w if and only if y' is derivable from x' in S'.

Q.E.D.

1-5.4 Post Correspondence Problem

A *Post system S over* $\Sigma = \{a, b\}$ consists of a set of k, $k \geqq 1$, ordered pairs (α_i, β_i) of words over Σ; that is,

$$S = \{(\alpha_1, \beta_1), (\alpha_2, \beta_2), \ldots, (\alpha_k, \beta_k)\}$$

A *solution to a Post system* is a nonempty sequence of integers $i_1, i_2, \ldots, i_m$

$(1 \leqq i_j \leqq k)$ such that

$$\alpha_{i_1}\alpha_{i_2} \ . \ . \ . \ \alpha_{i_m} = \beta_{i_1}\beta_{i_2} \ . \ . \ . \ \beta_{i_m}$$

The *Post correspondence problem* (*PCP*) *over* $\Sigma = \{a, b\}$ is a class of yes/no problems which can be stated as follows: Given an arbitrary Post system over $\Sigma = \{a, b\}$, does it have a solution?

EXAMPLE 1-23

1. Let $\Sigma = \{a, b\}$. The Post system

$$S = \{(b, bbb), (babbb, ba), (ba, a)\}$$

has a solution $i_1 = 2$, $i_2 = 1$, $i_3 = 1$, and $i_4 = 3$ (that is, $m = 4$) since

$$\underbrace{babbb}_{\alpha_2}\underbrace{b}_{\alpha_1}\underbrace{b}_{\alpha_1}\underbrace{ba}_{\alpha_3} = \underbrace{ba}_{\beta_2}\underbrace{bbb}_{\beta_1}\underbrace{bbb}_{\beta_1}\underbrace{a}_{\beta_3}$$

2. Let $\Sigma = \{a, b\}$. The Post system

$$S = \{(ab, abb), (b, ba), (b, bb)\}$$

has no solution. In each pair α_i is shorter than β_i; therefore, for any non-empty sequence of integers the string of α_i's will be shorter than the corresponding string of β_i's. □

We have the following theorem.

THEOREM 1-9 (Post). *The Post correspondence problem over* $\Sigma = \{a, b\}$ *is unsolvable.*

That is, there is no algorithm that takes arbitrary Post system over $\Sigma = \{a, b\}$ as input and determines whether or not it has a solution.

Proof (Scott). We show that the HP of Post machines is reducible to the PCP. For an arbitrary Post machine M over $\Sigma = \{a, b\}$ and input word $w \in \Sigma^*$, we construct a Post system S over $\Sigma = \{a, b\}$ such that M halts for input w if and only if S has a solution.

Suppose the Post machine M has m TEST and ASSIGNMENT statements labeled by $B_1, B_2, \ldots, B_m$ (see the proof of Theorem 1-8). Let B_0 be the START statement, and let B_{m+1} stand for any ACCEPT or REJECT halt. Suppose also that $w = \sigma_1\sigma_2 \ . \ . \ . \ \sigma_n$. Then the corresponding Post system S over the alphabet $\{a, b, \#, *, B_0, \ldots, B_{m+1}\}$ is

1. B_0 START B_1 yields $(B_0, B_0{*}\sigma_1{*}\sigma_2{*} \ . \ . \ . \ {*}\sigma_n{*}B_1{*})$

2. 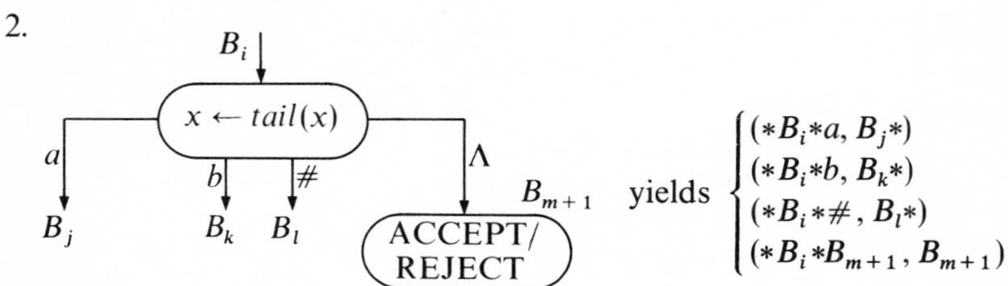

$$\text{yields} \begin{cases} ({*}B_i{*}a, B_j{*}) \\ ({*}B_i{*}b, B_k{*}) \\ ({*}B_i{*}\#, B_l{*}) \\ ({*}B_i{*}B_{m+1}, B_{m+1}) \end{cases}$$

3. B_i $x \leftarrow x\sigma$ B_j yields $({*}B_i, \sigma{*}B_j{*})$

where $\sigma \in \{a, b, \#\}$.

4. Cycling: $({*}\sigma, \sigma{*})$ for all $\sigma \in \{a, b, \#\}$.

It should now be verified that a concatenation of words from the first members of these pairs can equal a corresponding concatenation from the second members if and only if it transcribes word by word a terminating computation of the Post machine with input w. The terminating computation is described as a sequence of B_i's. Between two successive B_i's and B_j's, we have a string over $\{a, b, \#\}$ that represents the current value of x after the execution of B_i and before the execution of B_j. All letters are separated by $*$; the role of the $*$'s is to ensure that the current value of x will be copied between the B_i's.

Q.E.D.

The unsolvability of the Post correspondence problem is very often used to prove the unsolvability of other classes of yes/no problems. In particular, the Post correspondence problem can be reduced to many classes of yes/no problems in formal language theory, concluding, therefore, that they are unsolvable. For example, the following can be shown.

1. *The equivalence problem of context-free (type-2) grammars is unsolvable.* That is, there is no algorithm that takes any two context-free grammars over $\Sigma = \{a, b\}$ as input and determines whether or not they generate the same language. Note that the equivalence problem of regular (type-3) grammars is solvable.

2. *The emptiness problem of context-sensitive (type-1) grammars is unsolvable.* That is, there is no algorithm that takes any context-sensitive grammar G over $\Sigma = \{a, b\}$ as input and determines whether or not the language generated by G is empty. Note that the emptiness problem of context-free (type-2) grammars is solvable.

3. *The word problem of type-0 grammars is unsolvable.* That is, there is no algorithm that takes any type-0 grammar G over $\Sigma = \{a, b\}$ and word $w \in \Sigma^*$ as input and determines whether or not w is in the language of G. Note that the word problem of context-sensitive (type-1) grammars is solvable.

EXAMPLE 1-24 (Floyd)

A finite (nonempty) set of 3×3 matrices $\{M_i\}$ over the integers is said to be *mortal* with respect to $\langle j_1, j_2 \rangle$, $1 \leqq j_1, j_2 \leqq 3$, if there is a finite product of members of the set, $M = M_{i_1} \cdot M_{i_2} \cdot \ldots \cdot M_{i_k}$, such that the $\langle j_1, j_2 \rangle$ element of M is 0. We shall show that *the mortality problem of matrices is unsolvable*; that is, there is no algorithm that takes a finite set of 3×3 integer matrices $\{M_i\}$ and a pair $\langle j_1, j_2 \rangle$, $1 \leqq j_1, j_2 \leqq 3$, as input and decides whether or not $\{M_i\}$ is mortal with respect to $\langle j_1, j_2 \rangle$.

We prove the unsolvability of the mortality problem by reducing the Post correspondence problem to the mortality problem; i.e., for an arbitrary Post system S over Σ we construct a set of 3×3 integer matrices $\{M_i\}$ in such a way that S has a solution if and only if $\{M_i\}$ is mortal with respect to $\langle 3, 2 \rangle$. The idea is to construct for a given pair of words (u, v) over Σ a 3×3 integer matrix $M(u, v)$ in such a way that

1. The $\langle 3, 2 \rangle$ element of $M(u, v)$ is 0 if and only if $u = v$.
2. For all words $u_1, u_2, v_1, v_2 \in \Sigma^*$

$$M(u_1, v_1) \cdot M(u_2, v_2) = M(u_1 u_2, v_1 v_2)$$

Now, for a given Post system $S = \{(\alpha_i, \beta_i)\}$ over Σ, we construct a set of 3×3 integer matrices $\{M_i\}$ where each $M_i = M(\alpha_i, \beta_i)$. Then from properties 1 and 2 above, it is clear that S has a solution $i_1, i_2, \ldots, i_k$ if and only if the $\langle 3, 2 \rangle$ element of $M_{i_1} \cdot M_{i_2} \cdot \ldots \cdot M_{i_k}$ is 0.

To define the matrix $M(u, v)$ we use two functions c (code) and el (exponent of length) mapping words over Σ into integers:

$c(x) = i$	iff x is the ith word in the natural lexicographic ordering
$el(x) = n^{\|x\|}$	where $\|x\|$ is the length of x and n is the number of letters in Σ

It is easy to prove that

$$c(xy) = c(x) \cdot el(y) + c(y)$$
$$el(xy) = el(x) \cdot el(y)$$

Now, for a pair (u, v) of words over Σ, we define

$$M(u, v) = \begin{bmatrix} el(u) & el(v) - el(u) & 0 \\ 0 & el(v) & 0 \\ c(u) & c(v) - c(u) & 1 \end{bmatrix}$$

$M(u, v)$ has the desired properties:

1. The $\langle 3, 2\rangle$ element of $M(u, v)$ is 0 iff $u = v$ since $c(v) - c(u) = 0$ iff $u = v$.

2. For all words $u_1, u_2, v_1, v_2 \in \Sigma^*$, $M(u_1, v_1) \cdot M(u_2, v_2) = M(u_1u_2, v_1v_2)$ since

$$M(u_1, v_1) \cdot M(u_2, v_2)$$

$$= \begin{bmatrix} el(u_1) & el(v_1) - el(u_1) & 0 \\ 0 & el(v_1) & 0 \\ c(u_1) & c(v_1) - c(u_1) & 1 \end{bmatrix} \cdot \begin{bmatrix} el(u_2) & el(v_2) - el(u_2) & 0 \\ 0 & el(v_2) & 0 \\ c(u_2) & c(v_2) - c(u_2) & 1 \end{bmatrix}$$

$$= \begin{bmatrix} el(u_1)\,el(u_2) & el(v_1)\,el(v_2) - el(u_1)\,el(u_2) & 0 \\ 0 & el(v_1)\,el(v_2) & 0 \\ c(u_1)\,el(u_2) + c(u_2) & [c(v_1)\,el(v_2) + c(v_2)] - [c(u_1)\,el(u_2) + c(u_2)] & 1 \end{bmatrix}$$

$$= M(u_1u_2, v_1v_2)$$

□

1-5.5 Partial Solvability of Classes of Yes/No Problems

It is quite interesting to note that although the classes of yes/no problems discussed in the previous sections are unsolvable, many of them are partially solvable. For example, the *halting problem of Turing machines is partially solvable.* That is, there is an algorithm (Turing machine) that takes any Turing machine M over $\Sigma = \{a, b\}$ and any word $w \in \Sigma^*$ as input and

(1) if M halts for w, the algorithm will eventually reach an ACCEPT halt, but (2) if M does not halt for w, the algorithm either reaches a REJECT halt or never halts. The standard proof of this result proceeds by constructing an algorithm (Turing machine) that takes an arbitrary Turing machine M over $\Sigma = \{a, b\}$ and a word $w \in \Sigma^*$ as input and simulates the behavior of M for input w. We call such a Turing machine a *universal Turing machine.* We can think of a universal Turing machine as a general-purpose computer which is powerful enough to simulate any computer, including itself.

The relationship between the solvability and partial solvability of a class $\mathscr{P}$ of yes/no problems is best described by means of the complement class $\bar{\mathscr{P}}$, that is, the class of yes/no problems obtained from $\mathscr{P}$ just by taking the negation of each problem in the class. Then the key result can be stated as follows: *$\mathscr{P}$ is solvable if and only if both $\mathscr{P}$ and $\bar{\mathscr{P}}$ are partially solvable.* It is clear that if $\mathscr{P}$ is solvable, then so is $\bar{\mathscr{P}}$ (interchange all the ACCEPT and REJECT halts in the given algorithm), and therefore if $\mathscr{P}$ is solvable, both $\mathscr{P}$ and $\bar{\mathscr{P}}$ are partially solvable. To show the result in the other direction, let us assume that algorithms A and $\bar{A}$ partially solve $\mathscr{P}$ and $\bar{\mathscr{P}}$, respectively. Then construct an algorithm B which simulates the operations of both A and $\bar{A}$.† Whenever A reaches an ACCEPT halt, so will B; but whenever $\bar{A}$ reaches an ACCEPT halt, B is modified to reach a REJECT halt. Thus, for every problem of $\mathscr{P}$ as input, if the answer to the problem is "yes," B will reach an ACCEPT halt and if the answer to the problem is "no," B will reach a REJECT halt; in other words, B solves the problems in $\mathscr{P}$.

Since the halting problem of Turing machines is unsolvable but is partially solvable, an important consequence of the above result is that its complement is not partially solvable; i.e., the *nonhalting problem of Turing machines is not partially solvable.* That is, there is no algorithm (Turing machine) that will take any Turing machine M over $\Sigma = \{a, b\}$ and word $w \in \Sigma^*$ as input and (1) if M *does not halt* for w, the algorithm will reach an ACCEPT halt, but (2) if M halts for w, the algorithm either reaches a REJECT halt or never halts.

The reduction technique for solvability can be used for partial solvability as well because we have that *if a class $\mathscr{P}$ of yes/no problems is reducible to $\mathscr{P}'$ and $\mathscr{P}'$ is partially solvable, then so is $\mathscr{P}$*; in other words, *if a class $\mathscr{P}$ of yes/no problems is reducible to $\mathscr{P}'$ and $\mathscr{P}$ is not partially solvable, then neither is $\mathscr{P}'$.* We shall illustrate this technique with one example. (An important

† The simulations of A and $\bar{A}$ are done "in parallel" so that neither requires the termination of the other in order to have its behavior completely simulated.

application of the results presented in this example is discussed in Chap. 4, Sec. 4-2.1.)

EXAMPLE 1-25 (Paterson)

Let $\Sigma = \{a, b\}$. A *two-registered finite automaton* A over Σ is a machine with domain Σ^∞ (the set of all *infinite* tapes of letters from Σ) and is described by a flow-diagram such that each statement in it is of one of the following forms:

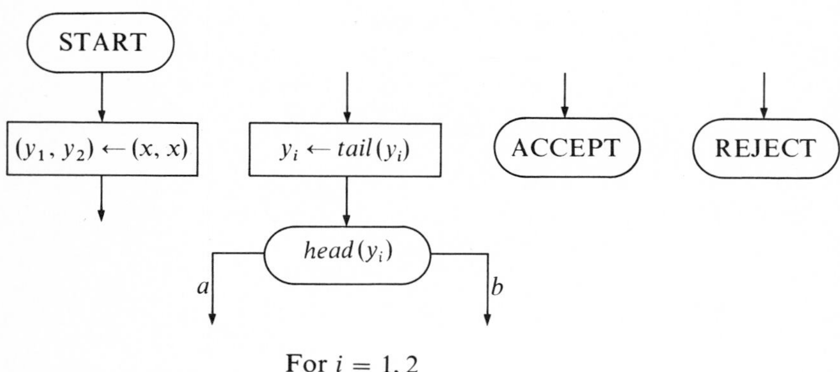

For $i = 1, 2$

where, for every $\sigma \in \Sigma$ and $w \in \Sigma^\infty$, $tail(\sigma w) = w$ and $head(\sigma w) = \sigma$. Note that the first letter of x is removed by the first application of *tail.*

For each input tape $\xi \in \Sigma^\infty$ for x, we distinguish between three possible computations: (1) If ACCEPT is reached, the tape is said to be *accepted*; (2) if REJECT is reached, the tape is said to be *rejected*; (3) otherwise, the automaton A is said to *loop* on the tape. Thus, a two-registered finite automaton A determines a threefold partition of Σ^∞ into $accept(A)$, $reject(A)$, and $loop(A)$, the classes of tapes of Σ^∞ which A accepts, rejects, and on which it loops, respectively.

We show the following results to be true.

1. *The nonacceptance problem of two-registered finite automata over* $\Sigma = \{a, b\}$ *is not partially solvable.* That is, there is no algorithm that takes any two-registered finite automaton A over $\Sigma = \{a, b\}$ as input and (1) if $accept(A) = \phi$, the algorithm will reach an ACCEPT halt, but (2) if $accept(A) \neq \phi$, the algorithm either reaches a REJECT halt or never halts.

2. *The looping problem of two-registered finite automata over* $\Sigma = \{a, b\}$ *is not partially solvable.* That is, there is no algorithm that takes any two-registered finite automaton A over $\Sigma = \{a, b\}$ as input and (1) if $loop(A) \neq \phi$,

the algorithm will reach an ACCEPT halt, but (2) if $loop(A) = \phi$, the algorithm either reaches a REJECT halt or never halts.

Both results are proved by reducing the nonhalting problem of Turing machines to the nonacceptance and the looping problems of two-registered finite automata.

Given a Turing machine M and an input word w over $\Sigma = \{a, b\}$, there is an effective method [see Paterson (1968) and Luckham, Park, and Paterson (1970)] for constructing a two-registered finite automaton $A(M, w)$ over Σ which checks whether or not its input tape $\xi \in \Sigma^\infty$ describes a computation of M starting with input w. In other words, A accepts a tape $\xi \in \Sigma^\infty$ if and only if ξ has a finite initial segment which describes a complete computation of M starting with w; A loops on the tape if and only if ξ describes a nonterminating computation of M starting with w; otherwise, A rejects the tape ξ. Roughly speaking, this is done by assuming ξ to be of the form $\alpha_0\alpha_1\alpha_2\alpha_3 \ldots$, where each $\alpha_i \in \Sigma^*$ indicates the *configuration* of M (contents of tape, position of reading head, and current state) after the ith step of the computation. The checking is done by letting y_2 "read" along the string α_i while y_1 "verifies" that the following string α_{i+1} is indeed the next configuration of the computation of M starting with w.

Then, the automaton $A(M, w)$ has the following property: M fails to halt starting with input w if and only if $accept(A) = \phi$, or, equivalently, if and only if $loop(A) \neq \phi$. Now, since the nonhalting problem of Turing machines is not partially solvable, neither are the nonacceptance and looping problems of two-registered finite automata.

□

Bibliographic Remarks

Three excellent books on computability are those of Minsky (1967), Hopcroft and Ullman (1969), and Kain (1972). There are several more advanced books such as those of Davis (1958), Hermes (1965), and Rogers (1967). Our presentation benefitted from the excellent papers of Shepherdson and Sturgis (1963) and Scott (1967).

The notion of finite state devices is attributed to McCulloch and Pitts (1943). An important paper discussing this topic is the one by Rabin and Scott (1959). The notion of regular expressions and their relation to regular sets (Theorem 1-1) is due to Kleene (1956). The equivalence of regular sets (Theorem 1-2) was first discussed by Moore (1956). An excellent exposition of regular sets is given by Ginzburg (1968) and Salomaa (1969) [see also the selected papers in Moore (1964)].

The basic notion of computability by Turing machines appears in

Turing's pioneer paper (1936). Our Post machine (Theorem 1-3) is very similar to Post's normal system (1936). However, it was not defined by Post, but by Arbib (1963) and independently by Shepherdson and Sturgis (1963). The power of finite machines with two pushdown stores (Theorem 1-4) was first discovered by Minsky (1961) [see also Evey (1963)]. Formal languages are discussed in detail by Hopcroft and Ullman (1969). The relation between recursively enumerable sets and type-0 languages (Theorem 1-5) was first given by Chomsky (1959). The notion of partial recursive functions (Theorem 1-6) was first introduced by Kleene (1936).

The unsolvability of the halting problem of Turing machines (Theorem 1-7) is given in Turing (1936); our proof is based on the exposition of Minsky (1967). The unsolvability of the semi-Thue system (Theorem 1-8) is due to Post (1947). Post's correspondence problem (Theorem 1-9) was first formulated and shown to be unsolvable by Post (1946); our proof is due to Scott (1967).

REFERENCES

Arbib, M. A. (1963): "Monogenic Normal Systems are Universal," *J. Aust. Math. Soc.,* **3**:301–306.

Chomsky, N. (1959): "On Certain Formal Properties of Grammars," *Inf. & Control,* **2**(2):137–167.

Church, A. (1936): "An Unsolvable Problem of Elementary Number Theory," *Am. J. Math.,* **58**:345–363.

Davis, M. (1958): *Computability and Unsolvability,* McGraw-Hill Book Company, New York.

——— (1965): *The Undecidable,* Raven Press, Hewlett, N.Y.

Evey, R. J. (1963): "The Theory and Applications of Pushdown Store Machines," Ph.D. thesis, Harvard University, Cambridge, Mass.

Ginzburg, A. (1968): *Algebraic Theory of Automata,* Academic Press, Inc., N.Y.

Hermes, H. (1965): *Enumerability, Decidability, Computability,* Academic Press, Inc., New York.

Hopcroft, J. E., and J. D. Ullman (1969): *Formal Languages and their Relation to Automata,* Addison-Wesley Publishing Company, Inc., Reading, Mass.

Kain, R. Y. (1972): *Automata Theory, Machines and Languages,* McGraw-Hill Book Company, New York.

Kleene, S. C. (1936): "General Recursive Functions of Natural Numbers," *Mathematisch Ann.*, **112**: 727–742.

——— (1956): "Representation of Events in Nerve Nets and Finite Automata," in C. E. Shannon and J. McCarthy (eds.), *Automata Studies*, pp. 3–42, Princeton University Press, Princeton, N.J.

Luckham, D. C., D. M. R. Park, and M. S. Paterson (1970): "On Formalized Computer Programs," *J. CSS*, **4**(3): 220–249.

McCulloch, W. S. and W. Pitts (1943): "A Logical Calculus of the Ideas Immanent in Nervous Activity," *Bull. Math. Biophys.*, **5**: 115–133.

Minsky, M. L. (1961): "Recursive Unsolvability of Post's Problem of 'Tag' and Other Topics in Theory of Turing Machines," *Ann. Math.*, **74**(3): 437–454.

——— (1967): *Computation: Finite and Infinite Machines*, Prentice-Hall, Inc., Englewood Cliffs, N.J.

Moore, E. F. (1956): "Gedanken Experiments on Sequential Machines," in C. E. Shannon and J. McCarthy (eds.), *Automata Studies*, pp. 129–153, Princeton University Press, Princeton, N.J.

——— (1964): *Sequential Machines: Selected Papers*, Addison-Wesley Publishing Company, Inc., Reading, Mass.

Paterson, M. S. (1968): "Program Schemata," in D. Michie (ed.), *Machine Intelligence 3*, pp. 19–31, Edinburgh University Press, Edinburgh.

Post, E. L. (1936): "Finite Combinatory Processes—Formulation, I," *Symb. Logic*, **1**: 103–105.

——— (1946): "A Variant of a Recursively Unsolvable Problem," *Bull. Am. Math. Soc.*, **52**(4): 264–268.

——— (1947): "Recursive Unsolvability of a Problem of Thue," *Symb. Logic*, **12**: 1–11.

Rabin, M. and D. Scott (1959): "Finite Automata and Their Decision Problems," *IBM J. Res. & Dev.*, **3**(2): 114–125. [Reprinted in Moore (1964).]

Rogers, H. (1967): *Theory of Recursive Functions and Effective Computability*, McGraw-Hill Book Company, New York.

Salomaa, A. (1969): *Theory of Automata*, Pergamon Press, New York.

Scott, D. (1967): "Some Definitional Suggestions for Automata Theory," *J. CSS*, **1**(2): 187–212.

Shepherdson, J. C. and H. E. Sturgis (1963): "Computability of Recursive Functions," *J. ACM*, **10**: 217–255.

Turing, A. M. (1936): "On Computable Numbers, With an Application to the Entscheidungsproblem," *Proc. Lond. Math. Soc., Ser. 2*, **42**: 230–265; correction, *ibid.*, **43**: 544–546 (1937).

PROBLEMS

Prob. 1-1 Prove the following identities for any regular expressions R and S over Σ:

(a) $R^* = R^*R^* = (R^*)^* = (\Lambda + R)^* = \Lambda + RR^*$

(b) $(R + S)^* = (R^* + S^*)^* = (R^*S^*)^* = (R^*S)^* R^* = R^*(SR^*)^*$

(c) $R^*R = RR^*$

(d) $(R^*S)^* = \Lambda + (R + S)^* S$

Prob. 1-2 Let $E(R_1, \ldots, R_n)$ stand for any regular expression over Σ containing regular expressions $R_1, \ldots, R_n$ in addition to '*', '·' and '+'. Prove the following:

(a) $E(R_1, \ldots, R_n) + (R_1 + \cdots + R_n)^* = (R_1 + \cdots + R_n)^*$

(b) $(R_1 + \cdots + R_n + E(R_1, \ldots, R_n))^* = (R_1 + \cdots + R_n)^*$

Prob. 1-3 Use the identities given in Sec. 1-1.1 to prove the following:

(a) $\Lambda + b^*(abb)^* [b^*(abb)^*]^* = (b + abb)^*$

(b) $(ba)^* b + (ba)^* (bb + a) [a + b(ba)^* (bb + a)]^* b(ba)^* b =$
$[ba + (bb + a)a^*b]^*b$
Hint: Show $[a + b(ba)^* (bb + a)]^* b = a^*b[(ba)^* (bb + a) a^*b]^*$

(c) $(a + b + aa)^* = (a + b)^*$
Hint: Show $(a + b + aa)^* = [(a + b)^* + aa]^* = (a + b)^*$.

(d) $[(b^*a)^* ab^*]^* = \Lambda + a(a + b)^* + (a + b)^* aa(a + b)^*$
Hint: Show $[a + b + (a + b)^* aa]^* = (a + b)^*$.

***Prob. 1-4** [One-dimensional checkers (Reynolds)]. Consider a one-dimensional (infinite) checkerboard where each square contains the letter a or b, for example,

···	a	a	b	a	a	b	b	b	a	a	b	a	a	a	···

There is always some word, starting and ending with b, ($baabbbaab$ in the example above) with an infinite string of a's in both directions. A *move* in the game consists of jumping a b over a neighbor b to an a square, as follows:

	Before move	After move
	$b\ b\ a$	$a\ a\ b$
or	$a\ b\ b$	$b\ a\ a$

An *initial board* consists of a word w (starting and ending with b). w is said to be a *winning word* if there is a finite sequence of moves that will lead to a *final board* consisting of one b (and the rest a's).

(a) Express the set of all winning words as a regular expression over $\{a, b\}$.
Hint: Consider the final board and play *backwards*.

(b) Prove your result.

***Prob. 1-5** [Regular equations (Arden†)].

(a) Let r be a variable, and let S and T denote regular expressions over Σ. Consider the equation

$$r = Sr + T$$

A set $X \subseteq \Sigma^*$ is said to be a *fixpoint* (*solution*) of the equation if $X = \tilde{S}X \cup \tilde{T}$. In general, an equation may have several fixpoints. A fixpoint X of the equation is said to be a *least fixpoint* if for every fixpoint Y of the equation, $X \subseteq Y$. Clearly, there can be at most one least fixpoint.

(i) Show that if $\Lambda \notin \tilde{S}$ there is a unique fixpoint given by $\widetilde{S^*T}$.

(ii) Show that every equation has a (unique) least fixpoint given by $\widetilde{S^*T}$.

(iii) Find the fixpoints of the equation $r = (ba)^*\, r + b$ over $\Sigma = \{a, b\}$.

(b) The above definition can be extended to systems of equations

$$r_i = S_{i1}r_1 + S_{i2}r_2 + \cdots + S_{in}r_n + T_i$$

where $1 \leqq i \leqq n$. An n-tuple of sets $\overline{X} = (X_1, \ldots, X_n)$ is said to be a *fixpoint of the system* if

$$X_i = \tilde{S}_{i1}X_1 \cup \tilde{S}_{i2}X_2 \cup \ldots \cup \tilde{S}_{in}X_n \cup \tilde{T}_i$$

for $1 \leqq i \leqq n$. A fixpoint $\overline{X} = (X_1, \ldots, X_n)$ is said to be a *least fixpoint of the system* if for every fixpoint $\overline{Y} = (Y_1, \ldots, Y_n)$, $X_i \subseteq Y_i$ for $1 \leqq i \leqq n$.

(i) Show that if $\Lambda \notin \tilde{S}_{11} \cup \tilde{S}_{12} \cup \ldots \cup \tilde{S}_{nn}$, then there is a unique fixpoint for which each X_i is regular.

(ii) Use this result to prove that for every finite automaton A over Σ there exists a regular expression R such that $\tilde{R} = \tilde{A}$.

† D. N. Arden, "Delayed logic and finite state machines," in *Theory of Computing Machine Design*, pp. 1–35, University of Michigan Press, Ann Arbor, 1960.

(iii) Show that every system of equations has a (unique) least fixpoint $\bar{X} = (X_1, \ldots, X_n)$ such that each X_i, $1 \leq i \leq n$, is regular.

(iv) Find the least fixpoint of the system

$$r_1 = (a + b)\, r_1 + (bb)^* r_2 + b$$
$$r_2 = (aa)^* r_1 + (a + b)\, r_2 + a$$

Prob. 1-6 Write finite automata that accept the following regular expressions:

(*a*) $\Lambda + a(a + b)^* + (a + b)^*\, aa(a + b)^*$

(*b*) $[ba + (a + bb)\, a^*b]^*$

(*c*) $(ba)^*\, (ab)^*\, (aa + bb)^*$

Prob. 1-7 Suppose that L is a regular set over Σ. Prove that the following are also regular sets:

(*a*) $rev(L) = \{w | w \text{ reversed is in } L\}$

(*b*) $init(L) = \{w_1 | w_1 w_2 \in L \text{ for some } w_2 \in \Sigma^*\}$

(*c*) $comp(L) = \{w | w \in \Sigma^* \text{ and } w \notin L\}$

(*d*) $lefthalf(L) = \{w_1 | w_1 w_2 \in L \text{ for some } w_2 \in \Sigma^* \text{ where } |w_1| = |w_2|\}$

(*e*) $righthalf(L) = \{w_2 | w_1 w_2 \in L \text{ for some } w_1 \in \Sigma^* \text{ where } |w_1| = |w_2|\}$

Suppose L_1, L_2 are regular sets over Σ. Prove that the following is also a regular set.

(*f*) $and\,(L_1, L_2) = \{w | w \in L_1 \text{ and } w \in L_2\}$

Prob. 1-8 Find regular expressions, finite automata, and simple transition graphs representing the following regular sets over $\Sigma = \{a, b\}$:

(*a*) All words in Σ^* such that every a has a b immediately to its right

(*b*) All words in Σ^* that do not contain two consecutive b's

Prob. 1-9

(*a*) Describe an algorithm to determine whether or not an arbitrary transition graph T accepts every word $w \in \Sigma^*$, that is, $\tilde{T} = \Sigma^*$.

(*b*) Does the following transition graph over $\Sigma = \{a, b\}$ accept Σ^*?

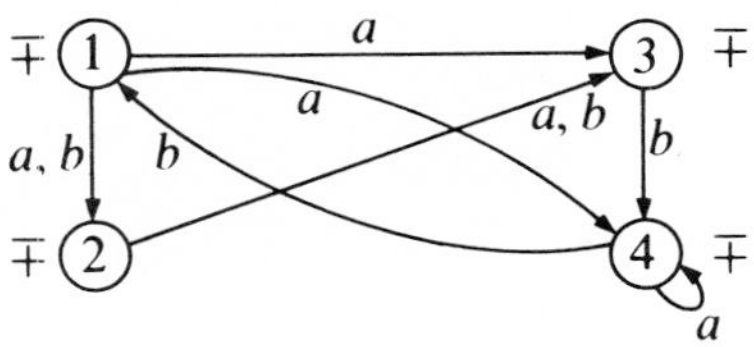

Prob. 1-10

(*a*) Consider the set L of words over $\Sigma = \{a, b\}$

$$L = \{a^n b a^n | n \geq 0\}$$

(i) Construct a Turing machine M_1, Post machine M_2, and finite machine M_3 (with one pushdown store) such that $accept(M_i) = L$ and $reject(M_i) = \Sigma^* - L$ for $1 \leqq i \leqq 3$.

(ii) Prove that there is no finite machine M with no pushdown stores such that $accept(M) = L$ and $reject(M) = \Sigma^* - L$.

(*b*) Do the same for $L = \{w | w$ consists of twice as many a's as b's$\}$.

Prob. 1-11 We define two different classes of boolean expressions.

(*a*) A *boolean expression* (be) is defined recursively as follows:

(i) T and F are be's.

(ii) If A and B are be's, so are $A \vee B$ and $A \wedge B$ (no parentheses!).

The computation rules of be's are

$$T \wedge T = T \qquad T \wedge F = F \wedge T = F \wedge F = F$$
$$F \vee F = F \qquad F \vee T = T \vee F = T \vee T = T$$

We assume that $\wedge$ is more binding than $\vee$. Construct a Turing machine M_1, Post machine M_2, and finite machine M_3 (with no pushdown stores) over $\Sigma = \{T, F, \wedge, \vee\}$ such that

$$accept(M_i) = \text{all be's with value } T$$
$$reject(M_i) = \text{all be's with value } F$$
$$loop(M_i) = \text{all words over } \Sigma \text{ which are not be's}$$

for $1 \leqq i \leqq 3$.

(*b*) Similarly construct a Turing machine M_1, Post machine M_2, and finite machine M_3 (with one pushdown store) over $\Sigma = \{T, F, \wedge, \vee, (,)\}$ for the following class of boolean expressions (be's):

(i) T and F are be's.

(ii) If A and B are be's, so are $A \vee B$ and $A \wedge B$.

(iii) If A is a be, so is (A).

***Prob. 1-12** (Finite machines with counters). A variable y_i is said to be a *counter over* $\Sigma = \{a, b\}$ if all the operations applied to y_i are of the form

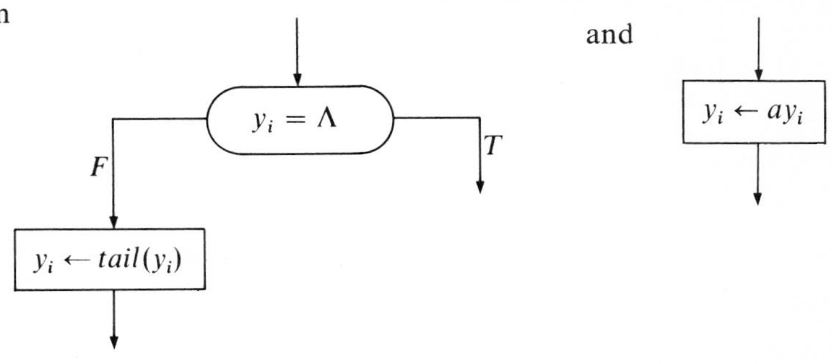

All counters are assumed to contain the empty word Λ initially. Thus a counter is actually a pushdown store which may contain only a's.

(a) Prove the following relations between the different classes of finite machines with counters over the same alphabet Σ

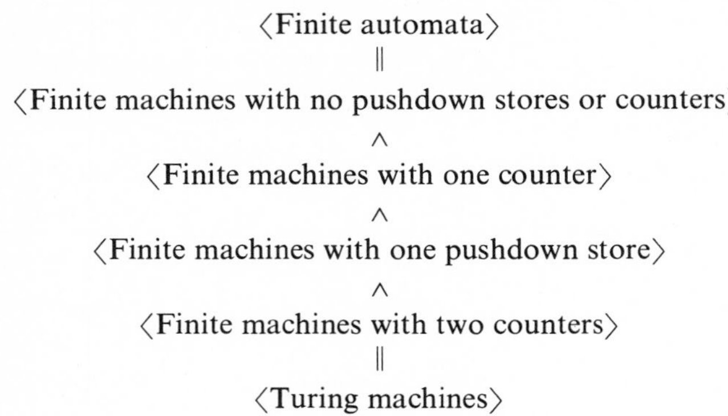

(b) How will the class of nondeterministic finite machines with one counter fit into this diagram?

Prob. 1-13 Describe a way for encoding every Turing machine over $\Sigma = \{a, b\}$ as a word over $\Sigma = \{a, b\}$ such that each word represents a unique Turing machine and vice versa.
Hint: Let every arrow of the form $(i) \xrightarrow{(\alpha,\beta,\gamma)} (j)$ be denoted by a 5-tuple $(i, \alpha, \beta, \gamma, j)$. Then express each Turing machine as a sequence of such 5-tuples followed by some indication as to what are the start and final states.

Prob. 1-14 Prove that a set of words over Σ is regular if and only if it is a type-3 language over Σ.

Prob. 1-15 Give grammars over $\Sigma = \{a, b, c\}$ that generate the following languages. In each case try to find a grammar of the highest possible type (i.e., a grammar of type-3 if possible; if not, then a grammar of type-2; and so on)

(a) $\{a^i b^i c^i | i \geqq 1\}$
(b) $\{a^i b^i c^k | i, k \geqq 1\}$
(c) $\{a^i b^k c^k | i, k \geqq 1\}$
(d) $\{a^i b^j c^k | i, j, k \geqq 1\}$
(e) $\{w \in \Sigma^* |$ number of a's, number of b's, and number of c's in w are all equal$\}$
(f) $\{ww^R | w \in \{a, b, c\}^*\}$.

Prob. 1-16 (Prefix-free language). A set L of words over Σ is called *prefix-free language* if there exists a set of words S over Σ such that

$$L = \Sigma^* S = \{w | w = w_1 w_2 \text{ where } w_1 \in \Sigma^* \text{ and } w_2 \in S\}$$

Denote by $\mathscr{L}$ the class of all prefix-free languages over Σ.

(*a*) Give an example of a prefix-free language L over $\Sigma = \{a, b\}$.

(*b*) Show that a necessary and sufficient condition for a language L to be in $\mathscr{L}$ is $L = \Sigma^* L$. What can you conclude about a prefix-free language containing Λ (the empty word)?

(*c*) Is $\mathscr{L}$ closed under complementation (that is, if $L \in \mathscr{L}$, then $\Sigma^* - L \in \mathscr{L}$)?

(*d*) Show that for any $L \in \mathscr{L}$, $L^* = \{\Lambda\} \cup L$. Is $\mathscr{L}$ closed under closure (that is, if $L \in \mathscr{L}$, then $L^* \in \mathscr{L}$)?

Prob. 1-17

(*a*) Prove that the following functions are primitive recursive:

(i) *length*(x) = "the binary representation (no leading 0's) of the number of letters in x, where a stands for 0 and b stands for 1."

(ii) *code*, *decode*, and *sub*, where $code(x) = a^i$ and $decode(a^i) = x$ iff x is the ith word in the natural lexicographic ordering ($i \geqq 0$) and $sub(a^i, a^j) = a^{i-j}$ (if $i \geqq j$). In all other cases *decode* and *sub* are defined arbitrarily to be Λ.

(*b*) Prove that the following predicates are primitive recursive:

(i) *substring*(x, y) = "is x a substring of y?"

(ii) *palindrom*$(x, \bar{y})$ = "does $x = append(y, reverse(y))$?"

(iii) *after*(x, y) = "does x follow y (not necessarily the next one) in the natural lexicographic ordering?"

Prob. 1-18 The class of partial recursive functions was defined in terms of the minimization operation:

$$\text{(1)} \quad \begin{aligned} &f(\bar{x}) = h(\bar{x}, \Lambda) \textit{ where} \\ &h(\bar{x}, y) \Leftarrow \textit{if } p(\bar{x}, y) \textit{ then } y \textit{ else } h(\bar{x}, next(y)) \end{aligned}$$

Prove that if we replace in this definition *next*(y) by *consa*(y), that is,

$$\text{(2)} \quad \begin{aligned} &f(\bar{x}) = h(\bar{x}, \Lambda) \quad \textit{where} \\ &h(\bar{x}, y) \Leftarrow \textit{if } p(\bar{x}, y) \textit{ then } y \textit{ else } h(\bar{x}, consa(y)) \end{aligned}$$

we still obtain exactly the class of all partial recursive functions. In other words, every partial recursive function which is expressed by definition 1 can be expressed by definition 2 and vice versa.

***Prob. 1-19** (The word problem of Thue systems). A *Thue system over* $\Sigma = \{a, b\}$ is a semi-Thue system S over Σ with the property that if $(\alpha_i, \beta_i) \in S$, then $(\beta_i, \alpha_i) \in S$. (Thus, in a Thue system, if y is derivable from x, then x is derivable from y.) Prove that the word problem of Thue systems is unsolvable.

Prob. 1-20 (Post correspondence problem). Let $\Sigma = \{a, b\}$.

(*a*) Prove that the Post system

$$S = \{(ba, bab), (abb, bb), (bab, abb)\}$$

has no solution.

(*b*) Find a solution for the Post system

$$S = \{(aab, a), (ab, abb), (ab, bab), (ba, aab)\}$$

Warning: The shortest solution is a sequence of 66 integers.

***Prob. 1-21** [Unsolvability in 3 × 3 matrices (Paterson†)]. A finite (nonempty) set of 3 × 3 matrices over the integers is said to be *mortal* if the zero matrix can be expressed as a finite (nonempty) product of members of the set. Prove that the problem of deciding whether a given finite set of 3 × 3 matrices is mortal is unsolvable.

Prob. 1-22 (Partial solvability). Consider all the unsolvable problems mentioned in Sec. 1-5.2 to 1-5.4. Indicate those problems among them that are not partially solvable.

† See M. S. Paterson, "Unsolvability in 3 × 3 matrices," *Stud. Appl. Math.*, **49**(1):105–107 (March 1970).

CHAPTER 2

Predicate Calculus

Introduction

The predicate calculus is a formal language whose essential purpose is to symbolize logical arguments in mathematics. The sentences in this language are called *well-formed formulas* (*wffs*). By "interpreting" the symbols in a wff we obtain a *statement* which is either true or false. We can associate many different interpretations with the same wff and therefore obtain a class of statements where each statement is either true or false. Our interest is mainly in a very restricted subclass of the wffs, those that yield a true statement for every possible interpretation.

The following is a typical wff of the predicate calculus

$$(\exists F)\{(F(a) = b) \wedge (\forall x)[p(x) \supset (F(x) = g(x, F(f(x))))]\}$$

Five of the symbols in this wff have fixed meaning:

1. $(\exists F) \ldots$ stands for "there exists a function F such that . . . is true," or, in other words, "for some function F, . . . is true."
2. $\cdots = \cdots$ stands for ". . . equals . . . is true."
3. $\cdots \wedge \cdots$ stands for ". . . and . . . are true."
4. $(\forall x) \ldots$ stands for "for every element x . . . is true."
5. $\cdots \supset \cdots$ stands for "if . . . is true, then . . . is true."

The wff can therefore be considered as representing the following English sentence:

> There exists a function F such that $F(a)$ equals b is true and for every x, if $p(x)$ is true, then $F(x)$ equals $g(x, F(f(x)))$ is true.

or in short

> There exists a function F such that $F(a) = b$ and for every x, if $p(x)$, then $F(x) = g(x, F(f(x)))$.

An interpretation of this wff is given by specifying a nonempty set D and then assigning an element of D to a, an element of D to b, a unary function (mapping D into D) to f, a binary function (mapping $D \times D$ into D) to g, and a unary predicate (mapping D into $\{true, false\}$) to p. For example, if we choose D to be the set N of all natural numbers and we let a be 0, b be 1, $f(x)$ be the predecessor function $x - 1$ (where $0 - 1 = 0$), $g(x, y)$ be the product function $x \cdot y$, and $p(x)$ be the predicate $x > 0$, then the interpreted wff yields the following statement:

> There exists a function F over N such that $F(0) = 1$ and for every $x \in N$, if $x > 0$, then $F(x) = x \cdot F(x - 1)$.

This is clearly a true statement. The factorial function $x!$ is an appropriate choice for F since $0! = 1$ and, for every $x > 0$, $x! = x \cdot (x - 1)!$.

Let us consider now another interpretation of the same wff. We choose D as the set of all words over the alphabet $\{\alpha, \beta\}$ and we let a and b be Λ (the empty word), $f(x)$ be $tail(x)$, $g(x, y)$ be $y * head(x)$,† and $p(x)$ be the predicate $x \neq \Lambda$. Then the interpreted wff yields the following statement:

> There exists a function F over Σ^* such that $F(\Lambda) = \Lambda$ and for every word $x \in \Sigma^*$, if $x \neq \Lambda$, then $F(x) = F(tail(x)) * head(x)$.

Again this is a true statement because if we take F to be the reverse function, $reverse(x)$, which reverses the order of the letters in any given word x, all the above requirements are satisfied; i.e., $reverse(\Lambda) = \Lambda$ and, for every $x \neq \Lambda$, $reverse(x) = reverse(tail(x)) * head(x)$.

However, the wff yields false statements for some other interpretations. For example, if we consider the interpretation in which D is the set N of all natural numbers, a is 0, b is 1, $f(x)$ is x (the identity function), $g(x, y)$ is $y + 1$, and $p(x)$ is $x > 0$, then we obtain the statement

> There exists a function F over N such that $F(0) = 1$ and for every $x \in N$, if $x > 0$, then $F(x) = F(x) + 1$.

† $w_1 * w_2$ stands for $append(w_1, w_2)$, that is, it concatenates the words w_1 and w_2 into one word $w_1 w_2$.

This is a false statement because there is no (total) function over N such that $F(x) = F(x) + 1$ for $x > 0$.

Note that F and x are *quantified* in the wff; i.e., they are preceded by the words "there exists . . ." or "for all . . .," and therefore there is no need to specify them in any interpretation of the wff. On the other hand, it is essential to specify all the *nonquantified* symbols a, b, f, g, and p in any interpretation. To distinguish between the two types of symbols, the quantified symbols F and x are called *variables* (F is a unary function variable and x is an individual variable), while the nonquantified symbols a, b, f, g, and p are called *constants* (a and b are individual constants, f is a unary function constant, g is a binary function constant, and p is a unary predicate constant).

As a second example, let us consider the following wff:

$$(\forall P)\{[P(a) \wedge (\forall x)[[\sim (x = a) \wedge P(f(x))] \supset P(x)]] \supset (\forall x)P(x)\}$$

Here we use one additional symbol which has a fixed meaning:

6. $\sim$ . . . stands for "not . . . is true," or, in other words, ". . . is false."

Therefore the wff can be read as follows:

> For every (unary) predicate P over D, if $P(a)$ is true, and for every $x \in D$, if $x \neq a$ and $P(f(x))$ are true then $P(x)$ is true, then for every $x \in D$, $P(x)$ is true.

Let us examine the meaning of this wff under two interpretations which are similar to those discussed earlier. First, if we consider the interpretation where D is N, a is 0, and $f(x)$ is $x - 1$, then we obtain the following statement:

> For every (unary) predicate P over N, if $P(0)$ is true, and for every $x \in N$, if $x \neq 0$ and $P(x - 1)$ are true then $P(x)$ is true, then for every $x \in N$, $P(x)$ is true.

This is a true statement because it is simply a version of the well-known induction principle over natural numbers.

Second, if we consider the interpretation in which $D = \Sigma^*$, where $\Sigma = \{\alpha, \beta\}$, a is Λ, and $f(x)$ is $tail(x)$, we obtain the statement

> For every (unary) predicate P over Σ^*, if $P(\Lambda)$ is true, and for every $x \in \Sigma^*$, if $x \neq \Lambda$ and $P(tail(x))$ is true then $P(x)$ is true, then for every $x \in \Sigma^*$, $P(x)$ is true.

Again this is a true statement because it is a version of the induction principle over strings.

One can easily find interpretations of this wff which yield false statements.

As a last example, let us consider the following wff:

$$\sim(x_1 = a) \wedge (\forall x_2)[(\exists x_3)(x_1 = f(x_2, x_3)) \supset [(x_2 = x_1) \vee (x_2 = a)]]$$

Here we use one additional symbol which has a fixed meaning:

7. $\cdots \vee \cdots$ stands for "... or ... is true."

Let us examine the meaning of this wff under the interpretation where D is the set of all positive integers, a is 1, and $f(x_2, x_3)$ is $x_2 \cdot x_3$; then we obtain the following statement:

> $x_1 \neq 1$ and for every positive integer x_2, if there exists a positive integer x_3 such that $x_1 = x_2 \cdot x_3$, then $x_2 = x_1$ or $x_2 = 1$.

or in short

> x_1 is a prime number.

In order to decide whether this statement is true or false, we have to extend the notion of interpretation and assign some positive integer to x_1. The reason is that although x_1 is a variable, it is not quantified (by "for all ..." or by "for some ..."); such nonquantified variables are called *free variables*. Thus, for example, if we let x_1 be 17 in our interpretation, we obtain

> 17 is a prime number,

which is a true statement.†

In Sec. 2-1 we introduce formally the notions of wffs and interpretations. The class of wffs we discuss is the so-called *second-order predicate calculus* (*with equality*). In our discussion we emphasize two subclasses of the wffs which are of special interest: the wffs of the *propositional calculus* and those of the *first-order predicate calculus* (*with equality*). A wff is said to be *valid* if it yields a true statement for all possible interpretations. This is a very strong requirement, and actually the three wffs discussed above are nonvalid. We are mainly concerned with the *validity problem* in predicate calculus, i.e., the existence of an algorithm (Turing machine) to determine whether or not a given wff is valid. We show that the validity problem of the propositional calculus is solvable, the validity problem of the first-order predicate calculus is unsolvable but partially solvable, while the

† Note that the role of free variables is actually identical to the role of constants. The need to distinguish between the two notions arises when we consider parts of wffs, as will be clarified later in Sec. 2-1.2.

validity problem of the second-order predicate calculus is not even partially solvable.

In Secs. 2-2 and 2-3 we describe two algorithms for partially solving the validity problem of the first-order predicate calculus. That is, each algorithm takes any first-order wff as input: If the wff is valid, the algorithm will eventually reach an ACCEPT halt; if the wff is not valid, the algorithm either reaches a REJECT halt or loops forever. The first algorithm is based on a common *natural deduction system*, while the second is based on the *resolution rule*.

2-1 BASIC NOTATIONS

2-1.1 Syntax

The symbols from which our sentences are constructed are listed below.†

1. *Truth symbols: T and F*
2. *Connectives:* $\sim$ (*not*), $\supset$ (*implication*), $\wedge$ (*and*), $\vee$ (*or*), $\equiv$ (*equivalence*), and IF-THEN-ELSE (*conditional connective*)
3. *Operators:* $=$ (*equality*) and *if-then-else* (*conditional operator*)
4. *Quantifiers:* $\forall$ (*universal quantifier*) and $\exists$ (*existential quantifier*)
5. *Constants:*
   (*a*) *n*-ary *function constants* f_i^n $(i \geqq 1, n \geqq 0)$; f_i^0 is called an *individual constant* and is also denoted by a_i
   (*b*) *n*-ary *predicate constants* p_i^n $(i \geqq 1, n \geqq 0)$; p_i^0 is called a *propositional constant*
6. *Variables:*
   (*a*) *n*-ary *function variables* F_i^n $(i \geqq 1, n \geqq 0)$; F_i^0 is called an *individual variable* and is also denoted by x_i
   (*b*) *n*-ary *predicate variables* P_i^n $(i \geqq 1, n \geqq 0)$; P_i^0 is called a *propositional variable*

Using these symbols we define recursively three classes of expressions: *terms*, *atomic formulas* (*atfs*), and *well-formed formulas* (*wffs*).

1. *Terms:*
   (*a*) Each individual constant a_i and each individual variable x_i is a term.
   (*b*) If $t_1, t_2, \ldots, t_n$ $(n \geqq 1)$ are terms, then so are $f_i^n(t_1, t_2, \ldots, t_n)$ and $F_i^n(t_1, t_2, \ldots, t_n)$.
   (*c*) If A is a wff (see below) and t_1 and t_2 are terms, then (*if* A *then* t_1 *else* t_2) is a term.

† In addition, we use punctuation marks ( ) and ,.

2. *Atomic formulas* (*atfs*)
   (*a*) T and F are atfs.
   (*b*) Each propositional constant p_i^0 and each propositional variable P_i^0 are atfs.
   (*c*) If $t_1, t_2, \ldots, t_n$ ($n \geqq 1$) are terms, then $p_i^n(t_1, t_2, \ldots, t_n)$ and $P_i^n(t_1, t_2, \ldots, t_n)$ are atfs.
   (*d*) If t_1, t_2 are terms, then $(t_1 = t_2)$ is an atf.
3. *Well-formed formulas* (*wffs*)
   (*a*) Each atf is a wff.
   (*b*) If A, B, and C are wffs, then so are $(\sim A)$, $(A \supset B)$, $(A \wedge B)$, $(A \vee B)$, $(A \equiv B)$, and (IF A THEN B ELSE C).
   (*c*) If v_i is a variable (that is, F_i or P_i) and A is a wff, then $((\forall v_i) A)$ and $((\exists v_i) A)$ are wffs. *For simplicity we assume that this step can be applied only if neither* $(\forall v_i)$ *nor* $(\exists v_i)$ *occurs already in* A.†

The reader should be aware that there is an essential difference in the use of the connective $\equiv$ (*equivalence*) and the operator $=$ (*equality*). The equivalence connective is used in expressions of the form

$$\langle \text{wff} \rangle \equiv \langle \text{wff} \rangle$$

yielding a wff, while the equality operator is used in expressions of the form

$$\langle \text{term} \rangle = \langle \text{term} \rangle$$

yielding an atf. Similarly, there is an essential difference in the use of the connective IF-THEN-ELSE (*conditional connective*) and the use of the operator *if-then-else* (*conditional operator*). The conditional connective is used in expressions of the form

$$\text{IF } \langle \text{wff} \rangle \text{ THEN } \langle \text{wff} \rangle \text{ ELSE } \langle \text{wff} \rangle$$

yielding a wff, while the conditional operator is used in expressions of the form

$$\textit{if } \langle \text{wff} \rangle \textit{ then } \langle \text{term} \rangle \textit{ else } \langle \text{term} \rangle$$

yielding a term.

In the following examples we use several straightforward abbreviations. Since the superscripts f_i^n, F_i^n, p_i^n, and P_i^n are used only to indicate the number of arguments, they are always omitted. The subscripts are used for enumerating the symbols and are omitted whenever their omission can cause no confusion. For simplicity we usually use additional symbols: a, b, and c for individual constants; f, g, and h for function constants; p, q, r, and s for predicate constants; x, y, and z for individual variables;

† This assumption is not essential and is added in order to simplify our discussion.

F, G, and H for function variables; and P, Q, R, and S for predicate variables.

Also we usually omit parentheses whenever their omission can cause no confusion; in particular, we usually write $(\exists v_i)$ and $(\forall v_i)$ as $\exists v_i$ and $\forall v_i$ without parentheses. Sometimes we use brackets [ ] or braces { } rather than parentheses ( ) to gain clarity. A wff of the form $\sim(t_1 = t_2)$ will usually be written as $t_1 \neq t_2$. We assume that $(\exists v_i)$, $(\forall v_i)$, and $\sim$ bind tighter than any other connective, i.e., they are always applied to the smallest possible scope (atf or a parenthesized expression). Thus

$\sim p \wedge \sim q$ stands for the wff $((\sim p) \wedge (\sim q))$,

$\sim(p \supset q) \supset q$ stands for $((\sim(p \supset q)) \supset q)$, and

$\sim\forall x p(x) \equiv \exists x \sim p(x)$ stands for $((\sim((\forall x)\, p(x))) \equiv ((\exists x)(\sim p(x))))$.

EXAMPLE 2-1

The following are wffs:

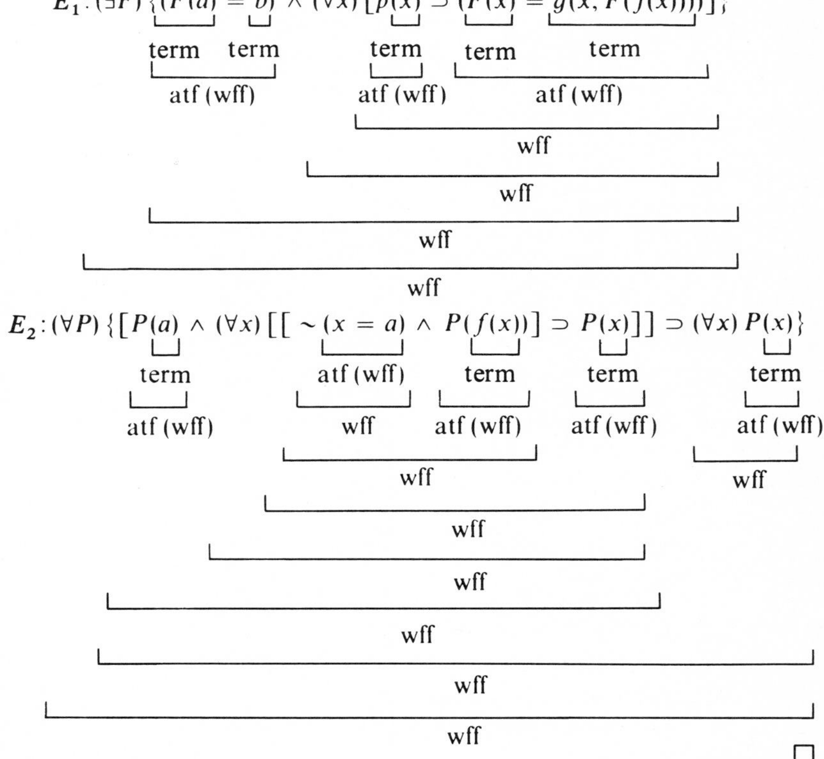

□

A wff which is a part of a wff A is said to be a *well-formed part* (*wfp*) *of A*. For example, there are seven wfps of the wff E_1 above:

$F(a) = b$
$p(x)$
$F(x) = g(x, F(f(x)))$
$p(x) \supset (F(x) = g(x, F(f(x))))$
$(\forall x)[p(x) \supset (F(x) = g(x, F(f(x))))]$
$(F(a) = b) \wedge (\forall x)[p(x) \supset (F(x) = g(x, F(f(x))))]$
and E_1 itself.

The capital letters $A, B, C, \ldots$, and so forth, usually indicate wffs or wfps. Thus an expression of the form $(A \supset B) \supset \forall x A$ stands for the class of all wffs having that form, for example, $(p(x) \supset q(x)) \supset \forall x p(x)$, $((x = y) \supset q) \supset \forall x(x = y)$, $(\exists y p(x, y) \supset x = y) \supset \forall x \exists y p(x, y)$, and so forth.

For a wfp of the form $(\forall v_i)A$, we say that the occurrence of the variable v_i in $(\forall v_i)$ is *universally quantified*, A is the *scope of* $(\forall v_i)$, and every occurrence of v_i in A is *bound by* $(\forall v_i)$. Similarly, for $(\exists v_i)A$ we say that the occurrence of the variable v_i in $(\exists v_i)$ is *existentially quantified*, A is the *scope of* $(\exists v_i)$, and every occurrence of v_i in A is *bound by* $(\exists v_i)$. Every occurrence of a variable v_i in a wff which is not quantified or bound is said to be a *free occurrence*. A variable v_i is said to be a *free variable of a wff* if there are free occurrences of v_i in the wff. A wff with no free variables is said to be *closed*. For example, the wffs E_1 and E_2 discussed above are closed wffs, while the following wff is not closed because x is a free variable of it:

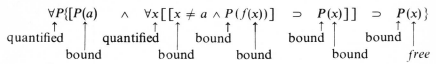

$$\forall P\{[P(a) \wedge \forall x[[x \neq a \wedge P(f(x))] \supset P(x)]] \supset P(x)\}$$

quantified, bound, quantified, bound, bound, bound, bound, bound, bound, *free*

The class of wffs described here is usually called *second-order predicate calculus (with equality)*. There are several subclasses of the wffs which are of special interest; these subclasses are obtained by restricting the set of constant and variable symbols that may occur in the wffs. We now describe four such subclasses. Each subclass is indicated by stating the admissible set of constant and variable symbols.

1. *Propositional calculus*:
   (*a*) Propositional constants p_i^0
2. *Quantified propositional calculus*:
   (*a*) Propositional constants p_i^0
   (*b*) Propositional variables P_i^0
3. *Equality calculus*:
   (*a*) Individual constants a_i
   (*b*) Individual variables x_i

4. *First-order predicate calculus (with equality)*:
   (*a*) n-ary ($n \geqq 0$) function constants f_i^n
   (*b*) n-ary ($n \geqq 0$) predicate constants p_i^n
   (*c*) Individual variables x_i

EXAMPLE 2-2
Consider the following wffs:

$$A:\ (\text{IF } p_1 \text{ THEN } p_2 \text{ ELSE } p_3) \equiv (\text{IF } \sim p_1 \text{ THEN } p_3 \text{ ELSE } p_2)$$
$$B:\ \forall P_1 (P_1 \equiv p) \supset \exists P_2 (P_2 \equiv \sim p)$$
$$C:\ \forall x_1 \forall x_2 \forall x_3 [(x_1 = x_2 \wedge x_2 = x_3) \supset x_1 = x_3]$$
$$D:\ (x_1 \neq a) \wedge \forall x_2 [\exists x_3 p(x_1, f(x_2, x_3)) \supset [p(x_2, x_1) \vee p(x_2, a)]]$$

The wffs A to D belong to subclasses 1 to 4, respectively. The two wffs E_1 and E_2 discussed previously are of the second-order predicate calculus but belong to none of the four subclasses.

□

Note that no function symbol (constant or variable) may occur in the propositional calculus. This implies that there are no terms in the propositional calculus, and therefore the operators = (*equality*) and *if-then-else* (*conditional operator*) can never be used. The same applies to the quantified propositional calculus. The most important subclass is the first-order predicate calculus. Note that it includes properly all the wffs of the propositional and equality calculus.

2-1.2 Semantics (Interpretations)

We can assign a meaning to each wff by "interpreting" the constant symbols and free variables in it. By associating different interpretations with a given wff, we obtain different *statements*, where each statement is either *true* or *false*. In this section we shall discuss the notion of an interpretation of a wff and the statement generated by it.

Let D be any nonempty set; then D^n ($n \geqq 1$) stands for the set of all ordered n-tuples of elements of D. An *n-ary function over D* ($n \geqq 1$) is a total function mapping D^n into D. An *n-ary predicate over D* ($n \geqq 1$) is a total function mapping D^n into $\{true, false\}$. In general, we also allow the case $n = 0$ where a 0-ary function over D denotes a fixed element of D, while a 0-ary predicate over D denotes a fixed truth value (*true* or *false*).

EXAMPLE 2-3

Let $D = I$ (the integers); then D^2 is the set of all ordered pairs of integers, and D^3 is the set of all ordered triples of integers. $x_2 + 1$, $x_1 + x_2$, and $(x_1 + x_2)\,x_3$ are unary, binary, and ternary functions over I, respectively; $x_1 = 0$, $x_1 > x_2$, and $x_1 + x_2 = x_3$ are unary, binary, and ternary predicates over I, respectively.

□

An *interpretation* $\mathscr{I}$ of a wff A is a triple $(D, \mathscr{I}_c, \mathscr{I}_v)$ where we have the following.

1. D is a nonempty set, which is called the *domain of the interpretation.*
2. $\mathscr{I}_c$ indicates the assignments to the *constants* of A:
   (*a*) To each function constant f_i^n $(n \geqq 0)$ which occurs in A, we assign an n-ary function over D. In particular (case $n = 0$), each individual constant a_i is assigned some element of D.
   (*b*) To each predicate constant p_i^n $(n \geqq 0)$ which occurs in A, we assign an n-ary predicate over D. In particular (case $n = 0$), each propositional constant is assigned the truth value *true* or *false.*
3. $\mathscr{I}_v$ indicates assignments to the *free variables* of A:
   (*a*) To each free function variable F_i^n $(n \geqq 0)$ of A, we assign an n-ary function over D. In particular (case $n = 0$), each free individual variable x_i in A is assigned some element of D.
   (*b*) To each free predicate variable P_i^n $(n \geqq 0)$ of A, we assign an n-ary predicate over D. In particular (case $n = 0$), each free propositional variable in A is assigned the truth value *true* or *false.*

For a given interpretation $\mathscr{I}$ of a wff A, the pair $\langle A, \mathscr{I}\rangle$ indicates a statement (sometimes called an *interpreted wff*) which has a truth value *true* or *false.* This truth value is obtained by first applying the assignments of $\mathscr{I}_c$ to all the constant symbols in A and the assignments of $\mathscr{I}_v$ to all free occurrences of variable symbols in A, and then using the meaning (semantics) of the truth symbols, connectives, operators, and quantifiers as explained below.

1. *The meaning of the truth symbols:*
   The meaning of T is *true* and of F is *false.*
2. *The meaning of the connectives:*
   (*a*) The connective $\sim$ (*not*) stands for a unary function mapping $\{true, false\}$ into $\{true, false\}$ as follows:

$$\sim \textit{true} \text{ is } \textit{false}$$
$$\sim \textit{false} \text{ is } \textit{true}$$

(*b*) The connectives $\supset$ (*implication*), $\wedge$ (*and*), $\vee$ (*or*), and $\equiv$ (*equivalence*) stand for binary functions mapping $\{true, false\}^2$ into $\{true, false\}$ as follows:

true $\supset$ *false* is *false*
true $\supset$ *true*, *false* $\supset$ *true*, and *false* $\supset$ *false* are *true*
true $\wedge$ *true* is *true*
true $\wedge$ *false*, *false* $\wedge$ *true*, and *false* $\wedge$ *false* are *false*
false $\vee$ *false* is *false*
true $\vee$ *true*, *true* $\vee$ *false*, and *false* $\vee$ *true* are *true*†
true $\equiv$ *true* and *false* $\equiv$ *false* are *true*
true $\equiv$ *false* and *false* $\equiv$ *true* are *false*.

(*c*) The connective IF-THEN-ELSE (*conditional connective*) stands for a ternary function mapping $\{true, false\}^3$ into $\{true, false\}$ as follows:

(IF *true* THEN α ELSE β) is α
(IF *false* THEN α ELSE β) is β

where α and β are either *true* or *false*.

Actually, the unary connective $\sim$ and all the binary connectives $\supset$, $\wedge$, $\vee$, and $\equiv$ are redundant because each one of them can be expressed in terms of the IF-THEN-ELSE connective and the truth symbols T and F:

$\sim A$	by	IF A THEN F ELSE T
$A \wedge B$	by	IF A THEN B ELSE F
$A \vee B$	by	IF A THEN T ELSE B
$A \supset B$	by	IF A THEN B ELSE T
$A \equiv B$	by	IF A THEN B ELSE $\sim B$ that is, IF A THEN B ELSE (IF B THEN F ELSE T)

3. *The meaning of the quantifiers*

We consider wfps of the form $(\forall F_i^n)\,A$, $(\forall P_i^n)\,A$, $(\exists F_i^n)\,A$, and $(\exists P_i^n)\,A$. Since such a wfp might have some free occurrences of variables, we have to consider its value for some fixed assignment of values to those free occurrences.

(*a*) The quantifier $\forall$ (*universal quantifier*) stands for the words "for all . . . is true". The value of $(\forall F_i^n)A$ is *true*, if for all

† Note that by our definition *true* $\vee$ *true* is *true*. Therefore the $\vee$ connective is sometimes called the *inclusive or* to distinguish it from the *exclusive or* for which *true* $\vee$ *true* is *false*.

n-ary functions Φ over D, the value of A (with Φ assigned to all occurrences of F_i^n) is *true*; otherwise, the value of $(\forall F_i^n)A$ is *false*. Similarly, the value of $(\forall P_i^n)A$ is *true* if for all n-ary predicates ψ over D, the value of A (with ψ assigned to all occurrences of P_i^n) is *true*; otherwise, the value of $(\forall P_i^n)\, A$ is *false*.

(*b*) The quantifier $\exists$ (*existential quantifier*) stands for the words "there exists . . . such that . . . is true." The value of $(\exists F_i^n)\, A$ is *true* if there exists an n-ary function Φ over D, such that the value of A (with Φ assigned to all occurrences of F_i^n) is *true*; otherwise, the value of $(\exists F_i^n)\, A$ is *false*. Similarly, the value of $(\exists P_i^n)\, A$ is *true* if there exists an n-ary predicate ψ over D, such that the value of A (with ψ assigned to all occurrences of P_i^n) is *true*; otherwise, the value of $(\exists P_i^n)\, A$ is *false*.

Note that one of the two quantifiers is actually redundant because each one of them can be expressed in terms of the other:

$$(\forall v_i)\, A \quad \text{by} \quad \sim (\exists v_i) \sim A$$
$$(\exists v_i)\, A \quad \text{by} \quad \sim (\forall v_i) \sim A$$

4. *The meaning of the operators*:

(*a*) The operator $=$ (*equality*) stands for a binary function mapping $D \times D$ into $\{true, false\}$ as follows:

For $d_1, d_2 \in D$, $d_1 = d_2$ is *true* if and only if d_1 and d_2 are the same element of D.

(*b*) The operator *if-then-else* (*conditional operator*) stands for a ternary function mapping $\{true, false\} \times D \times D$ into D as follows:

$$(\textit{if true then } d_1 \textit{ else } d_2) \quad \text{is} \quad d_1$$
$$(\textit{if false then } d_1 \textit{ else } d_2) \quad \text{is} \quad d_2,$$

where $d_1, d_2 \in D$.

Actually both operators are redundant because every atf of the form $t_1 = t_2$ can be replaced by $\forall P[P(t_1) \equiv P(t_2)]$ while every atf of the form $p(t_1, \ldots, t_{i-1}, \textit{if } A \textit{ then } t_i' \textit{ else } t_i'', t_{i+1}, \ldots, t_n)$ can be replaced by

$$\text{IF } A \text{ THEN } p(t_1, \ldots, t_{i-1}, t_i', t_{i+1}, \ldots, t_n) \quad \text{ELSE } p(t_1, \ldots, t_{i-1}, t_i'', t_{i+1}, \ldots, t_n)$$

EXAMPLE 2-4

1. The wff

$$\exists x \forall y [p(y) \supset x = y]$$

means "there exists x such that for all y, if $p(y)$ is true then $x = y$", or in short, "there is *at most one* x such that $p(x)$ is true." This wff yields the value *true* for any interpretation with an arbitrary domain D and an assignment of a unary predicate over D to p as long as $p(d)$ is *true* for at most one element d of D.

2. The wff

$$\exists x [p(x) \wedge \forall y [p(y) \supset x = y]]$$

means "there exists x such that $p(x)$ is true, and for all y, if $p(y)$ is true then $x = y$", or in short "there is a *unique* x such that $p(x)$ is true." This wff yields the value *true* for any interpretation with an arbitrary domain D and an assignment of a unary predicate over D to p as long as $p(d)$ is *true* for exactly one element d of D.

□

EXAMPLE 2-5

Consider the wff

$$\forall z \exists u \exists v [(z = u \vee z = v) \wedge u \neq v]$$
$$\wedge \forall x \forall y \forall P [x \neq y \vee (P(x, x) \vee \sim P(y, y))]$$

Since there are neither constant symbols nor free variables in this wff, each interpretation of the wff consists only of the specification of some nonempty set D (the domain of the interpretation). We show that this wff yields the truth value *false* for any domain with one element but yields the value *true* for any domain with two elements. (It can also be shown that it yields the value *true* for any domain with n, $n \geqq 3$, elements.)

1. *Suppose the domain D consists of one element, say, d.* In this case, in the process of interpreting the meaning of the quantifiers, only d can be assigned to any individual variable. Thus, $(z = u \vee z = v) \wedge u \neq v$ becomes $(true \vee true) \wedge false$, which is *false*. It is clear also that $\forall z \exists u \exists v [(z = u \vee z = v) \wedge u \neq v]$, which stands for "for all $z \in D$, there exists $u \in D$ and $v \in D$ such that . . ." also yields the value *false*. Therefore because of the meaning of the $\wedge$ (*and*) connective, it follows that the entire wff yields the value *false*.
2. *Now suppose D is composed of two elements d_1 and d_2.* We treat the two parts of the wff separately.

(*a*) First notice that $(z = u \vee z = v) \wedge u \neq v$ obtains the value *true* if and only if the elements of D assigned to u and v are different; for as there are only the elements d_1 and d_2, the element assigned to z is the same as one of the elements assigned to u or v. Then $z = u \vee z = v$ obtains always the value *true*, and therefore the truth value of this expression depends only on the truth value of $u \neq v$. Thus the value of $\forall z \exists u \exists v[(z = u \vee z = v) \wedge u \neq v]$ must be *true* because, for any choice (d_1 or d_2) for z, let u be d_1 and v be d_2.

(*b*) We show now that $\forall P[x \neq y \vee (P(x, x) \vee \sim P(y, y))]$ obtains the value *true* for any assignment of a pair of elements of D to x and y. If we assign two different elements to x and y, then $x \neq y$ is *true* and therefore, because of the meaning of the $\vee$ (*or*) connective, the entire expression is *true*. If we assign the same element to x and y, say, d_1, then $P(x, x)$ and $P(y, y)$ obtain the same value by any assignment of a binary predicate over D to P. Therefore, $P(x, x) \vee \sim P(y, y)$ is *true*; and because of the meaning of the $\vee$ (*or*) connective, $x \neq y \vee (P(x, x) \vee \sim P(y, y))$ obtains also the value *true*. Since the above discussion was independent of the assignment for P, it follows that $\forall P[x \neq y \vee (P(x, x) \vee \sim P(y, y))]$ obtains the value *true*. Thus, $\forall P[x \neq y \vee (P(x, x) \vee \sim P(y, y))]$ obtains the value *true* for any assignment of x and y; that is, $\forall x \forall y \forall P[x \neq y \vee (P(x, x) \vee \sim P(y, y))]$ obtains the value *true*.

□

2-1.3 Valid wffs

The examples just presented show that a wff may yield the value *true* for some interpretations and the value *false* for some other interpretations. We are interested mainly in two types of wffs: those that yield the value *true* for every possible interpretation, called *valid wffs*, and those that yield the value *false* for every possible interpretation, called *unsatisfiable wffs*. In other words:

1. A wff A is said to be *valid* if it yields the value *true* for every interpretation. Thus, a wff is *nonvalid* if and only if there exists some interpretation for which A yields the value *false*; such an interpretation is called a *countermodel for A*.

2. A wff A is said to be *unsatisfiable* if it yields the value *false* for every interpretation. Thus, a wff is *satisfiable* if and only if there exists some

interpretation for which A yields the value *true*; such an interpretation is called a *model for A*.

There is one important relation between the two notions: *A wff A is valid if and only if* $\sim A$ *is unsatisfiable.*

EXAMPLE 2-6

1. *The wff* $\forall x \forall y \forall P[x \neq y \vee (P(x, x) \vee \sim P(y, y))]$ *is valid.* For if we assign two different elements d_1 and d_2 to x and y, $x \neq y$ is *true* and therefore $\forall P[x \neq y \vee (P(x, x) \vee \sim P(y, y))]$ is *true*. If we assign the same element d to x and y, then $P(x, x)$ and $P(y, y)$ obtains the same value by any assignment of a binary predicate over D to P; that is, $P(x, x) \vee \sim P(y, y)$ is *true*. Therefore $\forall P[x \neq y \vee (P(x, x) \vee \sim P(y, y))]$ is *true*.

2. *The wff* $\exists P \forall x \exists y[P(x, x) \wedge \sim P(x, y)]$ *is neither valid nor unsatisfiable.* Actually, the wff obtains the value *false* for every interpretation with a domain of only one element and the value *true* for every interpretation with a domain of at least two elements. If there is only one element in D, $P(x, x) \wedge \sim P(x, y)$ obtains the value *false* by any assignment of a binary predicate over D to P because the elements assigned to x and y are the same. If there are at least two elements in D, we assign to P a binary predicate over D, the value of which is *true* only for ordered pairs of elements of the form (d, d), where $d \in D$ (that is, both members are the same). Then, given any assignment for x, an assignment for y can be found, namely, an element of D different from the element assigned to x, so that $P(x, x) \wedge \sim P(x, y)$ obtains the value *true*, which means that $\exists P \forall x \exists y[P(x, x) \wedge \sim P(x, y)]$ obtains the value *true*.

3. *The wff* $\exists P \exists x \exists y[(P(x, x) \wedge \sim P(x, y)) \wedge x = y]$ *is unsatisfiable.* If we assign to P an arbitrary binary predicate over D and the elements d_1 and d_2 of D to x and y, there are two cases: either d_1 and d_2 are not the same element, then $x = y$ obtains the value *false*, or d_1 and d_2 are the same element, then $P(x, x)$ and $P(x, y)$ obtain the same value, so that either $P(x, x)$ or $\sim P(x, y)$ obtains the value *false*. Thus, in both cases $(P(x, x) \wedge \sim P(x, y)) \wedge x = y$ obtains the value *false*.

□

EXAMPLE 2-7

We shall now list 11 valid first-order wffs; for each wff we shall give a "similar" nonvalid first-order wff.

VALID wffs	NONVALID wffs
A_1: $\forall x p_1(x) \supset \exists x p_1(x)$	B_1: $\exists x p_1(x) \supset \forall x p_1(x)$
A_2: $p_1(x) \supset p_1(x)$	B_2: $p_1(x) \supset p_1(a)$

A_3: $\forall x q_1(x) \supset q_1(a)$

A_4: $p_1(a) \supset \exists x p_1(x)$

A_5: $\forall x \forall y (p_2(x, y) \supset p_2(x, y))$

A_6: $\exists y \forall x p_2(x, y) \supset \forall x \exists y p_2(x, y)$

A_7: $\exists x p_2(x, x) \supset \exists x \exists y p_2(x, y)$

A_8: $\forall x \forall y q_2(x, y) \supset \forall x q_2(x, x)$

A_9: $[\forall x p_1(x) \vee \forall x q_1(x)] \supset \forall x (p_1(x) \vee q_1(x))$

A_{10}: $\exists x (p_1(x) \wedge q_1(x)) \supset [\exists x p_1(x) \wedge \exists x q_1(x)]$

A_{11}: $[\exists x p_1(x) \supset \forall x q_1(x)] \supset \forall x (p_1(x) \supset q_1(x))$

B_3: $q_1(a) \supset \forall x q_1(x)$

B_4: $\exists x p_1(x) \supset p_1(a)$

B_5: $\forall x \forall y (p_2(x, y) \supset p_2(y, x))$

B_6: $\forall x \exists y p_2(x, y) \supset \exists y \forall x p_2(x, y)$

B_7: $\exists x \exists y p_2(x, y) \supset \exists x p_2(x, x)$

B_8: $\forall x q_2(x, x) \supset \forall x \forall y q_2(x, y)$

B_9: $\forall x (p_1(x) \vee q_1(x)) \supset [\forall x p_1(x) \vee \forall x q_1(x)]$

B_{10}: $[\exists x p_1(x) \wedge \exists x q_1(x)] \supset \exists x (p_1(x) \wedge q_1(x))$

B_{11}: $\forall x (p_1(x) \supset p_1(x)) \supset [\exists x p_1(x) \supset \forall x p_1(x)]$

We can show the nonvalidity of wffs B_1 to B_{11} by stating appropriate countermodels. For this purpose, let $D = \{\text{all integers}\}$, $p_1(x)$ be $x > 0$, $q_1(x)$ be $x \leq 0$, $p_2(x, y)$ be $x > y$, $q_2(x, y)$ be $x = y$, a be 0, and the free x be 1. The interpretation is a countermodel for B_1 to B_{11} because (note that *true* $\supset$ *false* is *false*)

B_1: $\exists x(x > 0) \supset \forall x(x > 0)$ is *false.*

B_2: $(1 > 0) \supset (0 > 0)$ is *false.*

B_3: $(0 \leqq 0) \supset \forall x(x \leqq 0)$ is *false.*

B_4: $\exists x(x > 0) \supset (0 > 0)$ is *false.*

B_5: $\forall x \forall y(x > y \supset y > x)$ is *false.*

B_6: $\forall x \exists y(x > y) \supset \exists y \forall x(x > y)$ is *false* because for every integer x there is a y, say, $x - 1$, for which $x > y$, but there does not exist a y for which every integer x has the property $x > y$.

B_7: $\exists x \exists y(x > y) \supset \exists x(x > x)$ is *false.*

B_8: $\forall x(x = x) \supset \forall x \forall y(x = y)$ is *false.*

B_9: $\forall x(x > 0 \vee x \leqq 0) \supset [\forall x(x > 0) \vee \forall x(x \leqq 0)]$ is *false* because $\forall x(x > 0 \vee x \leqq 0)$ is *true*, but both $\forall x(x > 0)$ and $\forall x(x \leqq 0)$ are *false.*

B_{10}: $[\exists x(x > 0) \wedge \exists x(x \leqq 0)] \supset \exists x(x > 0 \wedge x \leqq 0)$ is *false* because both $\exists x(x > 0)$ and $\exists x(x \leqq 0)$ are *true*, but $\exists x(x > 0 \wedge x \leqq 0)$ is *false.*

B_{11}: $\forall x(x > 0 \supset x > 0) \supset [\exists x(x > 0) \supset \forall x(x > 0)]$ is *false* because both $\forall x(x > 0 \supset x > 0)$ and $\exists x(x > 0)$ are *true*, but $\forall x(x > 0)$ is *false.* [Note that *true* $\supset$ (*true* $\supset$ *false*) is *false.*]

The validity of wffs A_1 to A_{11} is best proved using the natural deduction technique or the resolution method (introduced later in this chapter). However, we can prove the validity of these wffs by contradiction. Let us prove, for example, that the wff

$$A_6: \quad \exists y \forall x p_2(x, y) \supset \forall x \exists y p_2(x, y)$$

is valid. For suppose A_6 is not valid; then there must exist a countermodel $\mathscr{I}$ of A_6. In other words, A_6 is *false* under $\mathscr{I}$, and therefore $\exists y \forall x p_2(x, y)$ is *true* while $\forall x \exists y p_2(x, y)$ is *false.* Since $\exists y \forall x p_2(x, y)$ is *true*, there must exist an element of D (the domain of $\mathscr{I}$), say, d_1, such that $\forall x p_2(x, d_1)$† is *true.* Since $\forall x \exists y p_2(x, y)$ is *false*, there must exist an element of D, say, d_2, such that $\exists y p_2(d_2, y)$ is *false.* Now, since $\forall x p_2(x, d_1)$ is *true*, then $p_2(d_2, d_1)$ must be *true*, which contradicts the fact that $\exists y p_2(d_2, y)$ is *false.*

□

EXAMPLE 2-8
The following wffs of the propositional calculus are valid:

$$p \supset p$$
$$p \vee (\sim p)$$
$$(p \wedge q) \supset p$$
$$((p \supset q) \supset p) \supset p$$
$$[((p \wedge q) \supset r) \wedge (p \supset q)] \supset (p \supset r)$$
$$\text{IF } p \text{ THEN } p \text{ ELSE } \sim p$$
$$\text{IF } F \text{ THEN } p \text{ ELSE } T$$

□

It is always possible and actually very easy to check the validity of wffs of the propositional calculus.

THEOREM 2-1 (Validity in the propositional calculus). *There are algorithms to decide the validity of wffs of the propositional calculus.*

Proof. We illustrate one algorithm (due to Quine, 1950) using the wff

$$A: \quad [((p \wedge q) \supset r) \wedge (p \supset q)] \supset (p \supset r)$$

By substituting T for p (left branch) and F for p (right branch), we obtain

$$[((p \wedge q) \supset r) \wedge (p \supset q)] \supset (p \supset r)$$

$$p = T \qquad\qquad p = F$$

$$[((T \wedge q) \supset r) \wedge (T \supset q)] \supset (T \supset r) \quad [((F \wedge q) \supset r) \wedge (F \supset q)] \supset (F \supset r)$$

† Note that this is not a wff because d_1 is an element of D and not a symbol of the predicate calculus. We shall sometimes use such expressions as part of the metalanguage as long as no confusion is caused.

Each such wff can be simplified by replacing

$\sim F$ by T	$\sim T$ by F
$T \supset A$ by A	$A \supset T$ by T
$F \supset A$ by T	$A \supset F$ by $\sim A$
$T \vee A$ or $A \vee T$ by T	$F \vee A$ or $A \vee F$ by A
$T \wedge A$ or $A \wedge T$ by A	$F \wedge A$ or $A \wedge F$ by F
$T \equiv A$ or $A \equiv T$ by A	$F \equiv A$ or $A \equiv F$ by $\sim A$
(IF T THEN A ELSE B) by A	(IF F THEN A ELSE B) by B
(IF A THEN T ELSE T) by T	(IF A THEN F ELSE F) by F
(IF A THEN T ELSE F) by A	(IF A THEN F ELSE T) by $\sim A$

Thus for our example we obtain, after applying all possible simplifications,

$$[((p \wedge q) \supset r) \wedge (p \supset q)] \supset (p \supset r)$$

$p = T$: $((q \supset r) \wedge q) \supset r$

$p = F$: T

We say that a wff is *terminal* if it consists of just T or F. Thus on the right branch we have reached a terminal wff T, while on the left we have reached a nonterminal wff. We continue the branching process of substituting T for q and F for q in the nonterminal wff $((q \supset r) \wedge q) \supset r$ and then applying all possible simplifications.

In general, we construct a binary tree of wffs, with the given wff as the root, substituting in each level T or F for one propositional letter and then applying all possible simplifications. The process terminates if either some terminal wff F is reached (which implies that the given wff is not valid) or all terminal wffs are T (which implies that the given wff is valid).

The complete binary tree obtained for the given wff A is

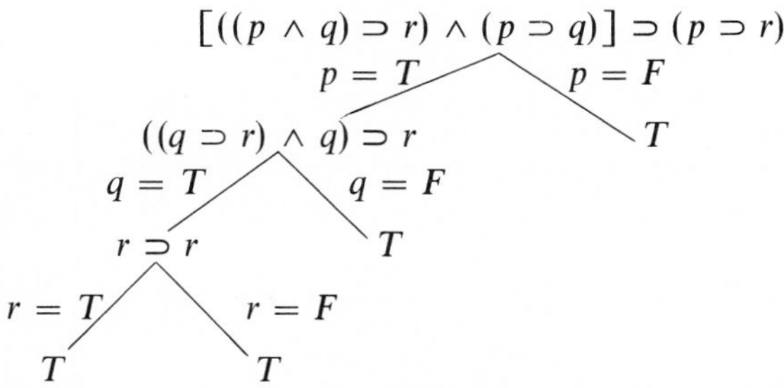

All terminal wffs are T; therefore A is valid. Q.E.D.

Actually, one can use the idea behind the proof of Theorem 2-1 to show a stronger result:

There are algorithms to decide the validity of wffs of the quantified propositional calculus.

Proof. Given any wff of the quantified propositional calculus, we first transform it into a wff containing no propositional variables by replacing every part in the wff of the form $(\forall P_i^0)\, B(P_i^0)$ by $B(T) \wedge B(F)$†, and every part of the form $(\exists P_i^0)\, B(P_i^0)$ by $B(T) \vee B(F)$. As the next step, each propositional constant p_i^0 occurring in the resulting wff A is eliminated by replacing the wff $A(p_i^0)$ by $A(T) \wedge A(F)$. This process is repeated now for the propositional constants in $A(T) \wedge A(F)$ until all the propositional constants are eliminated. If one keeps simplifying the resulting wff using the meaning of the connectives, the wff must reduce finally to T or F. The given wff is valid if and only if it reduces to T.

Q.E.D.

At this point it is worthwhile to introduce a theorem which enables us to reduce in certain cases the validity of wffs in predicate calculus to the validity of wffs in propositional calculus. The theorem can be stated as follows:‡

THEOREM 2-2 (The tautology theorem). *Let A be a wff in the propositional calculus with propositional constants $p_1, p_2, \ldots, p_n$. Let A' be the result of replacing each occurrence of p_i $(1 \leqq i \leqq n)$ in A by some wff B_i of the predicate calculus. If A is valid, then so is A'.*

For example, since $p \supset p$ is a valid wff of the propositional calculus, it implies that *any wff* of the predicate calculus of the form $B \supset B$ is valid. This is the reason why from now on we say that $B \supset B$ is valid (i.e., every wff of the predicate calculus having this form is valid) rather than saying that $p \supset p$ is valid.

2-1.4 Equivalence of wffs

We say that *two wffs A and B are equivalent* if both of them yield the same truth value for any interpretation which includes assignments to all the constants and free variables occurring in A and B. From the definition of

† We denote the wfp B by $B(P_i^0)$ so that $B(T)$ stands for the wfp obtained by replacing all free occurrences of P_i^0 in B by T and similarly, $B(F)$ stands for the result of replacing all free occurrences of P_i^0 in B by F.

‡ The theorem is called *the tautology theorem* because valid wffs of the propositional calculus are usually called *tautologies*. (The unsatisfiable wffs of the propositional calculus are usually called *contradictions*.)

validity and the meaning of the equivalence connective $\equiv$, it follows that two wffs A and B are equivalent if and only if the wff $(A \equiv B)$ is valid.

The following theorem is one of the most important results concerning equivalence of wffs.

THEOREM 2-3 (The replacement theorem). *If A' is a wff containing a wfp A, and B' is the result of replacing one or more occurrences of A in A' by B, then if A and B are equivalent, so are A' and B'.*

Another important property is the *transitivity* of the equivalence relation, that is:

If A and B are equivalent wffs and B and C are equivalent wffs, so are A and C.

It follows therefore that, in general, wffs can be transformed into simpler (shorter) equivalent wffs by successively replacing wfps of the wffs by equivalent wfps. Some of the standard simplification rules follow directly from the meaning of the connectives, operators, and quantifiers; for example, we can replace:

1.	(a) $T \supset B$ by B	$B \supset T$ by T
	(b) $F \supset B$ by T	$B \supset F$ by $\sim B$
	(c) $B \supset B$ by T	
	(d) $B \supset \sim B$ by $\sim B$	$\sim B \supset B$ by B
	(e) $\sim \sim B$ by B	
2.	(a) $T \vee B$ or $B \vee T$ by T	$F \vee B$ or $B \vee F$ by B
	(b) $B \vee B$ by B	$B \vee \sim B$ or $\sim B \vee B$ by T
	(c) $T \wedge B$ or $B \wedge T$ by B	$F \wedge B$ or $B \wedge F$ by F
	(d) $B \wedge B$ by B	$B \wedge \sim B$ or $\sim B \wedge B$ by F
	(e) $B \vee (B \wedge C)$ or $B \wedge (B \vee C)$ by B	
	(f) $(B \vee C) \wedge (\sim B \vee C)$ or $(B \wedge C) \vee (\sim B \wedge C)$ by C	
3.	(a) $T \equiv B$ or $B \equiv T$ by B	$F \equiv B$ or $B \equiv F$ by $\sim B$
	(b) $B \equiv B$ by T,	$B \equiv \sim B$ or $\sim B \equiv B$ by F
4.	(a) (IF T THEN B ELSE C) by B	(IF F THEN B ELSE C) by C
	(b) (IF B THEN T ELSE F) by B	(IF B THEN F ELSE T) by $\sim B$
	(c) (IF B THEN C ELSE C) by C	(*if* B *then* t *else* t) by t
	(d) (*if* T *then* t_1 *else* t_2) by t_1	(*if* F *then* t_1 *else* t_2) by t_2

5. (*a*) $\sim \forall x \sim A$ by $\exists x A$	$\sim \exists x \sim A$ by $\forall x A$
(*b*) $\exists P \forall x[(A \vee P(x)) \wedge (B \vee \sim P(x))]$ by $\forall x[A \vee B]$ (*c*) $\forall P \exists x[(A \wedge P(x)) \vee (B \wedge \sim P(x))]$ by $\exists x[A \wedge B]$	where A and B are assumed not to contain the predicate variable P
6. (*a*) $t = t$ by T	$t \neq t$ by F
(*b*) $\forall P[P(x) \equiv P(y)]$ by $x = y$	$\exists P[P(x) \wedge \sim P(y)]$ by $x \neq y$
(*c*) $\forall x[x \neq y \vee A]$ by A' (*d*) $\exists x[x = y \wedge A]$ by A'	where A' is the result of replacing all free occurrences of x in A by y

Several additional interesting equivalent pairs of wffs which follow from the meaning of the connectives are:

7. (*a*) $A \supset B$ and $\sim A \vee B$	$A \supset B$ and $\sim (A \wedge \sim B)$
(*b*) $A \equiv B$ and $(A \supset B) \wedge (B \supset A)$	
(*c*) (IF A THEN B ELSE C) and $(A \supset B) \wedge (\sim A \supset C)$	
8. (*a*) $\sim (A \supset B)$ and $A \wedge \sim B$	$\sim (A \equiv B)$ and $A \equiv \sim B$
(*b*) $\sim (A \vee B)$ and $\sim A \wedge \sim B$ (*c*) $\sim (A \wedge B)$ and $\sim A \vee \sim B$	de Morgan's laws
9. (*a*) $A \wedge (B \vee C)$ and $(A \wedge B) \vee (A \wedge C)$ (*b*) $A \vee (B \wedge C)$ and $(A \vee B) \wedge (A \vee C)$	Distributive laws
10. (*a*) $A \vee B$ and $B \vee A$ (*b*) $A \wedge B$ and $B \wedge A$ (*c*) $A \equiv B$ and $B \equiv A$	Commutative laws†
11. (*a*) $(A \vee B) \vee C$ and $A \vee (B \vee C)$ (*b*) $(A \wedge B) \wedge C$ and $A \wedge (B \wedge C)$ (*c*) $(A \equiv B) \equiv C$ and $A \equiv (B \equiv C)$	Associative laws
12. (*a*) $A \supset (B \supset C)$ and $(A \wedge B) \supset C$	$A \supset (B \supset C)$ and $B \supset (A \supset C)$
(*b*) $A \equiv B$ and $(\sim A \vee B) \wedge (A \vee \sim B)$	$A \equiv B$ and $(A \wedge B) \vee (\sim A \wedge \sim B)$
(*c*) $A \equiv B$ and $\sim A \equiv \sim B$	$A \supset B$ and $\sim B \supset \sim A$
(*d*) (IF $\sim A$ THEN B ELSE C) and (IF A THEN C ELSE B)	

† Note that $A \supset B$ is not equivalent to $B \supset A$.

The associative laws imply that we can write $A \vee B \vee C$ (called the *disjunction* of A, B, and C), $A \wedge B \wedge C$ (called the *conjunction* of A, B, and C), and $A \equiv B \equiv C$ without any parentheses. Note, however, that $(A \supset B) \supset C$ is not equivalent to $A \supset (B \supset C)$.

EXAMPLE 2-9

Consider the following wff of the propositional calculus:

$$A: \quad [((p \wedge q) \supset r) \wedge (p \supset q)] \supset (p \supset r)$$

Show that A is equivalent to the wff

$$B: \quad T$$

We first use $7a$ to eliminate $\supset$ in A, and get

$$\sim[(\sim(p \wedge q) \vee r) \wedge (\sim p \vee q)] \vee (\sim p \vee r)$$

Then by de Morgan's laws ($8b$ and $8c$), we have

$$[(\sim \sim(p \wedge q) \wedge \sim r) \vee (\sim \sim p \wedge \sim q)] \vee (\sim p \vee r)$$

Then by $1e$ and the associative laws ($11a$ and $11b$) we get

$$(p \wedge q \wedge \sim r) \vee (p \wedge \sim q) \vee \sim p \vee r$$

Applying repeatedly the distributive law $9b$ and the commutative law $10a$ we obtain

$$\begin{aligned} &(p \vee p \vee \sim p \vee r)\\ \wedge\ &(p \vee \sim q \vee \sim p \vee r)\\ \wedge\ &(q \vee p \vee \sim p \vee r)\\ \wedge\ &(q \vee \sim q \vee \sim p \vee r)\\ \wedge\ &(\sim r \vee p \vee \sim p \vee r)\\ \wedge\ &(\sim r \vee \sim q \vee \sim p \vee r) \end{aligned}$$

Then finally by the commutative law $10a$ and equivalences $2a$ to $2c$ we obtain the simple wff

$$B: \quad T$$

Any single step in the transformation is obtained by replacing some wfp by an equivalent wfp. Therefore, by the replacement theorem, any two successive wffs in the above transformation are equivalent. This implies, by the transitivity of the equivalence relation, that the given wff A and the wff B are equivalent. In other words, A is a valid wff. □

From the meaning of the quantifiers and connectives we obtain the result that the following pairs of wffs are equivalent. We distinguish between $B(v_i)$ and B to indicate that in the first case B may contain occurrences of v_i while in the second case no occurrences of v_i in B are allowed. Similarly, we distinguish between $A(v_i)$ and A.†

13.	(*a*) $(\forall v_i)\, B$	and	B
	(*b*) $(\exists v_i)\, B$	and	B
14.	(*a*) $\sim (\forall v_i)\, A(v_i)$	and	$(\exists v_i) \sim A(v_i)$
	(*b*) $\sim (\exists v_i)\, A(v_i)$	and	$(\forall v_i) \sim A(v_i)$
15.	(*a*) $(\exists v_i)\, A(v_i) \vee (\exists v_i)\, B(v_i)$	and	$(\exists v_i)\, [A(v_i) \vee B(v_i)]$ ‡
	(*b*) $(\exists v_i)\, A(v_i) \vee B$	and	$(\exists v_i)\, [A(v_i) \vee B]$
	(*c*) $B \vee (\exists v_i)\, A(v_i)$	and	$(\exists v_i)\, [B \vee A(v_i)]$
	(*d*) $(\forall v_i)\, A(v_i) \vee B$	and	$(\forall v_i)\, [A(v_i) \vee B]$
	(*e*) $B \vee (\forall v_i)\, A(v_i)$	and	$(\forall v_i)\, [B \vee A(v_i)]$
16.	(*a*) $(\forall v_i)\, A(v_i) \wedge (\forall v_i)\, B(v_i)$	and	$(\forall v_i)\, [A(v_i) \wedge B(v_i)]$ ‡‡
	(*b*) $(\exists v_i)\, A(v_i) \wedge B$	and	$(\exists v_i)\, [A(v_i) \wedge B]$
	(*c*) $B \wedge (\exists v_i)\, A(v_i)$	and	$(\exists v_i)\, [B \wedge A(v_i)]$
	(*d*) $(\forall v_i)\, A(v_i) \wedge B$	and	$(\forall v_i)\, [A(v_i) \wedge B]$
	(*e*) $B \wedge (\forall v_i)\, A(v_i)$	and	$(\forall v_i)\, [B \wedge A(v_i)]$
17.	(*a*) $(\forall v_i)\, A(v_i) \supset (\exists v_i)\, B(v_i)$	and	$(\exists v_i)\, [A(v_i) \supset B(v_i)]$
	(*b*) $(\exists v_i)\, A(v_i) \supset B$	and	$(\forall v_i)\, [A(v_i) \supset B]$
	(*c*) $B \supset (\exists v_i)\, A(v_i)$	and	$(\exists v_i)\, [B \supset A(v_i)]$
	(*d*) $(\forall v_i)\, A(v_i) \supset B$	and	$(\exists v_i)\, [A(v_i) \supset B]$
	(*e*) $B \supset (\forall v_i)\, A(v_i)$	and	$(\forall v_i)\, [B \supset A(v_i)]$
18.	(*a*) $(\forall v_i)(\forall v_j)\, A(v_i, v_j)$	and	$(\forall v_j)(\forall v_i)\, A(v_i, v_j)$
	(*b*) $(\exists v_i)(\exists v_j)\, A(v_i, v_j)$	and	$(\exists v_j)(\exists v_i)\, A(v_i, v_j)$

EXAMPLE 2-10

Consider the wff

$$A: \ \forall x \exists P \{\exists y [x \neq y \wedge P(y)] \wedge \exists z \forall u [x \neq z \wedge (z \neq u \vee \sim P(u))]\}$$

We would like to find a simpler wff, with no predicate variables, which is equivalent to it. First we use the equivalences 16*b* and *c* to place $\exists y$ and $\exists z$ at the beginning of the wff and then use 18*b* to change the succession of $\exists P$, $\exists y$, and $\exists z$ and get

$$\forall x \exists y \exists z \exists P \{[x \neq y \wedge P(y)] \wedge \forall u [x \neq z \wedge (z \neq u \vee \sim P(u))]\}$$

† We use this convention in a few other places in this chapter; however, whenever it is used, we state this fact explicitly.

‡ Note that $(\forall v_i)\, A(v_i) \vee (\forall v_i)\, B(v_i)$ and $(\forall v_i)\, [A(v_i) \vee B(v_i)]$ are not equivalent.

‡‡ Note that $(\exists v_i)\, A(v_i) \wedge (\exists v_i)\, B(v_i)$ and $(\exists v_i)\, [A(v_i) \wedge B(v_i)]$ are not equivalent.

We now use 16*e* to push $\forall u$ to the right and get the wff

$$\forall x \exists y \exists z \exists P[x \neq y \wedge P(y) \wedge x \neq z \wedge \forall u[z \neq u \vee \sim P(u)]]$$

Now we can use 6*c* to replace the part $\forall u\ [z \neq u \vee \sim P(u)]$ by $\sim P(z)$ and obtain

$$\forall x \exists y \exists z \exists P[x \neq y \wedge P(y) \wedge x \neq z \wedge \sim P(z)]$$

By 10*b* we get

$$\forall x \exists y \exists z \exists P[x \neq y \wedge x \neq z \wedge P(y) \wedge \sim P(z)]$$

Then by 16*c* we obtain

$$\forall x \exists y \exists z[x \neq y \wedge x \neq z \wedge \exists P[P(y) \wedge \sim P(z)]]$$

By 6*b* the part $\exists P[P(y) \wedge \sim P(z)]$ can be replaced by $y \neq z$, and therefore we obtain the wff

$$B\colon\ \forall x \exists y \exists z[x \neq y \wedge x \neq z \wedge y \neq z]$$

Again, by the replacement theorem, and the transitivity of the equivalence relation, it follows that the given wff A and the wff B obtained are equivalent.

□

Let $A(x)$ be any wff and $A(y)$ the result of substituting y for all free occurrences of x in A. We say that *$A(x)$ and $A(y)$ are similar* if $A(y)$ has free occurrences of y in exactly those places where $A(x)$ has free occurrences of x. For example, the wffs $A(x)$: $\exists z[x \neq z \wedge P(z, x)]$ and $A(y)$: $\exists z[y \neq z \wedge P(z, y)]$ are similar while the following wffs are not similar:

$$B(x)\colon\ \exists z(x \neq z) \wedge \forall y P(x, \underset{\substack{\uparrow \\ \text{free}}}{y}) \qquad \text{and} \qquad B(y)\colon\ \exists z(y \neq z) \wedge \forall y P(y, \underset{\substack{\uparrow \\ \text{bound}}}{y})$$

The following rule, called *alphabetic change of bound variables*, is often used:

> *If $A(x)$ and $A(y)$ are similar, then $\forall x A(x)$ and $\forall y A(y)$ are equivalent and $\exists x A(x)$ and $\exists y A(y)$ are equivalent.*

It is important to introduce two new notions at this point. Let A be a wff and let $v_1, v_2, \ldots, v_n$ be all the distinct free variables of A. The *universal closure of* A is the wff $\forall v_1 \forall v_2 \ldots \forall v_n A$, and the *existential closure of* A is the wff $\exists v_1 \exists v_2 \ldots \exists v_n A$. There is, however, one difficulty involved in obtaining the closure, because we do not allow our wffs to contain nested quantifiers having the same variable. Thus, to obtain the appropriate closure of A, we may have sometimes to do alphabetic change of bound variables.

For example, the universal closure of the wff $p(x) \supset q(y)$ is $\forall x \forall y [p(x) \supset q(y)]$. However, to obtain the universal closure of the wff $p(x) \supset \forall x q(x)$, we first replace $\forall x q(x)$ by $\forall y q(y)$ (alphabetic change of the bound variable x) and then, taking the universal closure of $p(x) \supset \forall y q(y)$, we obtain $\forall x [p(x) \supset \forall y q(y)]$.

It is straightforward to show that: (1) *a wff is valid if and only if its universal closure is valid*, and (2) *a wff is unsatisfiable if and only if its existential closure is unsatisfiable.*

Since an interpretation of a wff consists in general of a triple, $(D, \mathscr{I}_c, \mathscr{I}_v)$, while an interpretation of a closed wff consists only of a pair, $(D, \mathscr{I}_c)$, it is clear that we prefer whenever possible to consider closed wffs. Thus, whenever we discuss the validity of a wff, we prefer to consider its universal closure. Similarly, whenever we discuss the unsatisfiability of a wff, we prefer to consider its existential closure.

2-1.5 Normal Forms of wffs

In this section we describe two special forms of wffs: prenex-conjunctive normal form and prenex-disjunctive normal form. Both forms are called *normal* because they have the common property that every wff can be transformed into an equivalent wff having any one of these forms.

(*A*) Prenex-conjunctive normal form A wff is said to be in *prenex-conjunctive normal form* if it is of the form

$$\begin{aligned}(\Box v_1)(\Box v_2) \cdots (\Box v_n)\{&[A_{11} \vee A_{12} \vee \cdots \vee A_{1l_1}]\\ \wedge\, &[A_{21} \vee A_{22} \vee \cdots \vee A_{2l_2}]\\ &\cdots\cdots\cdots\cdots\cdots\cdots\\ \wedge\, &[A_{m1} \vee A_{m2} \vee \ldots \vee A_{ml_m}]\}\end{aligned}$$

where (1) each $\Box$ is either a universal $\forall$ quantifier or an existential $\exists$ quantifier; (2) the v_i's are all distinct function or predicate variables occurring among the A_{ij}'s; and (3) each A_{ij} is either an atomic formula or a negation of an atomic formula (with no occurrences of the *if-then-else* operator). For example, the following wff is in prenex-conjunctive normal form

$$\forall x \exists Q \forall y \{[\sim p \vee x \neq a \vee x = b] \wedge [Q(y) \vee a = b]\}$$

The first part of the wff, the succession of the quantifiers $(\Box v_1)$ $(\Box v_2)$ . . . $(\Box v_n)$, is called the *prefix* of the wff, while the rest of the wff is called the *matrix* of the wff. Note that it is not required that all the variables occurring in the matrix will appear in the prefix; in other words, a wff in prenex-conjunctive normal form is not necessarily closed.

We now prove the following theorem.

THEOREM 2-4*A*. *Every wff can be transformed into an equivalent wff in prenex-conjunctive normal form.*

Proof. Suppose the wff is D. We construct a wff D' in prenex-conjunctive normal form by successively replacing wfps of D by equivalent wfps. Thus, by the replacement theorem and the transitivity of the equivalence relation it follows that D is equivalent to D'. We proceed in steps:

Step 1: *Eliminate in D all redundant quantifiers.* That is, eliminate any quantifier $\forall v_i$ or $\exists v_i$ whose scope does not contain v_i.

Step 2: *Rename variables.* Pick out the leftmost wfp of D of the form $\forall v B(v)$ or $\exists v B(v)$, such that v occurs (free or bound) in some other part of D. Replace it by $\forall v' B(v')$ or $\exists v' B(v')$, respectively, where v' is a new variable. The new variable v' may be any variable of the same type as v (F_i^n or P_i^n) that does not already occur in the wff. This renaming process (alphabetic change of bound variables) is repeated until all quantifiers in the wff have different variables and no variable is both bound and free.

Step 3a: *Eliminate the if-then-else operator.* Replace any wfp A containing one or more occurrences of a term *if B then t′ else t″* by

$$\text{IF } B \text{ THEN } A' \text{ ELSE } A''$$

where A' (respectively, A'') results from A by replacing all occurrences of *if B then t′ else t″* by t' (respectively, t'').

Step 3b: *Eliminate all occurrences of connectives other than* $\wedge$, $\vee$, *and* $\sim$. Replace

$$(A \supset B) \quad \text{by} \quad (\sim A \vee B)$$
$$(A \equiv B) \quad \text{by} \quad (\sim A \vee B) \wedge (\sim B \vee A)$$
$$(\text{IF } A \text{ THEN } B \text{ ELSE } C) \quad \text{by} \quad (\sim A \vee B) \wedge (A \vee C)$$

Step 4. *Move* $\sim$ *all the way inward.* Replace

$$\sim (\forall v_i) A(v_i) \quad \text{by} \quad (\exists v_i) \sim A(v_i)$$
$$\sim (\exists v_i) A(v_i) \quad \text{by} \quad (\forall v_i) \sim A(v_i)$$
$$\sim (A \vee B) \quad \text{by} \quad \sim A \wedge \sim B$$
$$\sim (A \wedge B) \quad \text{by} \quad \sim A \vee \sim B$$
$$\sim \sim A \quad \text{by} \quad A$$

until each occurrence of $\sim$ immediately precedes an atomic formula.

Step 5. *Push quantifiers to the left.* Replace

$$
\begin{array}{lll}
(\exists v_i)\, A(v_i) \vee B & \text{by} & (\exists v_i)[A(v_i) \vee B] \\
B \vee (\exists v_i)\, A(v_i) & \text{by} & (\exists v_i)[B \vee A(v_i)] \\
(\forall v_i)\, A(v_i) \vee B & \text{by} & (\forall v_i)[A(v_i) \vee B] \\
B \vee (\forall v_i)\, A(v_i) & \text{by} & (\forall v_i)[B \vee A(v_i)]
\end{array}
$$

$$
\begin{array}{lll}
(\exists v_i)\, A(v_i) \wedge B & \text{by} & (\exists v_i)[A(v_i) \wedge B] \\
B \wedge (\exists v_i)\, A(v_i) & \text{by} & (\exists v_i)[B \wedge A(v_i)] \\
(\forall v_i)\, A(v_i) \wedge B & \text{by} & (\forall v_i)[A(v_i) \wedge B] \\
B \wedge (\forall v_i)\, A(v_i) & \text{by} & (\forall v_i)[B \wedge A(v_i)]
\end{array}
$$

Note that, by Step 2, B cannot have any occurrences of v_i. Very often the number of quantifiers can be reduced by replacing

$$
\begin{array}{lll}
(\exists v_i)\, A(v_i) \vee (\exists v_i)\, B(v_i) & \text{by} & (\exists v_i)[A(v_i) \vee B(v_i)] \\
(\forall v_i)\, A(v_i) \wedge (\forall v_i)\, B(v_i) & \text{by} & (\forall v_i)[A(v_i) \wedge B(v_i)]
\end{array}
$$

Step 6. *Distribute, whenever possible,* $\wedge$ *over* $\vee$. Replace

$$
\begin{array}{lll}
(A \wedge B) \vee C & \text{by} & (A \vee C) \wedge (B \vee C) \\
A \vee (B \wedge C) & \text{by} & (A \vee B) \wedge (A \vee C)
\end{array}
$$

The wff obtained is the desired wff D'. Q.E.D.

EXAMPLE 2-11

Consider the wff

$$D: \quad \forall x[(\forall y p(x) \vee \forall z q(z, y)) \supset \sim \forall y r(x, y)]$$

1. Eliminate the redundant quantifier $\forall y$:

$$D_1: \quad \forall x[(p(x) \vee \forall z q(z, y)) \supset \sim \forall y r(x, y)]$$

2. Rename y because it occurs both free and bound:

$$D_2: \quad \forall x[(p(x) \vee \forall z q(z, y)) \supset \sim \forall y_1 r(x, y_1)]$$

3. Eliminate the occurrence of $\supset$:

$$D_3: \quad \forall x[\sim (p(x) \vee \forall z q(z, y)) \vee \sim \forall y_1 r(x, y_1)]$$

4. Move $\sim$ all the way inward:

$$D_4: \quad \forall x[(\sim p(x) \wedge \exists z \sim q(z, y)) \vee \exists y_1 \sim r(x, y_1)]$$

5. Push quantifiers $\exists$ to the left:

$$D_5: \quad \forall x \exists z \exists y_1[(\sim p(x) \wedge \sim q(z, y)) \vee \sim r(x, y_1)]$$

6. Distribute $\wedge$ over $\vee$:

$$D': \quad \forall x \exists z \exists y_1[(\sim p(x) \vee \sim r(x, y_1)) \wedge (\sim q(z, y) \vee \sim r(x, y_1))]$$

Thus, D' is in prenex-conjunctive normal form, and is equivalent to D.

□

(*B*) Prenex-disjunctive normal form A wff is said to be in *prenex-disjunctive normal form* if it is of the form

$$\begin{aligned}(\Box v_1)(\Box v_2)\ \ldots\ (\Box v_n)\{&[A_{11} \wedge A_{12} \wedge \cdots \wedge A_{1l_1}]\\ \vee\ &[A_{21} \wedge A_{22} \wedge \cdots \wedge A_{2l_2}]\\ &\cdots\cdots\cdots\cdots\cdots\\ \vee\ &[A_{m1} \wedge A_{m2} \wedge \cdots \wedge A_{ml_m}]\}\end{aligned}$$

where the meaning of the $\Box$'s and the A_{ij}'s is exactly as in prenex-conjunctive normal form.

We have again the following theorem:

THEOREM 2-4*B*. *Every wff can be transformed into an equivalent wff in prenex-disjunctive normal form.*

We can simply follow the previous algorithm, but with one change: In Step 6 replace

$$(A \vee B) \wedge C \text{ by } (A \wedge C) \vee (B \wedge C)$$
$$A \wedge (B \vee C) \text{ by } (A \wedge B) \vee (A \wedge C)$$

There is a very important relation between wffs in both forms. Let B be a wff in prenex-conjunctive normal form

$$\begin{aligned}(\Box_1 v_1)(\Box_2 v_2)\ \ldots\ (\Box_n v_n)\{&[A_{11} \vee A_{12} \vee \cdots \vee A_{1l_1}]\\ \wedge\ &[A_{21} \vee A_{22} \vee \cdots \vee A_{2l_2}]\\ &\cdots\cdots\cdots\cdots\cdots\\ \wedge\ &[A_{m1} \vee A_{m2} \vee \cdots \vee A_{ml_m}]\}\end{aligned}$$

and let C be a wff in prenex-disjunctive normal form

$$\begin{aligned}(\Box'_1 v_1)(\Box'_2 v_2)\ \ldots\ (\Box'_n v_n)\{&[A'_{11} \wedge A'_{12} \wedge \cdots \wedge A'_{1l_1}]\\ \vee\ &[A'_{21} \wedge A'_{22} \wedge \cdots \wedge A'_{2l_2}]\\ &\cdots\cdots\cdots\cdots\cdots\\ \vee\ &[A'_{m1} \wedge A'_{m2} \wedge \cdots \wedge A'_{ml_m}]\}\end{aligned}$$

where $\Box'_i$ is the complement quantifier to $\Box_i$ (that is, $\forall$ and $\exists$ are interchanged) and A'_{ij} is the complement atomic formula to A_{ij} (that is, non-negated atomic formulas are now negated and vice versa). Then it is straightforward (using equivalences 14*a* and *b*, 8*b* and *c*, and 1*e*) to show that B and $\sim C$ are equivalent.

A wff is said to be in *prenex normal form* if it is of the form $(\Box v_1)(\Box v_2) \ldots (\Box v_n)A$ where (1) each $\Box$ is either a universal $\forall$ quantifier or an existential $\exists$ quantifier; (2) the v_i's are all distinct function or predicate variables occurring in A; and (3) there are no quantifiers in A.

As before, the succession of the quantifiers is called the *prefix* of the wff, while A is called the *matrix* of the wff. Note that both prenex-conjunctive and prenex-disjunctive normal forms are special cases of the prenex normal form.

2-1.6 The Validity Problem

Considering our interest in the class of valid wffs, it is quite natural to look for an algorithm (Turing machine) that will take any wff of the predicate calculus as input and determine whether or not the wff is valid. This is called *the validity problem of the predicate calculus.*

The following theorem is presented without proof.

THEOREM 2-5 (Gödel). *The validity problem of the (second-order) predicate calculus is not partially solvable.*

That is, there is no algorithm (Turing machine) that takes any second-order wff as input and reaches an ACCEPT halt if the wff is valid but may reach a REJECT halt or loop forever if the wff is nonvalid.

However, we still can obtain positive results if we consider appropriate subclasses of wffs. For example, the validity problem for the first-order predicate calculus is partially solvable although still unsolvable.

THEOREM 2-6 (Church). *The validity problem of the first-order predicate calculus is unsolvable, but partially solvable.*

That is, there is no algorithm (Turing machine) that takes any first-order wff as input and always halts, reaching an ACCEPT halt if the wff is valid and a REJECT halt if the wff is nonvalid. However, there exists an algorithm that takes an arbitrary first-order wff as input and always reaches an ACCEPT halt if the wff is valid but may reach a REJECT halt or loop forever if the wff is nonvalid. In the following sections we present two such algorithms.

Proof (Floyd). The unsolvability is best proved by showing that the Post correspondence problem is reducible to the validity problem in first-order predicate calculus. That is, there exists a Turing machine that takes as input any Post system S over $\Sigma = \{0, 1\}$ and yields as output a first-order wff W_S such that S has a solution if and only if the wff W_S is valid. Thus, since the Post correspondence problem is unsolvable, so is the validity problem of the first-order predicate calculus (see Chap. 1, Sec. 1-5.4).

In the construction of the wff W_S the only constant symbols we use are: one individual constant a, two unary function constants f_0 and f_1, and one binary predicate constant p. This implies that we actually show that the validity problem is unsolvable for a very restricted subclass of the first-order wffs. In the description of the wff W_S we make use of one abbreviation: we denote a term of the form $f_{\sigma_m}(\ldots(f_{\sigma_2}(f_{\sigma_1}(x)))\ldots)$, where $\sigma_i \in \{0, 1\}$, by $f_{\sigma_1\sigma_2\ldots\sigma_m}(x)$.

Let $S = \{(\alpha_1, \beta_1), (\alpha_2, \beta_2), \ldots, (\alpha_n, \beta_n)\}$, $n \geqq 1$, be any Post system over $\Sigma = \{0, 1\}$; then the wff W_S is

$$\left\{ \bigwedge_{i=1}^{n} p(f_{\alpha_i}(a), f_{\beta_i}(a)) \right. \tag{2-1}$$

$$\left. \wedge\ \forall x \forall y [p(x, y) \supset \bigwedge_{i=1}^{n} p(f_{\alpha_i}(x), f_{\beta_i}(y))] \right\} \tag{2-2}$$

$$\supset \exists z p(z, z) \tag{2-3}$$

We proceed to show that the given Post system S has a solution if and only if W_S is valid.

Part 1. Assume W_S is valid. Let $\mathscr{I}$ be the interpretation with domain $\{0, 1\}^*$ for which a is Λ (the empty word), $f_0(x)$ is the unary function $x0$ (the concatenation of the word $x \in \{0, 1\}^*$ with the letter 0), $f_1(x)$ is the unary function $x1$ (the concatenation of the word $x \in \{0, 1\}^*$ with the letter 1), and $p(x, y)$ is *true* iff $x = \alpha_{i_1}\alpha_{i_2}\ldots\alpha_{i_m}$ and $y = \beta_{i_1}\beta_{i_2}\ldots\beta_{i_m}$ for some nonempty sequence of integers $i_1, i_2, \ldots, i_m$ (where $1 \leqq i_j \leqq n$).

Since W_S is valid, in particular, it must be *true* for this interpretation. The antecedents of W_S [Eqs. (2-1) and (2-2)] are clearly *true* under this interpretation; therefore, the consequent of W_S [Eqs. (2-3)] must also be *true*. This means that there exists a word $z \in \{0, 1\}^*$ such that $p(z, z)$ is *true* under $\mathscr{I}$; that is, there is some nonempty sequence of integers $i_1, i_2, \ldots,$ i_m such that

$$\alpha_{i_1}\alpha_{i_2}\cdots\alpha_{i_m} = z = \beta_{i_1}\beta_{i_2}\cdots\beta_{i_m}$$

In other words, the given Post system S has a solution.

Part 2. Assume S has a solution $i_1, i_2, \ldots, i_m$; that is,

$$\alpha_{i_1}\alpha_{i_2}\ldots\alpha_{i_m} = \beta_{i_1}\beta_{i_2}\ldots\beta_{i_m}$$

We show that for every interpretation $\mathscr{I}$ of W_S if the antecedents of W_S [Eqs. (2-1) and (2-2)] are *true*, then so is the consequent of W_S [Eq. (2-3)]. This implies that W_S is *true* for every interpretation; that is, W_S is valid. Thus, let $\mathscr{I}$ be an arbitrary interpretation for which the antecedents of W_S [Eqs. (2-1) and (2-2)] are *true*. We can deduce then from Eq. (2-1) and repeated applications of Eq. (2-2) that $p(f_{\alpha_{i_1}\alpha_{i_2}\cdots\alpha_{i_m}}(a), f_{\beta_{i_1}\beta_{i_2}\cdots\beta_{i_m}}(a))$ is *true* under $\mathscr{I}$. But since by our assumption $\alpha_{i_1}\alpha_{i_2}\ldots\alpha_{i_m} = \beta_{i_1}\beta_{i_2}\ldots\beta_{i_m}$, it implies that the consequent of W_S [Eq. (2-3)] is *true* under $\mathscr{I}$.

Q.E.D.

Although the validity problem of the second-order predicate calculus in general is unsolvable (not even partially solvable), there are still several interesting restricted subclasses of wffs for which the validity problem is solvable, in addition to the propositional calculus (see Theorem 2-1). In the remainder of this section we discuss several such subclasses.

1. The most important class of wffs for which the validity problem is known to be solvable is the *unary (monadic) predicate calculus.* All wffs of the unary predicate calculus, called *unary wffs*, contain no constant or variable symbols other than individual constants and variables, propositional constants and variables, and unary predicate constants and variables. Note that the class of unary wffs contains all the wffs of the equality calculus and all the wffs of the quantified propositional calculus. We have the following result:

The validity problem of the unary predicate calculus is solvable.

That is, there exists an algorithm that takes any unary wff as input and determines whether or not it is valid.

2. We have shown before that the validity problem of the first-order predicate calculus is unsolvable. We present now several subclasses of the restricted first-order predicate calculus for which the validity problem is solvable. The *restricted first-order predicate calculus* consists of all wffs, called *restricted first-order wffs*, with no constant or variable symbols other than individual variables and predicate constants. We have the following theorem.

The validity problem is solvable for the classes of the restricted first-order wffs which are in prenex normal form and which have a prefix of one of the following forms ($m, n \geqq 0$):

(*a*) $\forall x_1 \ldots \forall x_m \exists y_1 \ldots \exists y_n$
(*b*) $\forall x_1 \ldots \forall x_m \exists y \forall z_1 \ldots \forall z_n$
(*c*) $\forall x_1 \ldots \forall x_m \exists y_1 \exists y_2 \forall z_1 \ldots \forall z_n$

It is quite interesting that the validity problem is *unsolvable* for the classes of restricted first-order wffs which are in prenex normal form and which have a prefix of one of the following forms ($m, n \geqq 0$):

(*d*) $\exists x_1 \ldots \exists x_m \forall y_1 \ldots \forall y_n$
(*e*) $\forall x_1 \ldots \forall x_m \exists y_1 \exists y_2 \exists y_3 \forall z_1 \ldots \forall z_n$

2-2 NATURAL DEDUCTION

A *deduction system* for the predicate calculus consists of a (possibly infinite) recursive set† of valid wffs, called *axioms*, and a finite set of mappings, called *rules of inference*; each rule of inference maps one or more valid wffs into a valid wff. A wff B is said to be *deducible* (*provable*) in such a system if there exists a finite sequence of wffs such that B is the last wff in the sequence and each wff in the sequence is either an axiom or derived from previous wffs in the sequence by one of the rules of inference. (Such a sequence of wffs is called a *proof* of B.) Thus, since each axiom is a valid wff and each rule of inference maps valid wffs into a valid wff, it follows that *every deducible wff is valid.*

The converse, however, is not always true; there may exist a deduction system in which some valid wffs cannot be deduced. We are interested mainly in *complete deduction systems*, i.e., deduction systems in which every valid wff can be deduced. Our interest arises from the fact that if we have a complete deduction system, then every valid wff can be proved to be valid by showing that it is deducible in the system. This suggests a very important and useful tool for proving the validity of wffs.

Unfortunately, we have the following theorem.

THEOREM 2-7 (Gödel) (*a*) *There is no complete deduction system for the second-order predicate calculus.* (*b*) *There are complete deduction systems for the first-order predicate calculus.*

In the remainder of this section we shall describe a complete deduction system for the first-order predicate calculus adapted from Gentzen's work. Such a deduction system is usually called a *natural deduction system* because its set of axioms and rules of inference is rich enough to enable valid wffs to be deduced in a very "natural" way. In order to discuss the natural deduction system, we must introduce some notation. We use expressions of the form $A_1, A_2, \ldots, A_n \Rightarrow B$, where each A_i and B are wffs, as abbreviated notation for the wff $A_1 \wedge A_2 \wedge \ldots \wedge A_n \supset B$; such expressions are called *assumption formulas*. Since in our discussion we are interested only in the validity or nonvalidity of the wff indicated by $A_1, A_2, \ldots, A_n \Rightarrow B$, it makes no difference if we reorder the A_i's or eliminate duplicate occurrences of them. It is therefore most convenient to consider the sequence $A_1, A_2, \ldots, A_n$ as a set of wffs, allowing the special case of the empty set; in this special case, the assumption formula

† That is, there is an algorithm (Turing machine) that takes an arbitrary wff as input and determines whether or not it is an axiom.

$\Rightarrow B$ stands for the wff B itself. We often use the Greek letter Γ to indicate any finite set of zero or more wffs.

We shall now list the axioms and rules of inference of our natural deduction system. These are divided into four parts: (1) *the axioms and basic rules*, (2) *rules for the connectives*, (3) *rules for the quantifiers*, and (4) *rules for the operators*. All the axioms and rules of inference are expressed in terms of the assumption formulas. Each rule of inference is of the form

$$\frac{\langle \text{assumption formula} \rangle \text{ and } \ldots \text{ and } \langle \text{assumption formula} \rangle}{\langle \text{assumption formula} \rangle}$$

which indicates that from the assumption formulas given above the line we can infer the one given below the line. We leave it to the reader to verify that each axiom is a valid wff and each rule of inference indeed maps valid wffs into a valid wff.

The most important point to note is that:

our deduction system is a complete deduction system for the first-order predicate calculus.

That is, for every given valid first-order wff B it is possible to construct a finite sequence of assumption formulas of the form

$$\Gamma_1 \Rightarrow B_1 \qquad \Gamma_2 \Rightarrow B_2 \qquad \cdots \qquad \Gamma_n \Rightarrow B_n$$

where (1) each assumption formula $\Gamma_i \Rightarrow B_i$ is either one of the given axioms or can be derived from previous assumption formulas in the sequence by one of the rules of inference, and (2) the final assumption formula in the sequence, $\Gamma_n \Rightarrow B_n$, is of the form $\Rightarrow B$, which stands for the given wff B.

I. The axioms and basic rules

(*a*) Assumptions

$\Gamma, A \Rightarrow A$ — *Assumption axiom*

$$\frac{\Gamma \Rightarrow B}{\Gamma, A \Rightarrow B}$$ *Introduction of assumption*

$$\frac{\Gamma, A \Rightarrow B \quad \text{and} \quad \Gamma, \sim A \Rightarrow B}{\Gamma \Rightarrow B}$$ *Elimination of assumption*

(*b*) Truth-symbols axioms

$\Gamma \Rightarrow T$ — *T axiom*

$\Gamma \Rightarrow \sim F$ — *F axiom*

Note that there are infinitely many axioms, since every assumption formula of the form $\Gamma, A \Rightarrow A$, $\Gamma \Rightarrow T$ or $\Gamma \Rightarrow \sim F$ is an axiom.

2-2.1 Rules for the Connectives

II. Rules for the connectives

(*a*) $\vee$ rules

$$\frac{\Gamma \Rightarrow A}{\Gamma \Rightarrow A \vee B} \qquad \frac{\Gamma \Rightarrow B}{\Gamma \Rightarrow A \vee B} \qquad \vee \textit{ introduction}$$

$$\frac{\Gamma, A \Rightarrow C \quad \text{and} \quad \Gamma, B \Rightarrow C \quad \text{and} \quad \Gamma \Rightarrow A \vee B}{\Gamma \Rightarrow C} \qquad \vee \textit{ elimination}$$

(*b*) $\wedge$ rules

$$\frac{\Gamma \Rightarrow A \quad \text{and} \quad \Gamma \Rightarrow B}{\Gamma \Rightarrow A \wedge B} \qquad \wedge \textit{ introduction}$$

$$\frac{\Gamma \Rightarrow A \wedge B}{\Gamma \Rightarrow A} \qquad \frac{\Gamma \Rightarrow A \wedge B}{\Gamma \Rightarrow B} \qquad \wedge \textit{ elimination}$$

(*c*) $\supset$ rules

$$\frac{\Gamma, A \Rightarrow B}{\Gamma \Rightarrow A \supset B} \qquad \supset \textit{ introduction (discharge rule)}$$

$$\frac{\Gamma \Rightarrow A \quad \text{and} \quad \Gamma \Rightarrow A \supset B}{\Gamma \Rightarrow B} \qquad \supset \textit{ elimination (modus ponens)}$$

(*d*) $\sim$ rules

$$\frac{\Gamma, A \Rightarrow B \quad \text{and} \quad \Gamma, A \Rightarrow \sim B}{\Gamma \Rightarrow \sim A} \qquad \sim \textit{ introduction (reductio ad absurdum)}$$

$$\frac{\Gamma \Rightarrow A \quad \text{and} \quad \Gamma \Rightarrow \sim A}{\Gamma \Rightarrow B} \qquad \sim \textit{ elimination}$$

(*e*) $\sim\sim$ rules

$$\frac{\Gamma \Rightarrow A}{\Gamma \Rightarrow \sim\sim A} \qquad \sim\sim \textit{ introduction}$$

$$\frac{\Gamma \Rightarrow \sim\sim A}{\Gamma \Rightarrow A} \qquad \sim\sim \textit{ elimination}$$

(*f*) $\equiv$ rules

$$\frac{\Gamma \Rightarrow A \supset B \quad \text{and} \quad \Gamma \Rightarrow B \supset A}{\Gamma \Rightarrow A \equiv B} \qquad \equiv \textit{ introduction}$$

$$\frac{\Gamma \Rightarrow A \equiv B}{\Gamma \Rightarrow A \supset B} \qquad \frac{\Gamma \Rightarrow A \equiv B}{\Gamma \Rightarrow B \supset A} \qquad \equiv \textit{ elimination}$$

(*g*) IF-THEN-ELSE rules

$$\frac{\Gamma \Rightarrow A \supset B \quad \text{and} \quad \Gamma \Rightarrow \sim A \supset C}{\Gamma \Rightarrow \text{IF } A \text{ THEN } B \text{ ELSE } C}$$ IF-THEN-ELSE *introduction*

$$\left.\begin{array}{c} \dfrac{\Gamma \Rightarrow \text{IF } A \text{ THEN } B \text{ ELSE } C}{\Gamma \Rightarrow A \supset B} \\[2ex] \dfrac{\Gamma \Rightarrow \text{IF } A \text{ THEN } B \text{ ELSE } C}{\Gamma \Rightarrow \sim A \supset C} \end{array}\right\}$$ IF-THEN-ELSE *elimination*

It can be shown that the set of axioms and rules of inference stated so far form a complete deduction system for the propositional calculus; that is, every valid wff of the propositional calculus can be deduced in this system (see Prob. 2-15).

At this point let us illustrate the deduction mechanism for a few valid wffs of the propositional calculus.

EXAMPLE 2-12
Deduce the wff

$$p \vee \sim p$$

1. $p \Rightarrow p$	Assumption axiom
2. $p \Rightarrow p \vee \sim p$	$\vee$ introduction (line 1)
3. $\sim p \Rightarrow \sim p$	Assumption axiom
4. $\sim p \Rightarrow p \vee \sim p$	$\vee$ introduction (line 3)
5. $\Rightarrow p \vee \sim p$	Elimination of assumption (lines 2 and 4)

□

EXAMPLE 2-13
Deduce the wff

$$(p \supset q) \equiv (\sim q \supset \sim p)$$

We deduce both wffs $(p \supset q) \supset (\sim q \supset \sim p)$ and $(\sim q \supset \sim p) \supset (p \supset q)$; and therefore, using the $\equiv$ introduction rule, we deduce $(p \supset q) \equiv (\sim q \supset \sim p)$. For example, to deduce the wff $(p \supset q) \supset (\sim q \supset \sim p)$, we first deduce $(p \supset q), \sim q \Rightarrow \sim p$ and then apply the $\supset$ introduction (discharge) rule twice. We observe that the $\sim$ introduction rule is the only rule we can use to introduce $\sim p$. In order to apply this rule, we must find some wff B such that $p \supset q, \sim q, p \Rightarrow B$ and $p \supset q, \sim q, p \Rightarrow \sim B$. An appropriate B is q; therefore we deduce first $p \supset q, \sim q, p \Rightarrow q$ and $p \supset q, \sim q, p \Rightarrow \sim q$. The wff $(\sim q \supset \sim p) \supset (p \supset q)$ is deduced similarly.

1.	$p \supset q, \sim q, p \Rightarrow p$	Assumption axiom
2.	$p \supset q, \sim q, p \Rightarrow p \supset q$	Assumption axiom
3.	$p \supset q, \sim q, p \Rightarrow q$	$\supset$ elimination (lines 1 and 2)
4.	$p \supset q, \sim q, p \Rightarrow \sim q$	Assumption axiom
5.	$p \supset q, \sim q \Rightarrow \sim p$	$\sim$ introduction (lines 3 and 4)
6.	$p \supset q \Rightarrow \sim q \supset \sim p$	$\supset$ introduction (line 5)
7.	$\Rightarrow (p \supset q) \supset (\sim q \supset \sim p)$	$\supset$ introduction (line 6)
8.	$\sim q \supset \sim p, p, \sim q \Rightarrow \sim q$	Assumption axiom
9.	$\sim q \supset \sim p, p, \sim q \Rightarrow \sim q \supset \sim p$	Assumption axiom
10.	$\sim q \supset \sim p, p, \sim q \Rightarrow \sim p$	$\supset$ elimination (lines 8 and 9)
11.	$\sim q \supset \sim p, p, \sim q \Rightarrow p$	Assumption axiom
12.	$\sim q \supset \sim p, p \Rightarrow \sim \sim q$	$\sim$ introduction (lines 10 and 11)
13.	$\sim q \supset \sim p, p \Rightarrow q$	$\sim \sim$ elimination (line 12)
14.	$\sim q \supset \sim p \Rightarrow p \supset q$	$\supset$ introduction (line 13)
15.	$\Rightarrow (\sim q \supset \sim p) \supset (p \supset q)$	$\supset$ introduction (line 14)
16.	$\Rightarrow (p \supset q) \equiv (\sim q \supset \sim p)$	$\equiv$ introduction (lines 7 and 15)

□

EXAMPLE 2-14

Deduce the wff

$$(p \wedge \sim p) \equiv F$$

1.	$F \Rightarrow F$	Assumption axiom
2.	$F \Rightarrow \sim F$	F axiom
3.	$F \Rightarrow p \wedge \sim p$	$\sim$ elimination (lines 1 and 2)
4.	$\Rightarrow F \supset (p \wedge \sim p)$	$\supset$ introduction (line 3)
5.	$p \wedge \sim p \Rightarrow p \wedge \sim p$	Assumption axiom
6.	$p \wedge \sim p \Rightarrow p$	$\wedge$ elimination (line 5)
7.	$p \wedge \sim p \Rightarrow \sim p$	$\wedge$ elimination (line 5)
8.	$p \wedge \sim p \Rightarrow F$	$\sim$ elimination (lines 6 and 7)
9.	$\Rightarrow (p \wedge \sim p) \supset F$	$\supset$ introduction (line 8)
10.	$\Rightarrow (p \wedge \sim p) \equiv F$	$\equiv$ introduction (lines 4 and 9)

□

EXAMPLE 2-15

Deduce the wff

$$(\text{IF } \sim p \text{ THEN } q \text{ ELSE } r) \supset (\text{IF } p \text{ THEN } r \text{ ELSE } q)$$

1.	IF $\sim p$ THEN q ELSE $r \Rightarrow$ IF $\sim p$ THEN q ELSE r	Assumption axiom

2. IF $\sim p$ THEN q ELSE $r \Rightarrow$ $\sim p \supset q$	IF-THEN-ELSE elimination (line 1)
3. IF $\sim p$ THEN q ELSE $r \Rightarrow$ $\sim\sim p \supset r$	IF-THEN-ELSE elimination (line 1)
4. IF $\sim p$ THEN q ELSE $r, p \Rightarrow$ $\sim\sim p \supset r$	Introduction of assumption (line 3)
5. IF $\sim p$ THEN q ELSE $r, p \Rightarrow p$	Assumption axiom
6. IF $\sim p$ THEN q ELSE $r, p \Rightarrow$ $\sim\sim p$	$\sim\sim$ introduction (line 5)
7. IF $\sim p$ THEN q ELSE $r, p \Rightarrow r$	$\supset$ elimination (lines 4 and 6)
8. IF $\sim p$ THEN q ELSE $r \Rightarrow$ $p \supset r$	$\supset$ introduction (line 7)
9. IF $\sim p$ THEN q ELSE $r \Rightarrow$ IF p THEN r ELSE q	IF-THEN-ELSE introduction (lines 2 and 8)
10. $\Rightarrow$ (IF $\sim p$ THEN q ELSE $r \supset$ IF p THEN r ELSE q)	$\supset$ introduction (line 9)

□

Derived rules of inference

In order to be able to write shorter deductions for wffs in practice, it is most convenient to have a library of *derived rules of inference*. We list below a few useful derived rules of inference. Each such rule can be given an effective proof in the sense that we can show effectively how to replace any derived rule of inference whenever it is used in a deduction by an appropriate sequence of wffs using only the "primitive" rules of inference and axioms.

1. (*a*)
$$\frac{\Gamma \Rightarrow A \supset (B \supset C)}{\Gamma \Rightarrow (A \wedge B) \supset C}$$

Proof.

1. $\Gamma \Rightarrow A \supset (B \supset C)$	Given
2. $\Gamma, A \wedge B \Rightarrow A \supset (B \supset C)$	Introduction of assumption
3. $\Gamma, A \wedge B \Rightarrow A \wedge B$	Assumption axiom
4. $\Gamma, A \wedge B \Rightarrow A$	$\wedge$ elimination
5. $\Gamma, A \wedge B \Rightarrow B \supset C$	$\supset$ elimination (lines 2 and 4)
6. $\Gamma, A \wedge B \Rightarrow B$	$\wedge$ elimination (line 3)
7. $\Gamma, A \wedge B \Rightarrow C$	$\supset$ elimination (lines 5 and 6)
8. $\Gamma \Rightarrow (A \wedge B) \supset C$	$\supset$ introduction

(*b*)
$$\frac{\Gamma \Rightarrow (A \wedge B) \supset C}{\Gamma \Rightarrow A \supset (B \supset C)}$$

Hint: Show $\Gamma, A, B \Rightarrow C$; then use the $\supset$ introduction rule.

2. (*a*) $$\frac{\Gamma, A_1, \ldots, A_n \Rightarrow B}{\Gamma \Rightarrow (A_1 \wedge \cdots \wedge A_n) \supset B}$$ *Generalized $\supset$ introduction*

Hint: Use the derived rule 1*a* above.

(*b*) $$\frac{\Gamma \Rightarrow A_1 \text{ and} \ldots \text{and } \Gamma \Rightarrow A_n \text{ and } \Gamma \Rightarrow (A_1 \wedge \cdots \wedge A_n) \supset B}{\Gamma \Rightarrow B}$$

Generalized $\supset$ elimination

Hint: Show $\Gamma \Rightarrow A_1 \wedge \cdots \wedge A_n$; then use the $\supset$ elimination rule.

3. (*a*) $$\frac{\Gamma \Rightarrow A \vee B \text{ and } \Gamma \Rightarrow \sim A}{\Gamma \Rightarrow B}$$

modus tollendo ponens

$$\frac{\Gamma \Rightarrow A \vee B \text{ and } \Gamma \Rightarrow \sim B}{\Gamma \Rightarrow A}$$

Hint: Show $\Gamma, A \Rightarrow B$ and $\Gamma, B \Rightarrow B$ for the first rule, and $\Gamma, A \Rightarrow A$ and $\Gamma, B \Rightarrow A$ for the second rule; then use the $\vee$ elimination rule.

(*b*) $$\frac{\Gamma \Rightarrow A \supset B \text{ and } \Gamma \Rightarrow \sim B}{\Gamma \Rightarrow \sim A}$$ *modus tollens*

Hint: Show that $\Gamma, A \Rightarrow B$ and $\Gamma, A \Rightarrow \sim B$; then use the $\sim$ introduction rule.

(*c*) $$\frac{\Gamma, A \Rightarrow C \text{ and } \Gamma, B \Rightarrow C}{\Gamma, A \vee B \Rightarrow C}$$ *Proof by cases*

Hint: Show that $\Gamma, A \vee B \Rightarrow A \vee B$ and $\Gamma, A \vee B, A \Rightarrow C$ and $\Gamma, A \vee B, B \Rightarrow C$; then use the $\vee$ elimination rule.

4. (*a*) $$\frac{\Gamma \Rightarrow A \supset B \text{ and } \Gamma \Rightarrow B \supset C}{\Gamma \Rightarrow A \supset C}$$ *Transitivity of implication*

(*b*) $$\frac{\Gamma \Rightarrow A \equiv B \text{ and } \Gamma \Rightarrow B \equiv C}{\Gamma \Rightarrow A \equiv C}$$ *Transitivity of equivalence*

EXAMPLE 2-16

Deduce the wff

$$[((p \wedge q) \supset r) \wedge (p \supset q)] \supset (p \supset r)$$

First we deduce that $((p \wedge q) \supset r), (p \supset q), p \Rightarrow r$, and then, by applying the $\supset$ introduction and the generalized $\supset$ introduction rule, we obtain the given wff.

1. $(p \wedge q \supset r), (p \supset q), p \Rightarrow p$	Assumption axiom
2. $(p \wedge q \supset r), (p \supset q), p \Rightarrow p \supset q$	Assumption axiom
3. $(p \wedge q \supset r), (p \supset q), p \Rightarrow q$	$\supset$ elimination (lines 1 and 2)
4. $(p \wedge q \supset r), (p \supset q), p \Rightarrow p \wedge q$	$\wedge$ introduction (lines 1 and 3)
5. $(p \wedge q \supset r), (p \supset q), p \Rightarrow$ $p \wedge q \supset r$	Assumption axiom
6. $(p \wedge q \supset r), (p \supset q), p \Rightarrow r$	$\supset$ elimination (lines 4 and 5)
7. $(p \wedge q \supset r), (p \supset q) \Rightarrow p \supset r$	$\supset$ introduction (line 6)
8. $\Rightarrow [(p \wedge q \supset r) \wedge (p \supset q)] \supset$ $(p \supset r)$	Generalized $\supset$ introduction (line 7)

□

2-2.2 Rules for the Quantifiers

We shall now describe the third group of rules of inference in our natural deduction system: the *rules for handling the quantifiers.* The reader should be aware that in an assumption formula of the form $A_1, \ldots, A_n \Rightarrow B$ both the A_i's and B may contain free occurrences of individual variables. Therefore, the rules of inference given below for introducing or eliminating quantifiers may be applied only if certain conditions regarding the free occurrences of individual variables in the A_i's and B are satisfied.

In order to state the rules of inference in the third group, we need to establish a substitution notation. To indicate that a term t is substituted for all free occurrences (if any) of x in a wff A, we denote A by $A(x)$ and then use $A(t)$ to stand for the result of the substitution. For example,

$$\text{If}\quad A(x)\quad \text{is } p(\underset{\text{free}}{\underset{\uparrow}{x}}) \supset \forall y q(\underset{\text{free}}{\underset{\uparrow}{x}}, y)$$

$$\text{then}\quad A(f(y))\quad \text{is}\quad p(f(\underset{\text{free}}{\underset{\uparrow}{y}})) \supset \forall y q(f(\underset{\text{bound}}{\underset{\uparrow}{y}}), y)$$

Here, both free occurrences of x were replaced by $f(y)$. In the new wff $A(f(y))$, the occurrence of y in the first $f(y)$ is free while the second is bound. In general, we would like to exclude substitutions which introduce new bound occurrences, and therefore we make use of the following definition.

We say that a *term t is free for x in a wff A* if, by substituting t for all free occurrences (if any) of x in A, we do not introduce new bound occurrences of variables.

Note that the condition is trivially satisfied whenever t is x itself, or t does not contain individual variables, or there are no free occurrences of x in A.

III. Rules for the quantifiers

(*a*) $\forall$ rules

$$\frac{\Gamma \Rightarrow A(x)}{\Gamma \Rightarrow \forall x A(x)} \qquad \forall \textit{ introduction (generalization)}$$

where x is not free in any member of Γ.

$$\frac{\Gamma \Rightarrow \forall x A(x)}{\Gamma \Rightarrow A(t)} \qquad \forall \textit{ elimination}$$

where t is free for x in $A(x)$.

Special cases:

$$\frac{\Gamma \Rightarrow \forall x A(x)}{\Gamma \Rightarrow A(x)} \quad \text{and} \quad \frac{\Gamma \Rightarrow \forall x A(x)}{\Gamma \Rightarrow A(a)}$$

(*b*) $\exists$ rules

$$\frac{\Gamma \Rightarrow A(t)}{\Gamma \Rightarrow \exists x A(x)} \qquad \exists \textit{ introduction}$$

where t is free for x in $A(x)$.

Special cases:

$$\frac{\Gamma \Rightarrow A(x)}{\Gamma \Rightarrow \exists x A(x)} \quad \text{and} \quad \frac{\Gamma \Rightarrow A(a)}{\Gamma \Rightarrow \exists x A(x)}$$

$$\frac{\Gamma \Rightarrow \exists x A(x) \text{ and } \Gamma, A(b) \Rightarrow C}{\Gamma \Rightarrow C} \qquad \exists \textit{ elimination}$$

where b is an individual constant not occurring in any member of Γ, in $\exists x A(x)$, or in C.

Note that in the $\exists$ introduction rule $A(t)$ stands for the result of substituting t for all free occurrences of x in $A(x)$. Thus, as a special case, from $\Gamma \Rightarrow p(a, a)$, we can deduce $\Gamma \Rightarrow \exists x p(x, a)$, or $\Gamma \Rightarrow \exists x p(a, x)$, or $\Gamma \Rightarrow \exists x p(x, x)$.

EXAMPLE 2-17

Deduce the wff

$$\forall x A(x) \supset \exists x A(x)$$

1. $\forall x A(x) \Rightarrow \forall x A(x)$	Assumption axiom
2. $\forall x A(x) \Rightarrow A(x)$	$\forall$ elimination
3. $\forall x A(x) \Rightarrow \exists x A(x)$	$\exists$ introduction
4. $\Rightarrow \forall x A(x) \supset \exists x A(x)$	$\supset$ introduction

□

Note again that $\forall x A(x) \supset \exists x A(x)$ is not really a wff but represents an infinite class of wffs each having this form, for example, $\forall x p(x) \supset \exists x p(x)$ and $\forall x \exists y p(x, y) \supset \exists x \exists y p(x, y)$. Every one of the wffs in the class can be deduced by following the deduction above with $A(x)$ being replaced by the appropriate wfp. We shall use this notation throughout the remaining sections of this chapter.

EXAMPLE 2-18

Deduce the wff

$$\exists x \forall y A(x, y) \supset \forall y \exists x A(x, y)$$

The basic step is to deduce $\exists x \forall y A(x, y) \Rightarrow \exists x A(x, y)$. For this purpose, we use the $\exists$ elimination rule, where Γ is $\{\exists x \forall y A(x, y)\}$, $\exists x A(x)$ is $\exists x \forall y A(x, y)$, $A(b)$ is $\forall y A(b, y)$, and C is $\exists x A(x, y)$.

1. $\exists x \forall y A(x, y) \Rightarrow \exists x \forall y A(x, y)$	Assumption axiom
2. $\exists x \forall y A(x, y), \forall y A(b, y) \Rightarrow \forall y A(b, y)$	Assumption axiom
3. $\exists x \forall y A(x, y), \forall y A(b, y) \Rightarrow A(b, y)$	$\forall$ elimination
4. $\exists x \forall y A(x, y), \forall y A(b, y) \Rightarrow \exists x A(x, y)$	$\exists$ introduction
5. $\exists x \forall y A(x, y) \Rightarrow \exists x A(x, y)$	$\exists$ elimination (lines 1 and 4)
6. $\exists x \forall y A(x, y) \Rightarrow \forall y \exists x A(x, y)$	$\forall$ introduction
7. $\Rightarrow \exists x \forall y A(x, y) \supset \forall y \exists x A(x, y)$	$\supset$ introduction

□

EXAMPLE 2-19

Deduce the wff

$$(\forall x A(x) \vee \forall x B(x)) \supset \forall x (A(x) \vee B(x))$$

1. $\forall x A(x) \Rightarrow A(x)$	Assumption rule and $\forall$ elimination
2. $\forall x A(x) \Rightarrow A(x) \vee B(x)$	$\vee$ introduction
3. $\forall x A(x) \Rightarrow \forall x (A(x) \vee B(x))$	$\forall$ introduction
4. $\forall x B(x) \Rightarrow B(x)$	Assumption rule and $\forall$ elimination

5. $\forall x B(x) \Rightarrow A(x) \vee B(x)$	$\vee$ introduction
6. $\forall x B(x) \Rightarrow \forall x (A(x) \vee B(x))$	$\forall$ introduction
7. $\forall x A(x) \vee \forall x B(x) \Rightarrow \forall x (A(x) \vee B(x))$	Proof by cases (a derived rule of inference), lines 3 and 6
8. $\Rightarrow (\forall x A(x) \vee \forall x B(x)) \supset \forall x (A(x) \vee B(x))$	$\supset$ introduction

□

EXAMPLE 2-20

Deduce the wff

$$\forall x (A \supset B(x)) \equiv (A \supset \forall x B(x))$$

where x is not free in A.

1. $A \supset \forall x B(x), A \Rightarrow \forall x B(x)$	Assumption axiom and $\supset$ elimination
2. $A \supset \forall x B(x), A \Rightarrow B(x)$	$\forall$ elimination
3. $A \supset \forall x B(x) \Rightarrow A \supset B(x)$	$\supset$ introduction
4. $A \supset \forall x B(x) \Rightarrow \forall x (A \supset B(x))$	$\forall$ introduction (since x is not free in A)
5. $\Rightarrow (A \supset \forall x B(x)) \supset \forall x (A \supset B(x))$	$\supset$ introduction
6. $\forall x (A \supset B(x)), A \Rightarrow A \supset B(x)$	Assumption axiom and $\forall$ elimination
7. $\forall x (A \supset B(x)), A \Rightarrow B(x)$	Assumption axiom and $\supset$ elimination
8. $\forall x (A \supset B(x)), A \Rightarrow \forall x B(x)$	$\forall$ introduction (since x is not free in A)
9. $\forall x (A \supset B(x)) \Rightarrow A \supset \forall x B(x)$	$\supset$ introduction
10. $\Rightarrow \forall x (A \supset B(x)) \supset (A \supset \forall x B(x))$	$\supset$ introduction
11. $\Rightarrow \forall x (A \supset B(x)) \equiv (A \supset \forall x B(x))$	$\equiv$ introduction (lines 5 and 10)

□

EXAMPLE 2-21

Deduce the wff

$$\sim \exists x A(x) \equiv \forall x \sim A(x)$$

1. $\sim \exists x A(x), A(x) \Rightarrow \exists x A(x)$	Assumption axiom and $\exists$ introduction
2. $\sim \exists x A(x), A(x) \Rightarrow \sim \exists x A(x)$	Assumption axiom
3. $\sim \exists x A(x) \Rightarrow \sim A(x)$	$\sim$ introduction (lines 1 and 2)

4. $\sim \exists x A(x) \Rightarrow \forall x \sim A(x)$	$\forall$ introduction
5. $\Rightarrow (\sim \exists x A(x)) \supset \forall x \sim A(x)$	$\supset$ introduction
6. $\forall x \sim A(x), \exists x A(x), A(b) \Rightarrow A(b)$	Assumption axiom
7. $\forall x \sim A(x), \exists x A(x), A(b) \Rightarrow \sim A(b)$	Assumption axiom and $\forall$ elimination
8. $\forall x \sim A(x), \exists x A(x), A(b) \Rightarrow F$	$\sim$ elimination (lines 6 and 7)
9. $\forall x \sim A(x), \exists x A(x) \Rightarrow \exists x A(x)$	Assumption axiom
10. $\forall x \sim A(x), \exists x A(x) \Rightarrow F$	$\exists$ elimination (lines 8 and 9)
11. $\forall x \sim A(x), \exists x A(x) \Rightarrow \sim F$	F axiom
12. $\forall x \sim A(x) \Rightarrow \sim \exists x A(x)$	$\sim$ introduction (lines 10 and 11)
13. $\Rightarrow \forall x \sim A(x) \supset \sim \exists x A(x)$	$\supset$ introduction
14. $\Rightarrow \sim \exists x A(x) \equiv \forall x \sim A(x)$	$\equiv$ introduction (lines 5 and 13)

□

The reader should be aware of the importance of the special restrictions attached to the rules. The rules, without the special restrictions, may map valid wffs into nonvalid wffs; thus, one may deduce *nonvalid* wffs just by applying one of these rules, ignoring the special restriction induced on its use. We shall illustrate this point with two examples.

EXAMPLE 2-22

1. $\forall x \exists y p(x, y) \Rightarrow \forall x \exists y p(x, y)$	Assumption axiom
2. $\forall x \exists y p(x, y) \Rightarrow \exists y p(y, y)$	$\forall$ *elimination* (*line* 1)
3. $\Rightarrow \forall x \exists y p(x, y) \supset \exists y p(y, y)$	$\supset$ introduction (line 2)

Thus, we have deduced the wff $\forall x \exists y p(x, y) \supset \exists y p(y, y)$, which is clearly *nonvalid*. Countermodel: Let D be the set of all integers and $p(x, y)$ be $x \neq y$. Then, since $\forall x \exists y (x \neq y)$ is *true* but $\exists y (y \neq y)$ is *false*, it follows that $\forall x \exists y (x \neq y) \supset \exists y (y \neq y)$ is *false*.

The reason that we have managed to deduce a nonvalid wff is that line 2 of our deduction is illegal. The $\forall$ elimination may not be applied in this case because y (which stands for the term t) is *not* free for x in $\exists y p(x, y)$ (which stands for the wff $A(x)$).

□

EXAMPLE 2-23

1. $\forall x \exists y p(x, y) \Rightarrow \forall x \exists y p(x, y)$	Assumption axiom
2. $\forall x \exists y p(x, y) \Rightarrow \exists y p(x, y)$	$\forall$ elimination (line 1)
3. $\forall x \exists y p(x, y), p(x, b) \Rightarrow p(x, b)$	Assumption axiom (line 2)
4. $\forall x \exists y p(x, y), p(x, b) \Rightarrow \forall x p(x, b)$	$\forall$ *introduction* (*line* 3)
5. $\forall x \exists y p(x, y), p(x, b) \Rightarrow \exists y \forall x p(x, y)$	$\exists$ introduction (line 4)
6. $\forall x \exists y p(x, y) \Rightarrow \exists y \forall x p(x, y)$	$\exists$ elimination (lines 2 and 5)
7. $\Rightarrow \forall x \exists y p(x, y) \supset \exists y \forall x p(x, y)$	$\supset$ introduction (line 6)

Thus we have deduced the wff $\forall x \exists y p(x, y) \supset \exists y \forall x p(x, y)$, which is also *nonvalid*. Countermodel: Let D be the set of all integers and $p(x, y)$ be $x > y$. Then $\forall x \exists y (x > y)$ is *true* (for every given integer x there is a y, say, $x - 1$, for which $x > y$), but $\exists y \forall x (x > y)$ is *false* (there does not exist a y for which every integer x has the property $x > y$); thus, $\forall x \exists y (x > y) \supset \exists y \forall x (x > y)$ is *false*.

The reason that we have managed to deduce a nonvalid wff in this case is that line 4 of our deduction sequence is illegal. Since Γ contains the wff $p(x, b)$ and x is free in $p(x,b)$, it is forbidden to apply the $\forall$ introduction rule on x.

□

Derived rules of inference

The following are several useful derived rules of inference for handling quantifiers. We leave it to the reader to verify that they can indeed be derived from the basic rules of inference.

1. (*a*) $$\frac{\Gamma, A(x) \Rightarrow B(x)}{\Gamma, \forall x A(x) \Rightarrow B(x)}$$ *Left $\forall$ introduction*

Proof:

1. $\Gamma, A(x) \Rightarrow B(x)$	Given
2. $\Gamma \Rightarrow A(x) \supset B(x)$	$\supset$ introduction
3. $\Gamma, \forall x A(x) \Rightarrow A(x) \supset B(x)$	Introduction of assumption
4. $\Gamma, \forall x A(x) \Rightarrow \forall x A(x)$	Assumption axiom
5. $\Gamma, \forall x A(x) \Rightarrow A(x)$	$\forall$ elimination
6. $\Gamma, \forall x A(x) \Rightarrow B(x)$	$\supset$ elimination (lines 3 and 5)

(*b*) $$\frac{\Gamma, A(x) \Rightarrow B(x)}{\Gamma, \forall x A(x) \Rightarrow \forall x B(x)}$$ *$\forall\forall$ introduction*

where x is not free in any member of Γ.
Hint: Deduce $\Gamma, \forall x A(x) \Rightarrow B(x)$ and then use the $\forall$ introduction rule (x is not free in any member of Γ).

2. (*a*) $$\frac{\Gamma, A(x) \Rightarrow B}{\Gamma, \exists x A(x) \Rightarrow B}$$ *Left $\exists$ introduction*

where x is not free in any member of Γ or in B.
Hint: Deduce $\Gamma, \exists x A(x), A(b) \Rightarrow B$ and then use the $\exists$ elimination rule.

(*b*) $$\frac{\Gamma, A(x) \Rightarrow B(x)}{\Gamma, \exists x A(x) \Rightarrow \exists x B(x)}$$ *∃∃ introduction*

where x is not free in any member of Γ.
Hint: Deduce $\Gamma,\ A(x) \Rightarrow \exists x B(x)$ and then use the left ∃ introduction rule.

EXAMPLE 2-24
Deduce the wff

$$\exists x(A(x) \wedge B(x)) \supset (\exists x A(x) \wedge \exists x B(x)).$$

Proof:

1. $A(x) \wedge B(x) \Rightarrow A(x)$	Assumption rule and ∧ elimination
2. $\exists x(A(x) \wedge B(x)) \Rightarrow \exists x A(x)$	∃∃ introduction
3. $A(x) \wedge B(x) \Rightarrow B(x)$	Assumption rule and ∧ elimination
4. $\exists x(A(x) \wedge B(x)) \Rightarrow \exists x B(x)$	∃∃ introduction
5. $\exists x(A(x) \wedge B(x)) \Rightarrow \exists x A(x) \wedge \exists x B(x)$	∧ introduction (lines 2 and 4)
6. $\Rightarrow \exists x(A(x) \wedge B(x)) \supset (\exists x A(x) \wedge \exists x B(x))$	⊃ introduction

□

EXAMPLE 2-25
Deduce the wff

$$\forall x(A(x) \equiv B(x)) \supset (\forall x A(x) \equiv \forall x B(x))$$

1. $\forall x(A(x) \equiv B(x)), A(x) \Rightarrow A(x) \equiv B(x)$	Assumption axiom and ∀ elimination
2. $\forall x(A(x) \equiv B(x)), A(x) \Rightarrow A(x) \supset B(x)$	≡ elimination
3. $\forall x(A(x) \equiv B(x)), A(x) \Rightarrow A(x)$	Assumption axiom
4. $\forall x(A(x) \equiv B(x)), A(x) \Rightarrow B(x)$	⊃ elimination (lines 2 and 3)
5. $\forall x(A(x) \equiv B(x)), \forall x A(x) \Rightarrow \forall x B(x)$	∀∀ introduction
6. $\forall x(A(x) \equiv B(x)) \Rightarrow \forall x A(x) \supset \forall x B(x)$	⊃ introduction
7. $\forall x(A(x) \equiv B(x)), B(x) \Rightarrow A(x) \equiv B(x)$	Assumption axiom and ∀ elimination
8. $\forall x(A(x) \equiv B(x)), B(x) \Rightarrow B(x) \supset A(x)$	≡ elimination
9. $\forall x(A(x) \equiv B(x)), B(x) \Rightarrow B(x)$	Assumption axiom
10. $\forall x(A(x) \equiv B(x)), B(x) \Rightarrow A(x)$	⊃ elimination (lines 8 and 9)

11. $\forall x(A(x) \equiv B(x)), \forall xB(x) \Rightarrow \forall xA(x)$ — $\forall\forall$ introduction
12. $\forall x(A(x) \equiv B(x)) \Rightarrow \forall xB(x) \supset \forall xA(x)$ — $\supset$ introduction
13. $\forall x(A(x) \equiv B(x)) \Rightarrow \forall xA(x) \equiv \forall xB(x)$ — $\equiv$ introduction (lines 6 and 12)
14. $\Rightarrow \forall x(A(x) \equiv B(x)) \supset (\forall xA(x) \equiv \forall xB(x))$ — $\supset$ introduction

□

2-2.3 Rules for the Operators

Finally we shall proceed to describe the last group of rules of inference: *the rules for handling the operators.* Recall that for a wff $B(x)$ and term t, the expression $B(t)$ stands for the result of replacing all free occurrences (if any) of x in $B(x)$ by t. Similarly, for a term $\tau(x)$, the expression $\tau(t)$ stands for the result of replacing all free occurrences (if any) of x in $\tau(x)$ by t.

IV. Rules for the operators

(*a*) *If-then-else* rules

$$\frac{\Gamma \Rightarrow A \supset B(t_1) \text{ and } \Gamma \Rightarrow \sim A \supset B(t_2)}{\Gamma \Rightarrow B(\textit{if } A \textit{ then } t_1 \textit{ else } t_2)}$$ *If-then-else introduction*

$$\frac{\Gamma \Rightarrow B(\textit{if } A \textit{ then } t_1 \textit{ else } t_2)}{\Gamma \Rightarrow A \supset B(t_1)}$$

$$\frac{\Gamma \Rightarrow B(\textit{if } A \textit{ then } t_1 \textit{ else } t_2)}{\Gamma \Rightarrow \sim A \supset B(t_2)}$$ *If-then-else elimination*

(*b*) $=$ rules

$$\Gamma \Rightarrow t = t$$ *= axiom*

$$\frac{\Gamma \Rightarrow t_1 = t_2}{\Gamma \Rightarrow A(t_1) \equiv A(t_2)}$$ *= rule*

where t_1 and t_2 are free for x in $A(x)$.

EXAMPLE 2-26

Deduce the wff

$$A(t) \equiv \forall x(x = t \supset A(x))$$

where t is free for x in $A(x)$ and x is not free in $A(t)$.

1. $A(t), x = t \Rightarrow x = t$	Assumption axiom
2. $A(t), x = t \Rightarrow A(x) \equiv A(t)$	$=$ rule (t is free for x in $A(x)$)
3. $A(t), x = t \Rightarrow A(t) \supset A(x)$	$\equiv$ elimination
4. $A(t), x = t \Rightarrow A(t)$	Assumption axiom
5. $A(t), x = t \Rightarrow A(x)$	$\supset$ elimination (lines 3 and 4)
6. $A(t) \Rightarrow x = t \supset A(x)$	$\supset$ introduction
7. $A(t) \Rightarrow \forall x(x = t \supset A(x))$	$\forall$ introduction (x is not free in $A(t)$)
8. $\Rightarrow A(t) \supset \forall x(x = t \supset A(x))$	$\supset$ introduction
9. $\forall x(x = t \supset A(x)) \Rightarrow \forall x(x = t \supset A(x))$	Assumption axiom
10. $\forall x(x = t \supset A(x)) \Rightarrow t = t \supset A(t)$	$\forall$ elimination (t is free for x in $x = t \supset A(x)$)
11. $\forall x(x = t \supset A(x)) \Rightarrow t = t$	$=$ axiom
12. $\forall x(x = t \supset A(x)) \Rightarrow A(t)$	$\supset$ elimination (lines 10 and 11)
13. $\Rightarrow \forall x(x = t \supset A(x)) \supset A(t)$	$\supset$ introduction
14. $\Rightarrow A(t) \equiv \forall x(x = t \supset A(x))$	$\equiv$ introduction (lines 8 and 13)

□

EXAMPLE 2-27

Deduce the wff

$$A(t) \equiv \exists x(x = t \wedge A(x))$$

where t is free for x in $A(x)$.

1. $A(t) \Rightarrow A(t)$	Assumption axiom
2. $A(t) \Rightarrow t = t$	$=$ axiom
3. $A(t) \Rightarrow t = t \wedge A(t)$	$\wedge$ introduction (lines 1 and 2)
4. $A(t) \Rightarrow \exists x(x = t \wedge A(x))$	$\exists$ introduction (t is free for x in $x = t \wedge A(x)$)
5. $\Rightarrow A(t) \supset \exists x(x = t \wedge A(x))$	$\supset$ introduction
6. $\exists x(x = t \wedge A(x)) \Rightarrow \exists x(x = t \wedge A(x))$	Assumption axiom
7. $\exists x(x = t \wedge A(x)), b = t \wedge A(b) \Rightarrow b = t \wedge A(b)$	Assumption axiom
8. $\exists x(x = t \wedge A(x)), b = t \wedge A(b) \Rightarrow b = t$	$\wedge$ elimination (line 7)

9. $\exists x(x = t \wedge A(x))$, $b = t \wedge A(b) \Rightarrow A(b)$	$\wedge$ elimination (line 7)
10. $\exists x(x = t \wedge A(x))$, $b = t \wedge A(b) \Rightarrow A(b) \equiv A(t)$	$=$ rule (line 8, t is free for x in $A(x)$)
11. $\exists x(x = t \wedge A(x))$, $b = t \wedge A(b) \Rightarrow A(b) \supset A(t)$	$\equiv$ elimination
12. $\exists x(x = t \wedge A(x))$, $b = t \wedge A(b) \Rightarrow A(t)$	$\supset$ elimination (lines 9 and 11)
13. $\exists x(x = t \wedge A(x)) \Rightarrow A(t)$	$\exists$ elimination (lines 6 and 12)
14. $\Rightarrow \exists x(x = t \wedge A(x)) \supset A(t)$	$\supset$ introduction
15. $\Rightarrow A(t) \equiv \exists x(x = t \wedge A(x))$	$\equiv$ introduction (lines 5 and 14)

□

Derived rules of inference:

1.
$$\frac{\Gamma \Rightarrow t_1 = t_2}{\Gamma \Rightarrow t_2 = t_1}$$

Proof:

(a) $\Gamma \Rightarrow t_1 = t_2$	Given
(b) $\Gamma \Rightarrow (t_1 = t_1) \equiv (t_2 = t_1)$	$=$ rule (where $A(x)$ is $x = t_1$)
(c) $\Gamma \Rightarrow (t_1 = t_1) \supset (t_2 = t_1)$	$\equiv$ elimination
(d) $\Gamma \Rightarrow t_1 = t_1$	$=$ axiom
(e) $\Gamma \Rightarrow t_2 = t_1$	$\supset$ elimination (lines c and d)

2.
$$\frac{\Gamma \Rightarrow t_1 = t_2 \text{ and } \Gamma \Rightarrow t_2 = t_3}{\Gamma \Rightarrow t_1 = t_3}$$

Proof:

(a) $\Gamma \Rightarrow t_1 = t_2$	Given
(b) $\Gamma \Rightarrow (t_1 = t_3) \equiv (t_2 = t_3)$	$=$ rule (where $A(x)$ is $x = t_3$)
(c) $\Gamma \Rightarrow (t_2 = t_3) \supset (t_1 = t_3)$	$\equiv$ elimination
(d) $\Gamma \Rightarrow t_2 = t_3$	Given
(e) $\Gamma \Rightarrow t_1 = t_3$	$\supset$ elimination (lines c and d)

3.
$$\frac{\Gamma \Rightarrow t_1 = t_2}{\Gamma \Rightarrow \tau(t_1) = \tau(t_2)}$$

Proof:

(a) $\Gamma \Rightarrow t_1 = t_2$	Given
(b) $\Gamma \Rightarrow (\tau(t_1) = \tau(t_2)) \equiv (\tau(t_2) = \tau(t_2))$	$=$ rule (where $A(x)$ is $\tau(x) = \tau(t_2)$)

(c) $\Gamma \Rightarrow (\tau(t_2) = \tau(t_2)) \supset$ $(\tau(t_1) = \tau(t_2))$	$\equiv$ elimination
(d) $\Gamma \Rightarrow \tau(t_2) = \tau(t_2)$	$=$ axiom
(e) $\Gamma \Rightarrow \tau(t_1) = \tau(t_2)$	$\supset$ elimination (lines c and d)

2-3 THE RESOLUTION METHOD

The *resolution method* is a partial decision procedure (algorithm) for deciding whether a given wff of the first-order predicate calculus is unsatisfiable. That is, it takes a wff B of the first-order predicate calculus as input and if B is unsatisfiable it will eventually detect it and stop; otherwise, if B is satisfiable, the procedure may run forever.† Thus, to decide whether or not a given wff A is valid, we apply the resolution method to $\sim A$ and check whether or not $\sim A$ is unsatisfiable‡. If $\sim A$ is unsatisfiable (that is, A is valid), the procedure will eventually detect it and stop; otherwise, if $\sim A$ is satisfiable (that is, A is not valid), the procedure may run forever.

The resolution method can be applied only to wffs of a special form called the *clause form.* In this section, therefore, our first task is to show that every wff can be transformed effectively to a wff in clause form preserving the property of being or not being satisfiable. We then introduce *Herbrand's theorem,* which was the basis for most earlier decision procedures for proving the unsatisfiability of wffs of first-order predicate calculus. We describe two such Herbrand procedures: *Davis and Putnam's method* and the *ground resolution method.* Both methods are very inefficient; however, the ground resolution method can be generalized to a much more efficient method: the *resolution method.* The main part of the generalization is the application of the *unification algorithm.* For simplicity we introduce the resolution method for first-order predicate calculus *without* equality; however, the method can be extended to the first-order predicate calculus with equality as well.

2-3.1 Clause Form

A *literal* is an atomic formula or the negation of an atomic formula (with no occurrences of the *if-then-else* operator); for example, $p(f(x), a)$ and $\sim q(y)$ are literals. A *clause* is a disjunction of one or more literals; for

† Formally, the procedure can be simulated by a Turing machine that takes an arbitrary wff B of the first-order predicate calculus as input and if B is unsatisfiable, it will eventually reach an ACCEPT halt; otherwise, if B is satisfiable, it either reaches a REJECT halt or loops forever.

‡ In particular, rather than showing that a wff of the form $A_1 \wedge A_2 \wedge \ldots \wedge A_n \supset A_{n+1}$ is valid, we show that $A_1 \wedge A_2 \wedge \ldots \wedge A_n \wedge \sim A_{n+1}$ is unsatisfiable.

example, $p(f(x), a) \vee \sim q(y) \vee \sim p(a, y)$ is a clause. A wff is said to be in *clause form* if it is of the form

$$\forall x_{i_1} \forall x_{i_2} \ldots \forall x_{i_m} [C_1 \wedge C_2 \wedge \ldots \wedge C_k]$$

where each $C_i (1 \leqq i \leqq k)$ is a clause and $x_{i_1}, x_{i_2}, \ldots, x_{i_m}$ are all the distinct individual variables occurring in the C_i's. The succession of quantifiers $\forall x_{i_1} \forall x_{i_2} \ldots \forall x_{i_m}$ is called the *prefix* of the wff, and the conjunction of clauses $C_1 \wedge C_2 \wedge \ldots \wedge C_k$ is called the *matrix* of the wff. Note that a wff is in clause form if and only if it is closed and in prenex-conjunctive normal form (see Sec. 2-1.5) with the prefix consisting only of universal quantifiers.

We now prove the following theorem.

THEOREM 2-8 (Skolem). *Every wff D can be transformed into a wff D′ in clause form such that D is satisfiable if and only if D′ is satisfiable.*

Proof. The transformation is done by constructing a sequence of wffs $D_1, D_2, \ldots, D_n$ such that $D_1 = D$, $D_n = D'$ and for each i, $1 \leqq i < n$, D_i is satisfiable if and only if D_{i+1} is satisfiable. The main step during the process is the elimination of existential quantifiers. This is done by repeatedly eliminating an existential quantifier $\exists y$ and replacing all free occurrences of y in its scope by a new constant function f that does not already occur in the wff. These functions are called *Skolem functions*. For practical purposes it is important to minimize the number of arguments in the Skolem functions introduced during the process, which is the reason for Step 5 below. The main step, step 6, is justified later.

Given a wff D:

Step 1a. *Take the existential closure of D.*

Step 1b. *Eliminate in D all redundant quantifiers.* That is, eliminate any quantifier $\forall x_i$ or $\exists x_i$ whose scope does not contain x_i.

Step 2. *Rename any variable that is quantified in D more than once.* That is, choose one such quantifier and replace the quantified variable x_i, together with all free occurrences of x_i in the scope of the chosen quantifier, by a new variable x_j that does not already occur in the wff (alphabetic change of bound variables). This renaming process is repeated until all quantifiers in the wff have different variables.

Step 3a. *Eliminate the if-then-else operator.* Replace any atf A containing one or more occurrences of a term *if B then t′ else t″* by

$$\text{IF } B \text{ THEN } A' \text{ ELSE } A''$$

where A' (A'', respectively) results from A by replacing all occurrences of *if B then t′ else t″* with t' (t'', respectively).

Step 3b. *Eliminate all occurrences of connectives other than* $\wedge$, $\vee$, *and* $\sim$. Replace

$$\begin{array}{l} (A \supset B) \ \text{ by } \ (\sim A \vee B) \\ (A \equiv B) \ \text{ by } \ (\sim A \vee B) \wedge (\sim B \vee A) \\ (\text{IF } A \text{ THEN } B \text{ ELSE } C) \ \text{ by } \ (\sim A \vee B) \wedge (A \vee C) \end{array}$$

Step 4. *Move* $\sim$ *all the way inward.* Replace

$$\begin{array}{l} \sim \forall x A \ \text{ by } \ \exists x \sim A \\ \sim \exists x A \ \text{ by } \ \forall x \sim A \\ \sim (A \vee B) \ \text{ by } \ \sim A \wedge \sim B \\ \sim (A \wedge B) \ \text{ by } \ \sim A \vee \sim B \\ \sim \sim A \ \text{ by } \ A \end{array}$$

until each occurrence of $\sim$ immediately precedes an atomic formula.

Step 5. *Push quantifiers to the right.* Replace

$$\exists x(A \vee B) \text{ by } \begin{cases} A \vee \exists x B & \text{if } x \text{ is not free in } A \\ \exists x A \vee B & \text{if } x \text{ is not free in } B \end{cases}$$

$$\forall x(A \vee B) \text{ by } \begin{cases} A \vee \forall x B & \text{if } x \text{ is not free in } A \\ \forall x A \vee B & \text{if } x \text{ is not free in } B \end{cases}$$

$$\exists x(A \wedge B) \text{ by } \begin{cases} A \wedge \exists x B & \text{if } x \text{ is not free in } A \\ \exists x A \wedge B & \text{if } x \text{ is not free in } B \end{cases}$$

$$\forall x(A \wedge B) \text{ by } \begin{cases} A \wedge \forall x B & \text{if } x \text{ is not free in } A \\ \forall x A \wedge B & \text{if } x \text{ is not free in } B \end{cases}$$

Step 6. *Eliminate existential quantifiers.* Pick out the leftmost wfp $\exists y B(y)$ and replace it by $B(f(x_{i_1}, x_{i_2}, \ldots, x_{i_n}))$, where
(*a*) $x_{i_1}, x_{i_2}, \ldots, x_{i_n}$ are all the distinct free variables of $\exists y \mathrm{B}(y)$ which are universally quantified to the left of $\exists y B(y)$, and
(*b*) f is any n-ary function constant which does not already occur in the wff.
Repeat the process until there are no more existential quantifiers.
Special case: If $n = 0$, that is, there are no variables universally quantified

to the left of $\exists y B(y)$ which have free occurrence in $\exists y B(y)$, $\exists y B(y)$ is replaced by $B(a)$, where a is any individual constant (0-ary function constant) which does not already occur in the wff.

Step 7. *Advance universal quantifiers.* Move all universal quantifiers to the left.

Step 8. *Distribute, whenever possible,* $\wedge$ *over* $\vee$. Replace

$$(A \wedge B) \vee C \text{ by } (A \vee C) \wedge (B \vee C)$$
$$A \vee (B \wedge C) \text{ by } (A \vee B) \wedge (A \vee C)$$

Step 9. *Use simplification rules which preserve satisfiability.* (This step is optional.) Simplify the resulting wff without affecting its property of being or not being satisfiable. For example:

(*a*) *Factoring.* Eliminate all duplicate occurrences of the same literal in a clause; e.g., the clause $p(x, a) \vee q(y) \vee p(x, a)$ may be replaced by $p(x, a) \vee q(y)$.

(*b*) *Elimination of tautologies.* Eliminate any clause containing an atomic formula and its negation as literals; e.g., a clause such as $p(x, a) \vee q(y) \vee \sim p(x, a)$ may be eliminated.

The final wff is the desired D'.

Q.E.D.

EXAMPLE 2-28

Transform the following wff D into a wff D' in clause form such that D is satisfiable if and only if D' is satisfiable:

$$D\colon\ \forall x\{p(x) \supset \exists z\{\sim \forall y[q(x, y) \supset p(f(x_1))] \wedge \forall y[q(x, y) \supset p(x)]\}\}$$

1. Take the existential closure of D and eliminate the redundant quantifier $\exists z$:

$$\exists x_1 \forall x\{p(x) \supset \{\sim \forall y[q(x, y) \supset p(f(x_1))] \wedge \forall y[q(x, y) \supset p(x)]\}\}$$

2. Rename y because it is quantified twice:

$$\exists x_1 \forall x\{p(x) \supset \{\sim \forall y[q(x, y) \supset p(f(x_1))] \wedge \forall z[q(x, z) \supset p(x)]\}\}$$

3. Eliminate all occurrences of $\supset$;

$$\exists x_1 \forall x\{\sim p(x) \vee \{\sim \forall y[\sim q(x, y) \vee p(f(x_1))] \wedge \forall z[\sim q(x, z) \vee p(x)]\}\}$$

4. Move $\sim$ all the way inward:

$$\exists x_1 \forall x\{\sim p(x) \vee \{\exists y[q(x, y) \wedge \sim p(f(x_1))] \wedge \forall z[\sim q(x, z) \vee p(x)]\}\}$$

5. Push the quantifiers $\exists y$ and $\forall z$ to the right:

$$\exists x_1 \forall x \{\sim p(x) \vee \{[\exists y q(x, y) \wedge \sim p(f(x_1))] \wedge [\forall z \sim q(x, z) \vee p(x)]\}\}$$

6. Eliminate the existential quantifiers $\exists x_1$ and $\exists y$:

$$\forall x \{\sim p(x) \vee \{[q(x, g(x)) \wedge \sim p(f(a))] \wedge [\forall z \sim q(x, z) \vee p(x)]\}\}$$

7. Advance the universal quantifier $\forall z$ to the left:

$$\forall x \forall z \{\sim p(x) \vee \{[q(x, g(x)) \wedge \sim p(f(a))] \wedge [\sim q(x, z) \vee p(x)]\}\}$$

8. Distribute $\wedge$ over $\vee$:

$$\forall x \forall z \{[\sim p(x) \vee [q(x, g(x)) \wedge \sim p(f(a))]] \wedge [\sim p(x) \vee \sim q(x, z) \vee p(x)]\}$$

$$\forall x \forall z \{[\sim p(x) \vee q(x, g(x))] \wedge [\sim p(x) \vee \sim p(f(a))] \wedge [\sim p(x) \vee \sim q(x, z) \vee p(x)]\}$$

9. Simplify:
   (*a*) Eliminate the third clause (a tautology).
   (*b*) Remove the now redundant quantifier $\forall z$.
   (*c*) In the second clause eliminate the literal $\sim p(x)$ because the wff is satisfiable before the elimination if and only if the wff is satisfiable after the elimination.

Thus

$$D': \ \forall x \{[\sim p(x) \vee q(x, g(x))] \wedge \sim p(f(a))\}$$

□

Step 6. (elimination of existential quantifiers) may need some justification. Let D_i be a wff and D_{i+1} be the result of replacing the leftmost wfp $\exists y B(y)$ by $B(f(x_{i_1}, \ldots, x_{i_n}))$. If D_i is satisfiable, it must have a model $\mathscr{I}$ such that for each assignment of values to $x_{i_1}, \ldots, x_{i_n}$ there would be one or more values of y making D_i *true*. Hence, consider the interpretation $\mathscr{I}'$, which is identical to $\mathscr{I}$ but, in addition, assigns to f a function such that for each assignment of values to $x_{i_1}, \ldots, x_{i_n}, f(x_{i_1}, \ldots, x_{i_n})$ has one of those values of y which make D_i *true*. Then $\mathscr{I}'$ is a model for D_{i+1}; that is, D_{i+1} is satisfiable. A similar argument holds also in the other direction, showing that if D_{i+1} is satisfiable, then so is D_i.

It was mentioned previously that for practical purposes it is important to minimize the number of arguments in the Skolem functions introduced in Step 6, which is the reason for Step 5 of our algorithm. Let us consider, for example, the following wff:

$$D: \ \forall x_2 \exists y_1 \forall x_1 \exists y_2 [p(x_1, y_1) \wedge q(x_2, y_2)]$$

Applying the algorithm *without* Step 5, we obtain the wff

$$D': \quad \forall x_2 \forall x_1 [p(x_1, f(x_2)) \wedge q(x_2, g(x_2, x_1))]$$

where f and g are the Skolem functions introduced in the process. However, if we apply the algorithm *with* Step 5, we obtain first, by pushing quantifiers to the right,

$$\exists y_1 \forall x_1 p(x_1, y_1) \wedge \forall x_2 \exists y_2 q(x_2, y_2)$$

and then, by eliminating the existential quantifiers,

$$\forall x_1 p(x_1, a) \wedge \forall x_2 q(x_2, g(x_2))$$

Finally, moving the universal quantifiers to the left, we obtain

$$D': \quad \forall x_1 \forall x_2 [p(x_1, a) \wedge q(x_2, g(x_2))]$$

where a and g are the Skolem functions introduced in the process.

2-3.2 Herbrand's Procedures

By definition, a wff A is unsatisfiable if and only if its value is *false* for all interpretations over all domains. Clearly it would be of great help in proving that A is unsatisfiable if we could fix on one special domain D such that A is unsatisfiable if and only if A obtains the value *false* for all the interpretations with this domain D. And, indeed, for any wff A, there does exist such a domain, which is called the *Herbrand universe of A*, denoted by H_A. H_A is the set of all terms that can be constructed from the individual constants a_i and the function constants f_i occurring in A (if no individual constant occurs in A, we use an arbitrary individual constant, say, a). For clarity in the following discussion, we enclose every term in this set within quotation marks; for example, we write "$g(a, f(b))$" rather than $g(a, f(b))$. For simplicity we consider from now on only closed wffs.

EXAMPLE 2-29

If A is the *wff* $\forall x [p(a) \vee q(b) \supset p(f(x))]$, then

$$H_A = \{\text{“}a\text{”}, \text{“}b\text{”}, \text{“}f(a)\text{”}, \text{“}f(b)\text{”}, \text{“}f(f(a))\text{”}, \text{“}f(f(b))\text{”}, \ldots\}$$

If A is the wff $\forall x \forall y [p(f(x), y, g(x, y))]$, then

$$H_A = \{\text{“}a\text{”}, \text{“}f(a)\text{”}, \text{“}g(a, a)\text{”}, \text{“}f(f(a))\text{”}, \text{“}g(a, f(a))\text{”}, \text{“}g(f(a), a)\text{”}, \ldots\}$$

□

Now, for any given closed wff A, an interpretation over the Herbrand universe H_A of A consists of assignments to the constants of A as follows: (1) to each function constant f_i^n which occurs in A, we assign an n-ary function over H_A (in particular, each individual constant a_i is assigned some element of H_A); and (2) to each predicate constant p_i^n which occurs in A, we assign an n-ary predicate over H_A (in particular, each propositional constant is assigned the truth value *true* or *false*).

Among all those interpretations over H_A, we are interested in a special subclass of interpretations, called *Herbrand interpretations of A*, which satisfy the following conditions: (1) each individual constant a_i in A is assigned the term "a_i" of H_A; and (2) each constant function f_i^n occurring in A is assigned the n-ary function over H_A which maps the terms "t_1", "t_2", . . . , "t_n" of H_A into the term "$f_i^n(t_1, t_2, \ldots, t_n)$" of H_A. Note that there is no restriction on the assignments to the predicate constants of A.

The most important property of Herbrand interpretations is that for any interpretation $\mathscr{I}$ of a wff A in clause form, there exists a Herbrand interpretation $\mathscr{I}^*$ such that if $\langle A, \mathscr{I} \rangle$ is true—so is $\langle A, \mathscr{I}^* \rangle$. The appropriate Herbrand interpretation $\mathscr{I}^*$ of A is obtained by defining the truth value of p_i^n("t_1", "t_2", . . . , "t_n") as follows: If under interpretation $\mathscr{I}$ (with domain D), $(t_1, \ldots, t_n) = (d_1, \ldots, d_n)$ where $d_j \in D$ and $p_i^n(d_1, \ldots, d_n) = true$, then we let p_i^n("t_1", . . . , "t_n") $= true$ under interpretation $\mathscr{I}^*$; and if $p_i^n(d_1, \ldots, d_n) = false$, then p_i^n("t_1", . . . , "t_n") $=$ *false*. This property implies an important result which indicates that to show unsatisfiability of a wff A, it suffices to consider only Herbrand interpretations over H_A:

A wff A in clause form is unsatisfiable if and only if it yields the value false under all Herbrand interpretations of A.

Now we arrive at a very important theorem, *Herbrand's theorem*, which is the basis for the resolution method. Let A be a wff in clause form $\forall x_{i_1} \forall x_{i_2} \ldots \forall x_{i_n} [C_1 \wedge C_2 \wedge \ldots \wedge C_k]$. A *ground instance* of a clause C_i $(1 \leq i \leq k)$ of A is a clause obtained by replacing all individual variables in C_i by some terms of H_A (ignoring the quotation marks). Such clauses with no individual variables are called *ground clauses*.

THEOREM 2-9. *A wff A in clause form is unsatisfiable if and only if there is a finite conjunction of ground instances of its clauses which is unsatisfiable.*

Herbrand's theorem suggests a procedure, called *Herbrand's procedure*, for proving the unsatisfiability of wffs in clause form. For a given wff A in clause form, we can generate successively the ground instances G_i of the clauses of A and test successively whether their conjunction is unsatisfiable. By Herbrand's theorem, if A is unsatisfiable, the procedure will detect it after a finite number of steps; otherwise, if A is satisfiable, the procedure may never terminate (it could keep generating new ground instances and testing their conjunction). One of the problems in implementing this procedure is how to test the unsatisfiability of a finite conjunction $S = G_1 \wedge G_2 \wedge \cdots \wedge G_N$ of ground clauses G_i. We show two methods for testing the unsatisfiability of S: *Davis and Putnam's method* and the *ground resolution method.*

(A) Davis and Putnam's method Davis and Putnam's method for deciding whether a finite conjunction $S = G_1 \wedge G_2 \wedge \cdots \wedge G_N$ of ground clauses G_i is unsatisfiable consists essentially of applying repeatedly the rules listed below. In each step the conjunction S is transformed to a new conjunction S' such that S is unsatisfiable if and only if S' is unsatisfiable, or to a new pair of conjunctions S' and S'' such that S is unsatisfiable if and only if both S' and S'' are unsatisfiable. The process must terminate because the number of distinct literals occurring in S is reduced in each step.

1. *One-literal rules*:
   (*a*) If both the one-literal ground clauses $G_i = l$ and $G_j = \sim l$† occur in S, S is unsatisfiable.
   (*b*) If rule *a* does not apply and S contains a one-literal ground clause $G_i = l$, obtain S' from S by deleting all ground clauses in S containing l (including G_i) and then deleting all occurrences of the complement literal $\sim l$ from the remaining ground clauses. If S' is empty, S is satisfiable.
2. *Purity rule*:
   If rule 1 does not apply and a literal l occurs in S while its complement $\sim l$ does not occur in S, then delete all the ground clauses G_i containing l. The remaining conjunction S' is unsatisfiable if and only if S is unsatisfiable. If no clauses remain, S is satisfiable.
3. *Splitting rule*:
   Suppose that rules 1 and 2 do not apply. Then there must be a literal, say, l, such that both l and its complement $\sim l$ occur in S. Thus, S may be put into the form

$$\begin{aligned}&(A_1 \vee l) \wedge \cdots \wedge (A_{N_1} \vee l) \wedge\\&(B_1 \vee \sim l) \wedge \cdots \wedge (B_{N_2} \vee \sim l) \wedge\\&R_1 \wedge \cdots \wedge R_{N_3}\end{aligned}$$

† By $\sim l$ (the complement literal of l) we understand $\sim p(\ldots)$ if l is the literal $p(\ldots)$, and $p(\ldots)$ if l is the literal $\sim p(\ldots)$.

where A_i, B_i, and R_i are ground clauses free of l and $\sim l$. Then the conjunctions $S' = A_1 \wedge \cdots \wedge A_{N_1} \wedge R_1 \wedge \cdots \wedge R_{N_3}$ and $S'' = B_1 \wedge \cdots \wedge B_{N_2} \wedge R_1 \wedge \cdots \wedge R_{N_3}$ are obtained. S is unsatisfiable if and only if $(S' \vee S'')$ is unsatisfiable; that is, both S' and S'' are unsatisfiable.

EXAMPLE 2-30

Let S be

$$[p_1(a) \vee p_2(b)] \wedge [p_1(a) \vee \sim p_3(a)] \wedge [\sim p_1(a) \vee p_3(a)]$$
$$\wedge [\sim p_1(a) \vee \sim p_2(b)] \wedge [p_3(a) \vee \sim p_2(b)] \wedge [\sim p_3(a) \vee p_2(b)]$$

The following tree describes a proof that S is unsatisfiable:

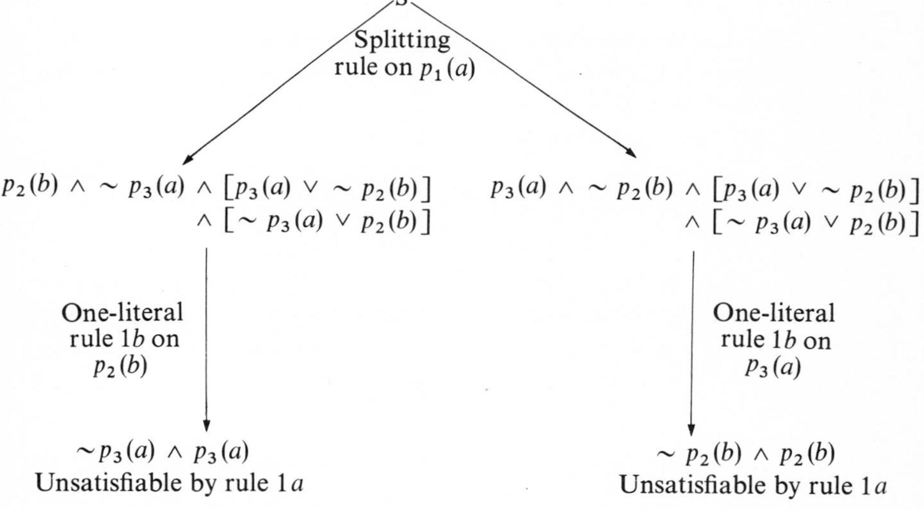

Hence S is unsatisfiable.

□

EXAMPLE 2-31

Let S be

$$[p_1(a) \vee p_2(b)] \wedge \sim p_2(b) \wedge [\sim p_1(a) \vee p_2(b) \vee \sim p_3(a)]$$

Then, by applying rule 1*b* on $\sim p_2(b)$, we obtain

$$p_1(a) \wedge [\sim p_1(a) \vee \sim p_3(a)]$$

Applying rule 1*b* on $p_1(a)$, we obtain

$$\sim p_3(a)$$

Finally, applying rule 1*b* on $\sim p_3(a)$, no clauses remain, which implies that S is satisfiable.

□

EXAMPLE 2-32
Let S be

$$[\sim p_1(a) \vee \sim p_2(b) \vee p_3(a)] \wedge [\sim p_1(a) \vee p_2(b)] \wedge p_1(a) \wedge \sim p_3(a)$$

Then, by applying rule $1b$ on $p_1(a)$, we obtain

$$[\sim p_2(b) \vee p_3(a)] \wedge p_2(b) \wedge \sim p_3(a)$$

Again applying rule $1b$ on $p_2(b)$, we have

$$p_3(a) \wedge \sim p_3(a)$$

which implies by rule $1a$ that S is unsatisfiable.

□

(B) The ground resolution method The ground resolution method consists of a single inference rule, called the *ground resolution rule*, which is essentially an extension of the one-literal rule of Davis and Putnam. The ground resolution rule can be stated as follows:

> For any two ground clauses G_1 and G_2 containing a literal l and its complement $\sim l$, respectively, construct a new clause G_3, called *the resolvent of* G_1 *and* G_2, obtained by first deleting all occurrences of l and $\sim l$ in G_1 and G_2, respectively, and then letting G_3 be the disjunction of the resulting clauses G_1' and G_2'. Eliminate duplicate occurrences of literals in G_3, and add G_3 to the list of ground clauses.

Special case: If there are two one-literal clauses, a literal l and its complement $\sim l$, then their resolvent is the *empty clause*, denoted by □.

The key result is that a *finite conjunction S of ground clauses is unsatisfiable if and only if* □ *(the empty clause) can be derived from S by repeated application of the ground resolution rule.* Clearly the process must always terminate because there are only finitely many distinct clauses (with no duplicate literals) that can be constructed from the literals of S. If the process terminates and □ (the empty clause) has not been derived, S is satisfiable. The idea behind the method is that $S = G_1 \wedge G_2 \wedge \cdots \wedge G_N$ is unsatisfiable if and only if $S' = G_1 \wedge G_2 \wedge \cdots \wedge G_{N+1}$ is unsatisfiable, where G_{N+1} is the resolvent of some G_i and G_j. Any satisfiability-preserving simplification rule may be applied during the process.

EXAMPLE 2-33
Let S be

$$[p_1(a) \vee p_2(b)] \wedge [p_1(a) \vee \sim p_3(a)] \wedge [\sim p_1(a) \vee p_3(a)]$$
$$\wedge [\sim p_1(a) \vee \sim p_2(b)] \wedge [p_3(a) \vee \sim p_2(b)] \wedge [\sim p_3(a) \vee p_2(b)]$$

We want to prove that S is unsatisfiable by the ground resolution method. First let us enumerate the clauses of S:

1. $p_1(a) \vee p_2(b)$
2. $p_1(a) \vee \sim p_3(a)$
3. $\sim p_1(a) \vee p_3(a)$
4. $\sim p_1(a) \vee \sim p_2(b)$
5. $p_3(a) \vee \sim p_2(b)$
6. $\sim p_3(a) \vee p_2(b)$

Using the ground resolution rule repeatedly, we produce new clauses:

7. $p_2(b) \vee p_3(a)$ — from 1 and 3 on $p_1(a)$
8. $p_2(b)$ — from 6 and 7 on $p_3(a)$
9. $\sim p_3(a) \vee \sim p_2(b)$ — from 2 and 4 on $p_1(a)$
10. $\sim p_2(b)$ — from 5 and 9 on $p_3(a)$
11. $\square$ — from 8 and 10 on $p_2(b)$

Thus S is unsatisfiable.

$\square$

EXAMPLE 2-34

Let S be

$$[p_1(a) \vee p_2(b)] \wedge \sim p_2(b) \wedge [\sim p_1(a) \vee p_2(b) \vee \sim p_3(a)]$$

The ground clauses of S are

1. $p_1(a) \vee p_2(b)$
2. $\sim p_2(b)$
3. $\sim p_1(a) \vee p_2(b) \vee \sim p_3(a)$

Using the ground resolution rule repeatedly, we obtain

4. $p_1(a)$ — from 1 and 2 on $p_2(b)$
5. $p_2(b) \vee \sim p_3(a)$ — from 1 and 3 on $p_1(a)$
6. $\sim p_1(a) \vee \sim p_3(a)$ — from 2 and 3 on $p_2(b)$
7. $\sim p_3(a)$ — from 2 and 5 on $p_2(b)$

Since no new clause can be produced, it follows that S is satisfiable.

$\square$

EXAMPLE 2-35

Let S be

$$[\sim p_1(a) \vee \sim p_2(b) \vee p_3(a)] \wedge [\sim p_1(a) \vee p_2(b)] \wedge p_1(a) \wedge \sim p_3(a)$$

The ground clauses of S are

1. $\sim p_1(a) \vee \sim p_2(b) \vee p_3(a)$
2. $\sim p_1(a) \vee p_2(b)$

3. $p_1(a)$
4. $\sim p_3(a)$

Applying the ground resolution rule repeatedly, we obtain

5. $\sim p_1(a) \vee p_3(a)$ from 1 and 2 on $p_2(b)$
6. $p_3(a)$ from 3 and 5 on $p_1(a)$
7. $\square$ from 4 and 6 on $p_3(a)$

Thus S is unsatisfiable.

$\square$

2-3.3 The Unification Algorithm

Testing the unsatisfiability of a finite conjunction of ground clauses was only one of the problems in implementing Herbrand's procedure. The major drawback with this procedure is that it needs to generate the ground instances of the given clauses. For most wffs, the number of ground instances that must be generated before an unsatisfiable conjunction is encountered is so large that it is impossible even to store all the ground instances in a computer, not to mention the time required for testing for unsatisfiability. In order to avoid the generation of ground instances as required in Herbrand's procedure, Robinson (1965) introduced the *resolution rule*, which is a generalization of the ground resolution rule. The main difference is that it can be applied directly to any conjunction S of clauses (not necessarily ground clauses) to test the unsatisfiability of S.

EXAMPLE 2-36

Suppose we want to use the ground resolution method to prove that the following wff A is valid:

$$A: \quad [\forall x \exists y p(x, y) \wedge \forall y \exists z q(y, z)] \supset \forall x \exists y \exists z (p(x, y) \wedge q(y, z))$$

For this purpose we show that $\sim A$ is unsatisfiable. First, we transform $\sim A$ to clause form and obtain the wff (check!)

$$B: \quad \forall x \forall y \forall y_1 \forall z [p(x, f(x)) \wedge q(y, g(y)) \wedge (\sim p(a, y_1) \vee \sim q(y_1, z))]$$

To prove that B is unsatisfiable using the ground resolution method, we generate successively the ground instances of the clauses of B and test successively whether their conjunction is unsatisfiable. We must keep repeating this procedure until we first encounter the following conjunction:

$$[p(a, f(a)) \wedge q(a, g(a)) \wedge [\sim p(a, a) \vee \sim q(a, a)]]$$

. . . .

$$\wedge\ [p(a, f(a)) \wedge q(f(a), g(f(a))) \wedge [\sim p(a, f(a)) \vee \sim q(f(a), g(f(a)))]]$$

where the last conjunction is obtained by replacing x by a, y and y_1 by $f(a)$, and z by $g(f(a))$. The empty clause □ is then derived from the above conjunction as follows:

1. $p(a, f(a))$
2. $q(f(a), g(f(a)))$
3. $\sim p(a, f(a)) \vee \sim q(f(a), g(f(a)))$

By resolving clauses 1 and 3 we obtain

4. $\sim q(f(a), g(f(a)))$

and then by resolving clauses 2 and 4 we obtain

5. □

The *general resolution method* suggests resolving the given clauses directly without actually looking at their ground instances. This method will be described in detail in the remainder of this section, but now let us illustrate how the method will be applied to prove the unsatisfiability of the wff B. The clauses of B are

1. $p(x, f(x))$
2. $q(y, g(y))$
3. $\sim p(a, y_1) \vee \sim q(y_1, z)$

Consider the clauses 1 and 3. The literal in 1 is not complementary to any literal of 3. However, complementary literals can be obtained if we replace x by a and y_1 by $f(a)$ to obtain

1′. $p(a, f(a))$
3′. $\sim p(a, f(a)) \vee \sim q(f(a), z)$

We denote such a substitution by $\{\langle x, a\rangle, \langle y_1, f(a)\rangle\}$; however, this is a very special substitution called a *unifier* because it unifies both $p(x, f(x))$ and $p(a, y_1)$ to yield the atomic formula $p(a, f(a))$. Note that if, in addition, we replace z by a, or z by $f(a)$, and so forth, we obtain a class of unifiers $\{\langle x,a\rangle,\langle y_1, f(a)\rangle,\langle z,a\rangle\}$, $\{\langle x,a\rangle,\langle y_1, f(a)\rangle,\langle z, f(a)\rangle\}$, ... The one we chose, $\{\langle x, a\rangle, \langle y_1, f(a)\rangle\}$, is the *most general unifier* among them, and it is best suited for our purpose.

If we resolve clauses 1′ and 3′, we obtain

4. $\sim q(f(a), z)$

Now let us consider clauses 2 and 4. In order to unify $q(y, g(y))$ and $\sim q(f(a), z)$, we need only replace y by $f(a)$ and z by $g(f(a))$; that is, we apply the substitution $\{\langle y, f(a)\rangle, \langle z, g(f(a))\rangle\}$ and obtain the clauses

2′. $q(f(a), g(f(a)))$
4′. $\sim q(f(a), g(f(a)))$

Clauses 2′ and 4′ can now be resolved to obtain the desired empty clause

5. $\square$

$\square$

In order to describe the (general) resolution method, we must first introduce a few definitions. We denote a *substitution* by a finite set (possibly empty) of pairs of the form $\alpha = \{\langle v_1, t_1\rangle, \langle v_2, t_2\rangle, \ldots, \langle v_n, t_n\rangle\}$, where the v_i's are distinct individual variables and each t_i is a term different from v_i. For any literal L, $L' = L\alpha$ is the literal obtained from L by replacing simultaneously each occurrence of the variable v_i, $1 \leqq i \leqq n$, in L by the term t_i. L' is called an *instance of* L. For example, if $\alpha = \{\langle x, f(y)\rangle, \langle y, g(b)\rangle\}$ and L is $p(x, y, f(y))$, then $L\alpha$ is $p(f(y), g(b), f(g(b)))$.

The *disagreement set* of a disjunction of atomic formulas $p(t_1^{(1)}, \ldots, t_n^{(1)}) \vee p(t_1^{(2)}, \ldots, t_n^{(2)}) \vee \ldots \vee p(t_1^{(N)}, \ldots, t_n^{(N)})$, or for short $A_1 \vee A_2 \vee \ldots \vee A_N$, is a set of subterms $\{\tau^{(1)}, \tau^{(2)}, \ldots, \tau^{(N)}\}$ obtained as follows: We regard each of the atomic formulas A_i as a string of symbols and detect the first symbol position in which not all the A_i's have the same symbol. Then, for each i $(1 \leqq i \leqq N)$, we let $\tau^{(i)}$ be the subterm of A_i that begins with this symbol position. For example, the disagreement set of the disjunction

$$p(x, g(\underline{f(y, z)}, x), y) \vee p(x, g(\underline{a}, b), b) \vee p(x, g(\underline{g(h(x), a)}, y), h(x))$$

is the set of subterms $\{f(y, z), a, g(h(x), a)\}$. Note that the disagreement set can have less than N elements because not all the $\tau^{(i)}$'s need be distinct.

A substitution α is called a *unifier* for a disjunction of atomic formulas $A_1 \vee A_2 \vee \cdots \vee A_N$ if $A_1\alpha = A_2\alpha = \cdots = A_N\alpha$. If there exists a unifier for a disjunction, the disjunction is said to be *unifiable*. A unifier β for a disjunction of atomic formulas $A_1 \vee A_2 \vee \cdots \vee A_N$ is a *most general unifier* if for each unifier α for the disjunction, $A_i\alpha$ is an instance of $A_i\beta$ (for all i, $1 \leqq i \leqq N$). The atomic formula B where $B = A_1\beta = A_2\beta = \cdots = A_N\beta$ obtained by any most general unifier β, called a *factor* of $A_1 \vee A_2 \vee \cdots \vee A_N$, is unique except for alphabetic variants. For example, the disjunctions $p(a, x) \vee p(b, y)$ and $p(a, f(x)) \vee p(x, f(b))$ are not unifiable. A unifier of the disjunction $p(a, f(x)) \vee p(y, z)$ is $\{\langle y, a\rangle, \langle x, b\rangle, \langle z, f(b)\rangle\}$. A most general unifier of the disjunction is $\{\langle y, a\rangle, \langle z, f(x)\rangle\}$. A most general unifier of the disjunction $p(a, x, f(g(y))) \vee p(z, h(z, w), f(w))$ is $\{\langle z, a\rangle, \langle x, h(a, g(y))\rangle, \langle w, g(y)\rangle\}$.

The basic part of the (general) resolution method is the application of the unification algorithm, which finds a most general unifier β for a given unifiable disjunction of atomic formulas $p(t_1^{(1)}, \ldots, t_n^{(1)}) \vee p(t_1^{(2)}, \ldots, t_n^{(2)}) \vee \cdots \vee p(t_1^{(N)}, \ldots, t_n^{(N)})$, denoted by $A_1 \vee A_2 \vee \cdots \vee A_N$, and reports a failure when the disjunction is not unifiable.

THE UNIFICATION ALGORITHM

Step 0. The algorithm starts with the empty substitution α_0 (the substitution that consists of no pairs) and constructs, in a step-by-step process, a most general unifier β if one exists.

Step $k+1$ ($k \geqq 0$). Suppose that at the kth step ($k \geqq 0$) the substitution produced so far is α_k. If all the atomic formulas $A_i\alpha_k$ are identical, then $\beta = \alpha_k$ is a most general unifier of $A_1 \vee A_2 \vee \cdots \vee A_N$ and the process is terminated. Otherwise, first we determine the disagreement set, say, D_k, of $A_1\alpha_k \vee A_2\alpha_k \vee \cdots \vee A_N\alpha_k$. Now the algorithm attempts to modify the substitution α_k (to obtain α_{k+1}) in such a way as to make two elements of the disagreement set equal. This can be done only if the disagreement set contains as members some variable, say, v_k, and some term, say, t_k, such that t_k does not contain v_k. (If no such members exist in D_k, we report a failure: the disjunct $A_1 \vee A_2 \vee \cdots \vee A_N$ is not unifiable.) Next we create the modified substitution α_{k+1}, which consists of all pairs of α_k obtained after replacing all occurrences of v_k in the terms of α_k by t_k, and add to α_{k+1} the pair $\langle v_k, t_k \rangle$. We then increment k and perform another step of the algorithm. □

Note that the process must always terminate because each α_k, $k \geqq 0$, contains substitutions for k distinct individual variables $v_1, v_2, \ldots, v_k$ and there are only finitely many distinct individual variables in the given disjunction $A_1 \vee A_2 \vee \cdots \vee A_N$.

EXAMPLE 2-37

To find a most general unifier of the disjunction

$$p(a, x, f(g(y))) \vee p(z, h(z, w), f(w)),$$

or for short, $A_1 \vee A_2$, we start with

$$\alpha_0 = \{\ \} \qquad \text{the empty substitution}$$

The disagreement set D_0 of $A_1 \vee A_2$ is $\{a, z\}$. Therefore we have

$$\alpha_1 = \{\langle z, a \rangle\}$$

Since the new disjunction $A_1\alpha_1 \vee A_2\alpha_1$ is $p(a, x, f(g(y))) \vee p(a, h(a, w), f(w))$, the disagreement set D_1 is $\{x, h(a, w)\}$. We now have

$$\alpha_2 = \{\langle z, a\rangle, \langle x, h(a, w)\rangle\}$$

The new disjunction $A_1\alpha_2 \vee A_2\alpha_2$ is $p(a, h(a, w), f(g(y))) \vee p(a, h(a, w), f(w))$, and the disagreement set D_2 is $\{g(y), w\}$. Therefore we have

$$\alpha_3 = \{\langle z, a\rangle, \langle x, h(a, g(y))\rangle, \langle w, g(y)\rangle\}$$

Since $A_1\alpha_3 = A_2\alpha_3 = p(a, h(a, g(y)), f(g(y)))$, $\beta = \alpha_3$ is a most general unifier.

□

2-3.4 The Resolution Rule

The general resolution method for proving the unsatisfiability of a wff S in clause form is based on repeated application of the *resolution rule*, which is a very powerful inference rule. We start by applying the resolution rule to a pair of clauses C_1 and C_2 from S to obtain a (general) resolvent C_3 of C_1 and C_2. We then add the new clause C_3 to S and apply the resolution rule again until □ (the empty clause) is derived. The essential result is the following theorem.

THEOREM 2-10 (Robinson). *A given wff S in clause form is unsatisfiable if and only if □ (the empty clause) can be derived eventually by repeated application of the resolution rule.*

THE RESOLUTION RULE

Let C_1 and C_2 be two clauses such that no individual variable is common to both C_1 and C_2. Suppose that

$$p(t_1^{(1)}, \ldots, t_n^{(1)}) \vee p(t_1^{(2)}, \ldots, t_n^{(2)}) \vee \cdots \vee p(t_1^{(N)}, \ldots, t_n^{(N)})$$

is a *subdisjunction*† of C_1 and

$$\sim p(\tau_1^{(1)}, \ldots, \tau_n^{(1)}) \vee \sim p(\tau_1^{(2)}, \ldots, \tau_n^{(2)}) \vee \cdots \vee \sim p(\tau_1^{(M)}, \ldots, \tau_n^{(M)})$$

is a subdisjunction of C_2 such that a most general unifier β exists for the disjunction

$$p(t_1^{(1)}, \ldots, t_n^{(1)}) \vee p(t_1^{(2)}, \ldots, t_n^{(2)}) \vee \cdots \vee p(t_1^{(N)}, \ldots, t_n^{(N)})$$
$$\vee\, p(\tau_1^{(1)}, \ldots, \tau_n^{(1)}) \vee p(\tau_1^{(2)}, \ldots, \tau_n^{(2)}) \vee \cdots \vee p(\tau_1^{(M)}, \ldots, \tau_n^{(M)})$$

† A *subdisjunction* of C_1 is a disjunction of some (or possibly all) of the literals of C_1.

Let us denote by $p(r_1, \ldots, r_n)$ the factor of this disjunction. Then we can construct a new clause C_3, called a *resolvent* of C_1 and C_2, by taking the disjunction of $C_1\beta$ and $C_2\beta$ after eliminating all occurrences of $p(r_1, \ldots, r_n)$ in $C_1\beta$ and all occurrences of $\sim p(r_1, \ldots, r_n)$ in $C_2\beta$.

□

The requirement that there are no common variables to C_1 and C_2 is not a real restriction because any set of clauses

$$C_1(x), C_2(x), \ldots, C_k(x)$$

can be replaced by an equivalent set of clauses

$$C_1(x_1), C_2(x_2), \ldots, C_k(x_k)$$

since the wffs

$$A\colon \quad \forall x[C_1(x) \wedge C_2(x) \wedge \cdots \wedge C_k(x)]$$

$$B\colon \quad \forall x_1 \forall x_2 \ldots \forall x_k[C_1(x_1) \wedge C_2(x_2) \wedge \cdots \wedge C_k(x_k)]$$

are equivalent. [Note that the wff A is equivalent to $A'\colon\ \forall x C_1(x) \wedge \forall x C_2(x) \wedge \cdots \wedge \forall x C_k(x)$, and the wff B is equivalent to $B'\colon\ \forall x_1 C_1(x_1) \wedge \forall x_2 C_2(x_2) \wedge \cdots \wedge \forall x_k C_k(x_k)$.] A similar argument holds when the clauses contain more than one variable.

EXAMPLE 2-38

Show that the following wff is valid:

$$A\colon \quad \sim \exists y \forall z[p(z, y) \equiv \sim \exists x[p(z, x) \wedge p(x, z)]]$$

We shall prove that $\sim A$, that is,

$$\exists y \forall z[p(z, y) \equiv \sim \exists x[p(z, x) \wedge p(x, z)]]$$

is unsatisfiable using the resolution method. First we transform the wff to clause form.

(*a*.) Eliminate the $\equiv$ connective:

$$\exists y \forall z\{[p(z, y) \supset \sim \exists x[p(z, x) \wedge p(x, z)]]$$
$$\wedge [\sim \exists x[p(z, x) \wedge p(x, z)] \supset p(z, y)]\}$$

(*b*.) Eliminate the $\supset$ connective:

$$\exists y \forall z\{[\sim p(z, y) \vee \sim \exists x[p(z, x) \wedge p(x, z)]]$$
$$\wedge [\exists x[p(z, x) \wedge p(x, z)] \vee p(z, y)]\}$$

(*c*.) Push $\sim$ all the way inward:

$$\exists y \forall z \{[\sim p(z, y) \vee \forall x[\sim p(z, x) \vee \sim p(x, z)]] \wedge [\exists x[p(z, x) \wedge p(x, z)] \vee p(z, y)]\}$$

(*d*.) Eliminate existential quantifiers:

$$\forall z \{[\sim p(z, a) \vee \forall x[\sim p(z, x) \vee \sim p(x, z)]] \wedge [[p(z, f(z)) \wedge p(f(z), z)] \vee p(z, a)]\}$$

(*e*.) Advance universal quantifiers:

$$\forall z \forall x \{[\sim p(z, a) \vee \sim p(z, x) \vee \sim p(x, z)] \wedge [[p(z, f(z)) \wedge p(f(z), z)] \vee p(z, a)]\}$$

(*f*.) Distribute $\wedge$ over $\vee$:

$$\forall z \forall x \{[\sim p(z, a) \vee \sim p(z, x) \vee \sim p(x, z)] \wedge [p(z, f(z)) \vee p(z, a)] \wedge [p(f(z), z) \vee p(z, a)]\}$$

The clauses are

1. $\sim p(z_1, a) \vee \sim p(z_1, x_1) \vee \sim p(x_1, z_1)$
2. $p(z_2, f(z_2)) \vee p(z_2, a)$
3. $p(f(z_3), z_3) \vee p(z_3, a)$

Note that we renamed the variables in each clause by adding appropriate subscripts. First we try to resolve clauses 1 and 2, taking the subdisjunctions $\sim p(z_1, a) \vee \sim p(z_1, x_1) \vee \sim p(x_1, z_1)$ in clause 1 and $p(z_2, a)$ in clause 2. Since the most general unifier of $p(z_1, a) \vee p(z_1, x_1) \vee p(x_1, z_1) \vee p(z_2, a)$ is $\{\langle x_1, a\rangle, \langle z_2, a\rangle, \langle z_1, a\rangle\}$, we obtain the resolvent

4. $p(a, f(a))$

Similarly, by resolving clauses 1 and 3 taking the subdisjunctions $\sim p(z_1, a) \vee \sim p(z_1, x_1) \vee \sim p(x_1, z_1)$ in clause 1 and $p(z_3, a)$ in clause 3, we find that the most general unifier is $\{\langle x_1, a\rangle, \langle z_1, a\rangle, \langle z_3, a\rangle\}$ and the resolvent is, therefore,

5. $p(f(a), a)$

Now resolving clauses 1 and 4 looking for the most general unifier of $p(x_1, z_1) \vee p(a, f(a))$, we find that it is $\{\langle x_1, a\rangle, \langle z_1, f(a)\rangle\}$, and the resolvent is therefore

6. $\sim p(f(a), a)$

From clauses 5 and 6 we obtain finally the empty clause

7. $\square$

It follows therefore that $\sim A$ is unsatisfiable; i.e., the given wff A is valid. $\square$

EXAMPLE 2-39
Show that the following wff is valid;

$$A: \quad \exists x \exists y \forall z \{[p(x, y) \supset [p(y, z) \wedge p(z, z)]] \wedge [[p(x, y) \wedge q(x, y)] \supset [q(x, z) \wedge q(z, z)]]\}$$

We shall prove that $\sim A$ is unsatisfiable using the resolution method. First we transform $\sim A$ to clause form.

(*a*) Eliminate the $\supset$ connective:

$$\sim \exists x \exists y \forall z \{[\sim p(x, y) \vee [p(y, z) \wedge p(z, z)]] \wedge [\sim [p(x, y) \wedge q(x, y)] \vee [q(x, z) \wedge q(z, z)]]\}$$

(*b*) Push $\sim$ all the way inward:

$$\forall x \forall y \exists z \{[p(x, y) \wedge [\sim p(y, z) \vee \sim p(z, z)]] \vee [p(x, y) \wedge q(x, y) \wedge [\sim q(x, z) \vee \sim q(z, z)]]\}$$

(*c*) Eliminate existential quantifiers:

$$\forall x \forall y \{[p(x, y) \wedge [\sim p(y, f(x, y)) \vee \sim p(f(x, y), f(x, y))]] \vee [p(x, y) \wedge q(x, y) \wedge [\sim q(x, f(x, y)) \vee \sim q(f(x, y), f(x, y))]]\}$$

(*d*) Distribute $\wedge$ over $\vee$: †

$$\begin{aligned} \forall x \forall y \{ & [p(x, y) \vee p(x, y)] \\ & \wedge [p(x, y) \vee q(x, y)] \\ & \wedge [p(x, y) \vee \sim q(x, f(x, y)) \vee \sim q(f(x, y), f(x, y))] \\ & \wedge [\sim p(y, f(x, y)) \vee \sim p(f(x, y), f(x, y)) \vee p(x, y)] \\ & \wedge [\sim p(y, f(x, y)) \vee \sim p(f(x, y), f(x, y)) \vee q(x, y)] \\ & \wedge [\sim p(y, f(x, y)) \vee \sim p(f(x, y), f(x, y)) \vee \sim q(x, f(x, y)) \\ & \qquad \vee \sim q(f(x, y), f(x, y))]\} \end{aligned}$$

† Note that the matrix is of the form $[A \wedge (B \vee C)] \vee [A \wedge D \wedge (E \vee F)]$ which is equivalent to

$$(A \vee A) \wedge (A \vee D) \wedge (A \vee E \vee F) \wedge (B \vee C \vee A) \wedge (B \vee C \vee D) \wedge (B \vee C \vee E \vee F)$$

(*e*) Simplify: Eliminate one occurrence of $p(x, y)$ from the first clause. Eliminate clauses 2 to 4 since the first clause $p(x, y)$ occurs as a subdisjunction in these clauses.†

Then, after renaming the variables in the remaining clauses, we have

1. $p(x_1, y_1)$
2. $\sim p(y_2, f(x_2, y_2)) \vee \sim p(f(x_2, y_2), f(x_2, y_2)) \vee q(x_2, y_2)$
3. $\sim p(y_3, f(x_3, y_3)) \vee \sim p(f(x_3, y_3), f(x_3, y_3)) \vee \sim q(x_3, f(x_3, y_3)) \vee \sim q(f(x_3, y_3), f(x_3, y_3))$

Applying the resolution rule, we obtain the following clauses. By clauses 1 and 2 with $\{\langle x_1, y_2\rangle, \langle y_1, f(x_2, y_2)\rangle\}$, we obtain

4. $\sim p(f(x_2, y_2), f(x_2, y_2)) \vee q(x_2, y_2)$

By clauses 1 and 4 with $\{\langle x_1, f(x_2, y_2)\rangle, \langle y_1, f(x_2, y_2)\rangle\}$, we obtain

5. $q(x_2, y_2)$

By clauses 3 and 5 with $\{\langle x_2, f(x_3, y_3)\rangle, \langle y_2, f(x_3, y_3)\rangle\}$, we obtain

6. $\sim p(y_3, f(x_3, y_3)) \vee \sim p(f(x_3, y_3), f(x_3, y_3)) \vee \sim q(x_3, f(x_3, y_3))$

By clauses 5 and 6 with $\{\langle x_2, x_3\rangle, \langle y_2, f(x_3, y_3)\rangle\}$ we obtain

7. $\sim p(y_3, f(x_3, y_3)) \vee \sim p(f(x_3, y_3), f(x_3, y_3))$

By clauses 1 and 7 with $\{\langle x_1, f(x_3, y_3)\rangle, \langle y_1, f(x_3, y_3)\rangle\}$, we obtain

8. $\sim p(y_3, f(x_3, y_3))$

Finally, by clauses 1 and 8 with $\{\langle x_1, y_3\rangle, \langle y_1, f(x_3, y_3)\rangle\}$, we obtain

9. $\square$

This implies that $\sim A$ is unsatisfiable; that is, A is valid.

Note that there was no need to rename the variables in clauses 4 to 8, because every pair of clauses C_1 and C_2 which were resolved did not have any variable in common.

$\square$

†Note that, for example, $\forall x \forall y[p(x, y) \wedge [p(x, y) \vee q(x, y)]]$ is satisfiable if and only if $\forall x \forall y[p(x, y)]$ is satisfiable.

Bibliographical Remarks

There exists quite a variety of textbooks on mathematical logic: elementary books like Hilbert and Ackermann (1950) and Rogers (1971), intermediate books like Mendelson (1964) and Kleene (1968), and advanced books like Church (1956) and Schoenfield (1967). We have tried to maintain an intermediate level in our own exposition.

Gödel (1931) was the first person to show that the second-order predicate calculus is incomplete and not partially solvable. The unsolvability of the first-order predicate calculus was discovered by Church (1936) and independently by Turing (1936–1937). Subclasses of wffs for which the decision problem is solvable are discussed in Church (1956) and Ackermann (1962).

Our natural deduction system for the first-order predicate calculus was adapted from Gentzen's work (1934–1935). Similar systems are discussed also in Kalish and Montague (1964), Smullyan (1968), and Kleene (1968). An early computer implementation is due to Wang (1960).

The resolution method, introduced in Sec. 2-3, is based on Herbrand's theorem (1930)† [see also Quine (1955)]. There were several efforts [Davis and Putnam (1960) and Gilmore (1960)] at direct implementation of Herbrand's procedure, but all of them turned out to be grossly inefficient. Improvements due to Prawitz (1960), Davis (1963), and others led to the resolution method of Robinson (1965). Excellent expositions of the resolution method are given in the books by Nilsson (1971) and Chang and Lee (1973).

Extension of the resolution method to first-order predicate calculus with equality is discussed by Robinson and Wos (1969), and Morris (1969). The possibility of extending the method to higher-order logic is discussed by Andrews (1971), Pietrzykowski (1973), and Huet (1973).

One part of the resolution method has remained unspecified: How to choose pairs of clauses and the subdisjunctions of these clauses to be resolved. An appropriate choice may significantly improve the efficiency of the method. Substantial effort has been devoted toward developing strategies for making this choice. The most important strategies are described in Nilsson (1971) and Chang and Lee (1973).

† This theorem is sometimes called the *Skolem-Herbrand-Gödel Theorem*. See their papers in: "From Frege to Gödel: A Survey Book in Mathematical Logic, 1879–1931," J. Van Heijenoort, ed., Harvard University Press, Cambridge, 1967.

REFERENCES

Ackermann, W. (1962): *Solvable Cases of the Decision Problem,* North-Holland Publishing Company, Amsterdam.

Andrews, P. (1972): "Resolution in Type Theory," *J. Symb. Logic,* **36:** 414–432.

Chang, C. L., and R. C. T. Lee (1973): *Symbolic Logic and Mechanical Theorem Proving,* Academic Press, New York.

Church, A. (1936): "An Unsolvable Problem with Elementary Number Theory," *Am. J. Math.,* **58:** 345–363.

——— (1956): *Introduction to Mathematical Logic,* vol. 1, Princeton University Press, Princeton, N.J.

Davis, M. (1963): "Eliminating the Irrelevant from Mechanical Proofs," *Proc. Symp. Appl. Math.,* **18:** 15–30, American Mathematical Society, Providence, R.I.

——— and H. Putnam (1960): "A Computing Procedure for Quantification Theory," *J.ACM,* **7**(3): 201–215.

Gentzen, G. (1934–1935): "Untersuchungen über das Logische Schliessen," in M. E. Szabo (ed.), *The Collected Papers of Gerhard Gentzen,* pp. 68–132, North-Holland Publishing Company, Amsterdam.

Gilmore, P. C. (1960): "A Proof Method for Quantification Theory," *IBM J. Res. & Dev.,* **4:** 28–35 (January).

Gödel, K. (1931): "On Formally Undecidable Propositions of Principia Mathematica and Related Systems I," in J. Heijenoort (ed.), *From Frege to Gödel,* pp. 592–617, Harvard University Press, Cambridge, Mass. (1967).

Herbrand, J. (1930): "Investigations in Proof Theory," in J. Heijenoort (ed.), *From Frege to Gödel,* pp. 525–581, Harvard University Press, Cambridge, Mass. (1967).

Hilbert, D., and W. Ackermann (1950): *Principles of Mathematical Logic,* Chelsea Publishing Company, New York.

Huet, G. P. (1973): "A Mechanization of Type Theory," Third International Joint Conference on Artificial Intelligence, Stanford, California (August 1973), pp. 139–146.

Kalish, D., and R. Montague (1964): *Techniques of Formal Reasoning,* Harcourt, Brace and World.

Kleene, S. C. (1968): *Mathematical Logic,* John Wiley & Sons, Inc., New York.

Mendelson, E. (1964): *Introduction to Mathematical Logic,* D. Van Nostrand Company, Inc., Princeton, N.J.

Morris, J. B. (1969): "E-resolution: Extension of Resolution to Include the Equality Relation," *Proc. Int. J. Conf. Artif. Intell.*

Nilsson, N. J. (1971): *Problem-Solving Methods in Artificial Intelligence,* McGraw-Hill Book Company, New York.

Pietrzykowski, T. (1973): "A Complete Mechanization of Second Order Type Theory," *J. ACM,* **20**(2): 333–364 (April).

Prawitz, D. (1960): "An Improved Proof Procedure," *Theoria,* **26:** 102–139.

Quine, W. V. (1950): *Methods of Logic,* Henry Holt and Company, Inc., New York.

——— (1955): "A Proof Procedure for Quantification Theory," *J. Symb. Logic,* **20:** 141–149.

Robinson, G. A., and L. Wos (1969): "Paramodulation and Theorem-proving in First-order Theories with Equality," in B. Meltzer and D. Michie (eds.), *Machine Intelligence 4,* pp. 135–150, American Elsevier Publishing Company, Inc., New York.

Robinson, J. A. (1965a): "A Machine-oriented Logic Based on the Resolution Principle," *J. ACM,* **12**(1): 23–41 (January).

Rogers, R. (1971): *Mathematical Logic and Formalized Theories,* North-Holland Publishing Company, Amsterdam.

Schoenfield, J. R. (1967): *Mathematical Logic,* Addison-Wesley Publishing Company, Inc., Reading, Mass.

Smullyan, R. M. (1968): *First-order Logic,* Springer-Verlag.

Turing, A. M. (1936–1937): "On Computable Numbers, with an Application to the Entscheidungsproblem," *Proc. Lond. Math. Soc.,* **42:** 230–265; correction, *ibid.,* **43:** 544–546 (1937).

Wang, H. (1960): "Toward Mechanical Mathematics," *IBM J. Res. & Dev.,* **4:** 2–22 (January).

PROBLEMS

Prob. 2-1

(*a*) In Sec. 2-1.2 we showed that any given n-ary ($n \geqq 0$) function mapping $\{true, false\}^n$ into $\{true, false\}$ can be expressed by the conditional connective (IF-THEN-ELSE) and the truth symbols (T or F) alone. Show that similarly any n-ary ($n \geqq 1$) function mapping $\{true, false\}^n$ into $\{true, false\}$ can be expressed using only the connectives $\wedge$ and $\sim$, or $\vee$ and $\sim$, or $\supset$ and $\sim$ (what about $\equiv$ and $\sim$?)

(*b*) There exist two binary connectives which are used only occasionally, but which are interesting because each alone suffices, by compound use, to yield any given n-ary ($n \geqq 1$) function mapping $\{true, false\}^n$ into $\{true, false\}$. These are:

(i) | (*Sheffer stroke*)

$$true|true \text{ is } false, \text{ while}$$

$$false|true,\ true|false \text{ and } false|false \text{ is } true$$

[Note that $A|B$ is equivalent to $\sim(A \wedge B)$ and therefore reads "not both A and B."]

(ii) ↓ (*Joint denial*)

$$false\downarrow false \text{ is } true, \text{ while}$$
$$true\downarrow true,\ true\downarrow false \text{ and } false\downarrow true \text{ is } false$$

[Note that $A\downarrow B$ is equivalent to $\sim(A \vee B)$ and therefore reads "neither A nor B."]

Prove that any given n-ary ($n \geqq 1$) function mapping $\{true, false\}^n$ into $\{true, false\}$ can be expressed by the Sheffer stroke alone and also by the joint denial alone (without using any other connective or the truth symbols T and F). Show that no other binary connective has this property. [see Mendelson (1964).]

Prob. 2-2 (Conditional form). The class of all wffs of the propositional calculus which are in *conditional form* is defined recursively as follows:

(*a*) The truth symbols T and F are in conditional form.

(*b*) If A and B are in conditional form and neither A nor B contains any occurrences of the propositional letter p, then

$$\text{IF } p \text{ THEN } A \text{ ELSE } B$$

is in conditional form.

For example, the following wff is in conditional form.†

```
IF p THEN IF q THEN T
               ELSE F
     ELSE IF q THEN F
               ELSE T
```

Describe an algorithm to transform every wff of the propositional calculus into an equivalent wff in conditional form.

† Note that instead of using parentheses we write each ELSE under the corresponding THEN.

Prob. 2-3 (Truth tables). For any given wff A of the propositional calculus, we are usually interested in the final values of A for all possible interpretations. This information is best described by a table, called the *truth table of A*. For example, the truth table of the wff $(p \vee q) \wedge \sim r$ is

p	q	r	$(p \vee q) \wedge \sim r$
true	*true*	*true*	*false*
true	*true*	*false*	*true*
true	*false*	*true*	*false*
true	*false*	*false*	*true*
false	*true*	*true*	*false*
false	*true*	*false*	*true*
false	*false*	*true*	*false*
false	*false*	*false*	*false*

Note that the wff contains three distinct propositional constants, and therefore its truth table has $2^3 = 8$ rows and $3 + 1$ columns. In general, each wff of the propositional calculus with n distinct propositional constants can be described by a truth table of 2^n rows and $n + 1$ columns. (The left n columns must clearly be of fixed form, while the right column is arbitrary.)

(*a*) Given any truth table of order n, $n \geqq 1$ (that is, of 2^n rows and $n + 1$ columns), give three algorithms for constructing three wffs (containing at most n distinct propositional constants) that yield this truth table such that

(i) The wff is in conditional form (see Prob. 2-2), or

(ii) The wff is in conjunctive normal form (i.e., a conjunction of disjunctions of literals), or

(iii) The wff is in disjunctive normal form (i.e., a disjunction of conjunctions of literals).

For example, for the truth table

p	q	r	?
true	*true*	*true*	*true*
true	*true*	*false*	*true*
true	*false*	*true*	*false*
true	*false*	*false*	*false*
false	*true*	*true*	*false*
false	*true*	*false*	*true*
false	*false*	*true*	*false*
false	*false*	*false*	*false*

the wffs will be

$$
\begin{aligned}
A:\ & \text{IF } p \text{ THEN IF } q \text{ THEN } T \\
& \qquad\qquad\qquad\qquad \text{ELSE } F \\
& \qquad \text{ELSE IF } q \text{ THEN IF } r \text{ THEN } F \\
& \qquad\qquad\qquad\qquad\qquad\qquad \text{ELSE } T \\
& \qquad\qquad\qquad\qquad \text{ELSE } F \\
B:\ & (p \wedge q) \vee (\sim p \wedge q \wedge \sim r) \\
C:\ & (\sim p \vee q) \wedge (p \vee \sim q \vee \sim r) \wedge (p \vee q)
\end{aligned}
$$

(*b*) Apply your algorithms to the following truth table:

p	q	r	?
true	*true*	*true*	*false*
true	*true*	*false*	*true*
true	*false*	*true*	*true*
true	*false*	*false*	*false*
false	*true*	*true*	*false*
false	*true*	*false*	*true*
false	*false*	*true*	*true*
false	*false*	*false*	*true*

Prob. 2-4 Prove that a wff of the propositional calculus containing only the connective $\equiv$ is valid if and only if each propositional constant occurs an even number of times. [For example, $(p \equiv q) \equiv (p \equiv (q \equiv p))$ is not valid because p occurs an odd number of times.]

Prob. 2-5 Determine whether each of the following wffs of the propositional calculus is valid, unsatisfiable, or neither valid nor unsatisfiable.

(*a*) (i) IF $p \supset q$ THEN $p \wedge \sim q$ ELSE q
(ii) IF $p \supset q$ THEN $\sim p \vee q$ ELSE p
(iii) IF $p \supset q$ THEN p ELSE q

(*b*) (i) IF $p \wedge q$ THEN q ELSE $p \supset \sim q$
(ii) IF $p \wedge q$ THEN q ELSE $\sim p$
(iii) IF $p \wedge q$ THEN $\sim p$ ELSE (IF p THEN $\sim p$ ELSE p)

(*c*) (i) IF $p \vee q$ THEN $\sim p$ ELSE $p \equiv q$
(ii) IF $p \vee q$ THEN $p \supset p$ ELSE $\sim q$
(iii) IF $p \vee q$ THEN $\sim p \wedge \sim q$ ELSE p

(*d*) (i) IF $\sim p$ THEN p ELSE (IF p THEN F ELSE T)
(ii) IF $\sim p$ THEN (IF p THEN F ELSE T) ELSE $p \vee q$
(iii) IF $\sim p$ THEN p ELSE p

(*e*) (i) IF $p \supset q$ THEN $q \supset r$ ELSE $p \supset r$
(ii) $(p \supset q) \supset [(q \supset r) \supset (p \supset r)]$
(iii) $[(p \supset q) \supset (q \supset r)] \supset (p \supset r)$
(iv) $(q \supset r) \supset [(p \supset q) \supset (p \supset r)]$

(*f*) (i) $\sim (p \supset q) \equiv (\sim p \vee q)$
(ii) $(p \supset q) \equiv \sim (p \wedge \sim q)$
(iii) $(p \supset q) \equiv (q \supset p)$
(iv) $(\sim p \supset q) \equiv (\sim q \supset p)$

Prob. 2-6 Given the following three statements as premises:

1. If Bill takes the bus and the bus is late, then Bill misses his appointment.
2. Bill should not go home if (i) Bill misses his appointment and (ii) Bill feels downcast.
3. If Bill does not get the job, then (i) Bill feels downcast and (ii) Bill should go home.

Is it valid to conclude the following?

(*a*) If Bill takes the bus and the bus is late, then Bill does get the job.
(*b*) Bill does get the job if (i) Bill misses his appointment and (ii) Bill should go home.
(*c*) If the bus is late, then either (i) Bill does not take the bus or (ii) Bill does not miss his appointment.
(*d*) Bill feels downcast if (i) the bus is late or if (ii) Bill misses his appointment.
(*e*) If (i) Bill should go home and Bill takes the bus, then (ii) Bill does not feel downcast if the bus is late.

Hint: Let p_1 stand for "Bill takes the bus," p_2 for "the bus is late," p_3 for "Bill misses his appointment," p_4 for "Bill feels downcast," p_5 for "Bill gets the job," and p_6 for "Bill should go home." Thus, to show statement (*a*) you have to prove that assumptions (1) to (3) imply $(p_1 \wedge p_2) \supset p_5$ for all possible interpretations. Note the difference between "either . . . or . . ." (exclusive or) and ". . . or . . ." (inclusive or).

Prob. 2-7 Use wffs of the propositional calculus to solve the following problems.

(*a*) A certain country is inhabited only by people who either always tell the truth or always tell lies, and who will respond to questions only with a "yes" or a "no." A tourist comes to a fork in the road, where one branch leads to the capital and the other does not. There is no sign indicating which branch to take, but there is an inhabitant, Mr. Z, standing at the fork. What single yes/no question should the tourist ask him to determine which branch to take? *Hint*: Let p stand for "Mr. Z always tells the truth," and let q stand for "the left-hand branch leads to the capital." By examining a suitable truth table, construct a wff A involving p and q such that Mr. Z's answer to the question "Is A true?" will be "yes" when and only when q is *true* (i.e., the left-hand branch leads to the capital).

*(*b*) A tourist is enjoying an afternoon refreshment in a local pub in England when the bartender says to him: "Do you see those three men over there? One is Mr. X, who always tells the truth, another is Mr. Y, who always lies, and the third is Mr. Z, who sometimes tells the truth and sometimes lies (that is, Mr. Z answers "yes" or "no" at random without regard to the question). You may ask them three yes/no questions, always indicating which man should answer. If, after asking these three questions, you correctly identify Mr. X, Mr. Y, and Mr. Z, they will buy you a drink." What yes/no questions should the thirsty tourist ask?
Hint: Use the first question to find some person of the three who is not Mr. Z. Ask him the other two questions.

Prob. 2-8

(*a*) A wff A is said to be *n valid* if it yields the value *true* for every interpretation with a domain of n elements.
(i) Find a wff which is 1 valid but not 2 valid.
(ii) Find a wff which is 1 valid and 2 valid but not 3 valid.
(iii) Find a wff which is 1, 2, and 3 valid but not 4 valid.

(*b*) Consider the wff A:

$$\{\forall x p(x,x) \wedge \forall x \forall y \forall z [(p(x,y) \wedge p(y,z)) \supset p(x,z)] \\ \wedge \forall x \forall y [p(x,y) \vee p(y,x)]\} \supset \exists y \forall x p(y,x)$$

(i) Show that A yields the value *true* for any interpretation with finite domain.
Hint: Use induction on the number of elements in the domain.
(ii) Find an interpretation with the set of natural numbers as domain for which the value of A is *false*.

(*c*) Consider the wff B;

$$\exists P [\forall x \exists y P(x,y) \wedge \forall x \sim P(x,x) \\ \wedge \forall x \forall y \forall z [(P(x,y) \wedge P(y,z)) \supset P(x,z)]]$$

Show that B yields the value *true* for any interpretation with infinite domain and the value *false* for any interpretation with finite domain.

Prob. 2-9 Give countermodels to show that the following wffs are not valid:

(*a*) $\exists x \forall y [(p(x, y) \wedge \sim p(y, x)) \supset (p(x, x) \equiv p(y, y))]$

(*b*) $[\forall x \forall y \forall z [(p(x, y) \wedge p(y, z)) \supset p(x, z)] \wedge \forall x \sim p(x, x)]$
$\supset \exists x \forall y \sim p(x, y)$

(*c*) $\forall x \forall y \forall z [p(x, x) \wedge [p(x, z) \supset (p(x, y) \vee p(y, z))]] \supset \exists y \forall z p(y, z)$

Prob. 2-10 Which of the following wffs are valid? Construct countermodels for those which are not valid and give informal proofs for the valid wffs.

(*a*) $p(x) \supset \exists x p(x)$

(*b*) $\exists x p(x) \supset p(x)$

(*c*) $p(x) \supset \forall x p(x)$

(*d*) $\forall x p(x) \supset p(x)$

(*e*) $\forall x \forall y p(x, y) \supset \forall y \forall x p(x, y)$

(*f*) $\forall x \forall y p(x, y) \supset \forall x \forall y p(y, x)$

(*g*) $\forall x [p(y) \supset q(x)] \supset [p(y) \supset \forall x q(x)]$

(*h*) $\forall x [p(x) \supset q(x)] \supset [p(x) \supset \forall x q(x)]$

(*i*) $\forall x \exists y p(x, y) \supset \exists y p(z, y)$

(*j*) $\forall x \exists y p(x, y) \supset \exists y p(y, y)$

(*k*) $\forall x [p(x) \supset p(x)]$

(*l*) $\forall x [p(x) \supset p(a)]$

(*m*) $\forall P [\forall x P(x) \supset \exists x P(x)]$

(*n*) $\exists P [\exists x P(x) \supset \forall x P(x)]$

(*o*) $\forall P [\exists x P(x) \supset \forall x P(x)]$

(*p*) $\forall P \forall x \forall y [P(x, y) \supset P(x, y)]$

(*q*) $\forall P \forall x \forall y [P(x, y) \supset P(y, x)]$

(*r*) $\exists P \forall x \forall y [P(x, y) \supset P(y, x)]$

(*s*) $\forall P \exists Q \forall x \forall y [P(x, y) \supset Q(y, x)]$

Prob. 2-11 Use the replacement theorem, the transitivity of the equivalence relation, and the equivalences given in Sec. 2-1.4 to show that the following pairs of wffs are equivalent:

(*a*) $(p \wedge q) \vee \sim (p \wedge r) \vee (q \wedge r \wedge s)$ and $(p \wedge q) \vee \sim (p \wedge r)$

(*b*) $(p \supset q) \supset [(r \supset q) \supset ((p \vee r) \supset q)]$ and T

Prob. 2-12 (The duality theorem). Let A and B be wffs which contain no operators and no connectives other than $\wedge$, $\vee$, and $\sim$. Let A^+ and B^+ result from A and B, respectively, by interchanging in each the connectives $\wedge$ and $\vee$, the truth symbols T and F, and the quantifiers $\forall$ and $\exists$. Show the following:

(*a*) A is valid if and only if $\sim A^+$ is valid.

(*b*) If $A \supset B$ is valid, so is $B^+ \supset A^+$.

(*c*) If $A \equiv B$ is valid, so is $A^+ \equiv B^+$.

Prob. 2-13 (Prenex-conjunctive/disjunctive normal form). Find wffs in prenex-conjunctive normal form and in prenex-disjunctive normal form which are equivalent to

(*a*) $[\exists x p(x) \vee \exists x q(x)] \supset \exists x [p(x) \vee q(x)]$

(*b*) $\forall x [p(x) \supset \forall y [\forall z q(x, y) \supset \sim \forall z r(y, x)]]$

(*c*) $\forall x p(x) \supset \exists x [\forall z q(x, z) \vee \forall z r(x, y, z)]$

(d) $\forall x[p(x) \supset q(x, y)] \supset [\exists y p(y) \wedge \exists z q(y, z)]$
(e) $\exists x p(x, z) \supset \forall z[\exists y p(x, z) \supset \sim \forall x \exists y p(x, y)]$

Prob. 2-14 Use our natural deduction system to deduce the following valid wffs of the propositional calculus:

(a) (i) $(\sim \sim A) \equiv A$ $\qquad A \equiv A$
(ii) $(A \supset (B \supset C)) \equiv (B \supset (A \supset C))$
(iii) $(A \wedge A) \equiv A$ $\qquad (A \wedge B) \equiv (B \wedge A)$
$((A \wedge B) \wedge C) \equiv (A \wedge (B \wedge C))$
(iv) $(A \vee A) \equiv A$ $\qquad (A \vee B) \equiv (B \vee A)$
$((A \vee B) \vee C) \equiv (A \vee (B \vee C))$
(v) $(A \equiv B) \equiv (B \equiv A)$
$((A \equiv B) \equiv C) \equiv (A \equiv (B \equiv C))$ $\qquad (A \equiv B) \equiv (\sim B \equiv \sim A)$
(vi) (IF A THEN B ELSE B) $\equiv B$

(b) (i) $(A \supset B) \equiv (\sim A \vee B)$ $\qquad (A \supset B) \equiv \sim (A \wedge \sim B)$
(ii) $(A \equiv B) \equiv ((A \supset B) \wedge (B \supset A))$ $\qquad (A \supset (B \supset C)) \equiv ((A \wedge B) \supset C)$
(iii) (IF A THEN B ELSE C) $\equiv ((A \supset B) \wedge (\sim A \supset C))$
(iv) $\sim (A \vee B) \equiv (\sim A \wedge \sim B)$ $\qquad \sim (A \wedge B) \equiv (\sim A \vee \sim B)$
(v) $(A \wedge (B \vee C)) \equiv ((A \wedge B) \vee (A \wedge C))$ $\qquad (A \vee (B \wedge C)) \equiv ((A \vee B) \wedge (A \vee C))$
(vi) $(A \vee (A \wedge B)) \equiv A$ $\qquad (A \wedge (A \vee B)) \equiv A$
(vii) $((A \vee B) \wedge (\sim A \vee B)) \equiv B$ $\qquad ((A \wedge B) \vee (\sim A \wedge B)) \equiv B$

(c) (i) $A \supset (B \supset A)$ $\qquad \sim A \supset (A \supset B)$
(ii) $(A \supset B) \vee (B \supset A)$ $\qquad (A \wedge (A \supset B)) \supset B$
(iii) $((A \vee B) \wedge \sim A) \supset B$ $\qquad ((A \supset B) \wedge \sim B) \supset \sim A$
(iv) $((A \supset B) \wedge (B \supset C)) \supset (A \supset C)$ $\qquad ((A \supset B) \supset A) \supset A$

(d) (i) (IF A THEN (IF A THEN B_1 ELSE B_2) ELSE B_3) $\equiv$ (IF A THEN B_1 ELSE B_3)
(ii) (IF A THEN B_1 ELSE (IF A THEN B_2 ELSE B_3)) $\equiv$ (IF A THEN B_1 ELSE B_3)
(iii) (IF (IF A_1 THEN A_2 ELSE A_3) THEN B_1 ELSE B_2) $\equiv$ (IF A_1 THEN (IF A_2 THEN B_1 ELSE B_2) ELSE (IF A_3 THEN B_1 ELSE B_2))
(iv) (IF A_1 THEN (IF A_2 THEN B_1 ELSE B_2) ELSE (IF A_2 THEN B_3 ELSE B_4)) $\equiv$ (IF A_2 THEN (IF A_1 THEN B_1 ELSE B_3) ELSE (IF A_1 THEN B_2 ELSE B_4))

***Prob. 2-15** (Completeness [Mendelson (1964)]). Prove the completeness of the natural deduction system for the propositional calculus; i.e., every valid wff of the propositional calculus can be deduced from the axioms, basic rules, and the rules for the connectives.
Hint: Consider, for example, the wff

$$A: \quad [((p \wedge q) \supset r) \wedge (p \supset q)] \supset (p \supset r)$$

Since there are three distinct propositional constants in A, there are eight possible combinations of literals to consider:

$$(p, q, r), (p, q, \sim r), (p, \sim q, r), \ \ldots, \ (\sim p, \sim q, \sim r)$$

Therefore deduce by our rules the following eight implications:

$$p, q, r \Rightarrow A$$
$$p, q, \sim r \Rightarrow A$$
$$\cdots\cdots$$
$$\sim p, \sim q, \sim r \Rightarrow A$$

Then, by applying repeatedly the elimination of assumption rule, finally deduce $\Rightarrow A$. [To show, for example, $p, \sim q, \sim r \Rightarrow A$, consider the way the truth value of A is computed by assigning *true* to p, *false* to q, and *false* to r.]

***Prob. 2-16** (System L [Mendelson (1964)]). The following is a complete deduction system for the wffs of the propositional calculus with no connectives other than $\supset$ and $\sim$:

$A1.$	$A \supset (B \supset A)$	Axiom $A1$
$A2.$	$(A \supset (B \supset C)) \supset ((A \supset B) \supset (A \supset C))$	Axiom $A2$
$A3.$	$(\sim B \supset \sim A) \supset ((\sim B \supset A) \supset B)$	Axiom $A3$
$MP.$	$\dfrac{A \text{ and } A \supset B}{B}$	*Modus ponens*

Deduce in this system the following valid wffs:
(*a*) $(q \supset r) \supset ((p \supset q) \supset (p \supset r))$
(*b*) $(p \supset q) \supset ((q \supset r) \supset (p \supset r))$
(*c*) $((p \supset q) \supset p) \supset (\sim p \supset p)$
(*d*) $((p \supset q) \supset p) \supset p$
Example: The wff $p \supset p$ is deduced in this system as follows:
1. $(p \supset ((p \supset p) \supset p)) \supset$ $((p \supset (p \supset p)) \supset (p \supset p))$ — Instance of axiom $A2$
2. $p \supset ((p \supset p) \supset p)$ — Instance of axiom $A1$

3. $(p \supset (p \supset p)) \supset (p \supset p)$ — *MP* (by 1 and 2)
4. $p \supset (p \supset p)$ — Instance of axiom *A*1
5. $p \supset p$ — *MP* (by 3 and 4)

Hint: Prove first the following derived rules of inference:

$$\frac{A}{B \supset A} \qquad \frac{A \supset B \text{ and } B \supset C}{A \supset C} \qquad \text{and} \qquad \frac{A \supset (B \supset C)}{B \supset (A \supset C)}$$

Prob. 2-17 (System *L* with deduction [Mendelson (1964)]). The following is a complete deduction system for the wffs of the propositional calculus with no connectives other than $\supset$ and $\sim$:

AA. $\Gamma, A \Rightarrow A$ — Assumption axiom

*A*1. $\Gamma \Rightarrow A \supset (B \supset A)$ — Axiom *A*1

*A*2. $\Gamma \Rightarrow (A \supset (B \supset C)) \supset ((A \supset B) \supset (A \supset C))$ — Axiom *A*2

*A*3. $\Gamma \Rightarrow (\sim B \supset \sim A) \supset ((\sim B \supset A) \supset B)$ — Axiom *A*3

MP. $\dfrac{\Gamma \Rightarrow A \text{ and } \Gamma \Rightarrow A \supset B}{\Gamma \Rightarrow B}$ — *Modus ponens*

DR. $\dfrac{\Gamma, A \Rightarrow B}{\Gamma \Rightarrow A \supset B}$ — Deduction rule

Deduce in this system the following valid wffs:

(*a*) $p \supset ((q \supset r) \supset ((p \supset q) \supset r))$
(*b*) $(p \supset q) \supset ((q \supset r) \supset (p \supset r))$
(*c*) $(p \supset (q \supset r)) \supset (q \supset (p \supset r))$
(*d*) $\sim\sim p \supset p$
(*e*) $p \supset \sim\sim p$
(*f*) $\sim p \supset (p \supset q)$
(*g*) $(\sim q \supset \sim p) \supset (p \supset q)$
(*h*) $(p \supset q) \supset (\sim q \supset \sim p)$
(*i*) $p \supset (\sim q \supset \sim (p \supset q))$
(*j*) $(p \supset q) \supset ((\sim p \supset q) \supset q)$

Prob. 2-18 (Wang's method (1960) for proving validity in the propositional calculus). We denote a wff of the form $(A_1 \wedge A_2 \wedge \cdots \wedge A_m) \supset (B_1 \vee B_2 \vee \cdots \vee B_n)$ by $A_1, A_2, \ldots, A_m \Rightarrow B_1, B_2, \ldots, B_n$. Note that for $n = 1$ we have $A_1, A_2, \ldots, A_m \Rightarrow B$, which is the form of the assumption formulas used in the text.

(*a*) Show that for any (finite) sets Γ_1 and Γ_2 of zero or more wffs and any wffs *A*, *B*, and *C*:

(i) $\Gamma_1, A \Rightarrow \Gamma_2, A$ is valid.

(ii) $\Gamma_1 \Rightarrow \Gamma_2, T$ is valid.
$\Gamma_1, T \Rightarrow \Gamma_2$ is valid if and only if $\Gamma_1 \Rightarrow \Gamma_2$ is valid.

(iii) $\Gamma_1, F \Rightarrow \Gamma_2$ is valid.
$\Gamma_1 \Rightarrow \Gamma_2, F$ is valid if and only if $\Gamma_1 \Rightarrow \Gamma_2$ is valid.

(iv) $\Gamma_1 \Rightarrow \Gamma_2, (\text{IF } A \text{ THEN } B \text{ ELSE } C)$ is valid if and only if $\Gamma_1, A \Rightarrow \Gamma_2, B$ and $\Gamma_1 \Rightarrow \Gamma_2, A, C$ are valid.

(v) Γ_1, (IF A THEN B ELSE C) $\Rightarrow \Gamma_2$ is valid if and only if $\Gamma_1, A, B \Rightarrow \Gamma_2$ and $\Gamma_1, C \Rightarrow \Gamma_2, A$ are valid.

(*b*) Show also that a wff of the form $A_1 \wedge \cdots \wedge A_m \supset B_1 \vee \cdots \vee B_n$, where each A_i and B_i is a propositional constant or a truth symbol, is valid if and only if either one of the A_i's is F, or one of the B_i's is T, or some propositional constant occurs in both sides of the implication.

(*c*) Give similar pairs of rules to eliminate the connectives $\sim$, $\wedge$, $\vee$, $\supset$, and $\equiv$ from the left- and right-hand sides of $\Rightarrow$.

(*d*) Use the above results to describe an algorithm for proving validity of wffs in propositional calculus. Apply the method to show the validity of the wff $[(p \wedge q \supset r) \wedge (p \supset q)] \supset (p \supset r)$.

Prob. 2-19 Let $A(x)$ and $B(x)$ be any wffs, and let A, B be any wffs not containing free occurrences of x. Use the natural deduction system to deduce the following wffs:

(*a*) (i) $\forall x(A \supset B(x)) \equiv (A \supset \forall x B(x))$

(ii) $\forall x(A(x) \supset B) \equiv (\exists x A(x) \supset B)$

*(iii) $\exists x(A(x) \supset B(x)) \equiv (\forall x A(x) \supset \exists x B(x))$

(iv) $\exists x(A \supset B(x)) \equiv (A \supset \exists x B(x))$

(v) $\exists x(A(x) \supset B) \equiv (\forall x A(x) \supset B)$

(*b*) (i) $\forall x(A \vee B(x)) \equiv (A \vee \forall x B(x))$

(ii) $\forall x(A(x) \vee B) \equiv (\forall x A(x) \vee B)$

(iii) $\exists x(A(x) \vee B(x)) \equiv (\exists x A(x) \vee \exists x B(x))$

(iv) $\exists x(A \vee B(x)) \equiv (A \vee \exists x B(x))$

(v) $\exists x(A(x) \vee B) \equiv (\exists x A(x) \vee B)$

(*c*) (i) $\exists x(A \wedge B(x)) \equiv (A \wedge \exists x B(x))$

(ii) $\exists x(A(x) \wedge B) \equiv (\exists x A(x) \wedge B)$

(iii) $\forall x(A(x) \wedge B(x)) \equiv (\forall x A(x) \wedge \forall x B(x))$

(iv) $\forall x(A \wedge B(x)) \equiv (A \wedge \forall x B(x))$

(v) $\forall x(A(x) \wedge B) \equiv (\forall x A(x) \wedge B)$

Prob. 2-20 Let $A(x)$ and $B(x)$ be any wffs. Use the natural deduction system to deduce the following wffs:

(*a*) (i) $\forall x(A(x) \equiv B(x)) \supset (\forall x A(x) \equiv \forall x B(x))$

(ii) $\forall x(A(x) \equiv B(x)) \supset (\exists x A(x) \equiv \exists x B(x))$

(*b*) (i) $(\exists x A(x) \supset \forall x B(x)) \supset \forall x(A(x) \supset B(x))$

(ii) $\exists x(A(x) \wedge B(x)) \supset (\exists x A(x) \wedge \exists x B(x))$

(iii) $(\forall x A(x) \vee \forall x B(x)) \supset \forall x(A(x) \vee B(x))$

(*c*) (i) $\forall x(A(x) \supset B(x)) \supset (\forall x A(x) \supset \exists x B(x))$

(ii) $\forall x(A(x) \supset B(x)) \supset (\forall x A(x) \supset \forall x B(x))$

(iii) $\forall x(A(x) \supset B(x)) \supset (\exists x A(x) \supset \exists x B(x))$

(*d*) (i) $\forall x A(x) \supset A(t)$
(ii) $A(t) \supset \exists x A(x)$ where t is free for x in $A(x)$

Give countermodels to show that the 10 wffs obtained from the above wffs by changing the direction of the main implication are nonvalid.

Prob. 2-21 Let $A(x)$ be any wff. Use the natural deduction system to deduce the following wffs:

(*a*) $\sim \exists x A(x) \equiv \forall x \sim A(x)$
(*b*) $\sim \forall x A(x) \equiv \exists x \sim A(x)$
(*c*) $\sim \forall x \sim A(x) \equiv \exists x A(x)$
(*d*) $\sim \exists x \sim A(x) \equiv \forall x A(x)$

Prob. 2-22 Given the following statements:

(*a*) Anyone who likes George will choose Nick for his team.
(*b*) Nick is not a friend of anyone who is a friend of Mike.
(*c*) Jay will choose no one but a friend of Ken for his team.

Prove that if Ken is a friend of Mike, then Jay does not like George. [Let g stand for George, n for Nick, j for Jay, k for Ken, m for Mike, $L(x, y)$ for "x likes y," $C(x, y)$ for "x will choose y for his team," and $F(x, y)$ for "x is a friend of y."]

Prob. 2-23 (Herbrand's theorem)

(*a*) Let S be a (possibly infinite) set of wffs of the propositional calculus. An interpretation $\mathscr{I}$ of S consists of an assignment of truth values to the propositional constants occurring in the wffs of S. S is said to be *satisfiable* if there exists an interpretation $\mathscr{I}$ of S under which every wff in S is *true*; otherwise, S is said to be *unsatisfiable*. For an infinite set S_0 of wffs, show that if every finite subset of S_0 is satisfiable, then S_0 is satisfiable; or, equivalently, if S_0 is unsatisfiable, then there exists a finite subset of S_0 which is unsatisfiable. *Hint*: Suppose $p_{i_1}, p_{i_2}, p_{i_3}, \ldots$, are all the propositional constants occurring in the wffs of S_0. Describe all possible truth-value assignments to these propositional constants by the following tree:

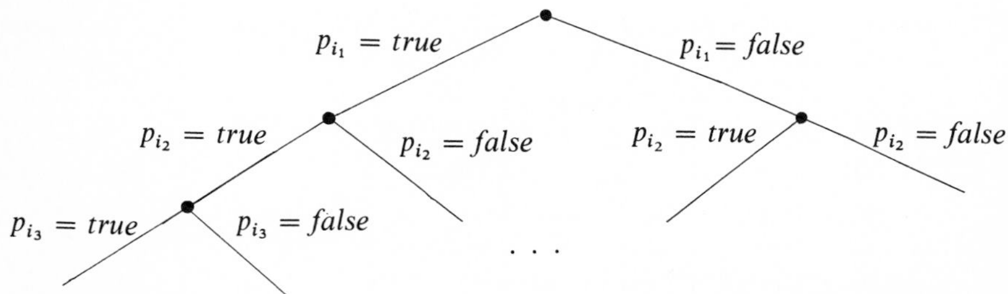

Then make use of König's infinity lemma; that is, a binary tree with no infinite paths must have only finitely many vertices.

(*b*) Use the above result to prove Herbrand's theorem (Theorem 2-9).

Prob. 2-24 (Davis and Putnam's method and the ground resolution method)

(*a*) Prove the correctness of Davis and Putnam's method; i.e., show that in each step of the process the conjunction S of ground clauses is transformed into a new conjunction S' such that S is unsatisfiable if and only if S' is unsatisfiable, or to a new pair of conjunctions S' and S'' such that S is unsatisfiable if and only if both S' and S'' are unsatisfiable.

(*b*) Prove the correctness of the ground resolution method; i.e., show that a conjunction S of ground clauses is unsatisfiable if and only if $\square$ (the empty clause) can be derived from S by repeated applications of the ground resolution rule.

Hint: Show that $S = G_1 \wedge G_2 \wedge \cdots \wedge G_N$ is unsatisfiable if and only if $S' = G_1 \wedge G_2 \wedge \cdots \wedge G_N \wedge G_{N+1}$ is unsatisfiable, where G_{N+1} is the resolvent of some G_i and G_j.

Prob. 2-25 Use Quine's method, Davis-Putnam's method, and the ground resolution method to prove that each of the following wffs of the propositional calculus is valid:

(*a*) $[(p \supset q) \wedge (p \supset r)] \supset [p \supset (q \wedge r)]$

(*b*) $[(p \supset q) \wedge (p \vee r)] \supset (q \vee r)$

(*c*) $[\sim (p \vee q)] \equiv [\sim p \wedge \sim q]$

(*d*) $[[p \supset (q \wedge (r \vee s))] \wedge (\sim q \vee \sim r)] \supset (p \supset s)$

Prob. 2-26 Use the resolution method to prove that the following wffs are valid:

(*a*) $\forall x_1 \forall x_2 \exists y \{[p(x_1) \supset q(x_2, y)] \supset \forall z[[q(x_2, y) \supset r(z)] \supset [p(x_1) \supset r(z)]]\}$

(*b*) $\exists x \exists y[p(x, y) \wedge \forall r \sim q(x, r)] \vee \forall s \forall t \exists z[\sim p(s, t) \vee q(t, z) \vee [q(s, z) \wedge \sim p(t, z)]]$

Prob. 2-27

(*a*) Prove by resolution that every predicate p that has the following properties:

$H1$. $\forall x \forall y[p(x, y) \supset p(y, x)]$	Symmetry
$H2$. $\forall x \forall y \forall z[(p(x, y) \wedge p(y, z)) \supset p(x, z)]$	Transitivity
$H3$. $\forall x \exists y p(x, y)$	

must be reflexive; that is,

C. $\forall x p(x, x)$

In other words, prove that $(H1 \wedge H2 \wedge H3) \supset C$ is a valid wff.

(*b*) Prove by resolution that for any ordered set, $x \leqq y$ and $y < z$ imply $x < z$ for all x, y, and z. For this purpose show that for any predicates E (stands for $=$) and L (stands for $<$) which have the following properties

$H1$. $\forall x E(x, x)$
$H2$. $\forall x \forall y \forall z[(E(x, y) \wedge E(y, z)) \supset E(x, z)]$
$H3$. $\forall x \forall y[E(x, y) \supset E(y, x)]$
$H4$. $\forall x \forall y \forall z[(L(x, y) \wedge L(y, z)) \supset L(x, z)]$
$H5$. $\forall x \forall y[L(x, y) \vee E(x, y) \vee L(y, x)]$
$H6$. $\forall x \forall y[E(x, y) \supset \sim L(x, y)]$
$H7$. $\forall x \forall y[L(x, y) \supset \sim L(y, x)]$

must satisfy

C. $\forall x \forall y \forall z\{[(L(x, y) \vee E(x, y)) \wedge L(y, z)] \supset L(x, z)\}$

In other words, prove that $(H1 \wedge H2 \wedge \cdots \wedge H7) \supset C$ is a valid wff.

(*c*) Formulate as predicate-calculus expressions the facts given and the question asked in the following puzzle. Use the resolution method to determine the answer to the question.

> Tony, Mike, and John belong to the Alpine Club. Every member of the Alpine Club is either a skier or a mountain climber or both. No mountain climber likes rain, and all skiers like snow. Mike dislikes whatever Tony likes and likes whatever Tony dislikes. Tony likes rain and snow. Is there a member of the Alpine Club who is a mountain climber but not a skier?

Use the following predicates: $AC(x)$ for "x belongs to the Alpine Club," $SK(x)$ for "x is a skier," $MC(x)$ for "x is a mountain climber," and $L(x, y)$ for "x likes y."

CHAPTER 3

Verification of Programs

Introduction

The purpose of this chapter is to describe methods for verifying computer programs. Suppose we are given a computer program with a description of its behavior, that is, a characteristic predicate (later called an *output predicate*), which describes the relationships among the program variables that must be satisfied at the completion of the program execution. Sometimes we are also given an *input predicate*, which defines the input restrictions that must be satisfied to make execution of the program meaningful. Our task is to prove that the program is correct with respect to such input and output predicates; that is, for all program executions with inputs satisfying the input predicate, we must guarantee that the program is terminated and that at the completion of execution the output predicate is satisfied. In this chapter we shall describe the construction of such proofs of correctness.

In order to discuss programs and their correctness we must specify a programming language. We shall consider flowchart programs without arrays (Sec. 3-1) and with arrays (Sec. 3-2), as well as simple Algol-like programs (Sec. 3-3). Methods for proving correctness of recursive programs are discussed in detail in Chap. 5.

3-1 FLOWCHART PROGRAMS

First let us consider a very simple class of flowchart programs. We distinguish among three types of variables (grouped as three vectors): (1) an *input vector* $\bar{x} = (x_1, x_2, \ldots, x_{\mathbf{a}})$, which consists of the given input values and therefore never changes during computation; (2) a *program vector* $\bar{y} =$

$(y_1, y_2, \ldots, y_b)$, which is used as temporary storage during computation; and (3) an *output vector* $\bar{z} = (z_1, z_2, \ldots, z_c)$, which yields the output values when computation terminates. Correspondingly, we also distinguish among three types of (nonempty) domains: (1) an *input domain* $D_{\bar{x}}$, (2) a *program domain* $D_{\bar{y}}$, and (3) an *output domain* $D_{\bar{z}}$. Each domain is actually a cartesian product of subdomains:

$$D_{\bar{x}} = D_{x_1} \times D_{x_2} \times \cdots \times D_{x_a}$$

$$D_{\bar{y}} = D_{y_1} \times D_{y_2} \times \cdots \times D_{y_b}$$

$$D_{\bar{z}} = D_{z_1} \times D_{z_2} \times \cdots \times D_{z_c}$$

We also distinguish among four types of statements:†

1. START statement

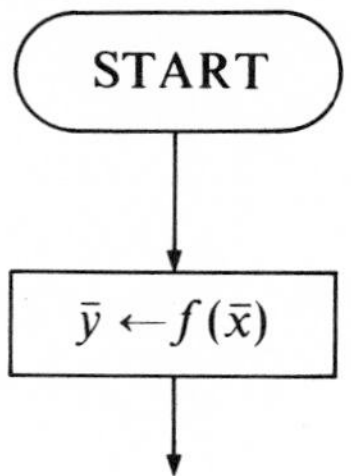

where $f(\bar{x})$ is a total function mapping $D_{\bar{x}}$ into $D_{\bar{y}}$.

2. ASSIGNMENT statement

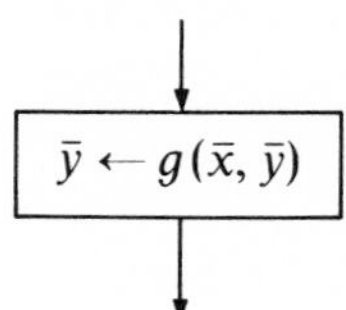

where $g(\bar{x}, \bar{y})$ is a total function mapping $D_{\bar{x}} \times D_{\bar{y}}$ into $D_{\bar{y}}$

3. TEST statement

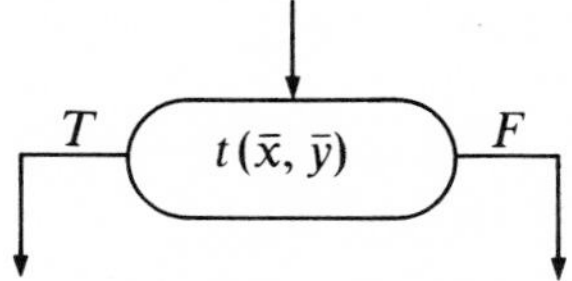

where $t(\bar{x}, \bar{y})$ is a total predicate over $D_{\bar{x}} \times D_{\bar{y}}$

† In addition, we clearly allow the JOINT statement for combining two or more arcs (arrows) into a single one.

4. HALT statement

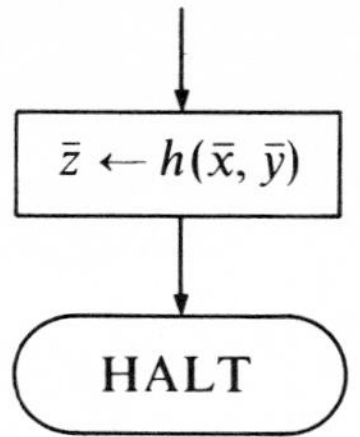

where $h(\bar{x}, \bar{y})$ is a total function mapping $D_{\bar{x}} \times D_{\bar{y}}$ into $D_{\bar{z}}$

A *flowchart program* is simply any flow-diagram constructed from these statements (with exactly one START statement) such that every ASSIGNMENT or TEST statement is on a path from the START statement to some HALT statement. In other words, flowchart programs are not allowed to include "dead-end" TEST statements such as

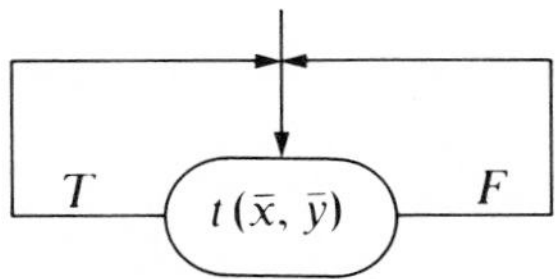

Given such a flowchart program P and an input value $\bar{\xi} \in D_{\bar{x}}$ for the input vector $\bar{x}$, the program can be executed. Execution always begins at the START statement by initializing the value of $\bar{y}$ to $f(\bar{\xi})$ and then proceeds in the normal way, following the arcs from statement to statement. Whenever an ASSIGNMENT statement is reached, the value of $\bar{y}$ is replaced by the value of $g(\bar{x}, \bar{y})$ for the current values $\bar{x}$ and $\bar{y}$. Whenever a TEST statement is reached, execution follows the T or F branch, depending on whether the current value of $t(\bar{x}, \bar{y})$ is *true* or *false*; the value of $\bar{y}$ is unchanged by a TEST statement. If the execution terminates (i.e., reaches a HALT statement), $\bar{z}$ is assigned the current value, say, $\bar{\zeta}$, of $h(\bar{x}, \bar{y})$ and we say that *$P(\bar{\xi})$ is defined and $P(\bar{\xi}) = \bar{\zeta}$*; otherwise, i.e., if the execution never terminates, we say that *$P(\bar{\xi})$ is undefined.* In other words, *the program P should be considered as representing a partial function $\bar{z} = P(\bar{x})$ mapping $D_{\bar{x}}$ into $D_{\bar{z}}$.*

For example, the flowchart program in Fig. 3-1 performs the integer division of x_1 by x_2, where $x_1 \geqq 0$ and $x_2 > 0$, yielding a quotient z_1 and a remainder z_2; that is, $z_1 = div(x_1, x_2)$, and $z_2 = rem(x_1, x_2)$. Here $\bar{x} = (x_1, x_2)$, $\bar{y} = (y_1, y_2)$, $\bar{z} = (z_1, z_2)$, and $D_{\bar{x}} = D_{\bar{y}} = D_{\bar{z}} = \{$all pairs of integers$\}$.

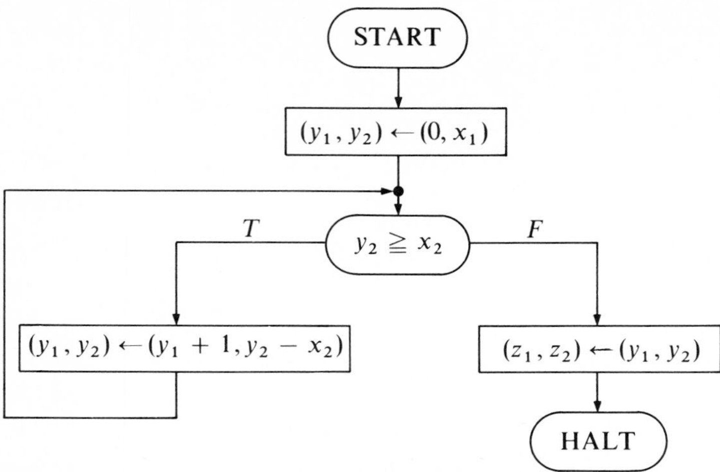

Figure 3-1 Flowchart program for performing integer division.

Note that $(y_1, y_2) \leftarrow (0, x_1)$ means that y_1 is replaced by 0 and y_2 is replaced by x_1; similarly $(y_1, y_2) \leftarrow (y_1 + 1, y_2 - x_2)$ means that y_1 is replaced by $y_1 + 1$ and y_2 is replaced by $y_2 - x_2$. In general, we shall use the notation $(y_1, y_2, \ldots, y_n) \leftarrow (g_1(\bar{x}, \bar{y}), g_2(\bar{x}, \bar{y}), \ldots, g_n(\bar{x}, \bar{y}))$ to indicate that the variables y_i, $1 \leqq i \leqq n$, are replaced by $g_i(x, y)$ *simultaneously*; that is, *all* the g_i's are evaluated before any y_i is changed. For example, if $y_1 = 1$ and $y_2 = 2$, the assignment $(y_1, y_2) \leftarrow (y_1 + 1, y_1 + y_2)$ yields $y_2 = 3$, not $y_2 = 4$. The assignment $(y_1, y_2) \leftarrow (y_2, y_1)$ has the effect of exchanging the contents of y_1 and y_2.

The *verification* of a flowchart program depends on two given predicates:

1. A total predicate $\varphi(\bar{x})$ over $D_{\bar{x}}$, called an *input predicate*, which describes those elements of $D_{\bar{x}}$ that may be used as inputs. In other words, we are interested in the program's performance only for those elements of $D_{\bar{x}}$ satisfying the predicate $\varphi(\bar{x})$. In the special case where we are interested in the program's performance for all elements of $D_{\bar{x}}$, we shall let $\varphi(\bar{x})$ be T; that is, $\varphi(\bar{x})$ is *true* for all elements of $D_{\bar{x}}$.

2. A total predicate $\psi(\bar{x}, \bar{z})$ over $D_{\bar{x}} \times D_{\bar{z}}$, called an *output predicate*, which describes the relationships that must be satisfied between the input variables and the output variables at the completion of program execution.

We may then define the following:

1. *P terminates over* φ if for every input $\bar{\xi}$, such that $\varphi(\bar{\xi})$ is *true*, the computation of the program terminates.

2. *P is partially correct with respect to* (*wrt*) φ *and* ψ if for every $\bar{\xi}$ such that $\varphi(\bar{\xi})$ is *true* and the computation of the program terminates, $\psi(\bar{\xi}, P(\bar{\xi}))$ is *true*.

3. *P is totally correct with respect to* (*wrt*) φ *and* ψ if for every $\bar{\xi}$ such that $\varphi(\bar{\xi})$ is *true*, the computation of the program terminates and $\psi(\bar{\xi}, P(\bar{\xi}))$ is *true*.

Thus, in partial correctness we "don't care" about termination, but in total correctness termination is essential. Verifying a program for a given input predicate $\varphi(\bar{x})$ and an output predicate $\psi(\bar{x}, \bar{z})$ means showing that it is totally correct wrt φ and ψ. However, usually it is most convenient to prove the program in two separate steps: first prove partial correctness wrt φ and ψ, and then prove termination over φ.

We shall now introduce methods for proving both partial correctness and termination of flowchart programs. Let us demonstrate the correctness of the division program introduced previously. First we show that the program is partially correct wrt the input predicate

$$\varphi(x_1, x_2): \quad x_1 \geqq 0 \wedge x_2 \geqq 0$$

(which asserts that we are interested in the program's performance when both x_1 and x_2 are nonnegative) and the output predicate

$$\psi(x_1, x_2, z_1, z_2): \quad x_1 = z_1 x_2 + z_2 \ \wedge 0 \leqq z_2 < x_2$$

(which is essentially a definition of integer division). Then we show that the program terminates over

$$\varphi'(x_1, x_2): \quad x_1 \geqq 0 \wedge x_2 > 0$$

Thus, since the program is partially correct wrt φ and ψ and terminates over φ', it follows that the program is totally correct wrt φ' and ψ. Note the difference between φ and φ'; it is essential to exclude the case $x_2 = 0$ when termination is discussed because the program does not terminate for $x_2 = 0$.

Partial correctness To prove the partial correctness of the division program wrt φ and ψ (see Fig. 3-2), we attach the input predicate φ to point A and the output predicate ψ to point C. The main problem in verifying programs is how to handle loops. The loop of this program becomes manageable by "cutting" the program at point B, which decomposes the program flow into three paths: the first path is from A to B (arcs 1 and 2); the second is from B around the loop and back to B (arcs 3, 4, and 5); and the third is from B to C (arcs 3, 6, and 7). We identify these three paths as

α (START), β (LOOP), and γ (HALT), respectively. All terminating executions of the program must first follow path α, then pass some number of times (possibly zero) around the loop β, and finally finish with path γ; thus all executions are "covered" by these three paths.

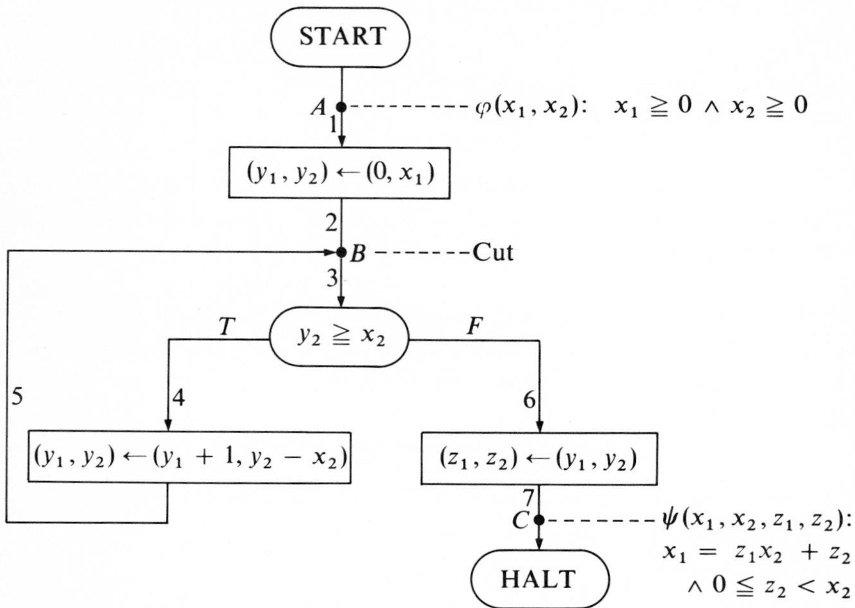

Figure 3-2 Flowchart program for performing integer division (with the input and output predicates).

In order to prove the partial correctness of the program, first we must find a predicate $p(x_1, x_2, y_1, y_2)$ describing the relationships among the program variables at cutpoint B. An appropriate predicate for this purpose is obtained by taking $p(x_1, x_2, y_1, y_2)$ to be

$$x_1 = y_1 x_2 + y_2 \ \wedge y_2 \geqq 0$$

Having obtained this predicate, we have covered the program by three paths, each of which begins and ends with a predicate. The partial correctness of the program is proved by verifying each one of the three paths α, β, and γ by showing that if its initial predicate is *true* for some values of $\bar{x}$ and $\bar{y}$, and the path is executed then its final predicate will be *true* for the new values of $\bar{x}$ and $\bar{y}$.

In the integer division program, verification of path α establishes that $p(x_1, x_2, y_1, y_2)$ is *true* on the first entrance to the loop of the program (assuming the input predicate of the program is satisfied). Verification of path β shows that if $p(x_1, x_2, y_1, y_2)$ is *true* at the entrance of the loop the first time, it will be *true* the second time; if it is *true* the second time, it will be *true* the third time; etc. Verification of path γ shows that when the loop is left with predicate $p(x_1, x_2, y_1, y_2)$ *true*, then the output predicate of the program is *true*. In other words, verification of paths α and β guarantees that $p(x_1, x_2, y_1, y_2)$ has the property that whenever the computation of the program reaches the cutpoint B, $p(x_1, x_2, y_1, y_2)$ is *true* for the current values of x_1, x_2, y_1, and y_2. Therefore, verification of path γ implies that *whenever* the computation of the program reaches point C, the output predicate of the program is *true*.

In order to complete the proof of the partial correctness of the division program, we must verify the paths α, β, and γ. The verification of a path is performed in two steps: First we construct a verification condition for each path in terms of the given predicates, and then we prove it.

Constructing a verification condition of a path is usually done by moving *backward* through the path, considering each statement in turn.

Path α: Let's consider first path α of Fig. 3-2.

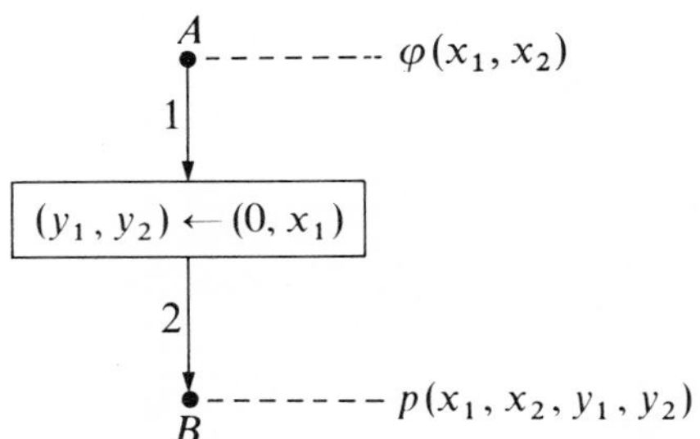

What must be *true* at point A, that is, before the execution of the statement $(y_1, y_2) \leftarrow (0, x_1)$, to ensure that $p(x_1, x_2, y_1, y_2)$ is *true* after its execution? The answer is $p(x_1, x_2, 0, x_1)$, which is formed by substituting 0 for all occurrences of y_1 in the predicate and x_1 for all occurrences of y_2. Thus, the verification condition of this path is

$$\varphi(x_1, x_2) \supset p(x_1, x_2, 0, x_1)$$

that is,

$$[x_1 \geqq 0 \wedge x_2 \geqq 0] \supset [x_1 = 0 \cdot x_2 + x_1 \ \wedge x_1 \geqq 0]$$

Path β: To construct the verification condition of path β, the TEST statement must be handled. As we follow path β, the TEST statement finds $y_2 \geqq x_2$, which can be shown as an annotated piece of flowchart:

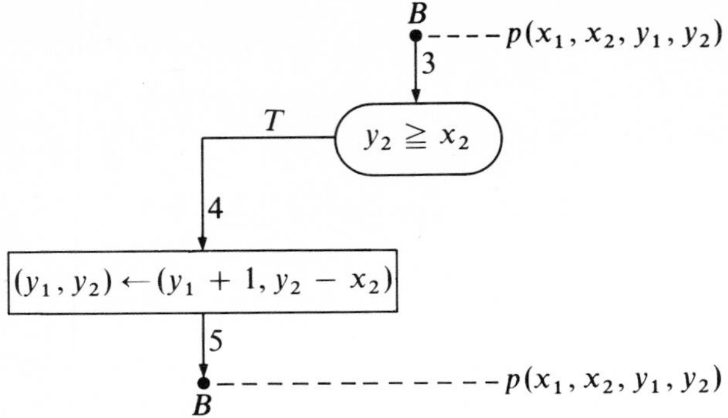

Deriving the predicate $p(x_1, x_2, y_1, y_2)$ backward past the ASSIGNMENT statement yields $p(x_1, x_2, y_1 + 1, y_2 - x_2)$ at arc 4. Although the TEST statement does not change the value of any program variable, it does supply additional useful information because, after the test, it is clear that $y_2 \geqq x_2$. To handle this case, the same question used on ASSIGNMENT statements is asked: What must be *true* at arc 3 so that when control takes the T branch of the TEST statement, that is, when $y_2 \geqq x_2$ is *true*, the predicate $p(x_1, x_2, y_1 + 1, y_2 - x_2)$ will be *true* at arc 4? In this case, the answer is simply $y_2 \geqq x_2 \supset p(x_1, x_2, y_1 + 1, y_2 - x_2)$. Thus, the complete analysis of path β is

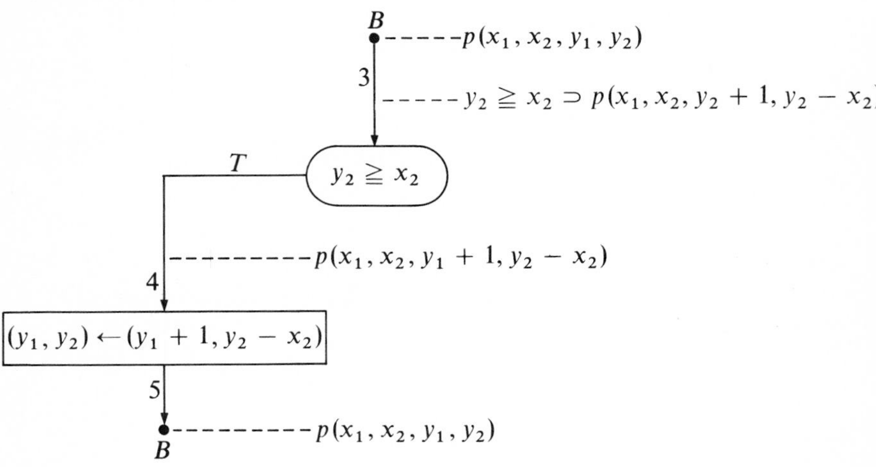

In this case the verification condition to be proved is

$$p(x_1, x_2, y_1, y_2) \supset [y_2 \geqq x_2 \supset p(x_1, x_2, y_1 + 1, y_2 - x_2)]$$

or, equivalently,

$$p(x_1, x_2, y_1, y_2) \wedge y_2 \geqq x_2 \supset p(x_1, x_2, y_1 + 1, y_2 - x_2)\dagger$$

Path γ: The analysis of path γ results in

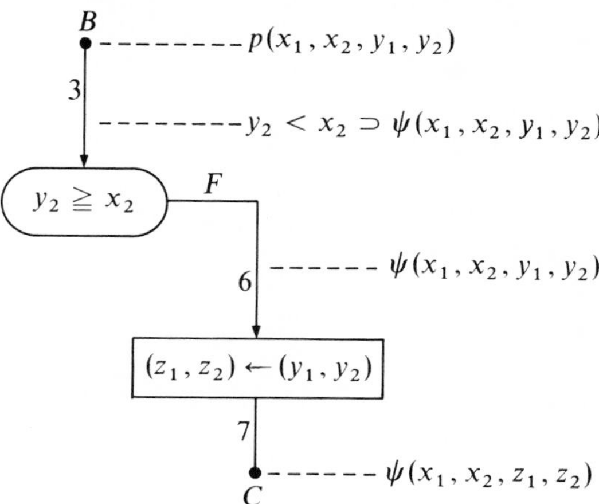

The verification condition to be proved is

$$p(x_1, x_2, y_1, y_2) \supset [y_2 < x_2 \supset \psi(x_1, x_2, y_1, y_2)]$$

or equivalently,

$$p(x_1, x_2, y_1, y_2) \wedge y_2 < x_2 \supset \psi(x_1, x_2, y_1, y_2)$$

Thus, we have formed the three verification conditions:

$\varphi(x_1, x_2) \supset p(x_1, x_2, 0, x_1)$ (α)

$p(x_1, x_2, y_1, y_2) \wedge y_2 \geqq x_2 \supset p(x_1, x_2, y_1 + 1, y_2 - x_2)$ (β)

$p(x_1, x_2, y_1, y_2) \wedge y_2 < x_2 \supset \psi(x_1, x_2, y_1, y_2)$ (γ)

where

$\varphi(x_1, x_2)$ is $x_1 \geqq 0 \wedge x_2 \geqq 0$

$p(x_1, x_2, y_1, y_2)$ is $x_1 = y_1 x_2 + y_2 \wedge y_2 \geqq 0$

$\psi(x_1, x_2, z_1, z_2)$ is $x_1 = z_1 x_2 + z_2 \wedge 0 \leqq z_2 < x_2$

The reader can check for himself that for all integers x_1, x_2, y_1, and y_2, the three verification conditions are *true*; thus, the program is partially correct wrt φ and ψ.

†Throughout this chapter it should be understood that an expression of the form $A_1 \wedge A_2 \supset B$ stands for $(A_1 \wedge A_2) \supset B$ and, in general, $A_1 \wedge A_2 \wedge \ldots \wedge A_n \supset B$ stands for $(A_1 \wedge A_2 \wedge \ldots \wedge A_n) \supset B$.

Termination Actually, so far we have only partially verified our program: We have proved that whenever a computation of the program terminates (that is, reaches a HALT statement), the output predicate is *true*; however, we have not proved at all that the computation of the program indeed terminates. Thus, in order to complete the verification of the division program, we must prove termination as well.

We shall now prove that the program terminates for every input x_1 and x_2 where

$$\varphi'(x_1, x_2): \quad x_1 \geqq 0 \wedge x_2 > 0$$

(Note, again, that the program does not terminate for $x_2 = 0$.) First we show that the predicate

$$q(x_1, x_2, y_1, y_2): \quad y_2 \geqq 0 \wedge x_2 > 0$$

has the property that whenever we reach point B during the computation, $q(x_1, x_2, y_1, y_2)$ is *true* for the current values of the variables. For this purpose, we must prove the following two verification conditions:

$$\varphi'(x_1, x_2) \supset q(x_1, x_2, 0, x_1) \qquad (\alpha)$$

$$q(x_1, x_2, y_1, y_2) \wedge y_2 \geqq x_2 \supset q(x_1, x_2, y_1 + 1, y_2 - x_2) \qquad (\beta)$$

that is,

$$(x_1 \geqq 0 \wedge x_2 > 0) \supset (x_1 \geqq 0 \wedge x_2 > 0)$$

$$(y_2 \geqq 0 \wedge x_2 > 0 \wedge y_2 \geqq x_2) \supset (y_2 - x_2 \geqq 0 \wedge x_2 > 0)$$

which are clearly *true*.

We observe now that since we always have $x_2 > 0$ at point B, whenever we go around the loop (from B back to B), *the value of* y_2 *decreases*. Also, we know that $y_2 \geqq 0$ whenever we reach point B. Thus, since there is no infinite decreasing sequence of natural numbers, we cannot go infinitely many times around the loop; in other words, the computation must terminate. Using this approach, we present a general technique for proving termination of programs in Sec. 3-1.2.

3-1.1 Partial Correctness

Let us generalize the technique demonstrated in verifying the division program. Suppose we are given a flowchart program P, an input predicate φ, and an output predicate ψ; to prove that P is partially correct wrt φ and ψ we proceed as follows.

Step 1. *Cutpoints.* The first step is to cut the loops of the program by choosing on the arcs of the flowchart a finite set of points, called *cutpoints*, in such a way that every loop includes at least one such cutpoint. To this set of cutpoints we add a point on the arc leading from the START box, called the *START point*, and, for each HALT statement, a point on the arc leading to the HALT box, called a *HALT* point.

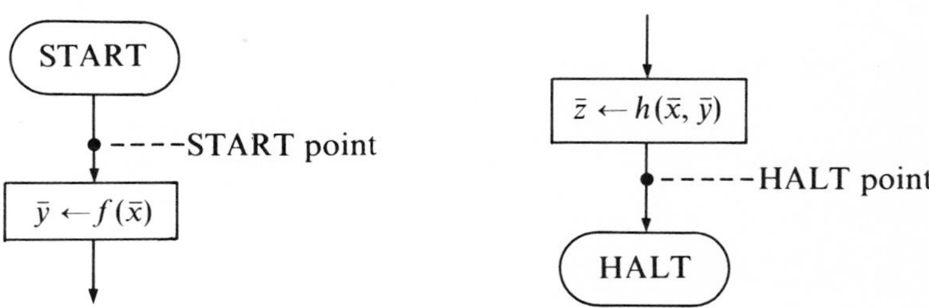

We consider only paths which start and end at cutpoints and which have no intermediate cutpoints. Each such path is finite because of the restriction that every loop includes a cutpoint, and there can be only a finite number of paths. Let α be a path leading from cutpoint i to j.† In the following discussion, we shall make use of the predicate $R_\alpha(\bar{x}, \bar{y})$, which indicates the condition for this path to be traversed, and $r_\alpha(\bar{x}, \bar{y})$, which describes the transformation of the values of $\bar{y}$ effected while the path is traversed. Thus, $R_\alpha(\bar{x}, \bar{y})$ is a predicate over $D_{\bar{x}} \times D_{\bar{y}}$, and $r_\alpha(\bar{x}, \bar{y})$ is a function mapping $D_{\bar{x}} \times D_{\bar{y}}$ into $D_{\bar{y}}$. Both R_α and r_α are expressed in terms of the functions and tests used in α; a simple method for deriving them is to use the *backward-substitution technique*.

Initially, $R(\bar{x}, \bar{y})$ is set to T and $r(\bar{x}, \bar{y})$ is set to $\bar{y}$, and both are attached to cutpoint j; then, in each step, the old R and r are used to construct the new R and r, moving *backward* toward cutpoint i. The final R and r obtained at cutpoint i are the desired R_α and r_α. The rules for constructing the new R and r in each step are:

†Note that $i = j$ is possible, as in the division example.

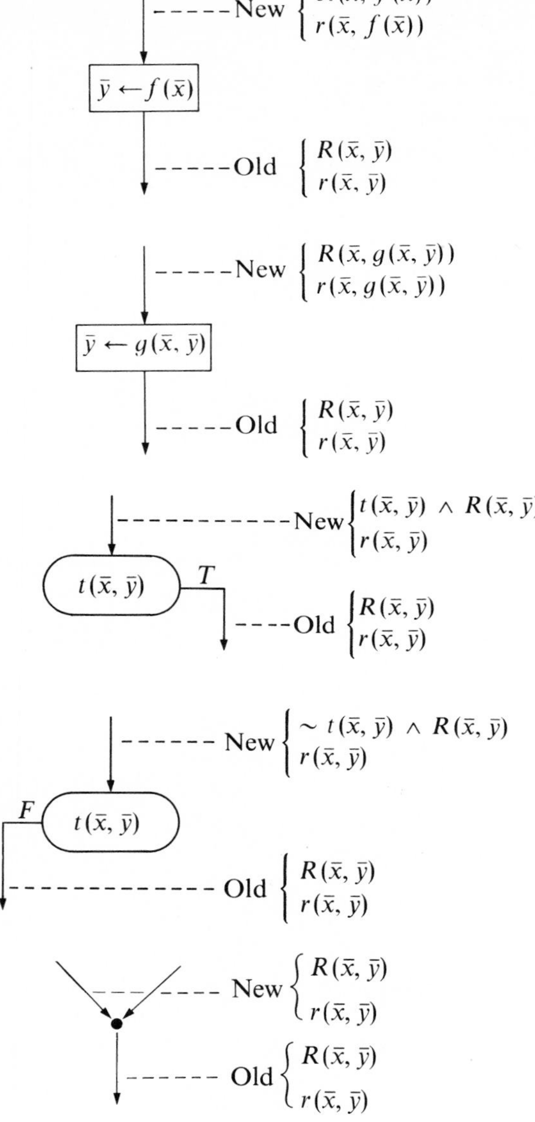

Consider, for example, the backward-substitution technique for path α described in Fig. 3-3. Starting with T for R and $\bar{y}$ for r at cutpoint j, we proceed backward and at cutpoint i finally obtain

$$R_\alpha(\bar{x}, \bar{y}): \; t_1(\bar{x}, g_1(\bar{x}, \bar{y})) \wedge \sim t_2(\bar{x}, g_2(\bar{x}, g_1(\bar{x}, \bar{y})))$$
$$r_\alpha(\bar{x}, \bar{y}): \; g_3(\bar{x}, g_2(\bar{x}, g_1(\bar{x}, \bar{y})))$$

In the special case that j is a HALT point, r is initialized to $\bar{z}$ and R to T; then in the first step of moving backward we obtain

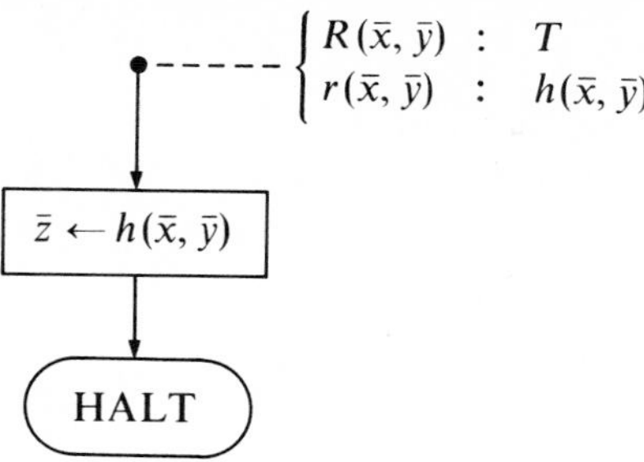

The process then continues by moving backward, as described previously. In the special case that i is the START point, both $R_\alpha(\bar{x}, \bar{y})$ and $r_\alpha(\bar{x}, \bar{y})$ contain no $\bar{y}$'s; R_α is a predicate over $D_{\bar{x}}$, and r_α is a function mapping $D_{\bar{x}}$ into $D_{\bar{y}}$.

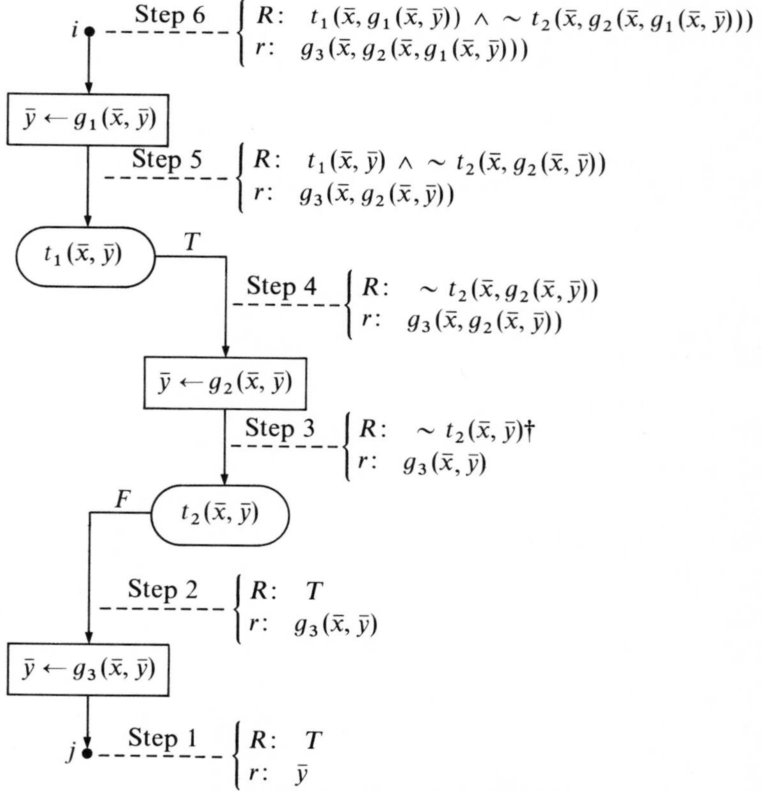

Figure 3-3 Backward-substitution technique.

†Note that we have used the fact that $\sim t_2(\bar{x}, \bar{y}) \wedge T$ is logically equivalent to $\sim t_2(\bar{x}, \bar{y})$.

Step 2. *Inductive assertions.* The second step is to associate with each cutpoint i of the program a predicate $p_i(\bar{x}, \bar{y})$ (often called *inductive assertion*), which purports to characterize the relation among the variables at this point; that is, $p_i(\bar{x}, \bar{y})$ will have the property that whenever control reaches point i, then $p_i(\bar{x}, \bar{y})$ must be *true* for the current values of $\bar{x}$ and $\bar{y}$ at this point. The input predicate $\varphi(\bar{x})$ is attached to the START point, and the output predicate $\psi(\bar{x}, \bar{z})$ is attached to the HALT points.

Step 3. *Verification conditions.* The third step is to construct for every path α leading from cutpoint i to j the verification condition:

$$\forall \bar{x} \forall \bar{y} [p_i(\bar{x}, \bar{y}) \wedge R_\alpha(\bar{x}, \bar{y}) \supset p_j(\bar{x}, r_\alpha(\bar{x}, \bar{y}))]$$

This condition states simply that if p_i is *true* for some values of $\bar{x}$ and $\bar{y}$, and $\bar{x}$ and $\bar{y}$ are such that starting with them at point i the path α will indeed be selected, then p_j is *true* for the new values of $\bar{x}$ and $\bar{y}$ after the path α is traversed.

In the special case that j is a HALT point, the verification condition is

$$\forall \bar{x} \forall \bar{y} [p_i(\bar{x}, \bar{y}) \wedge R_\alpha(\bar{x}, \bar{y}) \supset \psi(\bar{x}, r_\alpha(\bar{x}, \bar{y}))]$$

and in the case that i is the START point, the verification condition is

$$\forall \bar{x} [\varphi(\bar{x}) \wedge R_\alpha(\bar{x}) \supset p_j(\bar{x}, r_\alpha(\bar{x}))]$$

The final step is to prove that all these verification conditions for our choice of inductive assertions are *true.* Proving the verification conditions implies that each predicate attached to a cutpoint has the property that whenever control reaches the point, the predicate is *true* for the current values of the variables; in particular, whenever control reaches a HALT point, $\psi(\bar{x}, \bar{z})$ is *true* for the current values of $\bar{x}$ and $\bar{z}$. In other words, proving the verification conditions implies that the given program P is partially correct wrt φ and ψ.

To summarize, we have the following theorem.

THEOREM 3-1 [INDUCTIVE-ASSERTIONS METHOD (Floyd)] *For a given flowchart program P, an input predicate $\varphi(\bar{x})$, and an output predicate $\psi(\bar{x}, \bar{z})$, apply the following steps: (1) Cut the loops; (2) find an appropriate set of inductive assertions; and (3) construct the verification conditions. If all the verification conditions are true, then P is partially correct wrt φ and ψ.*

In general, all the steps are quite mechanical, except for step 2; discovering the proper inductive assertion requires a deep understanding of the program's performance. Let us illustrate the inductive-assertions method with a few examples.

EXAMPLE 3-1

The program P_1 over the integers (Fig. 3-4) computes $z = \lfloor\sqrt{x}\rfloor$ for every natural number x; that is, the final value of z is the largest integer k such that $k \leqq \sqrt{x}$. The computation method is based on the fact that $1 + 3 + 5 + \cdots + (2n + 1) = (n + 1)^2$ for every $n \geqq 0$; n is computed in y_1, the odd number $2n + 1$ in y_3, and the sum $1 + 3 + 5 + \cdots + (2n + 1)$ in y_2.

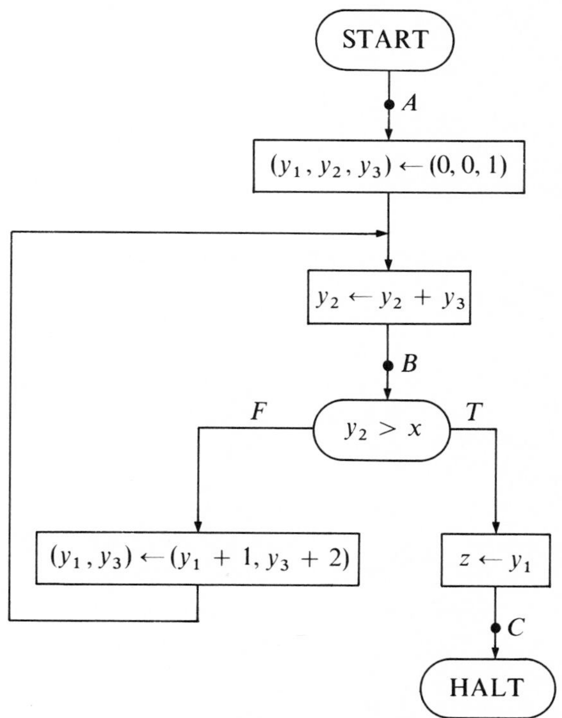

Figure 3-4 Program P_1 for computing $z = \lfloor\sqrt{x}\rfloor$

We shall prove that the program is partially correct wrt the input predicate $\varphi(x)$: $x \geqq 0$ and the output predicate $\psi(x, z)$: $z^2 \leqq x < (z + 1)^2$. For this purpose first we cut the only loop of the program at point B and therefore have three control paths to consider. Using the backward-substitution technique, we obtain the predicate R and term r for each path as follows.

Path α (*from A to B*):

A
Step 3
R: T
r: (0, 0 + 1, 1)
(y1, y2, y3) ← (0, 0, 1)
Step 2
R: T
r: (y1, y2 + y3, y3)
y2 ← y2 + y3
Step 1
R: T
r: (y1, y2, y3)
B

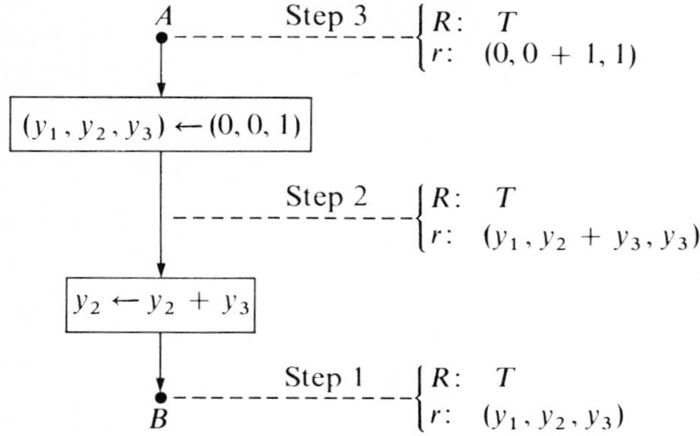

Thus, R_α is T, and r_α is (0, 1, 1).

Path β (*from B to B*):

B
Step 4
R: y2 ≦ x
r: (y1 + 1, y2 + y3 + 2, y3 + 2)
y2 > x
F
Step 3
R: T
r: (y1 + 1, y2 + y3 + 2, y3 + 2)
(y1, y3) ← (y1 + 1, y3 + 2)
Step 2
R: T
r: (y1, y2 + y3, y3)
y2 ← y2 + y3
Step 1
R: T
r: (y1, y2, y3)
B

Thus, R_β is $y_2 \leqq x$, and r_β is $(y_1 + 1, y_2 + y_3 + 2, y_3 + 2)$.

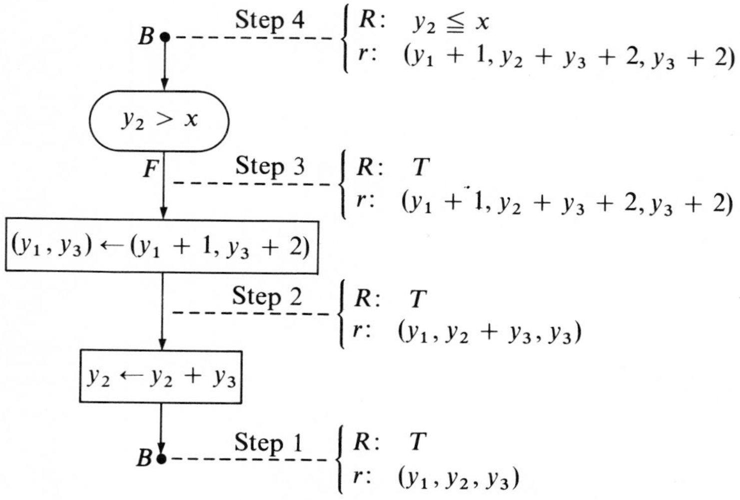

Path γ (from B to C):

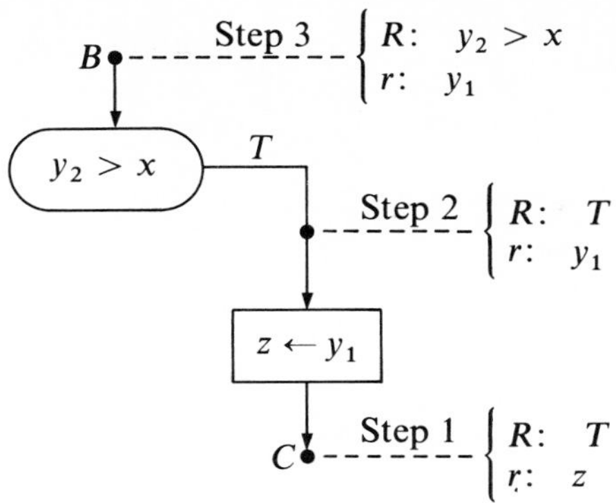

Thus, R_γ is $y_2 > x$, and r_γ is y_1.

Now we are ready to verify the given program. For this purpose we attach the inductive assertion

$$p(x, y_1, y_2, y_3):\quad y_1^2 \leqq x \wedge y_2 = (y_1 + 1)^2 \wedge y_3 = 2y_1 + 1$$

to cutpoint B, in addition to attaching the input predicate $\varphi(x)$: $x \geqq 0$ to cutpoint A and the output predicate $\psi(x, z)$: $z^2 \leqq x < (z + 1)^2$ to cutpoint C (see Fig. 3-5).

The three verification conditions to be proved (for all integers x, y_1, y_2, and y_3) are:

1. For path α

   $$[\varphi(x) \wedge T] \supset p(x, 0, 1, 1)$$

   that is,

   $$x \geqq 0 \supset [0^2 \leqq x \wedge 1 = (0 + 1)^2 \wedge 1 = 2 \cdot 0 + 1]$$

2. For path β

   $$[p(x, y_1, y_2, y_3) \wedge y_2 \leqq x] \supset p(x, y_1 + 1, y_2 + y_3 + 2, y_3 + 2)$$

   that is,

   $$[y_1^2 \leqq x \wedge y_2 = (y_1 + 1)^2 \wedge y_3 = 2y_1 + 1 \wedge y_2 \leqq x]$$

   $$\supset [(y_1 + 1)^2 \leqq x \wedge y_2 + y_3 + 2 = (y_1 + 2)^2$$

   $$\wedge\ y_3 + 2 = 2(y_1 + 1) + 1]$$

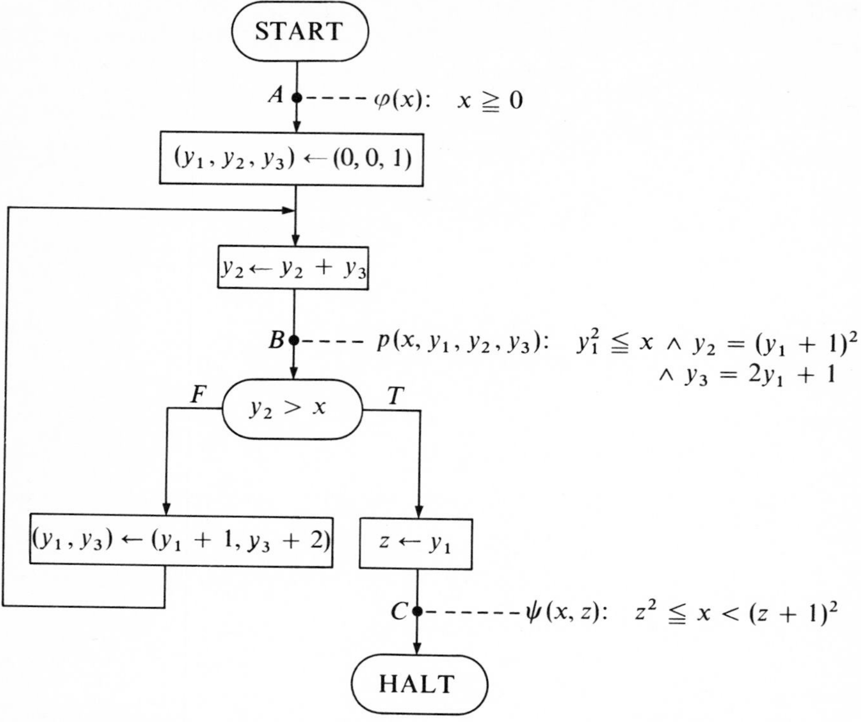

Figure 3-5 Program P_1 for computing $z = \lfloor\sqrt{x}\rfloor$ (partial correctness).

3. For path γ

   $$[p(x, y_1, y_2, y_3) \land y_2 > x] \supset \psi(x, y_1)$$

   that is,

   $$[y_1^2 \leqq x \land y_2 = (y_1 + 1)^2 \land y_3 = 2y_1 + 1 \land y_2 > x]$$
   $$\supset y_1^2 \leqq x < (y_1 + 1)^2$$

Since the three verification conditions are *true*, it follows that the given program P_1 is partially correct wrt the input predicate $x \geqq 0$ and the output predicate $z^2 \leqq x < (z + 1)^2$.

□

EXAMPLE 3-2

The program P_2 over the integers (Fig. 3-6) computes $z = x_1^{x_2}$ for any integer x_1 and any natural number x_2 (we define 0^0 as equal to 1). The computation is based on the binary expansion of x_2, i.e., that for every $y_2 \geqq 0$

$$y_1^{y_2} = y_1 \cdot y_1^{y_2 - 1} \quad \text{if } y_2 \text{ is odd}$$
$$y_1^{y_2} = (y_1 \cdot y_1)^{y_2/2} \quad \text{if } y_2 \text{ is even}$$

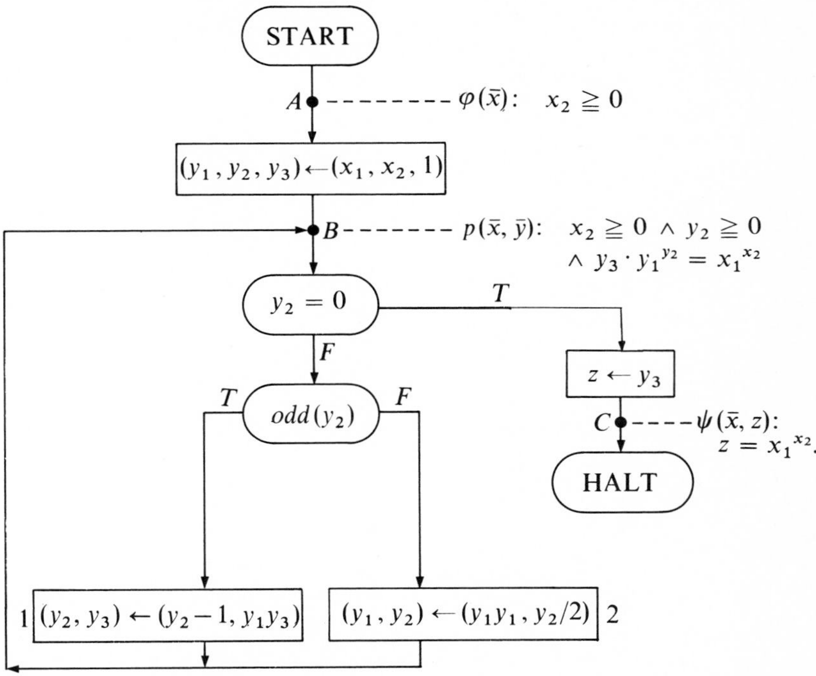

Figure 3-6 Program P_2 for computing $z = x_1^{x_2}$ (partial correctness).

We shall prove that the program is partially correct wrt the input predicate $\varphi(\bar{x})$: $x_2 \geqq 0$ and the output predicate $\psi(\bar{x}, z)$: $z = x_1^{x_2}$. For this purpose we cut both loops of the program at point B and attach to it the inductive assertion

$$p(\bar{x}, \bar{y}):\quad x_2 \geqq 0 \wedge y_2 \geqq 0 \wedge y_3 \cdot y_1^{y_2} = x_1^{x_2}$$

The verification conditions to be proved (for all integers x_1, x_2, y_1, y_2, and y_3) are:

1. For path α (from A to B)

$$\varphi(\bar{x}) \supset p(\bar{x}, x_1, x_2, 1)$$

that is,

$$x_2 \geqq 0 \supset [x_2 \geqq 0 \wedge x_2 \geqq 0 \wedge 1 \cdot {x_1}^{x_2} = {x_1}^{x_2}]$$

2. For path β_1 (from B to B via statement 1)

$$[p(\bar{x}, \bar{y}) \wedge y_2 \neq 0 \wedge odd(y_2)] \supset p(\bar{x}, y_1, y_2 - 1, y_1 y_3)$$

that is,

$$[x_2 \geqq 0 \wedge y_2 \geqq 0 \wedge y_3 \cdot {y_1}^{y_2} = {x_1}^{x_2} \wedge y_2 \neq 0 \wedge odd(y_2)]$$
$$\supset [x_2 \geqq 0 \wedge y_2 - 1 \geqq 0 \wedge (y_1 y_3) \cdot {y_1}^{y_2 - 1} = {x_1}^{x_2}]$$

3. For path β_2 (from B to B via statement 2)

$$[p(\bar{x}, \bar{y}) \wedge y_2 \neq 0 \wedge even(y_2)] \supset p(\bar{x}, y_1 y_1, y_2/2, y_3)$$

that is,

$$[x_2 \geqq 0 \wedge y_2 \geqq 0 \wedge y_3 \cdot {y_1}^{y_2} = {x_1}^{x_2} \wedge y_2 \neq 0 \wedge even(y_2)]$$
$$\supset [x_2 \geqq 0 \wedge y_2/2 \geqq 0 \wedge y_3 \cdot (y_1 y_1)^{y_2/2} = {x_1}^{x_2}]$$

4. For path γ (from B to C)

$$[p(\bar{x}, \bar{y}) \wedge y_2 = 0] \supset \psi(\bar{x}, y_3)$$

that is,

$$[x_2 \geqq 0 \wedge y_2 \geqq 0 \wedge y_3 \cdot {y_1}^{y_2} = {x_1}^{x_2} \wedge y_2 = 0] \supset y_3 = {x_1}^{x_2}$$

Since the four verification conditions are *true*, it follows that the program is partially correct wrt the input predicate $x_2 \geqq 0$ and the output predicate $z = {x_1}^{x_2}$.

□

EXAMPLE 3-3

The program P_3 over the integers (Fig. 3-7) computes $z = gcd(x_1, x_2)$ for every pair of positive integers x_1 and x_2; that is, z is the greatest common divisor of x_1 and x_2 [for example, $gcd(14, 21) = 7$, and $gcd(13, 21) = 1$]. The computation method is based on the fact that

If $y_1 > y_2$, then $gcd(y_1, y_2) = gcd(y_1 - y_2, y_2)$
If $y_1 < y_2$, then $gcd(y_1, y_2) = gcd(y_1, y_2 - y_1)$
If $y_1 = y_2$, then $gcd(y_1, y_2) = y_1 = y_2$

We shall prove that the program is partially correct wrt the input predicate $\varphi(\bar{x})$: $x_1 > 0 \wedge x_2 > 0$ and the output predicate $\psi(\bar{x}, z)$: $z = gcd(x_1, x_2)$. For this purpose we cut the two loops of the program at point B and attach to the cutpoint B the assertion

$$p(\bar{x}, \bar{y}):\quad x_1 > 0 \wedge x_2 > 0 \wedge y_1 > 0 \wedge y_2 > 0 \wedge gcd(y_1, y_2) = gcd(x_1, x_2)$$

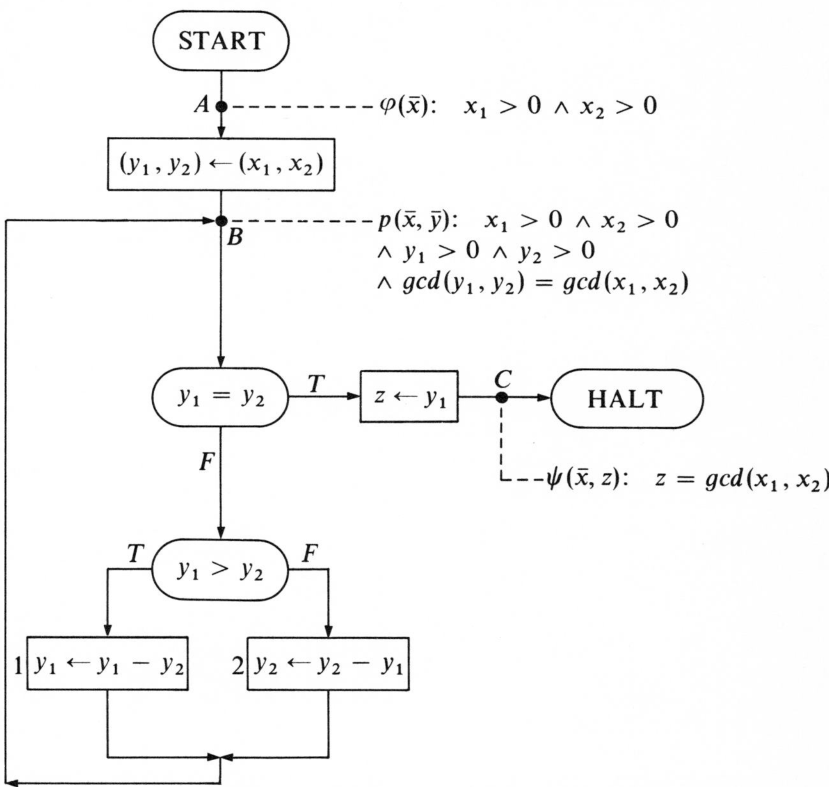

Figure 3-7 Program P_3 for computing $z = gcd(x_1, x_2)$ (partial correctness).

The verification conditions to be proved (for all integers x_1, x_2, y_1, and y_2) are:

1. For path α (from A to B)
   $\varphi(\bar{x}) \supset p(\bar{x}, x_1, x_2)$
   that is,

   $$[x_1 > 0 \wedge x_2 > 0] \supset [x_1 > 0 \wedge x_2 > 0 \wedge x_1 > 0 \wedge x_2 > 0 \wedge gcd(x_1, x_2) = gcd(x_1, x_2)]$$

2. For path β_1 (from B to B via statement 1)

$$[p(\bar{x}, \bar{y}) \wedge y_1 \neq y_2 \wedge y_1 > y_2] \supset p(\bar{x}, y_1 - y_2, y_2)$$

that is,

$$\begin{aligned}&[x_1 > 0 \wedge x_2 > 0 \wedge y_1 > 0 \wedge y_2 > 0\\ &\wedge gcd(y_1, y_2) = gcd(x_1, x_2) \wedge y_1 \neq y_2 \wedge y_1 > y_2]\\ &\supset [x_1 > 0 \wedge x_2 > 0 \wedge y_1 - y_2 > 0 \wedge y_2 > 0\\ &\wedge gcd(y_1 - y_2, y_2) = gcd(x_1, x_2)]\end{aligned}$$

3. For path β_2 (from B to B via statement 2)

$$[p(\bar{x}, \bar{y}) \wedge y_1 \neq y_2 \wedge y_1 \leqq y_2] \supset p(\bar{x}, y_1, y_2 - y_1)$$

that is,

$$\begin{aligned}&[x_1 > 0 \wedge x_2 > 0 \wedge y_1 > 0 \wedge y_2 > 0\\ &\wedge gcd(y_1, y_2) = gcd(x_1, x_2) \wedge y_1 \neq y_2 \wedge y_1 \leqq y_2]\\ &\supset [x_1 > 0 \wedge x_2 > 0 \wedge y_1 > 0 \wedge y_2 - y_1 > 0\\ &\wedge gcd(y_1, y_2 - y_1) = gcd(x_1, x_2)]\end{aligned}$$

4. For path γ (from B to C)

$$[p(\bar{x}, \bar{y}) \wedge y_1 = y_2] \supset \psi(\bar{x}, y_1)$$

that is,

$$\begin{aligned}&[x_1 > 0 \wedge x_2 > 0 \wedge y_1 > 0 \wedge y_2 > 0\\ &\wedge gcd(y_1, y_2) = gcd(x_1, x_2) \wedge y_1 = y_2]\\ &\supset y_1 = gcd(x_1, x_2)\end{aligned}$$

Since the four verification conditions are *true*, it follows that the program is partially correct wrt the input predicate $x_1 > 0 \wedge x_2 > 0$ and the output predicate $z = gcd(x_1, x_2)$.

□

3-1.2 Termination

Next we shall describe a method for proving the termination of flowchart programs. We simply use an ordered set with no infinite decreasing sequences to establish that the program cannot go through a loop indefinitely. The most common ordered set used for this purpose is the set of natural numbers ordered with the usual $>$ (*greater than*) relation. Since, for any

n, we have $n > \cdots > 2 > 1 > 0$, there are no infinite decreasing sequences of natural numbers. Note that we may not use the set of all integers with the same ordering because it has infinite decreasing sequences such as $n > \cdots > 2 > 1 > 0 > -1 > -2 > \cdots$. In general, every well-founded set can be used for the purpose of proving the termination of flowchart programs as we shall demonstrate.

A *partially ordered set* $(W, \prec)$ consists of a nonempty set W and any binary relation $\prec$ on elements of W which satisfies the following properties:

1. For all $a, b, c \in W$, if $a \prec b$ and $b \prec c$, then $a \prec c$ (*transitivity*).
2. For all $a, b \in W$, if $a \prec b$, then $b \nprec a$ (*asymmetry*).
3. For all $a \in W$, $a \nprec a$ (*irreflexivity*).

As usual, we write $a \prec b$ or $b \succ a$; $a \nprec b$ means "a does not precede b." Note that the ordering need not be total, i.e., it is possible that for some $a, b \in W$, neither $a \prec b$ nor $b \prec a$ holds.

A partially ordered set $(W, \prec)$ which contains no infinite decreasing sequences, $a_0 \succ a_1 \succ a_2 \succ \cdots$, of elements of W is called a *well-founded set*. For example:

(a) The set of all real numbers between 0 and 1, with the usual ordering $<$, is partially ordered but not well-founded (consider the infinite decreasing sequence $\frac{1}{2} > \frac{1}{3} > \frac{1}{4} > \cdots$).

(b) The set I of integers, with the usual ordering $<$, is partially ordered but not well-founded (consider the infinite decreasing sequence $0 > -1 > -2 > \cdots$).

(c) The set N of natural numbers, with the usual ordering $<$, is well-founded.

(d) If Σ is any alphabet, then the set Σ^* of all words over Σ with the substring relation $\prec$ (that is, $w_1 \prec w_2$ iff w_1 is a proper substring of w_2), is well-founded.

Now, suppose we are given a flowchart program P and an input predicate φ. To show that P terminates over φ, we propose the following procedure:

1. Choose a well-founded set $(W, \prec)$.
2. Select a set of cutpoints to cut the loops of the program.
3. With every cutpoint i, associate a function $u_i(\bar{x}, \bar{y})$ mapping $D_{\bar{x}} \times D_{\bar{y}}$ into W; that is,

$$(*) \qquad \forall\bar{x}\forall\bar{y}[u_i(\bar{x}, \bar{y}) \in W]$$

If for every path α from cutpoint i to j with no intermediate cutpoints which is a part of some loop (i.e., there is also some path from j to i), we have

(**) $\qquad \forall\bar{x}\forall\bar{y}\{\varphi(\bar{x}) \wedge R_\alpha(\bar{x}, \bar{y}) \supset [u_i(\bar{x}, \bar{y}) \succ u_j(\bar{x}, r_\alpha(\bar{x}, \bar{y}))]\}$

then P terminates over φ.

In other words, for any computation, when we move from one cutpoint to another, there is associated a smaller and smaller element $u_i(\bar{x}, \bar{y})$ of W. Since W is a well-founded set, there is no infinite decreasing sequence of elements of W, which, in turn, implies that any computation of P must be finite.

The main drawback of the procedure just described is that conditions (*) and (**) are too restrictive, and it is possible only rarely to find an appropriate set of functions $u_i(\bar{x}, \bar{y})$ that will satisfy both conditions. The problem is that we require that the conditions will be *true* for all $\bar{x}$ and $\bar{y}$, while, in general, it suffices to show (*) and (**) only for those values of $\bar{x}$ and $\bar{y}$ which can indeed be reached at point i at some stage of the computation. This problem suggests attaching an inductive assertion $q_i(\bar{x}, \bar{y})$ to each cutpoint i in such a way that $q_i(\bar{x}, \bar{y})$ has the property that whenever the computation of the program reaches cutpoint i, $q_i(\bar{x}, \bar{y})$ is *true* for the current values of $\bar{x}$ and $\bar{y}$. Then we can state a more powerful method for proving termination, as follows.

Step 1. Select a set of cutpoints to cut the loops of the program and with every cutpoint i associate an assertion $q_i(\bar{x}, \bar{y})$ such that $q_i(\bar{x}, \bar{y})$ *are good assertions*. That is, for every path α from the START point to cutpoint j (with no intermediate cutpoints), we have

$$\forall\bar{x}[\varphi(\bar{x}) \wedge R_\alpha(\bar{x}) \supset q_j(\bar{x}, r_\alpha(\bar{x}))]$$

and for every path α from cutpoint i to j (with no intermediate cutpoints), we have

$$\forall\bar{x}\forall\bar{y}[q_i(\bar{x}, \bar{y}) \wedge R_\alpha(\bar{x}, \bar{y}) \supset q_j(\bar{x}, r_\alpha(\bar{x}, \bar{y}))]$$

Step 2. Choose a well-founded set $(W, \prec)$ and with every cutpoint i associate a partial function $u_i(\bar{x}, \bar{y})$ mapping $D_{\bar{x}} \times D_{\bar{y}}$ into W such that $u_i(\bar{x}, \bar{y})$ *are good functions*. That is, for every cutpoint i, we have

$$\forall\bar{x}\,\forall\bar{y}[q_i(\bar{x}, \bar{y}) \supset u_i(\bar{x}, \bar{y}) \in W]$$

Step 3. Show that *the termination conditions hold*. That is, for every path α from cutpoint i to j (with no intermediate cutpoints) which is a part of some loop, we have

$$\forall\bar{x}\,\forall\bar{y}\{q_i(\bar{x}, \bar{y}) \wedge R_\alpha(\bar{x}, \bar{y}) \supset [u_i(\bar{x}, \bar{y}) \succ u_j(\bar{x}, r_\alpha(\bar{x}, \bar{y}))]\}$$

The method just described is summarized in the following theorem.

THEOREM 3-2 [WELL-FOUNDED-SETS METHOD (Floyd)]. *For a given flowchart program P and an input predicate $\varphi(\bar{x})$, apply the following steps: (1) Cut the loops and find "good" inductive assertions; and (2) choose a well-founded set and find "good" partial functions. If all the termination conditions are true, then P terminates over φ.*

EXAMPLE 3-4

First we prove that the program P_1 of Example 3-1 terminates for every natural number x. To show that the program terminates over $\varphi(x)$: $x \geqq 0$, we use the well-founded set $(N, <)$, that is, the set of natural numbers with the usual ordering $<$. We cut the single loop at point B and attach to it the assertion $q(x, \bar{y})$: $y_2 \leqq x \wedge y_3 > 0$ and the function $u(x, \bar{y})$: $x - y_2$ (see Fig. 3-8).

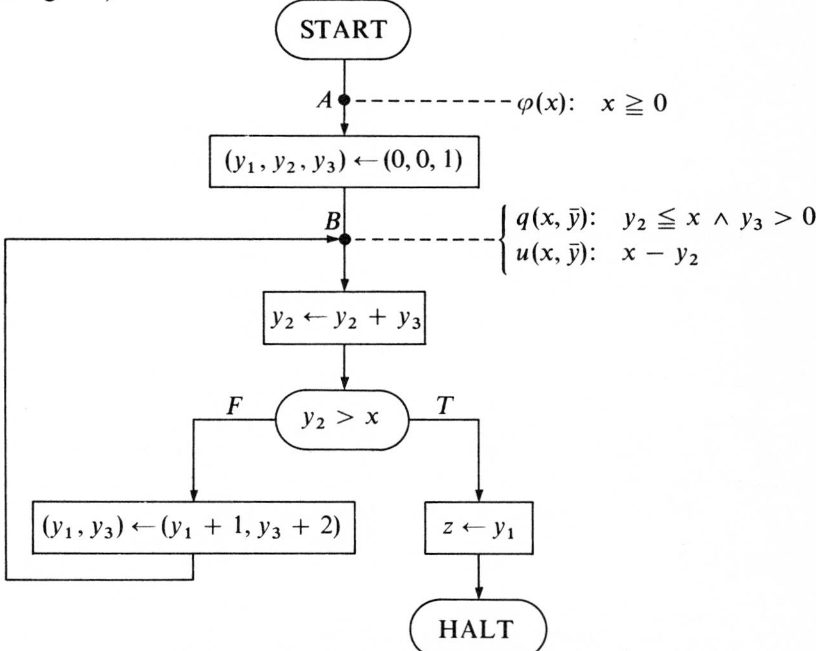

Figure 3-8 Program P_1 for computing $z = [\sqrt{x}]$ (termination).

Note that there are two paths of interest here:

Path α_1 (from A to B): R_{α_1} is T, and r_{α_1} is $(0, 0, 1)$.

Path α_2 (from B to B): R_{α_2} is $y_2 + y_3 \leqq x$, and r_{α_2} is $(y_1 + 1,\ y_2 + y_3, y_3 + 2)$.

Our proof consists of three steps. For all integers x, y_1, y_2, and y_3:

Step 1. *$q(x, \bar{y})$ is a good assertion.*
For path α_1

$$\varphi(x) \supset q(x, 0, 0, 1)$$

that is,

$$x \geqq 0 \supset [0 \leqq x \wedge 1 > 0]$$

For path α_2

$$[q(x, y_1, y_2, y_3) \wedge y_2 + y_3 \leqq x] \supset q(x, y_1 + 1, y_2 + y_3, y_3 + 2)$$

that is,

$$[y_2 \leqq x \wedge y_3 > 0 \wedge y_2 + y_3 \leqq x] \supset [y_2 + y_3 \leqq x \wedge y_3 + 2 > 0]$$

Step 2. *$u(x, \bar{y})$ is a good function.*

$$q(x, \bar{y}) \supset u(x, \bar{y}) \in N$$

that is,

$$[y_2 \leqq x \wedge y_3 > 0] \supset x - y_2 \geqq 0$$

Step 3. *The termination condition holds.*
For path α_2

$$[q(x, \bar{y}) \wedge y_2 + y_3 \leqq x]$$
$$\supset [u(x, y_1, y_2, y_3) > u(x, y_1 + 1, y_2 + y_3, y_3 + 2)]$$

that is,

$$[y_2 \leqq x \wedge y_3 > 0 \wedge y_2 + y_3 \leqq x] \supset [x - y_2 > x - (y_2 + y_3)]$$

(Note that path α_1 is not considered because it is not part of any loop.)

Since all three conditions are *true*, it follows that the program terminates for every natural number x.

□

It is straightforward to prove that the program P_2 of Example 3-2 terminates over $\varphi(\bar{x})$: $x_2 \geqq 0$ [let $q_B(\bar{x}, \bar{y})$ be $y_2 \geqq 0$ and $u_B(\bar{x}, \bar{y})$ be y_2] and that the program P_3 of Example 3-3 terminates over $\varphi(\bar{x})$: $x_1 > 0 \wedge x_2 > 0$ [let $q_B(\bar{x}, \bar{y})$ be $y_1 > 0 \wedge y_2 > 0$ and $u_B(\bar{x}, \bar{y})$ be $max(y_1, y_2)$]. We proceed with a less trivial example.

EXAMPLE 3-5 (Knuth)

The program P_4 over the integers (Fig. 3-9) also computes $z = gcd(x_1, x_2)$ for every pair of positive integers x_1 and x_2; that is, z is the greatest common divisor of x_1 and x_2. We leave it as an exercise for the reader to prove that the program is partially correct wrt the input predicate $\varphi(\bar{x})$: $x_1 > 0 \wedge x_2 > 0$ and the output predicate $\psi(\bar{x}, z)$: $z = gcd(x_1, x_2)$.† We would like to prove that P_4 terminates over φ.

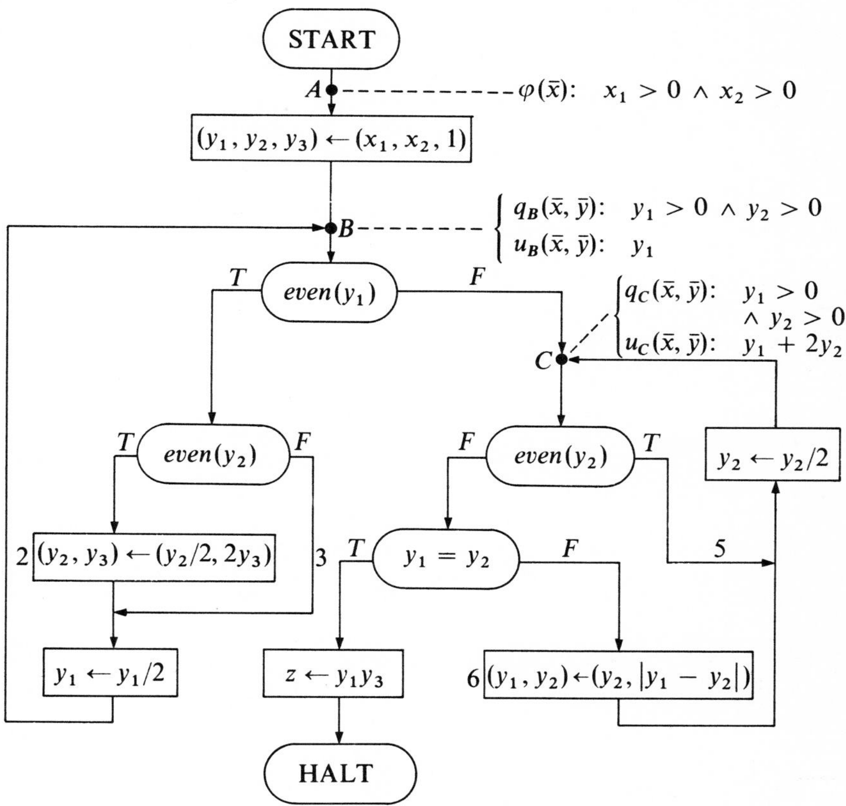

Figure 3-9 Program P_4 for computing $z = gcd(x_1, x_2)$ (termination).

Again we use the well-founded set $(N, <)$. We cut the loops of the program at points B and C and then attach to cutpoint B

$$q_B(\bar{x}, \bar{y}):\quad y_1 > 0 \wedge y_2 > 0 \qquad \text{and} \qquad u_B(\bar{x}, \bar{y}):\quad y_1$$

† Let $p_B(\bar{x}, \bar{y})$ be $x_1 > 0 \wedge x_2 > 0 \wedge y_1 > 0 \wedge y_2 > 0 \wedge y_3 \cdot gcd(y_1, y_2) = gcd(x_1, x_2)$ and let $p_C(\bar{x}, \bar{y})$ be $x_1 > 0 \wedge x_2 > 0 \wedge y_1 > 0 \wedge y_2 > 0 \wedge odd(y_1) \wedge y_3 \cdot gcd(y_1, y_2) = gcd(x_1, x_2)$.

and to cutpoint C

$$q_C(\bar{x}, \bar{y}):\ \ y_1 > 0 \wedge y_2 > 0 \qquad \text{and} \qquad u_C(\bar{x}, \bar{y}):\ \ y_1 + 2y_2$$

Note that there are six paths of interest in this program:

α_1 (from A to B): R_{α_1} is T, and r_{α_1} is $(x_1, x_2, 1)$.
α_2 (from B to B via statement 2): R_{α_2} is $even(y_1) \wedge even(y_2)$, and r_{α_2} is $(y_1/2, y_2/2, 2y_3)$.
α_3 (from B to B via arc 3): R_{α_3} is $even(y_1) \wedge odd(y_2)$, and r_{α_3} is $(y_1/2, y_2, y_3)$.
α_4 (from B to C): R_{α_4} is $odd(y_1)$, and r_{α_4} is (y_1, y_2, y_3).
α_5 (from C to C via arc 5): R_{α_5} is $even(y_2)$, and r_{α_5} is $(y_1, y_2/2, y_3)$.
α_6 (from C to C via statement 6): R_{α_6} is $odd(y_2) \wedge y_1 \neq y_2$, and r_{α_6} is $(y_2, |y_1 - y_2|/2, y_3)$.

Again our proof consists of three steps. For all integers x, y_1, y_2, and y_3:

Step 1. *q_B and q_C are good assertions.*
For path α_1

$$\varphi(\bar{x}) \supset q_B(\bar{x}, x_1, x_2, 1)$$

For path α_2

$$q_B(\bar{x}, \bar{y}) \wedge even(y_1) \wedge even(y_2) \supset q_B(\bar{x}, y_1/2, y_2/2, 2y_3)$$

For path α_3

$$q_B(\bar{x}, \bar{y}) \wedge even(y_1) \wedge odd(y_2) \supset q_B(\bar{x}, y_1/2, y_2, y_3)$$

For path α_4

$$q_B(\bar{x}, \bar{y}) \wedge odd(y_1) \supset q_C(\bar{x}, y_1, y_2, y_3)$$

For path α_5

$$q_C(\bar{x}, \bar{y}) \wedge even(y_2) \supset q_C(\bar{x}, y_1, y_2/2, y_3)$$

For path α_6

$$q_C(\bar{x}, \bar{y}) \wedge odd(y_2) \wedge y_1 \neq y_2 \supset q_C(\bar{x}, y_2, |y_1 - y_2|/2, y_3)$$

Step 2. *u_B and u_C are good functions.*

$$q_B(\bar{x}, \bar{y}) \supset u_B(\bar{x}, \bar{y}) \in N$$

$$q_C(\bar{x}, \bar{y}) \supset u_C(\bar{x}, \bar{y}) \in N$$

Step 3. *The termination conditions hold.*
For path α_2

$$[q_B(\bar{x}, \bar{y}) \wedge even(y_1) \wedge even(y_2)]$$
$$\supset [u_B(\bar{x}, y_1, y_2, y_3) > u_B(\bar{x}, y_1/2, y_2/2, 2y_3)]$$

For path α_3

$$[q_B(\bar{x}, \bar{y}) \wedge even(y_1) \wedge odd(y_2)]$$
$$\supset [u_B(\bar{x}, y_1, y_2, y_3) > u_B(\bar{x}, y_1/2, y_2, y_3)]$$

For path α_5

$$[q_C(\bar{x}, \bar{y}) \wedge even(y_2)] \supset [u_C(\bar{x}, y_1, y_2, y_3) > u_C(\bar{x}, y_1, y_2/2, y_3)]$$

For path α_6

$$[q_C(\bar{x}, \bar{y}) \wedge odd(y_2) \wedge y_1 \neq y_2]$$
$$\supset [u_C(\bar{x}, y_1, y_2, y_3) > u_C(\bar{x}, y_2, |y_1 - y_2|/2, y_3)]$$

Substituting the given assertions q_B and q_C and the given functions u_B and u_C, all the above statements can easily be verified; therefore it follows that the program terminates for every pair of positive integers x_1 and x_2.

□

3-2 FLOWCHART PROGRAMS WITH ARRAYS

An *array* is a programming feature used for describing a large family of related program variables. For example, to describe a group of 21 integer variables, instead of using letters $A, B, C, \ldots, T, U$, we prefer to identify the variables as $S[0], S[1], \ldots, S[20]$, where S is a 21-element array; this notation corresponds to the mathematical subscript notation S_0, $S_1, \ldots, S_{20}$. An expression like $S[i+j]$ indicates the $(i+j)$th element $(0 \leqq i+j \leqq 20)$ in this family, depending on the current value of $i+j$.

3-2.1 Partial Correctness

In this section we shall prove the partial correctness of several flowchart programs which use arrays and discuss some of the difficulties involved in treating arrays. However, in our examples we shall ignore one problem concerning the correctness of flowchart programs with arrays: We shall not verify that the array subscript actually lies within the boundaries of the array. For instance, suppose that a program uses an array S of 21 elements $S[0], S[1], \ldots, S[20]$ and a statement in the program is $y \leftarrow S[i+j]$. Then we must prove that whenever we reach this statement, $0 \leqq i+j \leqq 20$, that is, the current value of $i+j$ is within the boundaries of the array. We may perform this proof simply by attaching the assertion $0 \leqq i+j \leqq 20$ to the arc leading to this statement and verifying it using the inductive-assertions approach.

EXAMPLE 3-6

Consider the program P_5 described in Fig. 3-10 (for a moment ignore the attached assertions) for *bubble-sorting* into increasing order an array X of $n+1$ $(n \geqq 0)$ real numbers $X[0], X[1], \ldots, X[n]$. First we transfer the elements of X to an array S and then rearrange the order of the elements of S. Note that the operation

$$(S[j], S[j+1]) \leftarrow (S[j+1], S[j])$$

has the effect of exchanging the contents of $S[j]$ and $S[j+1]$. Finally we transfer the elements of S to the output array Z.

We wish to prove that whenever this program terminates:

1. The $n+1$ elements of the array Z are a permutation of the elements of the original array X. We denote this property by $perm(X, Z, 0, n)$, where the predicate $perm(X, Z, k, l)$ is taken to mean that the elements $Z[k]$, $Z[k+1], \ldots, Z[l]$ are a permutation of the elements $X[k], X[k+1], \ldots, X[l]$. (This is considered to be vacuously true if $k \geqq l$.)
2. The elements of the array Z are in increasing order. We denote this property by $ordered(Z, 0, n)$, where the predicate $ordered(Z, k, l)$ is taken to mean that the elements $Z[k], Z[k+1], \ldots, Z[l]$ are in increasing order; that is, $Z[k] \leqq Z[k+1] \leqq \cdots \leqq Z[l]$. (This is considered to be vacuously true if $k \geqq l$.)

Thus, we must prove that the program is partially correct wrt the input predicate

$$\varphi(n, X): \quad n \geqq 0$$

and the output predicate

$$\psi(n, X, Z): \quad perm(X, Z, 0, n) \wedge ordered(Z, 0, n)$$

Note that it is quite straightforward that $perm(X, Z, 0, n)$ holds because $(S[j], S[j+1]) \leftarrow (S[j+1], S[j])$ is the only operation applied to S and it leaves the contents of the array S unchanged except for order.

To show that $ordered(Z, 0, n)$ holds, we cut the three loops of the

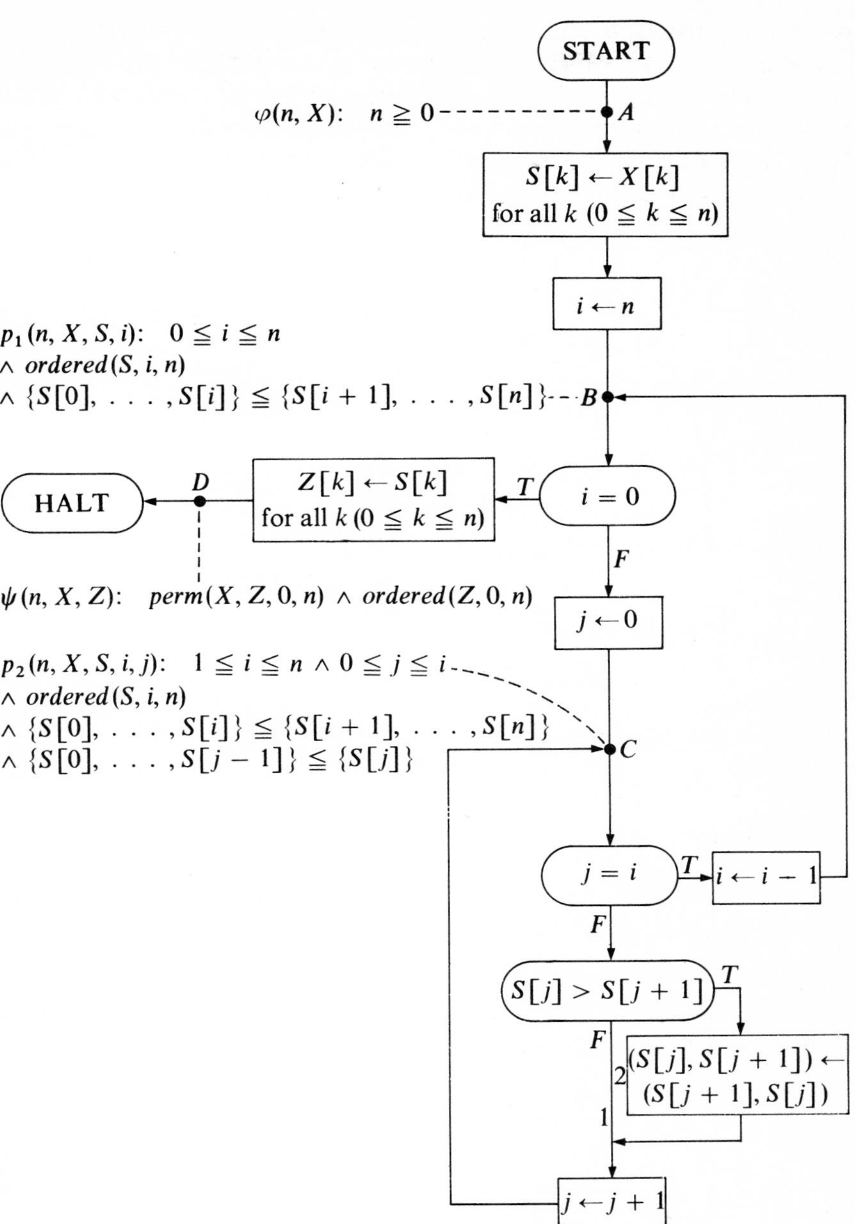

Figure 3-10 Program P_5 for bubble-sorting an array of real numbers (partial correctness).

program at points B and C and attach to them appropriate inductive assertions. To express the inductive assertions, we use $\{S[k], \ldots, S[l]\}$ to represent the set of all elements $S[m]$, $k \leqq m \leqq l$ (note that this set is empty if $k > l$). Furthermore, for any two sets of real numbers T_1 and T_2, $T_1 \leqq T_2$ means that every element of T_1 is less than or equal to any element of T_2 (which is vacuously true if either T_1 or T_2 is empty).

Now the inductive assertions can be expressed as follows:

$p_1(n, X, S, i)$ at cutpoint B:

$$0 \leqq i \leqq n \wedge ordered(S, i, n) \\ \wedge \{S[0], \ldots, S[i]\} \leqq \{S[i+1], \ldots, S[n]\}$$

$p_2(n, X, S, i, j)$ at cutpoint C:

$$1 \leqq i \leqq n \wedge 0 \leqq j \leqq i \wedge ordered(S, i, n) \\ \wedge \{S[0], \ldots, S[i]\} \leqq \{S[i+1], \ldots, S[n]\} \\ \wedge \{S[0], \ldots, S[j-1]\} \leqq \{S[j]\}$$

Six verification conditions must be proved:

1. For path α (from A to B)

$$\varphi(n, X) \supset p_1(n, X, X, n)$$

2. For path γ (from B to D)

$$[p_1(n, X, S, i) \wedge i = 0] \supset \psi(n, X, S)$$

3. For path β_1 (from B to C)

$$[p_1(n, X, S, i) \wedge i \neq 0] \supset p_2(n, X, S, i, 0)$$

4. For path β_2 (from C to C via arc 1)

$$[p_2(n, X, S, i, j) \wedge (S[j] \leqq S[j+1]) \wedge j \neq i] \supset \\ p_2(n, X, S, i, j+1)$$

5. For path β_3 (from C to C via statement 2)

$$[p_2(n, X, S, i, j) \wedge (S[j] > S[j+1]) \wedge j \neq i] \supset \\ p_2(n, X, S^*, i, j+1)$$

where S^* represents the array S after exchanging the values of $S[j]$ and $S[j+1]$.

6. For path β_4 (from C to B)

$$[p_2(n, X, S, i, j) \wedge j = i] \supset p_1(n, X, S, i-1)$$

It is straightforward to prove the six verification conditions. For example, to prove verification condition 6, we must show

$$[p_2(n, X, S, i, j) \wedge j = i] \supset p_1(n, X, S, i - 1)$$

that is,

$$\begin{aligned}
&[1 \leqq i \leqq n \wedge 0 \leqq j \leqq i \wedge \mathit{ordered}(S, i, n) \\
&\qquad \wedge \{S[0], \ldots, S[i]\} \leqq \{S[i+1], \ldots, S[n]\} \\
&\qquad \wedge \{S[0], \ldots, S[j-1]\} \leqq \{S[j]\} \wedge j = i] \\
&\supset [0 \leqq i - 1 \leqq n \wedge \mathit{ordered}(S, i-1, n) \\
&\qquad \wedge \{S[0], \ldots, S[i-1]\} \leqq \{S[i], \ldots, S[n]\}]
\end{aligned}$$

First, it is clear that $1 \leqq i \leqq n$ implies $0 \leqq i - 1 \leqq n$; in addition, *ordered*(S, i, n) and $S[i-1] \leqq S[i]$ (we have $S[j-1] \leqq S[j]$ and $j = i$) imply *ordered*$(S, i-1, n)$; finally, $\{S[0], \ldots, S[i]\} \leqq \{S[i+1], \ldots, S[n]\}$ and $\{S[0], \ldots, S[i-1]\} \leqq \{S[i]\}$ imply $\{S[0], \ldots, S[i-1]\} \leqq \{S[i], \ldots, S[n]\}$.

□

In Example 3-6 the inductive assertions were expressed in a very informal manner. For a more formal treatment of such assertions, quantifiers might be used; e.g., the part of assertion p_2

$$\{S[0], \ldots, S[j-1]\} \leqq \{S[j]\}$$

should be expressed formally as

$$\forall k[0 \leqq k < j \supset S[k] \leqq S[j]]$$

The verification conditions of the example were also constructed in quite an informal manner. In general, special care should be taken in the construction of the verification conditions for programs with ASSIGNMENT statements which change the value of some element of an array.

As an illustration, consider the ASSIGNMENT statement which exchanges the values of $S[j]$ and $S[j+1]$

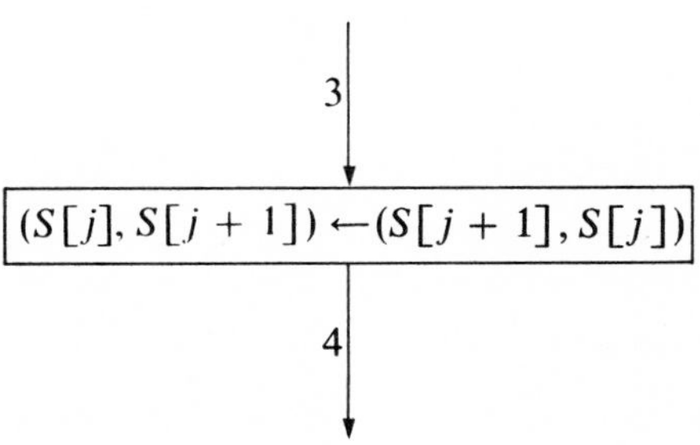

where the assertion

$$\forall k[0 \leqq k \leqq j \supset S[k] \leqq S[j+1]]$$

is assumed to be *true* at arc 4. (Note that this would actually be a part of the construction of verification condition 5 of Example 3-6.) The construction of the appropriate assertion at arc 3 requires the substitution of $S[j]$ for $S[j+1]$ and of $S[j+1]$ for $S[j]$ *simultaneously*. There are two possible places for the substitution to occur, namely, $S[k]$ and $S[j+1]$: $S[k]$ is replaced by the expression "*if* $k = j$ *then* $S[j+1]$ *else* (*if* $k = j+1$ *then* $S[j]$ *else* $S[k]$)," while $S[j+1]$ is replaced simply by $S[j]$ because it appears explicitly in the assertion. Thus, we obtain

$$\forall k[0 \leqq k \leqq j$$
$$\supset (\textit{if } k = j \textit{ then } S[j+1] \textit{ else } (\textit{if } k = j+1 \textit{ then } S[j] \textit{ else } S[k])) \leqq S[j]]$$

which, by considering the two cases $k = j$ and $0 \leqq k < j$ (note that $0 \leqq k \leqq j$ implies that $k \neq j+1$), can be simplified to

$$S[j+1] \leqq S[j] \wedge \forall k[0 \leqq k < j \supset S[k] \leqq S[j]]$$

Another approach for handling arrays is the use of the special functions c (*contents*) and a (*assign*), which were introduced by McCarthy (1962). An array, say, $S[0], S[1], \ldots$, is described as a single variable S whose value represents some coding of all the information contained in the array in such a way that

1. The function $c(S, i)$ extracts the value (contents) of $S[i]$.
2. The function $a(S, i_1, x_1, i_2, x_2, \ldots, i_n, x_n)$, $n \geqq 1$, yields a new coded value representing the array S after applying the assignments $S[i_1] \leftarrow x_1; S[i_2] \leftarrow x_2; \ldots; S[i_n] \leftarrow x_n$ simultaneously.†

Thus, in this notation, the statement

$$S[i] \leftarrow S[j] + 2$$

would be written as

$$S \leftarrow a(S, i, c(S, j) + 2)$$

A new problem arises, however: How does one deal with c and a? The following axioms allow us to work with these functions:

1. If $i_1 \neq j, i_2 \neq j, \ldots$, and $i_n \neq j$, then $c(a(S, i_1, x_1, \ldots, i_n, x_n), j) = c(S, j)$.
2. If $i_k = j$, where $1 \leqq k \leqq n$, then $c(a(S, i_1, x_1, \ldots, i_n, x_n), j) = x_k$.

Kaplan (1968) actually showed that these two axioms are sufficient to handle all necessary operations with c and a.

Let us redo the previous example using the McCarthy notation. The ASSIGNMENT statement which exchanges the values of $S[j]$ and $S[j+1]$ will be expressed as

†We assume that the values of $i_1, i_2, \ldots, i_n$ are always distinct.

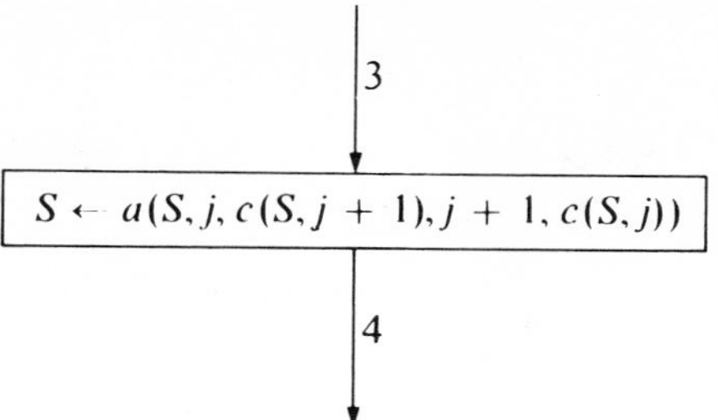

and the given assertion at arc 4 will be written as

$$\forall k[0 \leqq k \leqq j \supset c(S, k) \leqq c(S, j+1)]$$

Performing the substitution indicated by the statement, we obtain the following assertion at arc 3:

$$\forall k[0 \leqq k \leqq j \supset c(a(S, j, c(S, j+1), j+1, c(S, j)), k)$$
$$\leqq c(a(S, j, c(S, j+1), j+1, c(S, j)), j+1)]$$

By case analysis ($k = j$ and $0 \leqq k < j$), using axioms 1 and 2, this assertion can be simplified to

$$c(S, j+1) \leqq c(S, j) \land \forall k[0 \leqq k < j \supset c(S, k) \leqq c(S, j)]$$

3-2.2 Termination

In Sec. 3-1.2 we introduced a method for proving the termination of flowchart programs which was based on the use of well-founded sets. In practice, it is very convenient to use the following known result regarding well-founded sets:

If $(W, \prec)$ is a well-founded set, then so is $(W^n, {}_n\!\prec)$, where W^n is the set of all n-tuples of elements of W and ${}_n\!\prec$ is the regular lexicographic ordering on W^n; that is, $\langle a_1, \ldots, a_n \rangle {}_n\!\prec \langle b_1, \ldots, b_n \rangle$ iff $a_1 = b_1$, $a_2 = b_2, \ldots, a_{i-1} = b_{i-1}$, and $a_i \prec b_i$ for some i $(1 \leqq i \leqq n)$.

For example,

1. Since the set $(N, <)$ of natural numbers with the usual ordering $<$ is well-founded, so is the set $(N^2, {}_2\!<)$ of all pairs of natural numbers. Note that $\langle n_1, n_2 \rangle {}_2\!< \langle m_1, m_2 \rangle$ iff $n_1 < m_1$ or $(n_1 = m_1) \land (n_2 < m_2)$; for example, $\langle 1, 100 \rangle {}_2\!< \langle 2, 1 \rangle$.

2. Since the alphabet $\Sigma = \{A, B, \ldots, Z\}$ with the usual ordering $A \prec B \prec C \prec \cdots \prec Z$ is well-founded, so is the set $(\Sigma^3, {}_3\!\prec)$ of words of length 3. Note that ${}_3\!\prec$ gives the usual alphabetic order; for example, ANT ${}_3\!\prec$ BAT ${}_3\!\prec$ BEE.

We shall now illustrate the use of well-founded sets of the form $(W^n, \underset{n}{\prec})$ for proving the termination of three flowchart programs with arrays.

EXAMPLE 3-7

Let us prove the termination of the bubble-sorting program P_5 introduced in Example 3-6.

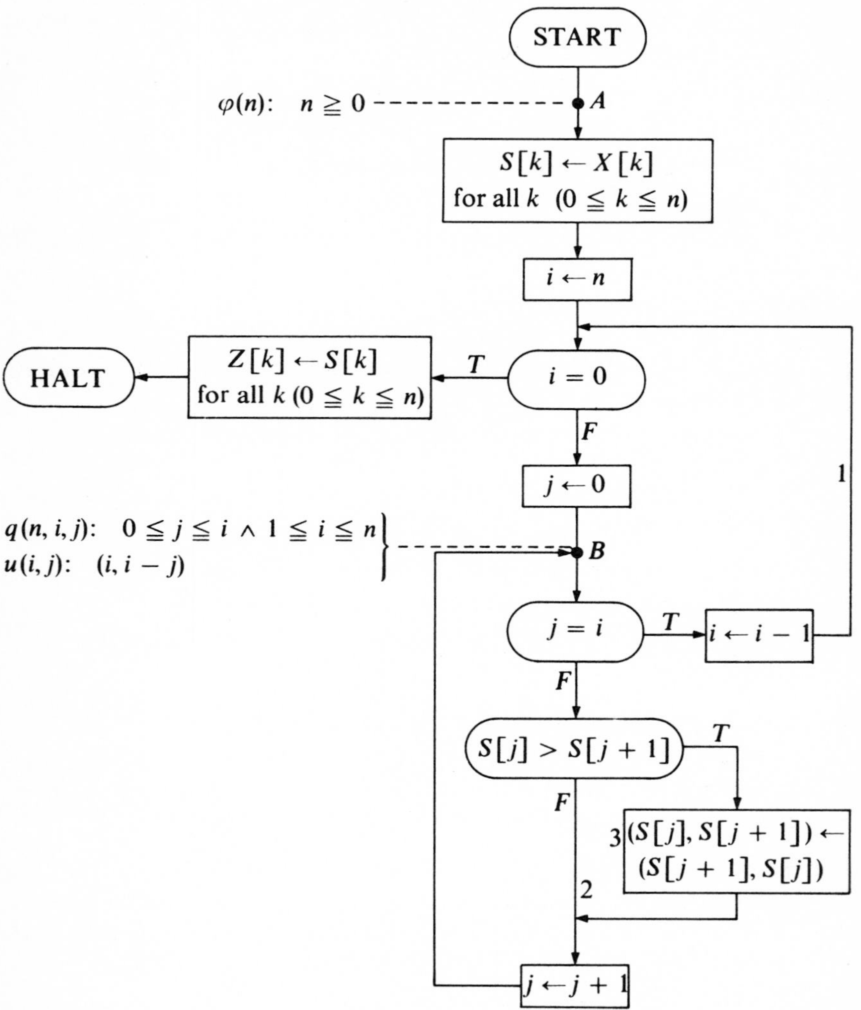

Figure 3-11 Program P_5 for bubble-sorting an array of real numbers (termination).

For this purpose we use the well-founded set $(N^2, {}_2<)$. We cut the three loops of the program at point B and attach to it the assertion

$$q(n, i, j): \quad 0 \leqq j \leqq i \wedge 1 \leqq i \leqq n$$

and the function

$$u(i, j): \quad (i, i - j)$$

(see Fig. 3-11). We proceed in the three steps. We must prove the following conditions for all integers i, j, and n:

Step 1. *q is a good assertion.*
For path A to B

$$[\varphi(n) \wedge n \neq 0] \supset q(n, n, 0)$$

For path B to B (via arc 1)

$$[q(n, i, j) \wedge j = i \wedge i - 1 \neq 0] \supset q(n, i - 1, 0)$$

For path B to B (via arc 2 or statement 3)

$$[q(n, i, j) \wedge j \neq i] \supset q(n, i, j + 1)$$

Step 2. *u is a good function.*

$$q(n, i, j) \supset u(i, j) \in N^2$$

that is,

$$[0 \leqq j \leqq i \wedge 1 \leqq i \leqq n] \supset [0 \leqq i \wedge 0 \leqq i - j]$$

Step 3. *The termination conditions hold.*
For path B to B (via arc 1)

$$[q(n, i, j) \wedge j = i \wedge i - 1 \neq 0] \supset [u(i, j) \succ_2 u(i - 1, 0)]$$

that is,

$$[0 \leqq j \leqq i \wedge 1 \leqq i \leqq n \wedge j = i \wedge i - 1 \neq 0] \supset [(i, i - j) \succ_2 (i - 1, i - 1)]$$

For path B to B (via arc 2 or statement 3)

$$[q(n, i, j) \wedge j \neq i] \supset [u(i, j) \succ_2 u(i, j + 1)]$$

that is,

$$[0 \leqq j \leqq i \wedge 1 \leqq i \leqq n \wedge j \neq i] \supset [(i, i - j) \succ_2 (i, i - (j + 1))]$$

The reader can verify easily that all these conditions are *true* for all integers i, j, and n. The first termination condition holds because the left component of u decreases from i to $i - 1$ and therefore we do not care what happens to the right component; the second termination condition holds because the right component of u decreases from $i - j$ to $i - (j + 1)$ while the left component remains unchanged. Therefore, it follows that the program terminates for every given real array $X[0], \ldots, X[n]$, where $n \geqq 0$. (Note that the proof that the program terminates depends only on the values of i, j, and n and has nothing to do with the given array X.)

□

EXAMPLE 3-8

Consider the program P_6 for evaluating the determinant $z = |X|$ of a two-dimensional real array X of order n ($n \geqq 1$) by gaussian elimination (Fig. 3-12).† For simplicity, we use X both as an input array and as a program array. We want to show that the program terminates for every positive integer n ($n \geqq 1$) and two-dimensional real array X of n^2 elements ($X[i, j]$ for $1 \leqq i, j \leqq n$). The program makes use of a real variable y and integer variables i, j, and k.

For this purpose we use the well-founded set $(N^3, \underset{3}{\prec})$. We cut the loops of the program at points B and C and attach to them the assertion q_B and q_C and the functions u_B and u_C, as indicated in Fig. 3-12. Again, we proceed in three steps. We must prove the following conditions for all integers i, j, k, and n:

Step 1. *q_B and q_C are good assertions.*
For path A to B

$$[\varphi(n) \wedge 1 \neq n] \supset q_B(n, 2, 1)$$

For path B to B

$$[q_B(n, i, k) \wedge k + 1 \neq n \wedge i = n + 1] \supset q_B(n, k + 2, k + 1)$$

For path B to C

$$[q_B(n, i, k) \wedge i \neq n + 1] \supset q_C(n, i, n, k)$$

For path C to B

$$[q_C(n, i, j, k) \wedge j = k] \supset q_B(n, i + 1, k)$$

For path C to C

$$[q_C(n, i, j, k) \wedge j \neq k] \supset q_C(n, i, j - 1, k)$$

Step 2. *u_B and u_C are good functions.*
For cutpoint B

$$q_B(n, i, k) \supset u_B(n, i, k) \in N^3$$

For cutpoint C

$$q_C(n, i, j, k) \supset u_C(n, i, j, k) \in N^3$$

†We consider the division operator over the real domain as a total function. (For example, interpret $r/0$ as $r/10^{-10}$ for every real r.)

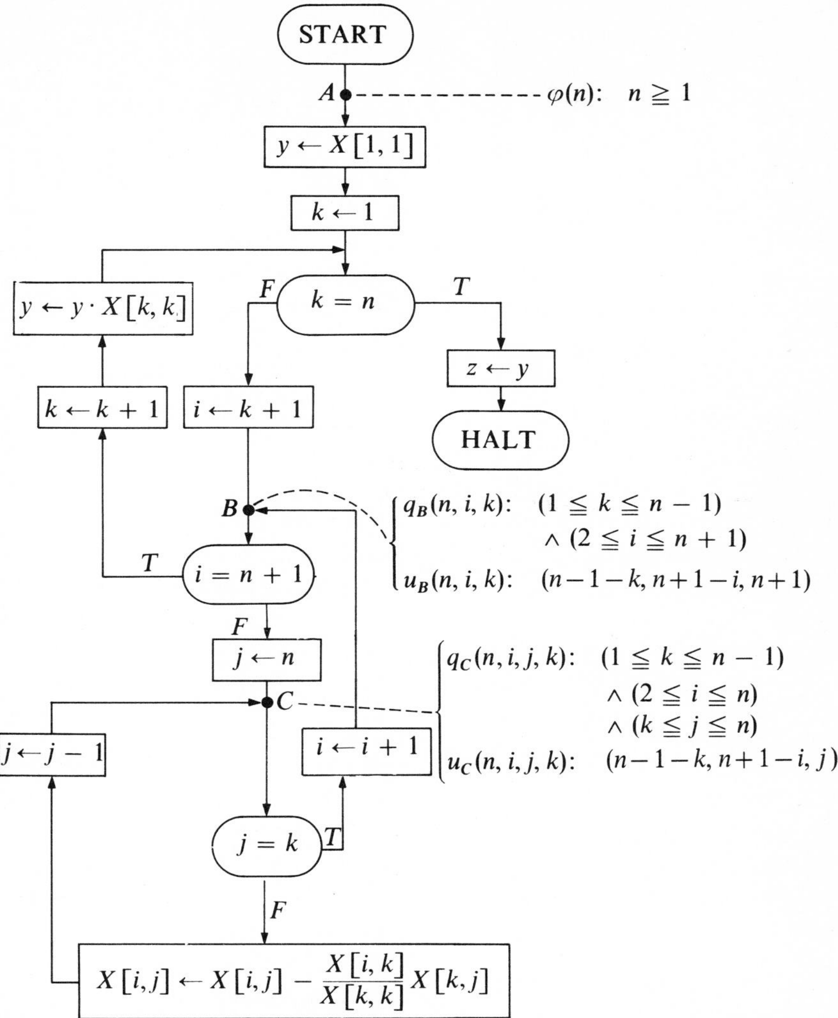

Figure 3-12 Program P_6 for evaluating the determinant $z = |X|$ (termination).

Step 3. *The termination conditions hold.*

For path B to B

$$[q_B(n, i, k) \wedge k + 1 \neq n \wedge i = n + 1] \supset$$
$$[u_B(n, i, k) \succ_3 u_B(n, k + 2, k + 1)]$$

For path B to C

$$[q_B(n, i, k) \wedge i \neq n + 1] \supset [u_B(n, i, k) \succ_3 u_C(n, i, n, k)]$$

For path C to B

$$[q_C(n, i, j, k) \wedge j = k] \supset [u_C(n, i, j, k) \underset{3}{\succ} u_B(n, i + 1, k)]$$

For path C to C

$$[q_C(n, i, j, k) \wedge j \neq k] \supset [u_C(n, i, j, k) \underset{3}{\succ} u_C(n, i, j - 1, k)]$$

The reader can show easily that all these conditions are *true* for all integers i, j, k, and n; therefore, it follows that the program terminates for every positive integer n and two-dimensional real array X.

□

EXAMPLE 3-9

The program P_7 (Fig. 3-13)† computes (without recursion) Ackermann's function $z = A(m, n)$ for a given pair of nonnegative integers (m, n); it uses the two integer arrays *place* and *value* to perform the computation. For a moment, ignore the initial ASSIGNMENT statement enclosed within dashed lines. A different version of Ackermann's function (mapping Σ^* into Σ^*) was discussed in Chap. 1, Sec. 1-4.2. Let us indicate again that this function is of special interest in recursive function theory because it grows faster than any primitive recursive function; for example, $A(0, 0) = 1$, $A(1, 1) = 3$, $A(2, 2) = 7$, $A(3, 3) = 61$, and $A(4, 4) = 2^{2^{2^{2^{16}}}} - 3$.

We would like to prove that the program terminates for any pair (m, n) of nonnegative integers. For this purpose we use the well-founded set $(N^{m+1}, \underset{m+1}{\succ})$, that is, the set of all $(m + 1)$-tuples of nonnegative integers ordered by the regular lexicographic ordering. (Note that the well-founded set used may differ from one computation to another, depending on the input value of m.) To simplify our proof, we assign the initial values

$$\left.\begin{array}{l} place[j] \leftarrow -1 \\ value[j] \leftarrow 1 \end{array}\right\} \quad \text{for all } j\ (1 \leqq j \leqq m + 1)$$

It can be verified easily that this assignment of values does not affect the performance of the program because the program does not make use of any initial values in *place*[j] or *value*[j].

There are five loops in the program, denoted by α, β, γ, δ, and ε. Since all the loops pass through point B, we choose B to be our cutpoint, and we attach to cutpoint B the predicate q and the function u, as indicated in

†This program is taken from H. G. Rice, "Recursion and Iteration," *C. ACM*, **8**(2): 114–115 (February 1965).

Fig. 3-13. Note that, according to the special initial values that were introduced, the value of the $(m + 1)$-tuple at the beginning of the program is $(n + 1, 2, 2, \ldots, 2)$. Note, also, that it can be shown easily that the values of all the variables in the program during computation are nonnegative except for the initial value of *place* $[j]$, which is -1.

The proof proceeds in three steps:

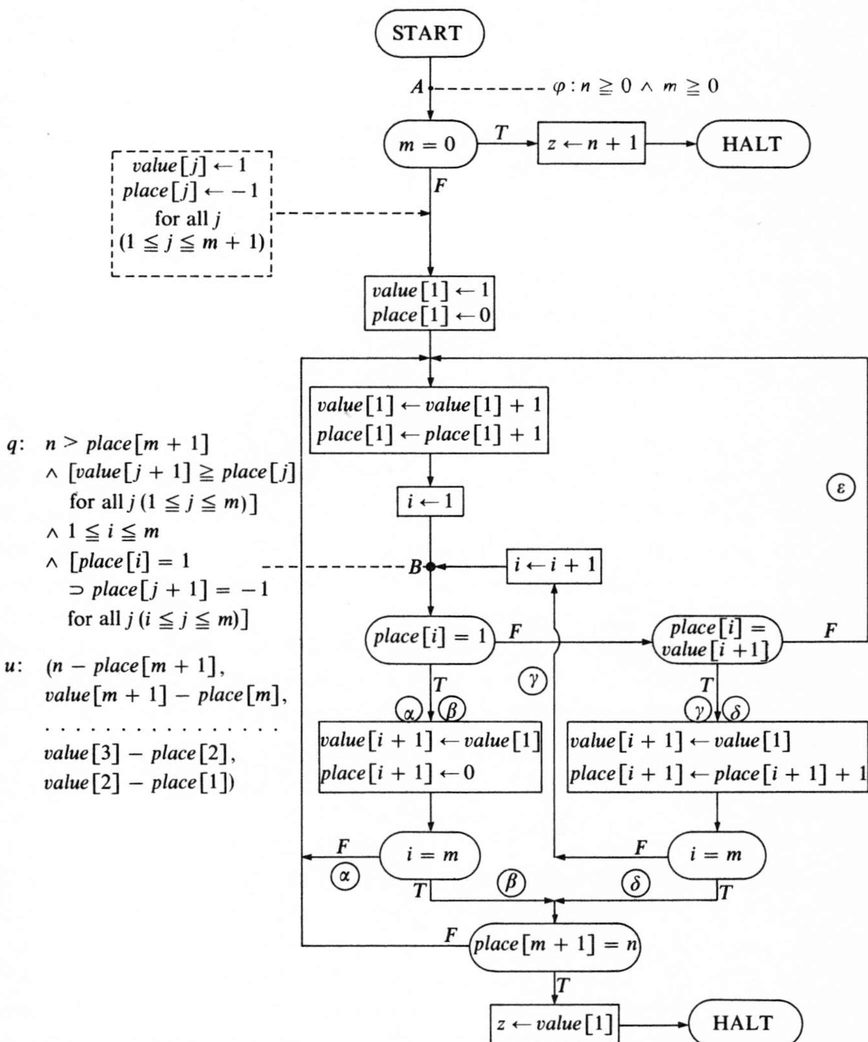

Figure 3-13 Program P_7 for computing Ackermann's function (termination).

Step 1. *q is a good predicate.* For this purpose six paths must be considered—A to B, and five paths from B to B ($\alpha, \beta, \gamma, \delta$, and ε)—and the corresponding six verification conditions must be verified. The details are left to the ambitious reader.

Step 2. *u is a good function.* This follows immediately because

$$[(n \geqq place[m+1]) \wedge (value[j+1] \geqq place[j] \text{ for all } j, 1 \leqq j \leqq m)]$$
$$\supset [(n - place[m+1] \geqq 0) \wedge (value[j+1] - place[j] \geqq 0 \text{ for all } j, 1 \leqq j \leqq m)]$$

Step 3. *The termination conditions hold.* The five paths from B to B ($\alpha, \beta, \gamma, \delta$, and ε) must be considered, and for each path we must show that the value of u decreases after going along that path.

(*a*) *Paths α and β*: Since $place[i] = 1$, it follows by q that $place[i+1] = -1$; thus, by $place[i+1] \leftarrow 0$, we have increased the value of $place[i+1]$. It is also given by q that $1 \leqq i \leqq m$. We distinguish between two cases. *If* $i = m$, then since $place[m+1]$ has been increased, $n - place[m+1]$ is decreased and the value of u is decreased in the lexicographic ordering, independent of how the other components are changed. *If* $1 \leqq i < m$, then since $place[i+1]$ has been increased while $value[i+2]$ is unchanged, $value[i+2] - place[i+1]$ is decreased. Thus, since all the components to the left of $value[i+2] - place[i+1]$ are unchanged, the value of u is decreased in the lexicographic ordering.

(*b*) *Paths γ and δ*: We use the same argument as in the previous paths because the value of $place[i+1]$ is increased by $place[i+1] \leftarrow place[i+1] + 1$.

(*c*) *Path ε*: The value of $place[1]$ is increased by $place[1] \leftarrow place[1] + 1$ while $value[2]$ is unchanged; hence, the value of $value[2] - place[1]$ is decreased. Thus, since all the other components are unchanged, the value of u is decreased in the lexicographic ordering.

□

3-3 ALGOL-LIKE PROGRAMS

So far we have discussed the class of flowchart programs (with or without arrays), and it is clear that the essential aspect in verifying such programs is the way loops are handled. In practice, programs are written in "linear forms," and loops are expressed in quite a variety of ways. In this section we shall discuss verification techniques for the class of while programs in which loops are expressed in terms of WHILE statements and no GO TO statements are allowed.

3-3.1 While Programs

First we introduce the class of while programs. A *while program* consists of a finite sequence of statements B_i separated by semicolons:

$$B_0; B_1; B_2; \ldots ; B_n$$

B_0 is the unique START statement

START
$\bar{y} \leftarrow f(\bar{x})$

and each B_i $(1 \leqq i \leqq n)$ is one of the following statements.

1. *ASSIGNMENT statement*:

$$\bar{y} \leftarrow g(\bar{x}, \bar{y})$$

2. *CONDITIONAL statement*:

$$\textbf{if } t(\bar{x}, \bar{y}) \textbf{ then } B \textbf{ else } B'$$

or

$$\textbf{if } t(\bar{x}, \bar{y}) \textbf{ do } B$$

where B and B' are any statements

3. *WHILE statement*:

$$\textbf{while } t(\bar{x}, \bar{y}) \textbf{ do } B$$

where B is any statement

4. *HALT statement*:

$$\bar{z} \leftarrow h(\bar{x}, \bar{y})$$

$$\text{HALT}$$

5. *COMPOUND statement*:

$$\textbf{begin } B'_1; B'_2; \ldots ; B'_k \textbf{ end}$$

where B'_j $(1 \leqq j \leqq k)$ are any statements

Given such a while program P and an input value $\bar{\xi} \in D_{\bar{x}}$ for the input vector $\bar{x}$, the program can be executed. Execution always begins at the START statement, initializing the value of $\bar{y}$ to be $f(\bar{\xi})$, and it then proceeds in the normal way following the sequence of statements. Whenever an ASSIGNMENT statement is reached, $\bar{y}$ is replaced by the current value of $g(\bar{x}, \bar{y})$. The execution of CONDITIONAL and WHILE statements can be described by the following pieces of flowcharts:

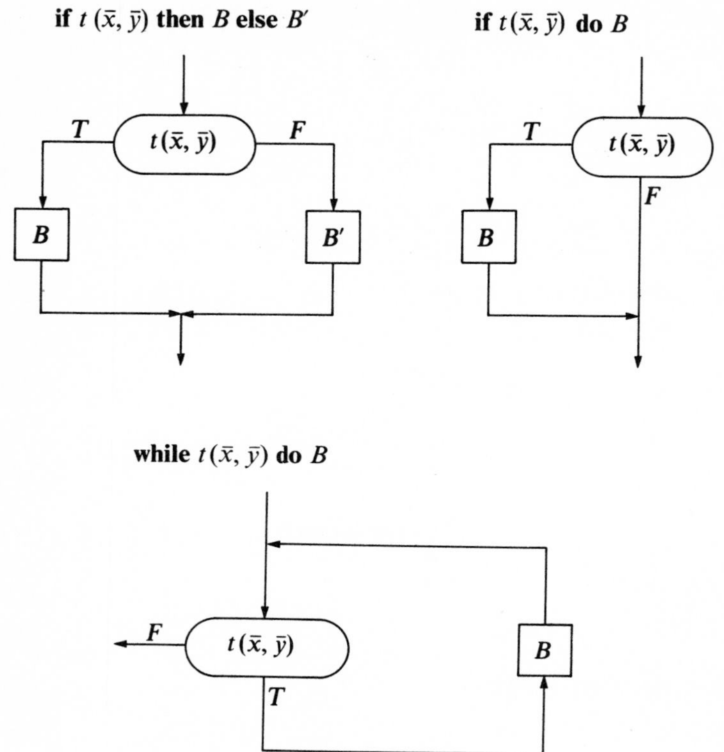

If execution terminates (i.e., reaches a HALT statement), $\bar{z}$ is assigned the current value $\bar{\zeta}$ of $h(\bar{x}, \bar{y})$ and we say that *$P(\bar{\xi})$ is defined and $P(\bar{\xi}) = \bar{\zeta}$*; otherwise, i.e., if the execution never terminates, we say that *$P(\bar{\xi})$ is undefined.*

EXAMPLE 3-10

1. The *square-root program P_1* of Example 3-1 can be expressed by

START
$(y_1, y_2, y_3) \leftarrow (0, 1, 1)$;
while $y_2 \leq x$ **do** $(y_1, y_2, y_3) \leftarrow (y_1 + 1, y_2 + y_3 + 2, y_3 + 2)$;
$z \leftarrow y_1$
HALT

2. The *gcd program* P_3 of Example 3-3 can be expressed by

START
$(y_1, y_2) \leftarrow (x_1, x_2)$;
while $y_1 \neq y_2$ **do if** $y_1 > y_2$ **then** $y_1 \leftarrow y_1 - y_2$ **else** $y_2 \leftarrow y_2 - y_1$;
$z \leftarrow y_1$
HALT

3. The *gcd program* P_4 of Example 3-5 can be expressed by

START
$(y_1, y_2, y_3) \leftarrow (x_1, x_2, 1)$;
while $even(y_1)$ **do**
  begin
  if $even(y_2)$ **do** $(y_2, y_3) \leftarrow (y_2/2, 2y_3)$;
  $y_1 \leftarrow y_1/2$
  end;
while $even(y_2) \vee y_1 \neq y_2$ **do**
  begin
  if $odd(y_2)$ **do** $(y_1, y_2) \leftarrow (y_2, |y_1 - y_2|)$;
  $y_2 \leftarrow y_2/2$
  end;
$z \leftarrow y_1 y_3$
HALT

□

3-3.2 Partial Correctness

In order to prove partial correctness of while programs, Hoare (1969) introduced the notation (called *inductive expression*)

$$\{p(\bar{x}, \bar{y})\}\ B\{q(\bar{x}, \bar{y})\}$$

where p, q are predicates and B is a program segment, meaning that if $p(\bar{x}, \bar{y})$ holds for the values of $\bar{x}$ and $\bar{y}$ immediately prior to execution of B and if execution of B terminates, then $q(\bar{x}, \bar{y})$ will hold for the values of $\bar{x}$ and $\bar{y}$ after execution of B.

Now, suppose we wish to prove the partial correctness of a given while program P with respect to an input predicate φ and an output predicate ψ; in other words, we would like to deduce

$$\{\varphi(\bar{x})\}\ P\{\psi(\bar{x}, \bar{z})\}$$

For this purpose we have *verification rules*, which consist of an *assignment axiom*, describing the transformation on program variables effected by ASSIGNMENT statements, and *inference rules*, by which expressions for small segments can be combined into one expression for a larger segment. To apply the rules, first we deduce inductive expressions of the form $\{p\}\, B\{q\}$ for each ASSIGNMENT statement B of the program, using the assignment axiom. Then we compose segments of the program, using the conditional rules, the while rule, the concatenation rule, and the consequence rules until we obtain the desired expression $\{\varphi\}\, P\{\psi\}$.

The inference rules will be described as

$$\frac{\alpha_1}{\beta} \quad \text{or} \quad \frac{\alpha_1 \text{ and } \alpha_2}{\beta}$$

where α_1 and α_2 are the *antecedents* (the conditions under which the rule is applicable) and β is the *consequent* (the inductive expression to be deduced). Each of the antecedents is either an inductive expression, which should have been previously established, or a logical expression, which should be proved separately as a *lemma*.

The verification rules are

1. *Assignment axiom*:

$$\{p(\bar{x}, g(\bar{x}, \bar{y}))\}\ \bar{y} \leftarrow g(\bar{x}, \bar{y})\ \{p(\bar{x}, \bar{y})\}$$

2. *Conditional rules*:

$$\frac{\{p \wedge t\}\, B_1\{q\} \qquad \text{and} \qquad \{p \wedge \sim t\}\, B_2\{q\}}{\{p\}\ \textbf{if}\ t\ \textbf{then}\ B_1\ \textbf{else}\ B_2\{q\}}$$

and

$$\frac{\{p \wedge t\}\, B\{q\} \qquad \text{and} \qquad (p \wedge \sim t) \supset q}{\{p\}\ \textbf{if}\ t\ \textbf{do}\ B\{q\}}$$

Note that $(p \wedge \sim t) \supset q$ is a logical expression. It should be considered as a closed wff with all free variables universally quantified. That is,

$$\forall\bar{x}\forall\bar{y}[(p(\bar{x}, \bar{y}) \wedge \sim t(\bar{x}, \bar{y})) \supset q(\bar{x}, \bar{y})]$$

3. *While rule*: The rule for WHILE statement is based on the simple fact that if the execution of the body B of the WHILE statement leaves the assertion p invariant (that is, p is always *true* on completion of B provided it is also *true* on initiation), p is *true* after any number of iterations

of B.

$$\frac{\{p \wedge t\}\, B\, \{p\}}{\{p\}\ \textbf{while}\ t\ \textbf{do}\ B\, \{p \wedge \sim t\}}$$

4. *Concatenation rule*:

$$\frac{\{p\}\, B_1\, \{q\} \quad \text{and} \quad \{q\}\, B_2\, \{r\}}{\{p\}\, B_1 ; B_2\, \{r\}}$$

5. *Consequence rules*:

$$\frac{p \supset q \quad \text{and} \quad \{q\}\, B\, \{r\}}{\{p\}\, B\, \{r\}} \quad \text{and} \quad \frac{\{p\}\, B\, \{q\} \quad \text{and} \quad q \supset r}{\{p\}\, B\, \{r\}}$$

Note again that $p \supset q$ and $q \supset r$ are logical expressions and should be proved separately as lemmas.

To summarize, we have the following theorem.

THEOREM 3-3 [VERIFICATION-RULES METHOD (Hoare)]. *Given a while program P, an input predicate $\varphi(\bar{x})$, and an output predicate $\psi(\bar{x}, \bar{z})$. If, by applying successively the verification rules just described, we can deduce*

$$\{\varphi(\bar{x})\}\, P\, \{\psi(\bar{x}, \bar{z})\}$$

then P is partially correct wrt φ and ψ.

Some of the verification rules can be combined to form new rules that are more convenient to use; such rules are usually called *derived verification rules*, four of which are the following.

1. *Assignment rule*: From the assignment axiom and the consequence rule, we obtain

$$\frac{p(\bar{x}, \bar{y}) \supset q(\bar{x}, g(\bar{x}, \bar{y}))}{\{p(\bar{x}, \bar{y})\}\ \bar{y} \leftarrow g(\bar{x}, \bar{y})\ \{q(\bar{x}, \bar{y})\}}$$

2. *Repeated assignment rule*: From the assignment and concatenation rules we obtain

$$\frac{p(\bar{x}, \bar{y}) \supset q(\bar{x}, g_n(\bar{x}, g_{n-1}(\bar{x}, \ldots, g_2(\bar{x}, g_1(\bar{x}, \bar{y}))\ \ldots)))}{\{p(\bar{x}, \bar{y})\}\ \bar{y} \leftarrow g_1(\bar{x}, \bar{y});\ \bar{y} \leftarrow g_2(\bar{x}, \bar{y});\ \ldots\ ;\bar{y} \leftarrow g_n(\bar{x}, \bar{y})\ \{q(\bar{x}, \bar{y})\}}$$

3. *Modified while rule*: From the while and consequence rules we obtain

$$\frac{\{p \wedge t\}\, B\, \{p\} \quad \text{and} \quad (p \wedge \sim t) \supset q}{\{p\}\ \textbf{while}\ t\ \textbf{do}\ B\, \{q\}}$$

4. *Modified concatenation rule*: From the concatenation and consequence rules we obtain

$$\frac{\{p\}\,B_1\,\{q\} \qquad \text{and} \qquad \{r\}\,B_2\,\{s\} \qquad \text{and} \qquad q \supset r}{\{p\}\,B_1;\,B_2\,\{s\}}$$

Note that for the START statement

$$\begin{array}{l}\text{START}\\ \bar{y} \leftarrow f(\bar{x})\end{array}$$

by the assignment axiom we obtain

$$\{p(\bar{x}, f(\bar{x}))\}\ \bar{y} \leftarrow f(\bar{x})\ \{p(\bar{x}, \bar{y})\}$$

and for the HALT statement

$$\begin{array}{l}\bar{z} \leftarrow h(\bar{x}, \bar{y})\\ \text{HALT}\end{array}$$

we obtain

$$\{p(\bar{x}, h(\bar{x}, \bar{y}))\}\ \bar{z} \leftarrow h(\bar{x}, \bar{y})\ \{p(\bar{x}, \bar{z})\}$$

EXAMPLE 3-11

Let us prove again the partial correctness of program P_1 of Example 3-1 wrt the input predicate $x \geqq 0$ and the output predicate $z^2 \leqq x < (z+1)^2$. The program is

START
$(y_1, y_2, y_3) \leftarrow (0, 1, 1)$;
while $y_2 \leqq x$ **do** $(y_1, y_2, y_3) \leftarrow (y_1 + 1, y_2 + y_3 + 2, y_3 + 2)$;
$z \leftarrow y_1$
HALT

In our proof we shall use the following assertion:

$$R(x, y_1, y_2, y_3)\text{:}\quad (y_1^2 \leqq x) \wedge (y_2 = (y_1 + 1)^2) \wedge (y_3 = 2y_1 + 1)$$

The proof can be stated formally as follows:

1. $x \geqq 0 \supset R(x, 0, 1, 1)$ — Lemma 1
2. $\{x \geqq 0\}$
   $(y_1, y_2, y_3) \leftarrow (0, 1, 1)$
   $\{R(x, y_1, y_2, y_3)\}$ — Assignment rule (line 1)
3. $R(x, y_1, y_2, y_3) \wedge y_2 \leqq x \supset R(x, y_1 + 1, y_2 + y_3 + 2, y_3 + 2)$
   Lemma 2

4. $\{R(x, y_1, y_2, y_3) \wedge y_2 \leqq x\}$
   $(y_1, y_2, y_3) \leftarrow (y_1 + 1, y_2 + y_3 + 2, y_3 + 2)$
   $\{R(x, y_1, y_2, y_3)\}$ Assignment rule (line 3)
5. $\{R(x, y_1, y_2, y_3)\}$
   while $y_2 \leqq x$ **do** $(y_1, y_2, y_3) \leftarrow (y_1 + 1, y_2 + y_3 + 2, y_3 + 2)$
   $\{R(x, y_1, y_2, y_3) \wedge y_2 > x\}$ While rule (line 4)
6. $\{x \geqq 0\}$
   $(y_1, y_2, y_3) \leftarrow (0, 1, 1);$
   while $y_2 \leqq x$ **do** $(y_1, y_2, y_3) \leftarrow (y_1 + 1, y_2 + y_3 + 2, y_3 + 2)$
   $\{R(x, y_1, y_2, y_3) \wedge y_2 > x\}$ Concatenation rule (lines 2 and 5)
7. $R(x, y_1, y_2, y_3) \wedge y_2 > x \supset y_1^2 \leqq x < (y_1 + 1)^2$ Lemma 3
8. $\{R(x, y_1, y_2, y_3) \wedge y_2 > x\}$
   $z \leftarrow y_1$
   $\{z^2 \leqq x < (z + 1)^2\}$ Assignment rule (line 7)
9. $\{x \geqq 0\}$
   $(y_1, y_2, y_3) \leftarrow (0, 1, 1);$
   while $y_2 \leqq x$ **do** $(y_1, y_2, y_3) \leftarrow (y_1 + 1, y_2 + y_3 + 2, y_3 + 2);$
   $z \leftarrow y_1$
   $\{z^2 \leqq x < (z + 1)^2\}$ Concatenation rule (lines 6 and 8).

Thus, since Lemmas 1, 2, and 3 are *true*, the proof implies that P_1 is partially correct wrt $x \geqq 0$ and $z^2 \leqq x < (z + 1)^2$.

As in the inductive-assertion method (described in Sec. 3-1.2), the choice of the assertion $R(x, y_1, y_2, y_3)$ is the most crucial part of the proof. In general, the process of finding such assertions requires a deep understanding of the program's performance. It is our hope that these assertions will be supplied by the programmer as comments in every program he writes; for example, if we enclose comments within braces, an appropriate way to express the square-root program would be

START
$\{x \geqq 0\}$
$(y_1, y_2, y_3) \leftarrow (0, 1, 1);$
while $y_2 \leqq x$ **do** $\{(y_1^2 \leqq x) \wedge (y_2 = (y_1 + 1)^2) \wedge (y_3 = 2y_1 + 1)\}$
$(y_1, y_2, y_3) \leftarrow (y_1 + 1, y_2 + y_3 + 2, y_3 + 2);$
$z \leftarrow y_1$
$\{z^2 \leqq x < (z + 1)^2\}$
HALT

□

EXAMPLE 3-12 [Hoare (1961), (1971)]

The purpose of the program P_8 in this example is to rearrange the elements of an array S of $n + 1$ ($n > 0$) real numbers $S[0], \ldots, S[n]$ and to find two integers i and j such that

$$0 \leqq j < i \leqq n$$

and

$$\forall a \forall b[(0 \leqq a < i \wedge j < b \leqq n) \supset S[a] \leqq S[b]]$$

In other words, we would like to rearrange the elements of S into two nonempty partitions such that those in the lower partition $S[0], \ldots, S[i-1]$ are less than or equal to those in the upper partition $S[j+1], \ldots, S[n]$, where $0 \leqq j < i \leqq n$. In the program, n is an input variable, r is a program variable, and i and j are output variables. For simplicity, S is used as an input and program array as well as an output array:

```
START
{n > 0}
r ← S[div(n, 2)]; (i, j) ← (0, n);
while i ≦ j do
      begin while S[i] < r do i ← i + 1;
            while r < S[j] do j ← j − 1;
            if i ≦ j then begin (S[i], S[j]) ← (S[j], S[i]);
                                (i, j) ← (i + 1, j − 1)
                          end

      end
{0 ≦ j < i ≦ n ∧ ∀a∀b[(0 ≦ a < i ∧ j < b ≦ n) ⊃ S[a] ≦ S[b]]}
HALT
```

The division into smaller and larger elements is done by selecting the element $r = S[div(n, 2)]$† and placing elements smaller than it in the lower partition and elements larger than it in the upper partition. Initially i is set to 0 and j to n, and i is stepped up for as long as $S[i] < r$ since these elements belong to the lower partition and may be left in position. When an $S[i]$ is encountered which is not less than r (and hence out of place), the stepping up of i is interrupted. The value of j is then stepped down while $r < S[j]$, and this stepping down is interrupted when an $S[j]$ not greater than r is met. The current $S[i]$ and $S[j]$ are now both in the wrong positions; the situation is corrected by exchanging them. If $i \leqq j$, i is stepped up by one and j is stepped down by one and the "i search" and "j search"

†Note that $div(n, 2)$ denotes the quotient of the integer division of n by 2.

are continued until the next out-of-place pair is found. If $j < i$, the lower and upper parts meet and the partition is complete.

We wish to prove that this program is partially correct; that is, when it terminates (if at all), (1) the elements of the array S are a permutation of the elements of the initial array† and (2) the following relation holds

$$(j < i) \wedge \forall a \forall b\, [(0 \leqq a < i \wedge j < b \leqq n) \supset S[a] \leqq S[b]]$$

We leave it as an exercise to the reader (Prob. 3-13) to prove that the stronger relation $0 \leqq j < i \leqq n$ holds. It is clear that relation 1 holds because $(S[i], S[j]) \leftarrow (S[j], S[i])$ is the only operation applied to S and it leaves the elements of the array S unchanged except for order.

Relation 2 can be verified in steps using the verification rules. Instead of giving a complete proof, we shall just describe the assertions that should be used in such a proof. The annotated program is

```
START
{n > 0}
r ← S[div(n, 2)]; (i, j) ← (0, n);
{0 ≦ i ∧ ∀a(0 ≦ a < i ⊃ S[a] ≦ r) ∧          (i invariant)
j ≦ n ∧ ∀b(j < b ≦ n ⊃ r ≦ S[b])}             (j invariant)
while i ≦ j do
     begin {i invariant ∧ j invariant}
          while S[i] < r do i ← i + 1;
          {i invariant ∧ j invariant ∧ r ≦ S[i]}
          while r < S[j] do j ← j − 1;
          {i invariant ∧ j invariant ∧ S[j] ≦ r ≦ S[i]}
          if i ≦ j then begin (S[i], S[j]) ← (S[j], S[i]);
                              (i, j) ← (i + 1, j − 1)
                        end
     end  {i invariant ∧ j invariant}

{j < i ∧ ∀a∀b[(0 ≦ a < i ∧ j < b ≦ n) ⊃ S[a] ≦ S[b]]}
HALT
```

□

3-3.3 Total Correctness

The verification-rules method (Theorem 3-3) enables us to prove only the partial correctness of while programs. In order to extend the method to prove the total correctness (including termination), Manna and Pnueli

†That is, $perm(S_{input}, S_{output}, 0, n)$ holds, where S_{input} indicates the value of S at the START statement and S_{output} indicates the value of S at the HALT statement.

(1974) have introduced the notation

$$\{p(\bar{x}, \bar{y})\}\ B\{q(\bar{x}, \bar{y}, \bar{y}')\}$$

meaning that for every $\bar{x}, \bar{y}$ if $p(\bar{x}, \bar{y})$ holds prior to execution of B, the execution of B terminates and (denoting the set of resulting values of $\bar{y}$ by $\bar{y}'$) $q(\bar{x}, \bar{y}, \bar{y}')$ holds. A new system of inference rules (called *termination rules*) can then be developed; they ensure that termination is hereditary from constituents to larger program segments. Using the termination rules, if we are able to deduce

$$\{\varphi(\bar{x})\}\ P\{\psi(\bar{x}, \bar{z})\}$$

then, in fact, we have shown that P is totally correct wrt φ and ψ.

First we present the straightforward termination rules dealing with assignments, conditionals, and concatenations, leaving the while rule (which is more complicated) to the end. For brevity, since $\bar{x}$ is never changed during the execution of the program, we express our predicates $p(\bar{x}, \bar{y})$ and $q(\bar{x}, \bar{y}, \bar{y}')$ as $p(\bar{y})$ and $q(\bar{y}, \bar{y}')$, respectively. The termination rules are

1. *Assignment rule*:

$$\frac{\forall \bar{y} \forall \bar{y}' [p(\bar{y}) \wedge \bar{y}' = f(\bar{y}) \supset q(\bar{y}, \bar{y}')]}{\{p(\bar{y})\}\ \bar{y} \leftarrow f(\bar{y})\ \{q(\bar{y}, \bar{y}')\}}$$

This rule is essentially an axiom because it uses only logical expressions to create an inductive expression.

2. *Conditional rules*:

$$\frac{\begin{array}{c}\{p(\bar{y}) \wedge t(\bar{y})\}\ B_1\ \{q(\bar{y}, \bar{y}')\} \\ \{p(\bar{y}) \wedge \sim t(\bar{y})\}\ B_2\ \{q(\bar{y}, \bar{y}')\}\end{array}}{\{p(\bar{y})\}\ \textbf{if}\ t(\bar{y})\ \textbf{then}\ B_1\ \textbf{else}\ B_2\ \{q(\bar{y}, \bar{y}')\}}$$

and

$$\frac{\begin{array}{c}\{p(\bar{y}) \wedge t(\bar{y})\}\ B\{q(\bar{y}, \bar{y}')\} \\ \forall \bar{y} \forall \bar{y}' [p(\bar{y}) \wedge \sim t(\bar{y}) \supset q(\bar{y}, \bar{y}')]\end{array}}{\{p(\bar{y})\}\ \textbf{if}\ t(\bar{y})\ \textbf{do}\ B\{q(\bar{y}, \bar{y}')\}}$$

3. *Concatenation rule*:

$$\{p_1(\bar{y})\}\ B_1\ \{q_1(\bar{y}, \bar{y}')\} \qquad (3\text{-}1)$$

$$\{p_2(\bar{y})\}\ B_2\ \{q_2(\bar{y}, \bar{y}')\} \qquad (3\text{-}2)$$

$$\forall \bar{y} \forall \bar{y}' [q_1(\bar{y}, \bar{y}') \supset p_2(\bar{y}')] \qquad (3\text{-}3)$$

$$\frac{\forall \bar{y} \forall \bar{y}' \forall \bar{y}'' [q_1(\bar{y}, \bar{y}') \wedge q_2(\bar{y}', \bar{y}'') \supset q(\bar{y}, \bar{y}'')]}{\{p_1(\bar{y})\}\ B_1; B_2\ \{q(\bar{y}, \bar{y}')\}} \qquad (3\text{-}4)$$

Condition (3-3) ensures that $\bar{y}'$ (the value of $\bar{y}$ after execution of B_1) satisfies p_2, the needed predicate for correct execution of B_2. Condition (3-4) characterizes $q(\bar{y}, \bar{y}'')$ as a transfer relation between $\bar{y}$ before execution and $\bar{y}''$ after execution of B_1; B_2. It requires an intermediate $\bar{y}'$, which appears temporarily after execution of B_1 and before execution of B_2.

4. *Consequence rules*:

$$\frac{\begin{array}{c}\{r(\bar{y})\}\, B\{q(\bar{y}, \bar{y}')\} \\ \forall \bar{y}[p(\bar{y}) \supset r(\bar{y})]\end{array}}{\{p(\bar{y})\}\, B\{q(\bar{y}, \bar{y}')\}}$$

and

$$\frac{\begin{array}{c}\{p(\bar{y})\}\, B\{s(\bar{y}, \bar{y}')\} \\ \forall \bar{y} \forall \bar{y}'[s(\bar{y}, \bar{y}') \supset q(\bar{y}, \bar{y}')]\end{array}}{\{p(\bar{y})\}\, B\{q(\bar{y}, \bar{y}')\}}$$

5. *Or rule*:

$$\frac{\begin{array}{c}\{p_1(\bar{y})\}\, B\{q(\bar{y}, \bar{y}')\} \\ \{p_2(\bar{y})\}\, B\{q(\bar{y}, \bar{y}')\}\end{array}}{\{p_1(\bar{y}) \vee p_2(\bar{y})\}\, B\{q(\bar{y}, \bar{y}')\}}$$

This rule creates the possibility for proof by case analysis.

6. *And rule*:

$$\frac{\begin{array}{c}\{p(\bar{y})\}\, B\{q_1(\bar{y}, \bar{y}')\} \\ \{p(\bar{y})\}\, B\{q_2(\bar{y}, \bar{y}')\}\end{array}}{\{p(\bar{y})\}\, B\{q_1(\bar{y}, \bar{y}') \wedge q_2(\bar{y}, \bar{y}')\}}$$

This rule enables us to generate incremental proofs.

7. *While rule*:

$$\frac{\begin{array}{cr}\{p(\bar{y}) \wedge t(\bar{y})\}\, B\{q(\bar{y}, \bar{y}') \wedge [u(\bar{y}) \succ u(\bar{y}')]\} & (3\text{–}5) \\ \forall \bar{y} \forall \bar{y}'[q(\bar{y}, \bar{y}') \wedge t(\bar{y}') \supset p(\bar{y}')] & (3\text{–}6) \\ \forall \bar{y} \forall \bar{y}' \forall \bar{y}''[q(\bar{y}, \bar{y}') \wedge q(\bar{y}', \bar{y}'') \supset q(\bar{y}, \bar{y}'')] & (3\text{–}7) \\ \forall \bar{y}[p(\bar{y}) \wedge \sim t(\bar{y}) \supset q(\bar{y}, \bar{y})] & (3\text{–}8)\end{array}}{\{p(\bar{y})\}\ \textbf{while}\ t(\bar{y})\ \textbf{do}\ B\{q(\bar{y}, \bar{y}') \wedge \sim t(\bar{y}')\}}$$

where $(W, \prec)$ is a well-founded set and u is a partial function mapping $D_{\bar{x}} \times D_{\bar{y}}$ into W.

Rule 7 (the while rule), which is seemingly complicated, is devised to overcome several difficulties caused by the need to prove termination. Termination of a looping WHILE statement is essentially ensured here by the well-founded-sets method (Theorem 3-2). Condition (3-5) requires establishing a well-founded set $(W, \prec)$ and a partial function u mapping $D_{\bar{x}} \times D_{\bar{y}}$ into W. If we were able to prove that after each execution of B, $u(\bar{y}) \succ u(\bar{y}')$ [where by writing this inequality we also mean that $u(\bar{y})$ and $u(\bar{y}')$ are both defined], then clearly B cannot be repeatedly executed an infinite number of times.

Let us review conditions (3-5) to (3-8) of the while rule:

1. Condition (3-5) ensures that if $t(\bar{y})$ holds, then the execution of B will establish $q(\bar{y}, \bar{y}')$ and a decrease in the value of $u(\bar{y})$, knowing that B will be executed at least once.

2. Condition (3-6) requires that having executed B at least once and having $t(\bar{y}')$ correct at this instance logically establishes $p(\bar{y}')$. $p(\bar{y})$ is exactly the predicate needed to use (3-5) once more and thus propagate the validity of q for all subsequent executions.

3. Condition (3-7) ensures that $q(\bar{y}, \bar{y}')$ bridges across, not only one execution of B, but any number of executions of B greater than one.

4. Condition (3-8) deals with the case of the initially vacant WHILE statement, where B was not executed even once. Here, also, we wish to establish the final outcome $q(\bar{y}, \bar{y}')$. [Note that $\bar{y}' = \bar{y}$ in this case.]

To summarize, we have the following theorem.

THEOREM 3-4 [TERMINATION-RULES METHOD (Manna and Pnueli)]. *Given a while program P, an input predicate $\varphi(\bar{x})$, and an output predicate $\psi(\bar{x}, \bar{z})$. If, by applying successively the termination rules, we can deduce*

$$\{\varphi(\bar{x})\}\ P\{\psi(\bar{x}, \bar{z})\}$$

then P is totally correct wrt φ and ψ.

Since a program P terminates over φ if and only if it is totally correct wrt φ and T [that is, $\psi(\bar{x}, \bar{z})$ is always *true*], we obtain the following corollary.

COROLLARY. *Given a while program P and an input predicate $\varphi(\bar{x})$. If, by applying successively the termination rules, we can deduce*

$$\{\varphi(\bar{x})\}\ P\{T\}$$

then P terminates over φ.

EXAMPLE 3-13

The following while program P_9 over the integers computes $z = gcd(x_1, x_2)$ for every pair of positive integers x_1 and x_2; that is, z is the greatest common divisor of x_1 and x_2 (see Example 3-3). In order to be able to refer to the program segments, we have labeled them with letters on the right.

```
START
(y1, y2) ← (x1, x2);                                    ⎤
while y1 ≠ y2 do                                   ⎤    ⎥
        begin                                  ⎤   ⎥    ⎥
        while y1 > y2 do               ⎤       ⎥   ⎥    ⎥
                  y1 ← y1 − y2 ;] a    ⎦ b     ⎥   ⎥    ⎥
        while y2 > y1 do               ⎤       e   f    g
                  y2 ← y2 − y1;] c     ⎦ d     ⎥   ⎥    ⎥
        end                                    ⎦   ⎦    ⎥
z ← y1                                                  ⎦
HALT
```

We would like to prove that the program P_9 is totally correct wrt

$$\varphi(x_1, x_2): \quad x_1 > 0 \wedge x_2 > 0$$

and

$$\psi(x_1, x_2, z): \quad z = gcd(x_1, x_2)$$

Because of the amount of detail involved, we shall concentrate on proving termination, with only general indication of the modifications required to add correctness. The well-founded set we shall use for proving termination is the domain of nonnegative integers with the ordinary $<$ relation. We shall use the same termination function $u(y_1, y_2)$: $y_1 + y_2$ for both the two inner WHILE loops and the outer WHILE loop. Our proof of termination distinguishes between two cases, according to whether $y_1 > y_2$ or $y_1 < y_2$ upon entrance to the compound statement e: In the first case, statement a is executed at least once ($y_1 + y_2$ decreasing) while statement c is executed zero or more times ($y_1 + y_2$ remaining the same or decreasing); in the second case, statement a is never executed ($y_1 + y_2$ remaining the same) while statement c is executed at least once ($y_1 + y_2$ decreasing). Therefore in our proof we shall analyze these two cases separately: Steps $a1$ to $e1$ for the case $y_1 > y_2$ and Steps $a2$ to $e2$ for the case $y_1 < y_2$. Their results will then be combined using the or rule (Step e).

In all the predicates of the following inductive expressions, the conjunction $y_1 > 0 \wedge y_2 > 0$ is omitted. We also use the consequence rules within while rule derivations without explicit indication.

$a1$. *Assignment rule*: Since $[y_1 > y_2 \wedge y_1' = y_1 - y_2 \wedge y_2' = y_2] \supset y_1 + y_2 > y_1' + y_2'$, by the assignment rule, we obtain

$$\{y_1 > y_2\}\, a\, \{y_1 + y_2 > y_1' + y_2'\}$$

$b1$. *While rule*: We use the while rule with the following predicates: $p(\bar{y})$ and $t(\bar{y})$ are $y_1 > y_2$; $u(\bar{y}) \succ u(\bar{y}')$ and $q(\bar{y}, \bar{y}')$ are $y_1 + y_2 > y_1' + y_2'$. Condition (3-5) of the while rule is justified by $a1$. We obtain

$$\{y_1 > y_2\}\, b\, \{y_1 + y_2 > y_1' + y_2'\}$$

$c1$. *Assignment rule*: Since $[y_2 > y_1 \wedge y_1' = y_1 \wedge y_2' = y_2 - y_1] \supset y_1 + y_2 > y_1' + y_2'$, by the assignment rule, we obtain

$$\{y_2 > y_1\}\, c\, \{y_1 + y_2 > y_1' + y_2'\}$$

$d1$. *While rule*: Assume the following substitution: $p(\bar{y})$ is T; $t(\bar{y})$ is $y_2 > y_1$; $u(\bar{y}) \succ u(\bar{y}')$ is $y_1 + y_2 > y_1' + y_2'$; and $q(\bar{y}, \bar{y}')$ is $y_1 + y_2 \geqq y_1' + y_2'$. Condition (3-5) of the while rule is justified by $c1$. We obtain

$$\{T\}\, d\, \{y_1 + y_2 \geqq y_1' + y_2'\}$$

$e1$. *Concatenation rule*: Combining $b1$ and $d1$ and using $[y_1 + y_2 > y_1' + y_2' \wedge y_1' + y_2' \geqq y_1'' + y_2''] \supset y_1 + y_2 > y_1'' + y_2''$, we obtain

$$\{y_1 > y_2\}\, e\, \{y_1 + y_2 > y_1' + y_2'\}$$

$a2$. *Assignment rule*: Since $[F \wedge y_1' = y_1 - y_2 \wedge y_2' = y_2] \supset F$, we have

$$\{F\}\, a\, \{F\}$$

$b2$. *While rule*: Let $t(\bar{y})$ be $y_1 > y_2$, $p(\bar{y})$ be $y_1 < y_2$, $u(\bar{y}) \succ u(\bar{y}')$ be $y_1 + y_2 > y_1' + y_2'$ and $q(\bar{y}, \bar{y}')$ be $y_1' < y_2' \wedge y_1 + y_2 = y_1' + y_2'$. By using $a2$, we obtain

$$\{y_1 < y_2\}\, b\, \{y_1' < y_2' \wedge y_1 + y_2 = y_1' + y_2'\}$$

$c2$. *Assignment rule*: By the assignment rule, we obtain

$$\{y_1 < y_2\}\, c\, \{y_1 + y_2 > y_1' + y_2'\}$$

$d2$. *While rule*: Let $p(\bar{y})$ and $t(\bar{y})$ be $y_2 > y_1$; $u(\bar{y}) \succ u(\bar{y}')$ and $q(\bar{y}, \bar{y}')$ be $y_1 + y_2 > y_1' + y_2'$. By using $c2$ we obtain

$$\{y_1 < y_2\}\, d\, \{y_1 + y_2 > y_1' + y_2'\}$$

$e2$. *Concatenation rule*: By combining $b2$ and $d2$, we obtain

$$\{y_1 < y_2\}\, e\, \{y_1 + y_2 > y_1' + y_2'\}$$

e. Or rule: Combining *e*1 and *e*2, we obtain

$$\{y_1 \neq y_2\}\, e\, \{y_1 + y_2 > y_1' + y_2'\}$$

f. While rule: Let $t(\bar{y})$ be $y_1 \neq y_2$, $p(\bar{y})$ be T, $u(\bar{y}) \succ u(\bar{y}')$ be $y_1 + y_2 > y_1' + y_2'$, and $q(\bar{y}, \bar{y}')$ be $y_1' = y_2'$. By using *e* for condition (3-5), we obtain [introducing the omitted conjunction $y_1 > 0 \wedge y_2 > 0$]

$$\{y_1 > 0 \wedge y_2 > 0\}\, f\, \{y_1' = y_2'\}$$

g. Assignment and concatenation rules: From *f* we obtain

$$\{x_1 > 0 \wedge x_2 > 0\}\, P_9\, \{y_1' = y_2'\}$$

Thus we have shown termination with the additional information that on exit $y_1' = y_2'$.

Trying to extend this result to prove correctness, we encounter the notion of *incremental proofs*: That is, having proved some properties of the program, including termination, how do we prove additional properties without repeating the whole proof process? For this particular example, we can use the following argument: Assume that instead of using the predicate $q(\bar{y}, \bar{y}')$ in any of the expressions, we used the predicate

$$q(\bar{y}, \bar{y}') \wedge gcd(y_1, y_2) = gcd(y_1', y_2')$$

It is not difficult to ascertain that all the steps remain valid, and consequently for the segment *f* we are able to prove

$$\{y_1 > 0 \wedge y_2 > 0\}\, f\, \{y_1' = y_2' \wedge gcd(y_1, y_2) = gcd(y_1', y_2')\}$$

that is,

$$\{y_1 > 0 \wedge y_2 > 0\}\, f\, \{y_1' = gcd(y_1, y_2)\}$$

Thus, for the complete program, we obtain

$$\{x_1 > 0 \wedge x_2 > 0\}\, P_9\, \{z = gcd(x_1, x_2)\}$$

□

Generalizing the previous argument, we obtain the following metatheorem.

METATHEOREM. *Suppose that the inductive expression*

$$\alpha\colon\quad \{\varphi(\bar{x})\}\, P\, \{\psi(\bar{x}, \bar{z})\}$$

had been deduced. Let $S(\bar{y}, \bar{y}')$ *be a reflexive and transitive relation; that is,*

$$\forall \bar{y}[S(\bar{y}, \bar{y})] \qquad \textit{and} \qquad \forall \bar{y}\forall \bar{y}'\forall \bar{y}''[S(\bar{y}, \bar{y}') \wedge S(\bar{y}', \bar{y}'') \supset S(\bar{y}, \bar{y}'')]$$

Suppose, also, that for any inductive expression of the form

$$\{p(\bar{y})\}\ \bar{y} \leftarrow g(\bar{x}, \bar{y})\ \{q(\bar{y}, \bar{y}')\}$$

used in the deduction of α, *it is possible to deduce*

$$\{p(\bar{y})\}\ \bar{y} \leftarrow g(\bar{x}, \bar{y})\ \{q(\bar{y}, \bar{y}') \wedge S(\bar{y}, \bar{y}')\}$$

Then the inductive expression

$$\alpha^{+}:\quad \{\varphi(\bar{x})\}\ P\ \{\psi(\bar{x}, \bar{z}) \wedge S(\bar{x}, \bar{z})\}$$

is also true for the complete program.

Thus, it is sufficient to treat ASSIGNMENT statements in order to extend the inductive expressions. In Example 3-13 above, the only ASSIGNMENT statements to be considered are

$$y_1 \leftarrow y_1 - y_2 \qquad \text{and} \qquad y_2 \leftarrow y_2 - y_1$$

which obviously preserve the *gcd* function. In order to prove the metatheorem, all the nonassignment termination rules must be inspected and it must be verified that if S was preserved in the constituents, it will be preserved in the bigger segment.

Bibliographic Remarks

The motivation for developing verification methods has existed since shortly after people began to write programs for computers. Some indication of the inductive-assertions method was mentioned as early as 1947 by Goldstine and von Neumann (1947) and later by Turing (1950) and Naur (1966). However, Floyd (1967) was the first to suggest explicitly the inductive-assertions method (Theorem 3-1) as a powerful verification technique. The method was formalized by Manna (1969), and it is briefly described also in Knuth (1968 pp. 14–20). Our exposition of the integer division example in Sec. 3-1 is based on King's IFIP paper (1971). Manna and Pnueli (1970), Ashcroft (1970), Burstall (1970), and others extended the method to higher-level programs.

The idea of using properties of well-founded sets for proving termination of programs (Theorem 3-2) was suggested by Floyd (1967) and was investigated further by Manna (1970).

The verification-rules method for proving the partial correctness of while programs (Theorem 3-3) is due to Hoare (1969), (1970). [See also Clint and Hoare (1972).] The termination-rules method for proving the total correctness of while programs (Theorem 3-4) was suggested by Manna and Pnueli (1974).

The practical aspects of the inductive-assertions method have been substantially pursued in three main directions:

1. *Machine implementation*: King (1969) was the first to use the technique for constructing an *automatic verification system*; other attempts in this direction include those of Good (1970), Gerhard (1972), Deutsch (1973), Waldinger and Levitt (1973), and Igarashi, London, and Luckham (1973). Some implementation techniques are discussed in Cooper (1971).

2. *Hand simulation*: Substantial effort has been devoted toward applying the inductive-assertions method to prove manually the correctness of "real" programs [see London (1970a)]. A typical example is the proof by London (1970b) of the correctness of Floyd's TREESORT3 algorithm.

3. *Heuristic approach*: Various heuristic techniques have been developed [Wegbreit (1973), Katz and Manna (1973), and others] to obtain automatically an appropriate set of inductive assertions.

One important topic has not been discussed in this chapter: *program synthesis*. This is the theory for constructing programs that are guaranteed to be correct and therefore do not require debugging or verification. There are three major approaches to the problem:

1. *Constructive approach*: The desired program is constructed step by step in such a way that it is guaranteed that each step preserves the desired properties of the program and therefore the final program must be correct. Several works along this line are those of Dijkstra (1968), Naur (1969), Wirth (1971), and Floyd (1971). This approach is also discussed in the excellent books by Dahl, Dijkstra, and Hoare (1972), and Wirth (1973).

2. *Theorem-proving approach*: To construct a program satisfying certain specifications, a theorem induced by those specifications is proved and the desired program is extracted from the proof. Early work in this direction by Green (1969) and Waldinger (1969) [see also Waldinger and Lee (1969)] considered essentially only loopfree programs. The possibility of constructing programs with loops and recursion is discussed by Manna and Waldinger (1971).

3. *Evolutionary approach*: A program is initially written which satisfies only part of the given specifications. The program is then debugged and modified in steps to satisfy more and more specifications, until we finally get the desired program which satisfies all the given specifications. The first attempt in this direction is due to Sussman (1973).

REFERENCES

Ashcroft, E. A. (1970): "Mathematical Logic Applied to the Semantics of Computer Programs," Ph.D. thesis, Imperial College, London.

Burstall, R. M. (1970): "Formal Description of Program Structure and Semantics of First-order Logic," in B. Meltzer and D. Michie (eds.), *Machine Intelligence 5,* pp. 79–98, Edinburgh University Press, Edinburgh.

Clint, M., and C. A. Hoare (1972): "Program Proving: Jumps and Functions," *Acta Inf.,* **1** (3): 214–224.

Cooper, D. C. (1971): "Programs for Mechanical Program Verification," in B. Meltzer and D. Michie (eds.), *Machine Intelligence 6,* pp. 43–59, Edinburgh University Press, Edinburgh.

Dahl, O. J., E. W. Dijkstra, and C. A. R. Hoare (1972): *Structured Programming*, Academic Press, New York.

Deutsch, L. P. (1973): "An Interactive Program Verifier," Ph.D. thesis, University of California, Berkeley, Cal. (May).

Dijkstra, E. W. (1968): "A Constructive Approach to the Problem of Program Correctness," *BIT,* **8:** 174–186.

Floyd, R. W. (1967): "Assigning Meanings to Programs," Proc. Symp. Appl. Math., **19;** in J. T. Schwartz (ed.), *Mathematical Aspects of Computer Science,* pp. 19–32, American Mathematical Society, Providence, R.I.

——— (1971): "Toward Interactive Design of Correct Programs," *Proc. IFIP,* pp. 7–10.

Gerhard, S. (1972): "Verification of APL Programs," Ph.D. Thesis, Carnegie-Mellon University, Pittsburgh, Pa. (November).

Goldstine, H. H., and J. von Neumann (1947): "Planning and Coding Problems for an Electronic Computer Instrument," in A. H. Traub (ed.), *Collected Works of John Von Neumann,* vol. 5, pp. 80–235, Pergamon Press, New York (1963).

Good, D. I. (1970): "Toward a Man-Machine System for Proving Program Correctness," Ph.D. thesis, Computer Sciences Department, University of Wisconsin, Madison (June).

Green, C. (1969): "The Application of Theorem Proving to Question-Answering Systems," Ph.D. thesis, Computer Science Department, Stanford University, Stanford, Cal.

Hoare, C. A. R. (1961): "Algorithm 65, Find," *C. ACM,* **4** (7): 321 (July).

——— (1969): "An Axiomatic Basis of Computer Programming," C.ACM, **12** (10): 576–580, 583 (October).

——— (1970): "Procedures and Parameters: An Axiomatic Approach," in E. Engeler (ed.), *Lecture Notes in Mathematics 188,* pp. 102–116, Springer-Verlag, Berlin.

——— (1971): "Proof of a Program: FIND," *C. ACM,* **14** (1): 39–45 (January)

Igarashi, S., R. L. London, and D. C. Luckham (1973): "Automatic Program Verification I: Logical Basis and its Implementation," Computer Science Report 365, Stanford University, Stanford, California (May).

Kaplan, D. (1968): "Some Completeness Results in the Mathematical Theory of Computation," *J. ACM,* **15**(1): 124–134 (January).

Katz, S. M., and Z. Manna (1973): "A Heuristic Approach to Program Verification," Third International Joint Conference on Artificial Intelligence, Stanford, Cal., pp. 500–512 (August).

King, J. C. (1969): "A Program Verifier," Ph.D. thesis, Carnegie-Mellon University, Pittsburgh, Pa.

——— (1971): "A Program Verifier," *Proc. IFIP,* pp. 234–249.

Knuth, D. E. (1968): *The Art of Computer Programming,* vol. 1, Addison-Wesley Publishing Company, Inc., Reading, Mass.

London, R. L. (1970a): "Proving Programs Correct: Some Techniques and Examples," *BIT,* **10:** 168–182.

——— (1970b): "Proof of Algorithms: A New Kind of Certification," *C. ACM,* **13**(6): 371–373 (June).

Manna, Z. (1969): "The Correctness of Programs," *J. CSS,* **3**(2): 119–127 (May).

——— (1970): "Termination of Programs Represented as Interpreted Graphs," *Proc. Spring J. Comput. Conf.,* pp. 83–89.

——— and Pnueli, A. (1970): "Formalization of Properties of Functional Programs," *J. ACM,* **17**(3): 555–569 (July).

——— and ——— (1974): "Axiomatic Approach to Total Correctness," *Acta Informatica* (to appear).

——— and Waldinger, R. J. (1971): "Towards Automatic Program Synthesis," *C. ACM,* **14**(3): 151–165 (March).

McCarthy, J. (1962): "Towards a Mathematical Science of Computation," in C. M. Popplewell (ed.), *Information Processing, Proceedings of IFIP Congress 62,* pp. 21–28, North-Holland Publishing Company, Amsterdam.

Naur, P. (1966): "Proof of Algorithms by General Snapshots," *BIT,* **6:** 310–316.

——— (1969): "Programming by Action Clusters," *BIT,* **9:** 250–258.

Sussman, G. J. (1973): "A Computational Model of Skill Acquisition," Ph.D. Thesis, M.I.T., Cambridge, Mass. (August).

Turing, A. (1950): "Checking a Large Routine," in *Rep. Conf. High Speed Automatic Calculating Machines,* Institute of Computer Science, McLennan Lab., University of Toronto, Toronto, Ont., Can. (January)

Waldinger, R. J. (1969): "Constructing Programs Automatically Using Theorem Proving," Ph.D. thesis, Carnegie-Mellon University, Pittsburgh, Pa. (May).

——— and Lee, R. C. T. (1969): "PROW: A Step Toward Automatic Program Writing," *Proc. Int. J. Conf. Artif. Intell.,* Washington, D.C. (May).

——— and Levitt, K. N. (1973): "Reasoning About Programs," Proceedings of the Symposium on Principles of Programming Languages, Boston (October).

Wegbreit, B. (1973): "Heuristic Methods for Mechanically Deriving Inductive Assertions," Third International Joint Conference on Artificial Intelligence, Stanford, Cal., pp. 524–536 (August).

Wirth, N. (1971): "Program Development by Stepwise Refinement," *C. ACM,* **14**(4): 221–227 (April).

——— (1973): *Systematic Programming: An Introduction,* Prentice Hall.

PROBLEMS

Prob. 3-1 Consider the flowchart program (Fig. 3-14) over the integers for computing $z = x!$. Prove that it is totally correct wrt $\varphi(x)$: $x \geqq 0$ and $\psi(x, z)$: $z = x!$.

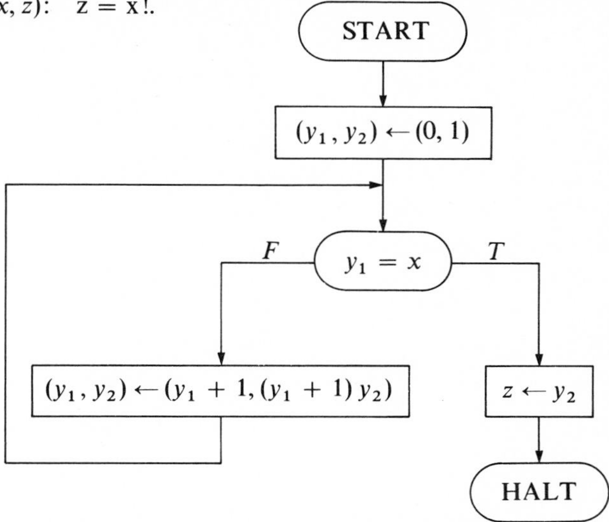

Figure 3-14 Flowchart program for computing $z = x!$.

Prob. 3-2 Consider the flowchart program (Fig. 3-15) over the natural numbers which computes $z_1 = div(x_1, x_2)$ and $z_2 = rem(x_1, x_2)$. Prove that it is totally correct wrt $\varphi(\bar{x})$: $x_1 > 0 \wedge x_2 > 0$ and $\psi(\bar{x}, \bar{z})$: $0 \leqq z_2 < x_2 \wedge x_1 = z_1 x_2 + z_2$.

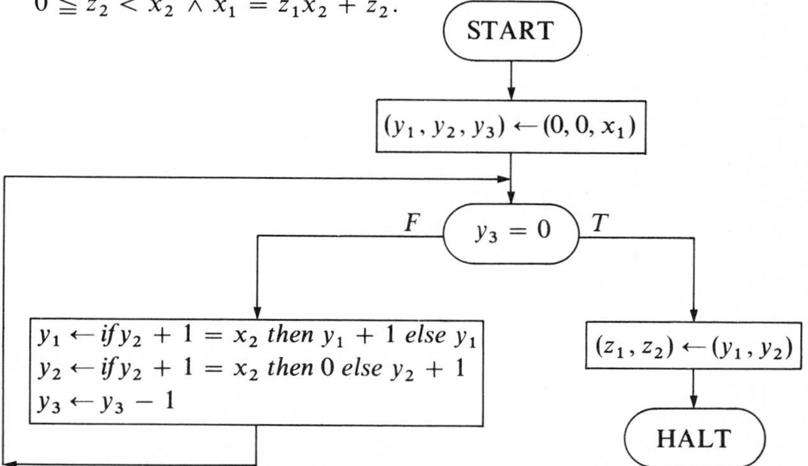

Figure 3-15 Flowchart program for performing integer division.

Prob. 3-3 Consider the flowchart program (Fig. 3-16) over the natural numbers for computing the greatest common divisor of x_1 and x_2. Prove that it is totally correct wrt $\varphi(x_1, x_2)$: $x_1 > 0 \wedge x_2 > 0$ and $\psi(x_1, x_2, z)$: $z = gcd(x_1, x_2)$.

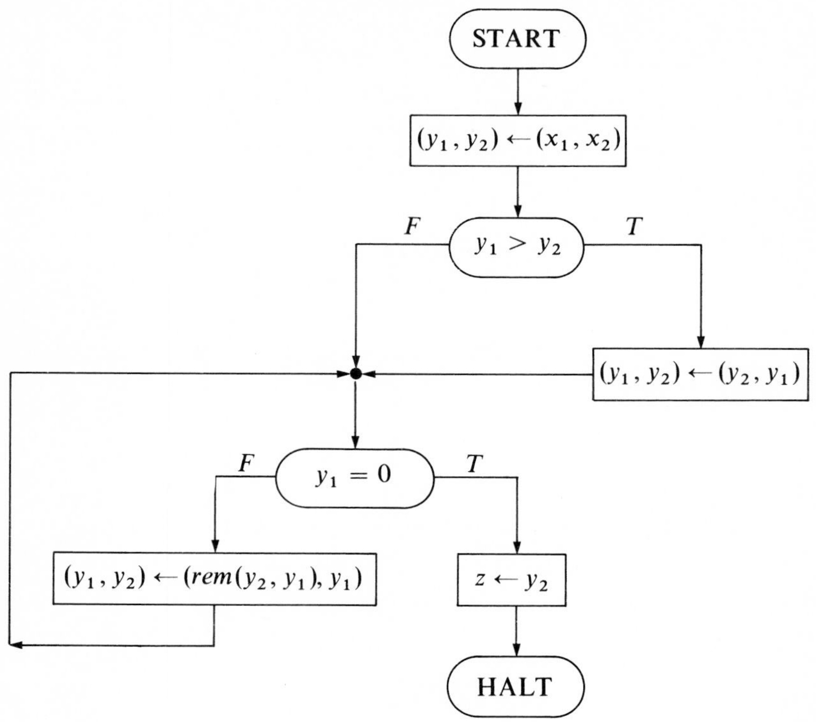

Figure 3-16 Flowchart program for computing $z = gcd(x_1, x_2)$.

Prob. 3-4 [Knuth (1968)]. Consider the flowchart program (Fig. 3-17) over the integers for computing the greatest common divisor of x_1 and x_2 and the appropriate multipliers. Prove that it is totally correct wrt $\varphi(\bar{x})$: $x_1 > 0 \wedge x_2 > 0$ and $\psi(\bar{x}, \bar{z})$: $z_3 = gcd(x_1, x_2) \wedge z_1 x_1 + z_2 x_2 = z_3$.

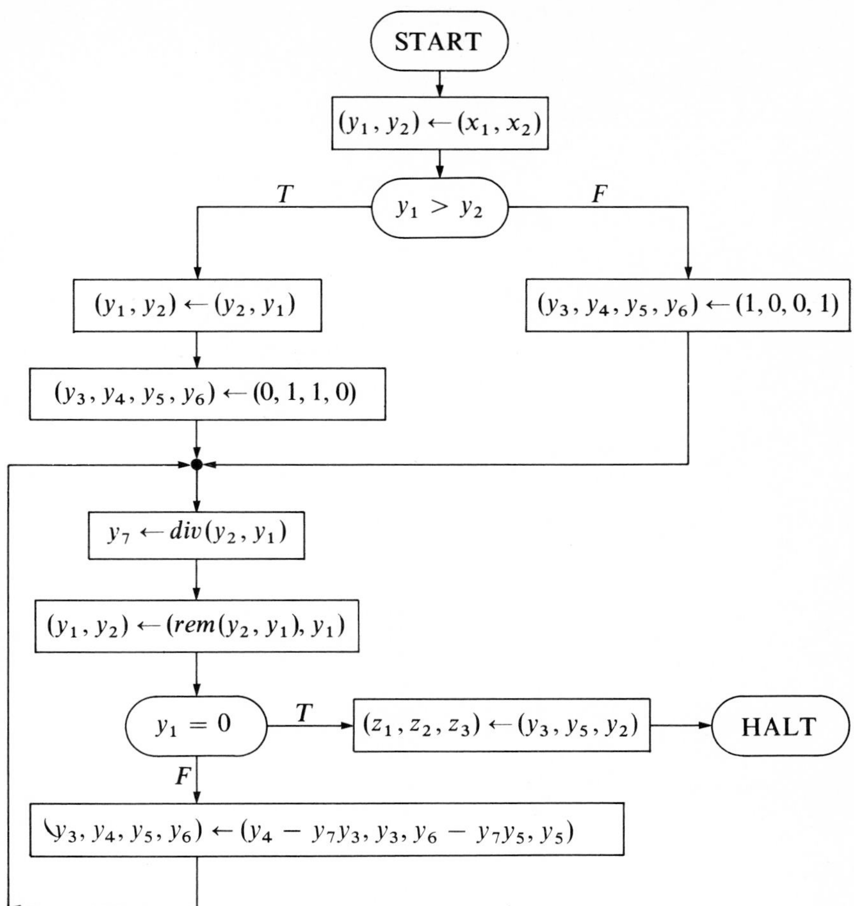

Figure 3-17 Flowchart program for computing $z_3 = gcd(x_1, x_2)$ and the appropriate multipliers.

***Prob. 3-5** Consider the flowchart program (Fig. 3-18) over the integers for computing *McCarthy's 91 function.* Prove that it is totally correct wrt $\varphi(x): T$ and $\psi(x, z): z = \textit{if } x > 100 \textit{ then } x - 10 \textit{ else } 91$.

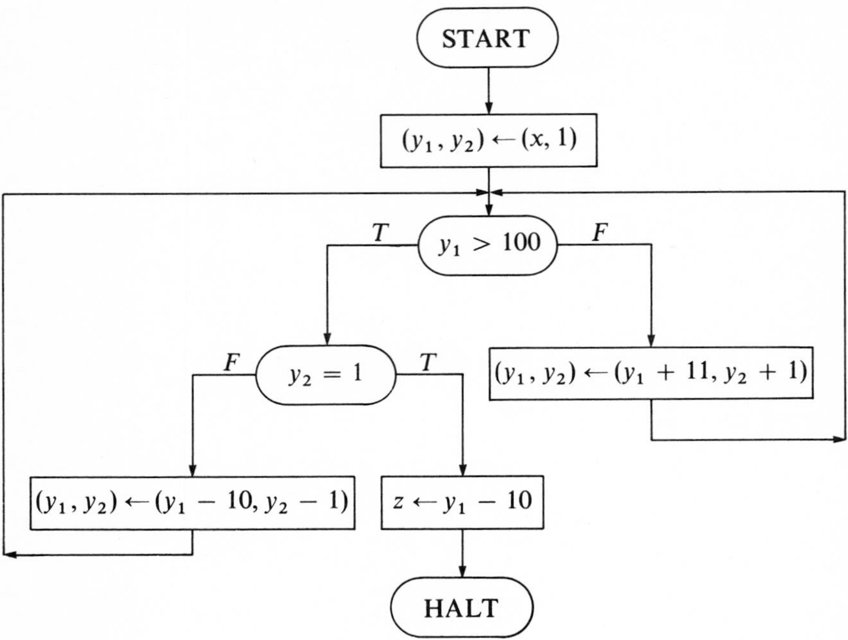

Figure 3-18 Flowchart program for computing McCarthy's 91 function.

Prob. 3-6 Consider the flowchart program (Fig. 3-19) over the integers for deciding whether or not a given integer x is a prime number. Prove that it is totally correct wrt $\varphi(x)$: $x \geqq 2$ and $\psi(x, z)$: $z \equiv prime(x)$, where $prime(x)$ is *true* if and only if x is a prime number; that is $\forall k[2 \leqq k < x \supset rem(x, k) \neq 0]$.

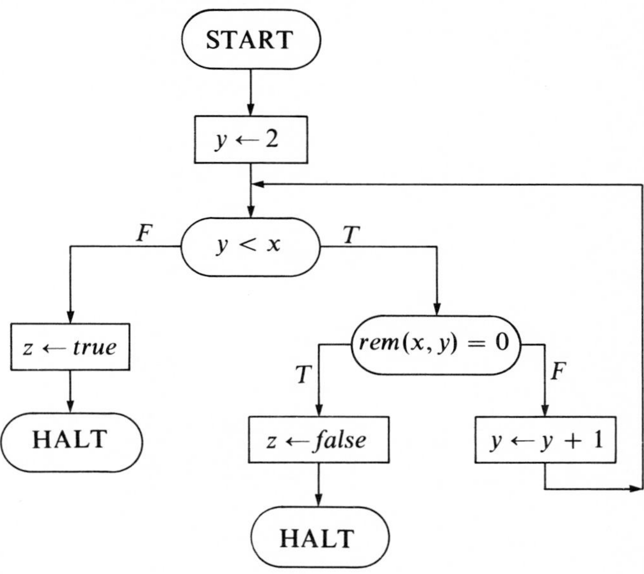

Figure 3-19 Flowchart program for deciding whether or not x is a prime number.

Prob. 3-7 Consider the flowchart program (Fig. 3-20) over the natural numbers for deciding whether or not a given positive integer x is a perfect number; that is, x is the sum of all t's such that $1 \leqq t < x$ and t divides x. For example, 6 and 28 are perfect numbers because $6 = 1 + 2 + 3$ and $28 = 1 + 2 + 4 + 7 + 14$. Prove that the program is totally correct wrt $\varphi(x)$: $x > 0$ and $\psi(x, z)$: z is *true* if and only if x is a perfect number.

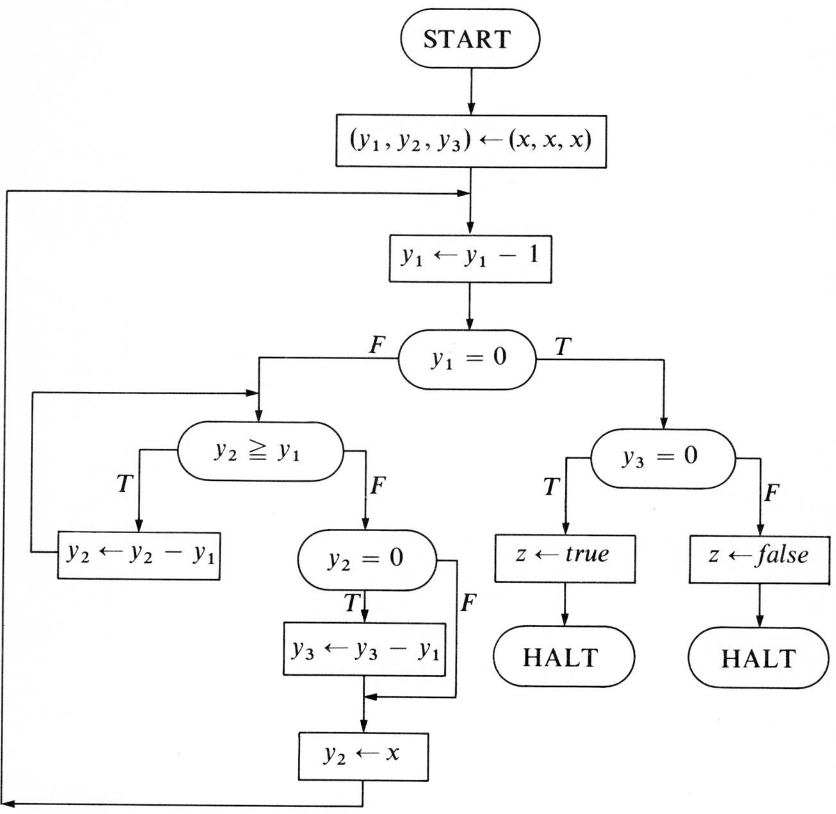

Figure 3-20 Flowchart program for deciding whether or not x is a perfect number.

Prob. 3-8 Consider the flowchart program (Fig. 3-21) over the integers for computing the quotient and the remainder of positive integers x_1 and x_2 using *hardware integer division.* Prove that it is totally correct wrt $\varphi(\bar{x})$: $x_1 \geqq 0 \wedge x_2 > 0$ and $\psi(\bar{x}, \bar{z})$: $0 \leqq z_1 < x_2 \wedge x_1 = z_2 x_2 + z_1$.

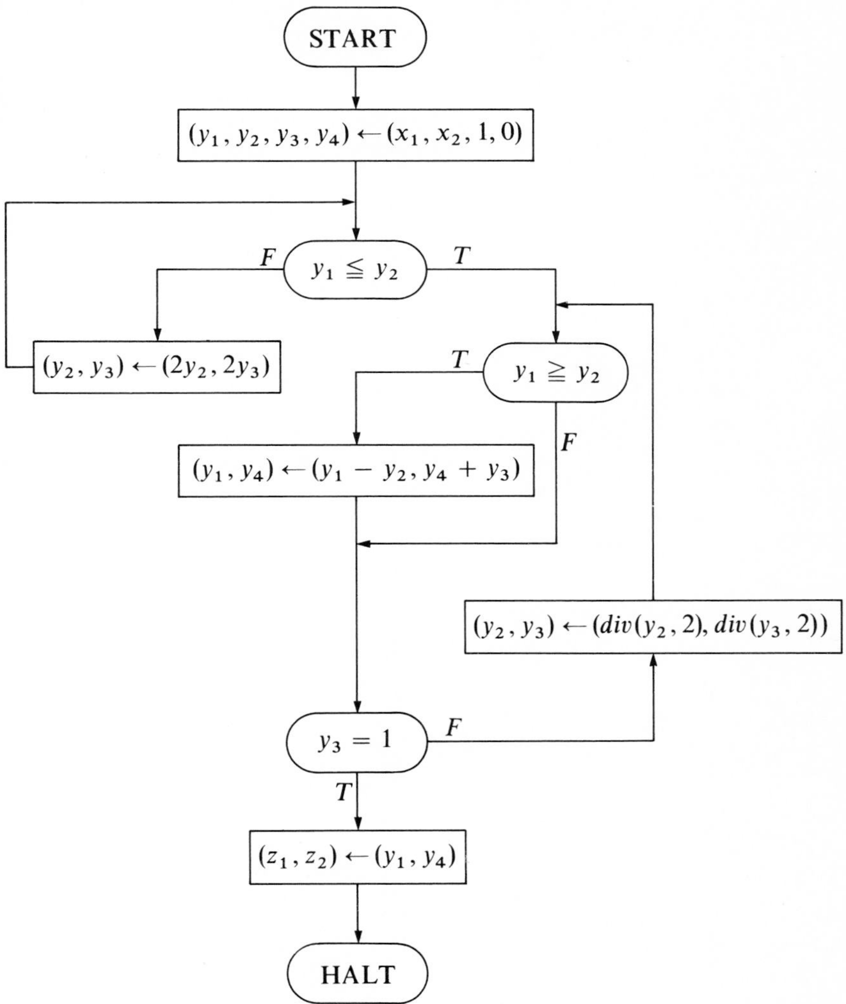

Figure 3-21 Flowchart program for performing hardware integer division.

Prob. 3-9 The flowchart program (Fig. 3-22) finds all the prime numbers between 2 and n, where $n \geqq 2$. It is based on the *sieve of Eratosthenes'* method. The program uses a boolean array S of $n - 1$ elements $S[2], S[3], \ldots, S[n]$; that is, each element in the array can take only two possible values: *true* or *false.* Prove that the program is totally correct wrt $\varphi(n)$: $n \geqq 2$ and $\psi(n, S): \forall k\, \{2 \leqq k \leqq n \supset S[k] \equiv prime(k)\}$.

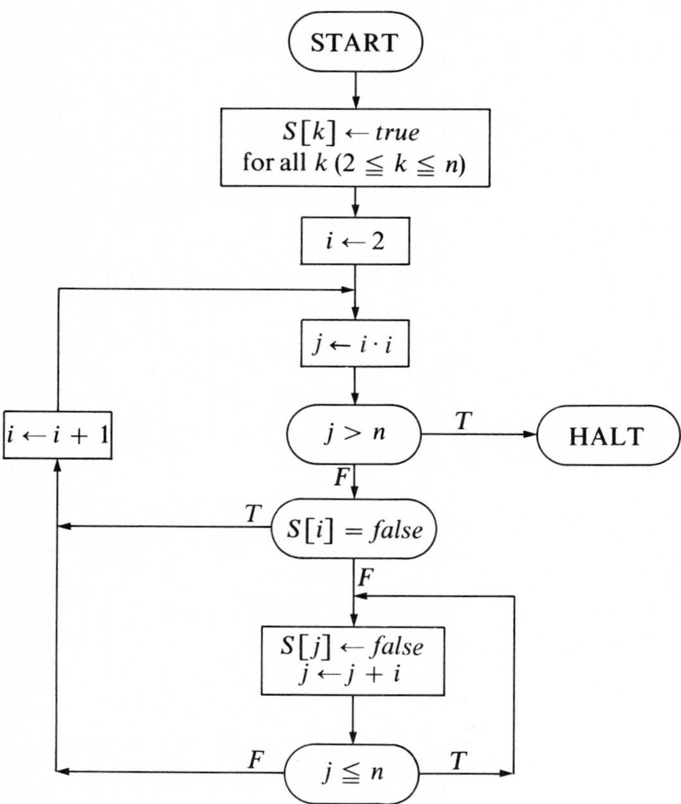

Figure 3-22 Flowchart program for finding all the prime numbers between 2 and n.

Prob. 3-10 The flowchart program (Fig. 3-23) sorts a given array $X[1]$, $\ldots, X[n]$ of real numbers, where $n \geqq 1$. Prove that it is totally correct wrt $\varphi(n, X)$: $n \geqq 1$ and $\psi(n, X, Z)$: $perm(X, Z, 1, n) \wedge ordered(Z, 1, n)$ [see Example 3-6 (Sec. 3-2.1)].

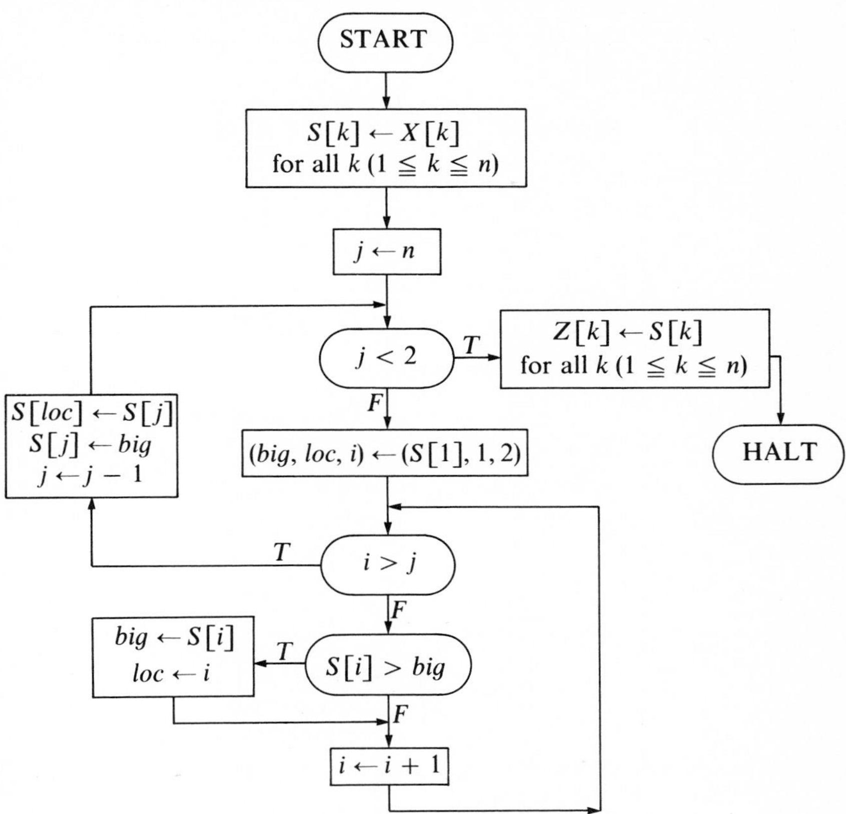

Figure 3-23 Flowchart program for sorting an array.

Prob. 3-11 The flowchart program (Fig. 3-24) takes an array X of $n + 1$, $n \geqq 0$, elements $X[0], X[1], \ldots, X[n]$ as input and yields as output an array Z of $n + 1$ elements $Z[0], Z[1], \ldots, Z[n]$ in such a way that the elements of Z are the elements of X in reverse order; that is, $Z[0] = X[n], Z[1] = X[n-1], \ldots,$ and $Z[n] = X[0]$. Prove that the program is totally correct wrt $\varphi(n, X)$: $n \geqq 0$ and $\psi(n, X, Z)$: $\forall k\{0 \leqq k \leqq n \supset Z[k] = X[n-k]\}$.

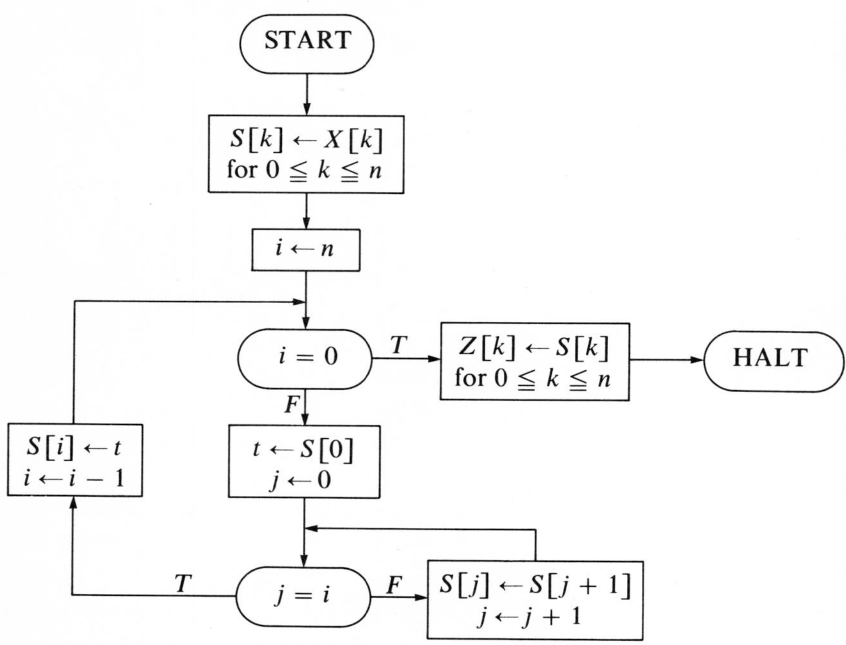

Figure 3-24 Flowchart program for reversing the order of the elements in an array.

Prob. 3-12 The flowchart program (Fig. 3-25) computes the minimum of a given real array $X[1], \ldots, X[n+1]$, $n \geqq 0$. Prove that it is partially correct wrt $\varphi(n, X)$: $n \geqq 0$ and $\psi(n, X, z)$: $z = min(X[1], \ldots, X[n+1])$.

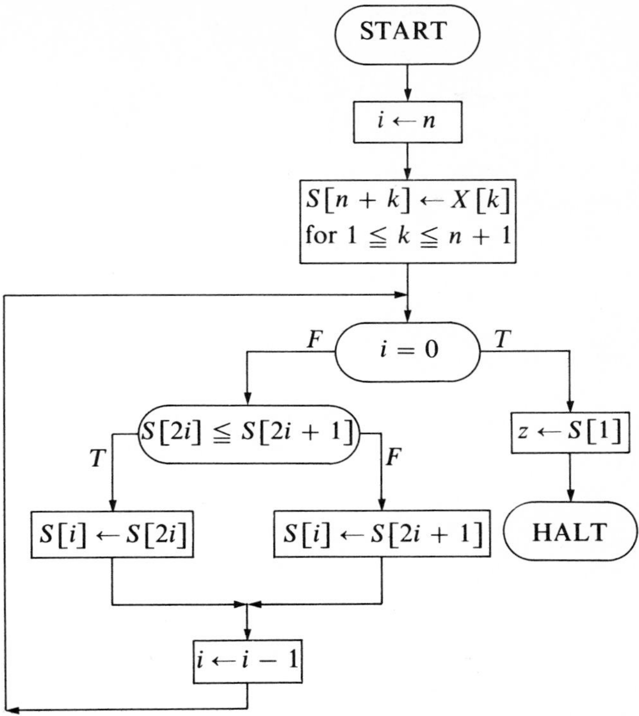

Figure 3-25 Flowchart program for computing the minimum of an array.

***Prob. 3-13** Consider the flowchart program P_8 for partitioning an array which was introduced in Example 3-12 (Sec. 3-3.2).

(*a*) Use the inductive-assertions method (Theorem 3-1) to prove that the following relation holds

$$(0 \leqq j < i \leqq n) \wedge \forall a \forall b[(0 \leqq a < i \wedge j < b \leqq n) \supset S[a] \leqq S[b]]$$

(*b*) Use the verification-rules method (Theorem 3-3) to prove that the following relation holds

$$(j < i) \wedge \forall a \forall b[(0 \leqq a < i \wedge j < b \leqq n) \supset S[a] \leqq S[b]]$$

(*c*) Use the termination-rules method (Theorem 3-4) to prove that the program terminates over $n \geqq 0$.

***Prob. 3-14** [Hoare (1971)]. The following program (called FIND) finds for a given array $S[1], \ldots, S[N]$ of integers and integer f $(1 \leqq f \leqq N)$ that element of the array whose value is the fth in order of magnitude.

It rearranges the elements of the array in such a way that

$$\forall a \forall b (1 \leqq a \leqq f \leqq b \leqq N \supset S[a] \leqq S[f] \leqq S[b])$$

Thus $S[f]$ contains the desired final result. [See also Example 3-12 (Sec. 3-3.2.)]

(*a*) Use the inductive-assertions method to prove partial correctness of the program.
(*b*) Use the verification-rules method to prove partial correctness of the program.
(*c*) Use the termination-rules method to prove termination of the program.

```
START
(m, n) ← (1, N);
while m < n do
begin (i, j) ← (m, n); r ← S[f];
      while i ≦ j do
      begin while S[i] < r do i ← i + 1;
            while r < S[j] do j ← j − 1;
            if i ≦ j do begin (S[i], S[j]) ← (S[j], S[i]);
                              (i, j) ← (i + 1, j − 1)
                        end
      end;
      if f ≦ j then n ← j
               else if i ≦ f then m ← i
                             else HALT
end
```

***Prob. 3-15** Consider the program P_7 (Fig. 3-13) in Sec. 3-2.2 for computing Ackermann's function $z = A(m, n)$. Prove that the function $A(m, n)$ computed by this program has the property that for every $m, n \geqq 0$:

$$A(m, n) = (\textit{if } m = 0 \textit{ then } n + 1 \;\; \textit{else if } n = 0 \textit{ then } A(m-1, 1) \;\; \textit{else } A(m-1, A(m, n-1)))$$

Prob. 3-16 Consider the flowchart program (Fig. 3-26) over the integers for computing Ackermann's function $z = A(m, n)$.

*(*a*) Prove that the program terminates over $\varphi(m, n)$: $m \geqq 0 \wedge n \geqq 0$.
(*b*) Prove that the function $A(m, n)$ computed by this program has the property that for every $m, n \geqq 0$:

$$A(m, n) = (\textit{if } m = 0 \textit{ then } n + 1 \;\; \textit{else if } n = 0 \textit{ then } A(m-1, 1) \;\; \textit{else } A(m-1, A(m, n-1)))$$

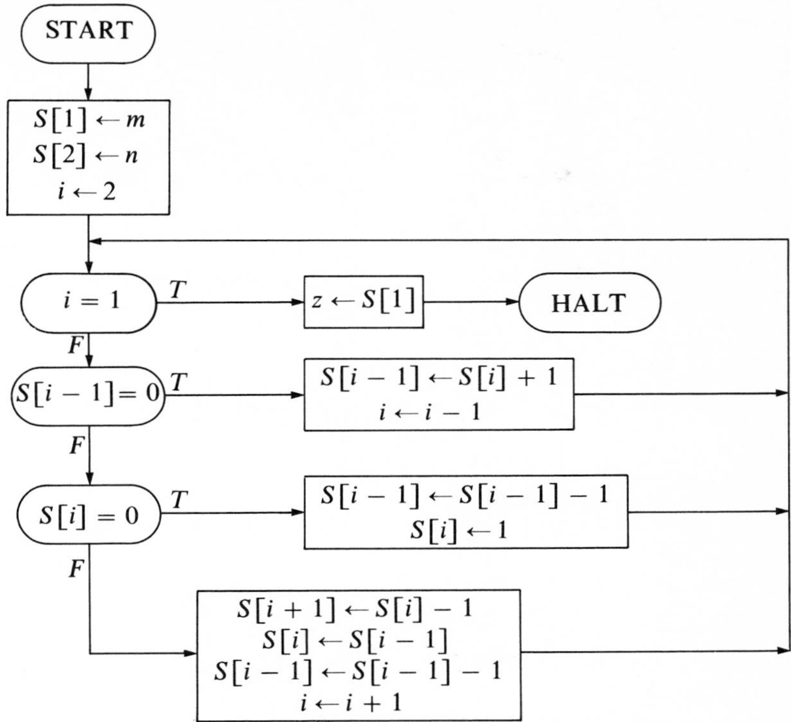

Figure 3-26 Flowchart program for computing Ackermann's function.

***Prob. 3-17** [London (1970b)]. The following is the Algol-60 program of TREESORT3.† Prove its total correctness (see the first comment in the program).

procedure TREESORT3 (M, n);
value n; **array** M; **integer** n;
comment The algorithm sorts the array $M[1:n]$, $n \geqq 1$. It is most easily followed if M is thought of as a tree, with $M[j \div 2]$ the father of $M[j]$ for $1 < j \leqq n$;

† R. W. Floyd, "Algorithm 245: Treesort 3," *C. ACM*, **7** (12): 701 (December 1964).

```
begin
    procedure exchange(x, y); real x, y;
        begin real t; t := x; x := y; y := t
        end exchange;
    procedure siftup(i, n); value i, n; integer i, n;
                M[i] is moved upward in the subtree of M[1 : n] of
          which it is the root;
    begin real copy; integer j;
        copy: = M[i];
    loop : j : = 2 × i;
        if j ≦ n then
        begin if j < n then
                begin if M[j + 1] > M[j] then j: = j + 1 end;
            if M[j] > copy then
                begin M[i]: = M[j]; i: = j; go to loop end
        end;
        M[i]: = copy
    end siftup;
    integer i;
    for i: = n ÷ 2 step − 1 until 2 do siftup(i, n);
    for i: = n step − 1 until 2 do
    begin siftup(1, i);
          comment M[j ÷ 2] ≧ M[j] for 1 < j ≦ i;
          exchange (M[1], M[i]);
          comment M[i:n] is fully sorted;
    end
end TREESORT3.
```

Prob. 3-18

(*a*) Find several distinct orderings to make the following sets well-founded:

(i) The set of all integers. [Note that the regular $<$ (greater than) relation is not an appropriate ordering.]

(ii) The set of all rational numbers a/b, where both a and b are positive integers.

(*b*) Prove the following:

(i) If $(W, \prec)$ is a well-founded set, so is $(W^n, {}_n\!\prec)$, that is, the set of all n-tuples of elements of W with the lexicographic ordering ${}_n\!\prec$.

(ii) If $(W_1, {}_1\!\prec)$ and $(W_2, {}_2\!\prec)$ are well-founded sets, so is $(W, \prec)$ where

(1) $W = W_1 \cup W_2$, that is, the union of all elements of W_1 and W_2

(2) $a \prec b$ iff $a, b \in W_1$ and $a \,{}_1\!\prec b$

or $a, b \in W_2$ and $a \,{}_2\!\prec b$

or $a \in W_1$ and $b \in W_2$.

Prob. 3-19 (*a*) Prove that Theorem 3-1 holds also in the other direction; that is, if P is partially correct wrt φ and ψ, then there exist cutpoints and inductive assertions such that the verification conditions are *true*. (*b*) Prove that Theorem 3-2 holds also in the other direction; that is, if P terminates over φ, then there exist cutpoints, "good" inductive assertions, and "good" partial functions such that the termination conditions are *true*.

Prob. 3-20 [Dijkstra]. Use the verification-rules method to prove the partial correctness of the following while programs over the integers:

(*a*)

START
$\{x_1 \geqq 0 \wedge x_2 > 0\}$
$(y_1, y_2) \leftarrow (x_1, 0)$;
while $x_2 \leqq y_1$ **do** $(y_1, y_2) \leftarrow (y_1 - x_2, y_2 + 1)$;
$(z_1, z_2) \leftarrow (y_1, y_2)$
$\{0 \leqq z_1 < x_2 \wedge x_1 = z_2 x_2 + z_1\}$
HALT

(*b*)

START
$\{x_1 \geqq 0 \wedge x_2 \geqq 0\}$
$(y_1, y_2, y_3) \leftarrow (x_1, x_2, 1)$;
while $y_2 \neq 0$ **do**
  begin if *odd* (y_2) **do** $(y_2, y_3) \leftarrow (y_2 - 1, y_3 y_1)$;
    $(y_1, y_2) \leftarrow (y_1 y_1, y_2/2)$
  end;
$z \leftarrow y_3$
$\{z = x_1{}^{x_2}\}$
HALT

(*c*)

START
$\{x_1 > 0 \wedge x_2 > 0\}$
$(y_1, y_2) \leftarrow (x_1, x_2)$;
while $y_1 \neq y_2$ **do**
  if $y_1 > y_2$ **then** $y_1 \leftarrow y_1 - y_2$ **else** $y_2 \leftarrow y_2 - y_1$;
$z \leftarrow y_1$
$\{z = gcd(x_1, x_2)\}$
HALT

(*d*)

START
$\{x_1 > 0 \wedge x_2 > 0\}$
$(y_1, y_2) \leftarrow (x_1, x_2)$;

```
while y₁ ≠ y₂ do
      begin while y₁ > y₂ do y₁ ← y₁ − y₂;
            while y₂ > y₁ do y₂ ← y₂ − y₁
      end;
z ← y₁
{z = gcd(x₁, x₂)}
HALT
```

(e)

```
START
{x₁ ≧ 0 ∧ x₂ > 0}
(y₁, y₂, y₃) ← (x₁, 0, x₂);
while y₃ ≦ y₁ do y₃ ← 2y₃;
while y₃ ≠ x₂ do
      begin (y₂, y₃) ← (2y₂, y₃/2);
            if y₃ ≦ y₁ do (y₁, y₂) ← (y₁ − y₃, y₂ + 1)
      end;
(z₁, z₂) ← (y₁, y₂)
{0 ≦ z₁ < x₂ ∧ x₁ = z₂x₂ + z₁}
HALT
```

(f)

```
START
{x₁ > 0 ∧ x₂ > 0}
(y₁, y₂, y₃, y₄) ← (x₁, x₂, x₂, 0);
while y₁ ≠ y₂ do
      begin while y₁ > y₂ do (y₁, y₄) ← (y₁ − y₂, y₄ + y₃);
            while y₂ > y₁ do (y₂, y₃) ← (y₂ − y₁, y₃ + y₄)
      end;
(z₁, z₂) ← (y₁, y₃ + y₄)
{z₁ = gcd(x₁, x₂) ∧ z₂ = scm(x₁, x₂)}
HALT
```

where $scm(x_1, x_2)$ is the smallest common multiple of x_1 and x_2; that is, it is their product divided by the greatest common divisor.

(g) The following program locates an integer x in a sorted array $A[1], \ldots, A[n]$, where $n \geqq 1$.

```
START
{n ≧ 1 ∧ A[1] ≦ A[2] ≦ ··· ≦ A[n] ∧ ∃i, 1 ≦ i ≦ n, such that x = A[i]}
(y₁, y₂) ← (1, n);
while y₁ ≠ y₂ do
      begin y₃ ← div(y₁ + y₂, 2);
            if x ≦ A[y₃] then y₂ ← y₃ else y₁ ← y₃ + 1
```

end;
$z \leftarrow y_1$
$\{1 \leqq z \leqq n \wedge x = A[z]\}$
HALT

***Prob. 3-21** Prove that the flowchart program (Fig. 3-27) computes the greatest common divisor of any array $X[1], \ldots, X[n]$, $n \geqq 1$, of nonnegative integers; that is, $z = gcd(X[1], \ldots, X[n])$. [It is assumed that 0's can be ignored; e.g., $gcd(5, 0, 0, 15, 0, 7) = gcd(5, 15, 7)$ and $gcd(0, 5, 0) = gcd(5)$.] For every non-negative integer a, $gcd(a) = a$.

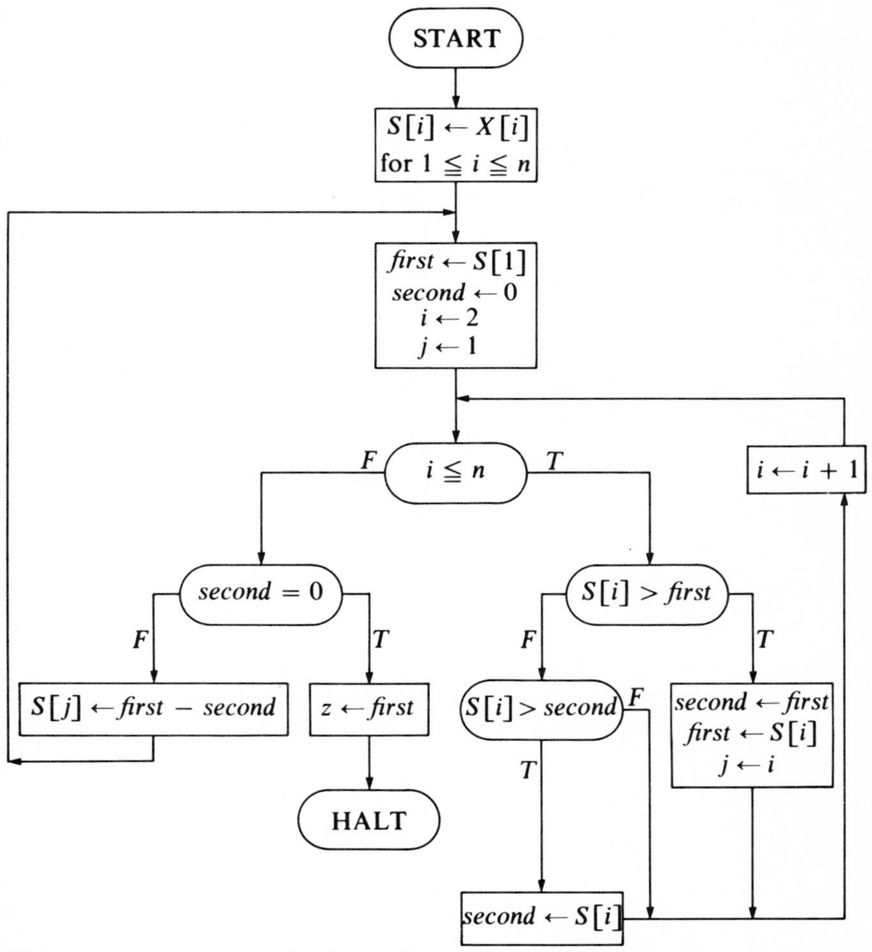

Figure 3-27 Flowchart program for computing the greatest common divisor of an array.

***Prob. 3-22†** The following program (*in-place permutation*) rearranges the elements of an array $S[1], S[2], \ldots, S[n]$, $n \geqq 1$, using a given permutation function $f(i)$ over the integers $1, 2, \ldots, n$; that is, the program rearranges the elements of S without using extra storage in such a way that $S_{\text{output}}[i] = S_{\text{input}}[f(i)]$ for $1 \leqq i \leqq n$. Prove that the program is totally correct wrt

$\varphi(n, f, S_{\text{input}})$: $n \geqq 1 \wedge (f$ is a permutation function over $1, 2, \ldots, n)$

and

$$\psi(n, f, S_{\text{input}}, S_{\text{output}}): \quad \forall i(1 \leqq i \leqq n \supset S_{\text{output}}[i] = S_{\text{input}}[f(i)]).$$

```
START
for k ← 1 step 1 until n do
   begin l ← f(k);
         while l < k do l ← f(l);
         (S[k], S[l]) ← (S[l], S[k])
   end
HALT
```

†See A. J. W. Duijvestijn, "Correctness Proof of an In-place Permutation," *BIT*, **12**(3): 318–324 (1972).

CHAPTER 4

Flowchart Schemas

Introduction

A *flowchart schema* is a flowchart program in which the domain of the variables is not specified (it is indicated by the symbol D) and the functions and predicates are left unspecified (they are denoted by the function symbols $f_1, f_2, \ldots$, and the predicate symbols $p_1, p_2, \ldots$). Thus a flowchart schema may be thought of as representing a family of flowchart programs. A program of the family is obtained by providing an interpretation for the symbols of the schema, i.e., a specific domain for D and specific functions and predicates for the symbols f_i and p_i. In Section 4-1 we introduce the basic notions and results regarding flowchart schemas.

In Sec. 4-2 we discuss the application of the theory of flowchart schemas for proving properties of programs. It often turns out that properties of a given program can be proved independent of the exact meaning of its functions and predicates; only the control structure of the program is really important in this case. Once the properties are proved for a schema, they apply immediately to all programs that can be obtained by specifying interpretations to the schema.

Flowchart programs are obtained from a given flowchart schema by specifying an interpretation in much the same way as interpreted wffs are obtained from a wff in the predicate calculus. In Sec. 4-3 we discuss first the relation between interpreted wffs of the predicate calculus and flowchart programs, and then the relation between (uninterpreted) wffs and flowchart schemas.

Essentially, a flowchart schema depicts the control structure of the program, leaving much of the details to be specified in an interpretation. This leads to a better understanding of program features because it allows for the separation of the effect of the specific properties of a given domain and the control mechanism used in the program. In Sec. 4-4 this idea is used to show that *recursion is more powerful than iteration.* For this purpose we define a class of recursive schemas and prove that every flowchart schema can be translated into an equivalent recursive schema but not vice versa.

4-1 BASIC NOTIONS

4-1.1 Syntax

An *alphabet* Σ_S of a flowchart schema S is a finite subset of the following set of symbols.

1. Constants:
   n-ary *functions constants* f_i^n $(i \geqq 1, n \geqq 0)$; f_i^0 is called an *individual constant* and is denoted by a_i.
   n-ary *predicate constants* p_i^n $(i \geqq 1, n \geqq 0)$; p_i^0 is called a *propositional constant.*

2. Individual variables:
   Input variables x_i $(i \geqq 1)$
   Program variables y_i $(i \geqq 1)$
   Output variables z_i $(i \geqq 1)$

The number of input variables $\bar{x}$, program variables $\bar{y}$, and output variables $\bar{z}$, in Σ_S is denoted by **a**, **b**, and **c**, respectively, where **a**, **b**, **c** $\geqq 0$. The subscripts of the symbols are used for enumerating the symbols and will be omitted whenever their omission causes no confusion. The superscripts of f_i^n and p_i^n are used only to indicate the number of arguments and therefore will always be omitted.

A *term* τ *over* Σ_S is constructed in the normal sense by composing individual variables, individual constants, and function constants of Σ_S. An *atomic formula* A *over* Σ_S is a propositional constant p_i^0 or an expression of the form $p_i^n(t_1, \ldots, t_n)$, $n \geqq 1$, where $t_1, \ldots, t_n$ are terms over Σ_S. We shall write $\tau(\bar{x})$ and $A(\bar{x})$ to indicate that the term τ and the atomic formula A contain no individual variables other than members of $\bar{x}$; similarly, we shall write $\tau(\bar{x}, \bar{y})$ and $A(\bar{x}, \bar{y})$ to indicate that the term τ and the atomic formula A contain no individual variables other than members of $\bar{x}$ and $\bar{y}$.

A *statement over* Σ_S is of one of the following five forms.

1. START statement:

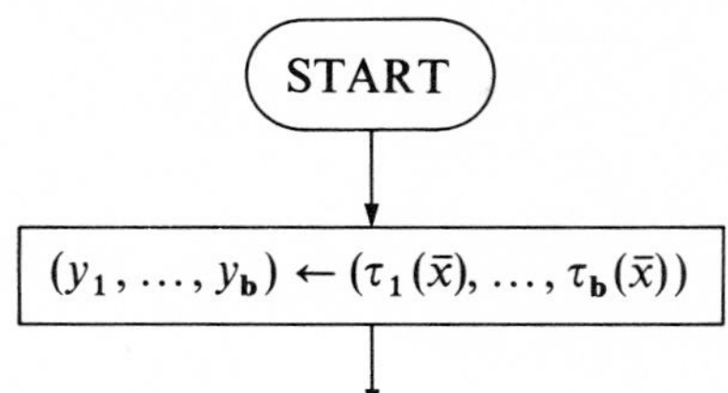

2. ASSIGNMENT statement:

$$(y_1, \ldots, y_{\mathbf{b}}) \leftarrow (\tau_1(\bar{x}, \bar{y}), \ldots, \tau_{\mathbf{b}}(\bar{x}, \bar{y}))$$

3. TEST statement:

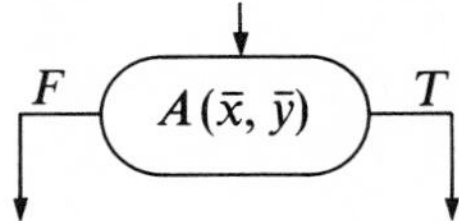

4. HALT statement:

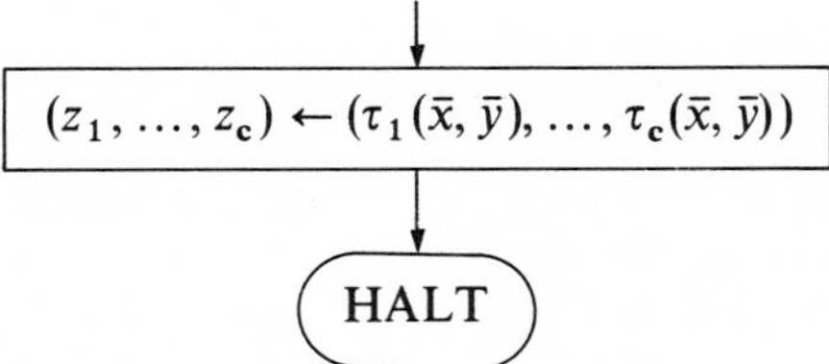

5. LOOP statement:

where all the terms and atomic formulas are over Σ_S.

A *flowchart schema S* over alphabet Σ_S (called *schema*, for short) is a finite flow-diagram constructed from statements over Σ_S, with one START statement, such that every ASSIGNMENT or TEST statement is on a path from the START statement to some HALT or LOOP statement.

EXAMPLE 4-1

In the sequel we shall discuss the schema S_1 described in Fig. 4-1. Σ_{S_1} consists of the individual constant a, the unary function constant f_1, the binary function constant f_2, the unary predicate constant p, the input variable x, the program variables y_1 and y_2, and the output variable z.

□

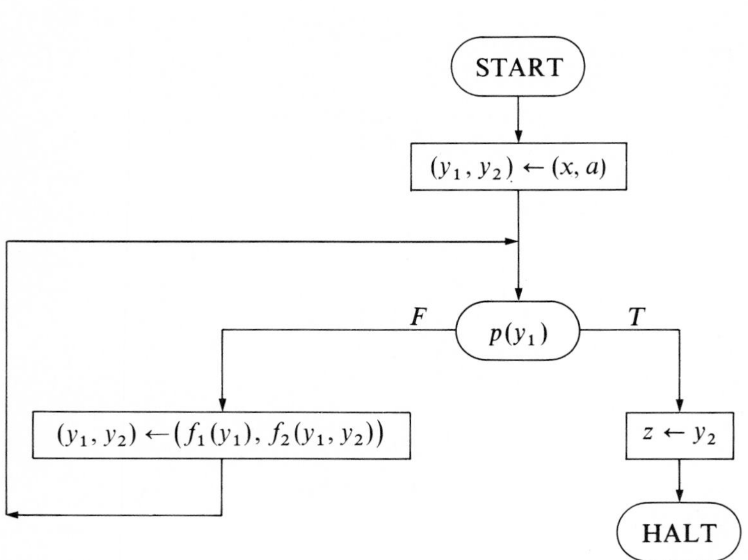

Figure 4-1 Schema S_1.

4-1.2 Semantics (Interpretations)

An *interpretation* $\mathscr{I}$ of a flowchart schema S consists of

1. A nonempty set of elements D (called the *domain* of the interpretation).
2. Assignments to the constants of Σ_S:
   (*a*) To each function constant f_i^n in Σ_S we assign a total function mapping D^n into D (if $n = 0$, the individual constant f_i^0 is assigned some fixed element of D).
   (*b*) To each predicate constant p_i^n in Σ_S we assign a total predicate mapping D^n into $\{true, false\}$ (if $n = 0$, the propositional constant p_i^0 is assigned the truth value *true* or *false*).

The pair $P = \langle S, \mathscr{I} \rangle$, where S is a flowchart schema and $\mathscr{I}$ is an interpretation of S, is called a *flowchart program* (or *program*, for short). Given initial values $\bar{\xi} \in D^{\mathbf{a}}$ for the input variables $\bar{x}$ of S, the program can be executed.

The *computation of* $\langle S, \mathscr{I}, \bar{\xi}\rangle$ proceeds in the normal sense, starting from the START statement, with $\bar{x} = \bar{\xi}$. The values of $(y_1, \ldots, y_\mathbf{b})$ are initialized in the START statement to $(\tau_1(\bar{\xi}), \ldots, \tau_\mathbf{b}(\bar{\xi}))$.† Note that if an ASSIGNMENT statement of the form $(y_1, \ldots, y_\mathbf{b}) \leftarrow (\tau_1(\bar{x}, \bar{y}), \ldots, \tau_\mathbf{b}(\bar{x}, \bar{y}))$ is reached with $\bar{y} = \bar{\eta}$ for some $\bar{\eta} \in D^\mathbf{b}$, the execution of the statement results in $(y_1, \ldots, y_\mathbf{b}) = (\tau_1(\bar{\xi}, \bar{\eta}), \ldots, \tau_\mathbf{b}(\bar{\xi}, \bar{\eta}))$; in other words, the new values of $y_1, \ldots, y_\mathbf{b}$ are computed simultaneously. Thus, for example, to interchange, the values of y_1 and y_2, we can write simply $(y_1, y_2) \leftarrow (y_2, y_1)$. The computation terminates as soon as a HALT statement is executed or a LOOP statement is reached: In the first case, if the execution of the HALT statement results in $\bar{z} = \bar{\zeta} \in D^\mathbf{c}$, we say that *val* $\langle S, \mathscr{I}, \bar{\xi}\rangle$ is defined and *val* $\langle S, \mathscr{I}, \bar{\xi}\rangle = \bar{\zeta}$; in the second case (i.e., if the computation reaches a LOOP statement) or if the computation never terminates, we say that *val* $\langle S, \mathscr{I}, \bar{\xi}\rangle$ is undefined. Thus a program P represents a partial function mapping $D^\mathbf{a}$ into $D^\mathbf{c}$.

EXAMPLE 4-2

Consider the schema S_1 (Figure 4-1) with the following interpretations.

1. Interpretation $\mathscr{I}_A$: $D = \{$the natural numbers$\}$; a is 1; $f_1(y_1)$ is $y_1 - 1$; $f_2(y_1, y_2)$ is $y_1 y_2$; and $p(y_1)$ is $y_1 = 0$. The program $P_A = \langle S_1, \mathscr{I}_A\rangle$, represented in Figure 4-2*a* clearly computes the factorial function; i.e., $z = factorial(x)$.

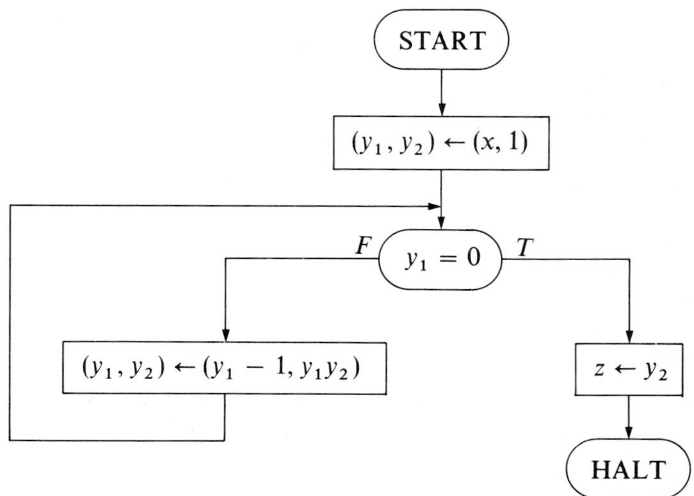

Figure 4-2*a* Program $P_A = \langle S_1, \mathscr{I}_A\rangle$ for computing $z = factorial(x)$.

† In some of the examples and problems in this chapter we do not initialize all the program variables in the START statement; however, the program variables are always assigned initial values before they are first needed.

2. Interpretation $\mathscr{I}_B$: This uses as domain the set Σ^* of all finite strings over the finite alphabet $\Sigma = \{A, B, \ldots, Z\}$, including the empty string Λ, thus $D = \{A, B, \ldots, Z\}^*$; a is Λ (the empty string); $f_1(y_1)$ is $tail(y_1)$; $f_2(y_1, y_2)$ is $head(y_1) \cdot y_2$; and $p(y_1)$ is $y_1 = \Lambda$. The program $P_B = \langle S_1, \mathscr{I}_B \rangle$ represented in Figure 4-2*b* clearly reverses the order of letters in a given string; i.e., $z = reverse(x)$. □

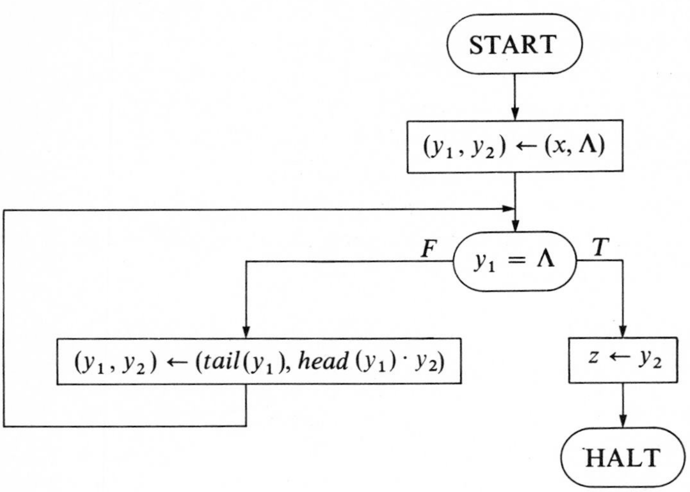

Figure 4-2*b* Program $P_B = \langle S_1, \mathscr{I}_B \rangle$ for computing $z = reverse(x)$.

EXAMPLE 4-3

Consider the schema S_3 (Fig. 4-3), where $y_1 \leftarrow f(y_1)$ abbreviates $(y_1, y_2) \leftarrow (f(y_1), y_2)$. Note that S_3 does not contain any input variable; thus, for a given interpretation $\mathscr{I}$ of S_3, the program $\langle S_3, \mathscr{I} \rangle$ can be executed without indicating any input value. Therefore, in this case we shall discuss the value of $val\langle S_3, \mathscr{I} \rangle$ rather than $val\langle S_3, \mathscr{I}, \bar{\xi} \rangle$. S_3 contains a dummy output variable (it is always assigned the individual constant a) because in this example we would like to know just whether or not $val\langle S_3, \mathscr{I} \rangle$ is defined rather than the value of $val\langle S_3, \mathscr{I} \rangle$.

Let us consider the following interpretation $\mathscr{I}^*$ of S_3:

1. The domain D consists of all strings of the form: $a, f(a), f(f(a)), f(f(f(a))), \ldots$. For clarity we enclose the strings within quotation marks and write

$$\text{“}a\text{”}, \quad \text{“}f(a)\text{”}, \quad \text{“}f(f(a))\text{”}, \quad \text{“}f(f(f(a)))\text{”}, \quad \ldots$$

† Here, $f^{(0)}(a)$ stands for a; $f^{(1)}(a)$ for $f(a)$; $f^{(2)}(a)$ for $f(f(a))$; $f^{(3)}(a)$ for $f(f(f(a)))$; and so forth.

2. The individual constant a of Σ_{S_3} is assigned the element "a" of D.

3. The unary function constant f of Σ_{S_3} is assigned a unary function mapping D into D as follows:† Any element "$f^{(n)}(a)$" of D ($n \geqq 0$) is mapped into "$f^{(n+1)}(a)$", which is also an element of D.

4. The unary predicate constant p of Σ_{S_3} is assigned a unary predicate mapping D into $\{true, false\}$ as follows: $p(\text{“}f^{(n)}(a)\text{”})$, $n \geqq 0$, takes the values (where t stands for *true* and f for *false*)

n:	0	1	2	3	4	5	6	7	8	9	10	11	12	13	14	15	
$p(\text{“}f^{(n)}(a)\text{”})$:	f	f	t	f	t	t	f	t	t	t	f	t	t	t	t	f	. . .

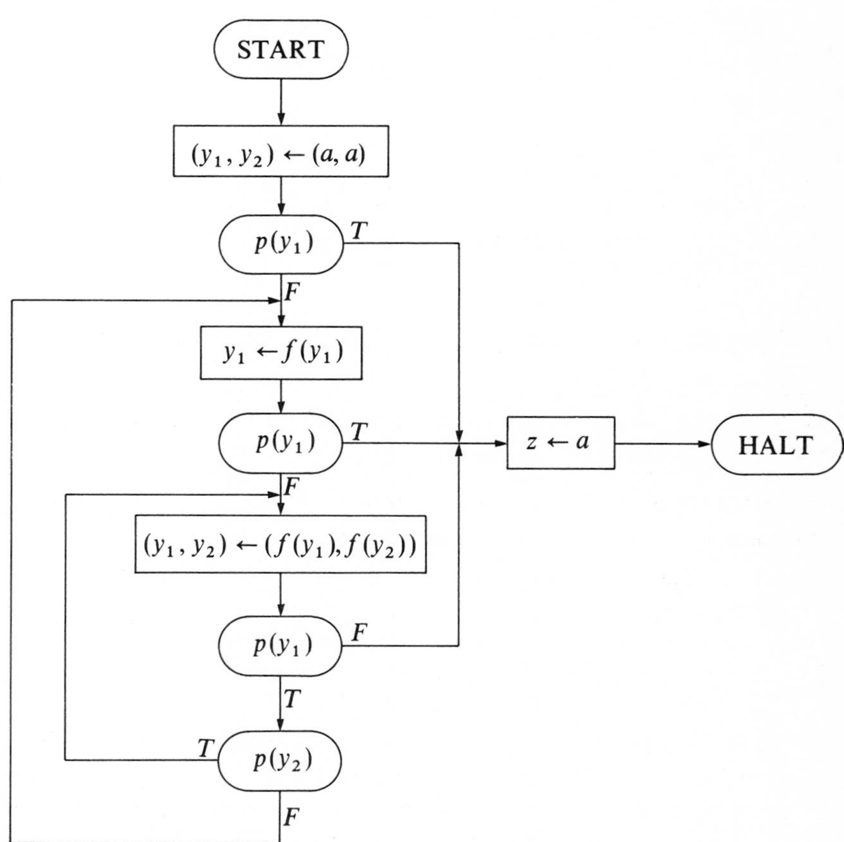

Figure 4-3 Schema S_3.

The computation of $\langle S_3, \mathscr{I}^* \rangle$ is best described by the following sequence of elements of $D \times D$ indicating the successive values of (y_1, y_2):

$$(\text{“}a\text{”}, \text{“}a\text{”}) \to (\text{“}f(a)\text{”}, \text{“}a\text{”}) \to (\text{“}f^{(2)}(a)\text{”}, \text{“}f(a)\text{”}) \to (\text{“}f^{(3)}(a)\text{”}, \text{“}f(a)\text{”})$$
$$\to (\text{“}f^{(4)}(a)\text{”}, \text{“}f^{(2)}(a)\text{”}) \to (\text{“}f^{(5)}(a)\text{”}, \text{“}f^{(3)}(a)\text{”})$$
$$\to (\text{“}f^{(6)}(a)\text{”}, \text{“}f^{(3)}(a)\text{”}) \to \dots\dots\dots\dots$$

It can be proved (by induction) that $val\langle S_3, \mathscr{I}^* \rangle$ is undefined. Interpretations similar to $\mathscr{I}^*$ are of special interest and will be discussed in Sec. 4-1.4.

Furthermore, it can be shown (see Prob. 4-1) that $val\langle S_3, \mathscr{I} \rangle$ is defined for every interpretation $\mathscr{I}$ with finite domain, and that it is also defined for every interpretation $\mathscr{I}$ with infinite domain unless $p(f^{(n)}(a))$, $n \geqq 0$, takes the following values under $\mathscr{I}$:

$$f,\ f,\ \underbrace{t,}\ f,\ \underbrace{t,\ t,}\ f,\ \underbrace{t,\ t,\ t,}\ f,\ \underbrace{t,\ t,\ t,\ t,}\ f,\ \dots$$

□

4-1.3 Basic Properties

After defining the syntax and the semantics of schemas, we shall now introduce a few basic properties of schemas which will be discussed in the rest of this chapter.

(A) Halting and divergence For a given program $\langle S, \mathscr{I} \rangle$ we say that

1. $\langle S, \mathscr{I} \rangle$ *halts* if for every input $\bar{\xi} \in D^{\mathbf{a}}$, $val\langle S, \mathscr{I}, \bar{\xi} \rangle$ is defined.
2. $\langle S, \mathscr{I} \rangle$ *diverges* if for every input $\bar{\xi} \in D^{\mathbf{a}}$, $val\langle S, \mathscr{I}, \bar{\xi} \rangle$ is undefined.

Note that a program $\langle S, \mathscr{I} \rangle$ may neither halt nor diverge if for some $\bar{\xi}_1 \in D^{\mathbf{a}}$, $val\langle S, \mathscr{I}, \bar{\xi}_1 \rangle$ is defined and for some other $\bar{\xi}_2 \in D^{\mathbf{a}}$, $val\langle S, \mathscr{I}, \bar{\xi}_2 \rangle$ is undefined. For a given schema S we say that

1. S *halts* if for every interpretation $\mathscr{I}$ of S, $\langle S, \mathscr{I} \rangle$ halts.
2. S *diverges* if for every interpretation $\mathscr{I}$ of S, $\langle S, \mathscr{I} \rangle$ diverges.

EXAMPLE 4-4

The schema S_4 in Fig. 4-4 halts (for every interpretation). It can be observed that (1) the LOOP statement can never be reached because whenever we reach TEST statement 1, $p(a)$ is *false*; and (2) we can never go through the loop more than once because whenever we reach TEST statement 2, either $p(a)$ is *true*, or $p(a)$ is *false* and $p(f(a))$ is *true*.

□

START
$y \leftarrow a$
T $p(y)$ F
1
F $p(y)$ T
$y \leftarrow f(y)$
LOOP
T $p(y)$ F
$y \leftarrow a$
HALT
2
F $p(y)$ T
$y \leftarrow f(y)$
HALT

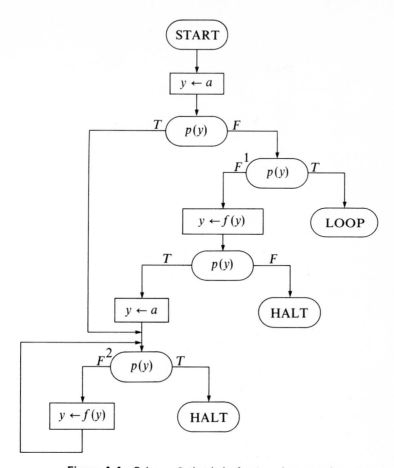

Figure 4-4 Schema S_4 that halts for every interpretation.

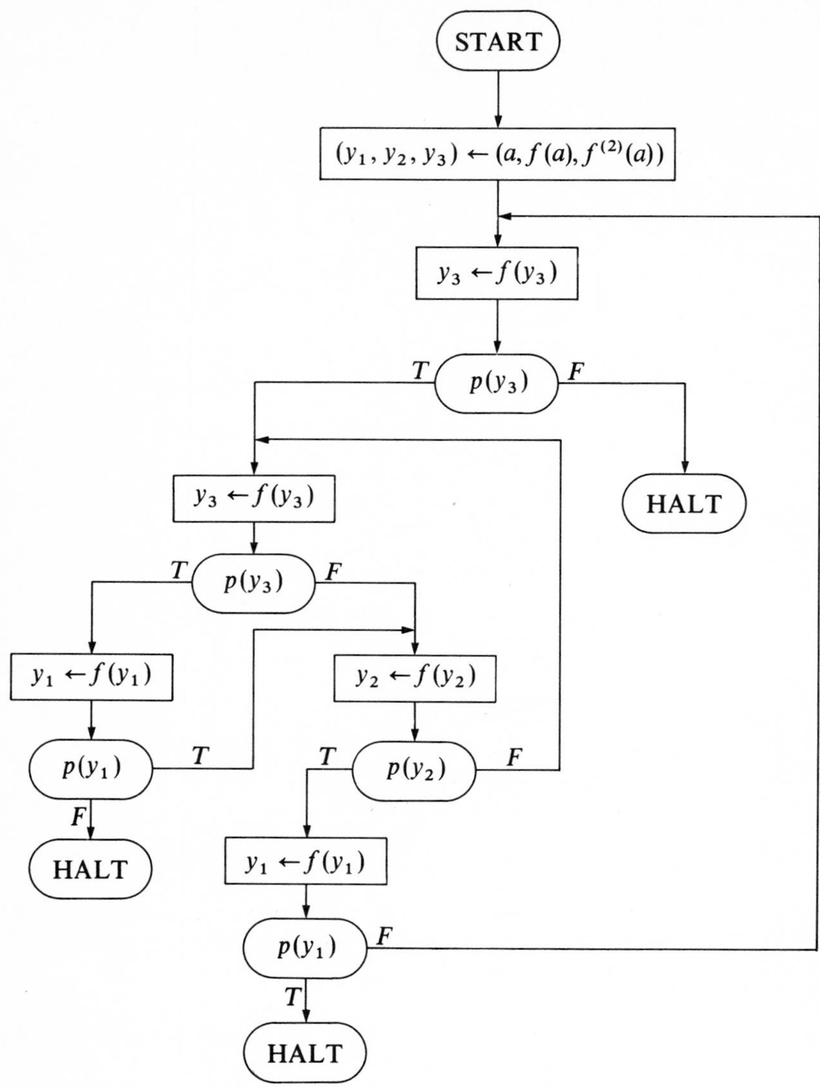

Figure 4-5 Schema S_5 that halts for every interpretation.

EXAMPLE 4-5 (Paterson)

The schema S_5 in Fig. 4-5 also halts (for every interpretation); however, it is very hard to prove it because there are some interpretations for which we must test $p(f^{(140)}(a))$ [but we shall never test $p(f^{(i)}(a))$ where $i > 140$].

□

(B) Equivalence The next property of schemas we shall discuss is the *equivalence of two schemas*, which is certainly the most important relation between schemas. Two schemas S and S' are said to be *compatible* if they have the same vector of input variables $\bar{x}$ and the same vector of output variables $\bar{z}$. Two programs $\langle S, \mathscr{I} \rangle$ and $\langle S', \mathscr{I}' \rangle$ are said to be *compatible* if the schemas S and S' are compatible and the interpretations $\mathscr{I}$ and $\mathscr{I}'$ have the same domain.

For two given compatible programs $\langle S, \mathscr{I} \rangle$ and $\langle S', \mathscr{I}' \rangle$, we say that *$\langle S, \mathscr{I} \rangle$ and $\langle S', \mathscr{I}' \rangle$ are equivalent* [notation: $\langle S, \mathscr{I} \rangle \approx \langle S', \mathscr{I}' \rangle$], if for every input $\bar{\xi} \in D^{\mathbf{a}}$, $val\langle S, \mathscr{I}, \bar{\xi} \rangle \equiv val\langle S', \mathscr{I}', \bar{\xi} \rangle$†, i.e., either both $val\langle S, \mathscr{I}, \bar{\xi} \rangle$ and $val\langle S', \mathscr{I}', \bar{\xi} \rangle$ are undefined, or both $val\langle S, \mathscr{I}, \bar{\xi} \rangle$ and $val\langle S', \mathscr{I}', \bar{\xi} \rangle$ are defined and $val\langle S, \mathscr{I}, \bar{\xi} \rangle = val\langle S', \mathscr{I}', \bar{\xi} \rangle$.

For two given compatible schemas S and S', we say that *S and S' are equivalent* [notation: $S \approx S'$] if for every interpretation‡ $\mathscr{I}$ of S and S', $\langle S, \mathscr{I} \rangle$ and $\langle S', \mathscr{I} \rangle$ are equivalent.

Note that the notion of equivalence is not only reflexive and symmetric but also transitive; i.e., it is really an equivalence relation. Thus one way to prove the equivalence of two schemas is by passing from one to the other by a chain of simple transformations, each of which obviously preserves equivalence. Some examples of such transformations are shown below. In each case it should be clear that equivalence is preserved.

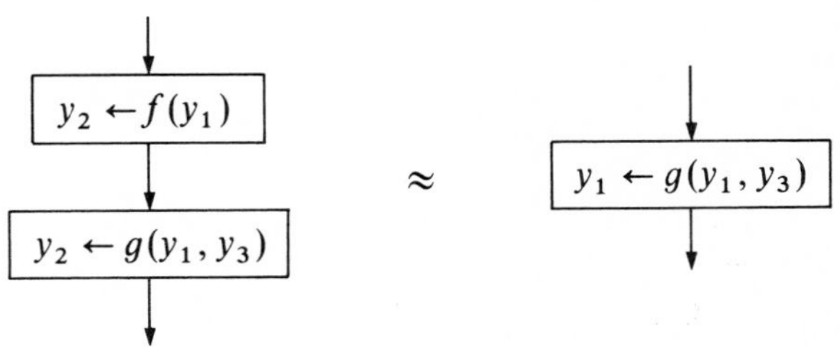

† $\equiv$ is the extension of the $=$ relation for handling undefined values: It is *true* if either both arguments are undefined or both are defined and equal; otherwise it is *false*. (Thus, the value is *false* if only one of the arguments is undefined.)

‡ That is, $\mathscr{I}$ includes assignments to all constant symbols occurring in $\Sigma_S \cup \Sigma_{S'}$.

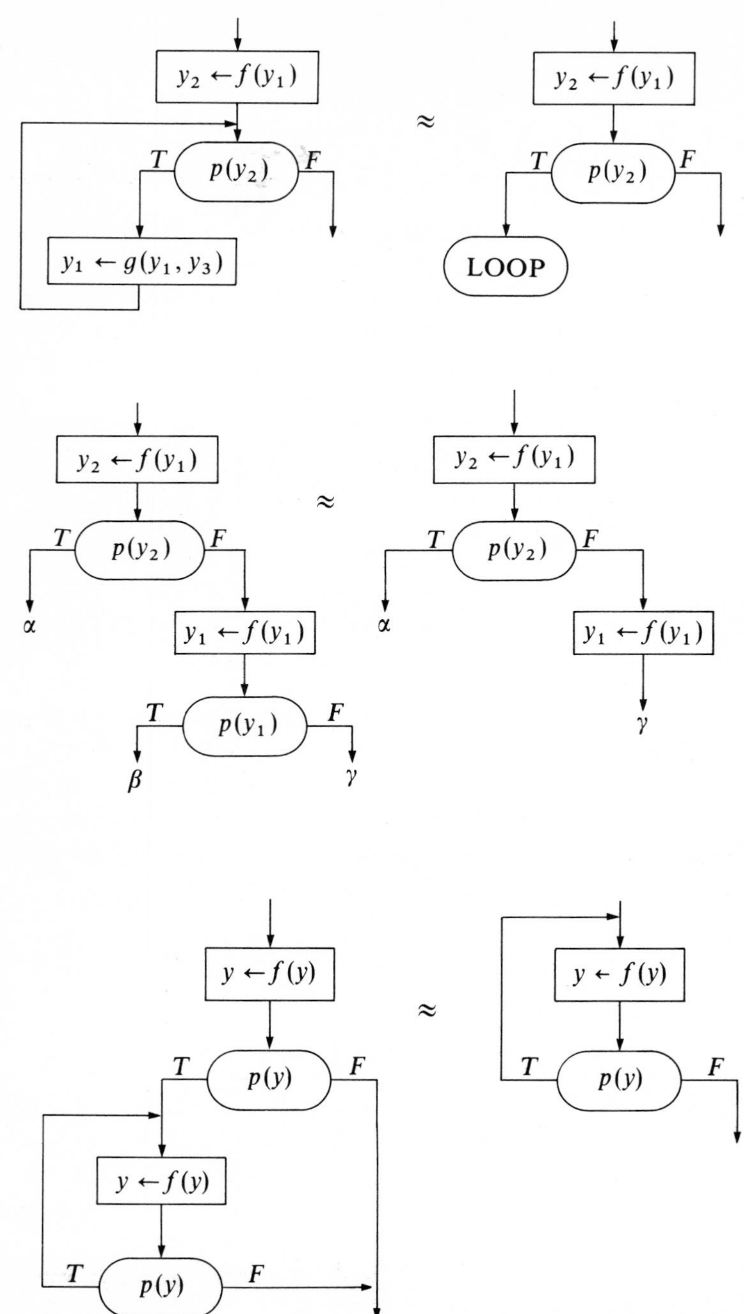

$y_2 \leftarrow f(y_1)$
$p(y_2)$
T
F
$y_1 \leftarrow g(y_1, y_3)$
≈
$y_2 \leftarrow f(y_1)$
$p(y_2)$
T
F
LOOP
$y_2 \leftarrow f(y_1)$
$p(y_2)$
T
F
α
$y_1 \leftarrow f(y_1)$
$p(y_1)$
T
F
β
γ
≈
$y_2 \leftarrow f(y_1)$
$p(y_2)$
T
F
α
$y_1 \leftarrow f(y_1)$
γ
$y \leftarrow f(y)$
$p(y)$
T
F
$y \leftarrow f(y)$
$p(y)$
T
F
≈
$y \leftarrow f(y)$
$p(y)$
T
F

EXAMPLE 4-6 (Paterson)

We shall apply some of these transformations to the schema S_{6A} (Fig. 4-6*a*) to show that it is equivalent to the schema S_{6E} (Fig. 4-6*e*). We proceed in 4 steps (see Figs 4-6*b* to *e*).

Step 1: $S_{6A} \approx S_{6B}$. Consider the schema S_{6A}. Note first that if at some stage we take the F branch of statement 7 (that is, $p(y_4) = \mathit{false}$), the schema gets into an infinite loop because the value of y_4 is not changed in statements 3, 4, and 6; note also that after execution of statements 2 and 3, we have $y_1 = y_4$. Thus, the first time we take the F branch of statement 5, either we get into an infinite loop through statements 3 and 4 or, if we get out of the loop, we get into an infinite loop when $p(y_4)$ is tested. Hence, let us replace the F branch of statement 5 by a LOOP statement; now, whenever we reach statement 5, we have $y_1 = y_4$. Thus whenever we reach statement 7, we must take its T branch; therefore statement 7 can be removed. Since at statement 4 we always have $y_1 = y_4$, we can replace y_4 by y_1 in this statement. Now, since y_4 is not used any longer, we can remove statement 2. Finally, we introduce the extra test statement 8′ just by unwinding once the loop through statements 8 and 9.

Step 2: $S_{6B} \approx S_{6C}$. Consider the schema S_{6B}. Since y_2 and y_3 are assigned the same values at statement 4, we have $y_2 = y_3$ when we first test $p(y_2)$ in statement 8. Therefore, if we take the T branch of $p(y_2)$, we can go directly to statement 11; however, if we take the F branch of $p(y_2)$ and later take the T branch of statement 8′ we return to statement 3 [since $p(y_3)$ is *false* (y_3 has not been modified)]. Thus, statement 10 can be removed (as shown in Fig. 4-6*c*), and y_3 can be replaced by y_2 in statement 6. Finally, since y_3 is now redundant, it can be eliminated.

Step 3: $S_{6C} \approx S_{6D}$. Consider the schema S_{6C}. Leaving the inner loop (8′–9), the value of y_2 is not used in statement 3 while we reset y_2 in statement 4; thus, the value of y_2 created in statement 9 serves no purpose. This suggests that we can remove the inner loop; however, there is the chance that we could loop indefinitely through statements 9 and 8′. In this case, if we reach statement 8 with some value $y_2 = \eta$, then $p(f^{(i)}(\eta)) = \mathit{false}$ for all i and especially $p(f^{(2)}(\eta)) = \mathit{false}$. Now, if we remove the inner loop, in statement 6 we set $y_1 = f(\eta)$ and then in statement 3 we set $y_1 = f^{(2)}(\eta)$. Thus $p(y_1)$ in statement 5 will be *false* leading to the LOOP statement. Thus, since the only possible use of statements 9 and 8′ is covered by the LOOP statement, the inner loop can be removed. Finally, since the value of y_2 is not used in statement 5, we can execute statement 4 after testing $p(y_1)$; similarly, since the value of y_1 is not used in statement 8, we can execute statement 6 after testing $p(y_2)$.

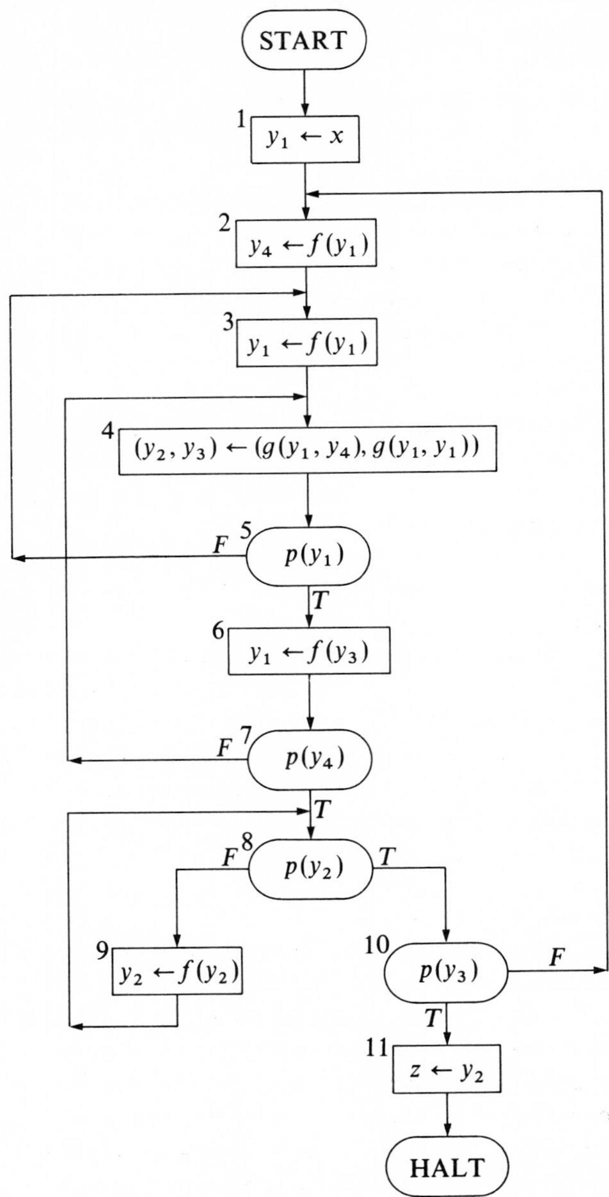

Figure 4-6a Schema S_{6A}.

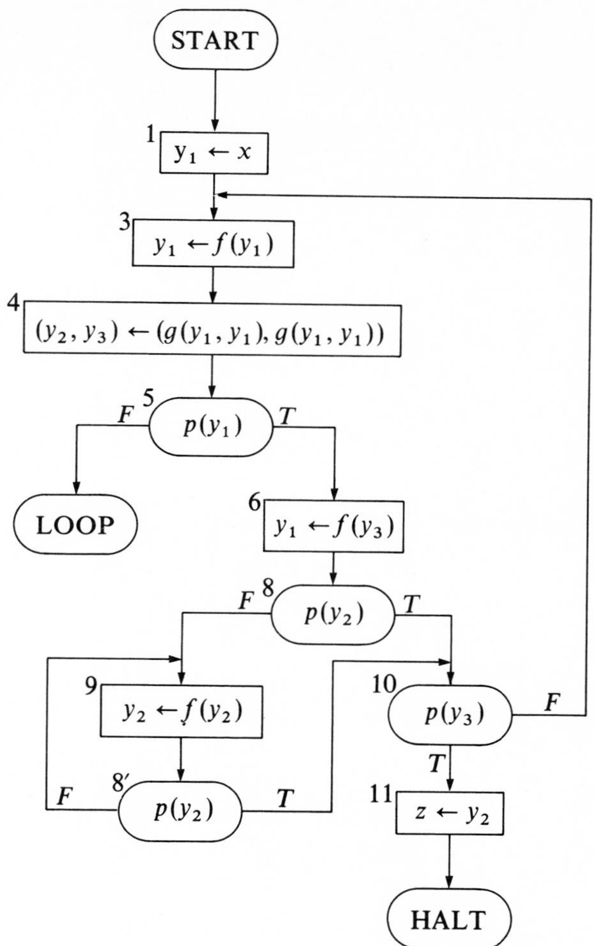

Figure 4-6*b* Schema S_{6B}.

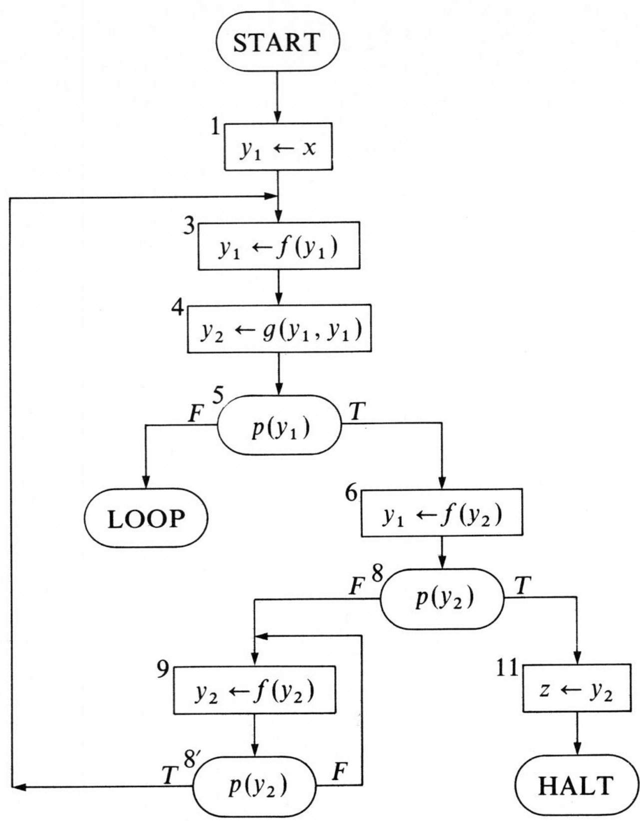

Figure 4-6c Schema S_{6C}.

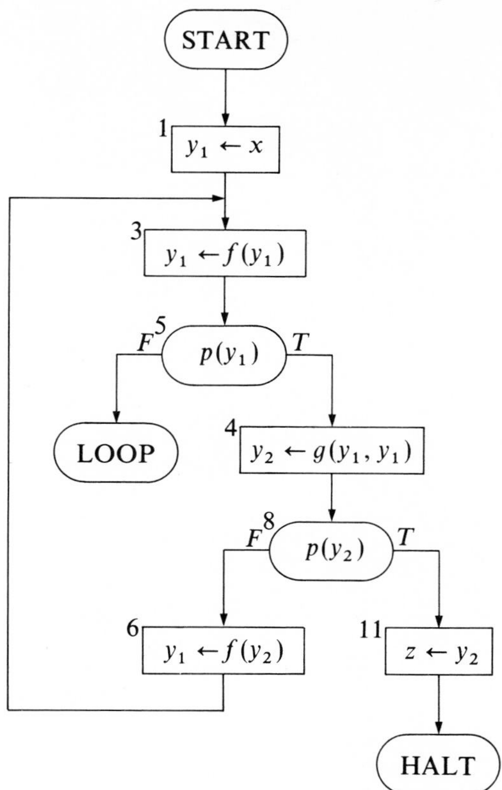

Figure 4-6*d* Schema S_{6D}.

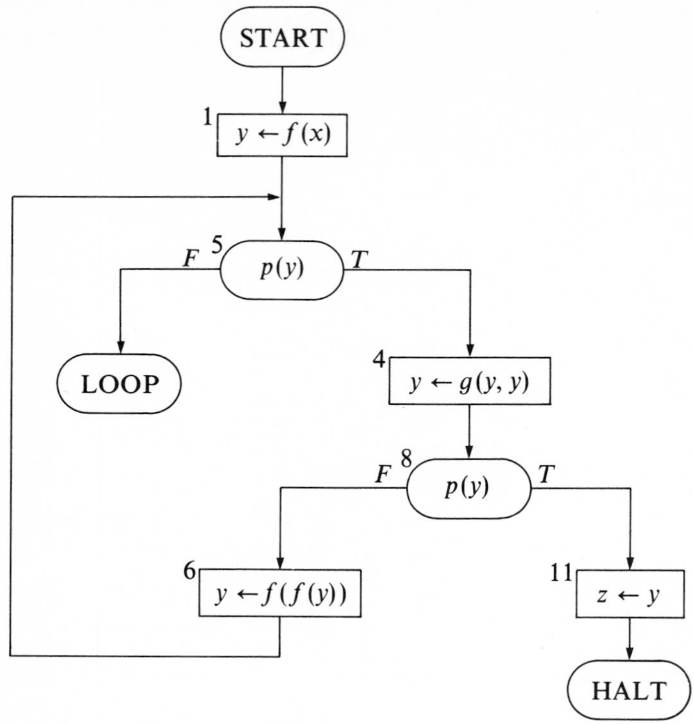

Figure 4-6*e* Schema S_{6E}

Step 4: $S_{6D} \approx S_{6E}$. Considering statements 4 and 6 in S_{6D}, we realize that y_2 is merely a dummy variable and can be replaced by y_1. Therefore, dropping the subscript and modifying statements 1, 3, and 6, we obtain S_{6E}. □

(C) Isomorphism Sometimes we would like to know, not only whether or not two schemas S and S' yield the same final value for the same interpretation, but also whether or not both schemas compute this value in the same manner. Therefore we introduce the stronger notion of equivalence called *isomorphism*. Two compatible schemas S and S' are said to be *isomorphic* (notation: $S \approxeq S'$) if for every interpretation $\mathscr{I}$ of S and S' and for every input $\bar{\xi} \in D^{\mathbf{a}}$, the (finite or infinite) sequence of statements executed in the computation of $\langle S, \mathscr{I}, \bar{\xi} \rangle$ is identical to the sequence of statements executed in the computation of $\langle S', \mathscr{I}, \bar{\xi} \rangle$.

EXAMPLE 4-7

The three schemas S_{7A}, S_{7B}, and S_{7C} (Fig. 4-7) are compatible. It is clear that $S_{7A} \approx S_{7B} \approx S_{7C}$, but $S_{7A} \approxeq S_{7B} \not\approxeq S_{7C}$.

□

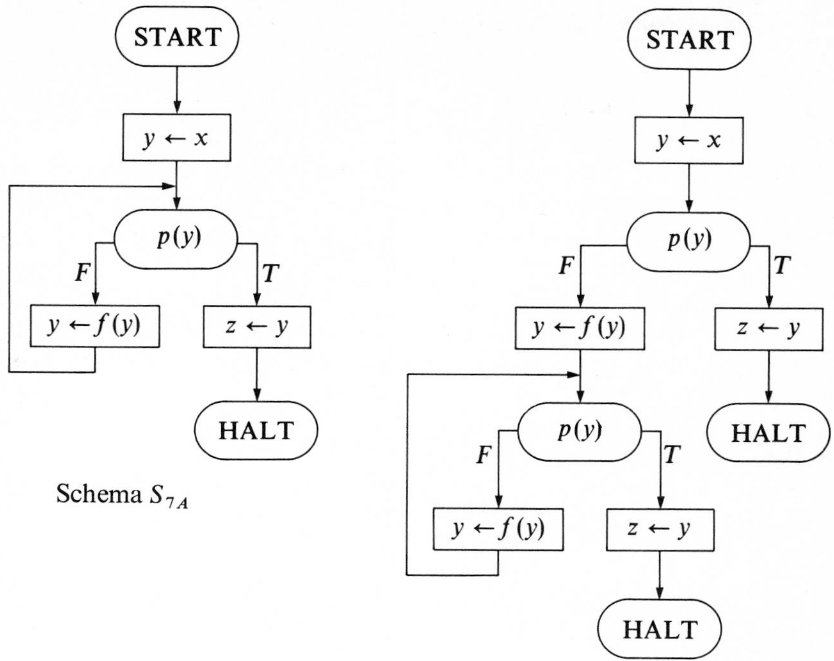

Schema S_{7A}

Schema S_{7B}

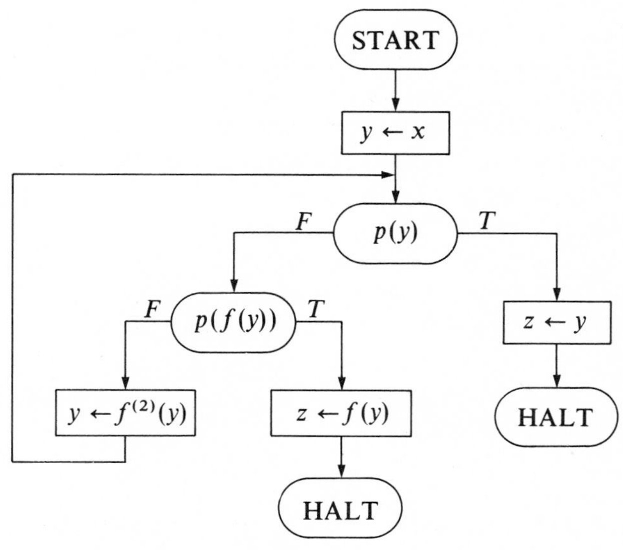

Schema S_{7C}

Figure 4-7

4-1.4 Herbrand Interpretations

The basic properties of schemas, such as halting, divergence, equivalence, or isomorphism, depend by definition on their behavior for all interpretations (over all domains). Clearly it would be of great help in proving properties of schemas if we could fix on one special domain such that the behavior of the schemas for all interpretations over this domain characterize their behavior for all interpretations over any domain. Fortunately, for any schema S, there does exist such a domain: It is called the *Herbrand universe of* S and is denoted by H_S. H_S consists of all strings of the following form: If x_i is an input variable and a_i is an individual constant occurring in S, then "x_i" and "a_i" are in H_S; if f_i^n is an n-ary function constant occurring in S and "t_1", "t_2", . . . , "t_n" are elements of H_S, then so is "$f_i^n(t_1, \ldots, t_n)$".

EXAMPLE 4-8

For the schema S_1 (Fig. 4-1), H_{S_1} consists of the strings

$$\text{"}a\text{"}, \text{"}x\text{"}, \text{"}f_1(a)\text{"}, \text{"}f_1(x)\text{"}, \text{"}f_2(a, a)\text{"}, \text{"}f_2(a, x)\text{"}, \text{"}f_2(x, a)\text{"}, \text{"}f_2(x, x)\text{"},$$
$$\text{"}f_1(f_1(a))\text{"}, \ldots$$

For the schema S_3 (Fig. 4-3), H_{S_3} consists of the strings

$$\text{"}a\text{"}, \text{"}f(a)\text{"}, \text{"}f(f(a))\text{"}, \text{"}f(f(f(a)))\text{"}, \ldots$$

□

Now, for any given schema S, an interpretation over the Herbrand universe H_S of S consists of assignments to the constants of S as follows: To each function constant f_i^n which occurs in S, we assign an n-ary function over H_S (in particular, each individual constant a_i is assigned some element of H_S); and to each predicate constant p_i^n which occurs in S, we assign an n-ary predicate over H_S (in particular, each propositional constant is assigned the truth value *true* or *false*). Among all these interpretations over H_S, we are interested in a special subclass of interpretations called *Herbrand interpretations of* S which satisfy the following conditions: Each individual constant a_i in S is assigned the string "a_i" of H_S; and each constant function f_i^n occurring in S is assigned the n-ary function over H_S which maps the strings "t_1", "t_2", . . . , and "t_n" of H_S into the string "$f_i^n(t_1, t_2, \ldots, t_n)$" of H_S. (Note that there is no restriction on the assignments to the predicate constants of S.)

EXAMPLE 4-9

The interpretation $\mathscr{I}^*$ described in Example 4-3 is a Herbrand interpretation of the schema S_3.

□

Note that H_S contains the strings "x_i" for all input variables x_i occurring in S. We let "$\bar{x}$" denote the vector of strings ("x_1", "x_2", . . . , "$x_{\mathbf{a}}$"). In general, among all possible computations of a schema S with Herbrand interpretation $\mathscr{I}^*$, the most interesting computation is $\langle S, \mathscr{I}^*, \text{"}\bar{x}\text{"}\rangle$, that is, the one in which the strings "x_i" of H_S are assigned to the input variables x_i. The reason is that for any interpretation $\mathscr{I}$ of a schema S and input $\bar{\xi} \in D^{\mathbf{a}}$, there exists a Herbrand interpretation $\mathscr{I}^*$ such that the (finite or infinite) sequence of statements executed in the computation of $\langle S, \mathscr{I}^*, \text{"}\bar{x}\text{"}\rangle$ is identical to the sequence of statements executed in the computation of $\langle S, \mathscr{I}, \bar{\xi}\rangle$.

The appropriate Herbrand interpretation $\mathscr{I}^*$ of S is obtained by defining the truth value of $p_i^n(\text{"}\tau_1\text{"}, \ldots, \text{"}\tau_n\text{"})$ as follows: Suppose that under interpretation $\mathscr{I}$ and input $\bar{\xi}$, $(\tau_1, \ldots, \tau_n) = (d_1, \ldots, d_n)$ where $d_i \in D$. Then, if $p(d_1, \ldots, d_n) = true$, we let $p(\text{"}\tau_1\text{"}, \ldots, \text{"}\tau_n\text{"}) = true$ under interpretation $\mathscr{I}^*$; and if $p(d_1, \ldots, d_n) = false$, we let $p(\text{"}\tau_1\text{"}, \ldots, \text{"}\tau_n\text{"}) = false$. This implies that many properties of schemas can be described and proved by considering just Herbrand interpretations rather than all interpretations, as suggested by the following theorem.

THEOREM 4-1 (Luckham-Park-Paterson).

(1) *For every schema S, S halts/diverges if and only if* $val\langle S, \mathscr{I}^*, \text{"}\bar{x}\text{"}\rangle$ *is defined/undefined for every Herbrand interpretation* $\mathscr{I}^*$ *of S.*

(2) *For every pair of compatible schemas S and S′, S and S′ are equivalent if and only if* $val\langle S, \mathscr{I}^*, \text{"}\bar{x}\text{"}\rangle \equiv val\langle S', \mathscr{I}^*, \text{"}\bar{x}\text{"}\rangle$ *for every Herbrand interpretation* $\mathscr{I}^*$ *of S and S′.*

(3) *For every pair of compatible schemas S and S′, S and S′ are isomorphic if and only if for every Herbrand interpretation* $\mathscr{I}^*$ *of S and S′ the sequence of statements executed in the computation of* $\langle S, \mathscr{I}^*, \text{"}\bar{x}\text{"}\rangle$ *is identical to the sequence of statements executed in the computation of* $\langle S', \mathscr{I}^*, \text{"}\bar{x}\text{"}\rangle$.

Proof. Let us sketch the proof of part (2). (Parts 1 and 3 can be proved similarly.) It is clear that if S and S' are equivalent, then $val\langle S, \mathscr{I}^*, \text{"}\bar{x}\text{"}\rangle \equiv val\langle S', \mathscr{I}^*, \text{"}\bar{x}\text{"}\rangle$ for every Herbrand interpretation $\mathscr{I}^*$. To prove the other direction, we assume that S and S' are not equivalent and show the existence of a Herbrand interpretation $\mathscr{I}^*$ such that $val\langle S, \mathscr{I}^*, \text{"}\bar{x}\text{"}\rangle \not\equiv val\langle S', \mathscr{I}^*, \text{"}\bar{x}\text{"}\rangle$. If S and S' are not equivalent, there must exist an interpretation $\mathscr{I}$ of S and S' and an input $\bar{\xi} \in D^{\mathbf{a}}$ such that $val\langle S, \mathscr{I}, \bar{\xi}\rangle \not\equiv val\langle S', \mathscr{I}, \bar{\xi}\rangle$. For this interpretation $\mathscr{I}$ and input $\bar{\xi}$, there exists a Herbrand interpretation $\mathscr{I}^*$ of S and S' such that the computations of $\langle S, \mathscr{I}^*, \text{"}\bar{x}\text{"}\rangle$ and $\langle S', \mathscr{I}^*, \text{"}\bar{x}\text{"}\rangle$ follow the same traces as the computations of $\langle S, \mathscr{I}, \bar{\xi}\rangle$ and $\langle S', \mathscr{I}, \bar{\xi}\rangle$, respectively. Now, suppose $val\langle S, \mathscr{I}^*, \text{"}\bar{x}\text{"}\rangle \equiv$

$val\langle S', \mathscr{I}^*, \text{“}\bar{x}\text{”}\rangle$, this means that both final values are either undefined or are an identical string over $H_S \cup H_{S'}$. This string is actually the term obtained by combining all the assignments along the computations of $\langle S, \mathscr{I}^*, \text{“}\bar{x}\text{”}\rangle$ or $\langle S', \mathscr{I}^*, \text{“}\bar{x}\text{”}\rangle$. Because of the correspondence between these computations and those of $\langle S, \mathscr{I}, \bar{\xi}\rangle$ and $\langle S', \mathscr{I}, \bar{\xi}\rangle$, it follows that† $val\langle S, \mathscr{I}, \bar{\xi}\rangle \equiv val\langle S', \mathscr{I}, \bar{\xi}\rangle$: a contradiction.

Q.E.D.

4-2 DECISION PROBLEMS

The notions of *solvable* and *partially solvable* were introduced in Chap. 1. Sec. 1-5. We say that a class of *yes/no problems* (that is, a class of problems, the answer to each one of which is either "yes" or "no") is *solvable*, if there exists an algorithm (Turing machine) that takes any problem in the class as input and always halts with the correct yes or no answer. We say that a class of yes/no problems is *partially solvable* if there exists an algorithm (Turing machine) that takes any problem in the class as input and: if it is a yes problem, the algorithm will eventually stop with a yes answer; otherwise, that is, if it is a no problem, the algorithm either stops with a no answer or loops forever. It is clear that if a class of yes/no problems is solvable then it is also partially solvable.

In this section we shall discuss four classes of yes/no problems.

1. *The halting problem for schemas*: Does there exist an algorithm that takes any schema S as input and always halts with a correct yes (S halts for every interpretation) or no (S does not halt for every interpretation) answer?

2. *The divergence problem for schemas*: Does there exist an algorithm that takes any schema S as input and always halts with a correct yes (S diverges for every interpretation) or no (S does not diverge for every interpretation) answer?

3. *The equivalence problem for schemas*: Does there exist an algorithm that takes any two compatible schemas S and S' as input and always halts with a correct yes (S and S' are equivalent) or no (S and S' are not equivalent) answer?

4. *The isomorphism problem for schemas*: Does there exist an algorithm that takes any two compatible schemas S and S' as input and always halts with a correct yes (S and S' are isomorphic) or no (S and S' are not isomorphic) answer?

† Note that $val\langle S, \mathscr{I}^*, \text{“}\bar{x}\text{”}\rangle \equiv val\langle S, \mathscr{I}^*, \text{“}\bar{x}\text{”}\rangle$ implies $val\langle S, \mathscr{I}, \bar{\xi}\rangle \equiv val\langle S', \mathscr{I}, \bar{\xi}\rangle$ but not necessarily vice versa!

We shall show that the halting problem for schemas is unsolvable but partially solvable while the divergence, equivalence, and isomorphism problems for schemas are not even partially solvable. It is quite surprising that all these unsolvability results can actually be shown for a very restricted class of schemas. For this purpose let us consider the class of schemas $\mathscr{S}_1$. We say that a schema S is in the class $\mathscr{S}_1$ if

1. Σ_S consists of a single individual constant a, a single unary function f, a single unary predicate p, two program variables y_1 and y_2, a single output variable z, but no input variables.
2. All statements in S are of one of the following forms:

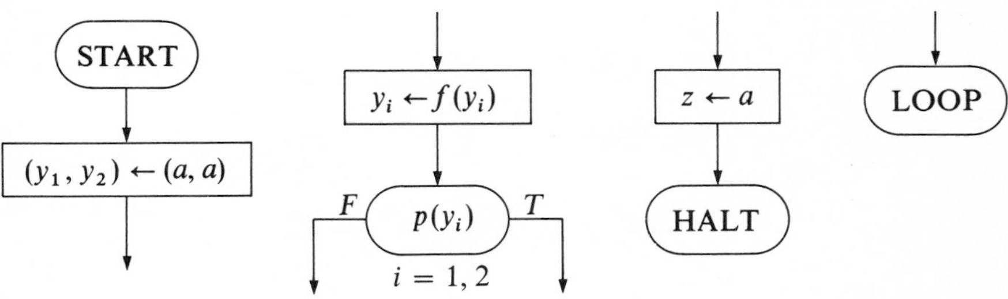

In Section 4-2.1 we shall show that

1. The halting problem for schemas in $\mathscr{S}_1$ is unsolvable.
2. The divergence problem for schemas in $\mathscr{S}_1$ is not partially solvable.
3. The equivalence problem for schemas in $\mathscr{S}_1$ is not partially solvable.
4. The isomorphism problem for schemas in $\mathscr{S}_1$ is not partially solvable.

In the rest of this chapter (Sec. 4-2.2 to 4-2.4) we shall discuss subclasses of schemas for which these problems are solvable. For example, it is very interesting to compare the four decision problems for $\mathscr{S}_1$ with those of a very "similar" class of schemas, namely, $\mathscr{S}_2$. Classes $\mathscr{S}_1$ and $\mathscr{S}_2$ differ only in that every schema in $\mathscr{S}_2$ contains two individual constants a and b and the START statement is of the form

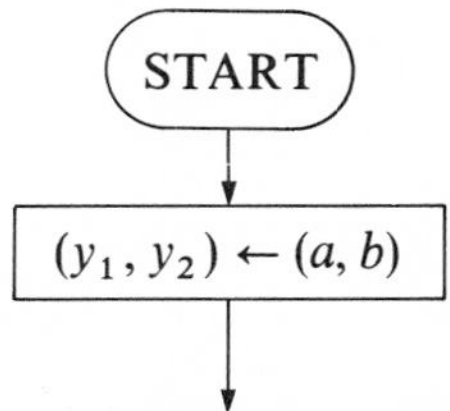

However, from our discussion in Sec. 4-2.3 it will follow that since every schema in $\mathscr{S}_2$ is "free", $\mathscr{S}_2$ has entirely different decision properties:

1. The halting problem for schemas in $\mathscr{S}_2$ is solvable.
2. The divergence problem for schemas in $\mathscr{S}_2$ is solvable.
3. The equivalence problem for schemas in $\mathscr{S}_2$ is solvable.†
4. The isomorphism problem for schemas in $\mathscr{S}_2$ is solvable.

4-2.1 Unsolvability of the Basic Properties

The main result is the following theorem.

THEOREM 4-2 (Luckham-Park-Paterson). *The following properties of schemas in $\mathscr{S}_1$ are not partially solvable:*

(1) $\langle S, \mathscr{I} \rangle$ *diverges for every interpretation* $\mathscr{I}$; *and*

(2) $\langle S, \mathscr{I} \rangle$ *diverges for some interpretation* $\mathscr{I}$.

Proof. The theorem is proved by showing that the nonacceptance/looping problem of two-registered finite automata (see Chap. 1, Example 1-25) is reducible to the divergence problem for every/some interpretation of schemas in $\mathscr{S}_1$. In Chap. 1, Example 1-25, we showed the following:

1. *The nonacceptance problem of two-registered finite automata over* $\Sigma = \{t, f\}$ *is not partially solvable.* That is, there is no algorithm that takes any two-registered finite automaton A over $\Sigma = \{t, f\}$ as input and if $accept(A) = \phi$, the algorithm will reach an ACCEPT halt; if $accept(A) \neq \phi$, the algorithm either reaches a REJECT halt or never halts.

2. *The looping problem of two-registered finite automata over* $\Sigma = \{t, f\}$ *is not partially solvable.* That is, there is no algorithm that takes any two-registered finite automaton A over $\Sigma = \{t, f\}$ as input and if $loop(A) \neq \phi$, the algorithm will reach an ACCEPT halt; if $loop(A) = \phi$, the algorithm either reaches a REJECT halt or never halts.

Now, for any given two-registered finite automaton A over $\{t, f\}$ we construct its corresponding schemas S'_A and S''_A, both in $\mathscr{S}_1$, as follows:

† This property follows from the recent work of Bird (1972).

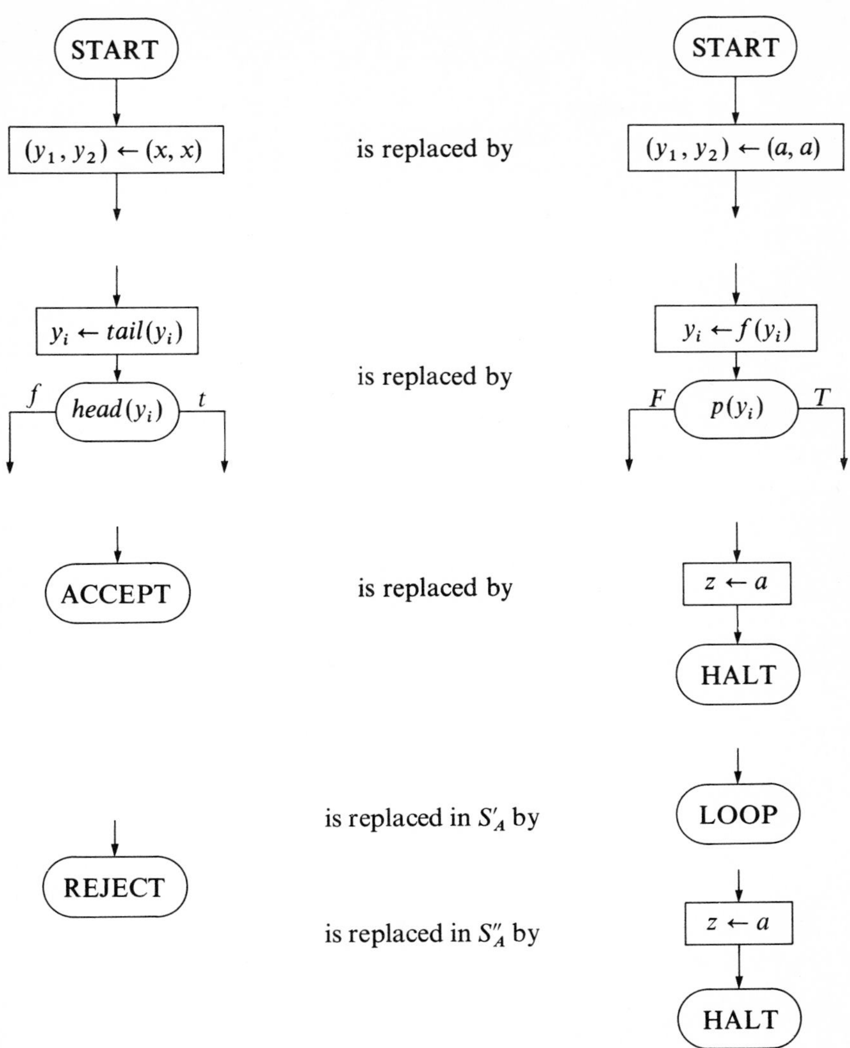

The desired result then follows from the fact that $accept(A) = \phi$ if and only if $\langle S'_A, \mathscr{I} \rangle$ diverges for every interpretation $\mathscr{I}$ and $loop(A) \neq \phi$ if and only if $\langle S''_A, \mathscr{I} \rangle$ diverges for some interpretation $\mathscr{I}$. The main idea in the proof is that every Herbrand interpretation $\mathscr{I}^*$ of a schema S in $\mathscr{S}_1$ can actually be described by an infinite string over $\{t, f\}$, where the ith ($i \geqq 0$) letter in the string indicates the truth value, *true* or *false*, of $p(``f^{(i)}(a)")$ under $\mathscr{I}^*$.

Q.E.D.

EXAMPLE 4-10

Consider the simple two-registered finite automaton A described in Fig. 4-8. It diverges only on the tapes

$$\alpha:\ t\ f\ \underbrace{t}\ f\ \underbrace{t\ t}\ f\ \underbrace{t\ t\ t}\ f\ \underbrace{t\ t\ t\ t}\ f\ \ldots$$

$$\alpha':\ f\ f\ \underbrace{t}\ f\ \underbrace{t\ t}\ f\ \underbrace{t\ t\ t}\ f\ \underbrace{t\ t\ t\ t}\ f\ \ldots$$

and it accepts/rejects all those tapes which first deviate from α or α' with an extra f/t. For example, any tape with prefix of the form $t\,f\,t\,f\,f\ldots$ will be accepted, while any tape with prefix of the form $t\,f\,t\,t\ldots$ will be rejected. When A is operating on such a tape, y_2 "reads" along a block of t's while y_1 verifies that the following block of t's contains precisely one more t. After this, y_2 is positioned to read the latter block and y_1 is positioned for the next block of t's. An extra t causes A to reject the tape, but an extra f causes A to accept the tape. The schemas S'_A and S''_A corresponding to A are described in Fig. 4-9. Note that they differ only in the LOOP/HALT statements. □

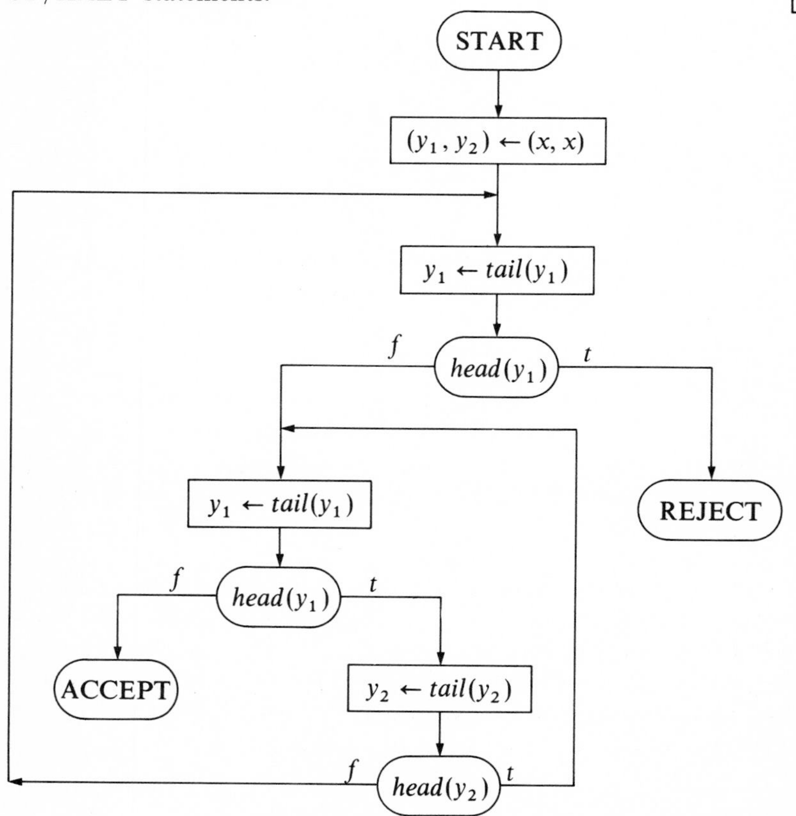

Figure 4-8 Two-registered finite automaton A.

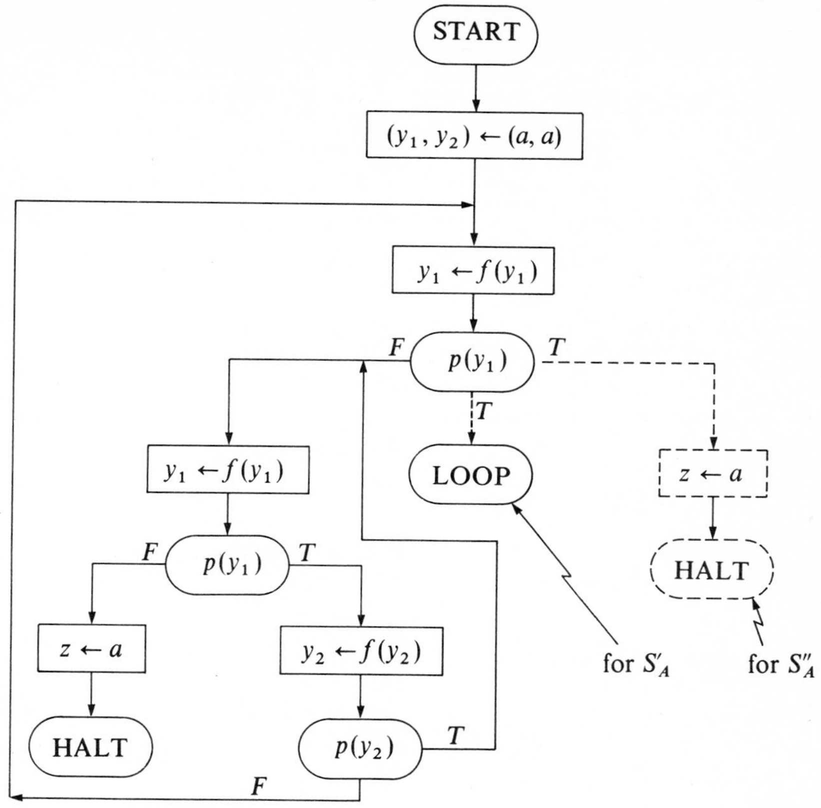

Figure 4-9 Schemas S'_A and S''_A

From Theorem 4-2 we obtain the following important corollary.

COROLLARY. (1) *The halting problem for schemas in* $\mathscr{S}_1$ *is unsolvable;*† (2) *the divergence problem for schemas in* $\mathscr{S}_1$ *is not partially solvable;* (3) *the equivalence problem for schemas in* $\mathscr{S}_1$ *is not partially solvable;* (4) *the isomorphism problem for schemas in* $\mathscr{S}_1$ *is not partially solvable.*

Part 1 of the corollary follows from part 2 of Theorem 4-2 because if the halting problem is solvable, its complement (the divergence problem for some interpretation) should be solvable also. Part 2 of the corollary is actually part 1 of Theorem 4-2. Part 3 of the corollary follows from Part 2 of the corollary because a schema S of $\mathscr{S}_1$ diverges if and only if it is equivalent to the following schema of $\mathscr{S}_1$:

† From our discussion in Sec. 4-2.3, it will actually follow that the halting problem of the class of all flowchart schemas is partially solvable.

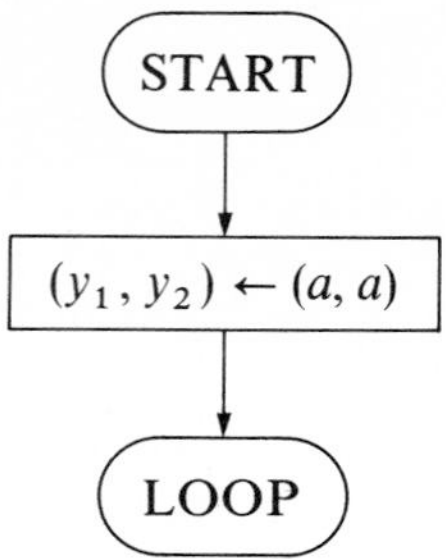

Thus, if the equivalence problem were partially solvable, the divergence problem would be partially solvable also. Part 4 of the corollary also follows from Part 2 of the corollary. For any schema S of $\mathscr{S}_1$, let $\bar{S}$ be the schema of $\mathscr{S}_1$ obtained by replacing all HALT statements in S by LOOP statements; then, S is isomorphic to $\bar{S}$ if and only if S diverges.

Q.E.D.

In the following sections we shall discuss subclasses of schemas for which the four problems are solvable.

4-2.2 Free Schemas

Freedom is an important notion because it is usually substantially simpler to prove the properties of free schemas rather than those of nonfree schemas. First let us consider the following example.

EXAMPLE 4-11

Consider the schema S_{11A} described in Fig. 4-10*a*. Note that no computation of S_{11A} includes a sequence of statements of the form $\cdots - 1 - 2 - 4 - 7 - \cdots$, or a sequence of statements of the form $\cdots - 1 - 2 - 5 - 8 - \cdots$, or a sequence of statements of the form $\cdots - 5 - 1 - 3 - \cdots$; in addition, no finite computation of S_{11A} includes the sequence of statements $1 - 2 - 5 - 1$. Therefore it follows that the schema S_{11B} (Figure 4-10*b*) is equivalent to S_{11A}. □

The schema S_{11A} had impossible sequences of statements in the sense that no computation could follow those sequences; schemas with such impossible sequences are said to be *nonfree*. The schema S_{11B} has no such impossible sequences and therefore is said to be *free*. Formally, a *schema S is said to be free if every finite path through its flow-diagram, from the START statement, is an initial segment of some computation.* This definition implies that for a free schema every infinite path through its flow-diagram, from the START statement, describes some computation [see Prob. 4-6(*b*)].

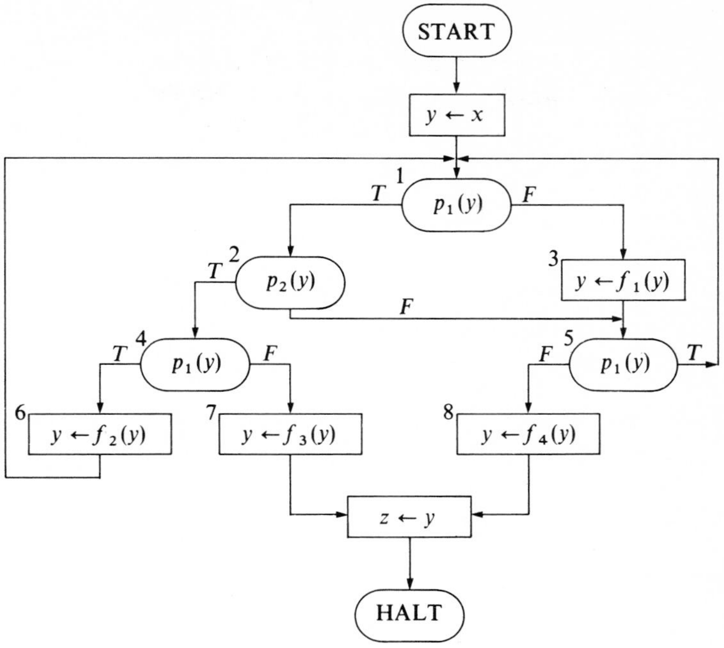

Figure 4-10*a* Schema S_{11A}.

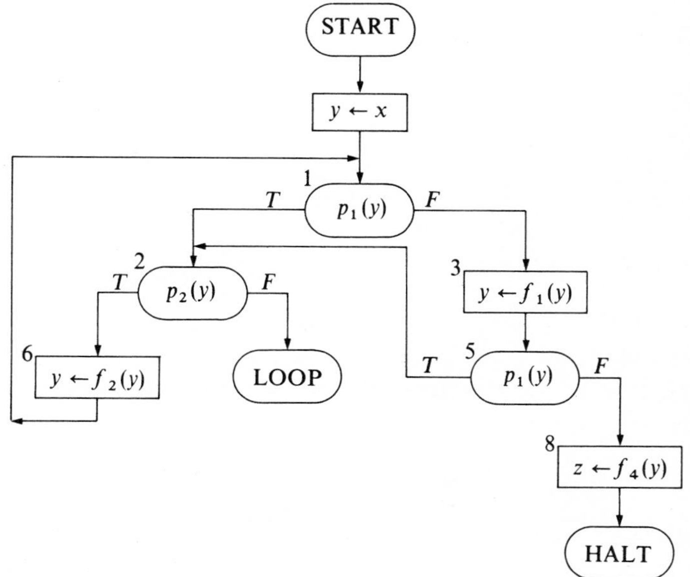

Figure 4-10*b* Schema S_{11B}.

EXAMPLE 4-12

The schema S_{12} (Fig. 4-11) is not free. Note that among all possible finite paths from the START to the HALT statements, only those that go through loop α the same number of times as through loop β describe possible computations of S_{12}. □

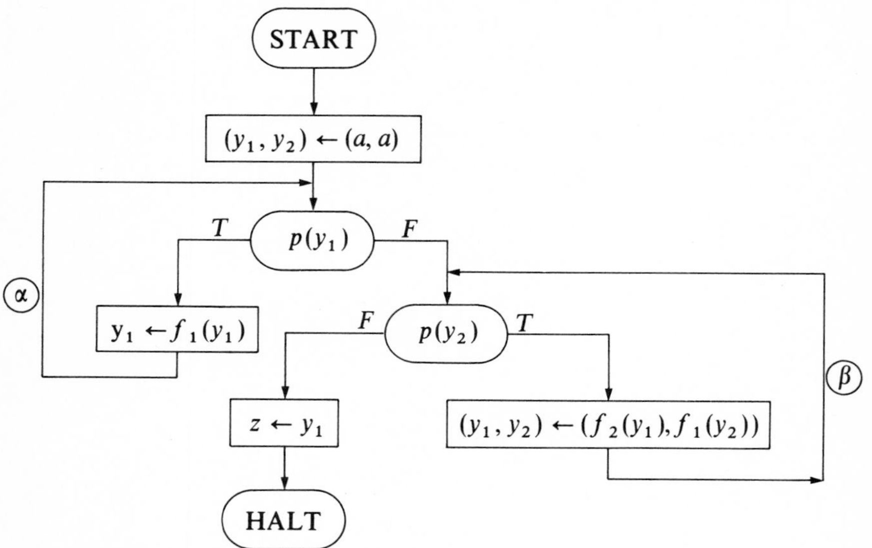

Figure 4-11 Nonfree schema S_{12}.

The following are several interesting properties of the class of free schemas:

1. *The halting problem for free schemas is solvable.* This follows from the fact that a free schema does not halt if and only if it contains a LOOP statement or its flow-diagram contains a loop in its structure.
2. *The divergence problem for free schemas is solvable.* This follows from the fact that a free schema does not diverge if and only if it contains a HALT statement.
3. *It is not partially solvable whether or not a schema is free* [Paterson (1967)].

We shall show that for every Post correspondence problem (PCP) C over Σ it is possible to construct a schema $S(C)$ such that $S(C)$ is free if and only if C has no solution. Since the PCP over Σ is unsolvable but partially solvable, it follows that its complement is not partially solvable (see

Chap. 1, Sec. 1-5.4). Then, since it is not partially solvable whether or not an arbitrary PCP does not have a solution, it is also not partially solvable whether or not an arbitrary schema is free.

Let C be a PCP which consists of a set of n pairs of strings $\{(u_i, v_i)\}_{1 \leq i \leq n}$ over an alphabet Σ. Then the corresponding schema $S(C)$ is constructed as follows: The function constants used in $S(C)$ are f and f_σ for every $\sigma \in \Sigma$. For any word $w = \sigma_1\sigma_2 \ldots \sigma_k \in \Sigma^*$, let

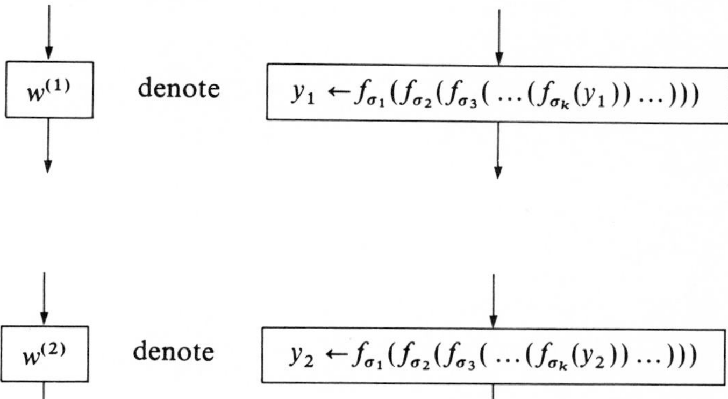
$w^{(1)}$
denote
$y_1 \leftarrow f_{\sigma_1}(f_{\sigma_2}(f_{\sigma_3}(\ldots(f_{\sigma_k}(y_1))\ldots)))$
and
$w^{(2)}$
denote
$y_2 \leftarrow f_{\sigma_1}(f_{\sigma_2}(f_{\sigma_3}(\ldots(f_{\sigma_k}(y_2))\ldots)))$

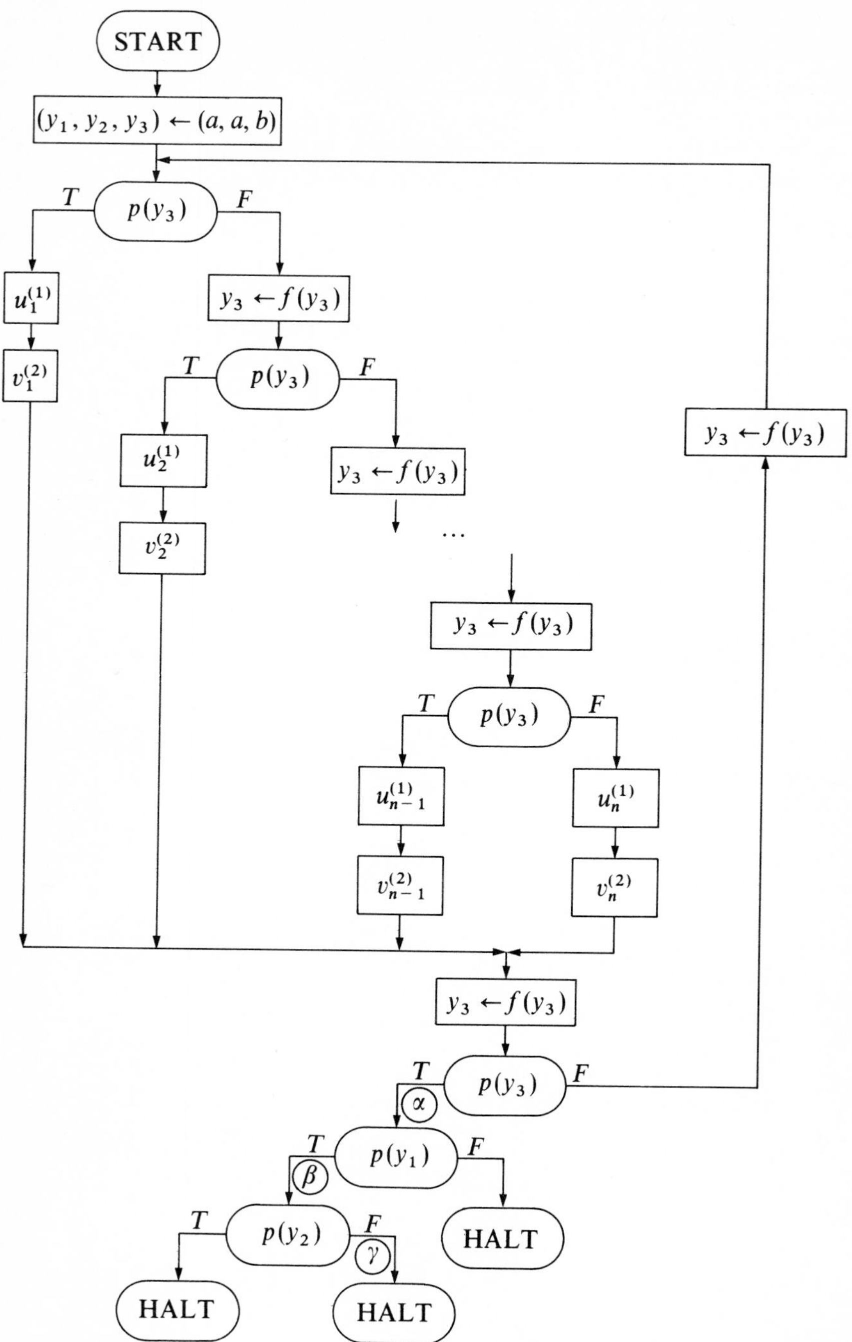

Figure 4-12 Schema $S(C)$ corresponding to the Post correspondence problem C.

The schema $S(C)$ (see Fig. 4-12) is constructed in such a way that the program variable y_1 simulates the composition of the u_i's while the program variable y_2 simulates the composition of the v_i's. Nonfreedom can only result from reaching α with $y_1 = y_2$, in which case the path . . . $\alpha\beta\gamma$ is impossible. Thus, $S(C)$ is not free if and only if the PCP C has a solution; or, equivalently, $S(C)$ is free if and only if C has no solution.

4. *It is unknown yet whether or not the equivalence problem for free schemas is solvable.*

5. *The isomorphism problem for free schemas is solvable.* To show this it is very convenient to express a schema by a regular expression which consists of statements rather than letters, as illustrated below.

EXAMPLE 4-13

The regular expression $\mathcal{R}(S_{13A})$ representing the schema S_{13A} (Figure 4-13) is

$$\text{START}\,[y \leftarrow x]\,\big([p(y) = F]\,[y \leftarrow f(y)]\big)^*\,[p(y) = T]\,[z \leftarrow y]\,\text{HALT}$$

and the regular expression $\mathcal{R}(S_{13B})$ representing the schema S_{13B} is

$$\begin{aligned}\text{START}\,[y \leftarrow x]\,\big([p(y) = T]\,[z \leftarrow y]\,\text{HALT}\\ + [p(y) = F]\,[y \leftarrow f(y)]\,\big([p(y) = F]\,[y \leftarrow f(y)]\big)^*\\ [p(y) = T]\,[z \leftarrow y]\,\text{HALT}\big)\end{aligned}$$ □

For any free schema S, every "word" in $\mathcal{R}(S)$ represents the sequence of statements of some *finite* computation $\langle S, \mathcal{I}^*, \text{“}\bar{x}\text{”}\rangle$ and vice versa. We leave to the reader to conclude that two compatible free schemas S and S' are isomorphic if and only if $\mathcal{R}(S) = \mathcal{R}(S')$. Since it is solvable whether or not two regular expressions define the same set of words (Chap. 1, Theorem 1-2), it follows that it is solvable whether or not two free schemas are isomorphic. For example, $\mathcal{R}(S_{13A})$ in Example 4-13 has the form $ab(cd)^*\,efg$ while $\mathcal{R}(S_{13B})$ has the form $ab\big(efg + cd(cd)^*\,efg\big)$. Since

$$ab\big(efg + cd(cd)^*\,efg\big) = ab\big(\Lambda + cd(cd)^*\big)\,efg = ab(cd)^*\,efg,$$

and since S_{13A} and S_{13B} are free schemas, it is implied that $S_{13A} \approx S_{13B}$.

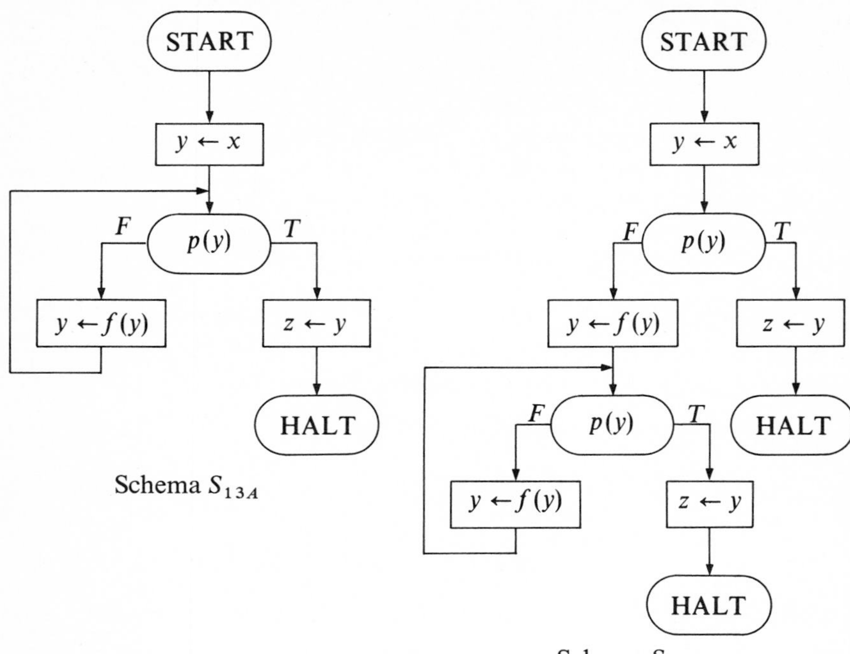

Figure 4-13 Isomorphic schemas S_{13A} and S_{13B}.

6. *The nonfree schema* S_{12} *(Fig.* 4-11) *has no equivalent free schema* [Chandra (1973)]. We shall sketch the proof of this result: Suppose there exists a free schema, say, S', which is equivalent to S_{12}. It can be proved that there must exist a free schema S'' which is equivalent to S' and contains no function constants other than the unary functions f_1 and f_2 (and the individual constant a). Then, since S'' is free and contains only unary function constants, it can be shown (see Prob. 4-7) that the set of all final terms (without parentheses) generated by S'' under all possible Herbrand interpretations can be expressed by a regular expression. But the set of all final terms generated by S_{12} is $f_2^{(i)}f_1^{(i)}a$, $i \geqq 0$, which cannot be expressed by any regular expression: contradiction.

The last result clearly implies that in general there cannot exist an algorithm for transforming a given schema into an equivalent free schema. The best we can do is to construct for any given schema an equivalent free *tree schema*. In Sec. 4-2.3 we shall discuss the class of tree schemas.

4-2.3 Tree Schemas

A *tree schema* T over a finite alphabet Σ_T is a (possibly infinite) treelike flow-diagram constructed from statements over Σ_T such that

1. There is exactly one START statement.
2. For each statement, there is exactly one way it can be reached from the START statement.
3. Each terminal statement is either a HALT or LOOP statement.

Note that every finite tree schema (that is, a tree schema with finitely many statements) is a flowchart schema. It is straightforward to show that *the halting problem, the divergence problem, the equivalence problem, and the isomorphism problem for finite tree schemas are solvable.*

We shall now illustrate the method for deciding whether or not two compatible finite tree schemas are equivalent.

EXAMPLE 4-14

Consider the finite tree schema S_{14A} (Fig. 4-14*a*) and S_{14B} (Fig. 4-14*b*). Here, e_1 is "$f(x_1, x_2)$", e_2 is "$g(x_2)$", and e_3 is "$f(f(x_1, x_2), g(x_2))$". The final value of z obtained by S_{14A} for all Herbrand interpretations can be described by

$$\textit{if} \quad p(e_2) = p(e_3) = \textit{false} \quad \textit{then} \quad \text{“}a\text{”} \quad \textit{else} \quad \text{“}b\text{”}$$

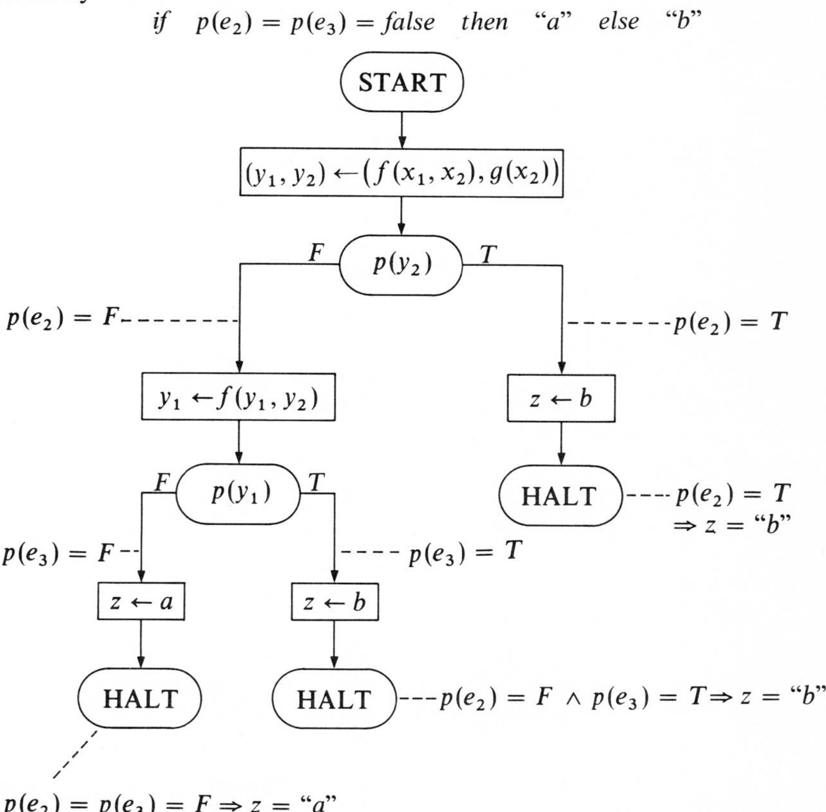

Figure 4-14*a* Finite tree schema S_{14A}

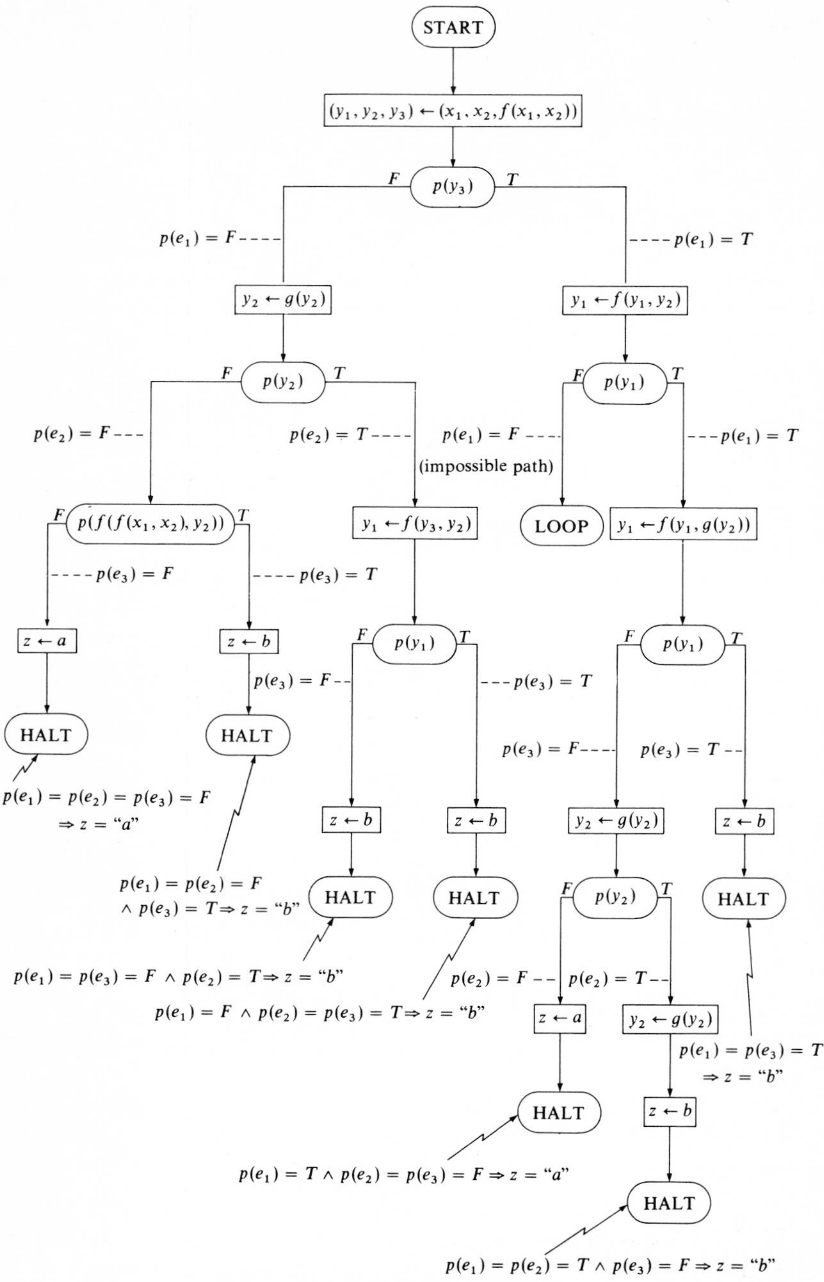

Figure 4-14*b* Finite tree schema S_{14B}

The final value of z obtained by S_{14B} can be summarized by the following table:

$p(e_1)$	$p(e_2)$	$p(e_3)$	z
true	*true*	*true*	"b"
true	*true*	*false*	"b"
true	*false*	*true*	"b"
true	*false*	*false*	"a"
false	*true*	*true*	"b"
false	*true*	*false*	"b"
false	*false*	*true*	"b"
false	*false*	*false*	"a"

or, equivalently,

$$\textit{if} \quad p(e_2) = p(e_3) = \textit{false} \quad \textit{then} \quad \text{“}a\text{”} \quad \textit{else} \quad \text{“}b\text{”}$$

This implies that $val(S_{14A}, \mathcal{I}^*, \text{“}\bar{x}\text{”}) \equiv val(S_{14B}, \mathcal{I}^*, \text{“}\bar{x}\text{”})$ for every Herbrand interpretation $\mathcal{I}^*$. Thus, S_{14A} and S_{14B} are equivalent.

□

Tree schemas and flowchart schemas are computed in the same manner, and therefore we can naturally define the freedom of tree schemas and discuss equivalence between compatible tree schemas and flowchart schemas. Furthermore, Theorem 4-1 (see Sec. 4-1.4) holds for tree schemas as well as for flowchart schemas. The main point concerning tree schemas is that *for any given flowchart schema S we can construct an equivalent free tree schema $T(S)$*, called the *tree schema of* S. Rather than giving a detailed algorithm, we shall illustrate the construction of $T(S)$ in the next example. (Note that by Theorem 4-1 it suffices to consider only Herbrand interpretations.)

EXAMPLE 4-15

Consider again the flowchart schema S_3 (Fig. 4-3). We can "unwind" the loops of S_3 to produce an equivalent infinite tree. While unwinding, we systematically look for impossible paths, which can be pruned. In this way for S_3 we construct the infinite tree schema described in Fig. 4-15a. The FAILURE statements indicate impossible computations; that is, no computation can reach these points. In the part of the tree that is shown in Fig. 4-15a there are two FAILURE statements because

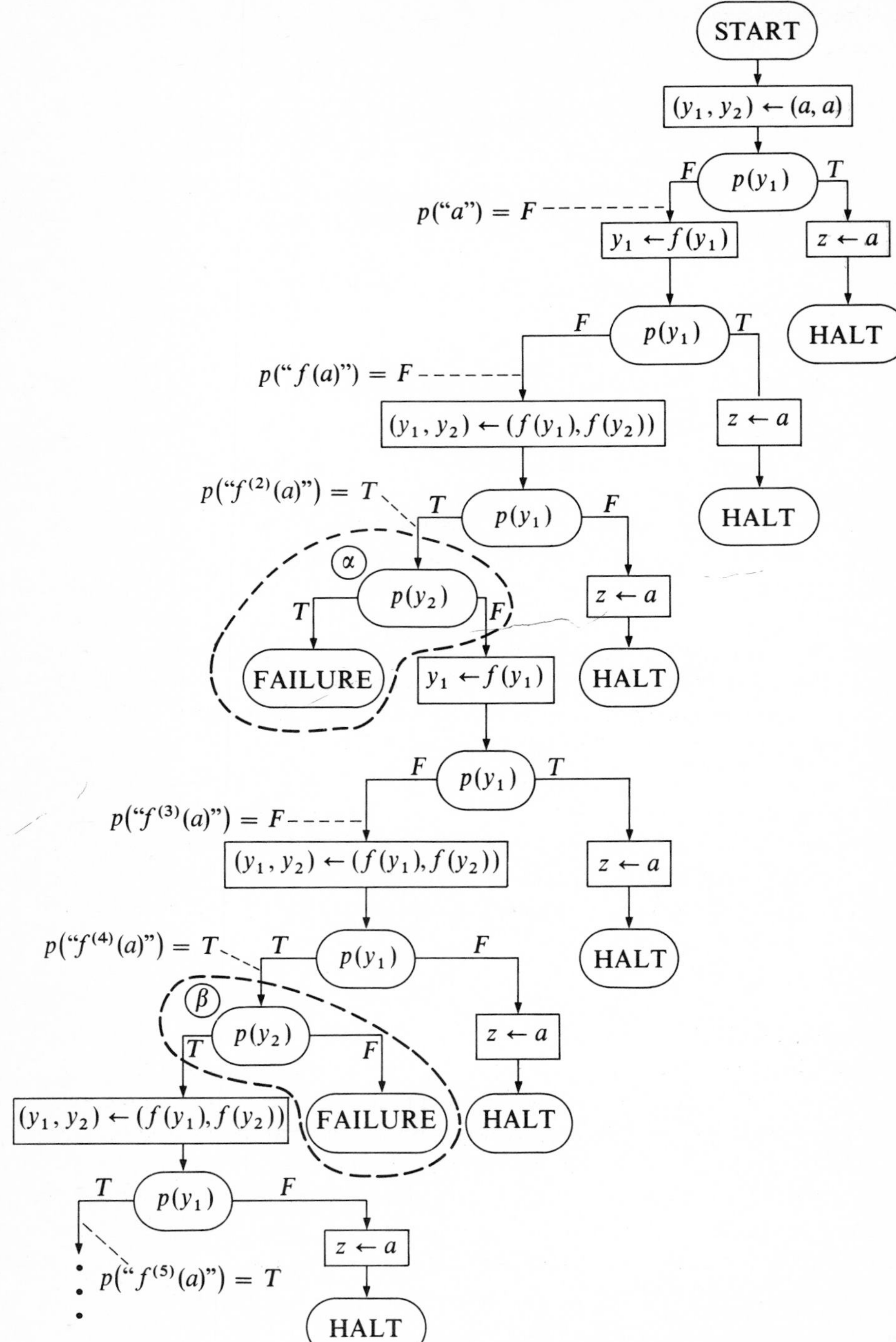

Figure 4-15a Intermediate step in the construction of $T(S_3)$.

1. Whenever we reach the TEST statement α, $(y_1, y_2) = (\text{“}f^{(2)}(a)\text{”}, \text{“}f(a)\text{”})$ and $p(\text{“}f(a)\text{”}) = false$; therefore it is impossible to take the T branch.

2. Whenever we reach the TEST statement β, $(y_1, y_2) = (\text{“}f^{(4)}(a)\text{”}, \text{“}f^{(2)}(a)\text{”})$ and $p(\text{“}f^{(2)}(a)\text{”}) = true$; therefore it is impossible to take the F branch.

The tree is pruned further (by removing those parts enclosed within broken lines) to obtain the free tree schema $T(S_3)$ (Fig. 4-15*b*). Thus, $T(S_3)$ is clearly equivalent to S_3.

□

Suppose that we translate in the same way a flowchart schema S which halts (for every interpretation) to obtain its equivalent free tree schema $T(S)$. Since every path in $T(S)$ corresponds to the trace of some computation of S, and since S halts for every interpretation, it follows that there are no infinite paths in $T(S)$. Moreover, every node (statement) in $T(S)$ has at most two branches leading from it. Thus by König's “infinity lemma,”† it follows that $T(S)$ has only finitely many statements; that is, $T(S)$ is finite. Therefore we can conclude that *for every flowchart schema which halts for every interpretation we can effectively construct an equivalent finite free tree schema.*‡

† See, for example, D. E. Knuth, *The Art of Computer Programming*, Vol. 1, Addison-Wesley Publishing Com., Reading, Mass. (1967), pp. 381–383.

‡ In Section 4-2.1 it was shown that the halting problem for flowchart schemas is unsolvable; however, this discussion implies that the halting problem for flowchart schemas is *partially solvable*.

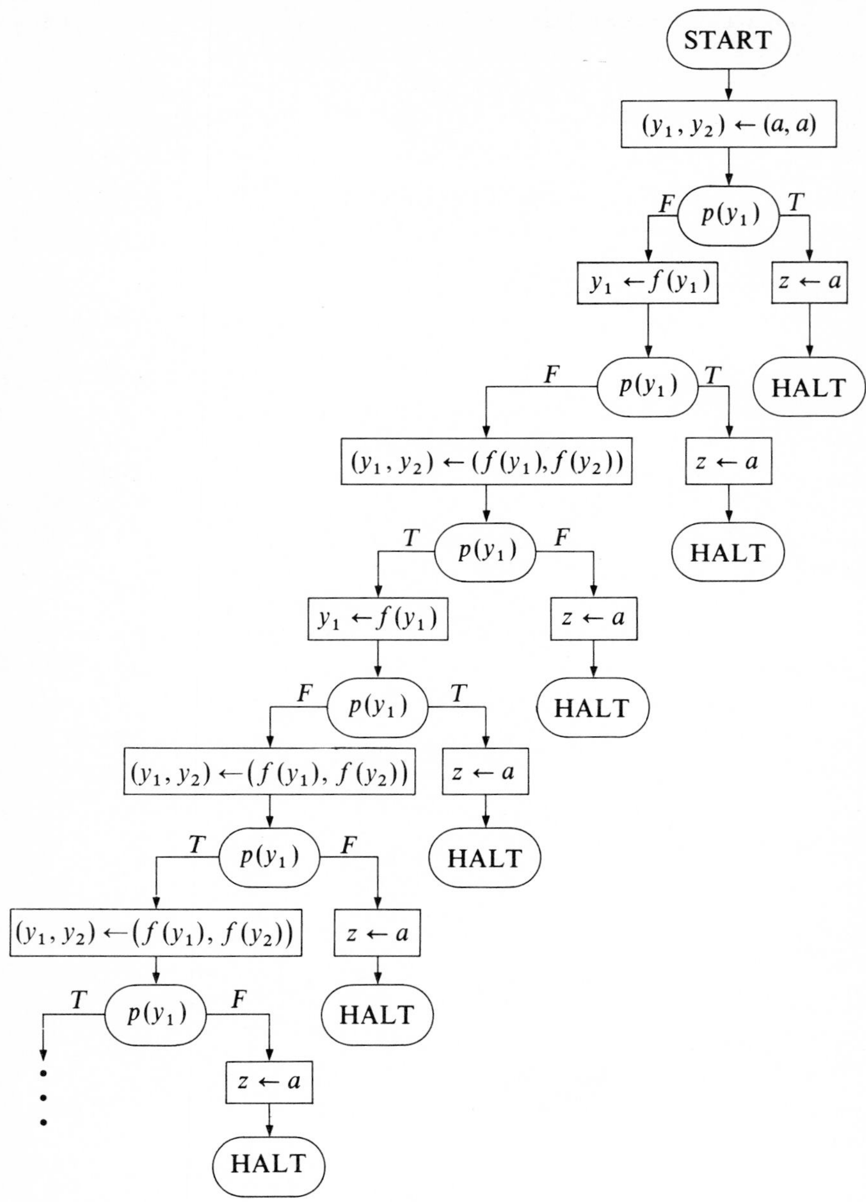

Figure 4-15*b* Tree schema $T(S_3)$.

This result is actually quite strong: It implies that for every flowchart schema S that halts for every interpretation, there exists a bound $b > 0$ such that no computation of S executes more than b statements. In other words, any flowchart schema S which has the property that for every positive integer i there is a computation of S that executes more than i statements, must have at least one infinite computation.

EXAMPLE 4-16

Consider the flowchart schema S_{16A} (Fig. 4-16*a*), which halts for every interpretation. First we construct the flowchart schema described in Fig. 4-16*b*. We have three FAILURE statements because

1. Whenever we reach the TEST statement α, $(y_1, y_2) = (\text{“}f(x)\text{”}, \text{“}f^{(2)}(x)\text{”})$ and $p(\text{“}f(x)\text{”}) = true$; therefore it is impossible to take the F branch.
2. Whenever we reach the TEST statement β, $(y_1, y_2) = (\text{“}f^{(2)}(x)\text{”}, \text{“}f^{(3)}(x)\text{”})$ and $p(\text{“}f^{(2)}(x)\text{”}) = false$; therefore it is impossible to take the T branch.
3. Whenever we reach the TEST statement γ, $(y_1, y_2) = (\text{“}f^{(2)}(x)\text{”}, \text{“}f^{(3)}(x)\text{”})$ and $p(\text{“}f^{(3)}(x)\text{”}) = false$; therefore it is impossible to take the T branch.

The tree is pruned further (by removing those parts enclosed within broken lines) to obtain the finite free tree schema S_{16B} (Fig. 4-16*c*).

□

The results achieved in this section can be used to show the following:

1. *The equivalence problem for flowchart schemas which halt for every interpretation is solvable.*
2. *The isomorphism problem for flowchart schemas which halt for every interpretation is solvable.*

Recall, however, that the halting problem for schemas is unsolvable; that is, there does not exist an algorithm that decides whether a given schema is a member of our class (halts for every interpretation) or not.

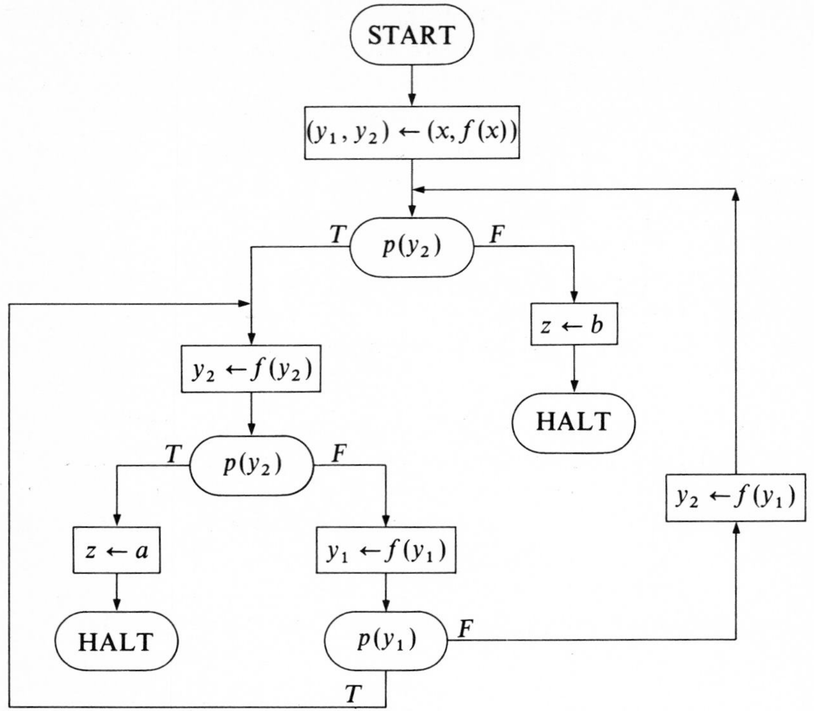

Figure 4-16a Flowchart schema S_{16A}.

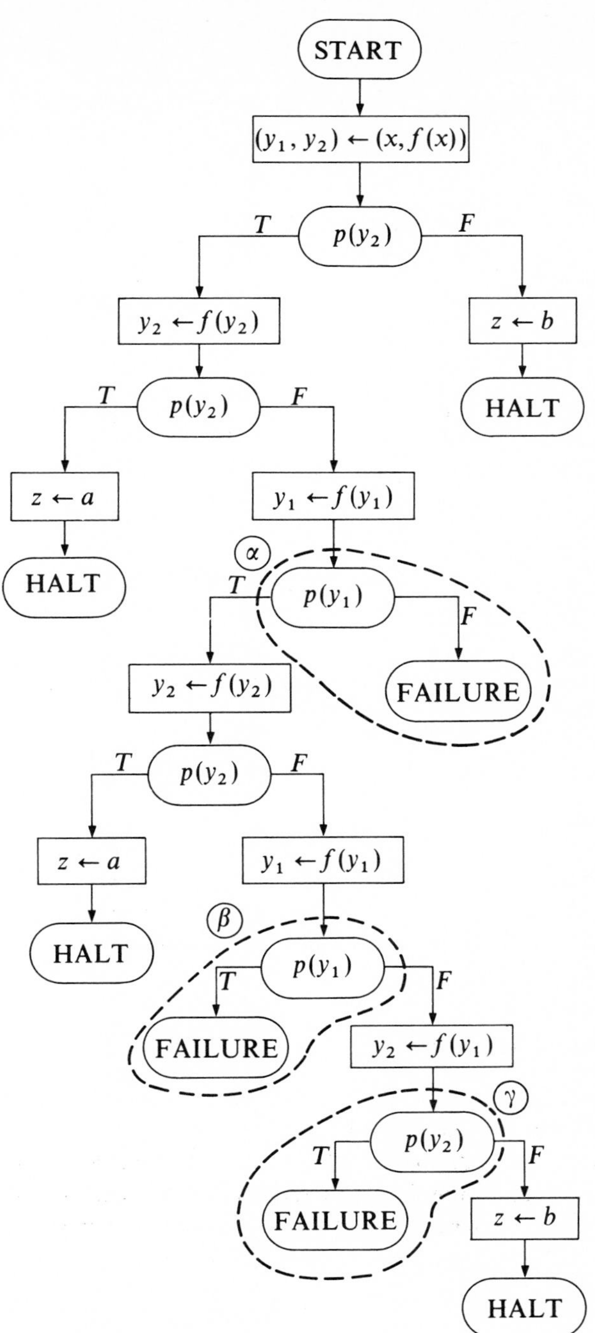

Figure 4-16*b* The intermediate step in the construction of S_{16B}.

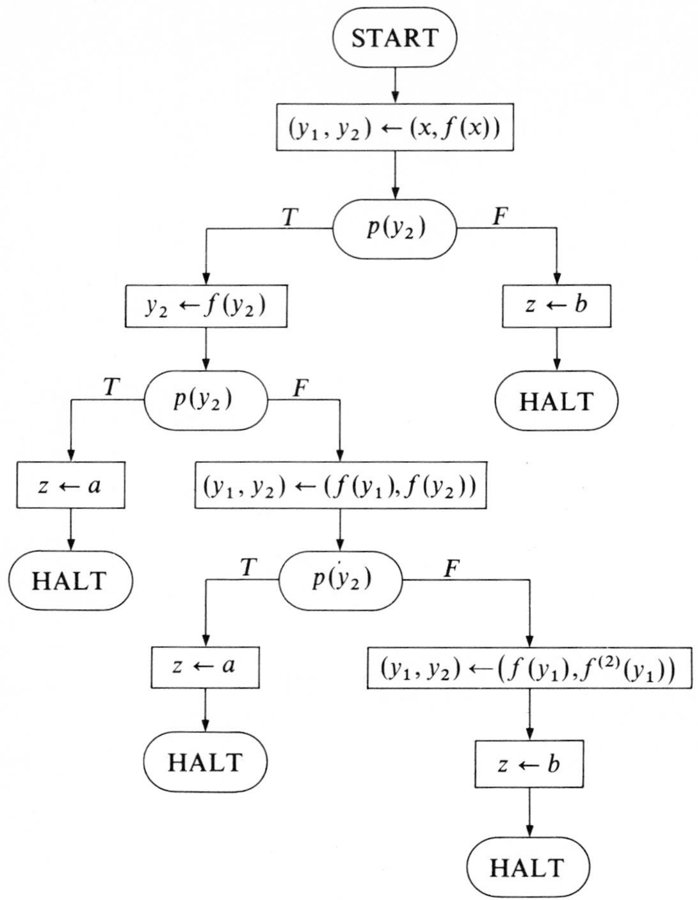

Figure 4-16c Finite free tree schema S_{16B}.

4-2.4 Ianov Schemas

In Sec. 4-2.3 it was stated that the equivalence and isomorphism problems are solvable for the class of all flowchart schemas which always halt. In this section we shall discuss another class of flowchart schemas, known as *Ianov schemas*, for which the four decision problems are solvable. The most important feature characterizing Ianov schemas is that they have a single program variable y. We say that a flowchart schema S is an *Ianov schema* if

1. Σ_S consists of a finite set of unary function constants $\{f_i\}$, a finite set of unary predicate constants $\{p_i\}$, a single input variable x, a single

program variable y, and a single output variable z. (Note that individual constants are not allowed.)

2. All statements in S are of one of the following forms:

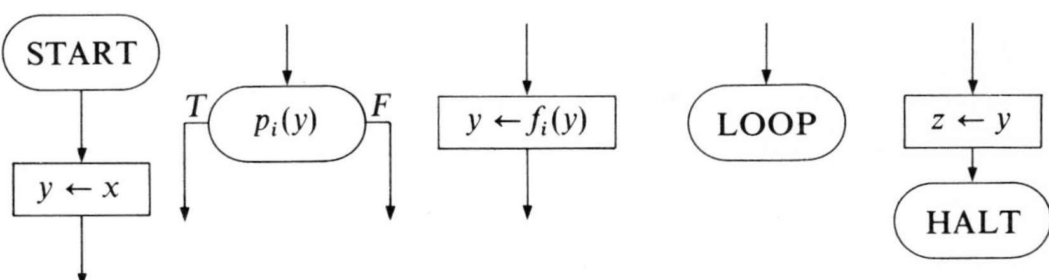

The following are several interesting properties of the class of Ianov schemas.

1. *It is solvable whether or not an Ianov schema is free.* This follows from the fact that an Ianov schema is nonfree if and only if it has a path with two identical tests and no ASSIGNMENT statement between the tests.

EXAMPLE 4-17

The schema S_{17A} (Fig. 4-17*a*) is an Ianov schema. It is not free because of the path from 1 to 2, the loop around 2, and the path from 1 to 3. The schema S_{17B} (Fig. 4-17*b*) is a free Ianov schema.

□

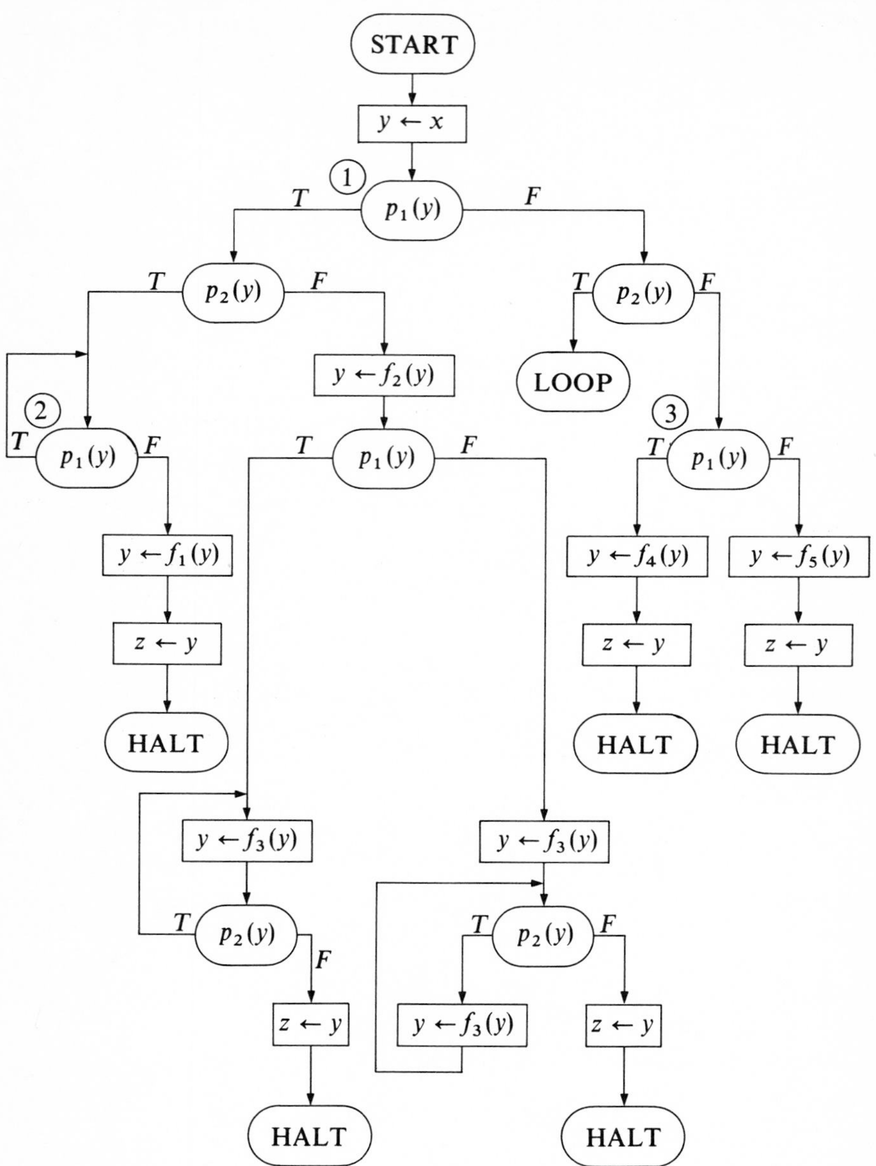

Figure 4-17*a* Ianov schema S_{17A}.

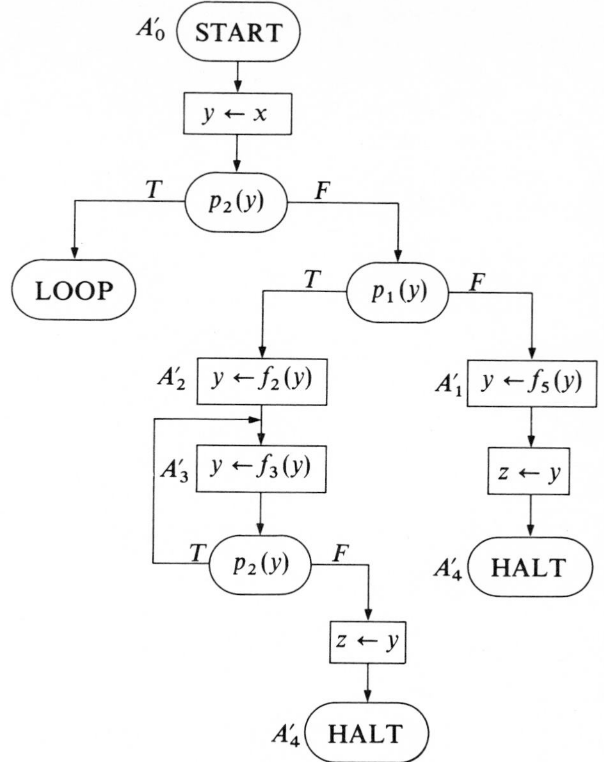

Figure 4-17*b* Ianov schema S_{17B}.

2. *Every nonfree Ianov schema S can be transformed effectively into an equivalent free Ianov schema S′.* We leave the formal proof of this property as an exercise to the reader [Prob. 4-9(*a*)]. However, let us sketch here one possible algorithm: Suppose the schema S consists of two predicate symbols p_1 and p_2. The idea is first to construct a free schema which consists of tests of the form

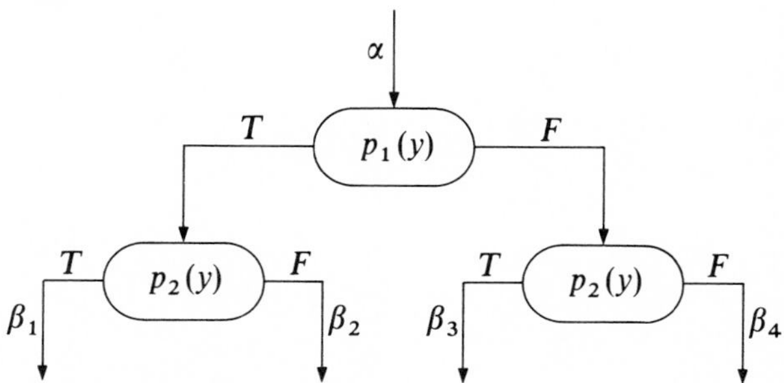

where the statement leading to arc α is the START statement or an ASSIGNMENT statement, and the first statement reachable from each β_i is a HALT, a LOOP, or an ASSIGNMENT statement.

The next step (recommended, but not required) is to simplify the free schema obtained by looking for two β's in the same test such that both β's lead to identical subschemas. For example, if β_1 and β_2 lead to identical subschemas, we can replace the test by

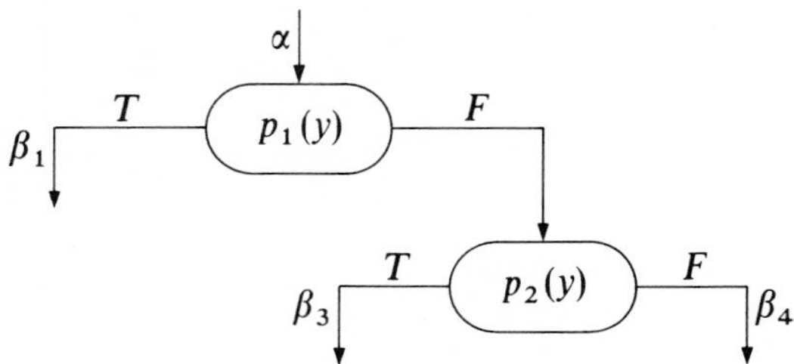

and if β_1 and β_3 lead to identical subschemas, we can replace the test by

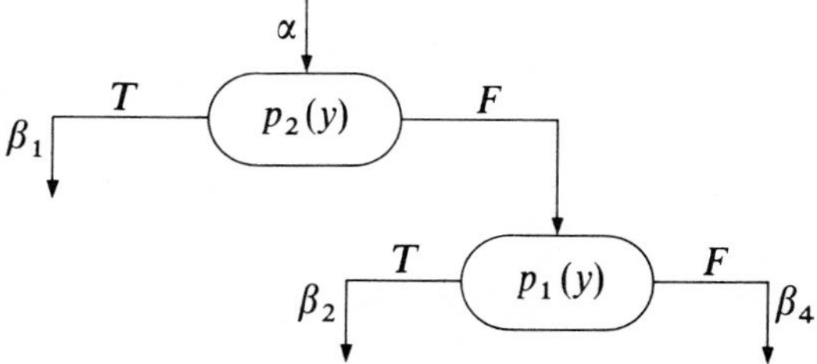

For the nonfree Ianov schema S_{17A} (Fig. 4-17*a*), the algorithm will yield the free schema S_{17C} (Fig. 4-17*c*), which is clearly equivalent to S_{17A}.

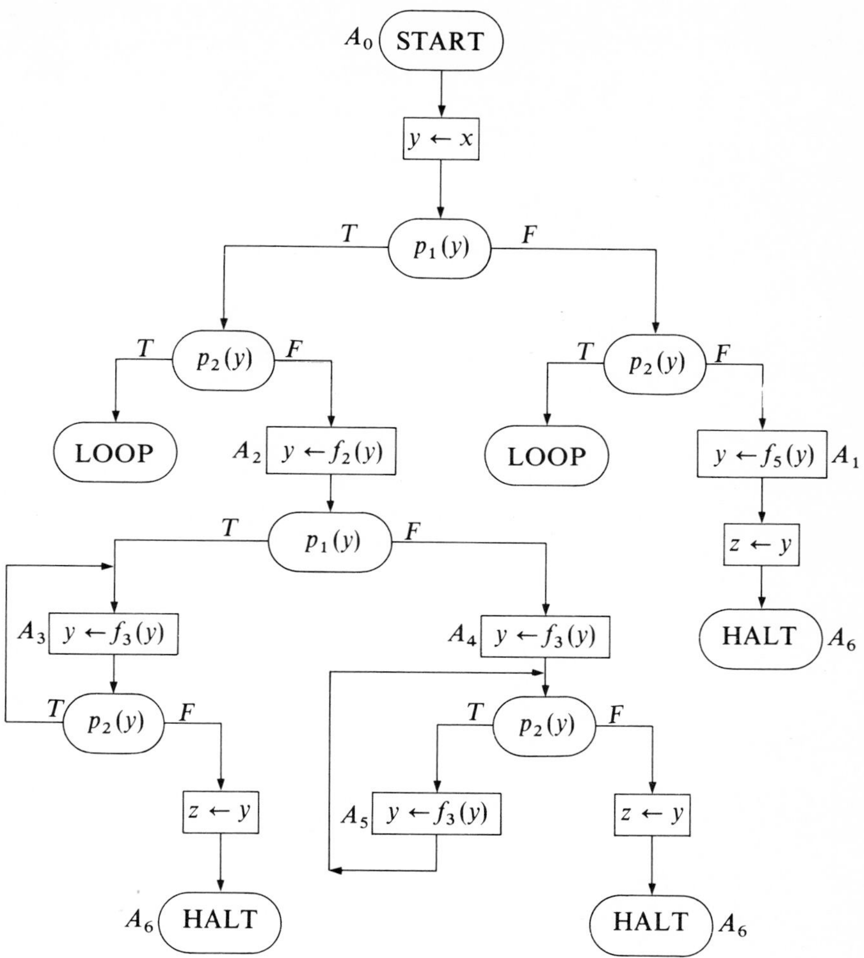

Figure 4-17c Ianov schema S_{17C}.

3. *The halting/divergence problems for Ianov schemas are solvable.* By property 2 every nonfree Ianov schema can be transformed effectively to an equivalent free Ianov schema, and the result then follows from the fact that these problems are solvable for free flowchart schemas.

4. *The equivalence problem for Ianov schemas is solvable* [Ianov (1960) and Kaplan (1969)]. Suppose that we are given a free Ianov schema S with a START statement labeled A_0 and ASSIGNMENT statements $A_1, \ldots, A_k$. Since every Ianov schema can be translated easily to an equivalent Ianov schema which has only one HALT statement, we can assume

that S has only one HALT statement, say, A_{k+1}. Suppose, also, that Σ_S consists of n function constants $f_1, \ldots, f_n$ and m predicate constants $p_1, \ldots, p_m$. We shall construct for S a transition graph G_S (see Chap. 1, Sec. 1-1.3) in such a way that G_S simulates the computations of S.

(*a*) The vertices (states) are

b_0 (representing the START statement)

a_i and b_i, $1 \leq i \leq k$ (representing the ASSIGNMENT statements)

a_{k+1} (representing the HALT statement)

The vertex b_0 is the only initial vertex (labeled by $-$), and the vertex a_{k+1} is the only final vertex (labeled by $+$). Note that we ignore the LOOP statements in S.

(*b*) The alphabet of G_S consists of the function constants $f_1, \ldots, f_n$ and the 2^m words of $\{T, F\}^m$. Intuitively, each such word (of length m) indicates the possible truth values *true* or *false* of the m predicate constants $p_1, \ldots, p_m$ for a given y.

(*c*) The arrows in G_S are constructed as follows:

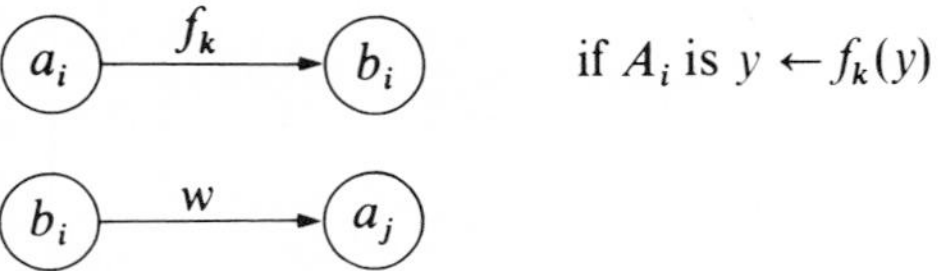

if A_i is $y \leftarrow f_k(y)$

where $w \in \{T, F\}^m$ if there is in S a path from A_i to A_j with no ASSIGNMENT statement such that the predicate values indicated by w do not contradict the tests along the path.

Now, for two given Ianov schemas S and S', we first translate them into equivalent free Ianov schemas and then construct the corresponding transition graphs G_S and $G_{S'}$. It is clear that S is equivalent to S' if and only if G_S is equivalent to $G_{S'}$. Since the equivalence problem for transition graphs is solvable (see Chap. 1, Theorem 1-2), the equivalence problem of Ianov schemas is solvable also.

EXAMPLE 4-18

Consider again the Ianov schemas S_{17A} (Fig. 4-17*a*) and S_{17B} (Fig. 4-17*b*). We would like to prove that S_{17A} is equivalent to S_{17B}. Informally it is easy to see this because:

1.

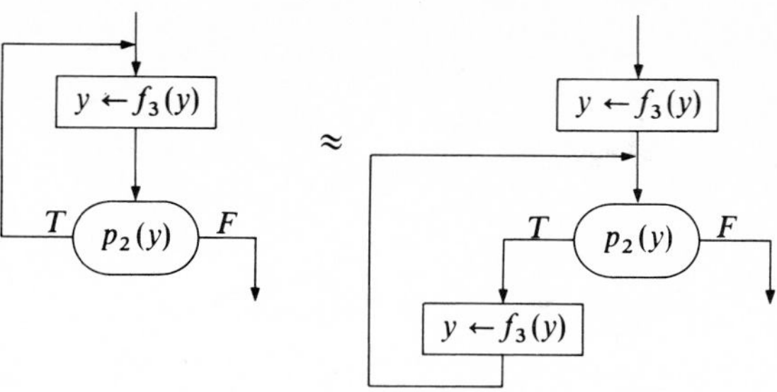

and therefore

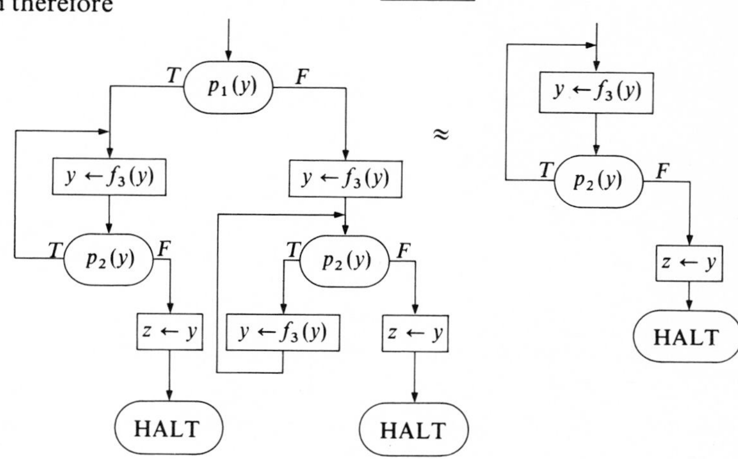

2.

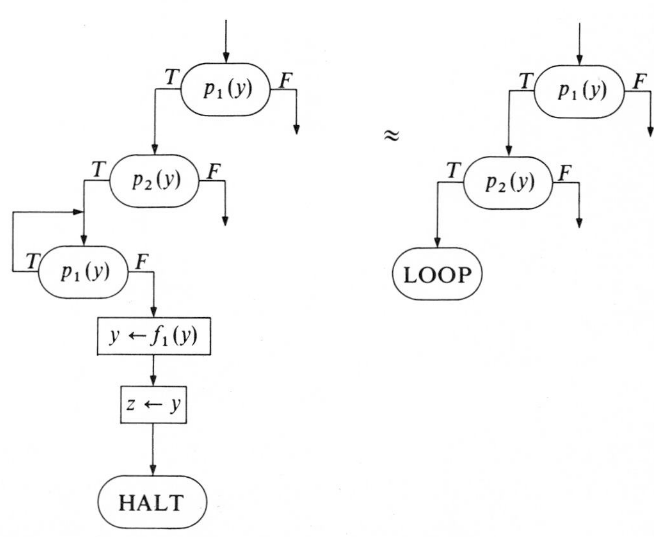

and therefore

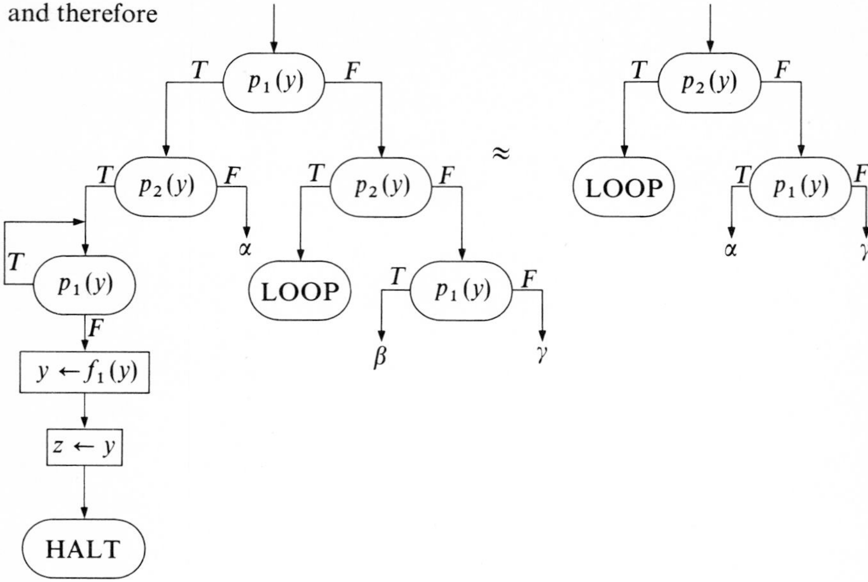

Let us show now the equivalence of S_{17A} and S_{17B} using the algorithm described previously. First we shall translate S_{17A} into the equivalent free Ianov schema S_{17C}. The transition graph G_{17A} for S_{17C} is described in Fig. 4-18*a* while the transition graph G_{17B} for S_{17B} is described in Fig. 4-18*b*. It is straightforward to show that G_{17A} is equivalent to G_{17B} following any one of the known algorithms for proving equivalence of transition graphs. □

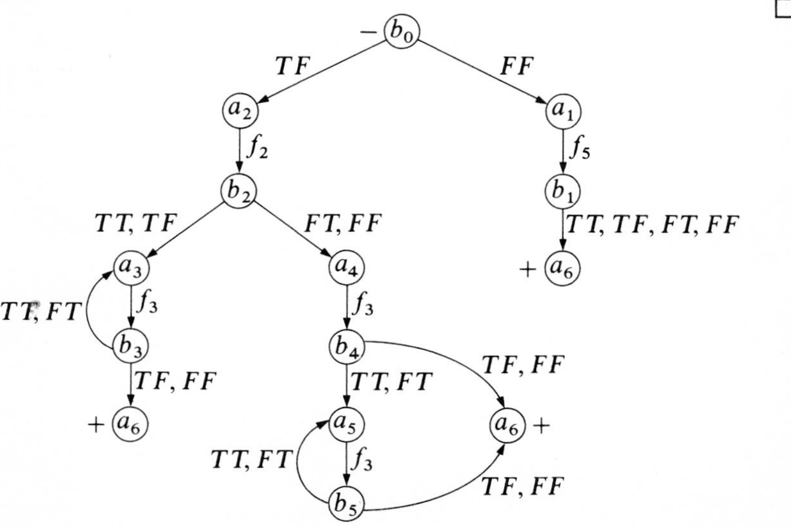

Figure 4-18*a* Transition graph G_{17A}.

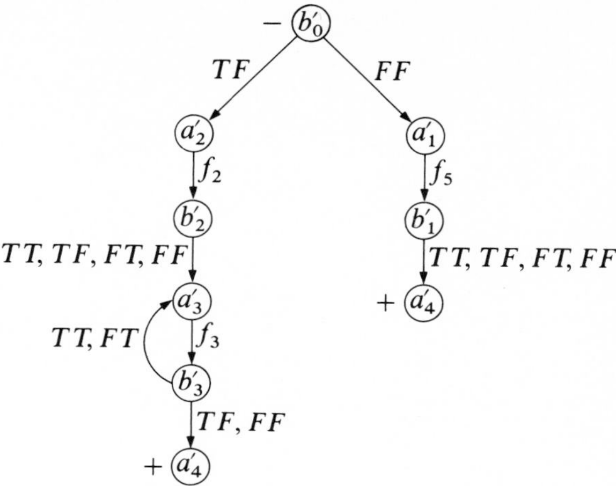

Figure 4-18*b* Transition graph G_{17B}.

5. *The isomorphism problem for Ianov schemas is solvable.* The proof is based again on the fact that the equivalence problem for transition graphs is solvable. For two given Ianov schemas S and S', we construct corresponding transition graphs $\tilde{G}_S$ and $\tilde{G}_{S'}$ in such a way that the transition graphs are equivalent if and only if S is isomorphic to S'. In Fig. 4-18*c* we illustrate the transition graph $\tilde{G}_{17A}$ for Ianov schema S_{17A} (Fig. 4-17*a*). Note that we have not transformed S_{17A} to an equivalent free schema as before. All the HALT and LOOP vertices are final vertices (denoted by +). Impossible paths in S_{17A} are eliminated, but the redundant tests (see vertices 1 and 2) remain.

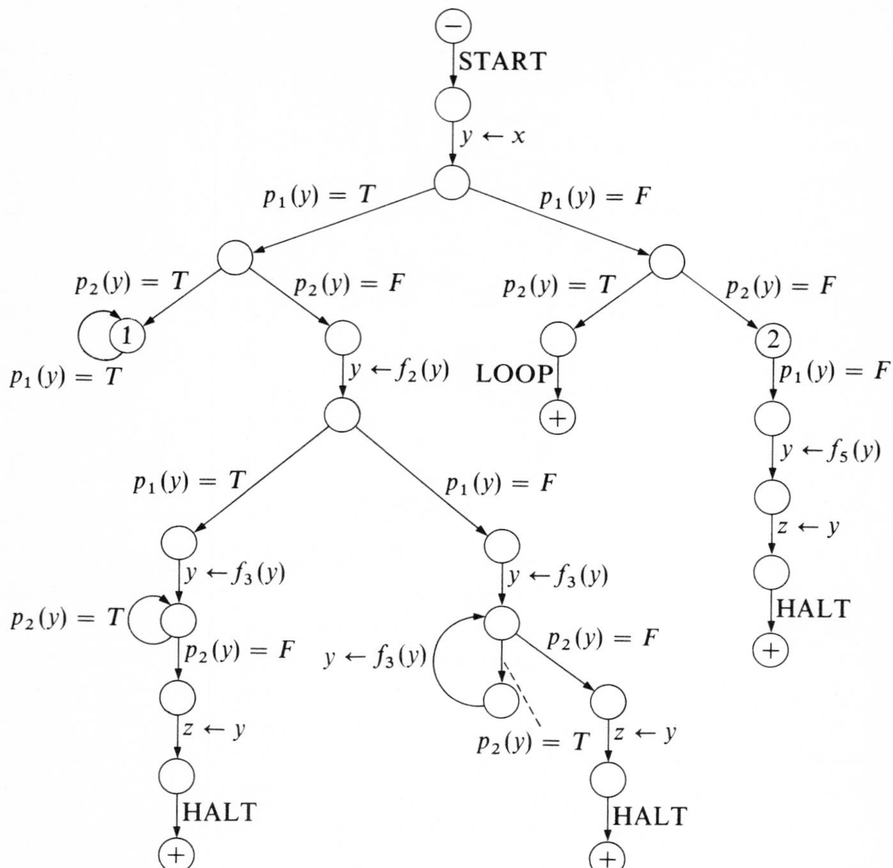

Figure 4-18c Transition graph $\tilde{G}_{17A}$.

4-3 FORMALIZATION IN PREDICATE CALCULUS

In this section we shall formalize the properties of both programs and schemas in the framework of predicate calculus. In addition to the properties of halting, divergence, and equivalence, discussed previously, we shall introduce and formalize two additional properties: *partial correctness* and *total correctness.*

The properties of schemas are formalized in terms of the validity of wffs, and, similarly, the properties of programs are formalized in terms of the truth of interpreted wffs. This formalization enables us to prove properties of schemas and programs by using the proof techniques of predicate calculus (for example, natural deduction or the resolution method).

First we shall describe an algorithm for constructing a wff W_S for any given schema S in such a way that for every program $P = \langle S, \mathscr{I} \rangle$, P is partially correct (that is, the input value of $\bar{x}$ and the output value of $\bar{z}$ satisfy some given relation, assuming that the program halts) if and only if the interpreted wff $W_P = \langle W_S, \mathscr{I} \rangle$ is *true*; then we shall use W_P to construct interpreted wffs which characterize the other properties of programs. Similarly, we shall use W_S to construct wffs which characterize the properties of schemas. The basic result—that P is partially correct if and only if W_P is *true*—is actually a formalization of the inductive-assertions method introduced in Chap. 3 (Theorem 3-1).

4-3.1 The Algorithm

In this section we shall describe an algorithm for constructing a wff W_S for any given schema S in such a way that for every program $P = \langle S, \mathscr{I} \rangle$ the interpreted wff $W_P = \langle W_S, \mathscr{I} \rangle$ characterizes the partial correctness of P. Given a schema S we can construct the wff W_S as follows.

Step 1. Choose a finite set of cutpoints on the arcs of S in such a way that every loop in the flow-diagram includes at least one such cutpoint. Associate a predicate variable $Q_i(\bar{x}, \bar{y})$ with each cutpoint. In addition, associate with each HALT box in S the predicate variable $H(\bar{x}, \bar{z})$.†

EXAMPLE 4-19

Consider again the schema S_3 (Fig. 4-19*a*). Note that S_3 has no input variables and that its output variable z is actually a "dummy variable": Whenever we halt, $z = a$. We associate the predicate variables $Q_1(y_1, y_2)$, $Q_2(y_1, y_2)$, and $Q_3(y_1, y_2)$ with the cutpoints A, B, and C, respectively. Note that S_3 contains two loops: The outer loop 1 includes the cutpoints B and C, and the inner loop 2 includes the cutpoint C. The predicate variable $H(z)$ is associated with the HALT box.

□

Step 2. Decompose the given schema into a set of *subtrees* such that

(*a*) The root of each subtree is either the START statement or a cutpoint.

† Note that $Q_i(\bar{x}, \bar{y})$ and $H(\bar{x}, \bar{z})$ are actually atomic formulas, while Q_i and H are predicate variables.

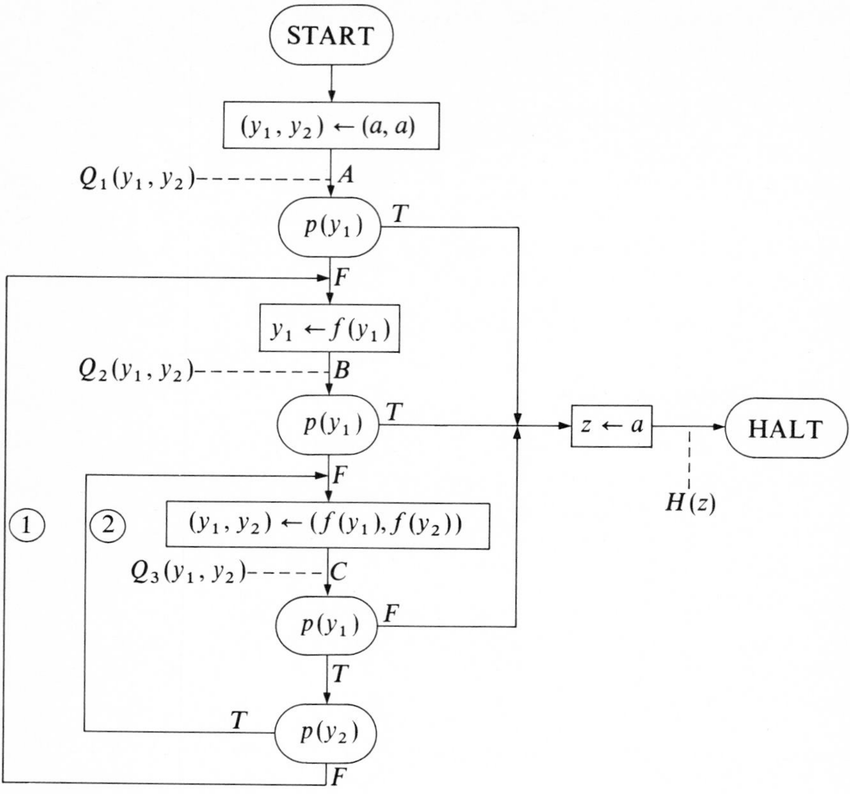

Figure 4-19a Schema S_3.

(*b*) Each terminal of a subtree is either a HALT statement, a LOOP statement, or a cutpoint.

(*c*) No other cutpoints are included in any subtree.

Since there are only finitely many cutpoints, there is always only a finite number of such subtrees. Each subtree must be finite because the set of cutpoints was chosen in such a way that every loop includes at least one cutpoint. Intuitively, the decomposition process is equivalent to cutting the flowchart at each cutpoint and converting the result to a set of subtrees.

EXAMPLE 4-19 (continued)

The four subtrees of the decomposition of schema S_3 are shown in Fig. 4-19*b*.

□

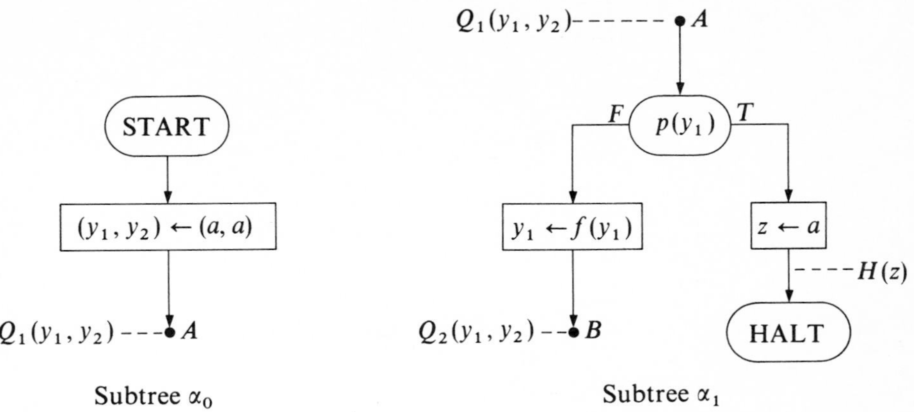

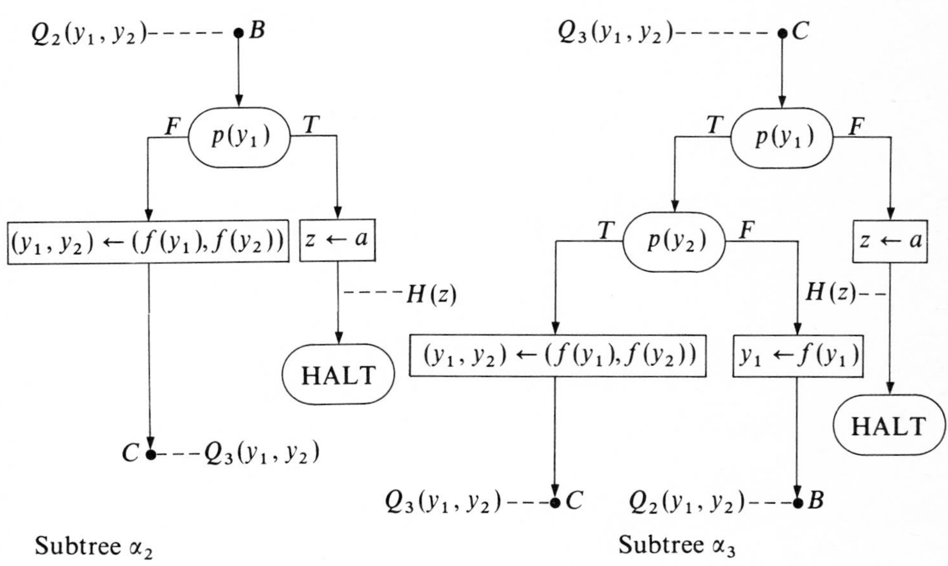

Figure 4-19*b* Decomposition of the schema S_3.

Step 3. To each subtree α of S there corresponds a wff W_α which will be used in the final construction of W_S. W_α is constructed in steps: First, W_{initial} is constructed, starting with the terminals of α; then, in each step W_{old} is used to construct W_{new} by moving *backward* toward the root; finally, W_{final}, which is the desired W_α, is constructed.

The construction proceeds as follows:

(*a*) The construction of W_{initial}:

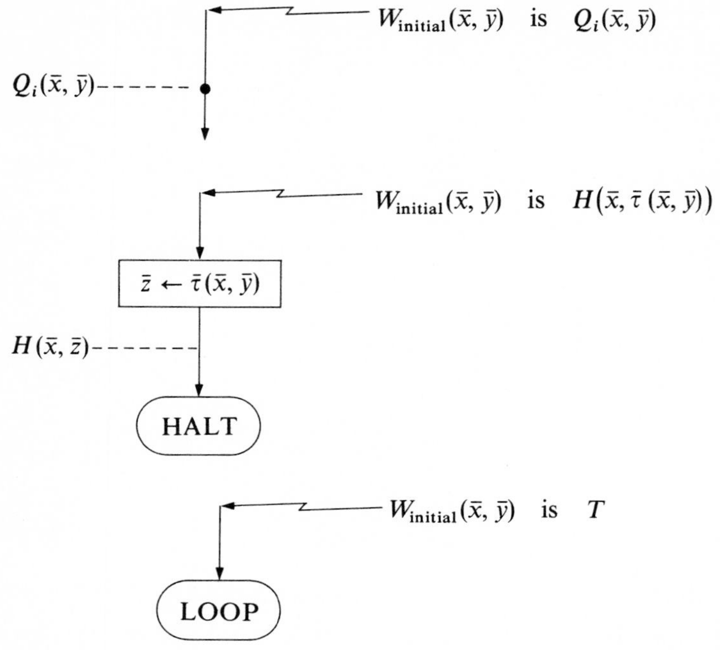

(*b*) The construction of W_{new} (using W_{old}):

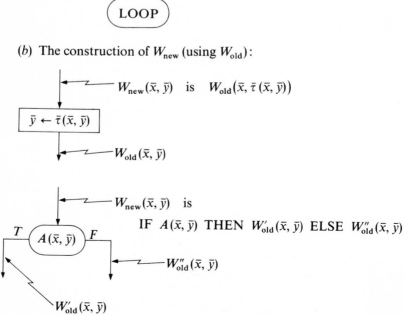

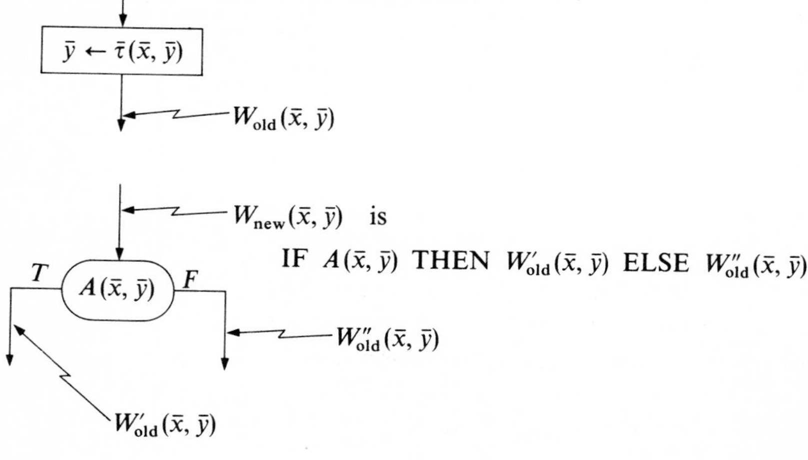

(*c*) The construction of W_{final} (that is, W_α):

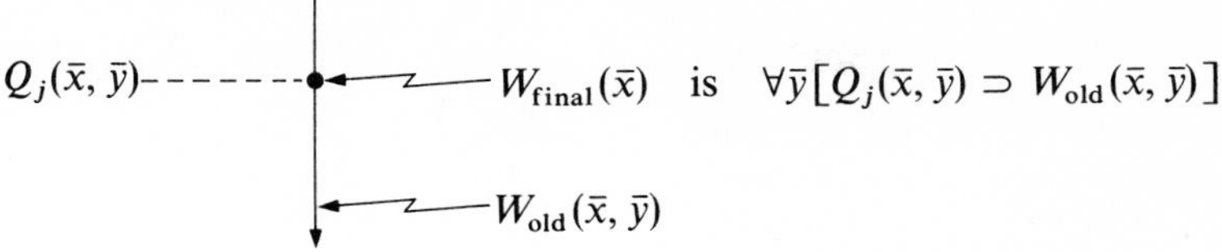

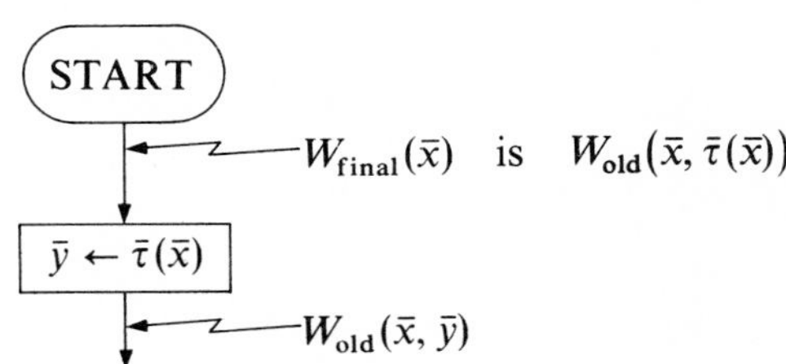

EXAMPLE 4-19 (continued)

The wffs for the four subtrees in Figure 4-19*b* are

W_{α_0} is $Q_1(a, a)$

W_{α_1} is $\forall y_1 \forall y_2 [Q_1(y_1, y_2) \supset \text{IF } p(y_1) \text{ THEN } H(a) \text{ ELSE } Q_2(f(y_1), y_2)]$

W_{α_2} is $\forall y_1 \forall y_2 [Q_2(y_1, y_2) \supset \text{IF } p(y_1) \text{ THEN } H(a) \text{ ELSE } Q_3(f(y_1), f(y_2))]$

W_{α_3} is $\forall y_1 \forall y_2 [Q_3(y_1, y_2) \supset \text{IF } p(y_1) \text{ THEN IF } p(y_2) \text{ THEN } Q_3(f(y_1), f(y_2))$

$\text{ELSE } Q_2(f(y_1), y_2)$

$\text{ELSE } H(a)]$

The construction of W_{α_1}, for example, proceeds backward as follows:

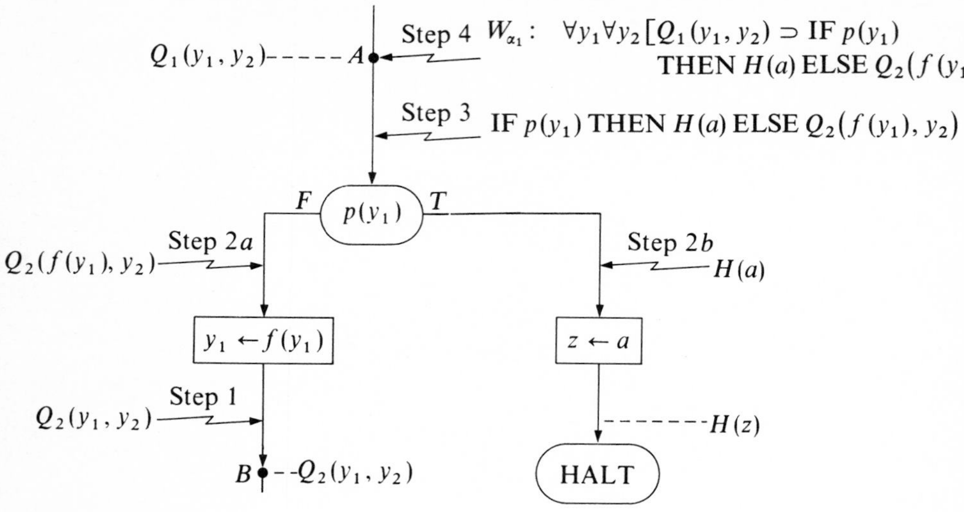

□

Step 4. Define W_S as $\exists \bar{Q}[\wedge_\alpha W_\alpha]$, where $\exists \bar{Q}$ means that all the predicate variables $Q_i(\bar{x}, \bar{y})$ associated with the cutpoints of S are existentially quantified; and $\wedge_\alpha W_\alpha$ stands for the conjunction of the W_α for all subtrees α in the decomposition of the schema S.

Usually, we write $W_S(\bar{x}, H)$ to emphasize that the input variables $\bar{x}$ and the predicate variable H are free (that is, unquantified) in W_S. Note that in general W_S is not unique because it depends on the choice of cutpoints made in Step 1.

EXAMPLE 4-19 (continued)

The wff W_{S_3} for the schema S_3 (Fig. 4-19a) is

$$\begin{aligned}
&\exists Q_1 \exists Q_2 \exists Q_3 \{Q_1(a, a) \\
&\wedge \forall y_1 \forall y_2 [Q_1(y_1, y_2) \supset \text{IF } p(y_1) \text{ THEN } H(a) \text{ ELSE } Q_2(f(y_1), y_2)] \\
&\wedge \forall y_1 \forall y_2 [Q_2(y_1, y_2) \supset \text{IF } p(y_1) \text{ THEN } H(a) \text{ ELSE } Q_3(f(y_1), f(y_2))] \\
&\wedge \forall y_1 \forall y_2 [Q_3(y_1, y_2) \supset \text{IF } p(y_1) \text{ THEN IF } p(y_2) \text{ THEN } Q_3(f(y_1), f(y_2)) \\
&\qquad\qquad\qquad\qquad\qquad\qquad\qquad\qquad \text{ELSE } Q_2(f(y_1), y_2) \\
&\qquad\qquad\qquad\qquad\qquad\qquad \text{ELSE } H(a)]\}
\end{aligned}$$

or, equivalently,†

$$\begin{aligned}
&\exists Q_1 \exists Q_2 \exists Q_3 \{Q_1(a, a)\\
&\wedge \forall y_1 \forall y_2 [Q_1(y_1, y_2) \wedge p(y_1) \supset H(a)]\\
&\wedge \forall y_1 \forall y_2 [Q_1(y_1, y_2) \wedge \sim p(y_1) \supset Q_2(f(y_1), y_2)]\\
&\wedge \forall y_1 \forall y_2 [Q_2(y_1, y_2) \wedge p(y_1) \supset H(a)]\\
&\wedge \forall y_1 \forall y_2 [Q_2(y_1, y_2) \wedge \sim p(y_1) \supset Q_3(f(y_1), f(y_2))]\\
&\wedge \forall y_1 \forall y_2 [Q_3(y_1, y_2) \wedge p(y_1) \wedge p(y_2) \supset Q_3(f(y_1), f(y_2))]\\
&\wedge \forall y_1 \forall y_2 [Q_3(y_1, y_2) \wedge p(y_1) \wedge \sim p(y_2) \supset Q_2(f(y_1), y_2)]\\
&\wedge \forall y_1 \forall y_2 [Q_3(y_1, y_2) \wedge \sim p(y_1) \supset H(a)]\}
\end{aligned}$$

□

EXAMPLE 4-20

Since both loops in the schema S_3 include point C, it suffices to choose C as the only cutpoint (see Fig. 4-20*a*). In this case there are only two subtrees in the decomposition of S_3 (Fig. 4-20*b*), and the wff W'_{S_3} obtained is

$$\begin{aligned}
&\exists Q \{[\text{IF } p(a) \text{ THEN } H(a)\\
&\qquad \text{ELSE IF } p(f(a)) \text{ THEN } H(a)\\
&\qquad\qquad \text{ELSE } Q(f^{(2)}(a), f(a))]\\
&\quad \wedge \forall y_1 \forall y_2 [Q(y_1, y_2) \supset\\
&\quad \text{IF } p(y_1) \text{ THEN IF } p(y_2) \text{ THEN } Q(f(y_1), f(y_2))\\
&\qquad\qquad \text{ELSE IF } p(f(y_1)) \text{ THEN } H(a)\\
&\qquad\qquad\qquad \text{ELSE } Q(f^{(2)}(y_1), f(y_2))\\
&\qquad \text{ELSE } H(a)]\}
\end{aligned}$$

□

† Note that $A \supset$ IF B THEN C ELSE D is logically equivalent to $(A \wedge B \supset C) \wedge (A \wedge \sim B \supset D)$

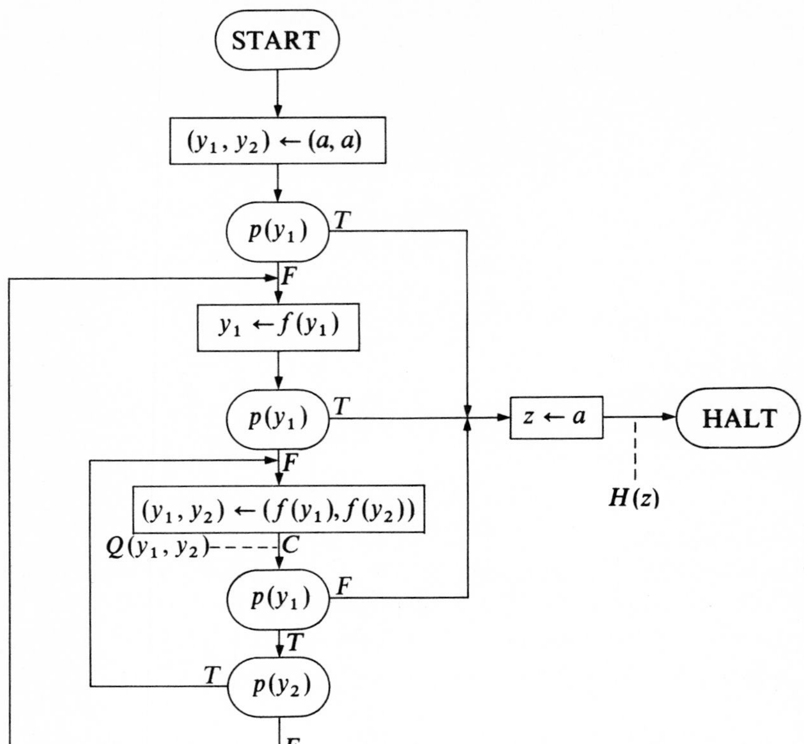

Figure 4-20*a* schema S_3.

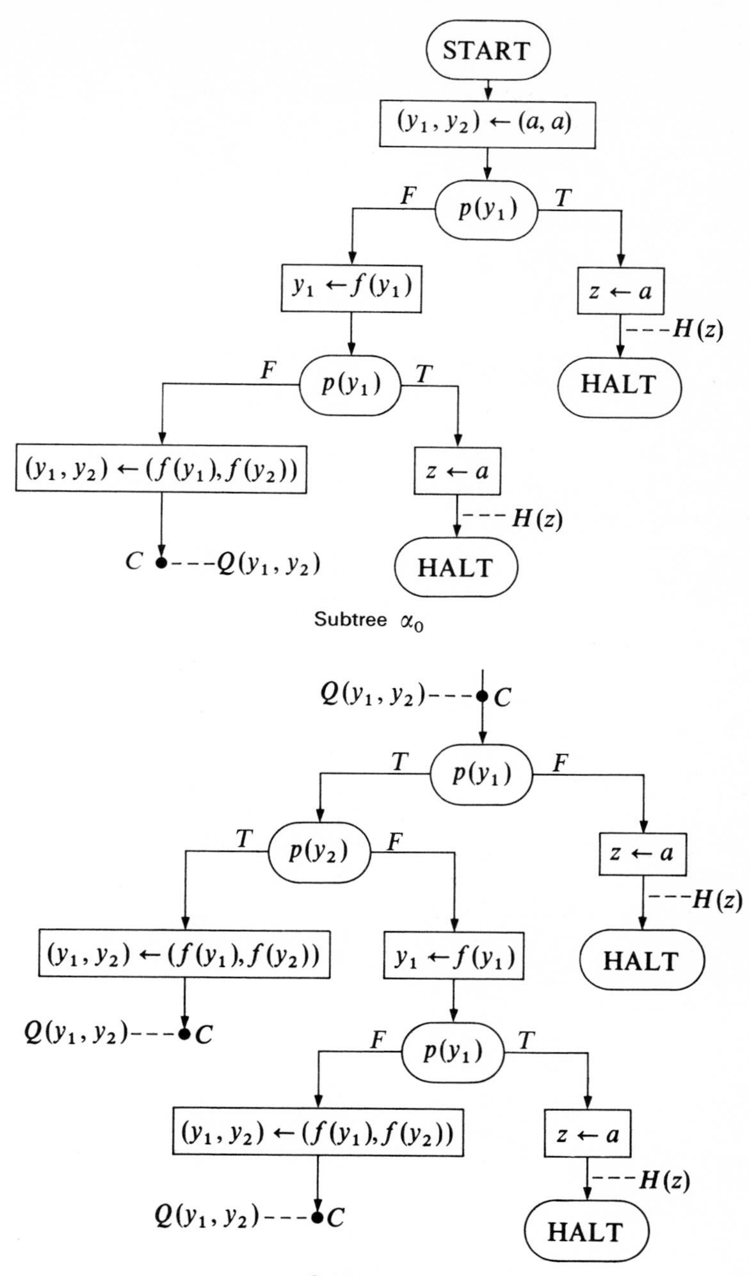

Figure 4-20*b* Another decomposition of schema S_3.

For a given program $P = \langle S, \mathscr{I} \rangle$, we denote by W_P the pair $\langle W_S, \mathscr{I} \rangle$, that is, the interpreted wff obtained from W_S under the interpretation $\mathscr{I}$. To emphasize that the input variables $\bar{x}$ and the predicate variable H are still free in W_P (that is, unquantified), we write $W_P(\bar{x}, H)$.

EXAMPLE 4-21

Consider the schema S_{21} (Fig. 4-21*a*). Since S_{21} has only one loop, it suffices to choose point A as the cutpoint. The wff $W_{S_{21}}(x, H)$ obtained is

$$(*) \quad \exists Q \{Q(x, x, a)$$
$$\wedge \forall y_1 \forall y_2 [Q(x, y_1, y_2) \supset \text{IF } p(y_1) \text{ THEN } H(x, y_2)$$
$$\text{ELSE } Q(x, f_1(y_1), f_2(y_1, y_2))]\}$$

Consider, now, the program $P_{21} = \langle S_{21}, \mathscr{I} \rangle$ (described in Fig. 4-21*b*) which computes $z = factorial(x)$ over the natural numbers (see Sec. 4-1.2). The corresponding interpreted wff $W_{P_{21}}(x, H)$ can be expressed as

$$(**) \; \exists Q \{Q(x, x, 1)$$
$$\wedge \forall y_1 \forall y_2 [Q(x, y_1, y_2) \supset \text{IF } y_1 = 0 \text{ THEN } H(x, y_2)$$
$$\text{ELSE } Q(x, y_1 - 1, y_1 y_2)]\}$$

□

For a given program P, input value $\bar{\xi} \in D^{\mathbf{a}}$, and output predicate $\psi(\bar{x}, \bar{z})$ mapping $D^{\mathbf{a}} \times D^{\mathbf{c}}$ into $\{true, false\}$ we say that $\langle P, \bar{\xi} \rangle$ is *partially correct wrt* ψ if either $val\langle P, \bar{\xi} \rangle$ is undefined or $val\langle P, \bar{\xi} \rangle$ is defined and $\psi(\bar{\xi}, val\langle P, \bar{\xi} \rangle) = true$. All the results presented in the rest of this section are based on the following lemma.

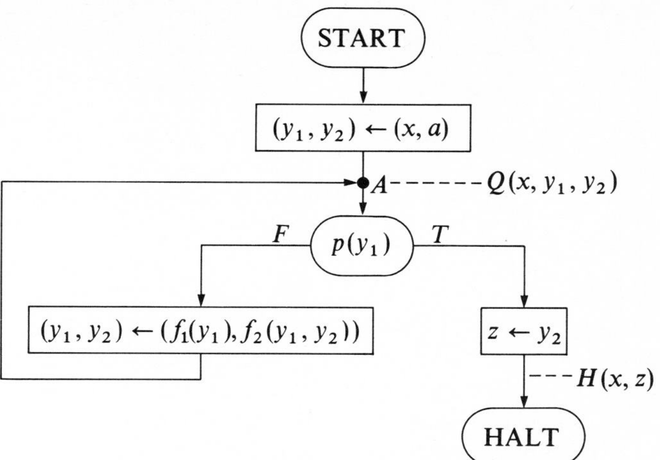

Figure 4-21*a* Schema S_{21}.

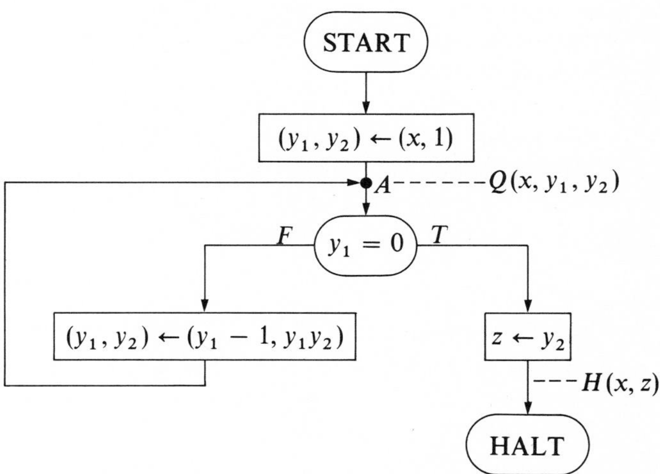

Figure 4-21 *b* Program $P_{21} = \langle S_{21}, \mathscr{I} \rangle$ for computing $z = factorial(x)$.

LEMMA (Manna). *For every program P, input value $\bar{\xi}$, and output predicate $\psi(\bar{x}, \bar{z})$, $\langle P, \bar{\xi} \rangle$ is partially correct wrt ψ if and only if $W_P(\bar{\xi}, \psi)$ is true.*

Proof. The lemma is proved by the use of the following definitions:

1. A predicate $q_i(\bar{y})$ over $D^{\mathbf{b}}$ is said to be a *valid predicate of cutpoint i* if for every $\bar{\eta} \in D^{\mathbf{b}}$, such that during the execution of $\langle P, \bar{\xi} \rangle$ we reach cutpoint i with $\bar{y} = \bar{\eta}$, $q_i(\bar{\eta}) = true$.

2. A predicate $q_i(\bar{y})$ over $D^{\mathbf{b}}$ is said to be *the minimal predicate of cutpoint i* if for every $\bar{\eta} \in D^{\mathbf{b}}$, such that during the execution of $\langle P, \bar{\xi} \rangle$ we reach cutpoint i with $\bar{y} = \bar{\eta}$, *and for no other* $\bar{\eta}$, $q_i(\bar{\eta}) = true$.

We shall now sketch the proof of the lemma.

$\Rightarrow$ For each predicate variable Q_i in $W_P(\bar{\xi}, \psi)$, let $Q_i(\bar{\xi}, \bar{y})$ be the minimal predicate of cutpoint i. Since $\langle P, \bar{\xi} \rangle$ is partially correct wrt ψ, by the construction of W_P it follows that $W_P(\bar{\xi}, \psi)$ is *true*.

$\Leftarrow$ If $W_P(\bar{\xi}, \psi)$ is *true*, it means that there exist predicates $q_i(\bar{y})$ over $D^{\mathbf{b}}$ for the predicate variables Q_i for which the formula is *true*. By construction of W_P, this implies that each q_i is a valid predicate of cutpoint i and therefore that $\langle P, \bar{\xi} \rangle$ is partially correct wrt ψ. Q.E.D.

Thus, to prove that $\langle P, \bar{\xi} \rangle$ is partially correct wrt a given output predicate ψ, it suffices to find an appropriate set of predicates (assertions) for the Q_i's to make the corresponding interpreted wff $W_P(\bar{\xi}, \psi)$ *true*. This is exactly the inductive-assertions method introduced in Chap. 3 (Theorem 3-1).

EXAMPLE 4-21 (continued)

Consider again the program $P_{21} = \langle S_{21}, \mathscr{I} \rangle$ (Fig. 4-21*b*) which computes $z = factorial(x)$ over the natural numbers. We want to show that for every natural number ξ, $\langle P_{21}, \xi \rangle$ is partially correct wrt the output predicate $z = x!$. For this purpose, in the interpreted wff (**) above we replace the predicate variable $Q(x, y_1, y_2)$ by $y_2 \cdot y_1! = x!$ and $H(x, z)$ by $z = x!$; thus, we obtain

$$1 \cdot x! = x!$$

$$\wedge\ \forall y_1 \forall y_2 [y_2 \cdot y_1! = x! \supset \text{IF } y_1 = 0 \text{ THEN } y_2 = x!$$

$$\text{ELSE } y_1 y_2 \cdot (y_1 - 1)! = x!]$$

which is clearly *true*. Therefore, from the previous lemma, it follows that for every natural number ξ, $\langle P_{21}, \xi \rangle$ is partially correct wrt the output predicate $z = x!$.

□

4-3.2 Formalization of Properties of Flowchart Programs

Thus far we have formalized in predicate calculus only the partial correctness of programs. In this section first we shall define other properties of programs which are of interest (most of these properties have been introduced previously in this chapter); then we shall show how these properties can be formalized in predicate calculus just by using the lemma presented in Sec. 4-3.1,

For a given program P, input value $\bar{\xi}$, and output predicate $\psi(\bar{x}, \bar{z})$, we say that

1. $\langle P, \bar{\xi}\rangle$ *is partially correct wrt* ψ if either $val\langle P, \bar{\xi}\rangle$ is undefined, or $val\langle P, \bar{\xi}\rangle$ is defined and $\psi(\bar{\xi}, val\langle P, \bar{\xi}\rangle) = true$.
2. $\langle P, \bar{\xi}\rangle$ *is totally correct wrt* ψ if $val\langle P, \bar{\xi}\rangle$ is defined and $\psi(\bar{\xi}, val\langle P, \bar{\xi}\rangle) = true$.

For a given program P and input value $\bar{\xi}$, we say that

1. $\langle P, \bar{\xi}\rangle$ *diverges* if $val\langle P, \bar{\xi}\rangle$ is undefined.
2. $\langle P, \bar{\xi}\rangle$ *halts* if $val\langle P, \bar{\xi}\rangle$ is defined.

For two given compatible programs P and P' and input value $\bar{\xi}$, we say that

1. $\langle P, \bar{\xi}\rangle$ *is an extension of* $\langle P', \bar{\xi}\rangle$ if whenever $val\langle P', \bar{\xi}\rangle$ is defined, then $val\langle P, \bar{\xi}\rangle$ is also defined and $val\langle P, \bar{\xi}\rangle = val\langle P', \bar{\xi}\rangle$.
2. $\langle P, \bar{\xi}\rangle$ *and* $\langle P', \bar{\xi}\rangle$ *are equivalent* if either both $val\langle P, \bar{\xi}\rangle$ and $val\langle P', \bar{\xi}\rangle$ are undefined, or both $val\langle P, \bar{\xi}\rangle$ and $val\langle P', \bar{\xi}\rangle$ are defined and $val\langle P, \bar{\xi}\rangle = val\langle P', \bar{\xi}\rangle$.

Before introducing our main theorem, we shall mention a few relations among these properties (some of them are used in the proof of the theorem): $\langle P, \bar{\xi}\rangle$ diverges if and only if $\langle P, \bar{\xi}\rangle$ is partially correct wrt the output predicate F; $\langle P, \bar{\xi}\rangle$ halts if and only if $\langle P, \bar{\xi}\rangle$ is totally correct wrt the output predicate T; $\langle P, \bar{\xi}\rangle$ is totally correct wrt ψ if and only if $\langle P, \bar{\xi}\rangle$ is not partially correct wrt $\sim\psi$; $\langle P, \bar{\xi}\rangle$ and $\langle P', \bar{\xi}\rangle$ are equivalent if and only if $\langle P, \bar{\xi}\rangle$ is an extension of $\langle P', \bar{\xi}\rangle$ and $\langle P', \bar{\xi}\rangle$ is an extension of $\langle P, \bar{\xi}\rangle$.

THEOREM 4-3 (Manna/Cooper)

For every program P, input value $\bar{\xi}$ and output predicate ψ: (1*a*) $\langle P, \bar{\xi}\rangle$ *is partially correct wrt ψ if and only if $W_P(\bar{\xi}, \psi)$ is true; and* (1*b*) $\langle P, \bar{\xi}\rangle$ *is totally correct wrt ψ if and only if $\sim W_P(\bar{\xi}, \sim\psi)$ is true* [*or, equivalently, $W_P(\bar{\xi}, \sim\psi)$ is false*].

For every program P and input value $\bar{\xi}$: (2*a*) $\langle P, \bar{\xi}\rangle$ *diverges if and only* *if* $W_P(\bar{\xi}, F)$ *is true; and* (2*b*) $\langle P, \bar{\xi} \rangle$ *halts if and only if* $\sim W_P(\bar{\xi}, F)$ *is true* [*or, equivalently,* $W_P(\bar{\xi}, F)$ *is false*].

For every pair of compatible programs P and P′ and for every input value $\bar{\xi}$: (3*a*) $\langle P, \bar{\xi} \rangle$ *is an extension of* $\langle P', \bar{\xi} \rangle$ *if and only if* $\forall H[W_P(\bar{\xi}, H) \supset W_{P'}(\bar{\xi}, H)]$ *is true; and* (3*b*) $\langle P, \bar{\xi} \rangle$ *and* $\langle P', \bar{\xi} \rangle$ *are equivalent if and only if* $\forall H[W_P(\bar{\xi}, H) \equiv W_{P'}(\bar{\xi}, H)]$ *is true.*

Proof.

1*a*. This is exactly the result of the lemma.

1.*b* $W_P(\bar{\xi}, \sim\psi)$ is *false*
if and only if (by 1*a*)
$\langle P, \bar{\xi} \rangle$ is *not* partially correct wrt $\sim\psi$
if and only if
$\langle P, \bar{\xi} \rangle$ is totally correct wrt ψ.

2*a*. This follows from (1*a*), taking ψ to be F.

2*b*. This follows from (1*b*), taking ψ to be T.

3*a*. $\forall H[W_P(\bar{\xi}, H) \supset W_{P'}(\bar{\xi}, H)]$ is *false*
if and only if
$\exists H[W_P(\bar{\xi}, H) \wedge \sim W_{P'}(\bar{\xi}, H)]$ is *true*
if and only if (by 1*a* and 1*b*)
There exists an output predicate ψ such that $\langle P, \bar{\xi} \rangle$ is partially correct wrt ψ and $\langle P', \bar{\xi} \rangle$ is totally correct wrt $\sim\psi$
if and only if
$\langle P', \bar{\xi} \rangle$ halts and if $\langle P, \bar{\xi} \rangle$ also halts then $val\langle P, \bar{\xi} \rangle \neq val\langle P', \bar{\xi} \rangle$
if and only if
$\langle P, \bar{\xi} \rangle$ is *not* an extension of $\langle P', \bar{\xi} \rangle$.

3*b*. $\forall H[W_P(\bar{\xi}, H) \equiv W_{P'}(\bar{\xi}, H)]$ is *true*
if and only if
$\forall H[W_P(\bar{\xi}, H) \supset W_{P'}(\bar{\xi}, H)] \wedge \forall H[W_{P'}(\bar{\xi}, H) \supset W_P(\bar{\xi}, H)]$ is *true*
if and only if (by 3*a*)
$\langle P, \bar{\xi} \rangle$ is an extension of $\langle P', \bar{\xi} \rangle$, and $\langle P', \bar{\xi} \rangle$ is an extension of $\langle P, \bar{\xi} \rangle$ if and only if
$\langle P, \bar{\xi} \rangle$ and $\langle P', \bar{\xi} \rangle$ are equivalent.

Q.E.D.

Note that the properties were defined and formalized for fixed input value $\bar{\xi}$. All the definitions and corresponding formulas can be extended to hold over some total input predicate $\phi(\bar{x})$; that is, we are interested in the program's performance for those $\bar{\xi} \in D^{\mathbf{a}}$ such that $\phi(\bar{\xi}) = true$. Thus, if some property is formalized for $\bar{\xi} \in D^{\mathbf{a}}$ by $W(\bar{\xi})$, then the property holds over input predicate $\phi(\bar{x})$ if and only if $\forall \bar{x}[\phi(\bar{x}) \supset W(\bar{x})]$ is *true.*

EXAMPLE 4-22

Consider the program P_{22} (Fig. 4-22) over the integers for multiplying an integer x_1 by a natural number x_2 by successive additions. We want to use part 1*b* of Theorem 4-3 to show directly that for every pair of integers (ξ_1, ξ_2) where $\xi_2 \geqq 0$, $\langle P_{22}, (\xi_1, \xi_2)\rangle$ is *totally correct* wrt the output predicate $z = x_1 x_2$. By Theorem 4-3, $\langle P_{22}, (\xi_1, \xi_2)\rangle$ is totally correct wrt the output predicate $z = x_1 x_2$ if and only if the interpreted wff $W_{P_{22}}(\xi_1, \xi_2, z \neq x_1 x_2)$ is *false*. This interpreted wff is

$$(*) \quad \exists Q\{Q(\xi_1, \xi_2, 0, \xi_2) \wedge \forall y_1 \forall y_2 [Q(\xi_1, \xi_2, y_1, y_2) \supset \text{IF } y_2 = 0 \text{ THEN } y_1 \neq \xi_1\xi_2 \text{ ELSE } Q(\xi_1, \xi_2, y_1 + \xi_1, y_2 - 1)]\}$$

We shall discuss two methods for showing that the interpreted wff $(*)$ is *false*; In Method 1 we assume the existence of a predicate Q for which the interpreted wff $(*)$ is *true* and then derive a contradiction; In Method 2 we show directly that the negation of $(*)$ is *true*.

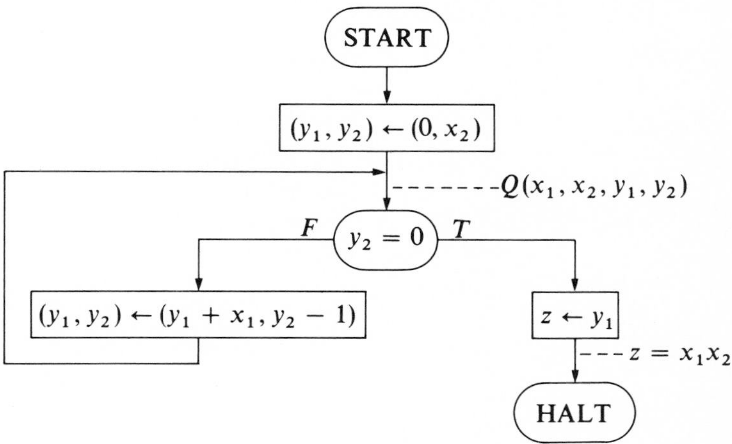

Figure 4-22 Program P_{22}.

Method 1. Suppose there exists a predicate Q, say, Q^*, for which the interpreted wff is *true*. We shall derive a contradiction from the following four clauses:

$$\xi_2 \geq 0 \tag{4-1}$$

$$Q^*(\xi_1, \xi_2, 0, \xi_2) \tag{4-2}$$

$$\forall y_1 \forall y_2 [Q^*(\xi_1, \xi_2, y_1, y_2) \wedge y_2 \neq 0 \supset Q^*(\xi_1, \xi_2, y_1 + \xi_1, y_2 - 1)] \tag{4-3}$$

$$\forall y_1 \forall y_2 [Q^*(\xi_1, \xi_2, y_1, y_2) \wedge y_2 = 0 \supset y_1 \neq \xi_1 \xi_2] \tag{4-4}$$

We shall make use of a special case of (4-3):

$$\forall y_1 \forall y_2 [Q^*(\xi_1, \xi_2, y_1, y_2) \wedge y_2 > 0 \supset Q^*(\xi_1, \xi_2, y_1 + \xi_1, y_2 - 1)] \tag{4-3$'$}$$

By substituting $\xi_1(\xi_2 - y_2)$ for y_1 in (4-3′), we obtain as a special case

$$\forall y_2 [Q^*(\xi_1, \xi_2, \xi_1(\xi_2 - y_2), y_2) \wedge y_2 > 0 \supset Q^*(\xi_1, \xi_2, \xi_1(\xi_2 - y_2) + \xi_1, y_2 - 1)] \tag{4-3$''$}$$

Using the *induction principle* in the form

$$\{[\xi_2 \geq 0 \wedge A(\xi_2)] \wedge \forall y_2 [A(y_2) \wedge y_2 > 0 \supset A(y_2 - 1)]\} \supset A(0)$$

with $A(t)$ being $Q^*(\xi_1, \xi_2, \xi_1(\xi_2 - t), t)$, we obtain by (4-1), (4-2) and (4-3″) that $A(0)$ is *true*; that is, $Q^*(\xi_1, \xi_2, \xi_1\xi_2, 0)$, which contradicts (4-4).

Method 2. We shall show that the negation of the interpreted wff (*) is *true*. Note that the negation of (*) can be expressed as

$$\forall Q \{Q(\xi_1, \xi_2, 0, \xi_2) \supset \exists y_1 \exists y_2 [Q(\xi_1, \xi_2, y_1, y_2) \wedge \text{IF } y_2 = 0 \text{ THEN } y_1 = \xi_1 \xi_2 \text{ ELSE } \sim Q(\xi_1, \xi_2, y_1 + \xi_1, y_2 - 1)]\}$$

If $Q(\xi_1, \xi_2, 0, \xi_2)$ is *false*, there is nothing to prove; otherwise we assume that $Q(\xi_1, \xi_2, 0, \xi_2)$ is *true* and show the existence of y_1 and y_2 for which the consequent of the interpreted wff is *true*. Define

$$y_2^* = min\, \{y_2 | y_2 \geq 0 \wedge \exists y_1 [Q(\xi_1, \xi_2, y_1, y_2) \wedge y_1 = \xi_1(\xi_2 - y_2)]\}$$

There is always such a y_2^* because $Q(\xi_1, \xi_2, 0, \xi_2)$ is *true* by assumption and $0 = \xi_1(\xi_2 - \xi_2)$.

Clearly $\exists y_1 [Q(\xi_1, \xi_2, y_1, y_2^*) \wedge y_1 = \xi_1(\xi_2 - y_2^*)]$ is *true*. Let y_1^* be one of these values of y_1; then, we have

$$Q(\xi_1, \xi_2, y_1^*, y_2^*) \wedge y_1^* = \xi_1(\xi_2 - y_2^*)$$

Now, since $y_1^* + \xi_1 = \xi_1(\xi_2 - (y_2^* - 1))$, it follows from the minimality condition in the definition of y_2^* that if $y_2^* > 0$,

$$Q(\xi_1, \xi_2, y_1^* + \xi_1, y_2^* - 1)$$

must be *false*. Thus, we have

$$Q(\xi_1, \xi_2, y_1^*, y_2^*) \wedge [\text{IF } y_2^* = 0 \text{ THEN } y_1^* = \xi_1 \xi_2 \text{ ELSE } \sim Q(\xi_1, \xi_2, y_1^* + \xi_1, y_2^* - 1)]$$

which is the desired consequence.

The reader should realize that in both methods we have used the predicate $y_1 = x_1(x_2 - y_2)$. In Method 1, one of the key steps was to substitute $\xi_1(\xi_2 - y_2)$ for y_1 in the interpreted wff (4-3′), while in Method 2 the predicate $y_1 = \xi_1(\xi_2 - y_2)$ appears in the definition of y_2^*. This is quite interesting because the predicate $y_1 = x_1(x_2 - y_2)$ is actually an appropriate assertion for proving the partial correctness of $\langle P_{22}, (\xi_1, \xi_2)\rangle$ wrt the output predicate $z = x_1 x_2$. In this case we obtain the interpreted wff

$$
\begin{aligned}
&0 = \xi_1(\xi_2 - \xi_2)\\
&\wedge\ \forall y_1 \forall y_2 [y_1 = \xi_1(\xi_2 - y_2) \supset \text{IF } y_2 = 0 \text{ THEN } y_1 = \xi_1\xi_2\\
&\qquad\qquad\qquad\qquad\qquad\qquad\qquad \text{ELSE } y_1 + \xi_1 = \xi_1(\xi_2 - (y_2 - 1))]
\end{aligned}
$$

which is clearly *true*.

□

4-3.3 Formalization of Properties of Flowchart Schemas

Thus far we have formalized properties of programs in predicate calculus; however, using Theorem 4-3, it is straightforward to extend the results to formalize properties of schemas. First we shall introduce several properties of schemas (most of them have been introduced previously).

For a given schema S and any wff $\tilde{\psi}(\bar{x}, \bar{z})$,† we say that

1. *S is partially correct wrt $\tilde{\psi}$* if for every interpretation $\mathscr{I}$ of S and $\tilde{\psi}$‡ and for every input value $\bar{\xi}$, $\langle S, \mathscr{I}, \bar{\xi}\rangle$ is partially correct wrt $\langle\tilde{\psi}, \mathscr{I}\rangle$.
2. *S is totally correct wrt $\tilde{\psi}$* if for every interpretation $\mathscr{I}$ of S and $\tilde{\psi}$ and for every input value $\bar{\xi}$, $\langle S, \mathscr{I}, \bar{\xi}\rangle$ is totally correct wrt $\langle\tilde{\psi}, \mathscr{I}\rangle$.

For a given schema S, we say that

1. *S diverges* if for every interpretation $\mathscr{I}$ of S and for every input value $\bar{\xi}$, $\langle S, \mathscr{I}, \bar{\xi}\rangle$ diverges.
2. *S halts* if for every interpretation $\mathscr{I}$ of S and for every input value $\bar{\xi}$, $\langle S, \mathscr{I}, \bar{\xi}\rangle$ halts.

For two compatible program schemas S and S', we say that

1. *S is an extension of S'* if for every interpretation $\mathscr{I}$ of S and S' and for every input value $\bar{\xi}$, $\langle S, \mathscr{I}, \bar{\xi}\rangle$ is an extension of $\langle S', \mathscr{I}, \bar{\xi}\rangle$.

† That is, $\tilde{\psi}$ contains no free individual variables other than $\bar{x}$ and $\bar{z}$.

‡ That is, $\mathscr{I}$ includes assignments to all constant symbols occuring in S or $\tilde{\psi}$.

2. *S and S′ are equivalent* if for every interpretation $\mathscr{I}$ of S and S' and for every input value $\bar{\xi}$, $\langle S, \mathscr{I}, \bar{\xi}\rangle$ and $\langle S', \mathscr{I}, \bar{\xi}\rangle$ are equivalent.

From Theorem 4-3, we have the following theorem.

THEOREM 4-4 (Manna/Cooper).

For every schema S and wff $\tilde{\psi}$: (1*a*) *S is partially correct wrt* $\tilde{\psi}$ *if and only if* $\forall\bar{x}W_S(\bar{x}, \tilde{\psi})$ *is valid;* (1*b*) *S is totally correct wrt* $\tilde{\psi}$ *if and only if* $\forall\bar{x} \sim W_S(\bar{x}, \sim\tilde{\psi})$ *is valid* [*or, equivalently,* $\exists\bar{x}W_S(\bar{x}, \sim\tilde{\psi})$ *is unsatisfiable*].

For every schema S: (2*a*) *S diverges if and only if* $\forall\bar{x}W_S(\bar{x}, F)$ *is valid; and* (2*b*) *S halts if and only if* $\forall\bar{x} \sim W_S(\bar{x}, F)$ *is valid* [*or, equivalently,* $\exists\bar{x}W_S(\bar{x}, F)$ *is unsatisfiable*].

For every pair of compatible schemas S and S′: (3*a*) *S is an extension of S′ if and only if* $\forall\bar{x}\forall H[W_S(\bar{x}, H) \supset W_{S'}(\bar{x}, H)]$ *is valid; and* (3*b*) *S and S′ are equivalent if and only if* $\forall\bar{x}\forall H[W_S(\bar{x}, H) \equiv W_{S'}(\bar{x}, H)]$ *is valid.*

We shall now illustrate two applications of Theorem 4-4: In Example 4-23 we shall use part 2*b* of the theorem to prove that a given schema halts, while in Example 4-24 we shall use part 3*b* to prove the equivalence of two given schemas.

EXAMPLE 4-23

Consider the schema S_{23} (Fig. 4-23). $W_{S_{23}}(x, H)$ is

$$\begin{aligned}&\exists\bar{Q}\{Q_1(x, x)\\ &\quad\wedge \forall y[Q_1(x, y) \supset \text{IF } p(y) \text{ THEN } Q_4(x, y) \text{ ELSE } Q_2(x, a)]\\ &\quad\wedge \forall y[Q_2(x, y) \supset \text{IF } p(y) \text{ THEN } Q_4(x, y) \text{ ELSE } Q_3(x, f(y))]\\ &\quad\wedge \forall y[Q_3(x, y) \supset \text{IF } p(y) \text{ THEN } Q_4(x, a) \text{ ELSE } H(x, c)]\\ &\quad\wedge \forall y[Q_4(x, y) \supset \text{IF } p(y) \text{ THEN } H(x, b) \text{ ELSE } Q_4(x, f(y))]\}\end{aligned}$$

By Theorem 4-4 (part 2*b*), S_{23} halts if and only if $\exists x W_{S_{23}}(x, F)$ is unsatisfiable. We shall prove that $\exists x W_{S_{23}}(x, F)$ is unsatisfiable using the resolution principle (see Chap. 2, Sec. 2-3.4). Since we consider the unsatisfiability of the wff, we can eliminate the existential quantifier $\exists\bar{Q}$ from the wff and consider the Q_i's as predicate constant, thus obtaining a first-order wff.

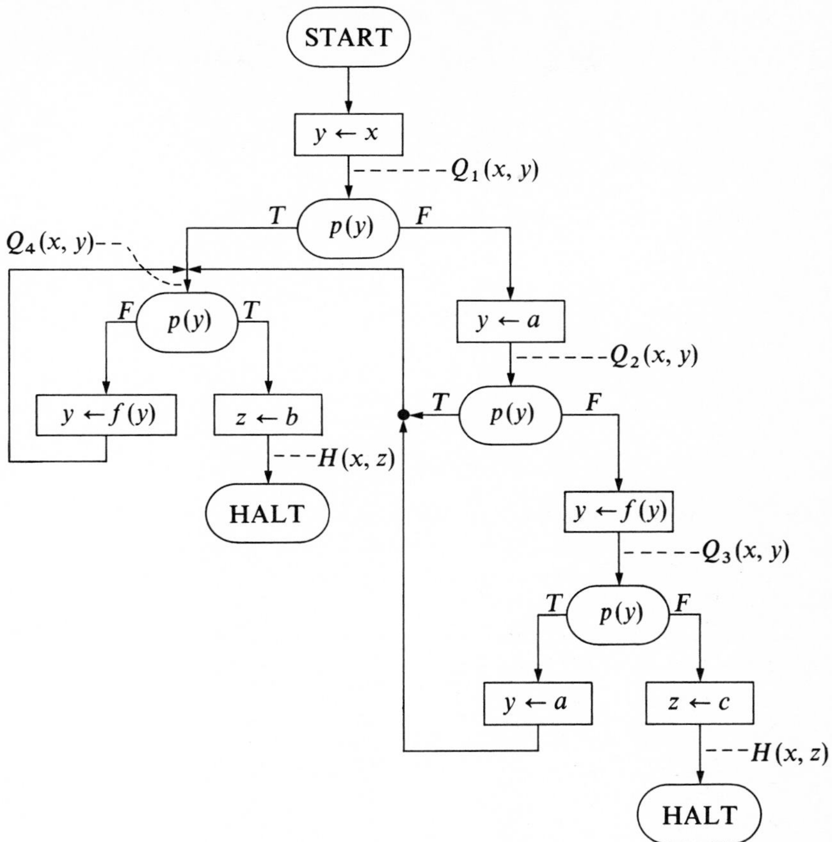

Figure 4-23 Schema S_{23}.

$\exists x W_{S_{23}}(x, F)$ can be written as

$$\begin{aligned}
\exists x \forall y \{ & Q_1(x, x) \\
& \wedge [Q_1(x, y) \wedge \quad p(y) \supset Q_4(x, y)] \\
& \wedge [Q_1(x, y) \wedge \sim p(y) \supset Q_2(x, a)] \\
& \wedge [Q_2(x, y) \wedge \quad p(y) \supset Q_4(x, y)] \\
& \wedge [Q_2(x, y) \wedge \sim p(y) \supset Q_3(x, f(y))] \\
& \wedge [Q_3(x, y) \wedge \quad p(y) \supset Q_4(x, a)] \\
& \wedge [Q_3(x, y) \wedge \sim p(y) \supset F] \\
& \wedge [Q_4(x, y) \wedge \quad p(y) \supset F] \\
& \wedge [Q_4(x, y) \wedge \sim p(y) \supset Q_4(x, f(y))]\}
\end{aligned}$$

which is equivalent in clause form to

0. $Q_1(d, d)$
1. $\sim Q_1(d, y), \sim p(y), Q_4(d, y)$
2. $\sim Q_1(d, y), \quad p(y), Q_2(d, a)$
3. $\sim Q_2(d, y), \sim p(y), Q_4(d, y)$
4. $\sim Q_2(d, y), \quad p(y), Q_3(d, f(y))$
5. $\sim Q_3(d, y), \sim p(y), Q_4(d, a)$
6. $\sim Q_3(d, y), \quad p(y)$
7. $\sim Q_4(d, y), \sim p(y)$
8. $\sim Q_4(d, y), \quad p(y), Q_4(d, f(y))$

Then, by resolving, we obtain

1*a*.	$\sim p(d), Q_4(d, d)$	by 0 and 1 (with $y = d$)
2*a*.	$p(d), Q_2(d, a)$	by 0 and 2 (with $y = d$)
9.	$\sim p(d)$	by 1*a* and 7 (with $y = d$)
10.	$Q_2(d, a)$	by 2*a* and 9
11.	$\sim p(a), Q_4(d, a)$	by 3 (with $y = a$) and 10
12.	$\sim p(a)$	by 7 (with $y = a$) and 11
13.	$p(a), Q_3(d, f(a))$	by 4 (with $y = a$) and 10
14.	$p(a), p(f(a))$	by 6 (with $y = f(a)$) and 13
15.	$p(a), \sim p(f(a)), Q_4(d, a)$	by 5 (with $y = f(a)$) and 13
16.	$p(a), \sim p(f(a)), Q_4(d, f(a))$	by 8 (with $y = a$) and 15
17.	$p(a), \sim p(f(a))$	by 7 (with $y = f(a)$) and 16
18.	$p(a)$	by 14 and 17
19.	$\square$	by 12 and 18

Thus, by resolving, we have inferred the empty clause □. Therefore $\exists x W_{S_{23}}(x, F)$ is unsatisfiable, which implies by Theorem 4-4 (part 2*b*) that S_{23} halts.

□

EXAMPLE 4-24 (Cooper)

Consider the schemas S_{24A} and S_{24B} (Fig. 4-24*a* and *b*).

$W_{S_{24A}}(x, H)$ is

$$\begin{aligned}\exists Q_1 \{Q_1(x, x) \\ \wedge \forall y[Q_1(x, y) \supset \text{IF } p_1(y) \text{ THEN IF } p_2(f(y)) \text{ THEN } H(x, f(y)) \\ \text{ELSE } Q_1(x, f(y)) \\ \text{ELSE } T]\}\end{aligned}$$

$W_{S_{24B}}(x, H)$ is

$$\begin{aligned}\exists Q_2 \exists Q_3 \{Q_2(x, x) \\ \wedge \forall y[Q_2(x, y) \supset \text{IF } p_1(y) \text{ THEN IF } p_2(f(y)) \text{ THEN } H(x, f(y)) \\ \text{ELSE } Q_3(x, f(y)) \\ \text{ELSE } T] \\ \wedge \forall y[Q_3(x, y) \supset \text{IF } p_1(y) \text{ THEN IF } p_2(f(y)) \text{ THEN } H(x, f(y)) \\ \text{ELSE } Q_3(x, f(y)) \\ \text{ELSE } T]\}\end{aligned}$$

By Theorem 4-4 (part 3*b*) S_{24A} and S_{24B} are equivalent if and only if the following wff is valid:

$$\forall x \forall H[W_{S_{24A}}(x, H) \equiv W_{S_{24B}}(x, H)]$$

or, equivalently,

$$\forall x \forall H[W_{S_{24A}}(x, H) \supset W_{S_{24B}}(x, H)] \wedge \forall x \forall H[W_{S_{24B}}(x, H) \supset W_{S_{24A}}(x, H)]$$

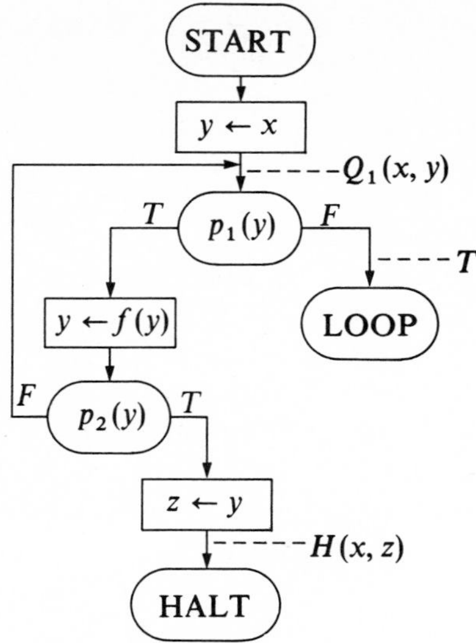

Figure 4-24*a* Schema S_{24A}.

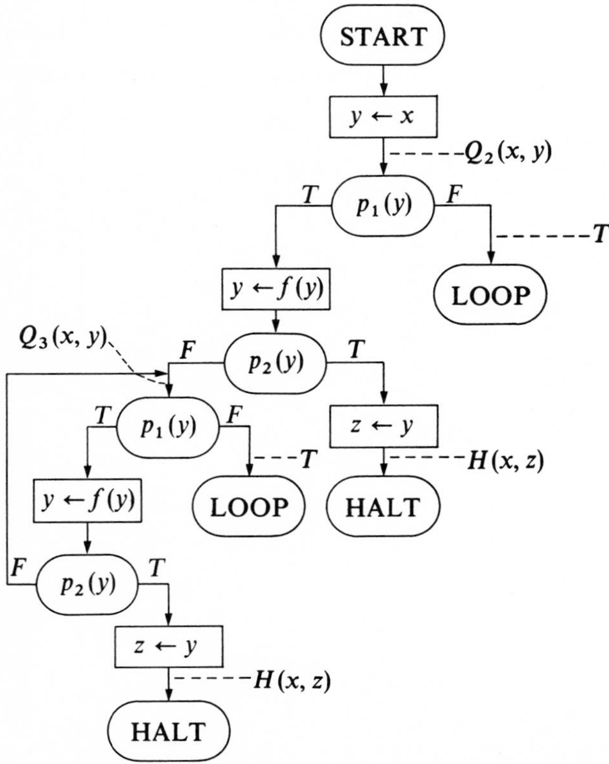

Figure 4-24*b* Schema S_{24B}.

The wff $\forall x \forall H[W_{S_{24A}}(x, H) \supset W_{S_{24B}}(x, H)]$ is of the form

$$\forall x \forall H[\exists Q_1 A \supset \exists Q_2 \exists Q_3 B]$$

or, equivalently,

$$\forall x \forall H \forall Q_1 \exists Q_2 \exists Q_3 [A \supset B]$$

If we guess the predicate variables Q_2 and Q_3 (in terms of x, H, Q_1, and the constant symbols of the schemas), we can eliminate the existential quantifiers on the predicate variables Q_2 and Q_3. Then, if we eliminate $\forall Q_1$ and $\forall H$ and consider them to be predicate constants, we have a first-order wff. In this case, the guessing is trivial: Take both Q_2 and Q_3 to be Q_1; each of the conjuncts of $W_{S_{24B}}$ is then a conjunct of $W_{S_{24A}}$, and so $W_{S_{24B}}$ follows from $W_{S_{24A}}$.

Similarly, the wff $\forall x \forall H[W_{S_{24B}}(x, H) \supset W_{S_{24A}}(x, H)]$ is of the form

$$\forall x \forall H[\exists Q_2 \exists Q_3 B \supset \exists Q_1 A]$$

or, equivalently,

$$\forall x \forall H \forall Q_2 \forall Q_3 \exists Q_1 [B \supset A]$$

Take Q_1 to be the disjunct $Q_2 \vee Q_3$; each of the conjuncts of $W_{S_{24A}}$ may then be proved *true* by using the conjuncts of $W_{S_{24B}}$.

□

4-4 TRANSLATION PROBLEMS

Ackermann's function $z = A(x)$ mapping natural numbers into natural numbers, is normally defined as follows: $z = F(x, x)$ where for every pair of natural numbers (y_1, y_2), $F(y_1, y_2)$ is defined recursively as:

$$\begin{aligned}
&\textit{if } y_1 = 0 \textit{ then } F(y_1, y_2) = y_2 + 1\\
&\qquad \textit{else if } y_2 = 0 \textit{ then } F(y_1, y_2) = F(y_1 - 1, 1)\\
&\qquad\qquad \textit{else } F(y_1, y_2) = F(y_1 - 1, F(y_1, y_2 - 1))
\end{aligned}$$

or, in short,

$$\begin{aligned}
&z = F(x, x) \textit{ where}\\
&F(y_1, y_2) \Leftarrow \textit{if } y_1 = 0 \textit{ then } y_2 + 1\\
&\qquad \textit{else if } y_2 = 0 \textit{ then } F(y_1 - 1, 1)\\
&\qquad\qquad \textit{else } F(y_1 - 1, F(y_1, y_2 - 1))
\end{aligned}$$

Such a definition is called a *recursive program:* x is an input variable, y_1 and y_2 are program variables, and z is an output variable.

Given a natural number ξ, the computation of the recursive program for $x = \xi$ is best described by a sequence of terms $\alpha_0, \alpha_1, \alpha_2, \ldots$, where α_0 is $F(\xi, \xi)$ and α_{i+1} $(i \geq 0)$ is constructed from α_i by applying a substitution rule and then all possible simplifications as illustrated below.

For $x = 1$, for example, first we have that

$$\alpha_0 \text{ is } F(1, 1)$$

To obtain α_1 we replace $F(1, 1)$ by its definition

$$\begin{aligned} &\textit{if } 1 = 0 \textit{ then } 1 + 1 \\ &\qquad \textit{else if } 1 = 0 \textit{ then } F(1 - 1, 1) \\ &\qquad\qquad \textit{else } F(1 - 1, F(1, 1 - 1)) \end{aligned}$$

which can be simplified to $F(0, F(1, 0))$; therefore

$$\alpha_1 \quad \text{is} \quad F(0, F(1, 0))$$

Now we replace $F(1, 0)$ by its definition

$$\begin{aligned} &\textit{if } 1 = 0 \textit{ then } 0 + 1 \\ &\qquad \textit{else if } 0 = 0 \textit{ then } F(1 - 1, 1) \\ &\qquad\qquad \textit{else } F(1 - 1, F(1, 0 - 1)) \end{aligned}$$

which can be simplified to $F(0, 1)$; therefore

$$\alpha_2 \quad \text{is} \quad F(0, F(0, 1))$$

Now we replace $F(0, 1)$ by its definition

$$\begin{aligned} &\textit{if } 0 = 0 \textit{ then } 1 + 1 \\ &\qquad \textit{else if } 1 = 0 \textit{ then } F(0 - 1, 1) \\ &\qquad\qquad \textit{else } F(0 - 1, F(0, 1 - 1)) \end{aligned}$$

which can be simplified to 2; therefore

$$\alpha_3 \quad \text{is} \quad F(0, 2)$$

Finally we replace $F(0, 2)$ by its definition

$$\begin{aligned} &\textit{if } 0 = 0 \textit{ then } 2 + 1 \\ &\qquad \textit{else if } 2 = 0 \textit{ then } F(0 - 1, 1) \\ &\qquad\qquad \textit{else } F(0 - 1, F(0, 2 - 1)) \end{aligned}$$

which can be simplified to 3. Therefore we say that $A(1)$ is defined and $A(1) = 3$.

The recursive program P for computing Ackermann's function can formally be described as a pair $P = \langle S, \mathscr{I} \rangle$, where

1. S is the recursive schema

$$z = F(x, x) \textit{ where}$$

$$F(y_1, y_2) \Leftarrow \textit{if } p(y_1) \textit{ then } f_1(y_2)$$

$$\textit{else if } p(y_2) \textit{ then } F(f_2(y_1), a_1)$$

$$\textit{else } F(f_2(y_1), F(y_1, f_2(y_2)))$$

2. $\mathscr{I}$ is an interpretation of S for which $D = \{\text{the natural numbers}\}$, a_1 is 1, $p(y)$ is $y = 0$, $f_1(y)$ is $y + 1$, and $f_2(y)$ is $y - 1$.

In this section we shall define the class of recursive schemas and discuss its relation to the class of flowchart schemas.

4-4.1 Recursive Schemas

An *alphabet* Σ_S of a recursive schema S is a finite subset of the following set of symbols:

1. Constants:

   n-ary *function constants* f_i^n $(i \geq 1, n \geq 0)$; f_i^0 is called *individual constant* and is also denoted by a_i.

   n-ary *predicate constants* p_i^n $(i \geq 1, n \geq 0)$; p_i^0 is called *propositional constant.*

2. Variables:

Input variables	$\{x_1, x_2, \ldots\}$
Program variables	$\{y_1, y_2, \ldots\}$
A single *output variable*	z†
Function variables	$\{F_1, F_2, \ldots\}$

A *quantifier-free wff* π *over* Σ_S is a quantifier-free wff in the normal sense constructed from function constants f_i^n, predicate constants p_i^n, and individual variables x_i, y_i, and z of Σ_S. (Note that π may not contain function

†For simplicity, we consider only recursive schemas with a single output variable z. The definition can be extended to recursive schemas with an arbitrary number of output variables.

variables). A *term t over* Σ_S is a term in the normal sense constructed from the function constants f_i^n, individual variables x_i, y_i, and z and the function variables F_i of Σ_S. A term with no occurrences of function variables is called a *constant term.*

A *conditional term* τ *over* Σ_S is defined recursively as follows:

1. Each term over Σ_S is a conditional term.

2. The special symbol ω, called the *undefined symbol,* is a conditional term over Σ_S.

3. If π is a quantifier-free wff over Σ_S, and τ_1 and τ_2 are conditional terms over Σ_S, then (*if* π *then* τ_1 *else* τ_2) is a conditional term over Σ_S. The conditional terms over Σ_S consists exactly of all finite expressions generated by repeated applications of rules 1 to 3. (Parentheses, subscripts, and superscripts are omitted whenever their omission causes no confusion.)

A *recursive schema S over* Σ_S is of the form

$$z = \tau_0(\bar{x}, \bar{F}) \textit{ where}$$

$$F_1(\bar{x}, \bar{y}) \Leftarrow \tau_1(\bar{x}, \bar{y}, \bar{F})$$

$$\cdots\cdots\cdots\cdots\cdots$$

$$F_N(\bar{x}, \bar{y}) \Leftarrow \tau_N(\bar{x}, \bar{y}, \bar{F})$$

Here, $\tau_0(\bar{x}, \bar{F})$ is a conditional term that contains no variables other than the input variables $\bar{x}$ and the function variables $\bar{F}$. Similarly, $\tau_i(\bar{x}, \bar{y}, \bar{F})$, $1 \le i \le N$, is a conditional term that contains no variables other than the input variables $\bar{x}$, the program variables $\bar{y}$, and the function variables $\bar{F}$.

An *interpretation* $\mathscr{I}$ of a recursive schema S consists of the following.

1. A nonempty set of elements D (called the *domain of the interpretation*).
2. Assignments to the constants of τ_i, $0 \le i \le N$:
   (*a*) To each function constant f_i^n we assign a total function mapping D^n into D. (If $n = 0$, the individual constant is assigned some fixed element of D.)
   (*b*) To each predicate constant p_i^n we assign a total predicate over D, that is, a total function mapping D^n into $\{true, false\}$. (If $n = 0$, the propositional constant is assigned the truth value *true* or *false*.)

Note that $\mathscr{I}$ does not include assignments to the variables of τ_i.

The pair $P = \langle S, \mathscr{I} \rangle$, where S is a recursive schema and $\mathscr{I}$ is an interpretation of S, is called a *recursive program.* Given values $\bar{\xi}$ for the input variables $\bar{x}$, the recursive program $P = \langle S, \mathscr{I} \rangle$ is executed by constructing a (finite or infinite) sequence of terms

$$\alpha_0, \alpha_1, \alpha_2, \alpha_3, \ldots$$

called the *computation sequence of* $\langle P, \bar{\xi} \rangle$, as follows:

1. α_0 is $\tau_0(\bar{x}, \bar{F})$ after *all possible* simplifications (see below).
2. α_{i+1} $(i \geq 0)$ is obtained from α_i by replacing in α_i the *leftmost-innermost* occurrence of $F_j(\bar{x}, \bar{t})$ by $\tau_j(\bar{x}, \bar{t}, \bar{F})$ and then applying *all possible* simplifications (see below). In other words, we replace in α_i the leftmost occurrence of $F_j(\bar{x}, \bar{t})$ in which all terms of $\bar{t}$ are free of $\bar{F}$'s and then apply the simplification rules until no more simplifications can be made.

The *simplification* rules are (using the assignment of $\bar{\xi}$ to $\bar{x}$ and the interpretation $\mathscr{I}$):

1. Replace any quantifier-free wff by its value (*true* or *false*).
2. Replace (*if true then A else B*) by A

   (*if false then A else B*) by B

(Note that B is not computed in the first case and A is not computed in the second case.)

3. Replace each occurrence of $f_i^n(t_1, \ldots, t_n)$, where each t_i is an element of the domain D, by its value.†

The computation sequence is finite and α_k is the final term in the sequence if and only if α_k is an element ζ of the domain D, or α_k contains the undefined symbol ω. In the first case we say that $val\langle P, \bar{\xi} \rangle$ is defined and $val\langle P, \bar{\xi} \rangle = \zeta$; otherwise, that is, if α_k contains ω or if the sequence is infinite, we say that $val\langle P, \bar{\xi} \rangle$ is undefined. Thus, the recursive program P defines a partial function mapping D^a into D denoted by $z = P(\bar{x})$.

EXAMPLE 4-25

Consider again the recursive program $P = \langle S, \mathscr{I} \rangle$ for computing Ackermann's function $z = A(x)$, where

1. The recursive schema S is

$$z = F(x, x) \textit{ where}$$

$$F(y_1, y_2) \Leftarrow \textit{if } p(y_1) \textit{ then } f_1(y_2)$$
$$\textit{else if } p(y_2) \textit{ then } F(f_2(y_1), a_1)$$
$$\textit{else } F(f_2(y_1), F(y_1, f_2(y_2)))$$

† For a more formal treatment, see Manna and Pnueli (1970).

2. The interpretation $\mathscr{I}$ of S is $D = \{\text{the natural numbers}\}$, a_1 is 1, $p(y)$ is $y = 0$, $f_1(y)$ is $y + 1$, and $f_2(y)$ is $y - 1$.

Informally,

$$z = F(x, x) \textit{ where}$$

$$F(y_1, y_2) \Leftarrow \textit{if } y_1 = 0 \textit{ then } y_2 + 1$$
$$\textit{else if } y_2 = 0 \textit{ then } F(y_1 - 1, 1)$$
$$\textit{else } F\big(y_1 - 1, F(y_1, y_2 - 1)\big)$$

The computation sequence of $\langle P, 1 \rangle$ is (see the introduction to this section)

α_0: $F(1, 1)$

α_1: $F\big(0, F(1, 0)\big)$

α_2: $F\big(0, F(0, 1)\big)$

α_3: $F(0, 2)$

α_4: 3

Thus $\textit{val}\langle P, 1 \rangle$ is defined and $\textit{val}\langle P, 1 \rangle = 3$. Usually we describe such a computation sequence informally as

$$F(1, 1) \to F\big(0, F(1, 0)\big) \to F\big(0, F(0, 1)\big) \to F(0, 2) \to 3$$

□

4-4.2 Flowchart Schemas versus Recursive Schemas

Consider the flowchart program P_{25} (Fig. 4-25*a*) over the natural numbers for computing $z = \textit{factorial}(x)$. Let us associate the function variable $F(x, y_1, y_2)$ with point A. If we define $F(x, y_1, y_2)$ recursively as

$$F(x, y_1, y_2) \Leftarrow \textit{if } y_1 = 0 \textit{ then } y_2 \textit{ else } F(x, y_1 - 1, y_1 y_2)$$

then clearly $F(\xi, \eta_1, \eta_2)$ represents the effect (that is, the final value of z) of the subprogram starting at A with $(x, y_1, y_2) = (\xi, \eta_1, \eta_2)$.

Thus, the flowchart program P_{25} is equivalent to the following recursive program over the natural numbers:

$$z = F(x, x, 1) \textit{ where}$$

$$F(x, y_1, y_2) \Leftarrow \textit{if } y_1 = 0 \textit{ then } y_2 \textit{ else } F(x, y_1 - 1, y_1 y_2)$$

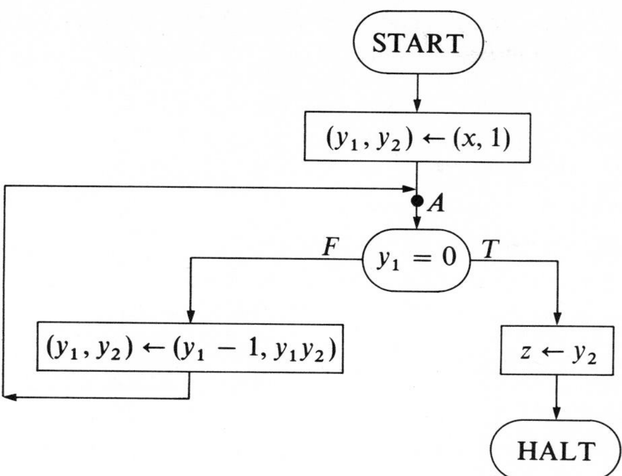

Figure 4-25*a* Flowchart program P_{25}.

In general, the flowchart schema S_{25} (Fig. 4-25*b*) is equivalent to the recursive schema

$$z = F(x, x, a) \textit{ where}$$

$$F(x, y_1, y_2) \Leftarrow \textit{if } p(y_1) \textit{ then } y_2 \textit{ else } F(x, f_1(y_1), f_2(y_1, y_2))$$

We shall now describe a detailed algorithm to perform such transformations.

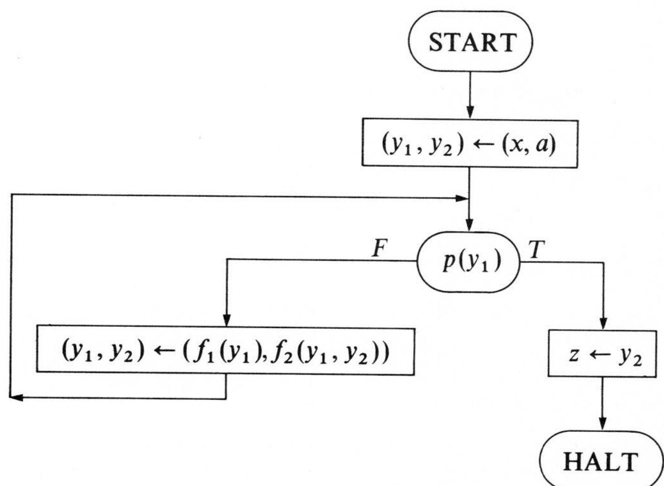

Figure 4-25*b* Flowchart schema S_{25}.

THEOREM 4-5 (McCarthy). *Every flowchart schema can be translated into an equivalent recursive schema.*

Proof. Given a flowchart schema S, an equivalent recursive schema S' can be constructed as follows.† Note the similarities between this algorithm and the one given in Sec. 4-3.1 for constructing the wff W_S.

Step 1. Choose a finite set of cutpoints on the arcs of S in such a way that every loop in the flow-diagram includes at least one such point. Associate a distinct function variable $F_i(\bar{x}, \bar{y})$ with each cutpoint.

Step 2. Decompose S into a finite set of finite subtrees such that (*a*) The root of each subtree is either the START statement or a cutpoint; (*b*) Each terminal of a subtree is either a HALT statement, a LOOP statement, or a cutpoint; and (*c*) no other cutpoints are included in any subtree.

Step 3. To each subtree α, an appropriate recursive equation E_α is constructed. The recursive equations are then combined to perform the desired recursive schema S'. To obtain E_α, a term τ is constructed in steps by *backward substitution*. First, the term τ_{initial} is constructed using the terminals of α. Then, in each step τ_{old} is used to construct τ_{new} by moving backward toward the root of α. Upon reaching the root, the recursive equation E_α is constructed.

† Since we have defined recursive schemas with only one output variable z, clearly we can transform only flowchart schemas with one output variable z. However, it is straightforward to define recursive schemas with an arbitrary output vector $\bar{z}$, and then describe the transformation for any flowchart schema.

1. Initial step. *The construction of* τ_{initial}:

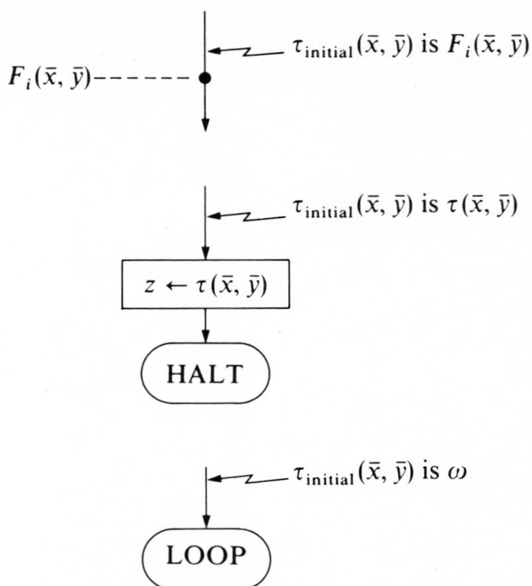

2. *The construction of* τ_{new} *from* τ_{old}:

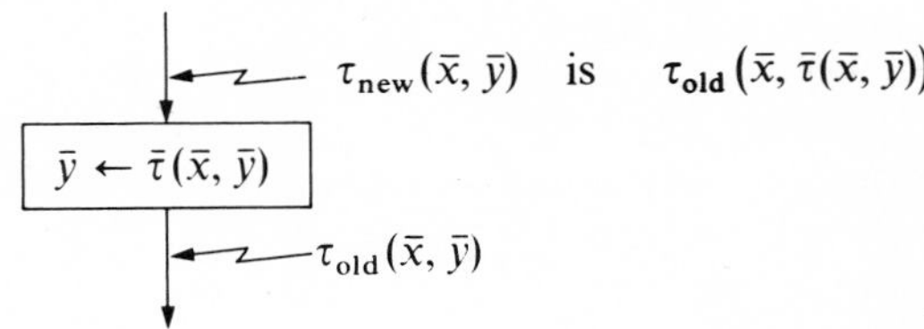

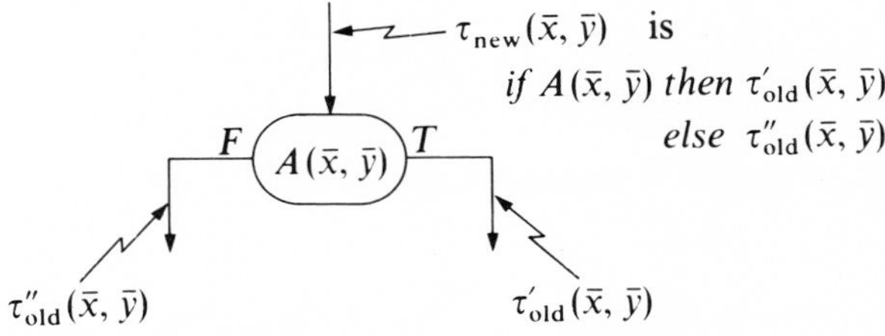

3. *Final step. The construction of the recursive equation* E_α:

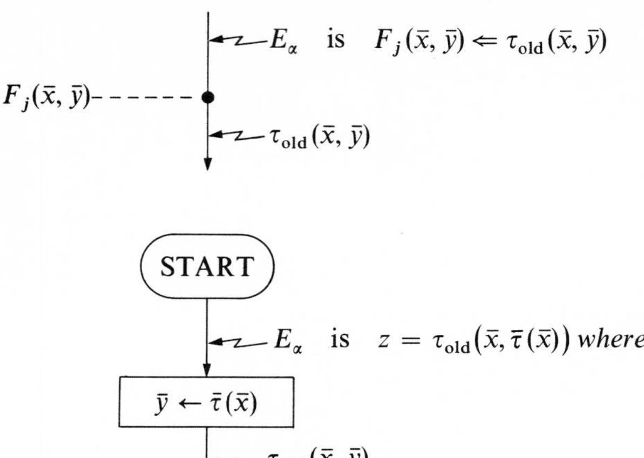

The set of all recursive equations together represent the desired recursive schema S'. Note that intuitively each $F_i(\bar{x}, \bar{y})$ represents the final value of z when the computation of S starts at cutpoint i with initial values $(\bar{x}, \bar{y})$.

Q.E.D.

EXAMPLE 4-26

Consider the flowchart schema S_{26} (Fig. 4-26). We would like to find a recursive schema S'_{26} which is equivalent to S_{26}. Let us associate with the cutpoints A, B, C, and D the function variables F_1, F_2, F_3, and F_4, as indicated in Fig. 4-26.

Applying the algorithm, we obtain in this case the recursive schema

S_{26}: $z = F_1(x, x, x)$ *where*

$$F_1(x, y_1, y_2) \Leftarrow \textit{if } p(y_1) \textit{ then } y_1 \textit{ else } F_2(x, f(y_1), y_2)$$

$$F_2(x, y_1, y_2) \Leftarrow \textit{if } p(y_1) \textit{ then } y_1 \textit{ else } F_3(x, f(y_1), f(y_2))$$

$$F_3(x, y_1, y_2) \Leftarrow \textit{if } p(y_1) \textit{ then } F_4(x, y_1, y_2) \textit{ else } y_1$$

$$F_4(x, y_1, y_2) \Leftarrow \textit{if } p(y_2) \textit{ then } F_3(x, f(y_1), f(y_2)) \textit{ else } F_2(x, f(y_1), y_2)$$

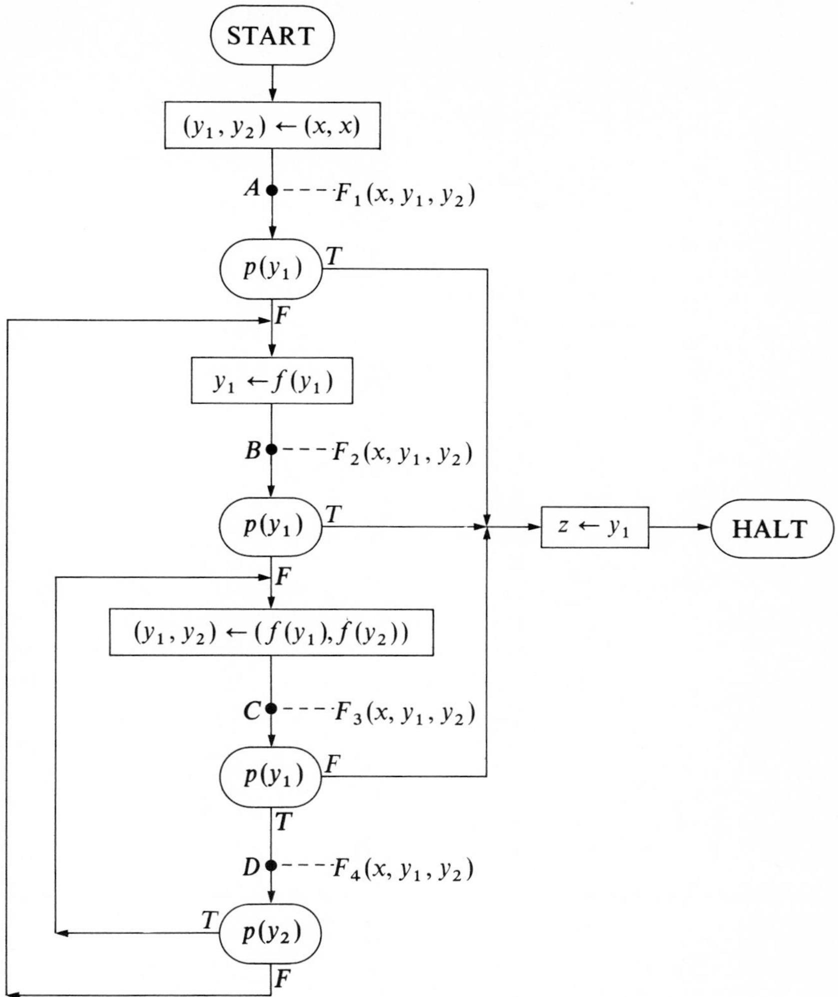

Figure 4-26 Flowchart schema S_{26}.

Note that since both loops in S_{26} include point C, it suffices to have only C as a cutpoint. Therefore, if we associate the function variable $F(x, y_1, y_2)$ with C and apply the algorithm we obtain the recursive schema

$$
\begin{aligned}
S''_{26}:\quad & z = \textit{if } p(x) \textit{ then } x \\
& \qquad \textit{else if } p(f(x)) \textit{ then } f(x) \\
& \qquad\qquad \textit{else } F(x, f^{(2)}(x), f(x)) \quad \textit{where} \\
& F(x, y_1, y_2) \Leftarrow \textit{if } p(y_1) \\
& \qquad \textit{then if } p(y_2) \textit{ then } F(x, f(y_1), f(y_2)) \\
& \qquad\qquad \textit{else if } p(f(y_1)) \textit{ then } f(y_1) \\
& \qquad\qquad\qquad \textit{else } F(x, f^{(2)}(y_1), f(y_2)) \\
& \qquad \textit{else } y_1
\end{aligned}
$$

□

Thus every flowchart schema can be translated into an equivalent recursive schema; however, on the other hand, we have the following theorem.

THEOREM 4-6 (Paterson and Hewitt). *There is no flowchart schema (with any number of program variables) which is equivalent to the recursive schema*

$$
\begin{aligned}
S_A:\quad & z = F(a) \textit{ where} \\
& F(y) \Leftarrow \textit{if } p(y) \textit{ then } f(y) \textit{ else } h(F(g_1(y)), F(g_2(y)))
\end{aligned}
$$

Proof. We shall describe a very restricted subclass of Herbrand interpretations $\{\mathscr{I}_n^*\}_{n \geq 0}$ of S_A such that for each n $(n \geq 0)$ $\mathscr{I}_n^*$ has the property that in order to compute the term $val\langle S_A, \mathscr{I}_n^*\rangle$ with a flowchart schema, at least $n + 1$ program variables are required. Thus, there is no flowchart schema (with any number of program variables) which is equivalent to S_A.

Without loss of generality we may restrict ourselves to flowchart schemas with only "primitive" ASSIGNMENT statements, that is, ASSIGNMENT statements in which the term contains at most one function constant. This follows from the fact that every "nonprimitive" ASSIGNMENT statement can always be replaced by a sequence of primitive ASSIGNMENT statements using extra program variables; for example, the ASSIGNMENT statement $y \leftarrow h(g_1(y), g_2(y))$ may be replaced by the sequence $y_1 \leftarrow g_1(y)$; $y_2 \leftarrow g_2(y)$; $y \leftarrow h(y_1, y_2)$.

The Herbrand universe H_{S_A} is the set of all constant terms constructed from a and the constant functions f, g_1, g_2, and h. The desired class of Herbrand interpretations $\{\mathscr{I}_n^*\}_{n \geq 0}$ is defined as follows: For every n ($n \geq 0$) and for every constant term t, the value of $p(t)$ under $\mathscr{I}_n^*$ is *true* if and only if the number of occurrences of g_i's in t is n.

We shall now describe the final term $val\langle S, \mathscr{I}_n^* \rangle$ for $n = 0, 1, 2$, and 3 (some of the parentheses are omitted for simplicity). We shall also illustrate how these expressions can be represented as binary trees, denoted by T_n.

$n = 0$: $z = f(a)$

T_0 is f

$n = 1$: $z = h(fg_1(a), fg_2(a))$

T_1 is

h

fg_1 $\quad$ fg_2

$n = 2$: $z = h(h(fg_1g_1(a), fg_2g_1(a)), h(fg_1g_2(a), fg_2g_2(a)))$

T_2 is

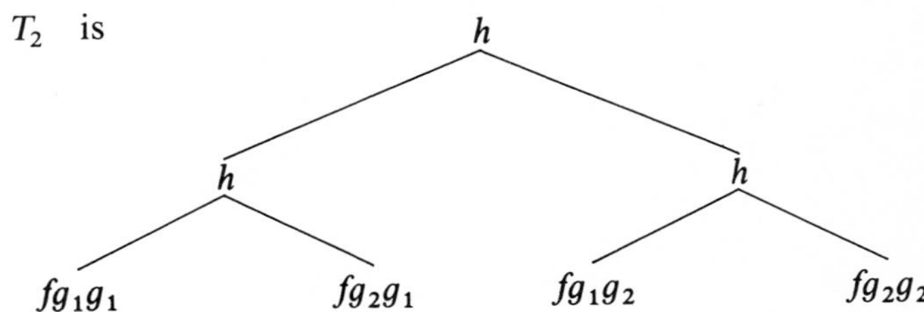

$n = 3$: $z = h(h(h(fg_1g_1g_1(a), fg_2g_1g_1(a)), h(fg_1g_2g_1(a), fg_2g_2g_1(a))),$
$h(h(fg_1g_1g_2(a), fg_2g_1g_2(a)), h(fg_1g_2g_2(a), fg_2g_2g_2(a))))$

T_3 is

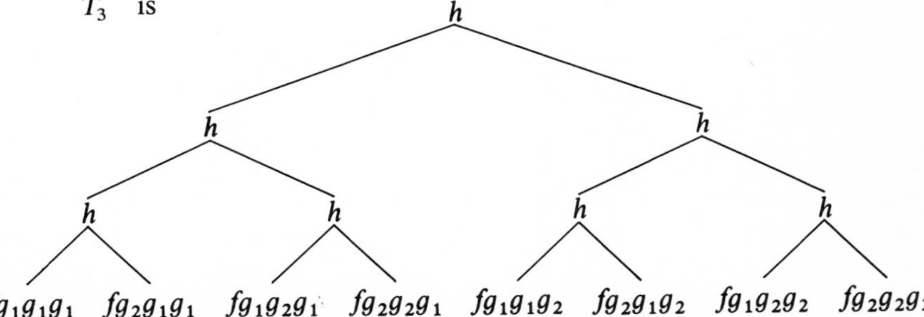

In their original proof Paterson and Hewitt (1970) showed why a flowchart schema is needed with at least $n + 1$ program variables. They did this by playing a game of placing movable tokens on T_n:

> The rules of the game are that any token may be put on a bottom node at any time. If the two nodes below a given node are covered, then the two tokens are removed and a token is put at the given node. How many tokens are needed to be able to reach the top node? It is easy to see that $n + 1$ are sufficient in general for T_n, and the following argument establishes their necessity.
>
> A tree will be said to be *closed* at a given stage of the game if there is at least one token on each path from top to bottom. Initially, the tree is devoid of tokens and so is not closed. Finally, there is a token at the top node and so it is closed. We concentrate our attention on the time at which the tree first becomes closed. This can only happen as a result of placing a token at a bottom node, closing off the last path. Now this path is otherwise empty of tokens and so each of the n subtrees sprouting immediately off this path must be independently closed. Since at least one token is needed to close any tree, there are at least $n + 1$ tokens on the tree at this time.

We assume that the relation between the assignments in a computation of a flowchart schema (with primitive ASSIGNMENT statements) and the moves in the game just described is self-evident. Note that one of the key points in the proof is that for any n $(n \geq 0)$ there is no subtree which occurs more than once in T_n.

Q.E.D.

It is quite essential that both F's occur as arguments of h in the definitions of S_A. For example, there are flowchart schemas which are equivalent to the recursive schemas:

$$S_B: \quad z = F(a) \textit{ where}$$

$$F(y) \Leftarrow \textit{if } p(y) \textit{ then } f(y) \textit{ else } h(F(g(y)))$$

and

$$S_C: \quad z = F(a) \textit{ where}$$

$$F(y) \Leftarrow \textit{if } p(y) \textit{ then } f(y) \textit{ else } h(y, F(g(y)))$$

1. *Flowchart schema S'_B (Fig. 4-27) is equivalent to the recursive schema*

S_B. For a given Herbrand interpretation $\mathscr{I}^*$, the computation of S'_B proceeds as follows: Suppose m ($m \geq 0$) is the least integer for which $p(\text{“}g^m(a)\text{”}) =$ *true* under $\mathscr{I}^*$; then $val\langle S_B, \mathscr{I}^*\rangle$ is “$h^{(m)}(f(g^{(m)}(a)))$”. This term is accumulated in y_1 as follows:

$$y_1 = \text{“}g^{(m)}(a)\text{”} \qquad \text{at point 1}$$

$$y_1 = \text{“}f(g^{(m)}(a))\text{”} \qquad \text{at point 2}$$

$$y_1 = \text{“}h^{(m)}(f(g^{(m)}(a)))\text{”} \qquad \text{at point 3}$$

y_2 is used as a counter to obtain m iterations in the second loop.

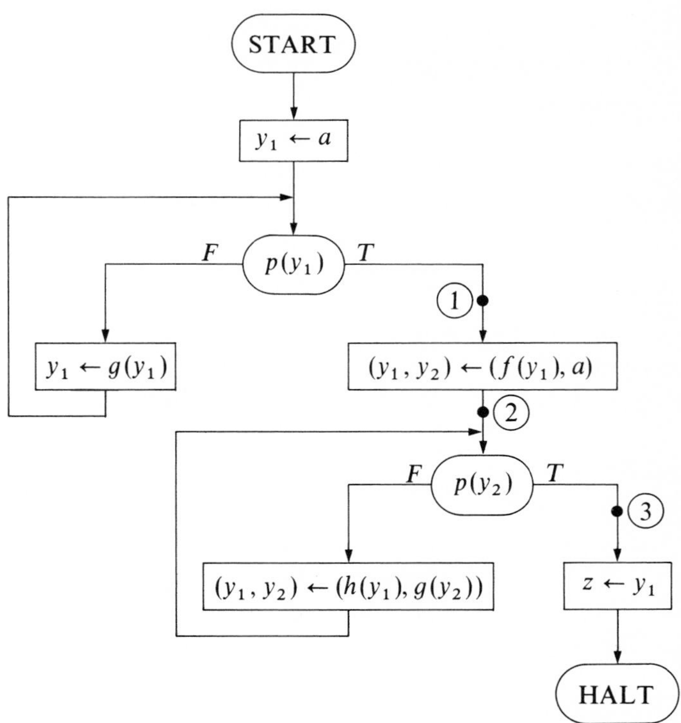

Figure 4-27 Flowchart schema S'_B.

2. *Flowchart schema S'_C (Fig. 4-28) is equivalent to the recursive schema S_C.* For a given Herbrand interpretation $\mathscr{I}^*$, if m ($m \geq 0$) is the least integer for which $p(\text{“}g^m(a)\text{”}) =$ *true* under $\mathscr{I}^*$, then $val\langle S_C, \mathscr{I}^*\rangle$ is

$$\text{“}h(a, h(g(a), h(g^{(2)}(a), \ldots, h(g^{(m-1)}(a), fg^{(m)}(a)) \ldots)))\text{”}$$

[In the special case when $m = 0$, $val\langle S_C, \mathscr{I}^*\rangle$ is $f(a)$.] This term is accumulated in y_1 as follows:

at point 1 ($i = 0$):

$$y_1 = \text{“}f(g^{(m)}(a))\text{”}$$

$$y_2 = \text{“}g^{(0)}(a)\text{”} = \text{“}a\text{”}$$

at point 2 ($0 \le i \le m$):

$$y_1 = \text{“}h(g^{(m-i)}(a), h(g^{(m-i+1)}(a), \ldots, h(g^{(m-1)}(a), fg^{(m)}(a)) \ldots))\text{”}$$

$$y_2 = \text{“}g^{(i)}(a)\text{”}$$

at point 3 ($i = m$):

$$y_1 = \text{“}h(a, h(g(a), h(g^{(2)}(a), \ldots, h(g^{(m-1)}(a), fg^{(m)}(a)) \ldots)))\text{”}$$

$$y_2 = \text{“}g^{(m)}(a)\text{”}$$

The value for y_4 which is used in the assignment $y_1 \leftarrow h(y_4, y_1)$ is obtained in the inner loop, since

$$y_3 : \text{“}g^{(i+1)}(a)\text{”}, \text{“}g^{(i+2)}(a)\text{”}, \ldots, \text{“}g^{(m)}(a)\text{”}$$

and at the same time

$$y_4 : \text{“}a\text{”}, \text{“}g(a)\text{”}, \ldots, \text{“}g^{(m-i-1)}(a)\text{”}$$

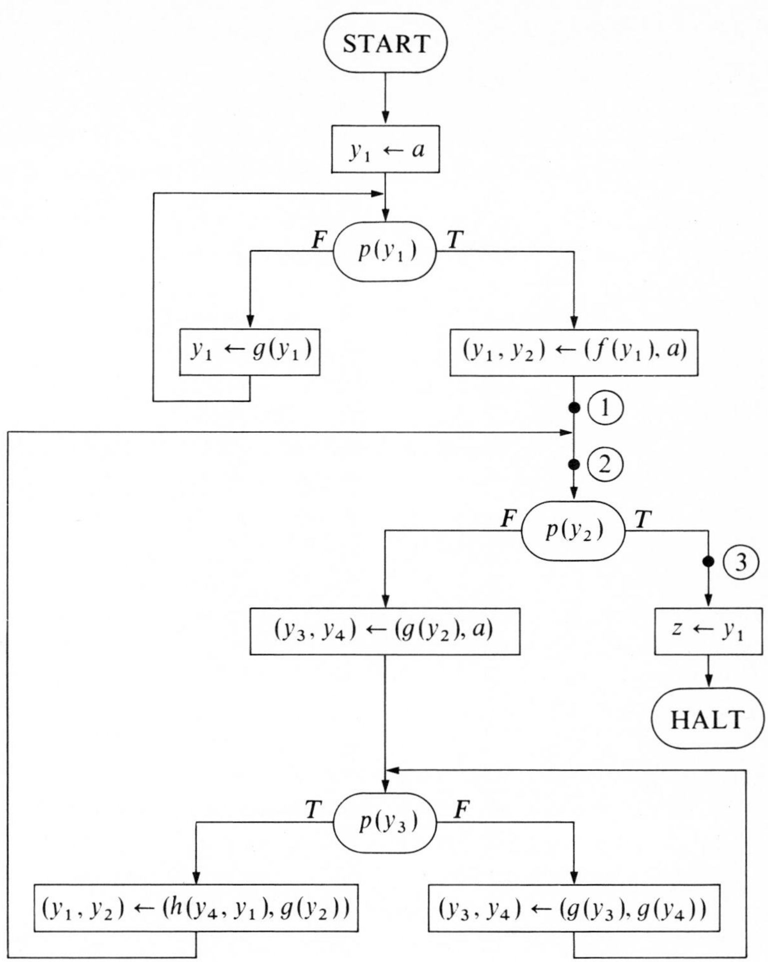

Figure 4-28 Flowchart schema S_C'.

Bibliographic Remarks

The pioneer work on flowchart schemas was done by Ianov (1960), who proved that the equivalence problem of Ianov schemas is solvable. This specific problem has been discussed further by Rutledge (1964) and Kaplan (1969). We shall distinguish here among several topics regarding schemas.

1. *Decision problems.* The most important works in this area are those of Paterson (1967, 1968) and Luckham, Park, and Paterson (1970); they introduced most of the basic results in this area, such as Herbrand's theorem (Theorem 4-1) and the unsolvability of the basic properties (Theorem 4-2). Similar work has been done for other types of schemas, such as parallel schemas [Karp and Miller (1969)] and recursive schemas [Ashcroft, Manna, and Pnueli (1973)]. Milner (1970) discussed the decision problems for schemas with *partial interpretations*, that is, interpretations in which functions and predicates may be partial rather than total. An excellent survey on the Russians' work in this area is presented by Ershov in IFIP (1971).

2. *Relation to predicate calculus.* Following Floyd's (1967) inductive-assertion method for proving partial correctness of programs, Manna (1969*a*, *b*) formalized the basic properties of flowchart programs (Theorem 4-3) and flowchart schemas (Theorem 4-4) in first-order predicate calculus. Cooper (1969, 1970) formalized the equivalence of flowchart schemas in second-order predicate calculus. Manna and Pnueli (1970) formalized similarly properties of recursive schemas. [See also Manna (1970).]

3. *Translation problems.* Recent work has considered more powerful types of flowchart schemas than those discussed in this text, that is, flowchart schemas with additional programming features like arrays [Constable and Gries (1972)], pushdown stacks [Brown, Gries and Szymanski (1972)], counters [Garland and Luckham (1973), Plaisted (1972)], and equality tests [Chandra and Manna (1972)]. These researchers were concerned mainly with the problem of translating program schemas from one class to another in an attempt to compare the "power" of those programming features. For this purpose, we introduced the class of recursive schemas. Since every flowchart schema can be translated to an equivalent recursive schema [Theorem 4-5, McCarthy (1962)], but not vice versa [Theorem 4-6, Paterson and Hewitt (1970)], it follows that *recursion is more powerful than iteration.* [See also Strong (1971).] An excellent survey of the above works together with many new results can be found in Chandra's thesis (1973).

REFERENCES

Ashcroft, E., and Z. Manna (1971): "The Translation of 'GOTO' Programs to 'WHILE' programs," *Proc. IFIP Cong.*, North-Holland pub. com., Amsterdam, pp. 250–255.

———, ———, and A. Pnueli (1973): "Decidable Properties of Monadic Functional Schemas," J. ACM, **20**(3): 489–499 (July).

Bird, M. (1972): "The Equivalence Problem for Deterministic Two-tape Automata," unpublished memo., Swansea, Glamorgan, U.K.

Brown, S., D. Gries, and T. Szymanski (1972): "Program Schemes with Pushdown Stores," *SIAM J. Computing,* **1**(4): 242–268 (December).

Chandra, A.K. (1973): "On the Properties and Applications of Program Schemas," Ph.D. thesis, Computer Science Department, Stanford University, Stanford, Calif.

——— and Z. Manna (1972): "Program Schemas with Equality," *Proc. 4th Ann. ACM Symp. Theory Comput.*, Denver, Colo. pp. 52–64 (May).

Cooper, D.C. (1969): "Program Scheme Equivalences and Second-order Logic," in B. Meltzer and D. Michie (eds.), *Machine Intelligence,* Vol. 4, pp. 3–15, Edinburgh University Press, Edinburgh.

——— (1970): "Program Schemes, Programs and Logic," in E. Engeler, (ed.), *Symposium on Semantics of Algorithmic Languages,* pp. 62–70, Springer-Verlag, Berlin.

——— (1971): "Programs for Mechanical Program Verification," in B. Meltzer and D. Michie (eds.), *Machine Intelligence*, Vol. 6, pp. 43–59, Edinburgh University Press, Edinburgh.

Constable, R.L., and D. Gries (1972): "On Classes of Program Schemata," *SIAM. Comput.*, **1**(1): 66–118 (March).

Engeler, E. (1971): "Structure and Meanings of Elementary Programs," in E. Engeler (ed.), *Symposium on Semantics of Algorithmic Languages,* pp. 89–101, Springer-Verlag, Berlin.

Ershov A. P. (1971): "Theory of Program Schemata," *Proc. IFIP Congr.*, North-Holland pub. com., Amsterdam, pp. 28–45.

Floyd, R.W. (1967): "Assigning meanings to programs," in J.T. Schwartz (ed.), *Proceedings of a Symposium in Applied Mathematics*, Vol. 19, *Mathematical Aspects of Computer Science*, pp. 19–32, American Mathematical Society, New York.

Garland, S.J. and D.C. Luckham (1973): "Program Schemes, Recursion Schemes, and Formal Languages," J. CSS, 7 (1): 119–160 (January).

Ianov, Y.I. (1960): "The Logical Schemes of Algorithms," in *Problems of Cybernetics,* vol. 1, pp. 82–140, Pergamon Press, New York (English translation).

Kaplan, D.M. (1969): "Regular expressions and the equivalence of programs," J.CSS, **3**(4): 361–385 (November).

Karp, R.M., and R.E. Miller (1969): "Parallel Program Schemata," *J.CSS*, **3**(2): 147–195 (May).

Knuth, D.E., and R.W. Floyd (1971): "Notes on Avoiding GOTO Statements," *Inf. Process. Lett.*, **1**(1): 23–31 (January).

Luckham, D.C., D.M.R. Park, and M.S. Paterson (1970): "On Formalized Computer Programs," *J.CSS*, **4**(3): 220–249 (June).

Manna, Z. (1969a): "Properties of Programs and First-order Predicate Calculus," *J.ACM*, **16**(2): 244–255 (April).

——— (1969b): "The Correctness of Programs," *J.CSS*, **3**(2): 119–127 (May).

——— (1970): "Second-order Mathematical Theory of Computation," *Proc. 2d. Ann. ACM Symp. Theory Comput.*, pp. 158–168 (May).

——— and A. Pnueli (1970): "Formalization of Properties of Functional Programs," *J.ACM*, **17**(3): 555–569 (July).

McCarthy, J. (1962): "Towards a Mathematical Science of Computation," in C.M. Popplewell (ed.), *Information Processing, Proceedings of IFIP Congress 1962*, pp. 21–28, North-Holland Publishing Company, Amsterdam.

Milner, R. (1970): "Equivalences on Program Schemes," *J.CSS*. **4**(3): 205–219 (June).

Paterson, M.S. (1967): "Equivalence Problems in a Model of Computation," Ph.D. thesis, University of Cambridge, Cambridge, Eng. (August). [Also: *Artificial Intelligence Memo No. 1,* M.I.T., Cambridge, Mass. (1970)].

——— (1968): "Program Schemata," in D. Michie (ed.), *Machine Intelligence*, Vol. 3, pp. 19–31, Edinburgh University Press, Edinburgh.

——— and C.E. Hewitt (1970): "Comparative Schematology," in *Record of Project MAC Conference on Concurrent Systems and Parallel Computation,* Association for Computer Machinery, New York, pp. 119–128 (December).

Plaisted, D.A. (1972): "Flowchart Schemes with Counters," *Proc. 4th Ann. Symp. Theory Comput.*, Denver, Colo. (May).

Rutledge, J.D. (1964): "On Ianov's Program Schemata," *J.ACM*, **11**(1): 1–9 (January).

Strong, H.R. (1971): "Translating Recursion Equations into Flowcharts." *J.CSS*, **5**(3): 254–285 (June).

PROBLEMS

Prob. 4-1 (Finite/infinite interpretation). *An interpretation is said to be finite/infinite if it has a finite/infinite domain.*

(*a*) Prove that the flowchart schema S_3 (Fig. 4-3) halts for every finite interpretation and also halts for every infinite interpretation $\mathscr{I}$ unless $p(f^{(n)}(a))$, $n \geq 0$, takes the following values under $\mathscr{I}$:

$$\begin{array}{rcccccccccccccccccc} n: & 0 & 1 & 2 & 3 & 4 & 5 & 6 & 7 & 8 & 9 & 10 & 11 & 12 & 13 & 14 & 15 \\ p(f^{(n)}(a)): & f & f & \underbrace{t} & f & \underbrace{t \; t} & & f & \underbrace{t \; t \; t} & & & f & \underbrace{t \quad t \quad t \quad t} & & & & f & \ldots \end{array}$$

(*b*) Consider the flowchart schema S_{29} (Fig. 4-29).

(i) Prove that for every finite interpretation $\mathscr{I}$, $\langle S_{29}, \mathscr{I} \rangle$ does not halt, that is, $\langle S_{29}, \mathscr{I}, \xi \rangle$ diverges for some ξ.

(ii) Does there exist an infinite interpretation $\mathscr{I}$ for which $\langle S_{29}, \mathscr{I} \rangle$ halts?

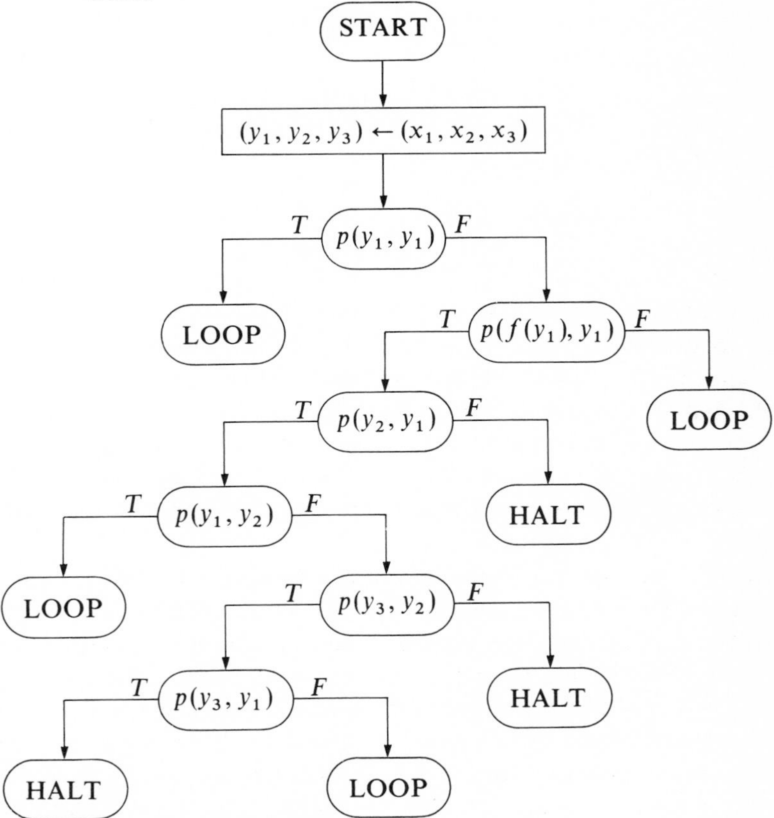

Figure 4-29 Flowchart schema S_{29}.

Prob. 4-2 (Equivalence under constraints). Consider the two structures of compatible flowchart schemas in Fig. 4-30

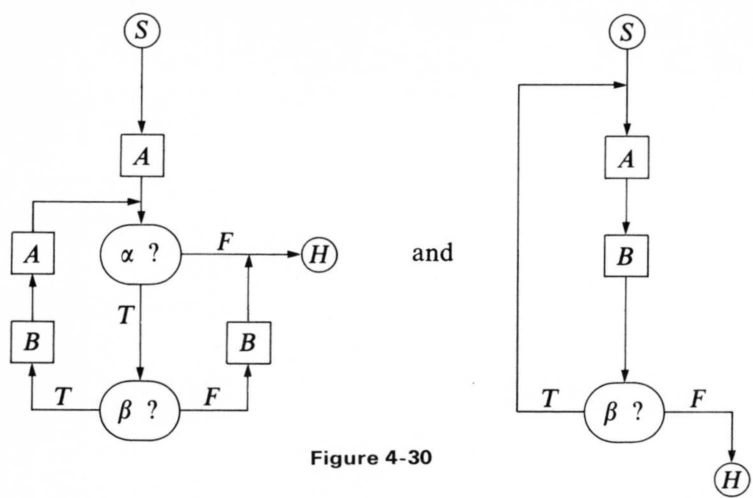

Figure 4-30

where S stands for a START statement, H stands for a HALT statement, A and B stand for ASSIGNMENT statements, and α and β stand for TEST statements. Note that for

$$A: \quad (y_1, y_2) \leftarrow (a, f(x, y_1, y_2)) \qquad \alpha: \quad y_1 = a$$

$$B: \quad (y_1, y_2) \leftarrow (f(x, y_1, y_2), y_2) \qquad \beta: \quad p(y_2)$$

the two flowchart schemas obtained are equivalent. Give a general condition on A, B, α, and β so that any two flowchart schemas with A, B, α, and β satisfying this condition will be equivalent.

Prob. 4-3 (Herbrand property, Chandra and Manna (1972)). All the flowchart schemas discussed in this chapter have one important common property (Theorem 4-1): For every interpretation there corresponds an Herbrand interpretation such that under both interpretations exactly the same path of computation is followed. Let us call this the *Herbrand property*. If we augment the class of our flowchart schemas and allow flowchart schemas with equality tests (that is, tests of the form $\tau_1(\bar{x}, \bar{y}) = \tau_2(\bar{x}, \bar{y})$, where τ_1 and τ_2 are terms), we may obtain flowchart schemas which do not have the Herbrand property.

(*a*) Prove that it is not partially solvable whether or not a given flowchart schema (with equality tests) has the Herbrand property.

(*b*) The flowchart schema S_{31} (Fig. 4-31) does not have the Herbrand property. Find an equivalent flowchart schema that has the Herbrand property.

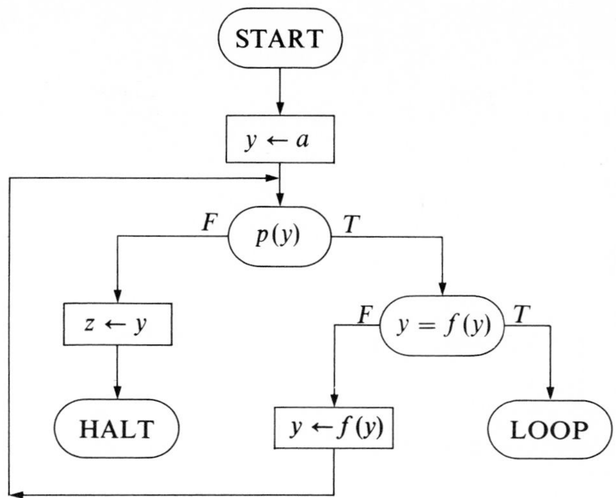

Figure 4-31 Flowchart schema S_{31}.

Prob. 4-4 (Decision problems).

(*a*) Show that the decision problem for the following properties is partially solvable: (i) nonfreedom,† (ii) nondivergence, and (iii) nonisomorphism.

(*b*) Show that the decision problem for the following properties is not partially solvable: (i) nonhalting, and (ii) nonequivalence.

(*c*) Discuss the decision problem for the following properties (and their complements):‡ (i) partial correctness, (ii) total correctness, and (iii) extension.

Prob. 4-5 (Finite interpretations—decision problems). Consider the class $\mathscr{S}_1$ of flowchart schemas introduced in Sec. 4-2. Show the following.

*(*a*) The following properties of flowchart schemas S in $\mathscr{S}_1$ are not partially solvable:

(i) S diverges for every finite interpretation.

(ii) S halts for every finite interpretation.

(*b*) The following properties of flowchart schemas S in $\mathscr{S}_1$ are unsolvable (but partially solvable for all flowchart schemas):

(i) S halts for some finite interpretation.

(ii) S diverges for some finite interpretation.

† That is, there exists an algorithm that takes any flowchart schema S as input and if S is not free, the algorithm will eventually halt with a yes answer; otherwise, that is, if S is free, the algorithm either halts with a no answer or loops forever.

‡ Note that the properties are defined in Section 4-3.2.

Prob. 4-6 (Free schemas).

(*a*) Find a free schema which is equivalent to the flowchart schema S_{32} (Fig. 4-32).

(*b*) Prove that for a free flowchart schema S every infinite path through its flow-diagram, from the START statement, describes some computation.

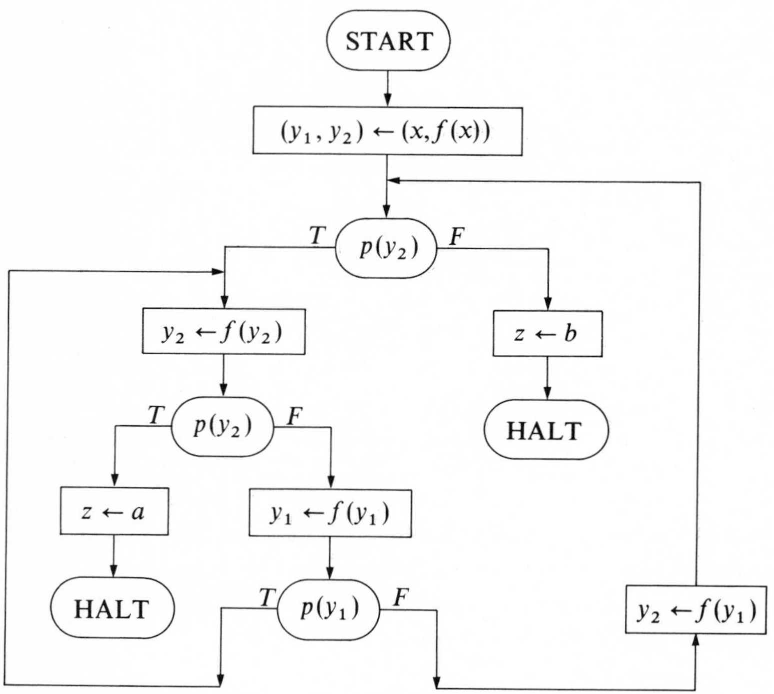

Figure 4-32 Flowchart schema S_{32}.

Prob. 4-7 (Outputs of free schemas are regular sets, Chandra (1973)). Let S be a free flowchart schema with one output variable z and with no function constants other than unary function constants and individual constants. Prove that the set of all final terms generated by S under all possible Herbrand interpretations is regular (consider terms as strings without parentheses).

Hint: Associate with each ASSIGNMENT or HALT statement i and program variable y_j a variable r_{ij}. Construct a system of regular equations (see Chap. 1, Prob. 1-5) in such a way that the corresponding least fixpoint R_{ij} represents the set of all possible values of y_j at statement i.

Prob. 4-8 (Tree schemas, Paterson (1967)).

(*a*) Prove that the flowchart schema S_{33} (Fig. 4-33) halts for every interpretation.

(*b*) Prove that the flowchart schema S_{14A} (Fig. 4-14*a*) is equivalent to the flowchart schema S_{34} (Fig. 4-34).

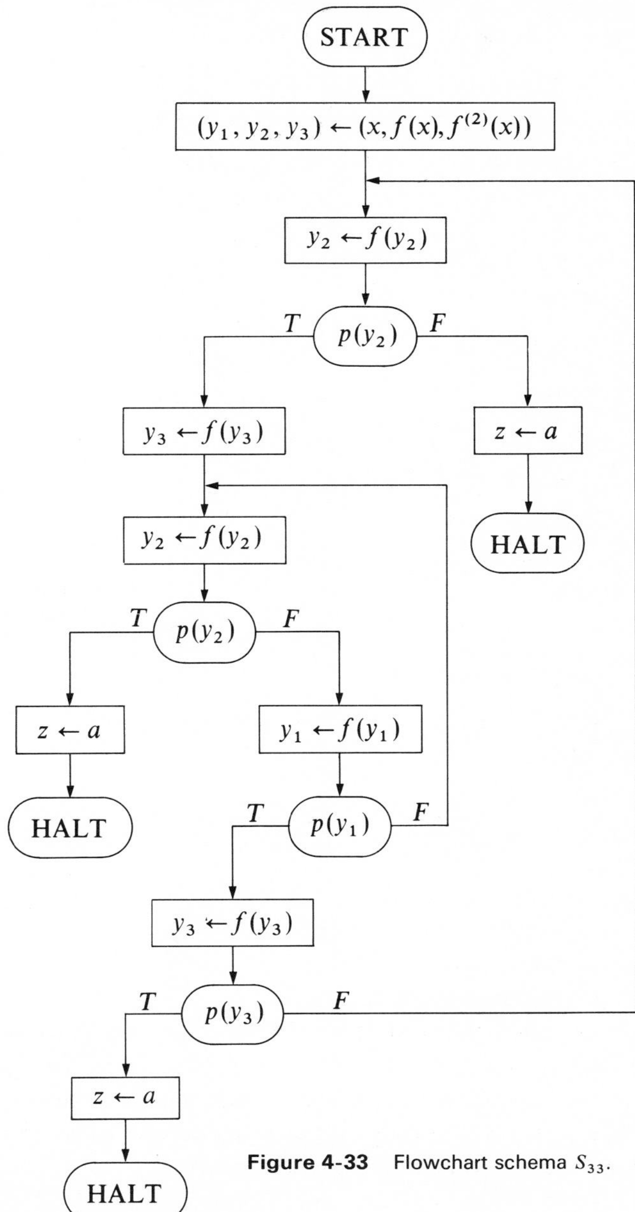

Figure 4-33 Flowchart schema S_{33}.

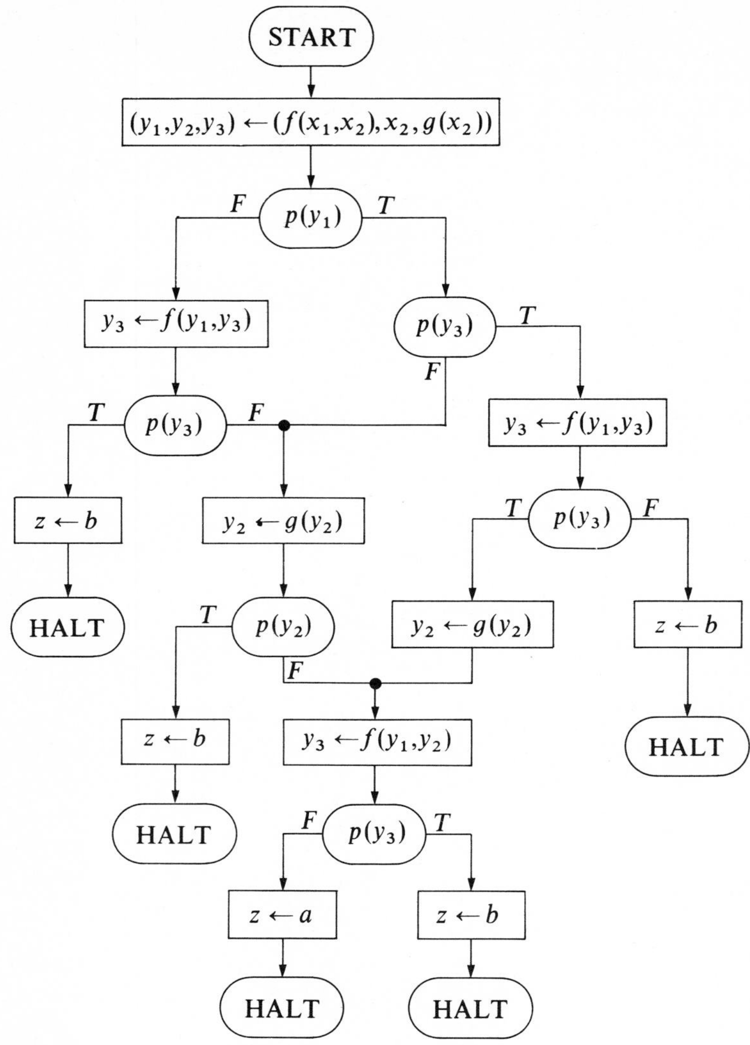

Figure 4-34 Flowchart schema S_{34}.

Prob. 4-9 (Ianov schemas—free schemas).

(*a*) Prove that every Ianov schema can be transformed to an equivalent free Ianov schema.

*(*b*) Prove that every one-variable flowchart schema (that is, any flowchart schema with only one program variable) can be transformed to an equivalent free flowchart schema.

Prob. 4-10 (Extended Ianov schemas, Chandra (1973)). Show that the halting, divergence, equivalence, and isomorphism problems for the following classes of flowchart schemas are solvable.

*(*a*) Ianov schemas with resets, that is, Ianov schemas with ASSIGNMENT statements of the form $y \leftarrow a_i$
Hint: Simulate the computations of the schemas from all resets simultaneously.

*(*b*) One-variable flowchart schemas, that is, flowchart schemas with one program variable (including individual constants, nonmonadic functions, and nonmonadic predicates).

*(*c*) Ianov schemas which may have equality tests of the form $y = a_i$.

Prob. 4-11 (Proving properties of programs). Consider the program P_{35} (Fig. 4-35) over the natural numbers. Use the two methods of Example 4-22 to prove that for every natural number ξ, $\langle P_{35}, \xi \rangle$ is totally correct wrt $z = x!$.

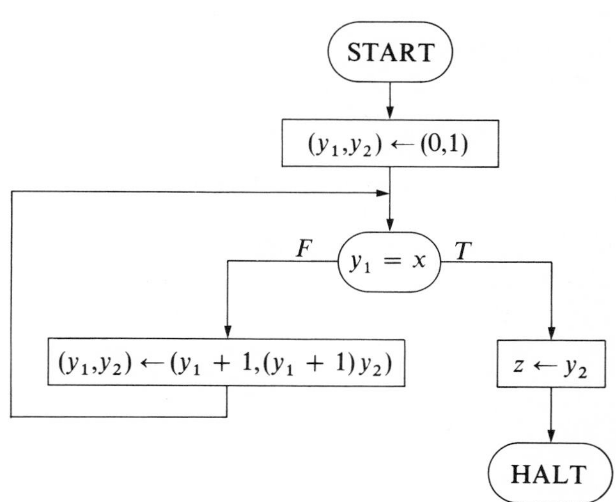

Figure 4-35 The program P_{35}.

Prob. 4-12 (Partial equivalence and total equivalence). For two compatible programs P and P' and input value ξ, we say that

1. $\langle P, \xi \rangle$ *and* $\langle P', \xi \rangle$ *are partially equivalent* if either at least one of $val\langle P, \xi \rangle$ or $val\langle P', \xi \rangle$ is undefined, or both $val\langle P, \xi \rangle$ and $val\langle P', \xi \rangle$ are defined and $val\langle P, \xi \rangle = val\langle P', \xi \rangle$;

2. $\langle P, \bar{\xi}\rangle$ *and* $\langle P', \bar{\xi}\rangle$ *are totally equivalent* if both $val\langle P, \bar{\xi}\rangle$ and $val\langle P', \bar{\xi}\rangle$ are defined and $val\langle P, \bar{\xi}\rangle = val\langle P', \bar{\xi}\rangle$.

For two compatible schemas S and S', we say that S *and* S' *are partially/totally equivalent* if for every interpretation $\mathscr{I}$ of S and S' and for every input value $\bar{\xi}$, $\langle S, \mathscr{I}, \bar{\xi}\rangle$ and $\langle S', \mathscr{I}, \bar{\xi}\rangle$ are partially/totally equivalent.

(*a*) Give interpreted wffs which formalize partial and total equivalence of programs as was done in Theorem 4-3 for the other properties.

(*b*) Give wffs which formalize partial and total equivalence of schemas as was done in Theorem 4-4 for the other properties.

(*c*) Show that partial equivalence is not a transitive relation and that total equivalence is not a reflexive relation.

(*d*) Show that

(i) The decision problem for partial equivalence is not partially solvable.

(ii) The decision problem for total equivalence is unsolvable but partially solvable.

Prob. 4-13 (Application of Theorem 4-4, Manna (1969a)). Considering the result of Theorem 4-4 (and Prob. 4-12), it follows that halting, total correctness, and total equivalence can be formalized by first-order wffs (since all quantifiers are universally quantified after being pushed to the left). Note that all the other properties are formalized in general by second-order wffs. Use this fact and the results of Sec. 2-1.6 (Chap. 2) to find subclasses of flowchart schemas for which halting, total correctness, and total equivalence are solvable.

Prob. 4-14 (Equivalence and predicate calculus, Cooper (1969)). Consider the flowchart schemas S_{36A} (Fig. 4-36*a*), S_{36B} (Fig. 4-36*b*) and S_{36C} (Fig. 4-36*c*). Prove that these flowchart schemas are equivalent by using

(*a*) Equivalence preserving transformations, and

*(*b*) the predicate calculus approach (Theorem 4-4).

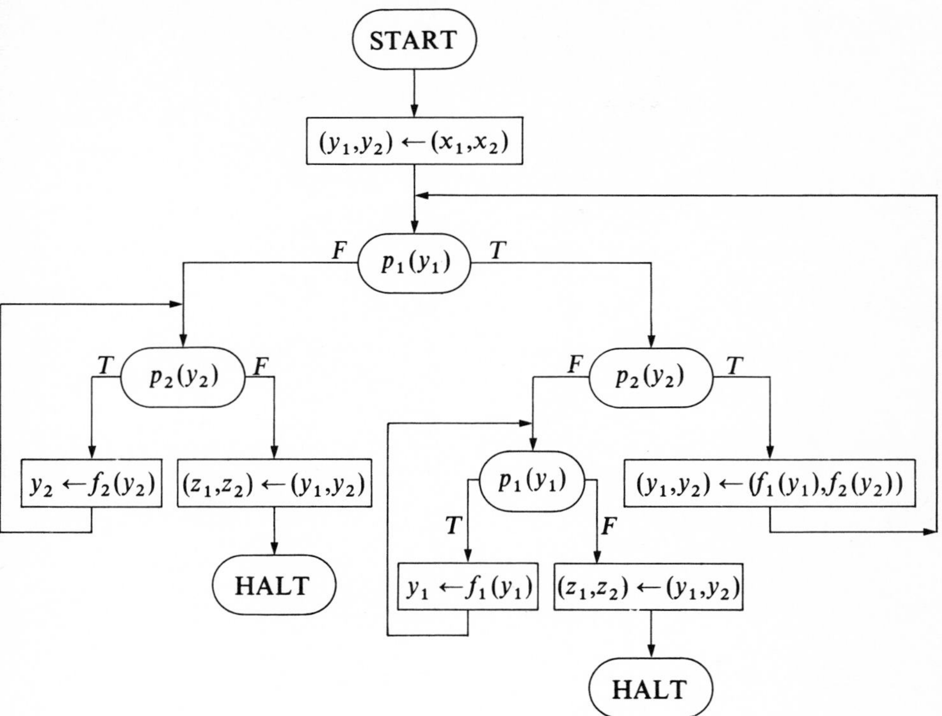

Figure 4-36a Flowchart schema S_{36A}.

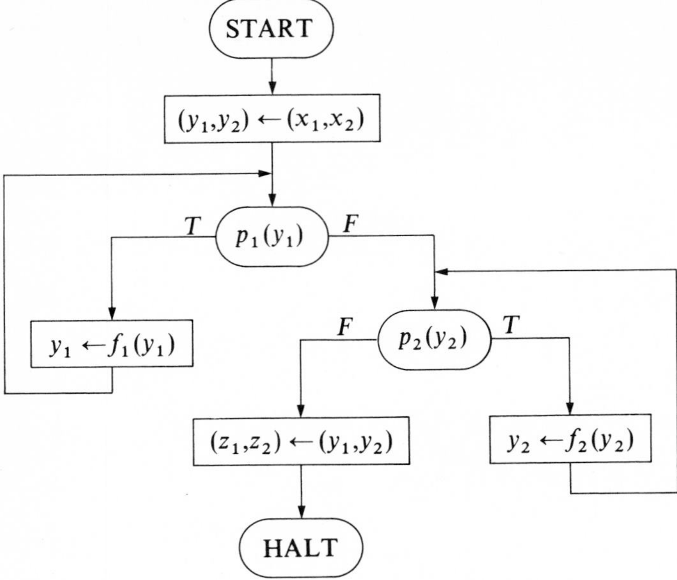

Figure 4-36*b* Flowchart schema S_{36B}.

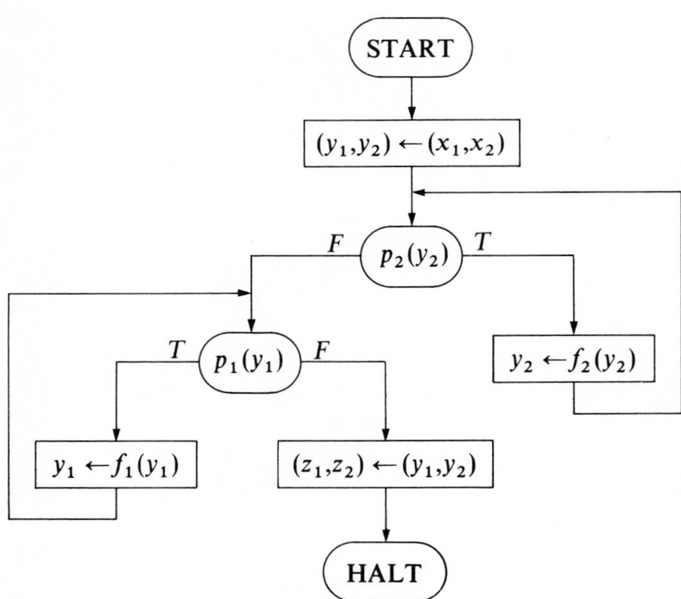

Figure 4-36*c* Flowchart schema S_{36C}.

Prob. 4-15 (Recursive schemas vs. flowchart schemas).

(*a*) Consider the recursive schema

$$S_A: \quad z = F(a) \quad where$$

$$F(y) \Leftarrow if\ p(y)\ \ then\ f(y)\ \ else\ \ h(F(g(y)))$$

Show that there is no flowchart schema with one program variable which is equivalent to S_A.

(*b*) Consider the flowchart schema S'_C (Fig. 4-28) with four program variables which is equivalent to the recursive schema

$$S_C: \quad z = F(a) \quad where$$

$$F(y) \Leftarrow if\ p(y)\ \ then\ f(y)\ \ else\ \ h(y, F(g(y)))$$

Give a flowchart schema with only three program variables which is equivalent to S'_C.

Hint: Use the variable y_2 to do also the job of y_3. To reset the value of y_2 to $g^{(i+1)}(a)$ at the end of the inner loop, use the fact that $y_4 = g^{(m-(i+1))}(a)$.

Prob. 4-16 (Noncompactness of flowchart schemas, Francez/Slutzky). Find an infinite class of schemas $\mathscr{S}$ such that for every finite subclass $\mathscr{S}'$ of $\mathscr{S}$, there is an interpretation for which all members of $\mathscr{S}'$ halt but there is no interpretation for which all members of $\mathscr{S}$ halt.

Prob. 4-17 (Flowchart schemas with additional programming features, Chandra (1973)). Consider the following problem: Given two unary function constants f and g and a unary predicate constant p, write a flowchart schema S (with one input variable and one output variable) that for every interpretation $\mathscr{I}$ and input ξ yields the output ζ, where $\zeta = f^{(i)}(g^{(j)}(\xi))$ for some $i, j \geqq 0$ and $p(\zeta)$ is *false*. If no such ζ exists, the computation of $\langle S, \mathscr{I}, \xi \rangle$ will loop forever.

(*a*) Show that no flowchart schema can solve the problem.

(*b*) Construct a flowchart schema with counters that solves the problem. [Counters are special variables. The values of counters are always nonnegative integers. The following operations can be applied to a counter c: $c \leftarrow c + 1$ (incrementing a counter), $c \leftarrow c - 1$ (decrementing a counter)†, $c \leftarrow 0$ (set a counter to 0) and $c = 0$? (test a counter for 0).]

(*c*) Construct a flowchart schema with equality tests (that is, tests of the form $\tau_1(\bar{x}, \bar{y}) = \tau_2(\bar{x}, \bar{y})$ where τ_1 and τ_2 are terms) that solves the problem.

† Where $0 - 1$ is 0.

Prob. 4-18 (Normal form, Cooper (1971) and Engeler (1971)). A flowchart schema is said to be in *normal form* if it is a finite tree-like schema in which branches may bend back only to ancestors. For example, the flowchart schema S_{37A} (Fig. 4-37*a*) is not in normal form because arc α bends back from a statement on the right branch to a statement on the left branch. The flowchart schema S_{37B} (Fig. 4-37*b*) is isomorphic to S_{37A} and it is in normal form.

(*a*) Prove that every flowchart schema can be transformed into an isomorphic flowchart schema which is in normal form.

(*b*) Prove that a flowchart schema is in normal form if and only if it is of the form

START statement

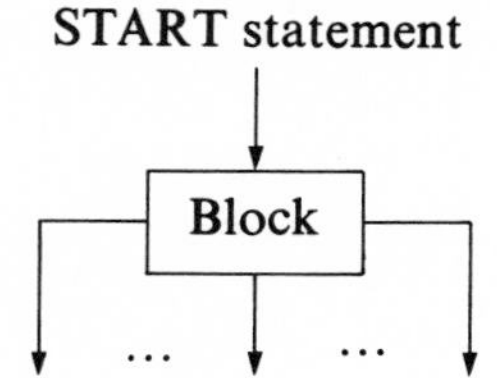

HALT or LOOP statements

where a block is defined recursively as follows:

(i) *Basic blocks:* Any TEST or ASSIGNMENT statement is a block. The *empty block* (with no statements at all) is also considered to be a basic block.

(ii) *Composition:*

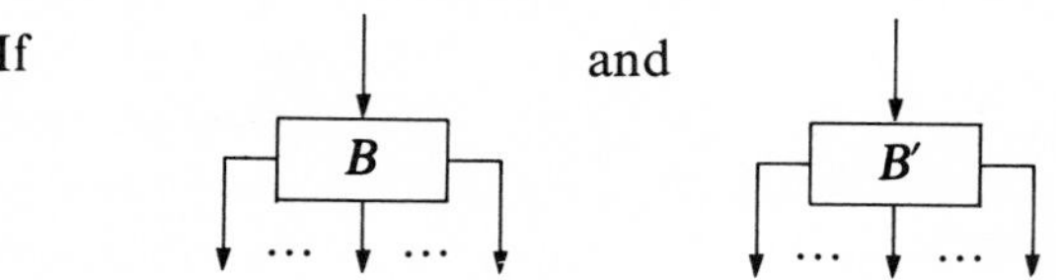

are blocks, then so is

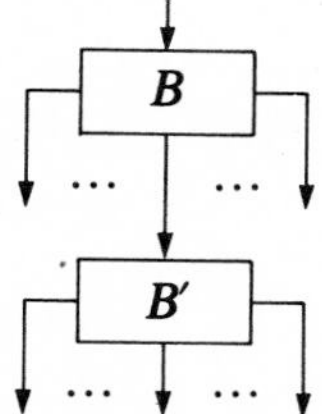

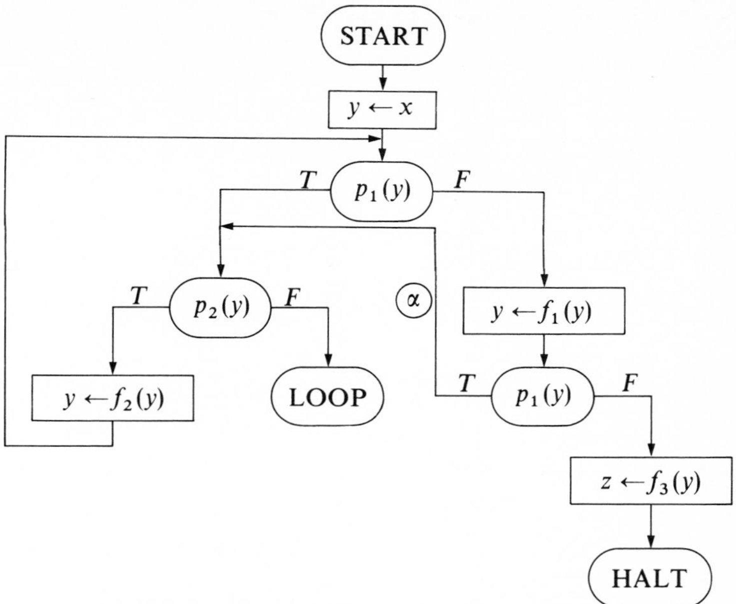

Figure 4-37*a* Flowchart schema S_{37A} (not in normal form).

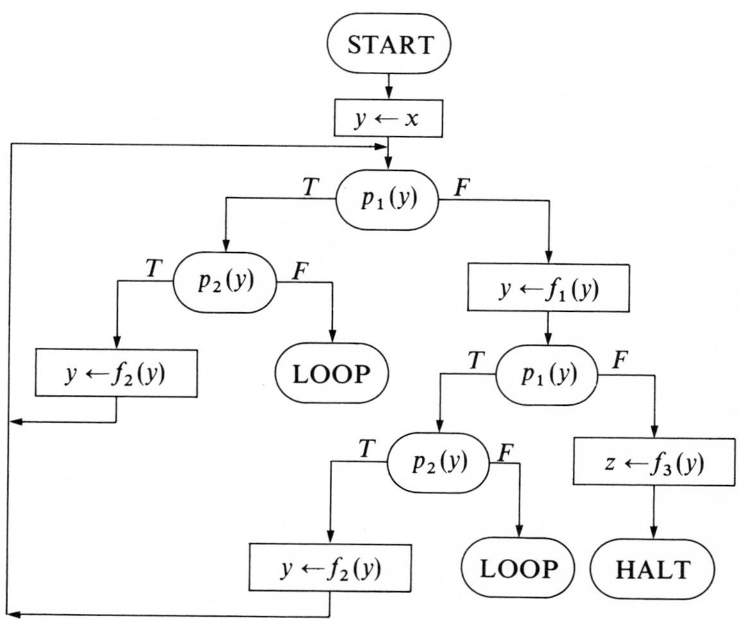

Figure 4-37*b* Flowchart schema S_{37B} (in normal form).

(iii) *Looping:*

if

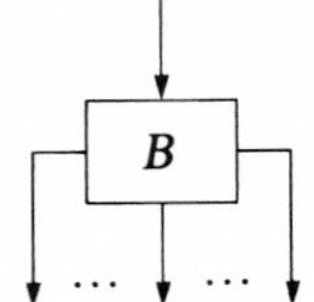

is a block, then so is

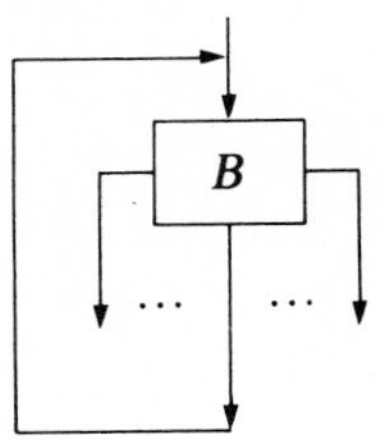

(*c*) Indicate the block structure of the flowchart schema S_{37B} (Fig. 4-37*b*).

Prob. 4-19 (While schemas—Knuth and Floyd (1971), Ashcroft and Manna (1971)). The class of *while schemas* is defined recursively as follows†

⟨while schemas⟩ : : =

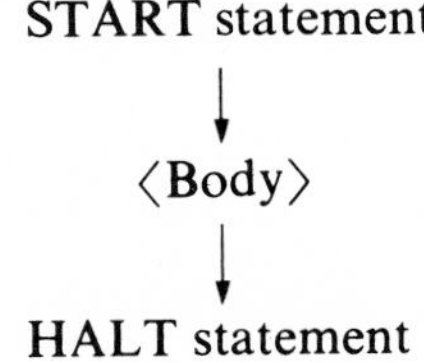

† Here, we allow a TEST statement to consist of any quantifier-free formula.

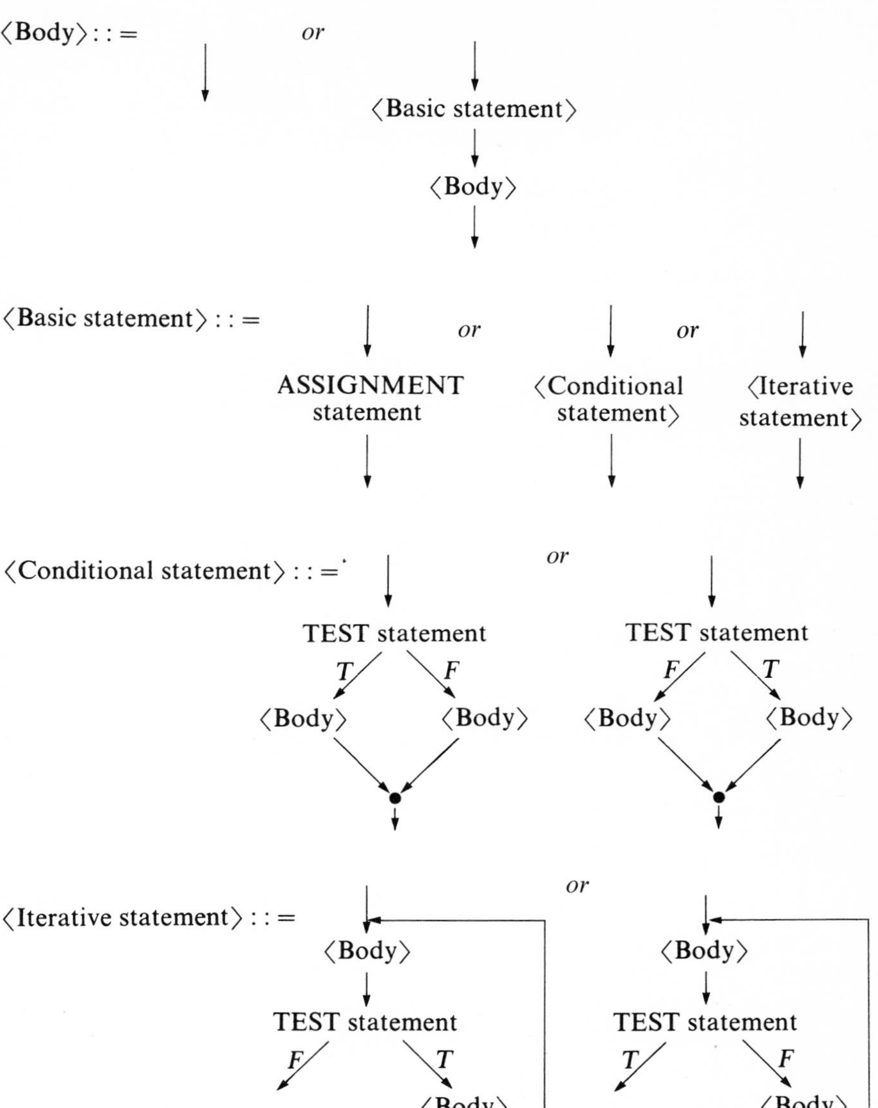

⟨Body⟩ : : =
or
⟨Basic statement⟩
⟨Body⟩
⟨Basic statement⟩ : : =
or
or
ASSIGNMENT statement
⟨Conditional statement⟩
⟨Iterative statement⟩
⟨Conditional statement⟩ : : =
or
TEST statement
T
F
⟨Body⟩
⟨Body⟩
TEST statement
F
T
⟨Body⟩
⟨Body⟩
⟨Iterative statement⟩ : : =
or
⟨Body⟩
TEST statement
F
T
⟨Body⟩
⟨Body⟩
TEST statement
T
F
⟨Body⟩

Note that each such while schema can be expressed an an Algol-like schema with ASSIGNMENT statements, IF-THEN-ELSE statements, WHILE statements and BEGIN-END blocks. (See Chap. 3, Sec. 3-3.1.) For example, the while schema S_{38} (Fig. 4-38) can be expressed as

$y \leftarrow x$;
while $p_1(y)$ **do begin** $y \leftarrow f_1(y)$;
  while $p_2(y)$ **do begin** $y \leftarrow f_3(y)$; $y \leftarrow f_1(y)$ **end**;
  $y \leftarrow f_4(y)$
end;
$y \leftarrow f_2(y)$;
if $p_3(y)$ **then begin** $y \leftarrow f_5(y)$;
  while $\sim p_4(y)$ **do** $y \leftarrow f_5(y)$
end
else $y \leftarrow f_6(y)$;
$z \leftarrow y$.

(*a*) Consider the flowchart schema S_{39} (Fig. 4-39). It is not a while schema.
   (i) Find a while schema which is equivalent to S_{39}.
   (ii) Prove that there is no while schema which is isomorphic to S_{39}.
   Hint: Express the class of while schemas as a class R of regular expressions. Show that S_{39} is not in R.

(*b*) Consider the flowchart schema S_{40} (Fig. 4-40). It is not a while schema. Find a while schema which is equivalent to S_{40}. (You may add extra program variables during the transformation.)

*(*c*) Prove that any flowchart schema can be transformed into an equivalent while schema. (You may add extra program variables during the transformation.)

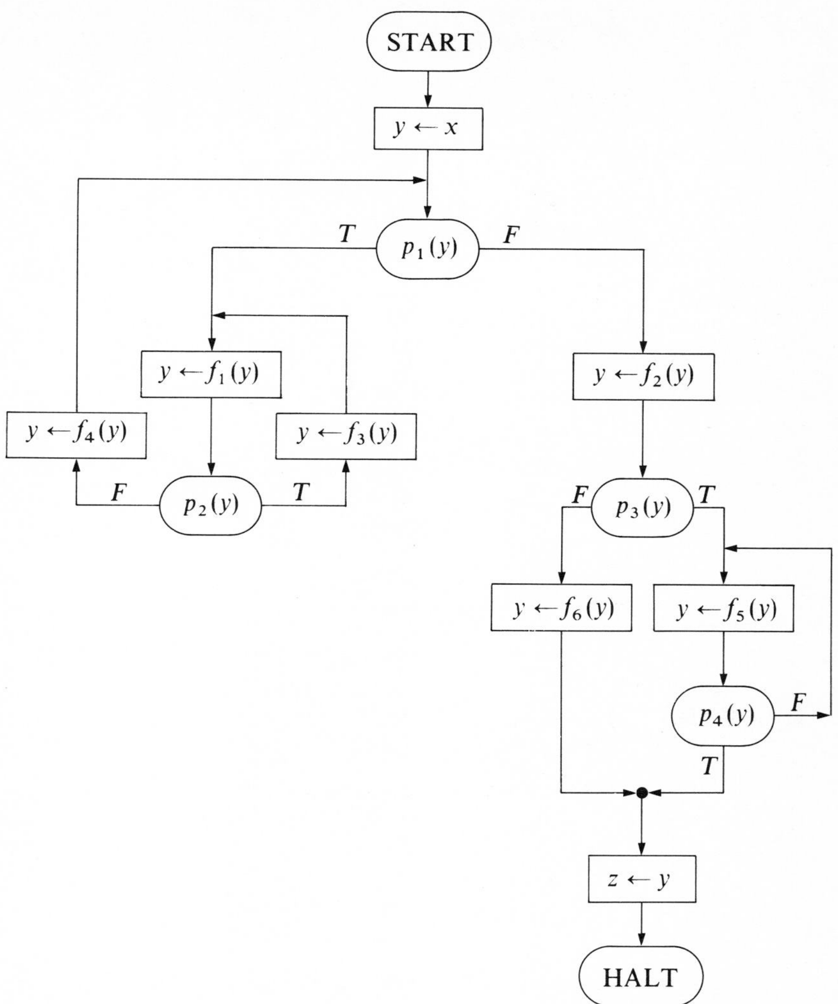

Figure 4-38 While schema S_{38}.

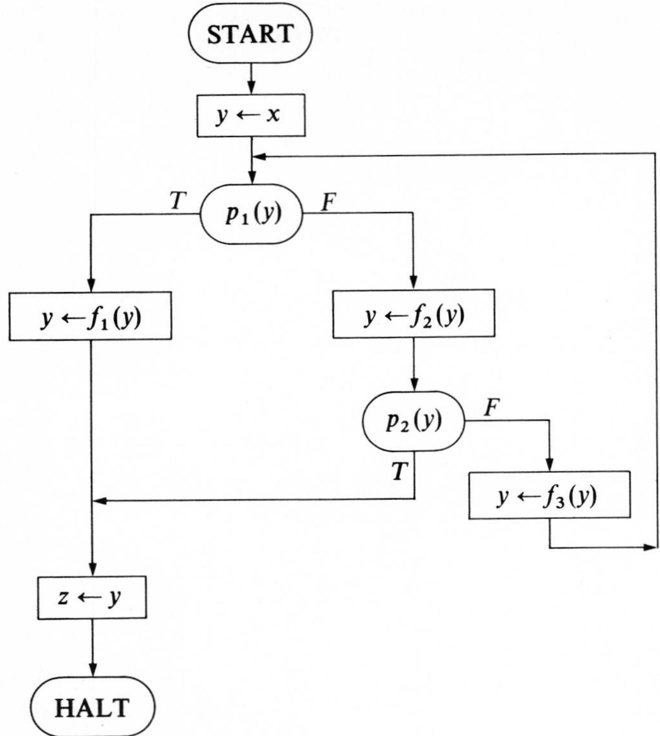

Figure 4-39 Flowchart schema S_{39}.

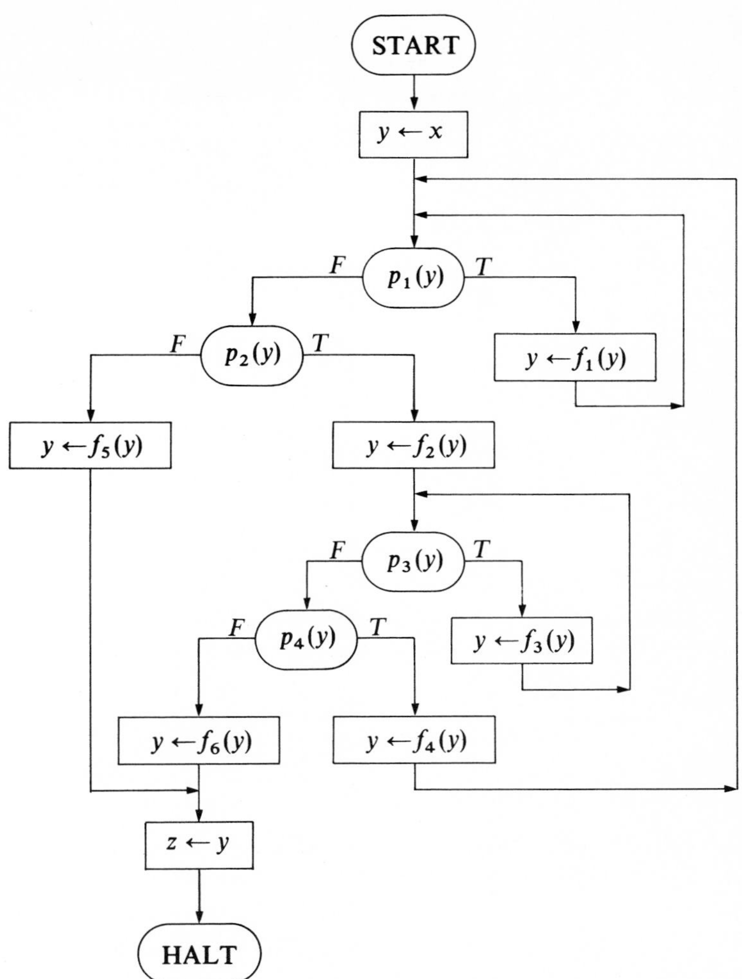

Figure 4-40 Flowchart schema S_{40}.

CHAPTER 5

The Fixpoint Theory of Programs

Introduction

In this chapter we shall present and discuss methods for proving properties of recursive programs. We shall consider a very restricted class of recursive programs, chosen because of its similarities to familiar programming languages such as Algol or Lisp. For example, the following is a recursive program over the integers:

$$P: \quad F(x, y) \Leftarrow \textit{if } x = y \textit{ then } y + 1$$
$$\textit{else } F(x, F(x - 1, y + 1))$$

The essential difference between the class of recursive programs we shall discuss in this chapter and those introduced in Chap. 4, Sec. 4-4.1, is that here we shall allow our base functions and predicates to be partial; that is, they may be undefined for some arguments. This is quite natural because they represent the result of some computation which, in general, may give results for some inputs and run indefinitely for others. We include as limiting cases the partial functions defined for all arguments (that is, the total functions), as well as the partial function undefined for all arguments.

Let us consider now the following functions:

$$f_1(x, y): \quad \textit{if } x = y \textit{ then } y + 1 \textit{ else } x + 1$$
$$f_2(x, y): \quad \textit{if } x \geq y \textit{ then } x + 1 \textit{ else } y - 1$$
$$f_3(x, y): \quad \textit{if } (x \geq y) \wedge (x - y \text{ even}) \textit{ then } x + 1 \textit{ else undefined}$$

These functions have an interesting common property: For each i $(1 \leq i \leq 3)$, if we replace all occurrences of F in the program P by f_i, the left- and right-hand sides of the symbol $\Leftarrow$ yield identical partial functions; that is,†

$$f_i(x, y) \equiv \textit{if } x = y \textit{ then } y + 1 \textit{ else } f_i(x, f_i(x - 1, y + 1))$$

We say that the functions f_1, f_2, and f_3 are *fixpoints* of the recursive program P.

Among the three functions, f_3 has one important special property: For any pair $\langle x, y \rangle$ of integers such that $f_3(x, y)$ is defined, that is, $x \geq y$ and $x - y$ is even, both $f_1(x, y)$ and $f_2(x, y)$ are also defined and have the same value as $f_3(x, y)$. We say that f_3 is *less defined than or equal to* f_1 and f_2 and denote this by $f_3 \sqsubseteq f_1$ and $f_3 \sqsubseteq f_2$. It can be shown that f_3 has this property, not only with respect to f_1 and f_2, but also with respect to all fixpoints of the recursive program P. Moreover, $f_3(x, y)$ is the *only* function having this property, and therefore f_3 is said to be *the least (defined) fixpoint of P*. One of the most important results related to this topic is due to Kleene, who showed that *every recursive program P has a unique least fixpoint, denoted by* f_P.

In discussing recursive programs, the key problem is: What is the partial function f defined by a recursive program P? There are two viewpoints:

1. *Fixpoint approach:* Let it be the unique least fixpoint f_P.
2. *Computational approach:* Let it be the computed function C_P for some given computation rule C.

In this chapter we shall discuss the theory of proving properties of recursive programs assuming that the function defined by a recursive program is exactly the least fixpoint f_P; that is, we shall adopt the fixpoint approach. This is a reasonable approach because in practice many implementations of recursive programs indeed lead to the least fixpoint.

5-1 FUNCTIONS AND FUNCTIONALS

We shall consider n-ary partial functions ($n \geq 0$) from a domain $D_1^n = D_1 \times D_1 \times \cdots \times D_1$ into a range D_2; that is, for every n-tuple of elements $\langle a_1, a_2, \ldots, a_n \rangle \in D_1^n$, $f(a_1, a_2, \ldots, a_n)$ either yields some element b in D_2 or is undefined. For example, the quotient function x/y mapping $R \times R$ (pairs of real numbers) into R (real numbers) is usually considered to be undefined for $y = 0$. A 0-ary partial function (the case

† There are two different ways to extend the regular equality relation: The natural extension, denoted by $=$, is *undefined* whenever at least one of its arguments is *undefined*; the other extension, denoted by $\equiv$, is *true* if both arguments are *undefined* and *false* if exactly one of them is *undefined*.

$n = 0$) is a function with no arguments yielding a constant value or undefined. We shall consider n-ary partial predicates as a special case because an n-ary partial predicate is actually an n-ary partial function mapping D_1^n into $\{true, false\}$.†

In developing a theory for handling partial functions it is convenient to introduce the special element ω to represent the value *undefined*. We let D_2^+ denote $D_2 \cup \{\omega\}$, assuming $\omega \notin D_2$ by convention. Any n-ary partial function f mapping D_1^n into D_2 may then be considered as a total function mapping D_1^n into D_2^+: *If f is undefined for $\langle a_1, \ldots, a_n \rangle \in D_1^n$, we let $f(a_1, \ldots, a_n)$ be ω.* For example, we consider the quotient function x/y as mapping $R \times R$ into R^+ by letting $x/0$ be ω for any x in R.

However, there is still one essential difficulty: Since we shall consider composition of functions, we may need to compute functions with some arguments being ω. For example, to compute $y/(x/0)$ we need the value of y/ω; thus we must extend every n-ary function mapping D_1^n into D_2^+ to a n-ary function mapping $(D_1^+)^n = D_1^+ \times \cdots \times D_1^+$ into D_2^+, where D_1^+ denotes $D_1 \cup \{\omega\}$.

There are many ways of performing the above extension. It turns out that the extensions which are satisfactory for our purposes always lead to *monotonic functions*. In Sec. 5-1.1, therefore, we define and discuss the class of n-ary monotonic functions mapping $(D_1^+)^n$ into D_2^+. We denote the class of all monotonic functions mapping $(D_1^+)^n$ into D_2^+ by $[(D_1^+)^n \to D_2^+]$. In Sec. 5-1.2 we introduce and discuss functionals mapping $[(D_1^+)^n \to D_2^+]$ into $[(D_1^+)^n \to D_2^+]$; that is, a functional τ maps every function from $[(D_1^+)^n \to D_2^+]$ into a function in $[(D_1^+)^n \to D_2^+]$. In that section we also introduce the notions of *monotonic functionals* and *continuous functionals*. In Sec. 5-1.3 we introduce the notions of *fixpoints* and *least fixpoints* of functionals. We conclude this section with a presentation of *Kleene's theorem*, which states that every continuous functional has a (unique) least fixpoint, and this result provides the key to our discussion throughout the rest of this chapter.

† For simplicity in our exposition, we consider only functions mapping D_1^n into D_2, and not the general case of functions mapping $A_1 \times A_2 \times \cdots \times A_n$ into $B_1 \times B_2 \times \cdots \times B_m (m \geq 1)$. All the results presented in this chapter hold for the general case, but some of the proofs must be modified. The *if-then-else* function that will be introduced in Example 5-3 is the only function used in this chapter which is of the general form.

5-1.1 Monotonic Functions

Partial ordering on D^+ To define *monotonicity*, we must first introduce the partial ordering† $\sqsubseteq$ on every extended domain $D^+ = D \cup \{\omega\}$. The partial ordering $\sqsubseteq$ is intended to correspond to the notion *is less defined than or equal to*, and accordingly we let

$$\omega \sqsubseteq d \quad \textit{and } d \sqsubseteq d \quad \textit{for all} \quad d \in D^+$$

Note that distinct elements of D are unrelated by $\sqsubseteq$; that is, for distinct a and b in D, neither $a \sqsubseteq b$ nor $b \sqsubseteq a$ hold. For $(D^+)^n$, we define

$$\langle a_1, \ldots, a_n \rangle \sqsubseteq \langle b_1, \ldots, b_n \rangle \quad \textit{iff} \quad a_i \sqsubseteq b_i \quad \textit{for each } i,\ 1 \le i \le n$$

EXAMPLE 5-1

1. If $D = \{a, b\}$, then $D^+ = \{a, b, \omega\}$ and the partial ordering on D^+ is

$$\omega \sqsubseteq \omega \qquad \omega \sqsubseteq a \qquad \omega \sqsubseteq b \qquad a \sqsubseteq a \qquad \text{and} \qquad b \sqsubseteq b$$

2. If $D = \{a, b\}$ then $D \times D = \{\langle a, a\rangle, \langle a, b\rangle, \langle b, a\rangle, \langle b, b\rangle\}$ and $D^+ \times D^+ = \{\langle \omega, \omega\rangle, \langle \omega, a\rangle, \langle a, \omega\rangle, \ldots, \langle a, b\rangle, \langle b, a\rangle, \langle b, b\rangle\}$. The partial ordering on $D^+ \times D^+$ is

$$\langle \omega, \omega\rangle \sqsubseteq \langle \omega, \omega\rangle, \langle \omega, a\rangle, \langle a, \omega\rangle, \ldots, \langle a, b\rangle, \langle b, a\rangle, \langle b, b\rangle$$

$$\langle a, \omega\rangle \sqsubseteq \langle a, \omega\rangle, \langle a, a\rangle, \langle a, b\rangle$$

$$\langle \omega, a\rangle \sqsubseteq \langle \omega, a\rangle, \langle a, a\rangle, \langle b, a\rangle$$

$$\langle \omega, b\rangle \sqsubseteq \langle \omega, b\rangle, \langle a, b\rangle, \langle b, b\rangle$$

$$\langle b, \omega\rangle \sqsubseteq \langle b, \omega\rangle, \langle b, a\rangle, \langle b, b\rangle$$

$$\langle a, a\rangle \sqsubseteq \langle a, a\rangle \qquad \langle a, b\rangle \sqsubseteq \langle a, b\rangle$$

$$\langle b, a\rangle \sqsubseteq \langle b, a\rangle \qquad \langle b, b\rangle \sqsubseteq \langle b, b\rangle$$

An alternative way to describe the partial ordering is by the following

† Recall that a partial ordering is a binary relation which is
Reflexive $(\forall a)[a \sqsubseteq a]$
Antisymmetric $(\forall a, b)[a \sqsubseteq b \wedge b \sqsubseteq a \Rightarrow a$ is identical to $b]$
Transitive $(\forall a, b, c)[a \sqsubseteq b \wedge b \sqsubseteq c \Rightarrow a \sqsubseteq c]$
As usual, we write $a \sqsubset b$ if $a \sqsubseteq b$ and a is not identical to b, and $a \not\sqsubseteq b$ if $a \sqsubseteq b$ does not hold.

diagram (here $A \to B$ stands for $B \sqsubseteq A$):

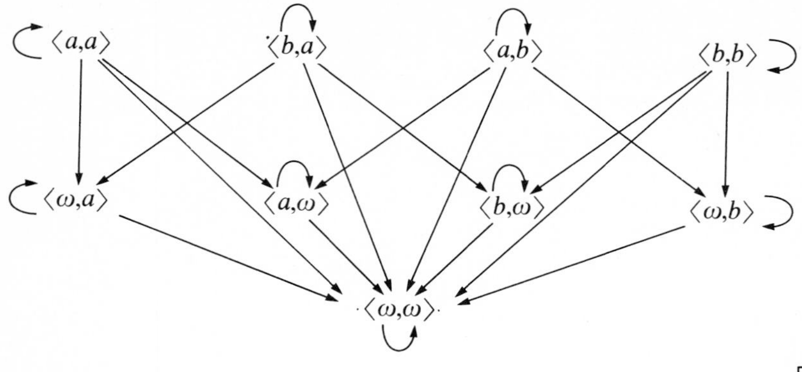

□

Monotonic functions We are ready now to define monotonicity:

An n-ary function f from $(D_1^+)^n$ into D_2^+ is said to be monotonic if $\bar{x} \sqsubseteq \bar{y}$ implies $f(\bar{x}) \sqsubseteq f(\bar{y})$ for all $\bar{x}, \bar{y} \in (D_1^+)^n$.

Intuitively, we require that whenever the "input" $\bar{x}$ is less defined than or equal to the input $\bar{y}$, the "output" $f(\bar{x})$ is less defined than or equal to the output $f(\bar{y})$. *The class of all monotonic functions mapping $(D_1^+)^n$ into D_2^+ is denoted by* $[(D_1^+)^n \to D_2^+]$.

EXAMPLE 5-2

1. The identity n-ary function I mapping any $\bar{x}$ in $(D_1^+)^n$ into itself is monotonic.

2. The totally undefined n-ary function Ω mapping any $\bar{x}$ in $(D_1^+)^n$ into ω is monotonic.

3. Every 0-ary function is monotonic.

4. Every n-ary constant function mapping any $\bar{x}$ in $(D_1^+)^n$ into a fixed element c of D_2^+ is monotonic.

□

Properties of monotonic functions We shall now describe several properties of monotonic functions, which will help us in deciding whether or not a given function mapping $(D_1^+)^n$ into D_2^+ is monotonic. (The proofs are straightforward and are left as an exercise to the reader.)

1. If f is a unary function mapping D_1^+ into D_2^+ (that is, if f has only one argument), then f is monotonic *if and only if*

either $f(\omega)$ is ω

or $f(a)$ is c for all $a \in D_1^+$

Thus, any unary constant function f, where $f(a)$ is c for all $a \in D_1$, can be extended to a monotonic function in two different ways: by letting $f(\omega)$ be either ω or c.

2. For $n \geq 2$, if an n-ary function f mapping $(D_1^+)^n$ into D_2^+ is monotonic, then

either $\quad f(\omega, \ldots, \omega) \quad$ is $\quad \omega$

or $\quad f(a_1, \ldots, a_n) \quad$ is $\quad c \quad$ for all $\langle a_1, \ldots, a_n \rangle \in (D_1^+)^n$

However, although every function satisfying the second condition is a constant function and therefore monotonic, there are functions which satisfy the first condition that are not monotonic. For example, the quotient function x/y over the real numbers extended as follows—x/ω is 0 for all $x \in R$, and ω/y is ω for all $y \in R^+$—is not monotonic; for although $\langle 1, \omega \rangle \sqsubseteq \langle 1, 1 \rangle$, $1/\omega$ is 0 and $1/1$ is 1, and thus $1/\omega \not\sqsubseteq 1/1$.

Natural extension An n-ary ($n \geq 1$) function f mapping $(D_1^+)^n$ into D_2^+ is said to be *naturally extended* if it has the following property: $f(a_1, \ldots, a_n)$ is ω *whenever at least one of the a_i's is ω*. The importance of natural extension can be seen in the following result.

LEMMA (The natural extension lemma). *Every naturally extended function is monotonic.*

Proof. (Proof by contradiction). Suppose the function $f(x_1, \ldots, x_n)$ is naturally extended but not monotonic. Since f is not monotonic, there must exist n-tuples $\langle a_1, \ldots, a_n \rangle$ and $\langle b_1, \ldots, b_n \rangle$ such that $\langle a_1, \ldots, a_n \rangle \sqsubseteq \langle b_1, \ldots, b_n \rangle$; that is, $a_i \sqsubseteq b_i$ for all i $(1 \leq i \leq n)$, and $f(a_1, \ldots, a_n) \not\sqsubseteq f(b_1, \ldots, b_n)$. This implies that $\langle a_1, \ldots, a_n \rangle \sqsubset \langle b_1, \ldots, b_n \rangle$, and therefore there must exist some i_0 $(1 \leq i_0 \leq n)$ such that $a_{i_0} \sqsubset b_{i_0}$. Thus, a_{i_0} must be ω. Since f is naturally extended, $f(a_1, \ldots, a_n)$ is ω. Thus, $f(a_1, \ldots, a_n) \sqsubseteq f(b_1, \ldots, b_n)$ independent of the value of $f(b_1, \ldots, b_n)$, which contradicts our previous conclusion that

$$f(a_1, \ldots, a_n) \not\sqsubseteq f(b_1, \ldots, b_n).$$

Q.E.D.

EXAMPLE 5-3

1. *The quotient function* mapping $\langle x, y \rangle \in R \times R$ into $x/y \in R$, extended to a total function by letting $x/0$ be ω for any x in R, becomes monotonic by the natural extension: Let x/ω and ω/y be ω for any x and y in R^+.

2. The *equality predicate* mapping $D \times D$ into $\{true, false\}$ can be extended in the following particularly interesting ways:

(*a*) *Weak equality* $=$ mapping $D^+ \times D^+$ into $\{true, false\}^+$, which yields the value ω whenever at least one of its arguments is ω. This is a natural extension, and therefore the weak equality predicate is monotonic.

(*b*) *Strong equality* $\equiv$ mapping $D^+ \times D^+$ into $\{true, false\}^+$, which yields the value *true* when both arguments are ω and *false* when exactly one argument is ω. The reader should be aware that *the strong equality predicate is not a monotonic function;* for example, $\langle \omega, d\rangle \sqsubseteq \langle d, d\rangle$ while $(\omega \equiv d) \not\sqsubseteq (d \equiv d)$ (that is, $false \not\sqsubseteq true$) for $d \in D$.

3. The *is-defined function def* mapping D^+ into $\{true, false\}^+$, defined by

$$def\,(d) \quad \text{is} \quad true \quad \text{for any } d \in D$$

$$def\,(\omega) \quad \text{is} \quad false$$

is not monotonic; for we have $\omega \sqsubseteq d$ while $def\,(\omega) \not\sqsubseteq def\,(d)$ (that is, $false \not\sqsubseteq true$) for $d \in D$.

4. The *if-then-else function* mapping $\{true, false\} \times D \times D$ into D is defined for any $a, b \in D$ as follows:

$$(\mathit{if}\ true\ \mathit{then}\ a\ \mathit{else}\ b) \quad \text{is} \quad a$$

$$(\mathit{if}\ false\ \mathit{then}\ a\ \mathit{else}\ b) \quad \text{is} \quad b$$

This function can be extended to a monotonic function mapping $\{true, false\}^+ \times D^+ \times D^+$ into D^+ by letting, for any $a, b \in D^+$,

$$(\mathit{if}\ true\ \mathit{then}\ a\ \mathit{else}\ \omega) \quad \text{be} \quad a$$

$$(\mathit{if}\ false\ \mathit{then}\ \omega\ \mathit{else}\ b) \quad \text{be} \quad b$$

$$(\mathit{if}\ \omega\ \mathit{then}\ a\ \mathit{else}\ b) \quad \text{be} \quad \omega$$

Note that this is a monotonic function although it is not the natural extension of if-then-else. To prove that the extended *if-then-else* function is monotonic, one must show that $(\mathit{if}\ v\ \mathit{then}\ a\ \mathit{else}\ b) \sqsubseteq (\mathit{if}\ v'\ \mathit{then}\ a'\ \mathit{else}\ b')$ whenever $\langle v, a, b\rangle \sqsubseteq \langle v', a', b'\rangle$, which is best done by considering the three cases where v is *true*, *false*, or ω.

□

From this point on we shall assume that all the base functions of our examples (other than constant functions and the if-then-else function) are naturally extended unless noted otherwise.

Composition of monotonic functions An important operation on functions is *composition*, which allows functions to be defined in terms of simpler functions. If f is a function from $(D_1^+)^n$ into D_2^+ and g is a function from D_2^+ into D_3^+, then the *composition of f and g* is the function from $(D_1^+)^n$ into D_3^+ defined by $g(f(\bar{x}))$ for every $\bar{x}$ in $(D_1^+)^n$. *If f and g are monotonic functions, then so is their composition.* The proof is straightforward because if f and g are monotonic, we have $\bar{a} \sqsubseteq \bar{b}$ implies $f(\bar{a}) \sqsubseteq f(\bar{b})$, which implies $g(f(\bar{a})) \sqsubseteq g(f(\bar{b}))$ for all $\bar{a}, \bar{b} \in (D_1^+)^n$; thus the composition of f and g is also a monotonic function.

EXAMPLE 5-4

1. The function f mapping N^+ into N^+ given by

$$f(x): \quad \textit{if } x = 0 \textit{ then } 1 \textit{ else } x$$

is defined by composition of the 0-ary functions 0 and 1, the identity function I, the weak equality predicate $=$, and the *if-then-else* function. Since all these functions are monotonic, then so is f.

2. The function f mapping N^+ into N^+ given by

$$f(x): \quad \textit{if } x \equiv \omega \textit{ then } 0 \textit{ else } 1$$

(note that we are using the nonmonotonic predicate $\equiv$) is not monotonic because $\omega \sqsubseteq 0$ but $f(\omega) \not\sqsubseteq f(0)$ (that is, $0 \not\sqsubseteq 1$).

3. The function f mapping N^+ into N^+ given by

$$f(x): \quad \textit{if } x = \omega \textit{ then } 0 \textit{ else } 1$$

is defined by composition of monotonic functions (ω here is a 0-ary function), and therefore it is a monotonic function. Note that we are using the weak equality $=$, not the strong equality $\equiv$; therefore the value of $f(\omega)$ is ω, not 0, as before; in fact, $f(x)$ is ω for all $x \in N^+$.

□

Distribution of monotonic functions over conditionals
Finally, we shall discuss an important corollary which follows from the properties of monotonic functions. Let us consider two functions f_1 and f_2 given by

$$f_1(\bar{x}): \quad g(\textit{if } p(\bar{x}) \textit{ then } h_1(\bar{x}) \textit{ else } h_2(\bar{x}))$$

and

$$f_2(\bar{x}): \quad \textit{if } p(\bar{x}) \textit{ then } g(h_1(\bar{x})) \textit{ else } g(h_2(\bar{x}))$$

where p, g, h_1, and h_2 are monotonic functions. Both f_1 and f_2 are monotonic because each is defined by a composition of monotonic functions. There is a very interesting relation between these two functions:

1. $f_2(\bar{x}) \sqsubseteq f_1(\bar{x})$ for any $\bar{x} \in (D_1^+)^n$.
2. If $g(\omega)$ is ω, then $f_2(\bar{x}) \equiv f_1(\bar{x})$ for any $\bar{x} \in (D_1^+)^n$.

Both of these properties are proved by considering the three cases where $p(\bar{x})$ is *true*, $p(\bar{x})$ is *false*, and $p(\bar{x})$ is ω. In the first two cases, $f_2(\bar{x}) \equiv f_1(\bar{x})$; and in the third case, [since $\omega \sqsubseteq g(\omega)$] $f_2(\bar{x}) \sqsubseteq f_1(\bar{x})$. Thus, in general, $f_2(\bar{x}) \sqsubseteq f_1(\bar{x})$ for any $\bar{x} \in (D_1^+)^n$; however, if $g(\omega)$ is ω, $f_2(\bar{x}) \equiv f_1(\bar{x})$ in the third case too and therefore $f_2(\bar{x}) \equiv f_1(\bar{x})$ for any $\bar{x} \in (D_1^+)^n$.

The preceding properties generalize to any n-ary ($n \geq 1$) monotonic function g. The functions f_1 and f_2 are given by

$$f_1(\bar{x}): \quad g(h_1(\bar{x}), \ldots, h_{i-1}(\bar{x}), \textit{if } p(\bar{x}) \textit{ then } h_i'(\bar{x}) \textit{ else } h_i''(\bar{x}), h_{i+1}(\bar{x}), \ldots, h_n(\bar{x}))$$

and

$$f_2(\bar{x}): \quad \textit{if } p(\bar{x}) \textit{ then } g(h_1(\bar{x}), \ldots, h_{i-1}(\bar{x}), h_i'(\bar{x}), h_{i+1}(\bar{x}), \ldots, h_n(\bar{x})) \textit{ else } g(h_1(\bar{x}), \ldots, h_{i-1}(\bar{x}), h_i''(\bar{x}), h_{i+1}(\bar{x}), \ldots, h_n(\bar{x}))$$

Then the following relations still hold:

1. $f_2(\bar{x}) \sqsubseteq f_1(\bar{x})$ for any $\bar{x} \in (D_1^+)^n$.
2. If $g(a_1, \ldots, a_{i-1}, \omega, a_{i+1}, \ldots, a_n)$ is ω for all values (including ω) of $a_1, \ldots, a_{i-1}, a_{i+1}, \ldots, a_n$, then $f_2(\bar{x}) \equiv f_1(\bar{x})$ for any $\bar{x} \in (D_1^+)^n$.

We shall often use this property in later proofs.

Least upper bound In order to introduce and discuss functionals, we must first define a few additional notions regarding monotonic functions. Note, again, that $[(D_1^+)^n \to D_2^+]$ indicates the set of all monotonic functions mapping $(D_1^+)^n$ into D_2^+,

1. Let $f, g \in [(D_1^+)^n \to D_2^+]$. *We say that* $f \sqsubseteq g$ *(read "f is less defined than or equal to g") if* $f(\bar{x}) \sqsubseteq g(\bar{x})$ *for all* $\bar{x}$ *in* $(D_1^+)^n$; this relation is actually a partial ordering on $[(D_1^+)^n \to D_2^+]$. (Note that $\Omega \sqsubseteq f$ for any $f \in [(D_1^+)^n \to D_2^+]$.)
2. Let $f, g \in [(D_1^+)^n \to D_2^+]$. *We say that* $f \equiv g$ *(read "f is equal to g") if* $f(\bar{x}) \equiv g(\bar{x})$ *for all* $\bar{x}$ *in* $(D_1^+)^n$; in other words, $f \equiv g$ if and only if $f \sqsubseteq g$ and $g \sqsubseteq f$.
3. Let $f_0, f_1, f_2, \ldots$, be a sequence of functions in $[(D_1^+)^n \to D_2^+]$, denoted, for short, by $\{f_i\}$; $\{f_i\}$ is called a *chain* if $f_0 \sqsubseteq f_1 \sqsubseteq f_2 \sqsubseteq f_3 \sqsubseteq \ldots$.

4. Let $\{f_i\}$ be a sequence of functions in $[(D_1^+)^n \to D_2^+]$, and let $f \in [(D_1^+)^n \to D_2^+]$. We say that f is an *upper bound of* $\{f_i\}$ if $f_i \sqsubseteq f$ for every $i \geq 0$. If, in addition, f is such that $f \sqsubseteq g$ for every upper bound g of $\{f_i\}$, then f is called the *least upper bound of* $\{f_i\}$, *denoted by* lub $\{f_i\}$. Note that by definition the lub of $\{f_i\}$ is unique (if it exists at all) because if both f and g are least upper bounds of $\{f_i\}$, then $f \sqsubseteq g$ and $g \sqsubseteq f$; therefore $f \equiv g$.

LEMMA (The lub lemma) *Every chain* $\{f_i\}$ *has a least upper bound.*

Proof. Let $\bar{a}$ be any element in $(D_1^+)^n$, and consider the sequence of elements

$$f_0(\bar{a}),\ f_1(\bar{a}),\ f_2(\bar{a}),\ \ldots$$

Since $\{f_i\}$ is a chain, there are only two possibilities: Either $f_i(\bar{a})$ is ω for all $i \geq 0$, or there exists some $i_0 \geq 0$ and some element $b \in D_2$ such that $f_i(\bar{a})$ is ω for all $i < i_0$ and $f_i(\bar{a})$ is b for all $i \geq i_0$. Therefore we can define unambiguously a function f as follows: *For every* $\bar{a} \in (D_1^+)^n$, $f(\bar{a})$ *is* ω *in the first case, and* $f(\bar{a})$ *is* b *in the second case.*

One can verify that f is monotonic, that is, that f is in $[(D_1^+)^n \to D_2^+]$. We shall show now that f is the lub of $\{f_i\}$.

Step 1. *f is an upper bound of* $\{f_i\}$. Consider any $\bar{a} \in (D_1^+)^n$ and $i \geq 0$. We distinguish between two possibilities: If $f_i(\bar{a})$ is ω, then clearly $f_i(\bar{a}) \sqsubseteq f(\bar{a})$; otherwise $f_i(\bar{a})$ is b (for some $b \in D_2$), and therefore $f_i(\bar{a}) \equiv f(\bar{a})$ by definition of f. It follows that $f_i \sqsubseteq f$ for all $i \geq 0$.

Step 2. *f is the lub of* $\{f_i\}$. Assume that g is any upper bound of $\{f_i\}$, that is, that $f_i \sqsubseteq g$ for all $i \geq 0$. Consider, now, any $\bar{a} \in (D_1^+)^n$. We distinguish between two possibilities: If $f(\bar{a})$ is ω, then clearly $f(\bar{a}) \sqsubseteq g(\bar{a})$; otherwise $f(\bar{a})$ is not ω and $f(\bar{a}) \equiv f_{i_0}(\bar{a})$, then since $f_{i_0} \sqsubseteq g$ it follows that $f(\bar{a}) \sqsubseteq g(\bar{a})$. Therefore $f \sqsubseteq g$.

Q.E.D.

EXAMPLE 5-5

Consider the sequence of functions $f_0, f_1, f_2, \ldots$ in $[N^+ \to N^+]$ defined by

$$f_i(x):\quad \textit{if } x < i \textit{ then } x! \textit{ else } \omega$$

This sequence is clearly a chain because $f_i \sqsubseteq f_{i+1}$ for every i. (Note that f_0 is Ω.) By the lub lemma it follows that the sequence has an lub; it is the factorial function $x!$ □

5-1.2 Continuous Functionals

We are now ready to introduce the notion of *functionals*. A *functional* τ *over* $[(D_1^+)^n \to D_2^+]$ *maps the set of functions* $[(D_1^+)^n \to D_2^+]$ *into itself*; that is, τ takes any monotonic function f (mapping $(D_1^+)^n$ into D_2^+) as its argument and yields a monotonic function $\tau[f]$ (mapping $(D_1^+)^n$ into D_2^+) as its value.

Two interesting properties of functionals are *monotonicity* and *continuity*:

1. *A functional* τ *over* $[(D_1^+)^n \to D_2^+]$ *is said to be monotonic if* $f \sqsubseteq g$ *implies* $\tau[f] \sqsubseteq \tau[g]$ *for all* $f, g \in [(D_1^+)^n \to D_2^+]$.
2. *A monotonic functional* τ *over* $[(D_1^+)^n \to D_2^+]$ *is said to be continuous if for any chain of functions* $\{f_i\}$, *we have*

$$\tau[lub\,\{f_i\}] \equiv lub\,\{\tau[f_i]\}.$$

Note that $\{f_i\}$ is a chain; that is, $f_0 \sqsubseteq f_1 \sqsubseteq f_2 \sqsubseteq \ldots$. Since τ is monotonic, we have $\tau[f_0] \sqsubseteq \tau[f_1] \sqsubseteq \tau[f_2] \sqsubseteq \cdots$; that is, $\{\tau[f_i]\}$ is also a chain. Therefore, by the lub lemma, both lub $\{f_i\}$ and lub $\{\tau[f_i]\}$ must exist.

EXAMPLE 5-6

1. The identity functional defined by

$$\tau[F]:\ F$$

mapping any f in $[(D_1^+)^n \to D_2^+]$ into itself is clearly monotonic because $f \sqsubseteq g$ implies $\tau[f] \equiv f \sqsubseteq g \equiv \tau[g]$. It is also continuous because $\tau[\text{lub}\{f_i\}] \equiv \text{lub}\,\{f_i\} \equiv \text{lub}\,\{\tau[f_i]\}$.

2. The constant functional defined by

$$\tau[F]:\ h$$

mapping any f in $[(D_1^+)^n \to D_2^+]$ into the function h is monotonic because $f \sqsubseteq g$ implies $\tau[f] \equiv h \equiv \tau[g]$. It is also continuous because $\tau[\text{lub}\,\{f_i\}] \equiv h \equiv \text{lub}\,\{h\} \equiv \text{lub}\,\{\tau[f_i]\}$.

□

Usually we specify a functional τ by the composition of known monotonic functions and the function variable F; when F is replaced by any known monotonic function f, the composition rules determine the function $\tau[f]$, which clearly is always monotonic. In all our examples we shall use the following important result.

THEOREM 5-1 *(Continuous functionals).* *Any functional τ defined by composition of monotonic functions and the function variable F, is continuous.*

Proof. We prove that τ is continuous by induction on the structure of τ. If τ consists of just F or h, where h is a monotonic function, then τ is clearly continuous, as shown in Example 5-6. To show the inductive step we distinguish between two cases:

1. $\tau[F]$ *is* $f(\tau_1[F], \ldots, \tau_n[F])$, where f is a monotonic function. We must show that if $\tau_1, \ldots, \tau_n$ are continuous, then so is τ. First, if $g \sqsubseteq h$, then, by the monotonicity of the functionals $\tau_1, \ldots, \tau_n$, it follows that $\tau_j[g] \sqsubseteq \tau_j[h]$ for $1 \leq j \leq n$. Then, by the monotonicity of f, it follows that $f(\tau_1[g], \ldots, \tau_n[g]) \sqsubseteq f(\tau_1[h], \ldots, \tau_n[h])$; that is, $\tau[g] \sqsubseteq \tau[h]$. Thus, τ is a monotonic functional.

Now, we shall show that $\tau[\text{lub}\{f_i\}] \equiv \text{lub}\,\{\tau[f_i]\}$ for any chain $\{f_i\}$. Since $f_i \sqsubseteq \text{lub}\,\{f_i\}$ for every $i \geq 0$, by the monotonicity of the functionals $\tau_1, \ldots, \tau_n$ and the function f, it follows that $\tau[f_i] \sqsubseteq \tau[\text{lub}\,\{f_i\}]$ for every $i \geq 0$. Therefore, $\text{lub}\,\{\tau[f_i]\} \sqsubseteq \tau[\text{lub}\,\{f_i\}]$.

To show the inequality in the other direction, let $\bar{x}_0 \in (D_1^+)^n$. Then by the definition of τ and the inductive hypothesis, we have:

$$\begin{aligned}
&\tau[\text{lub}\,\{f_i\}](\bar{x}_0)\\
&\equiv f(\tau_1[\text{lub}\,\{f_i\}](\bar{x}_0), \ldots, \tau_n[\text{lub}\,\{f_i\}](\bar{x}_0))\\
&\equiv f(\text{lub}\,\{\tau_1[f_i]\}(\bar{x}_0), \ldots, \text{lub}\,\{\tau_n[f_i]\}(\bar{x}_0)).
\end{aligned}$$

From the construction of the lub in the proof of the lub lemma (Sec. 5-1.1), it follows that for every j, $1 \leq j \leq n$, there exists a natural number i_j such that for every $k \geq i_j$:

$$\text{lub}\,\{\tau_j[f_i]\}(\bar{x}_0) \equiv \tau_j[f_k](\bar{x}_0).$$

Let i_0 be the maximum of $i_1, i_2, \ldots, i_n$. Then for every j, $1 \leq j \leq n$, we have

$$\text{lub}\,\{\tau_j[f_i]\}(\bar{x}_0) \equiv \tau_j[f_{i_0}](\bar{x}_0),$$

and therefore

$$\begin{aligned}
&f(\text{lub}\,\{\tau_1[f_i]\}(\bar{x}_0), \ldots, \text{lub}\,\{\tau_n[f_i]\}(\bar{x}_0))\\
&\equiv f(\tau_1[f_{i_0}](\bar{x}_0), \ldots, \tau_n[f_{i_0}](\bar{x}_0))\\
&\equiv f(\tau_1[f_{i_0}], \ldots, \tau_n[f_{i_0}])(\bar{x}_0)
\end{aligned}$$

$$\equiv \tau[f_{i_0}](\bar{x}_0)$$

$$\sqsubseteq \text{lub}\,\{\tau[f_i]\}(\bar{x}_0).$$

Thus, since $\bar{x}_0$ was an arbitrary element of $(D_1^+)^n$, we obtain

$$\tau[\text{lub}\,\{f_i\}] \sqsubseteq \text{lub}\,\{\tau[f_i]\}.$$

2. $\tau[F]$ *is* $F(\tau_1[F], \ldots, \tau_n[F])$. We must prove that if $\tau_1, \ldots, \tau_n$ are continuous functionals, then so is τ. The proof is very similar to the proof of case 1, but here we must use the monotonicity of f_i and lub $\{f_i\}$ rather than f.

Q.E.D.

EXAMPLE 5-7

1. The functional τ over $[N^+ \to N^+]$ defined by

$$\tau[F](x): \quad \textit{if } x = 0 \textit{ then } 1 \textit{ else } F(x+1)$$

is constructed by the composition of monotonic functions (*if-then-else*, identity, addition, weak equality, and the 0-ary functions 0 and 1) and the function variable F; *therefore it is continuous.*

2. The functional τ over $[N^+ \to N^+]$ defined by

$$\tau[F](x): \quad \textit{if } (\forall y \in N)[F(y) = y] \textit{ then } F(x) \textit{ else } \omega$$

is monotonic but not continuous; if we consider the chain $f_0 \sqsubseteq f_1 \sqsubseteq f_2 \sqsubseteq \ldots$, where

$$f_i(x): \quad \textit{if } x < i \textit{ then } x \textit{ else } \omega$$

then $\tau[f_i]$ is Ω for any i so that lub $\{\tau[f_i]\}$ is Ω, whereas lub $\{f_i\}$ and therefore also $\tau[\text{lub}\,\{f_i\}]$ are the identity function.

3. The functional τ over $[N^+ \to N^+]$ defined by

$$\tau[F](x): \quad \textit{if } F(x) \equiv \omega \textit{ then } 0 \textit{ else } \omega$$

is not even monotonic. For let Z denote the zero function; that is, $Z(x) \equiv 0$ for all $x \in N^+$. Then $\tau[Z]$ is Ω and $\tau[\Omega]$ is Z; thus while $\Omega \sqsubseteq Z$, we have $\tau[\Omega] \not\sqsubseteq \tau[Z]$ (since $Z \not\sqsubseteq \Omega$). Note that the functional τ' over $[N^+ \to N^+]$ defined by

$$\tau'[F](x): \quad \textit{if } F(x) = \omega \textit{ then } 0 \textit{ else } \omega$$

is continuous (and monotonic) because it is constructed by composition of monotonic functions and the function variable F.

□

Let us consider a functional τ which is defined by composition of monotonic functions and the function variable F. Suppose there are two occurrences of F in τ; we denote τ by $\tau[F, F]$ to distinguish between the two occurrences of F. It can be shown [see Prob. 5-2(c)] that τ must be *monotonic with respect to any occurrence of F;* that is, $f \sqsubseteq g$ implies $\tau[f, h] \sqsubseteq \tau[g, h]$ and $\tau[h, f] \sqsubseteq \tau[h, g]$ for any h, in addition to $\tau[f, f] \sqsubseteq \tau[g, g]$, which is the regular monotonicity condition. The result holds also in the general case when τ contains any number of occurrences of F.

5-1.3 Fixpoints of Functionals

We are now ready to introduce the notions of *fixpoints* and *least fixpoints* for continuous functionals. Let τ be a functional over $[(D_1^+)^n \to D_2^+]$. We say that a function $f \in [(D_1^+)^n \to D_2^+]$ is a *fixpoint of* τ if $\tau[f] \equiv f$, that is, if τ maps the function f into itself. If f is a fixpoint of τ and $f \sqsubseteq g$ for any other fixpoint g of τ, then f is called the *least fixpoint of* τ. A functional may have either no fixpoints at all, a finite number of fixpoints, or an infinite number of fixpoints; but a functional may have at most one least fixpoint because if both f_1 and f_2 are least fixpoints of τ, then $f_1 \sqsubseteq f_2$ and $f_2 \sqsubseteq f_1$ and therefore $f_1 \equiv f_2$.

Let τ be any monotonic functional over $[(D_1^+)^n \to D_2^+]$. Let us consider the sequence of functions $\tau^0[\Omega], \tau^1[\Omega], \tau^2[\Omega], \ldots$, where $\tau^0[\Omega]$ stands for Ω (the totally undefined function) and $\tau^{i+1}[\Omega]$ is $\tau[\tau^i[\Omega]]$ for $i \geq 0$. Each function $\tau^i[\Omega]$ is in $[(D_1^+)^n \to D_2^+]$; moreover, since $\Omega \sqsubseteq \tau[\Omega]$, and since τ is monotonic, $\{\tau^i[\Omega]\}$ must be a chain; that is,

$$\Omega \sqsubseteq \tau[\Omega] \sqsubseteq \tau^2[\Omega] \sqsubseteq \cdots$$

Therefore, by the lub lemma, lub $\{\tau^i[\Omega]\}$ must exist. In other words, *for every monotonic functional τ over $[(D_1^+)]^n \to D_2^+]$, the sequence $\{\tau^i[\Omega]\}$ is a chain and has an lub.*

EXAMPLE 5-8

1. For the functional τ over $[N^+ \to N^+]$

$$\tau[F](x): \quad \textit{if } x = 0 \textit{ then } 1 \textit{ else } x \cdot F(x-1)$$

we have, for $i \geq 0$,

$$\tau^i[\Omega](x): \quad \textit{if } x < i \textit{ then } x! \textit{ else } \omega$$

and

$$\text{lub}\,\{\tau^i[\Omega]\}(x): \quad x!$$

To justify $\tau^i[\Omega]$, we must show that $\tau[\tau^i[\Omega]] \equiv \tau^{i+1}[\Omega]$ for $i \geq 0$ (note that $\tau^0[\Omega] \equiv \Omega$):

$$\begin{aligned}\tau[\tau^i[\Omega]](x) &\equiv \textit{if } x = 0 \textit{ then } 1 \textit{ else } x \cdot (\textit{if } x - 1 < i \textit{ then } (x-1)! \textit{ else } \omega) \\ &\equiv \textit{if } x = 0 \textit{ then } 1 \textit{ else } (\textit{if } x < i + 1 \textit{ then } x! \textit{ else } \omega) \\ &\equiv \textit{if } x < i + 1 \textit{ then } x! \textit{ else } \omega \\ &\equiv \tau^{i+1}[\Omega](x)\end{aligned}$$

2. Let τ be the following functional over $[N^+ \to N^+]$:

$$\tau[F](x): \quad \textit{if } x > 100 \textit{ then } x - 10 \textit{ else } F(F(x+11))$$

For $1 \leq i \leq 11$ we have

$$\tau^i[\Omega](x): \quad \textit{if } x > 100 \textit{ then } x - 10 \quad \textit{else if } x > 101 - i \textit{ then } 91 \textit{ else } \omega$$

while for $i \geq 11$ we have

$$\tau^i[\Omega](x): \quad \textit{if } x > 100 \textit{ then } x - 10 \quad \textit{else if } x > 90 - 11(i-11) \textit{ then } 91 \textit{ else } \omega$$

Note that for $i = 11$ both definitions of τ^i are identical. It can be verified that $\tau^{i+1}[\Omega] \equiv \tau[\tau^i[\Omega]]$ for all $i \geq 0$. Clearly the lub of the sequence is

$$\text{lub}\,\{\tau^i[\Omega]\}(x): \quad \textit{if } x > 100 \textit{ then } x - 10 \textit{ else } 91$$

□

The last property leads us to Kleene's theorem.

THEOREM 5-2 **(First recursion theorem, Kleene).** *Every continuous functional τ has a least fixpoint denoted by f_τ. Actually, f_τ is lub $\{\tau^i[\Omega]\}$.*

Proof. Since τ is continuous, it is monotonic and therefore we know that $\{\tau^i[\Omega]\}$ is a chain and has an lub which we denote by f_τ. We shall show that f_τ is the least fixpoint of τ in two steps.

Step 1. *f_τ is a fixpoint of τ.* Since τ is continuous, we have

$$\tau[f_\tau] \equiv \tau[\text{lub}\,\{\tau^i[\Omega]\}] \equiv \text{lub}\,\{\tau^{i+1}[\Omega]\} \equiv \text{lub}\,\{\tau^i[\Omega]\} \equiv f_\tau$$

Thus $\tau[f_\tau] \equiv f_\tau$.

Step 2. $f_\tau \sqsubseteq g$ *for any fixpoint* g *of* τ. First we show that $\tau^i[\Omega] \sqsubseteq g$ for all $i \geq 0$ by induction on i. It is clear that $\tau^0[\Omega] \equiv \Omega \sqsubseteq g$. Now, if $\tau^{i-1}[\Omega] \sqsubseteq g$ for some $i \geqq 1$, then since τ is monotonic and g is a fixpoint of τ, we obtain

$$\tau^i[\Omega] \equiv \tau[\tau^{i-1}[\Omega]] \sqsubseteq \tau(g) \equiv g$$

Thus, $\tau^i[\Omega] \sqsubseteq g$ for all $i \geq 0$. This implies that g is an upper bound of $\{\tau^i[\Omega]\}$; but since f_τ is the lub of $\{\tau^i[\Omega]\}$, it follows that $f_\tau \sqsubseteq g$.

Q.E.D.

It is possible to show that the result of Theorem 5-2 holds for every monotonic (not necessarily continuous) functional. However, it is easy to see that monotonicity is an essential requirement in the proof just presented, as described in the following example.

EXAMPLE 5-9

1. The following nonmonotonic functional over $[I^+ \to I^+]$

$$\tau[F](x): \quad \textit{if } F(x) \equiv 0 \textit{ then } 1 \textit{ else } 0$$

has no fixpoints at all. For suppose $f(x)$ is a fixpoint of τ. Then if $f(0) \equiv 0$, we have $\tau[f](0) \equiv 1$; and if $f(0) \not\equiv 0$, we have $\tau[f](0) \equiv 0$.

2. The following nonmonotonic functional over $[I^+ \to I^+]$

$$\tau[F](x): \quad \textit{if } F(x) \equiv 0 \textit{ then } 0 \textit{ else } 1$$

has infinitely many fixpoints—all total functions with values 0 or 1, but it has no least fixpoint.

□

In Examples 5-10 to 5-12 we shall introduce functionals, all of which are defined by the composition of monotonic functions and the function variable F; therefore, all of these functionals are continuous. For each such functional we shall indicate its unique least fixpoint. The general technique that can be used to verify that a function f is the least fixpoint of a given continuous functional τ is to find $\tau^i[\Omega]$ for $i \geq 0$ and show that $f \equiv \text{lub}\,\{\tau^i[\Omega]\}$. (Additional methods will be described in Sec. 5-3.)

EXAMPLE 5-10

1. The functional τ over $[(D_1^+)^n \to D_2^+]$ given by

$$\tau[F](\bar{x}): \quad F(\bar{x})$$

has every function in $[(D_1^+)^n \to D_2^+]$ as fixpoint. Clearly, Ω, the totally undefined function, is the least fixpoint of τ.

2. The functional τ over $[(D_1^+)^n \to D_2^+]$ given by

$$\tau[F](\bar{x}): \quad \mathit{if}\ p(\bar{x})\ \mathit{then}\ F(\bar{x})\ \mathit{else}\ h(\bar{x})$$

where p and h are any fixed (naturally extended) functions, has as its fixpoints the functions

$$\mathit{if}\ p(\bar{x})\ \mathit{then}\ g(\bar{x})\ \mathit{else}\ h(\bar{x})$$

for any function g in $[(D_1^+)^n \to D_2^+]$. The function

$$\mathit{if}\ p(\bar{x})\ \mathit{then}\ \Omega(\bar{x})\ \mathit{else}\ h(\bar{x})$$

is the least fixpoint of τ.

□

EXAMPLE 5-11

1. Consider the functional τ over $[N^+ \to N^+]$

$$\tau[F](x): \quad \mathit{if}\ x = 0\ \mathit{then}\ 1\ \mathit{else}\ F(x+1)$$

The following functions are fixpoints of τ:

$$f_0(x): \quad \mathit{if}\ x = 0\ \mathit{then}\ 1\ \mathit{else}\ 0$$

$$f_1(x): \quad \mathit{if}\ x = 0\ \mathit{then}\ 1\ \mathit{else}\ 1$$

$$f_2(x): \quad \mathit{if}\ x = 0\ \mathit{then}\ 1\ \mathit{else}\ 2$$

and so forth. In general, all the fixpoints of τ are of the form (for all $n \in N^+$)

$$f_n(x): \quad \mathit{if}\ x = 0\ \mathit{then}\ 1\ \mathit{else}\ n$$

because for all $n \in N^+$ and $x \in N^+$,

$$\begin{aligned}\tau[f_n](x) &\equiv \mathit{if}\ x = 0\ \mathit{then}\ 1\ \mathit{else}\ (\mathit{if}\ x+1 = 0\ \mathit{then}\ 1\ \mathit{else}\ n)\\ &\equiv \mathit{if}\ x = 0\ \mathit{then}\ 1\ \mathit{else}\ n\\ &\equiv f_n(x)\end{aligned}$$

Therefore the least fixpoint is

$$f_\tau(x): \quad \mathit{if}\ x = 0\ \mathit{then}\ 1\ \mathit{else}\ \omega$$

2. The functional τ over $[I^+ \to I^+]$ given by

$$\tau[F](x): \quad \mathit{if}\ x > 100\ \mathit{then}\ x - 10\ \mathit{else}\ F(F(x+11))$$

has only one fixpoint

$$\textit{if } x > 100 \textit{ then } x - 10 \textit{ else } 91$$

which is therefore the least fixpoint f_τ, known as *McCarthy's* 91 *function*. (See Example 5-8, part 2.)

□

EXAMPLE 5-12

Some of the fixpoints of the functional τ over $[I^+ \to I^+]$ defined by

$$\tau[F](x, y): \quad \textit{if } x = y \textit{ then } y + 1 \textit{ else } F(x, F(x - 1, y + 1))$$

are

$$f(x, y): \quad \textit{if } x = y \textit{ then } y + 1 \textit{ else } x + 1$$

$$g(x, y): \quad \textit{if } x \geq y \textit{ then } x + 1 \textit{ else } y - 1$$

$$h(x, y): \quad \textit{if } (x \geq y) \wedge (x - y \text{ even}) \textit{ then } x + 1 \textit{ else } \omega$$

The function $f(x, y)$, for example, is a fixpoint of τ because

$$\begin{aligned}
\tau[f](x, y) &\equiv \textit{if } x = y \textit{ then } y + 1 \textit{ else } f(x, f(x - 1, y + 1)) \\
&\equiv \textit{if } x = y \textit{ then } y + 1 \textit{ else} \\
&\qquad (\textit{if } x = [\textit{if } x - 1 = y + 1 \textit{ then } y + 2 \textit{ else } x] \\
&\qquad \textit{then } [\textit{if } x - 1 = y + 1 \textit{ then } y + 2 \textit{ else } x] + 1 \\
&\qquad \textit{else } x + 1) \\
&\equiv \textit{if } x = y \textit{ then } y + 1 \textit{ else } (\textit{if } x = y + 2 \textit{ then } y + 3 \textit{ else } x + 1) \\
&\equiv \textit{if } x = y \textit{ then } y + 1 \textit{ else } x + 1 \\
&\equiv f(x, y)
\end{aligned}$$

Note that in performing such simplifications we must consider carefully the cases where x or y are ω. At this point the reader may wonder why we chose the strange $f(x, y)$ rather than $f'(x, y)$: $x + 1$. The reason is that $f'(x, y)$: $x + 1$ is not a fixpoint of τ because $\tau[f'](x, \omega)$ is ω while $f'(x, \omega)$ is $x + 1$.

The function $g(x, y)$ is also a fixpoint of τ because

$$\begin{aligned}
\tau[g](x, y) \equiv\ &\textit{if } x = y \textit{ then } y + 1 \\
&\qquad \textit{else } g(x, \textit{if } x - 1 \geq y + 1 \textit{ then } (x - 1) + 1 \\
&\qquad\qquad\qquad \textit{else } (y + 1) - 1)
\end{aligned}$$

$$\equiv \textit{if } x = y \textit{ then } y + 1$$
$$\textit{else} \left(\textit{if } x - 1 \geq y + 1 \textit{ then } g(x, x) \textit{ else } g(x, y)\right)$$
$$\equiv \textit{if } x = y \textit{ then } y + 1$$
$$\textit{else} \left(\textit{if } x - 1 \geq y + 1 \textit{ then } x + 1 \textit{ else } g(x, y)\right)$$
$$\equiv \textit{if } x = y \vee x \geq y + 2 \textit{ then } x + 1 \textit{ else } g(x, y)$$
$$\equiv g(x, y)$$

Similarly, it can be verified that $h(x, y)$ is also a fixpoint of τ and, in fact, that it is the least fixpoint of τ.

□

5-2 RECURSIVE PROGRAMS

We are ready now to define our class of recursive programs. In our class, a program called a *recursive definition*, or *recursive program*, over D is of the form†

$$F(\bar{x}) \Leftarrow \tau[F](\bar{x})$$

where $\tau[F](\bar{x})$ is a functional over $[(D^+)^n \to D^+]$ expressed by composition of known monotonic functions and predicates (called *base functions and predicates*) and the function variable F, applied to the individual variables $\bar{x} = \langle x_1, x_2, \ldots, x_n \rangle$.

Of course, our programs are meaningless until we describe the semantics of our language, that is, indicate the function defined by a program. We agree that *the function defined by a recursive program P*

$$P: \quad F(\bar{x}) \Leftarrow \tau[F](\bar{x})$$

is f_τ (the least fixpoint of τ) and denote it by f_P.‡ For example, the following recursive program over the natural numbers

$$P: \quad F(x) \Leftarrow \textit{if } x = 0 \textit{ then } 1 \textit{ else } x \cdot F(x - 1)$$

defines the factorial function (that is, $f_P(x)$ is $x!$) because this is the least fixpoint of the functional

$$\tau[F](x): \quad \textit{if } x = 0 \textit{ then } 1 \textit{ else } x \cdot F(x - 1)$$

† A more general notion of recursive programs which consist of systems of recursive definitions will be introduced in Sec. 5-2.3.

‡ Note that the existence of f_τ is assured by the results of Theorems 5-1 and 5-2.

In order for our programming language to have any practical use, we must describe how to compute the function defined by a recursive program. Therefore our next step is to give *computation rules* for executing recursive programs. However, we must remember that the computation rules should have one important characteristic: For every program P, the computed function should be identical to f_P. We call such computation rules *fixpoint computation rules.*

5-2.1 Computation Rules

Let $F(\bar{x}) \Leftarrow \tau[F](\bar{x})$ be a recursive program over some domain D. For a given input value $\bar{d} \in (D^+)^n$ for $\bar{x}$, the program is executed by constructing a sequence of terms $t_0, t_1, t_2, \ldots$, called *the computation sequence for* $\bar{d}$, or *the computation of* $F(\bar{d})$, as follows:

1. The first term t_0 is $F(\bar{d})$.
2. For each i $(i \geq 0)$, the term t_{i+1} is obtained from t_i in two steps.
   (*a*) *Substitution:* Some occurrences (see below) of F in t_i are replaced by $\tau[F]$ simultaneously:
   (*b*) *Simplification:* Base functions and predicates are replaced by their values *whenever possible* until no further simplifications can be made.

The sequence is finite, and t_k is the final term in the sequence if and only if t_k contains no occurrences of the symbol F, that is, when t_k is an element of D^+.

A *computation rule C* tells us which occurrences of $F(\bar{e})$ should be replaced by $\tau[F](\bar{e})$ in each substitution step. We are interested only in "reasonable" computation rules, which, for any term t_i arising in a computation and containing occurrences of F, will determine a nonempty substitution to be carried out. For a given computation rule C, the program defines a partial function C_P mapping $(D^+)^n$ into D^+ as follows: If for input $\bar{d} \in (D^+)^n$ the computation sequence for $\bar{d}$ is finite, we say that $C_P(\bar{d})$ is t_k; if the computation sequence for $\bar{d}$ is infinite, we say that $C_P(\bar{d})$ is ω.

The following are several computation rules which will be discussed later.

1 *Leftmost-innermost ("call-by-value") rule:* Replace only the leftmost-innermost occurrences of F (that is, the leftmost occurrence of F which has all its arguments free of F's). We denote the computed function by LI_P.

2. *Parallel-innermost rule:* Replace all the innermost occurrences of F (that is, all occurrences of F with all arguments free of F's) simultaneously. We denote the computed function by PI_P.

3. *Leftmost ("call-by-name") rule:* Replace only the leftmost occurrence of F. We denote the computed function by L_P.

4. *Parallel-outermost rule:* Replace all the outermost occurrences of F (that is, all occurrences of F which do not occur as arguments of other F's) simultaneously. We denote the computed function by PO_P.

5. *Free-argument rule:* Replace all occurrences of F which have at least one argument free of F's simultaneously. We denote the computed function by FA_P.

6. *Full-substitution rule:* Replace all occurrences of F simultaneously. We denote the computed function by FS_P.

EXAMPLE 5-13

Consider the term

$$F(0,\ F(1,1)) + F(F(2,2),\ F(3,3))$$

We shall indicate by arrows those occurrences of F that will be replaced under each one of the computation rules given previously:

```
Leftmost-innermost     F(0, F(1,1)) + F(F(2,2), F(3,3))
                            ↑
Parallel-innermost     F(0, F(1,1)) + F(F(2,2), F(3,3))
                            ↑            ↑        ↑
Leftmost               F(0, F(1,1)) + F(F(2,2), F(3,3))
                       ↑
Parallel-outermost     F(0, F(1,1)) + F(F(2,2), F(3,3))
                       ↑              ↑
Free-argument          F(0, F(1,1)) + F(F(2,2), F(3,3))
                       ↑    ↑            ↑        ↑
Full-substitution      F(0, F(1,1)) + F(F(2,2), F(3,3))
                       ↑    ↑         ↑  ↑        ↑
```

□

EXAMPLE 5-14

Let us consider the recursive program P over the integers:

$$F(x) \Leftarrow \textit{if } x > 100 \textit{ then } x - 10 \textit{ else } F(F(x + 11))$$

The least-fixpoint function is

$$f_P(x): \quad \textit{if } x > 100 \textit{ then } x - 10 \textit{ else } 91$$

We shall illustrate the computation sequences for $x = 99$ using three of the computation rules. (We shall indicate by arrows the occurrences of F used for substitution.)

1. Using the full-substitution rule,

$$t_0 \text{ is } \underset{\uparrow}{F}(99)$$

$$\textit{if } 99 > 100 \textit{ then } 99 - 10 \textit{ else } F(F(99 + 11))$$

$$t_1 \text{ is } \underset{\uparrow}{F}(\underset{\uparrow}{F}(110))$$

$$\begin{aligned}&\textit{if } [\textit{if } 110 > 100 \textit{ then } 110 - 10 \textit{ else } F(F(110 + 11))] > 100\\ &\textit{then } [\textit{if } 110 > 100 \textit{ then } 110 - 10 \textit{ else } F(F(110 + 11))] - 10\\ &\textit{else } F(F([\textit{if } 110 > 100 \textit{ then } 110 - 10 \textit{ else } F(F(110 + 11))] + 11))\end{aligned}$$

$$t_2 \text{ is } \underset{\uparrow}{F}(\underset{\uparrow}{F}(111))$$

$$\begin{aligned}&\textit{if } [\textit{if } 111 > 100 \textit{ then } 111 - 10 \textit{ else } F(F(111 + 11))] > 100\\ &\textit{then } [\textit{if } 111 > 100 \textit{ then } 111 - 10 \textit{ else } F(F(111 + 11))] - 10\\ &\textit{else } F(F([\textit{if } 111 > 100 \textit{ then } 111 - 10 \textit{ else } F(F(111 + 11))] + 11))\end{aligned}$$

$$t_3 \text{ is } 91$$

In short, the computation sequence is

$$\underset{\uparrow}{F}(99) \to \underset{\uparrow}{F}(\underset{\uparrow}{F}(110)) \to \underset{\uparrow}{F}(\underset{\uparrow}{F}(111)) \to 91$$

Thus, $FS_P(99)$ is 91.

2. Using the leftmost-innermost rule,

$$t_0 \text{ is } \underset{\uparrow}{F}(99)$$

$$\textit{if } 99 > 100 \textit{ then } 99 - 10 \textit{ else } F(F(99 + 11))$$

$$t_1 \text{ is } F(\underset{\uparrow}{F}(110))$$

$$F(\textit{if } 110 > 100 \textit{ then } 110 - 10 \textit{ else } F(F(110 + 11)))$$

$$t_2 \text{ is } \underset{\uparrow}{F}(100)$$

$$\mathit{if}\ 100 > 100\ \mathit{then}\ 100 - 10\ \mathit{else}\ F(F(100 + 11))$$

$$t_3 \text{ is } F(\underset{\uparrow}{F}(111))$$

$$F(\mathit{if}\ 111 > 100\ \mathit{then}\ 111 - 10\ \mathit{else}\ F(F(111 + 11)))$$

$$t_4 \text{ is } \underset{\uparrow}{F}(101)$$

$$\mathit{if}\ 101 > 100\ \mathit{then}\ 101 - 10\ \mathit{else}\ F(F(101 + 11))$$

$$t_5 \text{ is } 91$$

In short,

$$\underset{\uparrow}{F}(99) \to F(\underset{\uparrow}{F}(110)) \to \underset{\uparrow}{F}(100) \to F(\underset{\uparrow}{F}(111)) \to \underset{\uparrow}{F}(101) \to 91$$

Thus, $LI_P(99)$ is 91. Note that in this case the same computation sequence is obtained by using either the parallel-innermost or the free-argument rule; thus, both $PI_P(99)$ and $FA_P(99)$ are 91.

3. Using the leftmost rule,

$$t_0 \text{ is } \underset{\uparrow}{F}(99)$$

$$t_1 \text{ is } \underset{\uparrow}{F}(F(110))$$

$$t_2 \text{ is } \mathit{if}\ \underset{\uparrow}{F}(110) > 100\ \mathit{then}\ F(110) - 10\ \mathit{else}\ F(F(F(110) + 11))$$

$$t_3 \text{ is } \underset{\uparrow}{F}(F(F(110) + 11))$$

$$t_4 \text{ is } \mathit{if}\ \underset{\uparrow}{F}(F(110) + 11) > 100\ \mathit{then}\ F(F(110) + 11) - 10$$

$$\mathit{else}\ F(F(F(F(110) + 11) + 11))$$

$$t_5 \text{ is } \mathit{if}\ [\mathit{if}\ \underset{\uparrow}{F}(110) > 89\ \mathit{then}\ F(110) + 1\ \mathit{else}\ F(F(F(110) + 22))] > 100$$

$$\mathit{then}\ F(F(110) + 11) - 10\ \mathit{else}\ F(F(F(F(110) + 11) + 11))$$

$$t_6 \text{ is } \mathit{if}\ \underset{\uparrow}{F}(110) > 99\ \mathit{then}\ F(F(110) + 11) - 10$$

$$\mathit{else}\ F(F(F(F(110) + 11) + 11))$$

t_7 is $F(F(110) + 11) - 10$
$\uparrow$

t_8 is $[\mathit{if}\ F(110) > 89\ \mathit{then}\ F(110) + 1\ \mathit{else}\ F(F(F(110) + 22))] - 10$
$\uparrow$

t_9 is $F(110) - 9$
$\uparrow$

t_{10} is 91

Thus, $L_P(99)$ is 91.

□

Computation diagram Before discussing the relation between C_P (the computed functions for some computation rule C) and f_P (the least fixpoint of P), we shall introduce a few notations that will be used in the proofs of Sec. 5-2.2. Let us consider a recursive program P of the form $F(\bar{x}) \Leftarrow \tau[F](\bar{x})$. For simplicity, let us assume that the functional τ has only two occurrences of F, denoted by $\tau[F, F]$ to distinguish between them. Since τ is defined by the composition of monotonic base functions and predicates and the function variable F, it *must be monotonic with respect to any occurrence of* F; that is, $f \sqsubseteq g$ implies $\tau[f, h] \sqsubseteq \tau[g, h]$ and $\tau[h, f] \sqsubseteq \tau[h, g]$ for any h, and clearly $\tau[f, f] \sqsubseteq \tau[g, g]$.

Consider, now, the following diagram, called the *computation diagram of* τ:

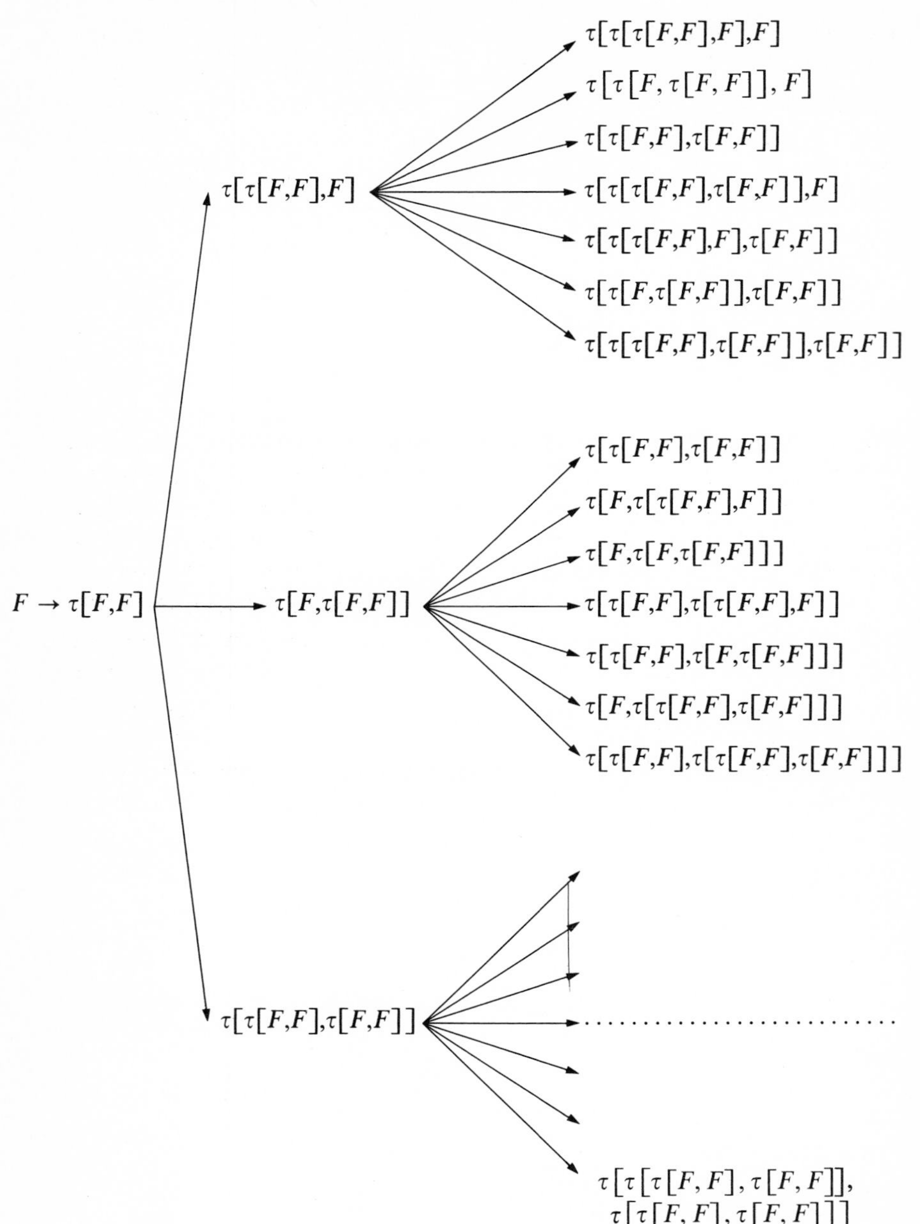

τ[τ[τ[F,F],F],F]
τ[τ[F, τ[F, F]], F]
τ[τ[F,F],τ[F,F]]
τ[τ[F,F],F]
τ[τ[τ[F,F],τ[F,F]],F]
τ[τ[τ[F,F],F],τ[F,F]]
τ[τ[F,τ[F,F]],τ[F,F]]
τ[τ[τ[F,F],τ[F,F]],τ[F,F]]
τ[τ[F,F],τ[F,F]]
τ[F,τ[τ[F,F],F]]
τ[F,τ[F,τ[F,F]]]
F → τ[F,F]
τ[F,τ[F,F]]
τ[τ[F,F],τ[τ[F,F],F]]
τ[τ[F,F],τ[F,τ[F,F]]]
τ[F,τ[τ[F,F],τ[F,F]]]
τ[τ[F,F],τ[τ[F,F],τ[F,F]]]
τ[τ[F,F],τ[F,F]]
τ[τ[τ[F, F], τ[F, F]],
τ[τ[F, F], τ[F, F]]]

This diagram is an *infinite tree.* Every element in it is obtained from its predecessor by replacing one or more occurrences of F by $\tau[F,F]$. Corresponding to each term in the computation diagram, we can obtain a function by substituting Ω for each F. A path of the diagram such that all F's in its terms are replaced by Ω's is called an Ω *path.* Since τ is monotonic with respect to any occurrence of F, and since $\Omega \sqsubseteq \tau[\Omega,\Omega]$, clearly we have

$$\tau[\Omega,\Omega] \sqsubseteq \tau[\tau[\Omega,\Omega],\Omega]$$
$$\tau[\Omega,\Omega] \sqsubseteq \tau[\Omega,\tau[\Omega,\Omega]]$$
$$\tau[\Omega,\Omega] \sqsubseteq \tau[\tau[\Omega,\Omega],\tau[\Omega,\Omega]]$$

and so forth, which implies that every Ω path in the computation diagram determines a chain of functions. For example,

$$\Omega \sqsubseteq \tau[\Omega,\Omega] \sqsubseteq \tau[\Omega,\tau[\Omega,\Omega]] \sqsubseteq \tau[\Omega,\tau[\tau[\Omega,\Omega],\Omega]] \sqsubseteq \cdots$$

Note that for the bottom path of the computation diagram

$$F \to \tau[F,F] \to \tau[\tau[F,F],\tau[F,F]] \to \cdots$$

obtained by replacing in each step all occurrences of F by $\tau[F,F]$, the corresponding Ω path is identical to the chain

$$\Omega \sqsubseteq \tau[\Omega] \sqsubseteq \tau^2[\Omega] \sqsubseteq \tau^3[\Omega] \sqsubseteq \cdots$$

which was introduced in the proof of Theorem 5-2.

There exists an important relation between the computation sequence $t_0, t_1, t_2, \ldots$ of a recursive program $F(\bar{x}) \Leftarrow \tau[F](\bar{x})$ and the Ω paths of the computation diagram of τ: *For any recursive program* $P: F(\bar{x}) \Leftarrow \tau[F](\bar{x})$, *element* $\bar{d}$ *and a computation rule* C, *there corresponds a (finite or infinite) path* $C_P^0[F], C_P^1[F], C_P^2[F], \ldots$, *in the computation diagram of* τ *such that*

$$C_P^i[F](\bar{d}) \equiv t_i$$

and †

$$\text{lub}\,\{C_P^i[\Omega]\}(\bar{d}) \equiv C_P(\bar{d})$$

To construct the path $\{C_P^i[F]\}$ we start from F and replace in each step some occurrences of F by $\tau[F,F]$. The choice of occurrences of F's which are substituted by $\tau[F,F]$ is determined by considering the computation sequence for $\bar{d}$. In each step we obtain $C_P^{i+1}[F]$ from $C_P^i[F]$ by replacing exactly those occurrences of F which are chosen to obtain t_{i+1} from t_i

† The lub of a finite chain is always the last element of the chain.

in the computation sequence for $\bar{d}$.† The path obtained, taken to be of the same length (finite or infinite) as the computation sequence for $\bar{d}$, is the desired path $C_P^0[F], C_P^1[F], \ldots$

EXAMPLE 5-15

Consider the following recursive program over the natural numbers (the *Fibonacci program*):

$$F(x) \Leftarrow \textit{if } x < 2 \textit{ then } 1 \textit{ else } [F(x-1) + F(x-2)]$$

We denote it by $F(x) \Leftarrow \tau[F, F](x)$ to distinguish between the two occurrences of F in τ.

In the following table, on the left we describe the computation of $F(3)$ by the leftmost computation rule while on the right we describe the corresponding path in the computation diagram of τ. (As before, we use arrows $\uparrow$ to indicate those occurrences of F which are being replaced.)

$F(3)$	$C_P^0[F]: \; F$
$\rightarrow \underset{\uparrow}{F}(2) + F(1)$	$C_P^1[F]: \; \tau[\underset{\uparrow}{F}, F]$
$\rightarrow [\underset{\uparrow}{F}(1) + F(0)] + F(1)$	$C_P^2[F]: \; \tau[\tau[\underset{\uparrow}{F}, F], F]$
$\rightarrow [1 + \underset{\uparrow}{F}(0)] + F(1)$	$C_P^3[F]: \; \tau[\tau[\tau[F, F], \underset{\uparrow}{F}], F]$
$\rightarrow 2 + \underset{\uparrow}{F}(1)$	$C_P^4[F]: \; \tau[\tau[\tau[F, F], \tau[F, F]], \underset{\uparrow}{F}]$
$\rightarrow 3$	$C_P^5[F]: \; \tau[\tau[\tau[F, F], \tau[F, F]], \tau[F, F]]$

Thus, the elements $C_P^i[F](x)$ of the path are

$$C_P^0[F](x): \; F(x)$$

$$C_P^1[F](x): \; \textit{if } x < 2 \textit{ then } 1 \textit{ else } [\underset{\uparrow}{F}(x-1) + F(x-2)]$$

$$C_P^2[F](x): \; \textit{if } x < 2 \textit{ then } 1 \; \textit{else } \{\textit{if } x - 1 < 2 \textit{ then } 1 \; \textit{else } [\underset{\uparrow}{F}(x-2) + F(x-3)] + F(x-2)\}$$

† Note that not all the occurrences of F in $C_P^i[F]$ will appear in the term t_i because some of them could have been eliminated by simplification during the computation.

$C_P^3[F](x)$:

$$
\begin{aligned}
& \textit{if } x < 2 \textit{ then } 1 \\
& \quad \textit{else } \{\textit{if } x - 1 < 2 \textit{ then } 1 \\
& \qquad \textit{else } \{\textit{if } x - 2 < 2 \textit{ then } 1 \\
& \qquad\quad \textit{else } [F(x-3) + F(x-4)] \\
& \qquad + F(x-3)\} \\
& \qquad\quad \uparrow \\
& \quad + F(x-2)\}
\end{aligned}
$$

$C_P^4[F](x)$:

$$
\begin{aligned}
& \textit{if } x < 2 \textit{ then } 1 \\
& \quad \textit{else } \{\textit{if } x - 1 < 2 \textit{ then } 1 \\
& \qquad \textit{else } \{\textit{if } x - 2 < 2 \textit{ then } 1 \\
& \qquad\quad \textit{else } [F(x-3) + F(x-4)] \\
& \qquad + \textit{if } x - 3 < 2 \textit{ then } 1 \\
& \qquad\quad \textit{else } [F(x-4) + F(x-5)]\} \\
& \quad + F(x-2)\} \\
& \qquad \uparrow
\end{aligned}
$$

$C_P^5[F](x)$:

$$
\begin{aligned}
& \textit{if } x < 2 \textit{ then } 1 \\
& \quad \textit{else } \{\textit{if } x - 1 < 2 \textit{ then } 1 \\
& \qquad \textit{else } \{\textit{if } x - 2 < 2 \textit{ then } 1 \\
& \qquad\quad \textit{else } [F(x-3) + F(x-4)] \\
& \qquad + \textit{if } x - 3 < 2 \textit{ then } 1 \\
& \qquad\quad \textit{else } [F(x-4) + F(x-5)]\} \\
& \quad + \textit{if } x - 2 < 2 \textit{ then } 1 \textit{ else } [F(x-3) + F(x-4)]\}
\end{aligned}
$$

The value of $C_P^5[\Omega](3)$ is

$$
\begin{aligned}
& \textit{if } 3 < 2 \textit{ then } 1 \\
& \quad \textit{else } \{\textit{if } 2 < 2 \textit{ then } 1 \\
& \qquad \textit{else } \{[\textit{if } 1 < 2 \textit{ then } 1 \textit{ else } \omega] \\
& \qquad\quad + [\textit{if } 0 < 2 \textit{ then } 1 \textit{ else } \omega]\} \\
& \quad + [\textit{if } 1 < 2 \textit{ then } 1 \textit{ else } \omega]\}
\end{aligned}
$$

which is indeed 3. □

5-2.2 Fixpoint Computation Rules

A computation rule C is said to be a *fixpoint computation rule* if for every recursive program P over D

$$C_P(\bar{d}) \equiv f_P(\bar{d}) \qquad \text{for all} \qquad \bar{d} \in (D^+)^n$$

The first three computation rules introduced in Sec. 5-2.1—*the leftmost-innermost* ("*call-by-value*"), *the parallel-innermost, and the leftmost* ("*call-by-name*") *rules*—*are not fixpoint rules.* The following example illustrates a recursive program P for which $LI_P \not\equiv f_P$, $PI_P \not\equiv f_P$, and $L_P \not\equiv f_P$.

EXAMPLE 5-16

Consider the recursive program P over the integers

$$F(x, y) \Leftarrow \textit{if } x = 0 \textit{ then } 0 \textit{ else } [F(x+1, F(x, y)) * F(x-1, F(x, y))]$$

where the multiplication function $*$ is extended as follows:

$0 * \omega$ and $\omega * 0$ are 0

$a * \omega$ and $\omega * a$ are ω (for any nonzero integer a)

$\omega * \omega$ *is* ω

Extended in this way, the multiplication function is a monotonic function and therefore can be used as a base function in our recursive definition.

The least fixpoint $f_P(x, y)$ is the binary zero function $Z(x, y)$, such that $Z(x, y)$ is 0 for all $x \in I$, $y \in I^+$ and $Z(\omega, y)$ is ω for all $y \in I^+$; thus, $f_P(1, 0)$ is 0. However, the computation of $F(1, 0)$ under the parallel-innermost rule yields the following infinite sequence:

$$\begin{aligned} F(1,0) &\to F(2, \underset{\uparrow}{F(1,0)}) * F(0, \underset{\uparrow}{F(1,0)}) \\ &\to F(2, F(2, \underset{\uparrow}{F(1,0)}) * F(0, \underset{\uparrow}{F(1,0)})) * F(0, F(2, \underset{\uparrow}{F(1,0)}) * F(0, \underset{\uparrow}{F(1,0)})) \\ &\to \cdots \end{aligned}$$

Similarly, we obtain infinite computation sequences for $F(1, 0)$ under the leftmost-innermost and the leftmost rules. Thus, the value of $LI_P(1, 0)$, $PI_P(1, 0)$, and $L_P(1, 0)$ is ω.

Note that the computation of $F(1, 0)$ under the parallel-outermost rule yields the following sequence:

$$\begin{aligned} F(1,0) &\to \underset{\uparrow}{F}(2, F(1,0)) * \underset{\uparrow}{F}(0, F(1,0)) \\ &\to [F(3, F(2, F(1,0))) * F(1, F(2, F(1,0)))] * 0 \\ &= 0 \end{aligned}$$

Similarly, we obtain that the value of $F(1,0)$ for the free-argument and full-substitution rules yield the value 0, not ω. The crucial point in these computations is that we are required to do simplifications *whenever possible*. Therefore, if we can determine the value of a function by having the value of some of its arguments, we must replace the function by its value *without waiting* for the other arguments to be calculated. Thus, the term

$$[F(3, F(2, F(1,0)))*F(1, F(2, F(1,0)))]*0$$

must be replaced by 0.

□

There is one important property of C_P that holds for any computation rule C.

THEOREM 5-3 (Cadiou) *For any computation rule C, the computed function C_P is less defined than or equal to the least fixpoint f_P; that is, $C_P \sqsubseteq f_P$.*

Proof. Let P be any recursive program $F(\bar{x}) \Leftarrow \tau[F, F](\bar{x})$ over D; let $\bar{d}$ be any element of $(D^+)^n$; and let C be any computation rule. Then we denote by $C_P^0[F], C_P^1[F], C_P^2[F], \ldots$, the corresponding path in the computation diagram of τ. Consider, in addition, the bottom path in the diagram: $\tau^0[F], \tau^1[F], \tau^2[F], \ldots$. Since for each i, $\tau^i[\Omega]$ can always be obtained from $C_P^i[\Omega]$ by replacing some occurrences of Ω by $\tau[\Omega, \Omega]$, it follows that

$$C_P^i[\Omega] \sqsubseteq \tau^i[\Omega] \qquad \text{for all} \qquad i \geq 0$$

Since $\tau^i[\Omega] \sqsubseteq \text{lub}\,\{\tau^i[\Omega]\}$, it follows that $C_P^i[\Omega] \sqsubseteq \text{lub}\,\{\tau^i[\Omega]\}$ for $i \geq 0$. Thus $\text{lub}\,\{\tau^i[\Omega]\}$ is an upper bound of $\{C_P^i[\Omega]\}$, and

$$\text{lub}\,\{C_P^i[\Omega]\} \sqsubseteq \text{lub}\,\{\tau^i[\Omega]\}$$

Now, since $C_P(\bar{d}) \equiv \text{lub}\,\{C_P^i[\Omega]\}(\bar{d})$, and since $f_P \equiv \text{lub}\,\{\tau^i[\Omega]\}$ (by Theorem 5-2), it follows that

$$C_P(\bar{d}) \sqsubseteq f_P(\bar{d})$$

Q.E.D.

We shall now describe a sufficient condition for a computation rule to be a fixpoint computation rule, which will imply that the parallel outer most, free-argument, and full-substitution rules are fixpoint computation rules. For this purpose, we shall need a few additional notations: Let

$\alpha[F^1, \ldots, F^i, F^{i+1}, \ldots, F^k](\bar{d})$ denote any term in the computation sequence for $\bar{d}$, where we use superscripts to distinguish the individual occurrences of F in α (however, the superscripts do not necessarily indicate the order of the occurrences). Suppose that, for substitution, we choose the occurrences $F^1, \ldots, F^i$ of F in α. We say that this is a *safe substitution* if

$$\alpha[\Omega, \ldots, \Omega, f_P, \ldots, f_P](\bar{d}) \equiv \omega$$

A computation rule is said to be safe if it always uses only safe substitutions.

THEOREM 5-4 (Vuillemin) *Any safe computation rule is a fixpoint computation rule.*

Proof. We assume that C is a safe computation rule but not a fixpoint computation rule and derive a contradiction. Let P be a recursive program $F(\bar{x}) \Leftarrow \tau[F, F](\bar{x})$ over D for which $C_P \not\equiv f_P$. From Theorem 5-3 we know that $C_P \sqsubseteq f_P$ for any computation rule C; therefore if C is not a fixpoint computation rule, we must have $C_P(\bar{d}) \equiv \omega$ and $f_P(\bar{d}) \not\equiv \omega$ for some $\bar{d} \in (D^+)^n$. Since, by Theorem 5-2, we have $f_P(\bar{d}) \equiv \text{lub}\,\{\tau^i[\Omega]\}(\bar{d})$, the assumption $f_P(\bar{d}) \not\equiv \omega$ implies that $\tau^n[\Omega](\bar{d}) \not\equiv \omega$ for some $n \geq 0$.

For the purpose of this proof it is convenient to express the elements of the computation diagram of τ as a binary tree in which every nonterminal vertex is labeled by τ and every terminal vertex is labeled by Ω. This method enables us to associate a depth with each occurrence of Ω in the term; for example, the term $\tau[\Omega, \tau[\tau[\Omega, \Omega], \Omega]]$ will be expressed as follows

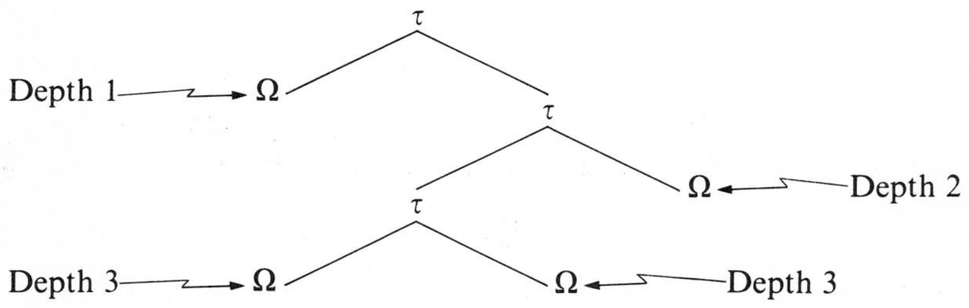

Let $C_P^0[F], C_P^1[F], C_P^2[F], \ldots,$ be the path in the computation diagram of τ which corresponds to the computation rule C and the input value $\bar{d}$. Since by our assumption $C_P(\bar{d}) \equiv \omega$, it follows that there are two possibilities: Either the computation sequence for $\bar{d}$ is finite and the last term is ω, or the computation sequence is infinite. In the first case, we derive the contradiction easily. Let us replace f_P for all occurrences of F in the terms of the computation sequence. Each term is now equivalent to its predecessor, while the first term is $f_P(\bar{d})$ and the last one is ω. Thus, $f_P(\bar{d}) \equiv \omega$, which contradicts our assumption that $f_P(\bar{d}) \not\equiv \omega$.

In the second case, the path $C_P^0[F], C_P^1[F], C_P^2[F], \ldots,$ must be infinite. Since each term $C_P^i[F]$ contains only finitely many F with depth $\leq n$, it follows that there must exist some N ($N \geq 0$) such that $C_P^{N+1}[F]$ is derived from $C_P^N[F]$ by substituting only F's of depth $> n$. Let us denote C_P^N by $\alpha[F^1, \ldots, F^i, F^{i+1}, \ldots, F^k]$, where $F^1, \ldots, F^i$ are the occurrences of F which are replaced in the process of obtaining $C_P^{N+1}[F]$. Now, consider the term

$$\alpha[\Omega, \ldots, \Omega, \tau^n[\Omega], \ldots, \tau^n[\Omega]]$$

All the first i occurrences of F are of a depth greater than n and are replaced by Ω; the remaining occurrences of F are replaced by $\tau^n[\Omega]$, which makes all occurrences of Ω in α to be of depth $\geq n$. Therefore

$$\tau^n[\Omega] \sqsubseteq \alpha[\Omega, \ldots, \Omega, \tau^n[\Omega], \ldots, \tau^n[\Omega]]$$

However, since $\tau^n[\Omega] \sqsubseteq f_P$ and α is monotonic with respect to any occurrence of F, it follows that

$$\alpha[\Omega, \ldots, \Omega, \tau^n[\Omega], \ldots, \tau^n[\Omega]] \sqsubseteq \alpha[\Omega, \ldots, \Omega, f_P, \ldots, f_P]$$

Thus $\tau^n[\Omega] \sqsubseteq \alpha[\Omega, \ldots, \Omega, f_P, \ldots, f_P]$. Since $\tau^n[\Omega](\bar{d}) \not\equiv \omega$, we obtain $\alpha[\Omega, \ldots, \Omega, f_P, \ldots, f_P](\bar{d}) \not\equiv \omega$, which contradicts our assumption that C is a safe computation rule.

Q.E.D.

COROLLARY. *The parallel-outermost, the free-argument,*† *and the full-substitution rules are safe rules and therefore are fixpoint computation rules.*

Proof. Instead of introducing a formal proof showing that the three rules are safe, we shall discuss a few problematic cases. To show that the parallel-outermost rule is a safe rule, let us consider a term of the form

$$g(a_1, \ldots, a_k, \underset{\uparrow}{F(t_1)}, \ldots, \underset{\uparrow}{F(t_n)})$$

where g is a base monotonic function, $a_i \in D^+$, and each t_i might contain further occurrences of F. If we reach such a term in a computation sequence, the next substitution will choose exactly those occurrences of F displayed above. Since we are required to do simplifications in the terms of the

† To show that the free-argument rule is safe, we need the restriction that f_P is not a constant function.

computation sequence whenever possible, it follows that

$$g(a_1, \ldots, a_k, \omega, \ldots, \omega) \equiv \omega.$$

For suppose $g(a_1, \ldots, a_k, \omega, \ldots, \omega) \not\equiv \omega$; then

$$g(a_1, \ldots, a_k, \omega, \ldots, \omega) \equiv d$$

for some $d \in D$. Therefore, by the monotonicity of g,

$$g(a_1, \ldots, a_k, b_1, \ldots, b_n) \equiv d$$

for all $b_i \in D^+$. Since the simplification rules require doing simplifications whenever possible, we had to replace the term

$$g(a_1, \ldots, a_k, F(t_1), \ldots, F(t_n))$$

by d in some previous step of the computation, and therefore it cannot be a term of a computation sequence. Thus, $g(a_1, \ldots, a_k, \omega, \ldots, \omega) \equiv \omega$, which is exactly the condition needed for safe substitution. Note that for any term of the form $F(\ldots)$ the substitution is clearly safe.

The fact that the parallel-outermost rule is safe implies immediately that the full-substitution rule is safe. The reason is that all occurrences of F replaced by the parallel-outermost rule are always included in the set of occurrences of F's replaced by the full-substitution rule.

To show that the free-argument rule is safe, consider a term of the form

$$F(\underset{\uparrow}{F(t_1)}, \underset{\uparrow}{F(t_2)}, \ldots, \underset{\uparrow}{F(t_n)})$$

where each t_i is free of F's. Since by the free-argument rule we replace only the inner occurrences of F, we have to check the value of

$$f_P(\Omega(t_1), \Omega(t_2), \ldots, \Omega(t_n))$$

Since f_P is monotonic and not a constant function (by our assumption), it follows that $f_P(\omega, \omega, \ldots, \omega) \equiv \omega$, which is the condition needed for safe substitution. (See Prob. 5-5(b).)

Q.E.D.

We have shown previously that the three computation rules—leftmost-innermost, parallel-innermost, and leftmost—are not fixpoint computation rules. Our counterexample (Example 5-16) made use of a base function (the multiplication function) which is not naturally extended. Since the base functions in most recursive programs are naturally extended, it is quite interesting to check to see what happens in this case:

For the restricted class of recursive programs, which use only naturally extended base functions (except for the if-then-else function), the leftmost-

innermost ("call-by-value") and the parallel-innermost rules are still not fixpoint rules, while the leftmost ("call-by-name") rule is safe and is therefore a fixpoint rule.

Consider any term in a computation sequence which is of the form

$$g(\underset{\uparrow}{F}(t_1), F(t_2))$$

where g is a naturally extended base function and each t_i may contain other occurrences of F. The leftmost rule will substitute the leftmost occurrence of F. Since g is naturally extended, $g(\omega, f_P(t_2)) \equiv \omega$ and the substitution is therefore safe. However, without this restriction (as was the case previously), we could have obtained $g(\omega, f_P(t_2)) \not\equiv \omega$, which makes our substitution unsafe. The only function allowed which is not naturally extended is the *if-then-else* function for which *if* ω *then* a *else* b is ω for all $a, b \in D^+$. This is the reason why the leftmost rule is the only rule that becomes now safe: It ensures that within *if* x *then* y *else* z we substitute first for x before trying to compute y or z.

The following example illustrates a recursive program P of the restricted class for which both $LI_P \not\equiv f_P$ and $PI_P \not\equiv f_P$.

EXAMPLE 5-17 (Morris)

Consider the recursive program P over the integers

$$F(x, y) \Leftarrow \textit{if } x = 0 \textit{ then } 1 \textit{ else } F(x - 1, F(x, y))$$

where the least fixpoint f_P is

$$f_P(x, y): \quad \textit{if } x \geq 0 \textit{ then } 1 \textit{ else } \omega$$

We compute $F(1, 0)$ using the leftmost-innermost computation rule:

$$\underset{\uparrow}{F}(1, 0) \to F(0, \underset{\uparrow}{F}(1, 0)) \to F(0, F(0, \underset{\uparrow}{F}(1, 0))) \to \cdots$$

and so on. The sequence is infinite, and therefore $LI_P(1, 0)$ is ω. In fact,

$$LI_P(x, y): \quad \textit{if } x = 0 \textit{ then } 1 \textit{ else } \omega$$

which is strictly less defined than f_P. The function PI_P for this program is identical to LI_P.

□

5-2.3 Systems of Recursive Definitions

The programming language discussed so far is very restrictive, mainly because we allow the use of only one function variable F and one recursive definition in every recursive program. In general, we would like a recursive program over D to consist of a system of recursive definitions of the form

$$F_1(\bar{x}) \Leftarrow \tau_1[F_1, \ldots, F_m](\bar{x})$$
$$F_2(\bar{x}) \Leftarrow \tau_2[F_1, \ldots, F_m](\bar{x})$$
$$\cdots\cdots\cdots\cdots\cdots\cdots$$
$$F_m(\bar{x}) \Leftarrow \tau_m[F_1, \ldots, F_m](\bar{x})$$

where each τ_i is a functional over $[(D^+)^n \to D^+]$ expressed by composition of known monotonic base functions and predicates and the function variables $F_1, F_2, \ldots, F_m$ applied to the individual variables $\bar{x} = \langle x_1, x_2, \ldots, x_n\rangle$. In order to discuss such a system of recursive definitions we must first extend some of the notions that were introduced in the first part of the chapter.

For m-tuples of functions $f = \langle f_1, \ldots, f_m\rangle$, we say that f *is monotonic* if each f_i is monotonic. For $f = \langle f_1, \ldots, f_m\rangle$ and $g = \langle g_1, \ldots, g_m\rangle$ we define $f \sqsubseteq g$ iff $f_i \sqsubseteq g_i$ for all i $(1 \le i \le m)$. Now we consider a functional $\tau[F_1, \ldots, F_m]$ over $[(D_1^+)^n \to D_2^+]^m$; that is, it maps an m-tuple of functions $\langle f_1, \ldots, f_m\rangle$ into an m-tuple of functions $\langle g_1, \ldots, g_m\rangle$, where each f_i and g_i are in $[(D_1^+)^n \to D_2^+]$. The best way to express such a functional is by coordinate functionals $\tau_1, \ldots, \tau_m$ so that $\tau[F_1, \ldots, F_m]$ is

$$\langle \tau_1[F_1, \ldots, F_m], \tau_2[F_1, \ldots, F_m], \ldots, \tau_m[F_1, \ldots, F_m]\rangle$$

An m-tuple of functions $f = \langle f_1, \ldots, f_m\rangle$ is said to be a *fixpoint of* τ if $f_i \equiv \tau_i[f_1, \ldots, f_m]$ for all i $(1 \le i \le m)$. If f is a fixpoint of τ and $f \sqsubseteq g$ for all other fixpoints $g = \langle g_1, \ldots, g_m\rangle$ of τ, then f is said to be the *least fixpoint of* τ.

A functional $\tau = \langle \tau_1, \ldots, \tau_m\rangle$ over $[(D_1^+)^n \to D_2^+]^m$ is said to be *continuous* if each τ_i is continuous. The results of Theorems 5-1 and 5-2 still hold: (1) *any functional* τ *defined by composition of monotonic functions and the function variables* $F_1, \ldots, F_m$ *is continuous, and* (2) *every continous functional* τ *has a unique least fixpoint, denoted by*

$$f_\tau = \langle f_{\tau_1}, \ldots, f_{\tau_m}\rangle.$$

EXAMPLE 5-18

Consider the functional over $[N^+ \to N^+]^2$

$$\tau[F_1, F_2] = \langle \tau_1[F_1, F_2], \tau_2[F_1, F_2]\rangle$$

where

$$\tau_1[F_1, F_2](x): \quad \textit{if } x = 0 \textit{ then } 1 \textit{ else } [F_1(x-1) + F_2(x-1)]$$

and

$$\tau_2[F_1, F_2](x): \quad \textit{if } x = 0 \textit{ then } 0 \textit{ else } F_2(x + 1)$$

For any $n \in N$, the pair $\langle g_n, h_n \rangle$ where

$$g_n(x): \quad \textit{if } x = 0 \vee x = 1 \textit{ then } 1 \textit{ else } [n(x - 1) + 1]$$

and

$$h_n(x): \quad \textit{if } x = 0 \textit{ then } 0 \textit{ else } n$$

is a fixpoint of τ since $g_n \equiv \tau_1[g_n, h_n]$ and $h_n \equiv \tau_2[g_n, h_n]$. The pair

$$\langle \textit{if } x = 0 \vee x = 1 \textit{ then } 1 \textit{ else } \omega, \textit{if } x = 0 \textit{ then } 0 \textit{ else } \omega \rangle$$

is the least fixpoint of τ. □

EXAMPLE 5-19

Consider the functional over $[N^+ \to N^+]^2$

$$\tau[F_1, F_2] = \langle \tau_1[F_1, F_2], \tau_2[F_1, F_2] \rangle$$

where

$$\tau_1[F_1, F_2](x): \quad \textit{if } x > 100 \textit{ then } x - 10 \textit{ else } F_1(F_2(x + 11))$$

and

$$\tau_2[F_1, F_2](x): \quad \textit{if } x > 100 \textit{ then } x - 10 \textit{ else } F_2(F_1(x + 11))$$

The only (and therefore also the least) fixpoint of τ is the pair

$$\langle \textit{if } x > 100 \textit{ then } x - 10 \textit{ else } 91, \textit{if } x > 100 \textit{ then } x - 10 \textit{ else } 91 \rangle$$

□

Similarly, we can generalize the computation rules to systems of recursive definitions. All the results relating the least fixpoint to the computed functions mentioned previously hold for systems of recursive definitions.

EXAMPLE 5-20

Let us consider again the recursive program over the natural numbers

$$F_1(x) \Leftarrow \textit{if } x = 0 \textit{ then } 1 \textit{ else } [F_1(x - 1) + F_2(x - 1)]$$

$$F_2(x) \Leftarrow \textit{if } x = 0 \textit{ then } 0 \textit{ else } F_2(x + 1)$$

The least fixpoint is the pair

$$\langle \textit{if } x = 0 \vee x = 1 \textit{ then } 1 \textit{ else } \omega, \textit{if } x = 0 \textit{ then } 0 \textit{ else } \omega \rangle$$

If we compute $F_1(2)$ using the leftmost rule we obtain

t_0 is $F_1(2)$
$\uparrow$

$if\ 2 = 0\ then\ 1\ else\ [F_1(2-1) + F_2(2-1)]$

t_1 is $F_1(1) + F_2(1)$
$\uparrow$

$[if\ 1 = 0\ then\ 1\ else\ [F_1(1-1) + F_2(1-1)]] + F_2(1)$

t_2 is $F_1(0) + F_2(0) + F_2(1)$
$\uparrow$

$[if\ 0 = 0\ then\ 1\ else\ [F_1(0-1) + F_2(0-1)]] + F_2(0) + F_2(1)$

t_3 is $1 + F_2(0) + F_2(1)$
$\uparrow$

$1 + [if\ 0 = 0\ then\ 0\ else\ F_2(0+1)] + F_2(1)$

t_4 is $1 + F_2(1)$
$\uparrow$

$1 + [if\ 1 = 0\ then\ 0\ else\ F_2(1+1)]$

t_5 is $1 + F_2(2)$
$\uparrow$

and so on. The computation never terminates, and therefore the value of $F_1(2)$ is ω, agreeing with the value of $f_{\tau_1}(2)$.

□

5-3 VERIFICATION METHODS

In this section we shall describe a few inductive methods for proving properties of the least fixpoint of recursive programs. The two main methods are the *computational induction method*, which is an induction on the level of recursion, and the *structural induction method*, which is essentially an induction on the depth of the data structure.

We shall concentrate on the computational induction and structural induction methods because they form a natural basis for future automatic program verifiers. In particular, most other known verification techniques can be justified directly by application of these methods.

5-3.1 Stepwise Computational Induction

The first method we shall describe for proving properties of recursive programs is the *stepwise computational induction method.* The idea of the method is essentially to prove properties of the least fixpoint f_P of a given recursive program P by induction on the level of recursion. For simplicity, first we shall explain the method for simple recursive programs, consisting of a single recursive definition; then we shall generalize to more complex programs.

Let P be a recursive program of the form $F(\bar{x}) \Leftarrow \tau[F](\bar{x})$. We shall consider the chain of functions $\{\tau^i[\Omega]\}$. By Kleene's theorem (Theorem 5-2) we know that

$$\text{lub}\,\{\tau^i[\Omega]\} \equiv f_\tau \equiv f_P$$

which suggests an induction rule for proving properties of f_P. To show that some property φ holds for f_P (that is, $\varphi(f_P)$ is *true*), we show that $\varphi(\tau^i[\Omega])$ holds for all $i \geq 0$, and that φ remains *true* for the lub. Therefore, we may conclude that $\varphi(\text{lub}\,\{\tau^i[\Omega]\})$, that is, $\varphi(f_P)$, holds. Unfortunately, in general it is not true that if $\varphi(\tau^i[\Omega])$ holds for all i, then $\varphi(\text{lub}\,\{\tau^i[\Omega]\})$ must hold, as illustrated in the following example.

EXAMPLE 5-21

Consider the recursive program over the natural numbers

$$P: \quad F(x) \Leftarrow \textit{if } x = 0 \textit{ then } 1 \textit{ else } x \cdot F(x-1)$$

As indicated in Example 5-8, part 1, we have for $i \geqq 0$

$$\tau^i[\Omega](x): \quad \textit{if } x < i \textit{ then } x! \textit{ else } \omega$$

and

$$\text{lub}\,\{\tau^i[\Omega]\}(x): \quad x!$$

Let us consider the predicate

$$\varphi(F): \quad (\exists x \in N)\,[F(x) \equiv \omega]$$

Then $\varphi(\tau^i[\Omega])$ holds for all $i \geq 0$; but since for all $x \in N$, $x! \not\equiv \omega$, $\varphi(\text{lub}\,\{\tau^i[\Omega]\})$ does not hold.

□

A predicate $\varphi(F)$ is said to be admissible if it has the property that for every continuous functional τ, if $\varphi(\tau^i[\Omega])$ holds for $i \geqq 0$, then $\varphi(\text{lub}\,\{\tau^i[\Omega]\})$ holds. The following lemma indicates one class of admissible predicates which will be used in all our examples. (In Problem 5-11 the reader is asked to prove the admissibility of a much wider class of predicates.)

LEMMA (The admissible predicates lemma). *Every predicate which is of the form* $\wedge_{i=1}^{n} (\alpha_i[F] \sqsubseteq \beta_i[F])$, *that is, a finite conjunction of inequalities* $\sqsubseteq$, *where* α_i *and* β_i *are continuous functionals, is admissible.*

Proof. Suppose $\varphi(F)$ is of the form $\alpha[F] \sqsubseteq \beta[F]$. We assume that $\alpha[\tau^i[\Omega]] \sqsubseteq \beta[\tau^i[\Omega]]$ holds for all $i \geq 0$. Since $\tau^i[\Omega] \sqsubseteq \text{lub}\{\tau^i[\Omega]\}$, it follows by the monotonicity of β that $\beta[\tau^i[\Omega]] \sqsubseteq \beta[\text{lub}\{\tau^i[\Omega]\}]$ and therefore that $\alpha[\tau^i[\Omega]] \sqsubseteq \beta[\text{lub}\{\tau^i[\Omega]\}]$ for all $i \geq 0$. Thus $\beta[\text{lub}\{\tau^i[\Omega]\}]$ is an upper bound of $\{\alpha[\tau^i[\Omega]]\}$, and therefore $\text{lub}\{\alpha[\tau^i[\Omega]]\} \sqsubseteq \beta[\text{lub}\{\tau^i[\Omega]\}]$. Since α is continuous, $\alpha[\text{lub}\{\tau^i[\Omega]\}] \equiv \text{lub}\{\alpha[\tau^i[\Omega]]\}$. Thus,

$$\alpha[\text{lub}\{\tau^i[\Omega]\}] \sqsubseteq \beta[\text{lub}\{\tau^i[\Omega]\}];$$

that is, $\varphi(\text{lub}\{\tau^i[\Omega]\})$ holds. (The extension of the proof for the case where φ is a finite conjunction of inequalities is straightforward.)

Q.E.D.

Note that the predicate $\alpha[F] \equiv \beta[F]$, where α and β are continuous functionals, is an admissible predicate by the lemma because it can be expressed as $(\alpha[F] \sqsubseteq \beta[F]) \wedge (\beta[F] \sqsubseteq \alpha[F])$.

From the definition of admissible predicates we obtain immediately the following important result.

THEOREM 5-5 (Stepwise computational induction, de Bakker and Scott). *For a recursive program* $P: F(\bar{x}) \Leftarrow \tau[F](\bar{x})$ *and an admissible predicate* $\varphi(F)$, *if* $\varphi(\Omega)$ *and* $\forall f[\varphi(f) \supset \varphi(\tau[f])]$ *hold, then* $\varphi(f_P)$ *holds.*

Note that the quantification $\forall f$ is $\forall f \in [(D^+)^n \to D^+]$, where D is the domain of P.

EXAMPLE 5-22

Consider the recursive program over D

$$P: \quad F(x) \Leftarrow \textit{if } p(x) \textit{ then } x \textit{ else } F(F(h(x)))$$

For our purpose there is no need to specify the domain D of the program or the meaning of p and h. However, as in all our examples, we shall assume that p and h are naturally extended; that is, $p(\omega)$ and $h(\omega)$ are ω. We wish to show that

$$f_P f_P \equiv f_P$$

that is†

$$\forall x[f_P(f_P(x)) \equiv f_P(x)]$$

† Note that $\forall x$ stands for *for all* $x \in D^+$ (and not just $x \in D$). This is the way all the universal quantifiers should be interpreted in the rest of this chapter.

Using computational induction, we prove that $\varphi(f_P)$ holds, where†

$$\varphi(F): \quad \forall x[f_P(F(x)) \equiv F(x)]$$

Note that $f_P(\omega)$ is ω because

$f_P(\omega) \equiv \textit{if } p(\omega) \textit{ then } \omega \textit{ else } f_P(f_P(h(\omega)))$	Since f_P is a fixpoint
$\equiv \textit{if } \omega \textit{ then } \omega \textit{ else } f_P(f_P(\omega))$	Since $p(\omega)$ is ω and $h(\omega)$ in ω
$\equiv \omega$	Definition of ($\textit{if } \omega \textit{ then } a \textit{ else } b$)

Step 1. $\varphi(\Omega)$: Prove $\forall x[f_P(\Omega(x)) \equiv \Omega(x)]$. For any x,

$$f_P(\Omega(x)) \equiv f_P(\omega) \equiv \omega \equiv \Omega(x)$$

Step 2. $\forall f[\varphi(f) \supset \varphi(\tau[f])]$: Assume $\forall x[f_P(f(x)) \equiv f(x)]$ and prove $\forall x[f_P(\tau[f](x)) \equiv \tau[f](x)]$. For any x,

$f_P(\tau[f](x))$

$\equiv f_P(\textit{if } p(x) \textit{ then } x \textit{ else } f(f(h(x))))$	Definition of τ
$\equiv \textit{if } p(x) \textit{ then } f_P(x) \textit{ else } f_P(f(f(h(x))))$	Distributing f_P over conditional ($f_P(\omega) \equiv \omega$)
$\equiv \textit{if } p(x) \textit{ then } (\textit{if } p(x) \textit{ then } x \textit{ else } f_P(f_P(h(x))))$ $\textit{else } f_P(f(f(h(x))))$	Definition of f_P
$\equiv \textit{if } p(x) \textit{ then } x \textit{ else } f_P(f(f(h(x))))$	Simplification
$\equiv \textit{if } p(x) \textit{ then } x \textit{ else } f(f(h(x)))$	Induction hypothesis
$\equiv \tau[f](x)$	Definition of τ

□

EXAMPLE 5-23

Consider the recursive program

$$P: \quad F(x, y) \Leftarrow \textit{if } p(x) \textit{ then } y \textit{ else } h(F(k(x), y))$$

We would like to prove that

$$\forall x \forall y[h(f_P(x, y)) \equiv f_P(x, h(y))]$$

For this purpose we let

$$\varphi(F) \quad \text{be} \quad \forall x \forall y[h(F(x, y)) \equiv F(x, h(y))]$$

Note that since $h(F(x, y))$ and $F(x, h(y))$ are continuous functionals, $\varphi(F)$ is an admissible predicate. We proceed in two steps.

† Note that it is essential to use this form of φ, not $\varphi'(F): \forall x[F(F(x)) \equiv F(x)]$, since the proof does not work for φ'.

Step 1. $\varphi(\Omega)$: Prove $\forall x \forall y[h(\Omega(x, y)) \equiv \Omega(x, h(y))]$. Clearly it holds because $h(\omega)$ is ω.

Step 2. $\forall f[\varphi(f) \supset \varphi(\tau[f])]$: Assume $\forall x \forall y[h(f(x, y)) \equiv f(x, h(y))]$ and prove $\forall x \forall y[h(\tau[f](x, y)) \equiv \tau[f](x, h(y))]$.

$$\begin{aligned} h(\tau[f](x, y)) &\equiv h(\mathit{if}\ p(x)\ \mathit{then}\ y\ \mathit{else}\ h(f(k(x), y))) \\ &\equiv \mathit{if}\ p(x)\ \mathit{then}\ h(y)\ \mathit{else}\ h(h(f(k(x), y))) && \text{since } h(\omega) \equiv \omega \\ &\equiv \mathit{if}\ p(x)\ \mathit{then}\ h(y)\ \mathit{else}\ h(f(k(x), h(y))) && \text{Induction hypothesis} \\ &\equiv \tau[f](x, h(y)) \end{aligned}$$

□

The next example uses as domain the set Σ^* of all words over a given finite alphabet Σ, including the empty word Λ. There are three basic functions (see Chap. 1, Sec. 1-2):

- *head*(x) gives the head of the nonempty word x (that is, the first letter of x)
- *tail*(x) gives the tail of the nonempty word x (that is, x with its first letter removed)
- $\sigma \cdot x$ concatenates the letter σ to the word x

EXAMPLE 5-24

The recursive program over Σ^*

$$P: \quad F(x, y) \Leftarrow \mathit{if}\ x = \Lambda\ \mathit{then}\ y\ \mathit{else}\ \mathit{head}(x) \cdot F(\mathit{tail}(x), y)$$

defines the *append* function $f_P(x, y)$, denoted by $x*y$. For example $AB*CD$ is $ABCD$. We would like to show that *append* is associative, that is, that

$$\forall x \forall y \forall z[(x*y)*z \equiv x*(y*z)]$$

For this purpose we prove $\varphi(f_P)$, where

$$\varphi(F): \quad \forall x \forall y \forall z[F(x, y)*z \equiv F(x, y*z)]$$

Note that both $F(x, y)*z$ and $F(x, y*z)$ are continuous functionals because they are expressed as a composition of the function variable F and the monotonic function $*$; therefore, $\varphi(F)$ is an admissible predicate.

In our proof we shall use the fact that $\omega*z \equiv \omega$ for all z because

$$\begin{aligned} \omega*z &\equiv \mathit{if}\ \omega = \Lambda\ \mathit{then}\ z\ \mathit{else}\ \mathit{head}(\omega) \cdot (\mathit{tail}(\omega)*z) \\ &\equiv \mathit{if}\ \omega\ \mathit{then}\ z\ \mathit{else}\ \mathit{head}(\omega) \cdot (\mathit{tail}(\omega)*z) \\ &\equiv \omega \end{aligned}$$

Step 1. $\varphi(\Omega)$: Prove $\forall x \forall y \forall z[\Omega(x, y)*z \equiv \Omega(x, y*z)]$.

$$\Omega(x, y)*z \equiv \omega*z \equiv \omega \equiv \Omega(x, y*z)$$

Step 2. $\forall f[\varphi(f) \supset \varphi(\tau[f])]$: Assume $\forall x \forall y \forall z[f(x, y)*z \equiv f(x, y*z)]$ and prove $\forall x \forall y \forall z[\tau[f](x, y)*z \equiv \tau[f](x, y*z)]$.

$\tau[f](x, y)*z$

$\equiv (\mathit{if}\ x = \Lambda\ \mathit{then}\ y\ \mathit{else}\ \mathit{head}(x) \cdot f(\mathit{tail}(x), y))*z$	Definition of τ
$\equiv \mathit{if}\ x = \Lambda\ \mathit{then}\ y*z\ \mathit{else}(\mathit{head}(x) \cdot f(\mathit{tail}(x), y))*z$	Distribution of $*z$ over conditional ($\omega*z$ is ω)
$\equiv \mathit{if}\ x = \Lambda\ \mathit{then}\ y*z\ \mathit{else}\ \mathit{head}(x) \cdot (f(\mathit{tail}(x), y)*z)$	Definition of $*$
$\equiv \mathit{if}\ x = \Lambda\ \mathit{then}\ y*z\ \mathit{else}\ \mathit{head}(x) \cdot f(\mathit{tail}(x), y*z)$	Induction hypothesis
$\equiv \tau[f](x, y*z)$	Definition of τ

□

The examples introduced so far demonstrate that computational induction is convenient and natural for proving many kinds of properties of recursive programs; however, certain difficulties are involved in proving termination and total correctness. To show that $g \sqsubseteq f_P$ for some fixed function g (which is not Ω), we cannot simply choose $\varphi(F)$ to be $g \sqsubseteq F$ because then $\varphi(\Omega)$ will always be *false*.

It is straightforward to extend the rules for proving some relation between two recursive programs. Suppose we are given the two recursive programs

$$P_1:\quad F_1(\bar{x}) \Leftarrow \tau_1[F_1](\bar{x})$$

and

$$P_2:\quad F_2(\bar{x}) \Leftarrow \tau_2[F_2](\bar{x})$$

Let $\varphi(F_1, F_2)$ be an admissible predicate, for example, a finite conjunction of inequalities $\alpha_i[F_1, F_2] \sqsubseteq \beta_i[F_1, F_2]$, where α_i and β_i are continuous functionals. To prove $\varphi(f_{P_1}, f_{P_2})$, we use the following rule.

If $\varphi(\Omega, \Omega)$ *and* $\forall f_1 \forall f_2[\varphi(f_1, f_2) \supset \varphi(\tau_1[f_1], \tau_2[f_2])]$ *hold then* $\varphi(f_{P_1}, f_{P_2})$ *holds.*

EXAMPLE 5-25

Consider the recursive programs over the natural numbers

$$P_1:\quad F_1(x, y, z) \Leftarrow \mathit{if}\ x = 0\ \mathit{then}\ y\ \mathit{else}\ F_1(x - 1, y + z, z)$$

and

$$P_2: \quad F_2(x, y) \Leftarrow \textit{if } x = 0 \textit{ then } y \textit{ else } F_2(x-1, y+2x-1)$$

We want to show that

$$\forall x[f_{P_1}(x, 0, x) \equiv f_{P_2}(x, 0)]$$

Both functions are actually identical to x^2, but we shall not show this.

We shall use computational induction on

$$\varphi(F_1, F_2): \quad \forall x \forall y[F_1(y, x(x-y), x) \equiv F_2(y, x^2 - y^2)]$$

to prove $\varphi(f_{P_1}, f_{P_2})$, which, for $y = x$, simplifies to $\forall x[f_{P_1}(x, 0, x) \equiv f_{P_2}(x,0)]$.

Step 1. $\varphi(\Omega, \Omega)$: Prove $\forall x \forall y[\Omega(y, x(x-y), x) \equiv \Omega(y, x^2 - y^2)]$. Clearly it holds because $\omega \equiv \omega$.

Step 2. $\forall f_1 \forall f_2[\varphi(f_1, f_2) \supset \varphi(\tau_1[f_1], \tau_2[f_2])]$:

Assume $\forall x \forall y[f_1(y, x(x-y), x) \equiv f_2(y, x^2 - y^2)]$

and show $\forall x \forall y[\tau_1[f_1](y, x(x-y), x) \equiv \tau_2[f_2](y, x^2 - y^2)]$:

$\tau_1[f_1](y, x(x-y), x)$

$\equiv \textit{if } y = 0 \textit{ then } x(x-y) \textit{ else } f_1(y-1, x(x-y)+x, x)$

$\equiv \textit{if } y = 0 \textit{ then } x^2 \textit{ else } f_1(y-1, x(x-(y-1)), x)$

$\equiv \textit{if } y = 0 \textit{ then } x^2 \textit{ else } f_2(y-1, x^2-(y-1)^2)$ Induction hypothesis

$\equiv \textit{if } y = 0 \textit{ then } x^2 - y^2 \textit{ else } f_2(y-1, (x^2-y^2)+2y-1)$

$\equiv \tau_2[f_2](y, x^2 - y^2)$.

□

The computational induction method can be generalized and be applied to any recursive program consisting of a system of recursive definitions of the form

$$F_1(\bar{x}) \Leftarrow \tau_1[F_1, F_2, \ldots, F_m](\bar{x})$$
$$F_2(\bar{x}) \Leftarrow \tau_2[F_1, F_2, \ldots, F_m](\bar{x})$$
$$\cdots\cdots\cdots\cdots\cdots\cdots$$
$$F_m(\bar{x}) \Leftarrow \tau_m[F_1, F_2, \ldots, F_m](\bar{x})$$

For example, to prove $\varphi(f_{\tau_1}, f_{\tau_2}, \ldots, f_{\tau_m})$, where $\varphi(F_1, F_2, \ldots, F_m)$ is an admissible predicate, we can use the following *stepwise computational induction rule:*

If $\varphi(\Omega, \Omega, \ldots, \Omega)$ *and* $\forall f_1 \forall f_2 \ldots \forall f_m[\varphi(f_1, f_2, \ldots, f_m) \supset \varphi(\tau_1[\bar{f}], \tau_2[\bar{f}], \ldots, \tau_m[\bar{f}])$ *hold, then* $\varphi(f_{\tau_1}, f_{\tau_2}, \ldots, f_{\tau_m})$ *holds.*

EXAMPLE 5-26

Consider the recursive program

$$F_1(x) \Leftarrow \textit{if } p(x) \textit{ then } F_1(F_2(h(x))) \textit{ else } F_2(g(x))$$

$$F_2(x) \Leftarrow \textit{if } q(x) \textit{ then } k(F_2(F_1(x))) \textit{ else } k(h(x))$$

$$F_3(x) \Leftarrow \textit{if } p(x) \textit{ then } F_3(k(F_4(h(x)))) \textit{ else } k(F_4(g(x)))$$

$$F_4(x) \Leftarrow \textit{if } q(x) \textit{ then } k(F_4(F_3(x))) \textit{ else } h(x)$$

We want to prove that $\forall x[f_{\tau_1}(x) \equiv f_{\tau_3}(x)]$. We let

$$\varphi(F_1, F_2, F_3, F_4) \quad \text{be} \quad \forall x\{[F_1(x) \equiv F_3(x)] \wedge [F_2(x) \equiv k(F_4(x))]\}$$

and show that $\varphi(f_{\tau_1}, f_{\tau_2}, f_{\tau_3}, f_{\tau_4})$ holds, as follows.

Step 1. $\varphi(\Omega, \Omega, \Omega, \Omega)$: Prove that $\forall x\{[\Omega(x) \equiv \Omega(x)] \wedge [\Omega(x) \equiv k(\Omega(x))]\}$. Clearly it holds because $k(\omega) \equiv \omega$.

Step 2. $\forall f_1 \forall f_2 \forall f_3 \forall f_4[\varphi(f_1, f_2, f_3, f_4) \supset \varphi(\tau_1[\bar{f}], \tau_2[\bar{f}], \tau_3[\bar{f}], \tau_4[\bar{f}])]$: Assume $\forall x\{[f_1(x) \equiv f_3(x)] \wedge [f_2(x) \equiv k(f_4(x))]\}$ and prove

$$\forall x\{[\tau_1[\bar{f}](x) \equiv \tau_3[\bar{f}](x)] \wedge [\tau_2[\bar{f}](x) \equiv k(\tau_4[\bar{f}](x))]\}.$$

$\tau_1[\bar{f}](x)$

$\equiv \textit{if } p(x) \textit{ then } f_1(f_2(h(x))) \textit{ else } f_2(g(x))$

$\equiv \textit{if } p(x) \textit{ then } f_3(k(f_4(h(x)))) \textit{ else } k(f_4(g(x)))$ Induction hypothesis

$\equiv \tau_3[\bar{f}](x)$

$\tau_2[\bar{f}](x)$

$\equiv \textit{if } q(x) \textit{ then } k(f_2(f_1(x))) \textit{ else } k(h(x))$

$\equiv k(\textit{if } q(x) \textit{ then } f_2(f_1(x)) \textit{ else } h(x))$

$\equiv k(\textit{if } q(x) \textit{ then } k(f_4(f_3(x))) \textit{ else } h(x))$ Induction hypothesis

$\equiv k(\tau_4[\bar{f}](x))$

□

5-3.2 Complete Computational Induction

We would like to express the stepwise computational induction rule (Theorem 5-5) using the usual mathematical induction over the natural numbers. For this purpose we denote $\tau^i[\Omega]$ by f^i; thus

$$f^0 \equiv \Omega$$

and
$$f^i \equiv \tau[f^{i-1}] \qquad \text{for } i \geq 1$$

We obtain the following theorem.

THEOREM 5-6 (Complete computational induction, Morris).

> *For a recursive program P and an admissible predicate $\varphi(F)$ if $\forall i\{[(\forall j$ such that $j < i)\ \varphi(f^j)] \supset \varphi(f^i)\}$ holds, then $\varphi(f_P)$ holds.*

That is, to prove $\varphi(f_P)$ it is sufficient to prove that for any $i \geq 0$, if $\varphi(f^j)$ holds for all $j < i$, then $\varphi(f^i)$ holds also. Note that the rule indicates implicitly the need to prove $\varphi(\Omega)$ unconditionally because for $i = 0$ there is no j such that $j < i$.

Theoretically, this result is stronger than the result of Theorem 5-5, because Theorem 5-5 requires $\varphi(f) \supset \varphi(\tau[f])$ to hold for all monotonic functions (over the domain of the program) rather than for just all functions of the form $\tau^i[\Omega]$; however, in practice both results have the same power.

The rule can be extended for proving some relation between two programs. For two recursive programs

$$P_1: \quad F_1(\bar{x}) \Leftarrow \tau_1[F_1](\bar{x})$$

and

$$P_2: \quad F_2(\bar{x}) \Leftarrow \tau_2[F_2](\bar{x})$$

and an admissible predicate $\varphi(F_1, F_2)$, we have the following rule:

> *If $\forall i\{[(\forall j$ such that $j < i)\ \varphi(f_1^j, f_2^j)] \supset \varphi(f_1^i, f_2^i)\}$ holds then $\varphi(f_{P_1}, f_{P_2})$ holds.*

EXAMPLE 5-27 (Morris)

Consider the two recursive programs (see Example 5-23)

$$P_1: \quad F_1(x, y) \Leftarrow \textit{if } p(x) \textit{ then } y \textit{ else } h(F_1(k(x), y))$$

$$P_2: \quad F_2(x, y) \Leftarrow \textit{if } p(x) \textit{ then } y \textit{ else } F_2(k(x), h(y))$$

Using the two forms of computational induction, we would like to prove that

$$\forall x \forall y [f_{P_1}(x, y) \equiv f_{P_2}(x, y)]$$

(A) Proof by stepwise computational induction If we restrict ourselves to the computational induction of Theorem 5-5, we must prove a stronger result than the desired one. (This happens very often in proofs by induction because we may use a stronger induction assumption). Thus, we actually show that

$$\forall x \forall y \{[f_{P_1}(x, y) \equiv f_{P_2}(x, y)] \wedge [f_{P_2}(x, h(y)) \equiv h(f_{P_2}(x, y))]\}$$

holds by computational induction on

$$\varphi(F_1, F_2): \quad \forall x \forall y \{[F_1(x, y) \equiv F_2(x, y)] \wedge [F_2(x, h(y)) \equiv h(F_2(x, y))]\}$$

We proceed in two steps.

Step 1. $\varphi(\Omega, \Omega)$: Prove

$$\forall x \forall y \{[\Omega(x, y) \equiv \Omega(x, y)] \wedge [\Omega(x, h(y)) \equiv h(\Omega(x, y))]\}.$$

Clearly it holds because $h(\omega) \equiv \omega$.

Step 2. $\forall f_1 \forall f_2 [\varphi(f_1, f_2) \supset \varphi(\tau_1[f_1], \tau_2[f_2])]$. Assume

$$\forall x \forall y \{[f_1(x, y) \equiv f_2(x, y)] \wedge [f_2(x, h(y)) \equiv h(f_2(x, y))]\}$$

and prove

$$\forall x \forall y \{[\tau_1[f_1](x, y) \equiv \tau_2[f_2](x, y)] \wedge [\tau_2[f_2](x, h(y)) \equiv h(\tau_2[f_2](x, y))]\}.$$

$\tau_1[f_1](x, y)$

$\equiv$ *if* $p(x)$ *then* y *else* $h(f_1(k(x), y))$

$\equiv$ *if* $p(x)$ *then* y *else* $h(f_2(k(x), y))$ Induction hypothesis

$\equiv$ *if* $p(x)$ *then* y *else* $f_2(k(x), h(y))$ Induction hypothesis

$\equiv \tau_2[f_2](x, y)$

$\tau_2[f_2](x, h(y))$

$\equiv$ *if* $p(x)$ *then* $h(y)$ *else* $f_2(k(x), h(h(y)))$

$\equiv$ *if* $p(x)$ *then* $h(y)$ *else* $h(f_2(k(x), h(y)))$ Induction hypothesis

$\equiv h($*if* $p(x)$ *then* y *else* $f_2(k(x), h(y)))$

$\equiv h(\tau_2[f_2](x, y))$

(B) Proof by complete computational induction Using complete computational induction we can prove the desired result directly;

that is, we prove that

$$\forall x \forall y[f_{P_1}(x, y) \equiv f_{P_2}(x, y)]$$

holds by complete computational induction on

$$\varphi(F_1, F_2): \quad \forall x \forall y[F_1(x, y) \equiv F_2(x, y)]$$

This is done by showing first that $\varphi(f_1^0, f_2^0)$ and $\varphi(f_1^1, f_2^1)$ hold and then that $\varphi\ (f_1^i, f_2^i)$ holds for all $i \geq 2$. [We treat the cases for $i = 0$ and $i = 1$ separately because to prove $\varphi(f_1^i, f_2^i)$ we use the induction hypotheses for both $i - 1$ and $i - 2$.]

Step 1. $\varphi(f_1^0, f_2^0)$: Prove $\forall x \forall y[f_1^0(x, y) \equiv f_2^0(x, y)]$. Clearly it holds.
Step 2. $\varphi(f_1^1, f_2^1)$: Prove $\forall x \forall y[f_1^1(x, y) \equiv f_2^1(x, y)]$.

$$\begin{aligned} f_1^1(x, y) &\equiv \textit{if } p(x) \textit{ then } y \textit{ else } h(f_1^0(k(x), y)) \\ &\equiv \textit{if } p(x) \textit{ then } y \textit{ else } \omega \qquad \text{since } h(\omega) \equiv \omega \\ &\equiv \textit{if } p(x) \textit{ then } y \textit{ else } f_2^0(k(x), h(y)) \\ &\equiv f_2^1(x, y) \end{aligned}$$

Step 3. $[(\forall j \textit{ such that } j < i)\, \varphi(f_1^j, f_2^j)] \supset \varphi(f_1^i, f_2^i) \textit{ for all } i \geq 2$:

Assume $\quad \forall x \forall y[f_1^{i-2}(x, y) \equiv f_2^{i-2}(x, y)]$

and $\quad \forall x \forall y[f_1^{i-1}(x, y) \equiv f_2^{i-1}(x, y)]$

and prove $\quad \forall x \forall y[f_1^i(x, y) \equiv f_2^i(x, y)]$:

$$\begin{aligned} f_1^i(x, y) &\equiv \textit{if } p(x) \textit{ then } y \textit{ else } h(f_1^{i-1}(k(x), y)) && \text{Definition of } f_1^i \\ &\equiv \textit{if } p(x) \textit{ then } y \textit{ else } h(f_2^{i-1}(k(x), y)) && \text{Induction hypothesis } (i-1) \\ &\equiv \textit{if } p(x) \textit{ then } y \textit{ else } h(\textit{if } p(k(x)) \textit{ then } y \\ &\qquad\qquad \textit{else } f_2^{i-2}(k(k(x)), h(y))) \\ & && \text{Definition of } f_2^{i-1} \\ &\equiv \textit{if } p(x) \textit{ then } y \textit{ else } h(\textit{if } p(k(x)) \textit{ then } y \\ &\qquad\qquad \textit{else } f_1^{i-2}(k(k(x)), h(y))) \\ & && \text{Induction hypothesis } (i-2) \\ &\equiv \textit{if } p(x) \textit{ then } y \textit{ else } (\textit{if } p(k(x)) \textit{ then } h(y) \\ &\qquad\qquad \textit{else } h(f_1^{i-2}(k(k(x)), h(y)))) \end{aligned}$$

$\equiv$ *if* $p(x)$ *then* y *else* $f_1^{i-1}(k(x), h(y))$ Definition of f_1^{i-1}

$\equiv$ *if* $p(x)$ *then* y *else* $f_2^{i-1}(k(x), h(y))$ Induction hypothesis $(i-1)$

$\equiv f_2^i(x, y)$ Definition of f_2^i

□

Similarly, we can generalize the complete computational induction rule for systems of recursive definitions. To prove $\varphi(f_{\tau_1}, f_{\tau_2}, \ldots, f_{\tau_m})$, where $\varphi(F_1, F_2, \ldots, F_m)$ is an admissible predicate, let

$$\langle f_1^0, f_2^0, \ldots, f_m^0 \rangle = \langle \Omega, \Omega, \ldots, \Omega \rangle$$

$$\langle f_1^{i+1}, f_2^{i+1}, \ldots, f_m^{i+1} \rangle = \langle \tau_1[\bar{f}^i], \tau_2[\bar{f}^i], \ldots, \tau_m[\bar{f}^i] \rangle$$

The complete computational induction rule can be stated as follows:

If $\forall i \{[(\forall j$ *such that* $j < i)\, \varphi(f_1^j, f_2^j, \ldots, f_m^j)] \supset \varphi(f_1^i, f_2^i, \ldots, f_m^i)\}$ *holds, then* $\varphi(f_{\tau_1}, f_{\tau_2}, \ldots, f_{\tau_m})$ *holds.*

5-3.3 Fixpoint Induction

The following result is very useful for proving properties of recursive programs.

THEOREM 5-7 (Fixpoint invariant transformations, Vuillemin).

Given two recursive programs $P: F(\bar{x}) \Leftarrow \tau[F](\bar{x})$ *and* $P': F(\bar{x}) \Leftarrow \tau'[F](\bar{x})$, *where* $\tau'[F]$ *is obtained from* $\tau[F]$ *by replacing some occurrences of* F *by either* f_τ *or* $\tau[F]$. *Then* $\forall \bar{x}[f_P(\bar{x}) \equiv f_{P'}(\bar{x})]$.

Proof. Let us write $\tau[F]$ as $\tau[F, F]$ where we use the second argument in $\tau[F, F]$ to distinguish the occurrences of F in τ which we wish to replace. We define

$$\tau_1[F] = \tau[F, \tau[F, F]]$$

and

$$\tau_2[F] = \tau[F, f_\tau]$$

Our goal is to prove that $f_\tau \equiv f_{\tau_1} \equiv f_{\tau_2}$, and we shall show this in two steps.

Step 1. $f_{\tau_1} \sqsubseteq f_\tau$ *and* $f_{\tau_2} \sqsubseteq f_\tau$: This part is easy because by definition of τ_1 and τ_2, $f_\tau \equiv \tau_1[f_\tau] \equiv \tau_2[f_\tau]$; that is, f_τ is a fixpoint of both τ_1 and τ_2, and therefore it is more defined than both f_{τ_1} and f_{τ_2}.

Step 2. $f_\tau \sqsubseteq f_{\tau_1}$ *and* $f_\tau \sqsubseteq f_{\tau_2}$: This is proved by stepwise computational induction using

$$\varphi(F, F_1, F_2): \quad (F \sqsubseteq F_1) \wedge (F \sqsubseteq F_2) \wedge (F \sqsubseteq f_\tau) \wedge (F \sqsubseteq \tau[F, F])$$

Clearly $\varphi(\Omega, \Omega, \Omega)$ holds. Let us assume that $\varphi(f, f_1, f_2)$ holds and show that $\varphi(\tau[f], \tau_1[f_1], \tau_2[f_2])$ must hold

Since $f \sqsubseteq \tau[f, f]$, by the monotonicity of τ with respect to the second argument, we have $\tau[f, f] \sqsubseteq \tau[f, \tau[f, f]]$. Since by the induction hypothesis $f \sqsubseteq f_1$, it follows by the monotonicity of τ that $\tau[f, \tau[f, f]] \sqsubseteq \tau[f_1, \tau[f_1, f_1]]$; that is,

$$\tau[f] \equiv \tau[f, f] \sqsubseteq \tau[f, \tau[f, f]] \sqsubseteq \tau[f_1, \tau[f_1, f_1]] \equiv \tau_1[f_1]$$

and thus $\tau[f] \sqsubseteq \tau_1[f_1]$. Similarly, since $f \sqsubseteq f_\tau$ and $f \sqsubseteq f_2$, we obtain

$$\tau[f] \equiv \tau[f, f] \sqsubseteq \tau[f, f_\tau] \sqsubseteq \tau[f_2, f_\tau] \equiv \tau_2[f_2]$$

and thus $\tau[f] \sqsubseteq \tau_2[f_2]$. Since $f \sqsubseteq f_\tau$, we obtain

$$\tau[f] \equiv \tau[f, f] \sqsubseteq \tau[f_\tau, f_\tau] \equiv f_\tau$$

and thus $\tau[f] \sqsubseteq f_\tau$. Finally, since $f \sqsubseteq \tau[f, f]$, we obtain

$$\tau[f, f] \sqsubseteq \tau[\tau[f, f], \tau[f, f]].$$

Q.E.D.

EXAMPLE 5-28

Consider the two recursive programs over the natural numbers

$$P_1: \quad F(x) \Leftarrow \textit{if } x > 10 \textit{ then } x - 10 \textit{ else } F(F(x + 13))$$

and $$P_2: \quad F(x) \Leftarrow \textit{if } x > 10 \textit{ then } x - 10 \textit{ else } F(x + 3)$$

We want to prove that

$$f_{P_1}(x) \equiv f_{P_2}(x) \qquad \text{for all} \quad x \in N$$

If we replace $F(x + 13)$ in P_1 by $\tau[F](x + 13)$, we obtain

$$P_1': \quad F(x) \Leftarrow \textit{if } x > 10 \textit{ then } x - 10 \textit{ else } F(\textit{if } x + 13 > 10$$
$$\textit{then } x + 13 - 10 \textit{ else } F(F(x + 13 + 13)))$$

By Theorem 5-7, $(\forall x \in N)[f_{P_1}(x) \equiv f_{P_1'}(x)]$. Since $x \geq 0$, we always have $x + 13 > 10$; therefore $F(\textit{if } x + 13 > 10 \textit{ then } x + 13 - 10 \textit{ else } F(F(x+13+13))$ can be simplified to $F(x + 3)$. Thus $(\forall x \in N)[f_{P_1'}(x) \equiv f_{P_2}(x)]$, and $(\forall x \in N)[f_{P_1}(x) \equiv f_{P_2}(x)]$ as desired.

□

EXAMPLE 5-29

Consider the recursive program

$$F_1(x) \Leftarrow if\ p(x)\ then\ F_3(F_2(F_2(f(x))))\ else\ g(x)$$

$$F_2(x) \Leftarrow if\ q(x)\ then\ F_3(h(x))\ else\ k(x)$$

$$F_3(x) \Leftarrow if\ p(x)\ then\ F_1(F_4(f(x)))\ else\ g(x)$$

$$F_4(x) \Leftarrow if\ q(x)\ then\ F_2(F_3(h(x)))\ else\ F_2(k(x))$$

We wish to prove that

$$\forall x[f_{\tau_1}(x) \equiv f_{\tau_3}(x)]$$

For this purpose first we change the definitions of F_1 and F_4 to

$$F_1(x) \Leftarrow if\ p(x)\ then\ F_3(f_{\tau_2}(F_2(f(x))))\ else\ g(x)$$

and $$F_4(x) \Leftarrow if\ q(x)\ then\ f_{\tau_2}(F_3(h(x)))\ else\ f_{\tau_2}(k(x))$$

respectively. By Theorem 5-7, the least fixpoints of the functionals have not been affected at all by this transformation. We are ready now to prove by computational induction that

$$\forall x\{[f_{\tau_1}(x) \equiv f_{\tau_3}(x)] \wedge [f_{\tau_2}(f_{\tau_2}(x)) \equiv f_{\tau_4}(x)]\}$$

using $$\varphi(F_1, F_2, F_3, F_4):\quad (F_1 \equiv F_3) \wedge (f_{\tau_2}F_2 \equiv F_4)$$

Step 1. $\varphi(\Omega, \Omega, \Omega, \Omega)$: Prove $\forall x\{[\Omega(x) \equiv \Omega(x)] \wedge [f_{\tau_2}(\Omega(x)) \equiv \Omega(x)]\}$. Clearly it holds because $f_{\tau_2}(\omega) \equiv \omega$.

Step 2. $\forall \bar{f}[\varphi(f_1, f_2, f_3, f_4) \supset \varphi(\tau_1'[\bar{f}], \tau_2[\bar{f}], \tau_3[\bar{f}], \tau_4'[\bar{f}])]$:†

Assume $\forall x\{[f_1(x) \equiv f_3(x)] \wedge [f_{\tau_2}(f_2(x)) \equiv f_4(x)]\}$

and prove $\forall x\{[\tau_1'[\bar{f}](x) \equiv \tau_3[\bar{f}](x)] \wedge [f_{\tau_2}(\tau_2[\bar{f}](x)) \equiv \tau_4'[\bar{f}](x)]\}$.

$$\begin{aligned}\tau_1'[\bar{f}](x) &\equiv if\ p(x)\ then\ f_3(f_{\tau_2}(f_2(f(x))))\ else\ g(x)\\ &\equiv if\ p(x)\ then\ f_1(f_4(f(x)))\ else\ g(x) \qquad \text{Induction hypothesis}\\ &\equiv \tau_3[\bar{f}](x)\end{aligned}$$

$$\begin{aligned}f_{\tau_2}(\tau_2[\bar{f}](x)) &\equiv f_{\tau_2}(if\ q(x)\ then\ f_3(h(x))\ else\ k(x))\\ &\equiv if\ q(x)\ then\ f_{\tau_2}(f_3(h(x)))\ else\ f_{\tau_2}(k(x))\\ &\equiv \tau_4'[\bar{f}](x)\end{aligned}$$

(The reader should be aware of the difficulties involved in proving directly that $\forall x[f_{\tau_1}(x) \equiv f_{\tau_3}(x)]$ without the previous transformations.)

□

† Here, $\forall \bar{f}$ stands for $\forall f_1 \forall f_2 \forall f_3 \forall f_4$, and $\tau_i[\bar{f}]$ stands for $\tau_i[f_1, f_2, f_3, f_4]$.

Another very useful result that can be proved using the computational induction rule is the fixpoint induction theorem:

THEOREM 5-8 (Fixpoint induction, Park). *Consider the recursive program $P: F(\bar{x}) \Leftarrow \tau[F](\bar{x})$ over D. Then $\tau[g] \sqsubseteq g$ implies $f_P \sqsubseteq g$ for every $g \in [(D^+)^n \to D^+]$.*

Proof. We use stepwise computational induction with

$$\varphi(F): \quad F \sqsubseteq g$$

First clearly $\varphi(\Omega)$ holds, and so we must prove that $\forall f\,[\varphi(f) \supset \varphi(\tau[f])]$. We assume $f \sqsubseteq g$ and show $\tau[f] \sqsubseteq g$. If $f \sqsubseteq g$, then because τ is monotonic, we obtain $\tau[f] \sqsubseteq \tau[g]$; and because it is given that $\tau[g] \sqsubseteq g$, we have $\tau[f] \sqsubseteq g$.

Q.E.D.

EXAMPLE 5-30

Let us consider the recursive program over the integers

$$P: \quad F(x) \Leftarrow \textit{if } x > 100 \textit{ then } x - 10 \textit{ else } F(F(x+11))$$

We would like to prove that

$$f_P(x) \sqsubseteq g(x) \qquad \text{for every integer } x$$

where

$$g(x): \quad \textit{if } x > 100 \textit{ then } x - 10 \textit{ else } 91.$$

By the fixpoint induction rule it is sufficient to show that $\tau[g] \sqsubseteq g$; that is,

$\textit{if } x > 100 \textit{ then } x - 10 \textit{ else}$

$$\begin{aligned}&[\textit{if } [\textit{if } x + 11 > 100 \textit{ then } x + 11 - 10 \textit{ else } 91] > 100\\ &\textit{then } [\textit{if } x + 11 > 100 \textit{ then } x + 11 - 10 \textit{ else } 91] - 10\\ &\textit{else } 91]\end{aligned}$$

$\sqsubseteq \textit{if } x > 100 \textit{ then } x - 10 \textit{ else } 91$

The proof is straightforward by case analysis: $x > 100$, $89 < x \leq 100$, and $x \leq 89$.

□

We shall now introduce another method, the *recursion induction method*, which actually was the first method proposed for proving properties of recursive programs.

THEOREM 5-9 (Recursion induction, McCarthy). *Given two functions $f_1, f_2 \in [(D_1^+)^n \to D_2^+]$ and subset $S \subseteq (D_1^+)^n$. To prove $f_1(\bar{x}) \equiv f_2(\bar{x})$ for all $\bar{x} \in S$, find a continuous functional τ so that* (1) $f_1 \equiv \tau[f_1]$, (2) $f_2 \equiv \tau[f_2]$, *and* (3) $f_\tau(\bar{x}) \not\equiv \omega$ *for all* $\bar{x} \in S$.

That is, we must show that both f_1 and f_2 are fixpoints of τ and that $f_\tau(x)$ is "defined" for all $\bar{x} \in S$.

Proof. Since f_τ is the least fixpoint of τ while f_1 and f_2 are fixpoints of τ, we know that $f_\tau(\bar{x}) \sqsubseteq f_1(\bar{x})$ and $f_\tau(\bar{x}) \sqsubseteq f_2(\bar{x})$ for any $\bar{x}$ in $(D_1^+)^n$. Therefore, since $f_\tau(\bar{x}) \not\equiv \omega$ for all $\bar{x}$ in S, we have

$$f_\tau(\bar{x}) \equiv f_1(\bar{x}) \equiv f_2(\bar{x}) \qquad \text{for all } \bar{x} \text{ in } S$$

Q.E.D.

Note that we can actually prove a stronger result: It is sufficient to find a monotonic τ satisfying the conditions (1) $f_1 \sqsupseteq \tau[f_1]$, (2) $f_2 \sqsupseteq \tau[f_2]$, and (3) $f_\tau(\bar{x}) \not\equiv \omega$ for all $\bar{x} \in S$. A major drawback of the recursion induction method is in condition (3): To prove the equivalence of two functions, an argument of termination is needed. This implies that recursion induction cannot be used to prove the equivalence of recursive programs for which the domain, predicates, and functions are not specified.

EXAMPLE 5-31

The function *reverse*(x) over Σ^* is defined as $f_P(x, \Lambda)$ where

$$P: \quad F(x, y) \Leftarrow \textit{if } x = \Lambda \textit{ then } y \textit{ else } F(\textit{tail}(x), \textit{head}(x) \cdot y)$$

We wish to prove by recursion induction that

$$\textit{reverse}(x*y) \equiv \textit{reverse}(y)*\textit{reverse}(x) \qquad \text{for all} \quad x, y \in \Sigma^*$$

where $*$ is the *append* function, that is, the least fixpoint of the recursive program

$$G(x, y) \Leftarrow \textit{if } x = \Lambda \textit{ then } y \textit{ else } \textit{head}(x) \cdot G(\textit{tail}(x), y)$$

For this purpose we choose the functional τ defined by

$$\tau[F](x, y): \quad \textit{if } x = \Lambda \textit{ then } \textit{reverse}(y) \textit{ else } F(\textit{tail}(x), y) * \textit{head}(x)$$

Then, using the known property of $*$ and *reverse* that $\textit{reverse}(\sigma \cdot w) \equiv \textit{reverse}(w)*\sigma$ for all $\sigma \in \Sigma$ and $w \in \Sigma^*$, we obtain the following.

Step 1. $reverse(x*y)$ is a fixpoint of τ because

$$\begin{aligned}
reverse(x*y) &\equiv reverse\big(\text{if } x = \Lambda \text{ then } y \text{ else } head(x)\cdot(tail(x)*y)\big)\\
&\equiv \text{if } x = \Lambda \text{ then } reverse(y) \text{ else } reverse\big(head(x)\cdot(tail(x)*y)\big)\\
&\equiv \text{if } x = \Lambda \text{ then } reverse(y) \text{ else } reverse\big(tail(x)*y\big)*head(x)
\end{aligned}$$

Step 2. $reverse(y) * reverse(x)$ is a fixpoint of τ because

$$\begin{aligned}
&reverse(y) * reverse(x)\\
&\quad\equiv \text{if } x = \Lambda \text{ then } reverse(y)*\Lambda \text{ else } reverse(y)*reverse(x)\\
&\quad\equiv \text{if } x = \Lambda \text{ then } reverse(y)\\
&\qquad\qquad \text{else } reverse(y)*\big(reverse(tail(x))*head(x)\big)\\
&\quad\equiv \text{if } x = \Lambda \text{ then } reverse(y)\\
&\qquad\qquad \text{else } \big(reverse(y)*reverse(tail(x))\big)*head(x)
\end{aligned}$$

by associativity of $*$.

Step 3. $f_\tau(x, y) \not\equiv \omega$ for every $x, y \in \Sigma^*$, as can be shown by a straightforward induction on x.

□

5-3.4 Structural Induction

The complete induction method for proving assertions on the domain N of natural numbers can be stated as follows: In order to prove that the statement $\psi(n)$ is *true* for every natural number n, we show that for any natural number i, the truth of $\psi(j)$ for all $j < i$ implies the truth of $\psi(i)$. That is, *if* $(\forall i \in N)\{[(\forall j \in N \text{ such that } j < i)\,\psi(j)] \supset \psi(i)\}$ *holds, then* $(\forall n \in N)\,\psi(n)$ *holds.* However, this induction rule is not necessarily valid for every ordered domain; for example, it is valid for the natural numbers with ordering $<$ but fails for the integers with the ordering $<$ [consider ψ, which is always *false*!].

In this section first we shall characterize the ordered domains on which such an induction is valid. Then we shall present a general rule, called *structural induction*, for proving assertions over these domains; complete induction, as well as stepwise induction, over natural numbers are just special cases of structural induction. Finally, we shall give several examples using structural induction to prove properties of recursive programs.

Every partially ordered set $(S, \prec)$ which is well-founded; that is, contains no infinite decreasing sequence $a_0 \succ a_1 \succ a_2 \succ \ldots$ of elements of S (see Chap. 3, Sec. 3-1.2), is suitable for our purpose. Therefore we shall state and prove the rule of structural induction on well-founded sets.

THEOREM 5-10 (Structural induction, Burstall). *Let $(S, \prec)$ be a well-founded set, and let φ be a total predicate over S: if $(\forall a \in S)\{[(\forall b \in S$ such that $b \prec a)\, \varphi(b)] \supset \varphi(a)\}$, then $(\forall c \in S)\, \varphi(c)$.*

That is, if for any a in S, we can prove that the truth of $\varphi(a)$ is implied by the truth of $\varphi(b)$ for all $b \prec a$, then $\varphi(c)$ is *true* for every c in S.†

Proof. To prove the validity of this rule, we shall show that if the assumption is satisfied, there can be no element in S for which φ is *false*. Consider the set A

$$A = \{a \mid a \in S \text{ and } \varphi(a) \text{ is } \textit{false}\}$$

Let us assume that A is nonempty. Then there is a least element a_0 in A such that $a \not\prec a_0$ for any $a \in A$; otherwise there would be an infinite descending sequence in S. Then, for any element b in S such that $b \prec a_0$, $\varphi(b)$ is *true*; that is, $(\forall b \in S$ such that $b \prec a_0)\, \varphi(b)$ holds. But the assumption then implies that $\varphi(a_0)$ is *true*, which contradicts the fact that $a_0 \in A$. Therefore A must be empty; that is, $\varphi(c)$ is *true* for all elements c in S.

Q.E.D.

Note that if there is no b in S such that $b \prec a$, the statement $(\forall b \in S$ such that $b \prec a)\, \varphi(b)$ holds vacuously. Therefore for such a's we must show $\varphi(a)$ unconditionally to establish the hypothesis needed for the structural induction.

We shall now give several examples using structural induction to prove properties of recursive programs. In many cases it is useful to use the *lexicographic ordering property* of well-founded sets (see Chap. 3, Sec 3-2.2). That is, if $(S, \prec)$ is a well-founded set, then so is $(S^n, \underset{n}{\prec})$, where S^n is the set of all n-tuples of elements of S, and $\underset{n}{\prec}$ is the lexicographic ordering defined as follows

$$\langle a_1, \ldots, a_n \rangle \underset{n}{\prec} \langle b_1, \ldots, b_n \rangle \textit{ iff}$$

$$a_1 = b_1, \ldots, a_{i-1} = b_{i-1} \quad \text{and} \quad a_i \prec b_i \qquad \text{for some} \quad i, 1 \le i \le n$$

In all the examples we use only the fixpoint property of f_P; that is, that $\tau[f_P] \equiv f_P$. Therefore, the results actually hold for all the fixpoints of τ and not only for the least fixpoint f_P.

† This is actually a version of the known *Noetherian induction*. See, for example, Cohn, P. M., *Universal Algebra*, Harper and Row, New York (1965).

EXAMPLE 5-32

Consider the recursive program over the natural numbers

$$P: \quad F(x, y) \Leftarrow \textit{if } x = 0 \textit{ then } y + 1$$
$$\textit{else if } y = 0 \textit{ then } F(x - 1, 1)$$
$$\textit{else } F(x - 1, F(x, y - 1))$$

$f_P(x, y)$ is known as *Ackermann's function* (see Chap. 3, Example 3-9). We wish to show that $f_P(x, y)$ is defined, that is, that $f_P(x, y) \not\equiv \omega$, for any $x, y \in N$. We shall use the structural induction rule applied on $(N^2, \underset{2}{\lneq})$, where $\underset{2}{\lneq}$ is the lexicographic ordering on pairs of natural numbers.

Assuming that $f_P(x', y')$ is defined for any $\langle x', y' \rangle$ such that $\langle x', y' \rangle \underset{2}{\lneq} \langle x, y \rangle$, we shall show that $f_P(x, y)$ must be defined also.

Step 1. If $x = 0$, obviously $f_P(x, y)$ is defined.
Step 2. If $x \neq 0$ and $y = 0$, we note that $\langle x - 1, 1 \rangle \underset{2}{\lneq} \langle x, y \rangle$, and so by the induction hypothesis, $f_P(x - 1, 1)$ is defined; thus $f_P(x, y)$ is defined also.
Step 3. Finally, if $x \neq 0$ and $y \neq 0$, $\langle x, y - 1 \rangle \underset{2}{\lneq} \langle x, y \rangle$ and $f_P(x, y - 1)$ is therefore defined by the induction hypothesis. Now, regardless of the value of $f_P(x, y - 1)$, we have $\langle x - 1, f_P(x, y - 1) \rangle \underset{2}{\lneq} \langle x, y \rangle$, and the desired result follows by another application of the induction hypothesis.

□

In the following example we shall use structural induction on the natural numbers N with the usual ordering $<$; that is, we shall use the regular complete induction on N.

EXAMPLE 5-33 (Cadiou)

Consider the two recursive programs over the natural numbers

$$P_1: \quad F_1(x) \Leftarrow \textit{if } x = 0 \textit{ then } 1 \textit{ else } x \cdot F_1(x - 1)$$

and P_2: $\quad F_2(x, y) \Leftarrow \textit{if } x = y \textit{ then } 1 \textit{ else } F_2(x, y + 1) \cdot (y + 1)$

$f_{P_1}(x)$ and $f_{P_2}(x, 0)$ compute $x! = 1 \cdot 2 \cdot \ldots \cdot x$ for every $x \in N$ in two different ways: $f_{P_1}(x)$ by "going down" from x to 0, and $f_{P_2}(x, 0)$ by "going up" from 0 to x. We wish to show that

$$f_{P_2}(x, 0) \equiv f_{P_1}(x) \qquad \text{for all} \quad x \in N$$

The proof uses the predicate

$$\varphi(x): \quad (\forall y \in N)\,[f_{P_2}(x + y, y) \cdot f_{P_1}(y) \equiv f_{P_1}(x + y)]$$

and the usual ordering on natural numbers.

Step 1. If $x = 0$, $\varphi(0)$ is $(\forall y \in N)\,[f_{P_2}(y, y) \cdot f_{P_1}(y) \equiv f_{P_1}(y)]$, which is clearly *true* by definition of f_{P_2}.

Step 2. If $x > 0$, we assume $\varphi(x')$ for all $x' < x$ and show $\varphi(x)$. For any $y \in N$,

$f_{P_2}(x + y, y) \cdot f_{P_1}(y)$	
$\equiv f_{P_2}(x + y, y + 1) \cdot (y + 1) \cdot f_{P_1}(y)$	Definition of f_{P_2} (since $x + y > y$)
$\equiv f_{P_2}(x + y, y + 1) \cdot f_{P_1}(y + 1)$	Definition of f_{P_1} (since $y + 1 > 0$)
$\equiv f_{P_2}((x - 1) + (y + 1), y + 1) \cdot f_{P_1}(y + 1)$	since $x > 0$
$\equiv f_{P_1}((x - 1) + (y + 1))$	Induction hypothesis (since $x - 1 < x$)
$\equiv f_{P_1}(x + y)$	

By complete induction we then obtain that $\varphi(x)$ holds for all $x \in N$. In particular, for $y = 0$, $f_{P_2}(x + 0, 0) \cdot f_{P_1}(0) \equiv f_{P_1}(x + 0)$. Since $f_{P_1}(0) \equiv 1$, we have $f_{P_2}(x, 0) \equiv f_{P_1}(x)$ for all $x \in N$, as desired.

□

In Examples 5-32 and 5-33 we used the most natural ordering on the domain to perform structural induction. In Example 5-34 it is convenient to use somewhat surprising ordering.

EXAMPLE 5-34 (Burstall)
The 91 function is defined as the least fixpoint f_P of the following recursive program over the integers I:

$$P:\quad F(x) \Leftarrow \textit{if } x > 100 \textit{ then } x - 10 \textit{ else } F(F(x + 11))$$

We wish to show that

$$f_P(x) \equiv g(x) \qquad \text{for every integer } x$$

where

$$g(x) \quad \text{is} \quad \textit{if } x > 100 \textit{ then } x - 10 \textit{ else } 91.$$

The proof is by structural induction on the well-founded set $(I, \prec)$, where $\prec$ is defined as follows:

$$x \prec y \quad \text{iff} \quad y < x \leq 101$$

(here $<$ is the usual ordering on the integers); thus $101 \prec 100 \prec 99 \prec \ldots$, but, for example, $102 \nprec 101$. We can easily check that $(I, \prec)$ is a well-founded set.

Suppose $f_P(y) \equiv g(y)$ for all $y \in I$ such that $y \prec x$. We must show that $f_P(x) \equiv g(x)$.

Step 1. If $x > 100$, $f_P(x) \equiv x - 10 \equiv g(x)$ directly.

Step 2. If $100 \geq x \geq 90$, $f_P(x) \equiv f_P(f_P(x + 11)) \equiv f_P(x + 1)$ by definition of f_P; and since $x + 1 \prec x$, we have $f_P(x) \equiv f_P(x + 1) \equiv g(x + 1)$ by the induction assumption. But since $x + 1 \leq 101$, $g(x + 1) \equiv 91 \equiv g(x)$ by definition of g; therefore $f_P(x) \equiv g(x)$.

Step 3. Finally, if $x < 90$, $f_P(x) \equiv f_P(f_P(x + 11))$ by definition of f_P; and since $x + 11 \prec x$, we have $f_P(x) \equiv f_P(f_P(x + 11)) \equiv f_P(g(x + 11))$ by induction. But since $x + 11 \leq 100$, $g(x + 11) \equiv 91$ by definition of g and we have $f_P(x) \equiv f_P(91)$. By induction we know that $f_P(91) = g(91)$, and by the definition of g we know that $g(91) \equiv 91 \equiv g(x)$. Thus $f_P(x) \equiv f_P(91) \equiv g(91) \equiv 91 \equiv g(x)$, as desired.

We could prove the previous property alternatively by structural induction on the natural numbers with the usual ordering $<$, using the more complicated predicate

$$\varphi(n): \quad (\forall x \in I)\,[x > 100 - n \supset f_P(x) \equiv g(x)]$$

The details of this proof and those of the previous one are precisely the same.

□

Since the set $(\Sigma^*, \prec)$ of finite strings over Σ with the substring relation $\prec$ is well-founded, we may use it for structural induction. In the following example we shall use an induction rule that can easily be derived from structural induction, namely: *If* $\varphi(\Lambda)$ and $(\forall x \in \Sigma^*)[x \neq \Lambda \wedge \varphi(tail(x)) \supset \varphi(x)]$, *then* $(\forall x \in \Sigma^*)\, \varphi(x)$.

EXAMPLE 5-35 (NESS)

Let us consider again the *reverse*(x) function which is $f_P(x, \Lambda)$ where

$$P: \quad F(x, y) \Leftarrow \textit{if } x = \Lambda \textit{ then } y \textit{ else } F(\textit{tail}(x), \textit{head}(x) \cdot y)$$

We wish to prove that *reverse*(x) is defined, that is, *reverse*$(x) \not\equiv \omega$, and *reverse*$($*reverse*$(x)) \equiv x$ for all $x \in \Sigma^*$. Of course, proving that *reverse*(x) has this property does not show that it actually reverses all words: Many other functions, for example, the identity function, also satisfy this property.

Step 1. To prove that *reverse*(x) is always defined, we let

$$\varphi(x) \text{ be } (\forall y \in \Sigma^*)\left[f_P(x, y) \text{ is defined}\right].$$

(*a*) *If* $x = \Lambda$, then $f_P(x, y) \equiv y$, and thus $f_P(x, y)$ is defined for all $y \in \Sigma^*$.

(*b*) *If* $x \neq \Lambda$, since $tail(x) \prec x$, we may assume that $f_P(tail(x), z)$ is defined for any $z \in \Sigma^*$; therefore, $f_P(tail(x), head(x) \cdot y)$ is defined for all $y \in \Sigma^*$. Thus $f_P(x, y)$ is defined for all $y \in \Sigma^*$.

By structural induction it follows that $f_P(x, y)$ is defined for all $x, y \in \Sigma^*$; in particular, since $reverse(x) \equiv f_P(x, \Lambda)$, *reverse*$(x)$ is defined for all $x \in \Sigma^*$.

Step 2. To prove $(\forall x \in \Sigma^*)\left[reverse(reverse(x)) \equiv x\right]$ we let

$$\varphi(x) \text{ be } (\forall y \in \Sigma^*)\left[reverse(f_P(x, y)) \equiv f_P(y, x)\right].$$

(*a*) *If* $x = \Lambda$, then for any $y \in \Sigma^*$ we have

$$reverse(f_P(\Lambda, y)) \equiv reverse(y) \equiv f_P(y, \Lambda)$$

(*b*) *If* $x \neq \Lambda$, then for any $y \in \Sigma^*$ we have

$$reverse(f_P(x, y))$$

$$\begin{aligned}
&\equiv reverse(f_P(tail(x), head(x) \cdot y)) && \text{Definition of } f_P \text{ (since } x \neq \Lambda) \\
&\equiv f_P(head(x) \cdot y, tail(x)) && \text{Induction hypothesis (since } tail(x) \prec x) \\
&\equiv f_P(y, head(x) \cdot tail(x)) && \text{Definition of } f_P \text{ (since } head(x) \cdot y \neq \Lambda) \\
&\equiv f_P(y, x)
\end{aligned}$$

Therefore, $reverse(f_P(x, y)) \equiv f_P(y, x)$ for all $x, y \in \Sigma^*$; in particular, for $y = \Lambda$, $reverse(f_P(x, \Lambda)) \equiv f_P(\Lambda, x)$. Thus,

$$reverse(reverse(x)) \equiv reverse(f_P(x, \Lambda)) \equiv f_P(\Lambda, x) \equiv x$$

for all $x \in \Sigma^*$, as desired.

□

Other properties of *reverse* may easily be proved by structural induction. In particular, Example 5-36 uses the properties that for any $a, b \in \Sigma$ and $w \in \Sigma^*$

1. $reverse(w * a) \equiv a \cdot reverse(w)$
2. $reverse(a \cdot w) \equiv reverse(w) * a$
3. $reverse(a \cdot (w * b)) \equiv b \cdot (reverse(w) * a)$

where $*$ is the *append* function (defined in Example 5-24.)

EXAMPLE 5-36 (Ashcroft)
Let us consider the recursive program over Σ^*

$$P: \quad F(x) \Leftarrow \textit{if } x = \Lambda$$
$$\textit{then } \Lambda$$
$$\textit{else if } tail(x) = \Lambda$$
$$\textit{then } x$$
$$\textit{else } head(F(tail(x))) \cdot F(head(x) \cdot F(tail(F(tail(x)))))$$

We wish to show that the least fixpoint f_P also defines a reversing function on Σ^*, that is, that

$$f_P(x) \equiv reverse(x) \qquad \text{for all } x \in \Sigma^*$$

Note that this definition does not use any auxiliary functions.

The intuitive idea behind the program is very simple: The expression

$$\alpha: \quad reverse(tail(reverse(tail(x))))$$

is the word x without its first and last letters; therefore

$$\beta: \quad head(x) \cdot \alpha$$

is the word x without its last letter. This last letter is

$$\gamma: \quad head(reverse(tail(x)))$$

Thus, if $x \neq \Lambda$ and $tail(x) \neq \Lambda$, we have $reverse(x) \equiv \gamma \cdot reverse(\beta)$.

In the proof we shall use the following lemma, which characterizes the elements of Σ^*: *For any* $x \in \Sigma^*$, *either* $x = \Lambda$, *or* $x \in \Sigma$ [*that is,* $x \neq \Lambda$ *and* $tail(x) = \Lambda$], *or* $x = a \cdot (w * b)$ *for some* $a, b \in \Sigma$ *and* $w \in \Sigma^*$. (The lemma is easy to prove by a straightforward structural induction.) We shall prove that $(\forall x \in \Sigma^*)[f_P(x) \equiv reverse(x)]$ by structural induction on $(\Sigma^*, \prec)$ where $\prec$ is the following partial ordering: †

$$x \prec y \quad \text{if and only if} \quad |x| < |y|.$$

$(\Sigma^*, \prec)$ is clearly a well-founded set.

Using the lemma previously given, the proof may be performed in three steps:

Step 1. If $x = \Lambda$, $f_P(x) \equiv \Lambda \equiv reverse(x)$.
Step 2. If $x \in \Sigma$, $f_P(x) \equiv x \equiv reverse(x)$.

† Recall that for a string $w \in \Sigma^*$, $|w|$ indicates the *length* of w, that is, the number of letters in w. In particular, $|\Lambda| = 0$.

Step 3. If $x = a \cdot (w{*}b)$ for some $a, b \in \Sigma$, $w \in \Sigma^*$:

$f_P(x)$

$\equiv head(f_P(tail(x))) \cdot f_P(head(x) \cdot f_P(tail(f_P(tail(x)))))$	Definition of f_P
$\equiv head(f_P(w{*}b)) \cdot f_P(a \cdot f_P(tail(f_P(w{*}b))))$	Since *head*(x) is a and *tail*(x) is $w{*}b$
$\equiv head(reverse(w{*}b)) \cdot f_P(a \cdot f_P(tail(reverse(w{*}b))))$	Induction hypothesis (since $w{*}b \prec x$)
$\equiv head(b \cdot reverse(w)) \cdot f_P(a \cdot f_P(tail(b \cdot reverse(w))))$	Property 1 of *reverse*
$\equiv b \cdot f_P(a \cdot f_P(reverse(w)))$	Properties of *head* and *tail*
$\equiv b \cdot f_P(a \cdot reverse(reverse(w)))$	Induction hypothesis [since $reverse(w) \prec x$]
$\equiv b \cdot f_P(a \cdot w)$	Property of *reverse* proven in Example 5-35
$\equiv b \cdot reverse(a \cdot w)$	Induction hypothesis (since $a \cdot w \prec x$)
$\equiv b \cdot (reverse(w){*}a)$	Property 2 of *reverse*
$\equiv reverse(x)$	Property 3 of *reverse*

We conclude that $f_P(x) \equiv reverse(x)$ for all $x \in \Sigma^*$, as desired.

□

Bibliographic Remarks

The discussion in Sec. 5-1 is based on the expository paper by Manna, Ness, and Vuillemin (1973). This topic is also discussed in the works by Kleene (1952), Scott (1970), and deBakker (1971) and in several unpublished works by Scott. Theorem 5-2 is due to Kleene (1952), and the extension of its result for monotonic functionals was suggested by Hitchcock and Park (1972).

The notion of recursive programs was introduced by McCarthy (1963a). Fixpoint computation rules were investigated in the Ph.D. dissertations of Morris (1968) (who showed that "call by value" is not a fixpoint computation rule), Cadiou (1972) (Theorem 5-3), and Vuillemin (1973) (Theorem 5-4). The relation of this topic to the semantics of programming languages is discussed in the works of Landin (1964), Strachey (1964), Scott and

Strachey (1971), Weyhrauch and Milner (1972), and Manna and Vuillemin (1972).

Most of the examples presented in Sec. 5-3 are from Manna, Ness, and Vuillemin (1973). The stepwise computational induction rule (Theorem 5-5) is essentially the *μ rule* suggested by deBakker and Scott (1969); and the complete computational induction rule (Theorem 5-6) is the *truncation induction rule* originated by Morris (1971). A machine implementation of proofs by computational induction is described by Milner (1972).

The fixpoint invariant transformations (Theorem 5-7) were suggested by Vuillemin (1973), and the fixpoint induction method (Theorem 5-8) was suggested by Park (1969). McCarthy's (1963b) recursion induction (Theorem 5-9) was the first method proposed for proving properties of recursive programs. It was Burstall (1969) who first suggested the structural induction method explicitly (Theorem 5-10), although it was often used previously [for example, by McCarthy and Painter (1967) for proving the correctness of a compiler and by Floyd (1967) for proving the termination of flowchart programs (see Chap. 3)]. A machine implementation of proofs by structural induction is described by Boyer and Moore (1973). Greif (1972), Milner (1972), and Vuillemin (1973) have discussed and compared the "power" of the different induction methods.

REFERENCES

Boyer, R. S. and J. S. Moore (1973): "Proving Theorems about Lisp Programs," in *Proceedings of the Third International Joint Conference on Artificial Intelligence,* Stanford, Cal., pp. 486–493 (August).

Burstall, R. M. (1969): "Proving Properties of Programs by Structural Induction," *Comput. J.,* **12** (1): 41–48 (February).

Cadiou, J. M. (1972): "Recursive Definitions of partial Functions and Their Computations," Ph.D. thesis, Computer Science Deparment, Stanford University, Stanford, Calif. (March).

DeBakker, J. W. (1971): *Recursive Procedures*, Mathematical Center, Amsterdam, Holland.

——— and D. Scott (1969): "A Theory of Programs," IBM Seminar, Vienna, Austria (August), unpublished notes.

Floyd, R. W. (1967): "Assigning Meanings to Programs," in J. T. Schwartz (ed.), *Proceedings of a Symposium in Applied Mathematics,* vol. 19, *Mathematical Aspects of Computer Science,* pp. 19–32, American Mathematical Society, New York.

Greif, I. G. (1972): "Induction in Proofs about Programs," M.Sc. thesis, M.I.T., Cambridge, Mass.

Hitchcock, P. and D. Park (1972): "Induction Rules and Proofs of Termination," *IRIA Conf. Autom. Lang. & Program. Theory,* France (July).

Kleene, S. C. (1952): *Introduction to Meta-mathematics,* D. Van Nostrand, Inc, Princeton, N.J.

Knaster, B. (1928): "Un théorème sur les functions d'ensembles," *Ann. Soc. Pol. Math.,* **6**: 133–134.

Landin, J. P. (1964): "The Mechanical Evaluation of Expressions," *Comput. J.* **6**(4): 308–320 (January).

Manna, Z., S. Ness, and J. Vuillemin (1973): "Inductive Methods for Proving Properties of Programs," C. ACM, **16** (8): 491–502 (August).

——— and J. Vuillemin (1972): "Fixpoint Approach to the Theory of Computation," *C.ACM,* **15**(7): 528–536 (July).

McCarthy, J. (1963a): "A basis for a mathematical theory of computation," in P. Braffort and D. Hirschberg (eds.), *Computer Programming and Formal Systems,* pp. 33–70. North-Holland Publishing Company, Amsterdam.

——— (1963b): "Towards a Mathematical Science of Computation," in C. M. Popplewell (ed.), *Information Processing: Proceedings of IFIP 1962,* pp. 21–28, North Holland Publishing Company, Amsterdam.

——— and J. A. Painter (1967): "Correctness of a Compiler for Arithmetic Expressions," in J. T. Schwartz (ed.), *Proceedings of a Symposium in Applied Mathematics,* vol. 19, *Mathematical Aspects of Computer Science,* pp. 33–41, American Mathematical Society, New York.

Milner, R. (1972): "Implementation and Applications of Scott's Logic for Computable Functions," in *Proc. ACM Conf. Proving Assertions about Programs,* Las Cruces, New Mexico (January).

Morris, J. H. (1968): "Lambda-Calculus Models of Programming Languages," Ph.D. thesis, Project MAC, MAC-TR-57, M.I.T., Cambridge, Mass. (December).

——— (1971): "Another Recursion Induction Principle," *C.ACM,* **14**(5): 351–354 (May).

Park, D. (1969): "Fixpoint Induction and Proofs of Program Properties," in B. Meltzer and D. Michie (eds.), *Machine Intelligence,* Vol. 5, pp. 59–78, Edinburgh University Press, Edinburgh.

Scott, D. (1970): "Outline of a Mathematical Theory of Computation," *4th Annu. Princeton Conf. Inform. Sciences & Syst.,* pp. 169–176.

——— and C. Strachey (1971): "Towards a Mathematical Semantics for Computer Languages," *Tech. Mono.* PRC-6, Oxford University, Oxford, Eng. (August).

Strachey, C. (1964): "Towards a Formal Semantics," in T. B. Steel (ed.), *Formal Description Languages for Computer Programming,* pp. 198–200, North-Holland Publishing Company, Amsterdam *(Proc. IFIP Working Conf. 1964)*.

Tarski, A. (1955): "A Lattice-Theoretical Fixpoint Theorem and its Applications," *Pacific J. Math.,* **5**: 285–309.

Vuillemin, J. (1973): "Proof Techniques for Recursive Programs," Ph.D. thesis, Computer Science Department, Stanford University, Stanford, Calif.

Weyhrauch, R., and R. Milner (1972): "Program Semantics and Correctness in a Mechanized Logic," paper presented at U.S.A.–Japan Computer Conference, Tokyo, Japan (October).

PROBLEMS

Prob. 5-1 (Monotonic functions). Show that the following functions are monotonic:

(*a*) Sequential *if-then-else* (see Example 5-3)

(*b*) Parallel *if-then-else*, which is defined like the sequential *if-then-else* but with one exception: (*if* ω *then d else d*) $\equiv d$ for all $d \in D^+$

(*c*) Parallel multiplication over the integers, where

$$(0 * \omega) \equiv (\omega * 0) \equiv 0$$

$$(a * \omega) \equiv (\omega * a) \equiv \omega \qquad \text{for any nonzero integer } a$$

$$(\omega * \omega) \equiv \omega$$

(*d*) Symmetric *or* and *and* predicates, where

$$(\mathit{true}\ \mathit{or}\ \omega) \equiv (\omega\ \mathit{or}\ \mathit{true}) \equiv \mathit{true} \qquad (\mathit{true}\ \mathit{and}\ \omega) \equiv (\omega\ \mathit{and}\ \mathit{true}) \equiv \omega$$

$$(\mathit{false}\ \mathit{or}\ \omega) \equiv (\omega\ \mathit{or}\ \mathit{false}) \equiv \omega \qquad (\mathit{false}\ \mathit{and}\ \omega) \equiv (\omega\ \mathit{and}\ \mathit{false}) \equiv \mathit{false}$$

$$(\omega\ \mathit{or}\ \omega) \equiv \omega \qquad (\omega\ \mathit{and}\ \omega) \equiv \omega$$

Prob. 5-2 (functionals).

(*a*) Are the following functionals over $[I^+ \to I^+]$ monotonic? continous?

(i) *if* (F is total) *then* ω *else* 0

(ii) *if* (F is total) *then* 0 *else* ω

(iii) *if* (F is total) *then* 0 *else* 0

where F *is total* means $F(x) \not\equiv \omega$ for every $x \in I^+$.

(*b*) Consider the functional $\tau[F](x)$: $F(F(x))$. Let

$$f(x): \quad \mathit{if}\ x \equiv \omega\ \mathit{then}\ 0\ \mathit{else}\ \omega$$

$$g(x): \quad \mathit{if}\ x \equiv \omega\ \mathit{then}\ 0\ \mathit{else}\ 1$$

Clearly $f \sqsubseteq g$. But

$$\tau[f](1) \equiv f(f(1)) \equiv f(\omega) \equiv 0$$
$$\tau[g](1) \equiv g(g(1)) \equiv g(1) \equiv 1$$

and thus $\tau[f] \not\sqsubseteq \tau[g]$. In other words, although τ is defined by composition of the function variable F, it is not monotonic (and therefore not continuous) in contrast with Theorem 5-1. What is wrong?

(*c*) Prove that every functional τ defined by composition of monotonic functions and the function variable F is monotonic with respect to any occurrence of F.

Prob. 5-3 (Least fixpoints).

(*a*) Find the least fixpoints of the following functionals over $[I^+ \to I^+]$. Prove your results.

(i) *If* $x = 0$ *then* 0 *else* $[1 + F(x - 1, F(y - 2, x))]$
(ii) *if* $x = 0$ *then* 1 *else* $F(x - 1, F(x - y, y))$

(*b*) Do the following two functionals have the same least fixpoint?

(i) *if* $x = 0$ *then* y *else if* $x > 0$ *then* $F_1(x - 1, y + 1)$
else $F_1(x + 1, y - 1)$
(ii) *if* $x = 0$ *then* y *else if* $x > 0$ *then* $F_2(x - 2, y + 2)$
else $F_2(x + 2, y - 2)$

Prob. 5-4 (Relation between the computation rules). Consider the following program over the integers

$$P: \quad F(x, y) \Leftarrow \textit{if } x = 0 \textit{ then } 1 \textit{ else } F(x - 1, F(x - y, y))$$

(*a*) Compute $F(2, 1)$ and $F(3, 2)$ using the six different computation rules introduced in Sec. 5-2.1.

(*b*) Find the computed function for each one of the six computation rules.

Prob. 5-5 (Safe computation rules, Vuillemin (1972))

(*a*) Describe a fixpoint computation rule which is not safe.

(*b*) Prove that the parallel-outermost, free-argument, and full-substitution rules are safe.

Prob. 5-6 Prove that the following functions are the least fixpoints of the corresponding recursive programs over the natural numbers:

(*a*) (i) $P: F(x, y) \Leftarrow$ *if* $xy = 0$ *then* $x + y$ *else* $F(x - 1, F(x, y - 1))$
$f_P(x, y)$: *if* $xy = 0$ *then* $x + y$ *else* 1

(ii) $P: F(x, y) \Leftarrow \textit{if}\ xy = 0\ \textit{then}\ x + y + 1\ \textit{else}\ F(F(x-1, 1), y-1)$
$f_P(x, y): x + y + 1$

(iii) $P: F(x, y) \Leftarrow \textit{if}\ xy = 0\ \textit{then}\ x + y + 1\ \textit{else}\ F(x-1, F(x, y-1))$
$f_P(0, y) \equiv 1 + y,\quad f_P(1, y) \equiv 2 + y,\quad f_P(2, y) \equiv 2y + 3,$
$f_P(3, y) \equiv 7 \cdot 2^y - 3.$

(*b*) (i) $P: \quad F(x, y) \Leftarrow \textit{if}\ x = 0\ \textit{then}\ y$
$\qquad \textit{else if}\ y = 0\ \textit{then}\ F(x-1, 1)$
$\qquad \textit{else}\ F(x-1, F(x, y-1))$

$f_P(x, y): \quad \textit{if}\ x = 0\ \textit{then}\ y\ \textit{else}\ 1$

(ii) $P: \quad F(x, y) \Leftarrow \textit{if}\ x = 0\ \textit{then}\ y + 1$
$\qquad \textit{else if}\ y = 0\ \textit{then}\ F(x-1, 1)$
$\qquad \textit{else}\ F(x-1, F(x, y-1))$

$$f_P(0, y) \equiv y + 1, \qquad f_P(1, y) \equiv y + 2, \qquad f_P(2, y) \equiv 2y + 3$$

$$f_P(3, y) \equiv 2^{y+3} - 3$$

Prob. 5-7

(*a*) Given the following program P over the integers

$$P: \quad F(x) \Leftarrow \textit{if}\ x > a\ \textit{then}\ x - b\ \textit{else}\ F(F(x + b + c))$$

where a, b, and c are integers ($b, c > 0$), show that†

$$f_P(x) \quad \text{is} \quad \textit{if}\ x > a\ \textit{then}\ x - b\ \textit{else}\ [a - b + c - \textit{rem}(a - x, c)]$$

(*b*) Given the recursive program P over the natural numbers

$$P: \quad F(x) \Leftarrow \textit{if}\ x > 10\ \textit{then}\ x - 10\ \textit{else}\ F(F(x + 13))$$

show that

$$f_P(x) \quad \text{is} \quad \textit{if}\ x > 10\ \textit{then}\ x - 10\ \textit{else}\ [\textit{rem}(x + 1, 3) + 1]$$

(*c*) Given the recursive program P over the integers

$$P: \quad F(x) \Leftarrow \textit{if}\ x < 0\ \textit{then}\ x + 1\ \textit{else}\ F(F(x - 2))$$

show that

$$f_P(x) \quad \text{is} \quad \textit{if}\ x < 0\ \textit{then}\ x + 1\ \textit{else}\ 0$$

Prob. 5-8 Consider the following class of recursive programs P_k over the integers:

$$\textit{if}\ x > 100\ \textit{then}\ x - 10\ \textit{else}\ \underbrace{F(F(\ \ldots\ (F}_{k\ \text{times}}(x + 10(k-1) + 1))\ \ldots\ ))$$

† Note that the meaning of $\textit{rem}(a - x, c)$ over the integers is $a - x = c \cdot \textit{div}(a - x, c) + \textit{rem}(a - x, c)$, where $0 \le \textit{rem}(a - x, c) < c$.

where $k \geq 2$. Prove that the least fixpoint of each program in this class is the *91 function*: *if* $x > 100$ *then* $x - 10$ *else* 91.

Prob. 5-9

(*a*) Given the recursive programs P_1 and P_2 over the natural numbers

$$P_1: \quad F_1(x) \Leftarrow \textit{if } x=0 \vee x=1 \textit{ then } 1 \textit{ else } [F_1(x-1)+F_1(x-2)]$$

$$P_2: \quad F_2(x) \Leftarrow \textit{if } x=0 \vee x=1 \textit{ then } 1 \textit{ else } 2F_2(x-2)$$

show that if $x_1 \geq x_2$, then $f_{P_1}(x_1) \geq f_{P_2}(x_2) \geq 1$.

(*b*) Given the recursive program P over the natural numbers

$$\begin{aligned} P: \quad F(x, y) \Leftarrow\ & \textit{if } x = 0 \textit{ then } y + 1 \\ & \textit{else if } y = 0 \textit{ then } F(x-1, 1) \\ & \textit{else } F(x-1, F(x, y-1)) \end{aligned}$$

show that if $x_1 > x_2$, then $f_P(x_1, x_1) > f_P(x_2, x_2)$.

(*c*) [Morris (1971).] Given the recursive program P over the integers

$$\begin{aligned} P: \quad F(x) \Leftarrow\ & \textit{if } x \leq 1 \textit{ then } 1 \\ & \textit{else if } even(x) \textit{ then } x/2 \\ & \textit{else } F(F(3 \cdot div(x, 2) + 2)) \end{aligned}$$

show that for every $x > 1$, if $f_P(x)$ is defined, then $f_P(x) \leq x/2$.

Prob. 5-10 (Manna and Vuillemin (1972)). Consider the two recursive programs over the natural numbers

$$P_1: \quad F_1(x) \Leftarrow \textit{if } x = 0 \textit{ then } 1 \textit{ else } x \cdot F_1(x-1)$$

$$P_2: \quad F_2(x, y, z) \Leftarrow \textit{if } x = y \textit{ then } z \textit{ else } F_2(x, y+1, (y+1)\, z)$$

Note that both $f_{P_1}(x)$ and $f_{P_2}(x, 0, 1)$ computes $x!$. Use the stepwise computational induction to prove that

$$\forall x [f_{P_1}(x) \equiv f_{P_2}(x, 0, 1)]$$

Hint: Consider the predicate $x \geq y$ over the natural numbers to be characterized by the least fixpoint $ge(x, y)$ of the recursive program $G(x, y) \Leftarrow \textit{if } x = y \textit{ then true else } G(x, y+1)$, then by computational induction show that $\forall x \forall y [ge(x, y) \sqsubseteq [f_{P_1}(x) = f_{P_2}(x, y, f_{P_1}(y))]]$.

Prob. 5-11 (Admissible predicates). In Sec. 5-3.1 we showed (the *admissible predicates lemma*) that any predicate $\varphi(F)$ which is a finite conjunction of inequalities $\alpha[F] \sqsubseteq \beta[F]$, where α and β are continuous functionals, is admissible. Show that the result holds for a more general class of predicates $\langle AP \rangle$, defined as follows

$$\langle AP \rangle \quad \textit{is} \quad \langle AP \rangle \wedge \langle AP \rangle \quad \textit{or} \quad \forall \bar{x} \langle EP \rangle$$

$$\langle EP \rangle \quad \textit{is} \quad \langle EP \rangle \vee \langle EP \rangle \quad \textit{or} \quad Q(\bar{x}) \quad \textit{or} \quad \alpha[F](\bar{x}) \sqsubseteq \beta[F](\bar{x})$$

where $Q(\bar{x})$ is any total predicate (mapping $(D_1^+)^n$ into $\{true, false\}$) which is free of F's, and α and β are continuous functionals.

Prob. 5-12 Use several different methods (such as computational induction, structural induction, and recursion induction) to prove the following results.

(*a*) Consider the system over the natural numbers in which the primitives are the predicate $zero(x)$ [true only when x is 0], the predecessor function $pred(x)$ [where $pred(0)$ is 0], and the successor function $succ(x)$. In this system we define the addition function $add(x, y)$ to be the least fixpoint of the following recursive program:

$$F(x, y) \Leftarrow \textit{if } zero(x) \textit{ then } y \textit{ else } F(pred(x), succ(y))$$

Prove that

(i) $\forall x, y \in N, succ(add(x, y)) \equiv add(x, succ(y))$
(ii) $\forall x, y \in N, add(add(x, y), z) \equiv add(add(x, z), y)$

(*b*) Consider the set of all words over an alphabet Σ with the primitive operations *head*, *tail*, and $\cdot$ (*concatenate*). The only properties of these functions you may use are

$$head(\sigma \cdot w) \equiv \sigma \qquad tail(\sigma \cdot w) \equiv w \qquad \sigma \cdot w \not\equiv \Lambda$$

$$w \neq \Lambda \supset head(w) \cdot tail(w) \equiv w \quad \text{where} \quad \sigma \in \Sigma \quad \text{and} \quad w \in \Sigma^*$$

The append function $x*y$ for concatenating two words x and y is defined as the least fixpoint of the following recursive program:

$$F(x, y) \Leftarrow \textit{if } x = \Lambda \textit{ then } y \textit{ else } head(x) \cdot F(tail(x), y)$$

The reverse function $reverse(x)$ for reversing the order of letters in a word x is defined as $f_P(x, \Lambda)$ where

$$P\colon \quad G(x, y) \Leftarrow \textit{if } x = \Lambda \textit{ then } y \textit{ else } G(tail(x), head(x) \cdot y)$$

Prove that

(i) $\forall x, y \in \Sigma^*, x*(y*z) \equiv (x*y)*z$ (see Example 5-24).
(ii) $\forall x, y \in \Sigma^*, reverse(x*y) \equiv reverse(y)*reverse(x)$ (see Example 5-31).
(iii) $\forall x \in \Sigma^*, reverse(reverse(x)) \equiv x$ (see Example 5-35).

Prob. 5-13 (The $3x + 1$ problem).

(*a*) Given the following recursive program P over the natural numbers

$$P: \quad F(x) \Leftarrow \textit{if } even(x) \textit{ then } x/2 \textit{ else } F(F(3x+1))$$

prove that f_P is defined for all natural numbers.
Hint: Look at the binary representation of the numbers.

**(*b*) *Open problem.* Given the following recursive program P over the natural numbers

$$\begin{aligned} P: \quad F(x) \Leftarrow \textit{if } x = 1 \textit{ then } 0 \\ \textit{else if } even(x) \textit{ then } F(x/2) \\ \textit{else } F(3x+1) \end{aligned}$$

Is f_P defined for all positive integers?
Warning: This is a "famous" open problem. A computer program has checked that it is defined for all positive integers up to $x = 3*10^8$.

Prob. 5-14 [The fixpoint theorem, Knaster (1928), Tarski (1955), and Park (1969)]. Let M be any subset of functions from $[(D_1^+)^n \to D_2^+]$. A function $f \in [(D_1^+)^n \to D_2^+]$ is said to be *a lower bound of M* if $f \sqsubseteq m$ for every function m in M. If, in addition, every lower bound g of M is such that $g \sqsubseteq f$, then f is called the *greatest lower bound of M*, denoted by glb(M). Note that by definition, the glb of M is unique (if it exists at all). Prove the following results:

(*a*) *The glb lemma:* Every nonempty subset M of $[(D_1^+)^n \to D_2^+]$ has a greatest lower bound.

(*b*) *The fixpoint theorem:* If τ is a monotonic functional over $[(D_1^+)^n \to D_2^+]$ and f_τ exists,† then

$$f_\tau \equiv \text{glb}\,\{f \in [(D_1^+)^n \to D_2^+] \mid \tau[f] \sqsubseteq f\}$$

(*c*) *The fixpoint induction rule:* If τ is a monotonic functional over $[(D_1^+)^n \to D_2^+]$, then

$$\tau[g] \sqsubseteq g \quad \text{implies} \quad f_\tau \sqsubseteq g \qquad \text{for every} \quad g \in [(D_1^+)^n \to D_2^+]$$

Prob. 5-15

(*a*) Consider the recursive schema

$$P: \quad F(x, y) \Leftarrow \textit{if } p(x) \textit{ then } y \textit{ else } F(k(x), h(y))$$

† Note that this is not a real requirement because f_τ exists for every monotonic functional (as indicated in the text).

Show that

$$\forall x \forall y [f_P(x, h(y)) \equiv h(f_P(x, y))]$$

(*b*) Consider the recursive schema

$$F_1(x, y) \Leftarrow \textit{if } p(x) \textit{ then } F_2(y) \textit{ else } F_1(h(x), y)$$
$$F_2(x) \Leftarrow \textit{if } p(x) \textit{ then } x \textit{ else } F_2(h(x))$$

Show that

$$\forall x [f_{\tau_1}(x, x) \equiv f_{\tau_2}(x)]$$

Prob. 5-16

(*a*) Consider the following recursive schema:

$$F_1(x) \Leftarrow \textit{if } q(x) \textit{ then } g(x) \textit{ else } F_3(F_4(f(x)))$$
$$F_2(x) \Leftarrow \textit{if } p(x) \textit{ then } x \textit{ else } F_2(f(x))$$
$$F_3(x) \Leftarrow \textit{if } p(x) \textit{ then } g(x) \textit{ else } F_1(F_2(f(x)))$$
$$F_4(x) \Leftarrow \textit{if } q(x) \textit{ then } x \textit{ else } F_4(f(x))$$

Show that

$$\forall x [f_{\tau_1}(f_{\tau_2}(x)) \equiv f_{\tau_3}(f_{\tau_4}(x))]$$

(*b*) Consider the following recursive schema:

$$F_1(x) \Leftarrow \textit{if } p(x) \textit{ then if } q(x) \textit{ then } F_3(F_2(g(x))) \textit{ else } F_2(F_3(g(x)))$$
$$\textit{else } h(x)$$
$$F_2(x) \Leftarrow \textit{if } q(x) \textit{ then } F_1(f(x)) \textit{ else } k(x)$$
$$F_3(x) \Leftarrow \textit{if } q(x) \textit{ then } F_4(f(x)) \textit{ else } k(x)$$
$$F_4(x) \Leftarrow \textit{if } p(x) \textit{ then } F_5(g(x)) \textit{ else } h(x)$$
$$F_5(x) \Leftarrow \textit{if } q(x) \textit{ then } F_2(F_4(f(x))) \textit{ else } F_3(k(x))$$

Show that

$$\forall x [f_{\tau_1}(x) \equiv f_{\tau_4}(x)]$$

Hint: Note that $\forall x [f_{\tau_5}(x) \equiv f_{\tau_3}(f_{\tau_2}(x)) \equiv f_{\tau_2}(f_{\tau_3}(x))]$ and that $\forall x [f_{\tau_3}(x) \equiv f_{\tau_2}(x)]$.

Quite often we define a recursive program P in terms of a system of recursive definitions, but actually we are interested, not in the m-tuple of least fixpoints $\langle f_{\tau_1}, \ldots, f_{\tau_m} \rangle$, but only in one of them, say, f_{τ_1}; that is, f_P is f_{τ_1}. To indicate such a case we shall write the recursive program P as

$$
\begin{aligned}
P:\quad & F_1(\bar{x}) \textit{ where} \\
& F_1(\bar{x}) \Leftarrow \tau_1[F_1, \ldots, F_m](\bar{x}) \\
& F_2(\bar{x}) \Leftarrow \tau_2[F_1, \ldots, F_m](\bar{x}) \\
& \ldots\ldots\ldots\ldots\ldots\ldots \\
& F_m(\bar{x}) \Leftarrow \tau_m[F_1, \ldots, F_m](\bar{x})
\end{aligned}
$$

This notation will be used in the following problems.

Prob. 5-17 (Morris (1971)). Consider the following two recursive programs over the natural numbers:

$$
\begin{aligned}
P_1:\quad & F(x) \Leftarrow \textit{if } x = 1 \textit{ then } 0 \\
& \qquad\qquad \textit{else if } even(x) \textit{ then } F(x/2) \\
& \qquad\qquad\qquad\qquad \textit{else } F(3x+1)
\end{aligned}
$$

$$
\begin{aligned}
P_2:\quad & F_1(x) \textit{ where} \\
& F_1(x) \Leftarrow \textit{if } x = 1 \textit{ then } 0 \textit{ else } F_1(F_2(x)) \\
& F_2(x) \Leftarrow \textit{if } x = 1 \textit{ then } 1 \\
& \qquad\qquad \textit{else if } even(x) \textit{ then } x/2 \\
& \qquad\qquad\qquad\qquad \textit{else } F_2(F_2((3x+1)/2))
\end{aligned}
$$

Prove that $f_{P_1}(x) \equiv f_{P_2}(x)$ for all $x > 0$.

Prob. 5-18 Consider the following pairs (P_1, P_2) of recursive programs over the natural numbers and prove that for each pair $f_{P_1} \equiv f_{P_2}$:

(a) $P_1:\quad F(x) \Leftarrow \textit{if } x = 0 \textit{ then } 0 \textit{ else } F(h(x))$

$$
\begin{aligned}
P_2:\quad & F_1(x) \textit{ where} \\
& F_1(x) \Leftarrow \textit{if } x = 0 \textit{ then } 0 \textit{ else } F_1(F_2(x)) \\
& F_2(x) \Leftarrow \textit{if } x = 0 \textit{ then } 0 \textit{ else } F_2(F_2(h(x)))
\end{aligned}
$$

(b) $P_1:\quad F(x) \Leftarrow \textit{if } x = 0 \textit{ then } 0$

$$\qquad\qquad \textit{else if } p(x) \textit{ then } F(g(x)) \textit{ else } F(h(x))$$

P_2: $F_1(x)$ *where*

$$F_1(x) \Leftarrow \textit{if } x = 0 \textit{ then } 0 \textit{ else } F_1(F_2(x))$$

$$F_2(x) \Leftarrow \textit{if } x = 0 \textit{ then } 0$$

$$\textit{else if } p(x) \textit{ then } g(x) \textit{ else } F_2(F_2(h(x)))$$

Prob. 5-19 Show that the following pairs of recursive schemas are equivalent; that is, for each pair $f_{P_1} \equiv f_{P_2}$:

(*a*) P_1: $F(x) \Leftarrow \textit{if } p(x) \textit{ then } F(F(f(x))) \textit{ else } x$

P_2: $F(x) \Leftarrow \textit{if } p(x) \textit{ then } F(f(x)) \textit{ else } x$

(*b*) P_1: $F_1(x)$ *where*

$$F_1(x) \Leftarrow \textit{if } p(x) \textit{ then } F_2(F_1(f(x))) \textit{ else } x$$

$$F_2(x) \Leftarrow \textit{if } p(x) \textit{ then } x \textit{ else } F_1(g(x))$$

P_2: $F(x) \Leftarrow \textit{if } p(x) \textit{ then } F(g(F(f(x)))) \textit{ else } x$

(*c*) P_1: $F_1(x)$ *where*

$$F_1(x) \Leftarrow \textit{if } p(x) \textit{ then } F_1(F_2(f(x))) \textit{ else } g(x)$$

$$F_2(x) \Leftarrow \textit{if } p(x) \textit{ then } F_2(h(x)) \textit{ else } x$$

P_2: $F_1(x)$ *where*

$$F_1(x) \Leftarrow \textit{if } p(x) \textit{ then } F_2(f(x)) \textit{ else } g(x)$$

$$F_2(x) \Leftarrow \textit{if } p(x) \textit{ then } F_2(h(x)) \textit{ else } g(x)$$

(*d*) P_1: $F_1(x)$ *where*

$$F_1(x) \Leftarrow \textit{if } p(x) \textit{ then } F_1(F_2(h(x))) \textit{ else } F_3(x)$$

$$F_2(x) \Leftarrow \textit{if } q(x) \textit{ then } f(F_2(F_1(x))) \textit{ else } f(h(x))$$

$$F_3(x) \Leftarrow \textit{if } q(g(x)) \textit{ then } F_3(x) \textit{ else } l(g(g(x)))$$

P_2: $F_1(x)$ *where*

$$F_1(x) \Leftarrow \textit{if } p(x) \textit{ then } F_1(f(F_2(h(x)))) \textit{ else } l(F_3(g(x)))$$

$$F_2(x) \Leftarrow \textit{if } q(x) \textit{ then } f(F_2(F_1(x))) \textit{ else } h(x)$$

$$F_3(x) \Leftarrow \textit{if } q(x) \textit{ then } F_3(x) \textit{ else } g(x)$$

(*e*) P_1: $F_1(x)$ *where*

$$F_1(x) \Leftarrow \textit{if } p(x) \textit{ then } F_2(F_3(f(x))) \textit{ else } F_2(f(F_4(g(x))))$$

$F_2(x) \Leftarrow if\ q(x)\ then\ F_2(f(x))\ else\ h(x)$

$F_3(x) \Leftarrow if\ r(x)\ then\ f(F_4(g(F_5(f(x)))))\ else\ F_5(g(k(x)))$

$F_4(x) \Leftarrow if\ s(x)\ then\ F_4(k(x))\ else\ g(x)$

$F_5(x) \Leftarrow if\ s(x)\ then\ F_5(k(x))\ else\ f(g(x))$

P_2: $F_1(x)$ *where*

$F_1(x) \Leftarrow if\ p(x)\ then\ F_2(g(F_3(f(x))))\ else\ F_2(g(x))$

$F_2(x) \Leftarrow if\ s(x)\ then\ F_2(k(x))\ else\ F_4(f(g(x)))$

$F_3(x) \Leftarrow if\ r(x)\ then\ F_5(f(x))\ else\ k(x)$

$F_4(x) \Leftarrow if\ q(x)\ then\ F_4(f(x))\ else\ h(x)$

$F_5(x) \Leftarrow if\ s(x)\ then\ F_5(k(x))\ else\ f(g(x))$

(*f*) P_1: $F_1(x)$ *where*

$F_1(x) \Leftarrow if\ p(x)\ then\ if\ q(x)\ then\ F_3(F_2(g(x)))\ else\ F_2(F_3(g(x)))$
$else\ h(x)$

$F_2(x) \Leftarrow if\ q(x)\ then\ F_1(f(x))\ else\ k(x)$

$F_3(x) \Leftarrow if\ q(x)\ then\ F_4(f(x))\ else\ k(x)$

$F_4(x) \Leftarrow if\ p(x)\ then\ F_5(g(x))\ else\ h(x)$

$F_5(x) \Leftarrow if\ q(x)\ then\ F_2(F_4(f(x)))\ else\ F_3(k(x))$

P_2: $F_1(x)$ *where*

$F_1(x) \Leftarrow if\ p(x)\ then\ F_2(F_2(g(x)))\ else\ h(x)$

$F_2(x) \Leftarrow if\ q(x)\ then\ F_1(f(x))\ else\ k(x)$

Now we must introduce a new notation. Consider, for example, the *reverse*(x) function over Σ^*, which was defined as $f_P(x, \Lambda)$ where

$$P:\quad F(x, y) \Leftarrow if\ x = \Lambda\ then\ y\ else\ F(tail(x), head(x) \cdot y)$$

Another way to say this is that *reverse*(x) is the least fixpoint of the following modified recursive program:

P: $F(x, \Lambda)$ *where*

$F(x, y) \Leftarrow if\ x = \Lambda\ then\ y\ else\ F(tail(x), head(x) \cdot y)$

This notation will be used in the next problem.

Prob. 5-20 Consider the following groups of recursive programs, and show that in each group the recursive programs are equivalent; that is, that $f_{P_1} \equiv f_{P_2} \equiv \ldots$.

(*a*) Compute 2^x over the natural numbers:

$$P_1: \quad F(x) \Leftarrow \textit{if } x = 0 \textit{ then } 1 \textit{ else } 2 \cdot F(x - 1)$$

$$P_2: \quad F(x) \Leftarrow \textit{if } x = 0 \textit{ then } 1 \textit{ else if } odd(x) \textit{ then } 2 \cdot [F((x-1)/2)]^2 \textit{ else } [F(x/2)]^2$$

(*b*) Compute x^3 over the natural numbers:

$$P_1: \quad F(x, 0, 0) \textit{ where}$$

$$F(x, y_1, y_2) \Leftarrow \textit{if } y_1 = x \textit{ then } y_2 \textit{ else } F(x, y_1 + 1, y_2 + 3y_1(y_1 + 1) + 1)$$

$$P_2: \quad F(x, 0) \textit{ where}$$

$$F(x, y) \Leftarrow \textit{if } x = 0 \textit{ then } y \textit{ else } F(x - 1, y + 3x(x - 1) + 1)$$

(*c*) Compute $(x^2 + x)/2$ over the natural numbers:

$$P_1: \quad F(x) \Leftarrow \textit{if } x = 0 \textit{ then } 0 \textit{ else } x + F(x - 1)$$

$$P_2: \quad F(x, 0) \textit{ where}$$

$$F(x, y) \Leftarrow \textit{if } x = 0 \textit{ then } y \textit{ else } F(x - 1, x + y)$$

$$P_3: \quad F(x, 1, 0) \textit{ where}$$

$$F(x, y_1, y_2) \Leftarrow \textit{if } y_1 = x + 1 \textit{ then } y_2 \textit{ else } F(x, y_1 + 1, y_1 + y_2)$$

(*d*) Compute $rem(x_1, x_2)$, the remainder of x_1/x_2, for positive integers x_1 and x_2:

$$P_1: \quad F(x_1, x_2) \Leftarrow \textit{if } x_1 = 0 \textit{ then } 0 \textit{ else if } F(x_1 - 1, x_2) + 1 = x_2 \textit{ then } 0 \textit{ else } F(x_1 - 1, x_2) + 1$$

$$P_2: \quad F(x_1, x_2) \Leftarrow \textit{if } x_1 < x_2 \textit{ then } x_1 \textit{ else } F(x_1 - x_2, x_2)$$

(*e*) Compute $x!$ over the natural numbers:

$$P_1: \quad F(x) \Leftarrow \textit{if } x = 0 \textit{ then } 1 \textit{ else } x \cdot F(x - 1)$$

P_2: $F(x, 1)$ *where*

$$F(x, y) \Leftarrow \textit{if } x = 0 \textit{ then } y \textit{ else } F(x - 1, xy)$$

P_3: $F(x, 0)$ *where*

$$F(x, y) \Leftarrow \textit{if } y = x \textit{ then } 1 \textit{ else } (y + 1) \cdot F(x, y + 1)$$

P_4: $F(x, 0, 1)$ *where*

$$F(x, y_1, y_2) \Leftarrow \textit{if } y_1 = x \textit{ then } y_2 \textit{ else } F(x, y_1 + 1, (y_1 + 1)\, y_2)$$

(*f*) Reverse the order of the letters in a given string $x \in \Sigma^*$:

P_1: $F(x, \Lambda)$ *where*

$$F(x, y) \Leftarrow \textit{if } x = \Lambda \textit{ then } y \textit{ else } F(\textit{tail}(x), \textit{head}(x) \cdot y)$$

P_2: $F_1(x)$ *where*

$$F_1(x) \Leftarrow \textit{if } x = \Lambda \textit{ then } x \textit{ else } F_2(\textit{head}(x), F_1(\textit{tail}(x)))$$

$$F_2(x, y) \Leftarrow \textit{if } y = \Lambda \textit{ then } x \textit{ else } \textit{head}(y) \cdot F_2(x, \textit{tail}(y))$$

(*g*) "Flatten" a given Lisp list x;† for example, the list $(a\,(b\ \ c)\,(d\,e))$ is transferred to the "flat" list $(a\,b\,c\,d\,e)$:

P_1: $F(x) \Leftarrow \textit{if } \textit{atom}(x) \textit{ then } \textit{cons}(x, \textit{NIL})$

$$\textit{else } \textit{append}(F(\textit{car}(x)), F(\textit{cdr}(x)))$$

P_2: $F(x, \textit{NIL})$ *where*

$$F(x, y) \Leftarrow \textit{if } \textit{atom}(x) \textit{ then } \textit{cons}(x, y)$$

$$\textit{else } F(\textit{car}(x), F(\textit{cdr}(x), y))$$

† This problem requires knowledge of Lisplike languages.

INDEXES

NAME INDEX

Ackermann, W., 145
Andrews, P., 145
Arbib, M. A., 68
Arden, D. N., 71
Ashcroft, E. A., 218, 334, 350, 414

Bird, M., 264*n.*
Boyer, R. S., 416
Brown, S., 334
Burstall, R. M., 218, 409, 411, 416

Cadiou, J. M., 385, 410, 415
Chandra, A. K., 274, 334, 338, 343, 347
Chang, C. L., 145
Chomsky, N., 42, 68
Church, A., 1, 105, 145
Clint, M., 218
Cohn, P. M., 409
Constable, R. L., 334
Cooper, D. C., 219, 307, 312, 315, 334, 344, 348

Dahl, O. J., 219
Davis, M., 1, 67, 145
deBakker, J. W., 394, 415, 416
Deutsch, L. P., 219
Dijkstra, E. W., 219, 237
Duijvestijn, A. J. W., 240*n.*

Engeler, E., 348
Ershov, A. P., 334
Evey, R. J., 68

Floyd, R. W., 63, 105, 174, 185, 218, 219, 235*n.*, 334, 350, 416
Francez, N., 347

Garland, S. J., 334
Gentzen, G., 108, 145
Gerhard, S., 219
Gilmore, P. C., 145
Ginzburg, A., 67

Gödel, K., 105, 108, 145
Goldstine, H. H., 218
Good, D. I., 219
Green, C., 219
Greif, I. G., 416
Gries, D., 334

Herbrand, J., 145
Hermes, H., 53, 67
Hewitt, C. E., 328, 330, 334
Hilbert, D., 53, 145
Hitchcock, P., 415
Hoare, C. A. R., 205, 207, 210, 218, 219
Hopcroft, J. E., 43, 67, 68
Huet, G. P., 145

Ianov, Y. I., 289, 334
Igarashi, S., 219

Kain, R. Y., 67
Kalish, D., 145
Kaplan, D. M., 194, 289, 334
Karp, R. M., 334
Katz, S. M., 219
King, J. C., 218, 219
Kleene, S. C., 1, 11, 52, 67, 68, 145, 357, 370, 415
Knaster, B., 423
Knuth, D. E., 187, 218, 224, 279*n.*, 350

Landin, J. P., 415
Lee, R. C. T., 145, 219
Levitt, K. N., 219
London, R. L., 219, 235
Luckham, D. C., 67, 219, 261, 264, 334

McCarthy, J., 194, 324, 334, 407, 415, 416
McCulloch, W. S., 67
Manna, Z., 211, 214, 306, 307, 312, 321*n.*, 338, 344, 350, 421
Matijasevic, Ju. V., 54
Mendelson, E., 145, 148, 155, 156
Miller, R. E., 334
Milner, R., 334, 416
Minsky, M. L., 33, 56, 67, 68
Montague, R., 145
Moore, E. F., 17, 67
Moore, J. S., 416
Morris, J. B., 145
Morris, J. H., 389, 400, 415, 416, 421, 425

Naur, P., 218, 219
Ness, S., 412, 415, 416
Nilsson, N. J., 145

Painter, J. A., 416
Park, D. M. R., 67, 261, 264, 334, 406, 415, 416, 423
Paterson, M. S., 66, 67, 76, 253, 261, 264, 270, 328, 330, 334, 341
Pietrzykowski, T., 145
Pitts, W., 67
Plaisted, D. A., 334
Pnueli, A., 211, 214, 218, 219, 321*n.*, 334
Post, E. L., 1, 27, 59, 61, 68
Prawitz, D., 145
Putnam, H., 145

Quine, W. V., 93, 145

Rabin, M., 67
Reynolds, J. C., 70
Rice, H. G., 200
Robinson, G. A., 145
Robinson, J. A., 136, 140, 145
Rogers, H., 67
Rogers, R., 145
Rutledge, J. D., 334

Salomaa, A., 67
Schoenfield, J. R., 145
Scott, D., 61, 67, 68, 394, 415, 416
Shepherdson, J. C., 67, 68
Skolem, 126, 145*n*.
Slutzky, G., 347
Smullyan, R. M., 145
Strachey, C., 415, 416
Strong, H. R., 334
Sturgis, H. E., 67, 68
Sussman, G. J., 219
Szymanski, T., 334

Tarski, A., 423
Turing, A. M., 1, 56, 68, 145, 218

Ullman, J. D., 43, 67, 68

Von Neumann, J., 218
Vuillemin, J., 386, 403, 415, 416, 419, 421

Waldinger, R. J., 219
Wang, H., 145, 156
Wegbreit, B., 219
Weyhrauch, R., 416
Wirth, N., 219
Wos, L., 145

SUBJECT INDEX

Ackerman's function (program), 53, 200–202, 234–235, 317–319, 321–322, 410
Admissible predicate (for computational induction), 393–403, 421–422
Algol-like programs (*see* While programs)
Algol-like schemas (*see* While schemas)
Algorithms (*see* Turing machines)
Alphabet, 2, 20, 396
Alphabetic change of bound variables, 100–102, 126
And connective ($\wedge$), 49, 77, 81, 87, 110
And rule, 213
append function (program), 46, 78*n*., 396–397, 407–408, 413, 422
Arden rule, 6
Array manipulation programs:
  minimum, 232–233
  partition, 210–211, 233
Array manipulation programs:
  permutation, 240
  reversing, 232
  sorting, 231
  (*See also* Bubble sorting program; FIND program; TREESORT3 program)
Arrays:
  in flowchart programs, 189
  in flowchart schemas, 334
Assertions (*see* Inductive assertions)
assign function, 194–195
Assignment axiom, 206
Assignment rule, 207–209, 212, 216–217
Associative laws, 97–98
Assumption:
  axiom, 109
  formulas, 108–109, 156
  rules, 109
Atomic formulas (atfs), 81–83, 125, 138–141
  complement, 104

Atomic formulas (atfs):
  in flowchart schemas, 242–243, 295*n.*
Automata (*see* Finite automata)

Backward substitution:
  in flowchart programs, 167–169, 171–173, 176–177
  in flowchart schemas, 297–300, 324–328
Base functions (of recursive programs), 356–358, 374
  (*See also* Monotonic functions; Natural extension)
Blocks (of flowchart schemas), 348–350
Boolean expressions, 73
Bound occurrences of variables (in wffs), 84, 100–102, 115, 126
Bubble-sorting program, 190–197

Call-by-name (*see* Leftmost computation rule)
Call-by-value (*see* Leftmost-innermost computation rule)
Chain (of monotonic functions), 364–366, 369–371, 381
Characteristic function (of primitive recursive predicates), 48–49
Choice branches (of nondeterministic machines), 35
Church's thesis, 1, 38, 44, 53
Clause form (of wffs), 125–131, 140–143
Clauses, 125–126, 136–137, 140–144
  empty, 134–136, 140, 143–144
  ground, 131–138
Closed wff, 84, 101, 126, 131
Commutative laws, 97–98
Compatibility:
  of flowchart programs, 251, 307–308
  of flowchart schemas, 251, 258–259, 261–262, 277, 311–312
Completeness, 108
  of first-order predicate calculus, 108–109
  of propositional calculus, 111, 155
  of second-order predicate calculus, 108, 145
Computable functions, 1, 44, 67
Computation diagram (of recursive programs), 379–383, 386–387
Computation rules (of recursive programs), 375–389, 391–392, 415, 419
  (*See also* Fixpoint computation rules; Safe computation rules)
Computation sequence (of recursive programs), 318–319, 321–322
Computational induction method, 392, 422
  complete, 400–403, 416
  stepwise, 393–401, 416, 421
Concatenation function, 20, 44–46
Concatenation rule, 207–209, 212–213, 216, 217
Conditional connective (IF-THEN-ELSE), 81, 82, 87, 111
Conditional form (of wffs), 148–149
Conditional operator (*if-then-else*), 81, 82, 85, 88, 122
Conditional rules, 206, 212
Conjunction:
  of ground instances, 131
  of wffs, 98

Connectives, 49, 81–83, 147–148
derived rules for, 113–115
meaning of, 86–87
rules for, 110–113
Consequence rules, 207, 213
Constant function, 360, 362
Constant functional, 366
Constants:
of flowchart schemas, 242, 311*n.*
of recursive schemas, 319–320
of well-formed formulas, 79, 80*n.*, 81, 85–86
contents function, 194–195
Context-free grammars, 42, 63
Context-free languages, 43
Context-sensitive grammars, 42, 54–55, 63
Context-sensitive languages, 43
Continuous functionals, 358, 366–371, 390, 407–408, 418
inequalities of, 394–403, 421–422
Contradiction, 95*n.*
Correctness (*see* Partial correctness; Termination; Total correctness; Verification)
Countermodel (for wffs), 90, 92, 119–120, 153, 158
Cutpoints, 165–166, 171–174, 183–185, 295–304, 324–328

Davis and Putnam's method, 125, 132–134, 159
Decidable problems (*see* Solvable problems)
Decision problems (*see* Partially solvable problems; Solvable problems; Unsolvable problems)
Decomposition of schemas (into subtrees), 295–303, 324–328
Deducible (provable) wff, 108
Deduction systems, 108
complete, 108–109, 111
natural (*see* Natural deduction)
De Morgan's laws, 97–98
Determinant evaluation program, 198–200
Determinism, 9
Disagreement set, 138–140
Discharge rule, 110
Disjunction:
of atomic formulas, 138–141
of wffs, 98
Distributive laws, 97–98
div function, 210*n.*
Divergence:
of finite-tree schemas, 275
of flowchart programs, 248, 307–308
of flowchart schemas, 248, 261–268, 311–312, 337, 339
of free flowchart schemas, 270
of Ianov schemas, 289, 343
Domain of interpretation (*see* Interpretation)
Duality theorem, 153

Emptiness problem (of context-sensitive grammars), 63
Empty-word halting problem (of Turing machines), 57
Equality calculus, 84–85, 107
Equality operator (=), 50, 77, 81–82, 85, 88, 122
(*See also* Weak equality; Strong equality)
Equality tests (in flowchart schemas), 334, 338, 343, 347
Equivalence:
of context-free grammars, 63
of finite automata, 17–20, 54
of finite tree schemas, 275–277

Equivalence:
of flowchart and free tree schemas, 277–281
of flowchart programs, 251, 307–308
of flowchart schemas, 251–259, 261–268, 281, 312, 315–317, 334, 338–339, 341, 344
of free flowchart schemas, 273
of Ianov schemas, 289–293, 334, 343
of recursive programs, 428–429
of recursive schemas, 426–427
of well-formed formulas, 95–101, 153
Equivalence connective (≡), 49, 81, 82, 87, 96, 110, 150
Existential closure (of wffs), 100–101
Existential quantifier (∃), 77, 81, 84, 88, 116, 120–121, 394*n.*
elimination of, 127–130
Exponent program, 178–180, 186
Extension:
of flowchart programs, 307–308
of flowchart schemas, 311–312, 339

Factor (of disjunction), 138, 141
Factorial function (program), 223, 245, 304–306, 322–323, 343, 365, 369, 374, 393, 410–411, 421, 428–429
FAILURE statement, 281
false value, 85–88
Fibonacci function (program), 382–383
FIND program, 233–234
(*See also* Partition program)
Finite automata, 1, 7–9, 14–17
acceptance by, 3, 7, 71–72

Finite automata:
equivalence of, 17–20, 54
power of, 33, 37, 74
two-registered, 66–67, 264–267
Finite directed graph, 7*n.*
Finite machines (with/without pushdown stores), 1, 20, 29–35
with counters, 73–74
halting problem of, 58
nondeterministic, 35–37, 43
power of, 33–35, 37, 68, 74
words accepted/rejected by, 31, 38–39, 43
First-order predicate calculus, 80–81, 85, 105–125, 145, 153, 157–158
(*See also* Completeness; Natural deduction; Resolution method; Validity)
Fixpoint:
of functionals, 356–357, 369–374, 390–391
of recursive programs, 374, 391–392, 409
of regular equations, 71–72
Fixpoint computation rules (of recursive programs), 384–389, 415, 419
Fixpoint induction method, 406, 416, 423
Fixpoint invariant transformations (of recursive programs), 403–405, 416
Flowchart programs, 161–202, 241–248, 294–311, 334
Flowchart schemas, 241–248, 334, 347–350
basic properties, 248–262
with counters, 334, 347
decision problems of, 262–294
with equality tests, 334, 338, 343, 347

Flowchart schemas:
  formalization in predicate calculus of, 294–317, 334
  versus recursive schemas, 242, 322–334, 347
  versus while schemas, 352
Flow-diagram, 24*n*.
Formal languages, 41–43, 62, 68
Free-argument computation rule, 376–378, 384–388, 419
Free occurrences of variables (in wffs), 84, 100, 115
Free schemas (*see* Freedom)
Free variables (of wffs), 80, 84–86, 116, 120
Freedom:
  of flowchart schemas, 264, 268–274, 339–340, 342
  of Ianov schemas, 285–289, 342
  of tree schemas, 274–284
Full-substitution computation rule, 376–377, 384–388, 419
Function constants:
  of flowchart schemas, 242, 244
  in predicate calculus, 79, 81–82, 85–86, 130
  of recursive schemas, 319–320
Function variables:
  in predicate calculus, 79, 81, 83, 86
  of recursive schemas, 319, 322–328
Functionals, 358, 366–374, 390, 418–419
  (*See also* Continuous functionals; Fixpoint of functionals; Least fixpoint of functionals; Monotonic functionals)

gcd (*see* Greatest common divisor program)
Generalization rule, 116
Grammars, 41, 63
  type-0, 41–43, 58, 63
  type-i, 42–43, 63, 74
Graph (*see* Finite directed graph)
Greatest common divisor (*gcd*) program, 180–182, 186–189, 205, 215–217, 224–225, 239
Greatest lower bound (*glb*) (of monotonic functions), 423
Ground instance, 131, 136
Ground resolution method (rule), 125, 132, 134–136, 159

Halt point, 171, 174
Halting problem (HP):
  of finite machines (with push-down stores), 58
  of finite tree schemas, 275
  of flowchart programs, 248, 307–308
    (*See also* Termination)
  of flowchart schemas, 248–251, 261–268, 279–284, 311–315, 337, 339, 341, 344
  of free flowchart schemas, 270
  of Ianov schemas, 289, 343
  of Post machines, 58–62
  of Turing machines, 55–58, 64, 68
head function, 20, 46–47, 66, 78
Herbrand interpretation:
  of flowchart schemas, 246–248, 260–262, 265, 275–277, 338
  in predicate calculus, 131
  of recursive schemas, 328–333
Herbrand procedure, 125, 130–132, 136, 145
Herbrand property, 338
Herbrand theorem, 125, 131–132, 145, 158–159

Herbrand universe, 130–131, 260–261
Hilbert's tenth problem, 53–54

Ianov schemas, 284–294, 334, 342–343
if-then-else function, 48–49, 358, 362–363, 418
Implication connective (⊃), 77, 81, 87, 110, 114
Incremental proof, 213, 217–218
Individual constants:
  of flowchart schemas, 242, 244
  in predicate calculus, 79, 81–82, 84, 86, 130
  of recursive schemas, 319–320
Individual variables:
  of flowchart schemas, 242, 311*n.*
  in predicate calculus, 79, 81–82, 84–86
  of recursive schemas, 319
Induction principle:
  over the natural numbers, 79, 310
  over strings, 80
Inductive assertions:
  for partial correctness, 166–169, 174, 177, 179, 181, 192–195, 208–209, 219, 311
  for termination, 184–186, 188, 197–198, 202
Inductive-assertions method, 174–182, 218, 219, 295, 306, 334
Inductive expressions, 205–206, 217–218
Input predicate, 161, 164–165, 174, 205, 308
Input variables ($\bar{x}$):
  of flowchart programs, 161–162
Input variables ($\bar{x}$):
  of flowchart schemas, 242, 244, 261, 284, 300, 304
  of recursive schemas, 319
Integer division program, 163–170, 223, 229
Integer square-root program, 175–178, 185–186, 204, 208–209
Interpretation:
  of flowchart schemas, 241–242, 244–248
    finite/infinite, 337, 339
  in predicate calculus, 77–80, 85–91, 101, 152
  of recursive schemas, 319–322
  (*See also* Herband interpretation; Partial interpretation)
Interpreted wffs, 85–90, 294–295, 304–311
Invariant assertions, 206–207
  (*See also* Inductive assertions)
Isomorphism:
  of finite tree schemas, 275
  of flowchart schemas, 258–259, 261–268, 281, 339, 348
  of free flowchart schemas, 273–274
  of Ianov schemas, 293–294, 343

Joint denial connective (|), 148
Joint statement, 162*n.*, 172

Kleene's theorem:
  equivalence of regular sets, 7, 9, 11–17
  least fixpoint of functionals, 358, 370–371, 393, 415
König's infinity lemma, 159, 279

Languages, 41
prefix-free, 75
type-0, 42, 58, 68
type-i, 43, 74
Least fixpoint:
of functionals, 356–357, 369–374, 390–391, 407–408, 419
of recursive programs, 357, 374–375, 379–385, 391, 409, 419–429
of regular equations, 71–72, 340
Least upper bound-*lub* (of monotonic functions), 364–365, 369–371, 381*n*.
Leftmost ("call-by-name") computation rule, 376–379, 382–384, 388–389, 391–392
Leftmost-innermost ("call-by-value") computation rule, 321, 375–378, 384, 388–389, 415
Lexicographic ordering (of well-founded sets), 195–196, 200, 409–410
Literals, 125
complement, 132*n*.
instance of, 138
LOOP statement (of flowchart schemas), 243
Looping problem (of two-registered finite automata), 66–67, 264–265
lub lemma, 365
(*See also* Least upper bound)

McCarthy's 91 function, 226, 370, 372–373, 376–379, 391, 406, 411–412, 421
Machines:
equivalence of, 20
nondeterministic, 20, 35–37
Machines:
power of, 20, 37
(*See also* Finite machines; Post machines; Turing machines)
Matrix (of wffs), 101–102, 104, 126
Minimization:
bounded, 50
unbounded, 51–52, 75
Model (for wffs), 91
Modus Ponens, 110, 155–156
Monotonic functionals, 358, 366–371, 390, 418–419
with respect to an occurrence of *F*, 369, 379, 419
Monotonic functions, 357–366, 390, 418
chain of, 364–366, 369–371, 381
equality of, 364, 394
inequality (less defined than) of, 359–360, 364, 385, 394
Mortality problem (of matrices), 63, 76
Multiplication program, 309–311

Natural deduction, 108
for first-order predicate calculus, 108–125, 145, 157–158
for propositional calculus, 109–115, 154–157
Natural extension (of functions), 361–362, 388–389, 394
Natural lexicographic ordering, 39
Noetherian induction, 409*n*.
Nonacceptance problem (of two-registered finite automata), 66–67, 264–265
Nondeterminism, 9, 20, 35–37
Nonhalting problem (of Turing machines), 65

Nonvalidity (of wffs), 90–93, 119–120, 158
Normal form:
  of flowchart programs, 348–350
  of wffs, 101–104, 107, 148–149, 153
Not connective (~), 49, 77, 81, 86, 110

Of connective ($\vee$), 49, 77, 81, 87, 110
  inclusive/exclusive, 87*n.*
Operators (of wffs), 81, 88, 122–125
Or rule, 213, 217
ordered predicate, 190–193
Output predicate, 161, 164–165, 174, 205, 304–306
Output variables ($\bar{z}$):
  of flowchart programs, 162
  of flowchart schemas, 242, 244, 285
  of recursive schemas, 319, 324

Parallel-innermost computation rule, 376–378, 384, 388–389
Parallel-outermost computation rule, 376, 384–388, 419
Parallel schemas, 334
Parallel simulation, 40*n.*, 65*n.*
Partial correctness:
  of flowchart programs, 165–169, 171–182, 189–195, 294–295, 304–308
  of flowchart schemas, 311–312, 339
  of while (Algol-like) programs, 205–211, 237–239
  (*See also* Verification)
Partial equivalence, 343–344
Partial functions, 44*n.*
  "good" for termination, 183–186, 188, 197, 198, 202, 213–214
Partial interpretation, 334
Partial recursive:
  functions, 1, 45, 50–53, 58, 68, 75
  predicates, 51
Partially ordered sets, 182–183, 359–360, 364
  (*See also* Well-founded sets)
Partially solvable problems, 54, 64–67, 76
  of flowchart schemas, 262–273, 279*n.*, 338–339, 344
  in predicate calculus, 105, 125, 145
Partition program, 210–211, 233
Path (of flowchart programs), 165–174
Perfect number program, 228
perm predicate, 190–191, 211*n.*
Post correspondence problem (PCP), 55, 60–64, 68, 76, 105, 270–273
Post machines, 1, 20, 24–28, 30, 68
  halting problem of, 58–62
  nondeterministic, 37
  power of, 27–28, 33, 37
  words accepted/rejected by, 25, 38, 39, 73
Post systems, 60–61, 68, 76, 105–106
Predicate calculus, 77–160
  (*See also* First-order predicate calculus; Propositional calculus; Second-order predicate calculus; Unary predicate calculus)

Predicate constants:
of flowchart schemas, 242, 244, 312, 317
in predicate calculus, 79, 81, 82, 85, 86
of recursive schemas, 319–320
Predicate variables (in predicate calculus), 81, 83, 86, 295*n.*
Prefix (of wffs), 101–102, 104, 107, 126
Prenex-conjunctive normal form, 101–104, 126, 149, 153
Prenex-disjunctive normal form, 101, 104, 149, 153
Prenex normal form, 104, 107
Prime number program, 227, 230
Primitive recursion, 46, 51
Primitive recursive:
functions, 45–50, 52–53, 75
predicates, 48–50, 75
Program synthesis, 219
Program variables ($\bar{y}$):
of flowchart programs, 161–162
of flowchart schemas, 242, 244, 284–285
of recursive schemas, 319, 328–333
Programs (*see* Flowchart programs; Recursive programs; While programs)
Propositional calculus, 80, 84, 85, 93–95, 109–115, 149–150, 154–157
(*See also* Completeness; Natural deduction; Validity)
Propositional constants:
of flowchart schemas, 242, 244
in predicate calculus, 81, 84, 86, 95
of recursive schemas, 319–320
Propositional variables (in predicate calculus), 81, 84, 86
Pushdown stores (*see* Finite machines)

Quantified propositional calculus, 84, 85, 95, 107
Quantifier-free wffs, 319–320
Quantifiers, 79–84, 87–90, 115–122
complement, 104
elimination of, 312, 317
scope of, 84

Recursion induction method, 407–408, 416, 422
Recursive definitions (*see* Recursive programs)
Recursive equations, 324–328
Recursive functions (*see* Partial recursive; Primitive recursive; Total recursive functions)
Recursive predicates (*see* Partial recursive; Primitive recursive)
Recursive programs, 317–322, 356–357, 374, 388–389, 415
defined by system of recursive definitions, 374*n.*, 389–392, 398–399, 403, 424–429
(*See also* Computation rules; Equivalence; Least fixpoint; Verification)
Recursive schemas, 242, 319–334, 394, 423–427
versus flowchart schemas, 242, 322–334, 347
Recursive sets, 1, 37–40, 43, 58, 108
Recursively enumerable sets, 1, 37–40, 42–43, 68

Recursiveness problem (of type-0 grammars), 58
Reductio ad absurdum, 110
Reduction (of yes/no problems), 55, 57–67, 105–106, 264–265, 270–273
Regular equations, 71–72, 340
Regular expressions, 3–7, 11–13, 16, 67, 70–72, 273–274, 352
Regular grammars, 42, 63
Regular languages, 43
Regular sets, 2–3, 5, 7–9, 11, 43, 67, 72, 74, 340
rem function, 420*n.*, 428
Replacement theorem, 96–98, 100, 102, 153
Resolution method (rule), 81, 92
  for first-order predicate calculus, 125, 136, 139–145, 159–160, 312–315
  for higher-order logic, 145
  (*See also* Ground resolution method)
Resolvent:
  of clauses, 140–145
  of ground clauses, 134–136
reverse function (program), 47, 78, 246, 407–408, 412–415, 422, 427, 429

Safe computation rules (of recursive programs), 386–389, 419
Satisfiability:
  of sets of wffs, 158–159
  of wffs, 90–91, 125–130, 132, 134, 144
Schemas (*see* Flowchart schemas; Recursive schemas; While schemas)
Second-order predicate calculus, 80–81, 84–85, 95, 105, 107, 108, 145
Second-order predicate calculus:
  (*See also* Completeness; Validity)
Semi-Thue systems, 55, 58–60, 68, 76
  (*See also* Recursive sets; Recursively enumerable sets; Regular sets)
Sheffer stroke connective (↓), 148
Similar wffs, 100
Skolem functions, 126, 129–130
Skolem-Herbrand-Gödel Theorem, 145*n.*
Solvable problems, 53–55, 63, 65
  of flowchart schemas, 262–264, 270, 273, 275, 281, 285, 289, 293, 334
  in predicate calculus, 93–95, 107, 145
Start point, 171, 173
Strong equality (≡), 251*n.*, 357*n.*, 362, 363
Structural induction method, 392, 408–416, 422
Subdisjunction (of atomic formulas), 140*n.*
Subtrees (of flowchart schemas), 295–303, 324–328
Synthesis of programs, 219
System *L*, 155–156

tail function, 20, 46–47, 66, 78–79
Tautology, 95*n.*
  elimination of, 128
  theorem, 95
Termination:
  of flowchart programs, 164, 165, 170, 182–189, 195–202, 218, 416
  of recursive programs, 397
  of while (Algol-like) programs, 212–217

Termination conditions, 183–186, 189, 197, 199–200, 202
Termination rules (for while programs), 212–214
Termination-rules method, 214–219
Terms, 81–83, 242–243, 320
  conditional, 320
  constant, 320
  free, 115–116, 119, 122
Thue systems, 76
Total correctness:
  of flowchart programs, 165, 307–311, 343
  of flowchart schemas, 311–312, 339, 344
  of while (Algol-like) programs, 211–218
Total equivalence, 343–344
Total functions, 44*n.*
Total recursive functions, 1, 52–53, 58
Totality problem (of partial recursive functions), 58
Transition graph, 3, 9–16, 72, 290–294
  generalized, 11–16
Transition table, 14–15
Tree schemas, 274–284, 341–342
  finite, 275–277
TREESORT3 program, 235–236
true value, 85–88
Truncation induction, 416
Truth symbols (T and F), 81, 86, 109
Truth tables, 149
Truth values (*true* and *false*), 85–88, 90–91
Turing computable functions, 43–45, 52–53, 67
Turing machines, 1, 20–23, 67–68
  as acceptors, 37–43
  as algorithms, 53–67
Turing machines:
  encoding of, 39, 55–56, 74
  as generators, 43–53
  nondeterministic, 35, 37
  power of, 27–28, 33–35, 37, 74
  reduction, 55
  universal, 65
  (*See also* Halting problem; Nonhalting problem)
Two-registered finite automata, 66–67, 264–267

Unary (monadic) predicate calculus, 107
Undecidable problems (*see* Unsolvable problems)
Undefined function (Ω), 360
Undefined symbol (ω), 320, 358
Unifiable disjunction (of atomic formulas), 138–140
Unification algorithm, 125, 139–140
Unifier, 138
  most general, 138–140, 142
Uniform halting problem (of Turing machines), 57
Universal closure (of wffs), 100–101
Universal quantifier ($\forall$), 77, 81, 84, 87–88, 116, 119–120, 126, 394*n.*
Unsatisfiability:
  of sets of wffs, 158–159
  of wffs, 90–91, 101, 125, 130–138, 140–144, 150, 312–315
Unsolvable problems, 53–64, 68, 76
  of flowchart schemas, 263, 267, 270, 279*n.*, 281, 334, 339, 344
  in predicate calculus, 105–107, 145

val of computation:
of flowchart programs, 245–248, 261–262
of recursive programs, 321–322, 328–332
Validity, 80–81, 90–95, 101, 105–107, 145, 152
of first-order predicate calculus, 105–109, 125, 153
of propositional calculus, 93–95, 111–115, 150
of quantified propositional calculus, 95
of second-order predicate calculus, 95, 105, 107, 108
of unary (monadic) predicate calculus, 107
Variables:
of flowchart schemas, 242
of recursive schemas, 319–320
of wffs, 79, 81
(*See also* Bound occurrences of variables; Free occurrences of variables; Free variables)
Verification, 161, 218
of flowchart programs, 164–169
of recursive programs, 392–416, 419–429
of while (Algol-like) programs, 202–218
(*See also* Partial correctness; Termination; Total correctness)
Verification conditions, 167–170, 174, 177–182, 192–195
Verification rules (for while programs), 206–208
Verification-rules method, 207–211, 218
Weak equality (=), 357*n.*, 362, 363
Well-formed formulas (wffs), 77, 81–90, 100–101, 294–301, 312–317
(*See also* Equivalence; Interpreted wffs; Nonvalidity; Normal form; Satisfiability; Unsatisfiability; Validity)
Well-formed parts (wfps), 83–84
Well-founded sets, 183–185, 187, 213–214, 236, 408–415
(*See also* Lexicographic ordering)
Well-founded-sets method, 185–189, 218
Wffs (*see* Well-formed formulas)
While programs, 202–218, 237–239
While rule, 206–207, 209, 213–214, 216, 217
While schemas, 350–355
Word problem (WP):
of context-sensitive grammars, 54–55, 63
of semi-Thue systems, 55, 58–60
of Thue systems, 76
of type-0 grammars, 63
Words, 2, 3*n.*, 20
length of, 6*n.*, 42*n.*, 414*n.*

Yes/no problems, 1, 53–67, 262
complement of, 65
(*See also* Partially solvable problems; Reduction; Solvable problems; Unsolvable problems)